CHURCH DOGMATICS

For further resources, including the forewords to the original 14-volume edition of the *Church Dogmatics*, log on to our website and sign up for the resources webpage: http://www.continuumbooks.com/dogmatics/

KARL BARTH

CHURCH DOGMATICS

VOLUME III

THE DOCTRINE
OF CREATION

§ 40–42

THE WORK OF CREATION

EDITED BY
G. W. BROMILEY
T. F. TORRANCE

t & t clark

Published by T&T Clark

A Continuum Imprint

The Tower Building, 11 York Road, London, SE1 7NX
80 Maiden Lane, Suite 704, New York, NY 10038

www.continuumbooks.com

Translated by G. W. Bromiley, J. W. Edwards, O. Bussey, Harold Knight, J. K. S. Reid, R. H. Fuller, R. J. Ehrlich, A. T. Mackey, T. H. L. Parker, H. A. Kennedy, J. Marks

Copyright © T&T Clark, 2010

Authorised translation of Karl Barth, *Die Kirchliche Dogmatik III*
Copyright © Theologischer Verlag Zürich, 1945–1951
All revisions to the original English translation and all translation of Greek, Latin and French
© Princeton Theological Seminary, 2009

British Library Cataloguing-in-Publication Data
A catalogue record for this book is available from the British Library

ISBN13: 978-0-567-19663-7

Typeset by Interactive Sciences Ltd, Gloucester, and Newgen Imaging Systems Pvt Ltd, Chennai
Printed and bound in Great Britain by CPI Antony Rowe, Chippenham, Wiltshire

PUBLISHER'S PREFACE TO
THE STUDY EDITION

Since the publication of the first English translation of *Church Dogmatics I.1* by Professor Thomson in 1936, T&T Clark has been closely linked with Karl Barth. An authorised translation of the whole of the *Kirchliche Dogmatik* was begun in the 1950s under the editorship of G. W. Bromiley and T. F. Torrance, a work which eventually replaced Professor Thomson's initial translation of *CD I.1*.

T&T Clark is now happy to present to the academic community this new *Study Edition* of the *Church Dogmatics*. Its aim is mainly to make this major work available to a generation of students and scholars with less familiarity with Latin, Greek, and French. For the first time this edition therefore presents the classic text of the translation edited by G. W. Bromiley and T. F. Torrance incorporating translations of the foreign language passages in Editorial Notes on each page.

The main body of the text remains unchanged. Only minor corrections with regard to grammar or spelling have been introduced. The text is presented in a new reader friendly format. We hope that the breakdown of the *Church Dogmatics* into 31 shorter fascicles will make this edition easier to use than its predecessors.

Completely new indexes of names, subjects and scriptural indexes have been created for the individual volumes of the *Study Edition.*

The publishers would like to thank the Center for Barth Studies at Princeton Theological Seminary for supplying a digital edition of the text of the *Church Dogmatics* and translations of the Greek and Latin quotations in the original T&T Clark edition made by Simon Gathercole and Ian McFarland.

London, April 2010

HOW TO USE THIS
STUDY EDITION

The *Study Edition* follows Barth's original volume structure. Individual paragraphs and sections should be easy to locate. A synopsis of the old and new edition can be found on the back cover of each fascicle.

All secondary literature on the *Church Dogmatics* currently refers to the classic 14-volume set (e.g. II.2 p. 520). In order to avoid confusion, we recommend that this practice should be kept for references to this *Study Edition*. The page numbers of the old edition can be found in the margins of this edition.

CONTENTS

§ 40–42

FAITH IN GOD THE CREATOR

The insight that man owes his existence and form, together with all the reality distinct from God, to God's creation, is achieved only in the reception and answer of the divine self-witness, that is, only in faith in Jesus Christ, i.e., in the knowledge of the unity of Creator and creature actualised in Him, and in the life in the present mediated by Him, under the right and in the experience of the goodness of the Creator towards His creature.

The first article of the "Apostles'" creed says: I believe in God the Father Almighty, Maker of heaven and earth, *creatorem coeli et terrae.* These last words—not by themselves, but together with what goes before, and with all that follows in the second and third articles—are the simplest and most comprehensive form of the teaching of the Church on creation. Though they speak of God, they do not speak only of God, but also of a reality which is distinct from God, i.e., of heaven and earth as the two great distinctive but related spheres, intersecting in man, of the whole being of the "world" as it exists apart from God. They say that He who alone is God the Father Almighty is not alone. And in order not to be alone and to have this other quite different reality before, with and near Him, He deliberately gave it an existence and definite form. They say that God is its Creator, that is, that heaven and earth and man between them owe to Him the fact as well as the content and manner of their being. Before these words, however, as before the whole creed, there stands the word *credo,* I believe.

Our first emphasis is on this final point that the doctrine of the creation no less than the whole remaining content of Christian confession is an article of faith, i.e., the rendering of a knowledge which no man has procured for himself or ever will; which is neither native to him nor accessible by way of observation and logical thinking; for which he has no organ and no ability; which he can in fact achieve only in faith; but which is actually consummated in faith, i.e., in the reception of and response to the divine witness, so that he is made to be strong in his weakness, to see in his blindness and to hear in his deafness [004] by the One who, according to the Easter story, goes through closed doors. It is a faith and doctrine of this kind which is expressed when in and with the whole of Christendom we confess that God is the Creator of heaven and earth.

This is stated clearly by the Epistle to the Hebrews (11^3): πίστει νοοῦμεν κατηρτίσθαι τοὺς αἰῶνας ῥήματι θεοῦ[EN1]. The statement does not stand at the head of a creed, but all

---

[EN1] through faith we understand that the ages were framed by the word of God

the more significantly as a sort of title at the beginning of a long recital of acts of faith on the part of men of the old covenant—a recital designed by the writer as an appeal to Christians not to cast away their confidence (10³⁵ᶠ·), but, in the presence of a great cloud of witnesses, to run with patience the race which is set before them, looking into Jesus, the author and finisher of the faith (12¹ᶠ). This recital (11³) of faith in God the Creator is obviously introduced by the writer as an illustration of the faith which, having its source and perfection in Jesus Christ, was tested by the ancients and has now to be tested by Christians. Whoever rightly and patiently, and therefore with certainty, believes in the fulfilment of the promise which was given in faith, believes that the world is created by God's Word. Accordingly Theophilus of Antioch (*Ad Autol.* II, 10) wrote that God's Logos descended on the prophets and through them proclaims τὰ περὶ τῆς ποιήσεως τοῦ κόσμου[EN2], so that with one voice (συμφώνως) they teach ὅτι ἐξ οὐκ ὄντων τὰ πάντα (ὁ θεὸς) ἐποίησεν[EN3]. And as the mouthpiece of this Logos, Moses said: "In the beginning God created heaven and earth." Later theology did, of course, think that it should and could distinguish between a conception of creation in general and as such on the one side, and its real consummation on the other, thus asserting that the insight that the world has not originated from itself, but has its origin and support from outside itself, may be attained *etiam ex rationis dictamine*[EN4]. But even in the framework of this retention of a certain natural theology Thomas Aquinas declared that at any rate the most important statement in the doctrine of creation—that of the *novitas mundi*[EN5] (that the world is not eternal but has a beginning)—is only *credibile, non autem scibile et demonstrabile*[EN6]. It is a matter of the free and as such inscrutable will of God, and it will only arouse the scorn of unbelievers if the attempt is made to find rational grounds for its decision (*S. theol.*, I, *qu.* 46, *art.* 2c). And very emphatically Polanus (*Synt. Theol. chr.*, 1609, *col.* 1700): *Creationis vera ac certa cognitio non philosophiae sed theologiae, non naturae sed fidei, non acumini mentis humanae, sed divino lumini, non humanae ratiocinationi, sed divinae revelationi, non rationibus et demonstrationibus physicis, sed autoritatibus et testimoniis divinis accepta est ferenda.*[EN7] And in a more exact definition Quenstedt (*Theol. did. pol.*, 1685, 1, *cap.* 10, *sect.* 2, *qu.* 1, *thes.* and *beb.* II): *Creatio mundi ex nihilo in tempore facta ex lumine naturae cognosci aut rationibus philosophicis apodictice et evidenter demonstrari nequit sed ex sola revelatione divina innotescit, adeoque est articulus purae fidei ac merae revelationis …. Nihil enim constat de liberis Dei actionibus nisi ex revelatione.*[EN8] The reliable testimony of Walter Koehler may be noted on this point: "Greek philosophy did not know the God who created the world" (*Dogm. Gesch.*, 1938, p. 92). On the basis of its conception of God (τὸ ἕν[EN9]) only the idea of an automatic emanation of the world is possible. In dogmatic history the Christian belief in the Creator reaches its climax in opposition to the Gnosis which tries to take up again the same conception of God and therefore this idea of the world's origin.

[EN2] the truth concerning the making of the world
[EN3] that from what is not (God) made all things
[EN4] also from the exercise of reason
[EN5] the contingency of the world
[EN6] a matter of belief, not of immediate knowledge or rational demonstration
[EN7] True and certain knowledge of creation is theological rather than philosophical, of faith rather than nature; it is grounded not in the power of the human mind, but in divine illumination; not in human reason, but in divine revelation; not in scientific reasoning or proof, but in divine authority and witness
[EN8] The creation of the world from nothing, as an event in time, cannot be known by the light of nature or demonstrated with clarity and certainty on the basis of philosophical reasoning, but is known by divine revelation alone, and so is an article of sheer faith and pure revelation …. For the free acts of God cannot be known except by revelation.
[EN9] the One

We must first try to realise why it is that the doctrine of creation is a doctrine of faith and its content a secret; why it is, therefore, that it belongs to the creed and to Church dogmatics. There are three reasons why it cannot be other than an *articulus fidei*[EN10], and there is then a positive and decisive reason why it is actually and necessarily an *articulus fidei*[EN11]. [005]

1. The proposition that God created heaven and earth and man asserts that the whole reality distinct from God truly is. Negatively, therefore, it asserts that God does not exist alone; that the divine being is not the only one to the exclusion of all others. And positively it asserts that another exists before, near and with God, having its own differentiated being quite distinct from that of God. Even this aspect of the creation dogma is not self-evident. The negative and positive assertion which is being made is certainly not impossible to the extent that it does not contain a palpable contradiction. But it is not demonstrable and can always be disputed. It cannot be shown that God must have created the world, that it exists necessarily as seen in relation to Him, and that, measured by His reality, it must itself therefore have reality, namely, its own special reality. Nor can it be shown in relation to the world that because God has created it, because it necessarily exists and has its being from Him, it is not an illusion, a dream, a mere figment of the imagination, but concept and reality. The positive counter-assertion that God exists alone, that this divine being is the only one to the exclusion of all others, and the negative counter-assertion that the world and we ourselves do not exist at all, that we do not have a being distinct from that of God, but that everything else apart from God is only supposition, are, of course, as contestable and as little demonstrable as the assertion. But they cannot be refuted by the assertion. On the contrary, they are refuted only if two conditions are fulfilled—and it is here that we see the real point of the dogma. The first is that it should be established on the basis of the divine self-witness—beyond all discussion of other possibilities suggested either in relation to God or the world—that God has in fact created the world; that it is, therefore, a reality by God's free will and contingent act. And the second is that we should have no less factual knowledge of this factual being of the world. Thus if we dare to take the not unimportant step of ascribing its own reality to that which is distinct from God, i.e., heaven and earth and ourselves; if we are of the bold opinion that we ourselves, and with us the so-called world, are and are not *not*, we have to realise that this is always an undemonstrable and contestable hypothesis, and that we must make up our minds to think and live and die on the basis of this hypothesis—unless we have accepted the divine self-witness and therefore confessed with the whole of Christendom that in the beginning God created heaven and earth and ourselves and therefore gave to the world distinct from Himself a demonstrable and indisputable reality.

[EN10] article of faith
[EN11] article of faith

The older theologians were right, therefore, when they understood the creation as a *libera actio Dei*^{EN12}, as a free act of the divine will, which can only be declared to man by God Himself and therefore *ex revelatione*^{EN13}, so that we can only believe it, proving and protecting it against attacks as the content of a statement of faith, but unable seriously and convincingly to maintain it on other grounds. It need only be added that the assertion of creation is a statement of faith, i.e., a statement which can never be more than a hypothesis apart from its foundation in God's self-witness, not only on the side which maintains that *God* is the Creator of the world, and which therefore asserts the reality of *God*, but also on that which asserts that God is the Creator of the *world*, and which therefore asserts the distinctive reality of the *world*. It is only too easy to suggest that, while the reality of God as the Creator is uncertain, and therefore needs proof or revelation, the reality of the creature is all the more certain, so that the one is to be treated as a factor which is not given but has still to be sought, whereas the other may be presupposed *rocher de bronce*^{EN14}. Even the older theologians were only partially consistent in this respect, according to the degree that they were sure of their subject, namely, the certain knowledge of God from His Word. To the extent that this was not the case, but they agreed with ancient philosophy in reflecting on God in relation to the world rather than with Holy Scripture in reflecting on the world in relation to God, their rational proofs of the existence of God and even their references to revelation necessarily take on a laboured and embarrassed character which might lead us, if we were so maliciously inclined, to agree with D. F. Strauss in his description and understanding of the whole history of theology as a continuous fighting retreat in face of the irresistible advance of a rational and empirical science which on the very different grounds of a triumphant human self-conceit is quite sure of its subject. In preoccupation with only one side of the question, there has been a dangerous failure to realise that the question of creation is not less but even more concerned with the reality of the creature than that of the Creator. Presupposing the certain knowledge of God in His Word, it is actually the case that the existence and being of the world are rendered far more problematical by the existence and being of God than *vice versa*. For how far do we know about the world and nature and history and above all ourselves with a certainty which makes quite indisputable the knowledge and statement that they and we really are, and really are what we are? How far can we ever of ourselves say that this is more than a plausible hypothesis? Are we so sure that the creature—heaven and earth and we ourselves—forms a sphere which is even possible side by side with God? What reasons have we for such a view? What place is there for another when God is there? How can there be another being side by side with His being? This is the question which must always be the first and more important concern of theology when it has the biblical witness to the relation between Creator and creature constantly and consistently before it. For according to this witness the transience and therefore the impossibility of the creature before its Creator is obviously a most urgent question. The statement : *Nihil constat de liberis actionibus Dei nisi ex revelatione*^{EN15}, was undoubtedly right; but it ought always to have been preceded by the statement: *Nihil constat de contingentia mundi nisi ex revelatione*^{EN16}. The following argument ought first to have been adduced against all science both ancient and modern. If the world is not created by God, it is not. If we do not recognise that it has been created by God, we do not recognise that it is. But we know that it has been created by God only on the ground of God's self-witness and therefore in faith. Therefore we know only in faith that the world is.

EN12 free act of God
EN13 by revelation
EN14 as a rock of certainty
EN15 The free acts of God cannot be known except by revelation
EN16 The objective reality of the world cannot be known except by revelation

The pressure exerted by science on theology could have been resisted if theology had been more energetically and effectively concerned with its own (*in thesi*^{EN17} solemnly enough affirmed) divine science; if it had realised that it is primarily the creature and not the Creator of whom we are not certain, and that in order to be certain of him we need proof or revelation. If it had said at once in this comprehensive sense that the creation of the world by God can be known only in faith, the unfortunate appearance of a rearguard action would have been avoided. Already in this delimitation faith would not only have been mentioned— [007] which might suggest a deliberate evasion—but confessed and vigorously and effectively exercised in the sense of Heb. 11³.

2. The proposition that God created heaven and earth and man asserts that this whole sphere is from God, willed and established by Him as a reality which is distinct from His own. In this respect, too, it contains within itself a negative and a positive. The negative is that the world is not alone—much less so than God. God could be alone; the world cannot. The world would not exist at all if God did not exist, and if it were not from Him. It is because it does not exist at all of itself, but only because God willed and created it, that it has no power over its existence and form; that it does not belong to itself; and that it cannot control itself. And the positive is that God is before the world; that He is an absolutely distinct and individual being in relation to it; that unlike the world He belongs to Himself and controls Himself; that He is completely self-sufficient because established and determined by Himself. And God is before the world in the strictest sense that He is its absolute origin, its purpose, the power which rules it, its Lord. For He created it. Through Him it came into being and through Him it is. Yet even this aspect of the creation dogma is not self-evident. The negative and positive assertions are possible, but again they are not necessary. The question of an external world-cause is pressing, but it is not unavoidable. Even the idea of an eternal world which is itself divine, and at the heart of which man can be the true place and bearer and content of its divinity, is not impossible. If it were true, then the world could also be alone. It could have come into being of its own accord, or it could be in a state of eternal becoming, and would thus control its own existence and form. There would then be no need for a God prior to it. It would require no external origin and purpose, no ruling power. No Creator would be needed. And if it is desired to regard the question of an external world-cause as unavoidable, the answer that God has created it would again be possible, but not so compelling as to exclude all kinds of other answers, or the assertion of other origins and lords. Even the claim that a wild chance, or the whim of a cosmic monster, has given it existence and made it its own master, cannot be described as a wholly unfounded hypothesis. In short, all sorts of negations of this aspect of the dogma and all sorts of counter-assertions are at least discussable, and will in fact be discussed as long as the world exists. It is true that they are also not demonstrable, but all very disputable hypotheses. But this is small comfort in view of the fact that the same is true of the statement of dogma so long as this is

---

^{EN17} in principle

5

not understood as a statement of faith—an answer to God's self-witness. Only if it is this is it futile to discuss what the world might be with or without an internal or external cause. Only if God is in fact its Creator, if it is in fact His

[008] creature, and if we have in fact to reckon with this because He Himself has told us, is the statement of dogma certain, demonstrable and indisputable on this side too. To believe that God has created the world is thus to take a bold step. If we take it, we must be careful that we are not merely advancing a plausible hypothesis besides which there can be many others that have a more or less good claim to be heard. We are in a sorry case if we are compelled to think and finally to live and die on the ground of this hypothesis. It is of little use if in answering the question of the origin of the world we can take steps which are only half certain—even if the hypothesis that we advance is a tolerably good one, and perhaps is in almost literal agreement with the statement of dogma. Understood and expressed as a mere opinion and hypothesis, the statement of dogma itself is poor comfort. Or is it the case that when we repeat this statement we are giving an answer to the divine self-witness, and therefore confessing a faith which puts an end once and for all to all other contradictory conjectures? We can only pray that this may be so. But it is a great and special thing to have and to confess the belief: *credo in Deum ... creatorem coeli et terrae*[EN18]. And we must not expect that a mere substitute will manifest the power which does, of course, reside in this confession.

It is extremely disturbing to read what the disciples of Schleiermacher thought it right and necessary to say on this matter. For example, A. Schweizer tells us: "When the absolute feeling of dependence with which we regard the whole world is applied to the objective notion that the world has a beginning, and developed *via causalitatis*[EN19], it gives rise to the doctrine of creation and determines God as the Creator. The conception thus arises, not merely of divine attributes, but also of divine functions; so that the omnipotence (to which all other attributes may already be reduced) is essentially creative in its actual expression" (*Gl.-Lehre d. ev. ref. Kirche* Vol. I, 1844, 296 f.). In R. A. Lipsius we read: "As man with his self-consciousness relates the world-consciousness posited with it to his God-consciousness, he places himself and his whole world in the relationship of dependence on God, and consequently regards the world as a creature" (*Lehrb. d. ev. prot. Dogmatik*[2], 1879, 294). "With reference to man and the world, the dogmatics of the Church attributes to God the three predicates of Creator, Sustainer and Ruler" (p. 237). "Thus to religious contemplation the world seems to be created, sustained and ruled by God, or, as regards its being, progress and teleology, grounded in divine causality" (p. 284). H. Lüdemann puts it in this way: "In virtue of his religious consciousness the Christian assumes that the world has arisen from God's creative power and, in accordance with the complete dependence of everything created, regards this creation as absolutely free and therefore also purely spiritual. He finds its motive, however, in the divine love. And in essentials he recognises the main features of his religious declaration in the biblical account of the Church's understanding of creation" (*Chr. Dogmatik* Vol. II, 1926, 282). It is hard to see why "the feeling of dependence should confine itself in its declarations entirely to its immediate self-experience. If the religious subject immediately extends its feeling of dependence to the world with which it finds itself in reciprocal oper-

---

[EN18] I believe in God ... maker of heaven and earth
[EN19] according to the argument from causation

ation, and therefore in the same position as itself, it must also say the same concerning it as its feeling of dependence compels it to say concerning itself. But this is not merely that it owes the continuation of its existence and preservation to God, but rather that its existence can only have its original source in God" (p. 283). For "if I am, my existence must have its basis in an existence which needs no basis." This is as such the unshakeable "egological" content of truth in the "cosmological" proof of God (p. 135f.). R. Seeberg may also be quoted to the same effect. If only one is certain of an "absolutely autonomous spirit which proves itself to be operative in the world," it must be admitted "that it is a justifiable logical postulate to enquire after a cause and purpose for the world. Now everything in the world is cause as well as effect. Thus nothing in the world can be only cause. Hence it is logical to postulate an extra-mundane cause which may rightly be described as self-caused. We have found such a cause, however, in the absolutely autonomous spirit of God. It is thus obvious that we must seek the desired first cause in the will of God" (*Chr. Dogm.* Vol. I. 1924, 351). [009]

All this is deeply disturbing because, although the statement of the dogma is formally approved and accepted, it is understood as a conception of man, who in this statement informs himself both about himself and also about the rest of the world, and whose task it is, as these theologians see it, to give himself this information. Constrained by his feeling of dependence, he finds his original source in God, and as he extends his feeling of dependence to the world, he makes the same discovery in relation to the world, namely, that it "seems to him" to be created, sustained and ruled by God. And so he "conceives" the creation dogma; he "determines" God as the Creator; he allows himself to "postulate" divine characteristics and functions, and to "attribute" to God the corresponding predicates; and he "puts" himself and his whole world in the relationship of dependence on God, as having "originated from God's creative power"; he "regards" it as creature, and its creation as free and spiritual, and motivated by God's love. As he sees it, he may and must "postulate" an extra-mundane cause of the world, and he makes the corresponding "religious statement," whose main features he "recognises" in essentials in the biblical account, and the Church's conception, of creation.

On the other hand, we will find in the details of this theology many of the vital points made by the Church about creation on the basis of what is stated in the Bible. But can they really be the same if they are made on this presupposition and in this form? Is it with impunity that we can translate the response to the divine self-witness—the statement of faith in creation (which is what the creation dogma really is)—into a postulate and declaration of the religious consciousness? The theology of the 19th century believed that in this way it could protect it against the attacks of certain opposing hypotheses concerning the origin of man and the world. But could it succeed in doing this by wrapping it in the garment of a hypothesis of this type? Is it surprising that this well meant and in every sense penetrating and painstaking attempt did not have the expected success with believing and unbelieving contemporaries? Is it surprising that in this translation the dogma could preserve only a small proportion of the impressive form in which once—in the time of the Church fathers and scholastics and even in the 16th and 17th centuries—it did not hesitate to confront as revealed truth and credal statement and mystery the clamant and hostile mythologies and philosophies of the day? When it is methodologically reduced to a level with these, being traced back to a profoundly pious discovery of man, who can obviously make very different discoveries, it is necessarily weakened and the Christian confession can only be uncertain— even though the translation says approximately the same as what has in fact to be said in reply to God's self-witness. The basis on which we make this statement is not without a bearing on its significance, and in the strict and ultimate sense on its meaning. No very solid structure can be built on the feeling of dependence.

[010]   In this connexion, it is worth remembering the very different example set in chapter 10, 6 of Augustine's *Confessions*. Augustine knew well enough the feeling of dependence—the recognition of the Creator in creation, in the world and in human consciousness. In face of this whole reality, overwhelmed by its lovable qualities and therefore in intimate communion with it, Augustine asks himself: *Quid autem amo, cum te amo*[EN20]? What do I love when I love my God? *Et quid est hoc? Interrogavi terram et dixit: Non sum, et quaecumque in eadem sunt, ista confessa sunt. Interrogavi mare et abyssos et reptilia animarum vivarum et responderunt: Non sumus Deus tuus; quaere super nos! Interrogavi auras flabiles, et inquit universus aer cum incolis suis: Fallitur Anaximenes; non sum Deus. Interrogavi coelum, solem, lunam, stellas; neque non sumus Deus quem quaeris, inquiunt. Et dixi omnibus iis quae circumstant fores carnis meae; dixistis mihi de Deo meo, quod vos non estis, dicite mihi de illo aliquid! Et exclamaverunt voce magna: Ipse fecit nos! ... Et direxi me ad me, et dixi mihi: Tu quis es? Et respondi: Homo!*[EN21] A man, who through the medium of his body has contact and communion with this universe of things, but more—a spirit, to whom physical messengers, his sense perceptions, brought, as to a president and judge, the great news: *Non sumus Deus, sed ipse fecit nos! Homo interior cognovit haec per exterioris ministerium; ego interior cognovi haec, ego, ego animus per sensus corporis mei*[EN22]. Up to this point the exposition of Augustine's could at a pinch be understood as a conception of the pious human consciousness. But all this—and it is here that Augustine's theology is already distinguished from that whose representatives we have just quoted—is not the real basis, but only a psychological description of the true knowledge of the Creator in contrast and relationship to His creation. The chapter begins, of course, with the supremely positive declaration: *Non dubia, sed certa conscientia, Domine, amo te. Percussisti cor meum verbo tuo, et amavi te*[EN23]. Heaven and earth and all that therein is do indeed summon him to love God. According to Rom. 1²⁰, they do not cease to deprive all men of any possible excuse. As a man, and therefore a physico-spiritual being, he is in a position to hear their voice and to give his approbation. *Altius autem tu misereberis cui misertus eris et misericordiam praestabis cui misericors fueris: alioquin coelum et terra surdis loquuntur laudes tuas.* [EN24] Augustine is well aware that the whole beauty of creation *non omnibus eadem loquitur*[EN25], although objectively its word is one and the same. He knows that it *aliter illi appareat, aliter huic;*[EN26] that it is silent for the one, and speaks for the other, although it does in fact speak to all. *Sed illi intelligunt qui euis vocem acceptam foris intus cum Veritate conferunt. Veritas enim dicit mihi: Non est Deus tuus coelum, et terra; neque omne*

[EN20] What do I love when I love you

[EN21] And what is it this God? I asked the earth, and it said: 'I am not,' and all that was in it confessed the same. I asked the sea and the depths and the living beings that swarm there, and they answered: 'We are not your God; seek Him above us!' I asked the airy breezes, and the whole realm of the atmosphere, with its inhabitants, said: 'Anaximenes was wrong; we are not God.' I asked the heavens, the sun, the moon, the stars: 'Neither are we the God whom you seek,' they said. And I spoke to everything surrounds my senses: 'You have spoken to me of my God, that you are not He. Tell me something about Him!' And they cried out with a loud voice: 'He made us!' ... And I turned to myself and said to myself: 'Who are you?' And I answered: 'A human being!'

[EN22] 'We are not God, but He made us!' The inner self came to know these things through the activity of the outer; the inner I came to know these things: I, myself, the soul through the senses of my body

[EN23] I love You, Lord, not with a doubtful but with a certain consciousness. You battered my heart with your word, and I loved You

[EN24] Indeed, You have mercy on whom You will have mercy and show compassion to whom You will be compassionate: otherwise heaven and earth speak Your praises to the deaf.

[EN25] does not speak the same things to everyone

[EN26] appears in one way to this person, in another to that *corpus*[EN27]. The *Veritas*[EN28], God Himself, has to speak directly to man, not through the voice of creation, but with its own voice, if his spirit as the *praeses et iudicans*[EN29] to whom the *carnales nuntii*[EN30] deliver that message of the universe is to hear and understand its voice and approve its message: *Non sumus Deus, sed ipse fecit nos*[EN31]! Hence it is the divine election of grace—He has mercy on whom He will have mercy—and the divine revelation (*Veritas dicit!*[EN32]) which open the way to the actual knowledge of the One who is more worthy to be loved than the whole universe of nature and spirit with all its lovable qualities. If the universe is not actually silent, it is still silent to those who are not participators in the truth, i.e., in the direct self-revelation of God. We obviously cannot say that Augustine's concept of *Veritas*[EN33] has all the theological clarity which is needed in its distinction from each and every human self-explanation. It is thus all the more important to see that even in the prevailing obscurity *Veritas*[EN34], being identical with God's spoken Word, is plainly a source of knowledge of a very different order from the witness which man tries to give himself in his unity and communion with heaven and earth. This very different witness is needed as a basis if the statement about God the Creator is to have greater content and significance than all its antitheses. In Augustine it has this foundation, and it is for this reason that in his writings it has an emphasis which it could not possibly have in the theological reinterpretation which has claimed our attention.

3. The statement which calls God the Creator of heaven and earth may be [011] traced back in all its explicit and implicit elements to the linguistic usage of Holy Scripture. The concept of creation to which it points and which may be gathered from it is thus pre-determined by this linguistic usage. If we are to honour this statement as an integral part of the Christian confession we are not in any sense free to fill it out at will even in respect of any one of its constituent elements. On the contrary, we must adhere to the biblical witness in its context of Old Testament and New Testament, of promise and fulfilment. The statement has reference to this context. Like the other credal statements, this too gathers up the witness to Christ which Christendom has heard from the very outset in the context of Scripture and by which it is constituted the Church. But in the context of the Old and New Testament the witness to Christ takes the form of revelation and self-witness, and it is in this way, if not always with equal consistency, that it has always been basically understood by the Christian Church. It is an appeal to faith. It can be understood and accepted only in faith. This also applies to the statement that God is the Creator of heaven and earth. In all its elements it is an answer to the witness to Christ, to the divine self-witness of the Old and New Testaments in its diversity and unity. It can be accepted and understood only on this basis and therefore in faith, or not at all. In view of what it says we have no alternative but to realise that it

---

[EN27] But they understand who join in its voice, received within their senses, with the Truth. For the Truth says to me: 'Your God is not heaven, or earth; neither is it any body at all.'
[EN28] Truth
[EN29] ruler and judge
[EN30] fleshy messengers
[EN31] 'We are not God, but He made us!'
[EN32] The Truth speaks!
[EN33] the Truth
[EN34] the Truth

speaks of the mystery which constitutes the Church. Otherwise we have not even the faintest realisation of what it really speaks. At this juncture we can only make anticipatory reference to the specific character given to its most important elements by this derivation.

(*a*) The subject "God" of which it speaks—and in the creed this obviously brackets all three articles—is not synonymous with the concept of a world-cause, rightly or wrongly postulated, disclosed or fulfilled. We may take any view we like of the existence or nature of a world-cause, but it is always posited by man, and therefore even if it is an uncreated, creative and supremely perfect being, it still belongs to the creaturely sphere. It is not God. It is a successful or unsuccessful product of the human mind. It is not identical with the *Creator coeli et terrae*[EN35]. Nor can it be subsequently identified with Him and given His titles and predicates. Whenever this happens, belief in the Creator loses its basis and therefore its certainty, its original meaning and therefore its credibility and practical import. The God who created heaven and earth is God "the Father," i.e., the Father of Jesus Christ, who as such in eternal generation posits Himself in the Son by the Holy Spirit, and is not therefore in any sense posited from without or elsewhere. It is as this Eternal Father, determined in the act of His free expression and therefore not from without but from within, determining Himself in His Son by the Holy Spirit and Himself [012] positing everything else, that He is also the Creator. And it is again as this Eternal Father, and not in any other way, that He reveals Himself as the Creator, i.e., in Jesus Christ His Son by the Holy Ghost, in exact correspondence to the way in which He has inwardly resolved and decided to be the Creator. As He cannot be the Creator except as the Father, He is not known at all unless He is known in this revelation of Himself.

It is unfortunately true that from the very first the Church has often missed this first and decisive point. One of the earliest examples of this is to be found in the *Apology of Aristides* (chapter 1): θεωρήσας τὸν οὐρανὸν καὶ τὴν γῆν καὶ τὴν θάλασσαν, ἥλιόν τε καὶ σελήνην καὶ τὰ λοιπά, ἐθαύμασα τὴν διακόσμησιν τούτων. ἰδὼν δὲ τὸν κόσμον καὶ τὰ ἐν αὐτῷ πάντα, ὅτι κατὰ ἀνάγκην κινεῖται, συνῆκα τὸν κινοῦντα καὶ διακρατοῦντα εἶναι θεόν. πᾶν γὰρ τὸ κινοῦν ἰσχυρότερον τοῦ κινουμένου, καὶ τὸ διακρατοῦν ἰσχυρότερον τοῦ διακρατουμένου ἐστίν. αὐτὸν οὖν λέγω εἶναι θεὸν τὸν συντησάμενον τὰ πάντα καὶ διακρατοῦντα, ἄναρχον καὶ ἀίδιον, ἀθάνατον καὶ ἀπροσδεῆ, ἀνώτερον πάντων τῶν παθῶν καὶ ἐλαττωμάτων, ὀργῆς τε καὶ λήθης καὶ ἀγνοίας καὶ τῶν λοιπῶν. δι᾽ αὐτοῦ δὲ τὰ πάντα συνέστηκεν[EN36].

[EN35] Maker of heaven and earth

[EN36] When I observed the heavens and the earth and the sea, the sun and the moon and the rest, I was amazed at their order. And when I saw the world and everything in it, that everything is moved by necessity, I understood that God was the one who moved and controlled things. For everything that causes motion is greater than that which is moved, and the director is greater than that which is directed. So I say that God is the one who frames and upholds all things, that He is without superior and eternal, immortal and without need, above all suffering and lack, above anger and forgetfulness and ignorance and all other passions. And through Him all things hold together

Note the θεωρήσας, the ἐθαύμασα, the ἰδών, the συνῆκα and the λέγω EN37. As the Christian philosopher does what other philosophers and inventors of myths have always been able to do and have in fact done, i.e., as he constructs a view of things by way of observation and reflection, he comes to the conclusion that the assumption of a principle which is superior to the world is unavoidable, and decides to accept the reality of this unavoidable principle and to call it God. In its main features this has happened time and again. It is obvious that in this process God's revelation and faith in it can be relevant only when the philosopher makes up his mind to give to the product of his speculation or poetic art the name of "God." It is equally obvious, however, that even at this point the relevance can only be theoretical. For the "God" who is here made out to be the Creator, or the "Creator" who is here made out to be God, whose being seems to consist decisively in the fact that it is absolutely different from the world and cannot be assailed by its frailties—what has this "God" to do with the Father Almighty of the creed? The way to the knowledge of this "Creator" was obvious from the very outset, and it was necessarily the way to the concept of the absolute. And this concept was maintained in being in view of the constant desire to go this way to the Creator, so that the whole history of dogma has known its ghostly shadow, continually hiding the real content of the Christian confession and threatening to destroy its credibility by its own incredibility, and to deprive it of any true meaning by its own meaninglessness in practice.

In face of it we have simply to remember that the God of the Christian confession, which undoubtedly goes back to Gen. 1^1, is *Elohim*, the God of Israel: that is, the God, who according to Jer. 18^{1-6} does with this people as the potter does with clay; who, according to Is. 22^{11} and 37^{26}, and 2 K. 19^{25}, long ago, from the "former days," willed and prepared what He would cause to come to pass in the history of this people with a view to the goal of this history. The beginning of this history is the history of the creation. And it is only in this way that this is the beginning of world history. And the Lord of this sphere is God the Creator; and it is only as such that He is the Lord of the sphere of the world. This relationship can tolerate no dissolution. The way it indicates cannot be circumvented. Every supposed short-cut leads elsewhere than to the God who created heaven and earth. We recall the *parallelismus membrorum*EN38 in Is. 17^7: "At that day shall a man look to his Maker, and his eyes shall have respect to the Holy One of Israel." We remember how the unity emerges in relation to the function of Cyrus in Is. 45^{1-13}, and particularly in vv. 6 and 7: "I am the Lord and there is none else. I form the light and create darkness: I make peace and create evil: I the Lord do all these things" (cf. also Is. 44^{24}). And we think of the scene in Rev. 4 where first and foremost the throne of God is surrounded, not by the four beasts representing the cosmos as such, but by Israel and the Church represented in their unity by the four and twenty elders—not forgetting the "seven lamps of fire which are the seven spirits of God." And if v. 9 tells us that the four beasts also give praise and honour and thanks to Him who sits on the throne and lives for ever and ever, according to v. 10 f. it is again the four and twenty elders that fall down before Him that sits on the throne and worship Him that lives for ever and ever, and cast their crowns before the throne and give voice and articulation as it were to creation's praise. It is obviously they alone who know and can say: "Thou art worthy, O Lord, to receive glory and honour and power: for thou hast created all things, and for thy pleasure they are and were created." To see the Holy One of Israel it is thus necessary to be called and to be in the community gathered around Him who sits upon the throne and to be able to make that statement about God the Creator. God the Creator is not the supreme being of our own choice and fancy. He is the Lord of the history of Israel. He is the One who sits upon this

[013]

EN37 I observed ... I was amazed ... I saw ... I understood ... I say
EN38 parallelism of the members

throne. And those who stand and fall down before this throne are those who know and confess Him, the participants in this history. The rest of creation with its praise of the Creator is also gathered around this throne; it exists for the sake of this history. The necessary connexion between the first and the other two articles of the creed, between the beginning and the continuation of the ways and works of the one God, must not be forgotten if in relation to dogma we are to maintain our birthright and not to sacrifice it for a mess of pottage. It is thus clear that when the dogma is genuinely understood in this respect it can be heard only as a summons to faith.

(*b*) When we come to the predicate "Creator" in the credal statement the main point to be made is that it encloses an event, a completed act. The *Creator* does not just "exist." He has done something: *creavit*[EN39]; He has accomplished the *creatio*[EN40]. The statement that God has created heaven and earth speaks of an incomparable perfect, and tells us that this perfect is the beginning of heaven and earth. It is also true that this beginning does not cease, but determines their duration; that the Creator remains Creator and as such is present as such to His creation—actively present, and not leaving His work behind, or abandoning it to someone else or to itself, like a shipbuilder his ship, or a watchmaker his watch. To the uniqueness of this perfect there belongs the fact that it also contains a present. But this does not alter the fact that it is a perfect, referring to something which has happened, and happened once and for all. In its own way the first article of the creed with its substantive *Creator* speaks no less historically than the second with its many verbal forms. It is for this very reason that the Creator cannot be changed into a world-cause, a supreme or first cause or a principle of being. All such concepts denote a timeless relationship, i.e., one which exists always and everywhere, analogous to the internal cosmic relationships of cause and effect. We must give them a new significance, therefore, if we are to use them to describe God the Creator. And this new meaning must be so radically different that the analogy to the internal cosmic relationships is completely broken. In contrast to everything that we know of origination and causation, creation denotes the divine action which has a real analogy, a genuine point of comparison, only in the eternal begetting of the Son by the Father, and therefore only in the inner life of God Himself, and not at all in the life of the creature. The historical secret of the creation is that outwith His own reality God willed and brought into being a correspondence to that which, as the constitutive act of His deity, forms the secret of His own existence and being. This is the incomparable perfect to which the creed looks back as the beginning of heaven and earth. Thus creation does also denote a relationship between God and the world, i.e., the relationship of absolute superiority and lordship on the one hand and of absolute dependence on the other. Creation does not signify, however, only a mythological or speculative intensification of the concept of this relationship, but its presupposition and decisive meaning. That is, creation speaks primarily

[014]

[EN39] he has created
[EN40] creation

of a basis which is beyond this relationship and makes it possible; of a unique, free creation of heaven and earth by the will and act of God.

This point of the dogma ought never to have been suppressed, or obscured and trivialised, by an overemphasising of the supra-temporal character of the act of creation on the one side, and the present character of the Creator-creature relationship on the other. It was a dangerous encroachment when some of the fathers (Theoph. of Antioch, *Ad Aut.*, 11, 10, Clement of Alex., *Strom.*, VI, 7, Ambrose, *Hexaem.*, 1, 4, 15, as well as Augustine. *Conf.*, XI, 8f., cf. 24) wanted to translate *b'reshith*[EN41], Gen. 1, ¹, by *ἐν Λόγῳ*[EN42]. It is true that creation took place by God's Word, but it certainly took place "in the beginning," i.e., as the beginning of all things. It was their historical entry into reality. Even Jn. 1¹ does not say that the Logos was the beginning, but that it was "in the beginning," i.e., that it was apart from Him, that it was with God and was God Himself; and it was also in and with the beginning of all that is distinct from God as created by Him. And His participation in creation is described in Jn. 1³, ⁹ by the same *ἐγένετο*[EN43] as in v. 14 describes His incarnation, and therefore surely denotes a unique historical act, and therefore (without detriment to its eternal basis and comprehensive significance for every age) not a mere timeless relationship between God and man. On very different presuppositions from those of the fathers, the Jewish commentator, B. Jacob, has also maintained (*Das erste Buch der Thora*, 1934, p. 20) that the *b'reshith* in Gen. 1¹ refers to "a unique, absolute pre-temporality," to "the pre-condition of all occurrence in time." In this case, however, the ensuing history of creation and the history of Israel which developed out of it confront it as time confronts eternity. The contingent, unique act of creation does not therefore belong to this history. It does not form its beginning. Indeed, strictly speaking, it is not even an event. It confronts history as an absolute transcendental origin. In view of the Jewish denial of the Messiahship of Jesus and the incarnation of the Word, this view of creation is supremely logical. In the Christian view, however, the circles which there confront one another in clear separation, touch and overlap—as they already touch and overlap and do not exclude one another in the person of Jesus Christ, and therefore in the concept of the Word of God, and indeed in the trinitarian concept and the understanding of the eternal will and decree of God. Because God created time, i.e., our time, with the world, it is not intrinsically alien to Him; for even eternity is His time, in the light of which He created our time. And as God founds and rules creaturely history as the salvation history resolved by Him, the reality of history again is not intrinsically alien to Him. Indeed even before the beginning of creaturely history it pre-exists originally in His own life as Father, Son and Holy Ghost, and indeed in the form of contingent history in His eternal decision regarding this creaturely history, in His election of grace as the eternal beginning of all His ways and works. Thus even this eternal beginning of all things in God does not exclude but includes the possibility that the completion of their creation may also be a historical secret, a beginning of the world with time and to that extent in time, a first history. And that this is what it was is what is actually maintained by the Christian confession concerning the Creator and His work. This assertion is based on the unity of God and man, eternity and time, God's absolute being and contingent will, as revealed and operative in the person of Jesus Christ. In it the Christian confession recognises the beginning of all the ways and works of God, the historicity of the eternal being and will of God, and therefore the diversity but not the separation of the inward life of God and His outward life which establishes, sustains and rules the world. It regards the beginning of the world, posited by the will and act

[015]

[EN41] in the beginning
[EN42] in the beginning ... in the Word
[EN43] was

of God, not merely as supra-historical, but also as historical. It is no mere accident that the substantive "Creator" occurs only once in the New Testament (1 Pet. 4^19), the normal rule being to use participles and relative clauses, thus explicitly understanding creation as a historical act of God. The result is, of course, that conversely the creed can regard the whole continuation and duration of creation as not merely historical but also, in the sense of this beginning, as supra-historical; as *creatio continua*^EN44 and not just as an immanent development on the basis of the transcendental origin of the whole. For the same reason it can also look forward to the creation of a new heaven and earth—no less contingently historical than the first. *Creator* means *creavit*^EN45, and this *creavit*^EN46 characterises the statement regarding creation as a statement of faith in the strictest sense of the term.

(*c*) In content, the predicate "Creator" speaks of an incomparable act. It tells us that God is the One who, although wholly self-sufficient in His possession of all perfections, and absolutely glorious and blessed in His inner life, did not as such will to be alone, and has not actually remained alone, but in accordance with His own will, and under no other inward constraint than that of the freedom of His love, has, in an act of the overflowing of His inward glory, posited as such a reality which is distinct from Himself. And it says of the world that it received through an act of God the reality, existence and form which it did not have and could not therefore give itself because it did not exist at all. It says that the world itself, in respect of its existence and essence, is an absolute gift of God. "Create" in the sense of the Christian creed denotes this act. Its *terminus a quo*^EN47 is the good-pleasure of the free omnipotence of the divine love. Its *terminus ad quem*^EN48 is the reality, elected and posited by this divine good-pleasure and established, determined and limited by this omnipotence of love, of something which is not divine and the existence and essence of which can be described only as absolute dependence on this act and therefore on God Himself, so that they can be understood only in this relationship to Him, and therefore as those of a "creature" which belongs wholly and utterly to Him. No matter how the relationship between the beginning and continuation of creation may be understood either exegetically or systematic-

[016] ally, there can be no doubt that in every case it can be understood only as this act with its very unequal counterpart and wholly dissimilar presuppositions; only in this irreversibility and this absolutely contingent event which we can comprehend and deduce neither from God nor from the world; only as the secret of the actuality of the Creator and the creature, of their association, and of the indissoluble order of their association. However things may stand between God on the one side and the world and man on the other, this presupposition is always the basis. And whatever may happen between these two, this act will always be the background. In this sense God will always be the Creator, and all reality which is distinct from Him will always be His creature. For this

---

EN44 continuing creation
EN45 He created
EN46 created
EN47 starting point
EN48 ending point

Creator-creature relationship—established, determined and limited by this act—corresponds externally to the inner life of the Father, the Son and the Holy Ghost. It is the execution of the contingent decision of God in His predestination. If the creation is this secret, it can be known only by the revelation of God Himself, and it can therefore be appropriated only in faith; that is, in the faith which has actually before it both aspects of this incomprehensible, indeducible and contingent act as presented to it by the act itself. A knowledge of the Creator and His work which is attained only by changing and weakening the real meaning of this predicate, and therefore otherwise than by revelation and faith, will have no reference to its true theme, and is in fact quite impossible as a knowledge of the Creator and His work.

Among the words used by the Bible to describe the divine creation (cf. for what follows the Art. κτίζειν by W. Foerster, *TWzNT*, III), the Old Testament *bara'*[EN49] is lexicographically unequivocal to the extent that in the strict sense—as in its immediate appearance in Gen. 1^1—it can denote only the divine creation in contrast to all other: the creation which does not work on an existing object or material which can be made by the Creator into something else; the *creatio ex nihilo*[EN50] whose Subject can only be God and no one apart from Him—no creature. B. Jacob (*op. cit.*, p. 22) calls the statement in Gen. 1^1, with reference to this *bara'*, "the first great act of the Torah, of the religious genius of Israel." But this of all statements surely cannot be understood when we think that we can say this of it, turning the glory of the God which this *bara'* proclaims and to which it obviously redounds into a glorification of Israel and its religious genius. Where is this genius in the LXX rendering of *bara'* as ἐποίησεν[EN51]? But be that as it may, the miracle of the will and act of God on the one side, and of the existence and essence of heaven and earth on the other, is not bound to this untranslateable word by which it is denoted. Both the Old and New Testaments are sparing in their use of ultimate and decisive words and more prodigal with penultimate terms. There is no reason for surprise, therefore, if in addition to the unique *bara'* other verbs are used to describe the creative activity of God—verbs which in themselves and apart from their context may not have the force of this *bara'*, but which stand in the light of it and may be interpreted by it: *qanah* (or κτίζειν), to acquire or procure or prepare for oneself; *yatsar* (or πλάσσειν), to fashion or form or shape in some way; *'asah* (or ποιεῖν), to manufacture or to make; and *yasad* (or θεμελιοῦν) to establish. When these terms are applied to the creative act of God, there can be no real doubt that they too denote that wonderful relationship between God and the object of His act—the incomprehensible, indeducible and contingent transition from the potentiality which has its basis only in God Himself to the actuality of another reality by the execution of His divine will and decree. The God of the Old Testament is the Creator in this sense, and everything that is not God is opposed to Him in this sense as creature. It is significant that without a single exception the LXX carefully avoided the familiar Greek verb δημιουργεῖν[EN52] as a rendering of the Hebrew words used to denote the creative activity of God to the Greeks. A δημιουργός[EN53] is really one who performs a definite work for the public, i.e., the seer, or doctor, or builder, or herald, or singer. More

[017]

[EN49] to create
[EN50] creation from nothing
[EN51] He made
[EN52] to fabricate or craft
[EN53] craftsman

commonly, he is the artisan, and even more commonly the expert in contrast to the lay-man—the man who unlike others can make something out of a given material. When δημιουργός EN54 is used of God in Greek literature it is to describe Him as the One who has transformed the world from ἀταξία EN55 into κόσμος EN56. The God of the Old Testament does, of course, fashion the world, but He does so as the Creator. In evident awareness of this, the LXX does not wish to equate Him with the demiurge of Greek philosophy and mythology. It was left to Christian Gnosticism to obliterate this distinction. Apart from this restraint, the positive fact is equally impressive that the LXX preferred κτίζειν EN57 to ποιεῖν, πλάσσειν EN58 and θεμελιοῦν EN59, so that this has become the true technical term for the divine creation. According to Foerster, κτίζειν EN60 signifies "the decisive act of will which underlies the erection, institution or foundation (e.g., of a city, theatre, temple, baths, etc.) and which is then followed by the actual execution (δημιουργεῖν EN61)''. Since the days of Alexander the Great, κτίζειν EN62 in the Hellenistic sense has had particular reference to the autocratic ruler with aspiration to divinity, who irrespective of what was there before causes a πόλις EN63 to arise by his word or command or will (backed by his power), thus acquiring divine honour in this city, since it owes its very existence wholly to him as its κτίστης EN64. The word *bara'* is not consistently translated κτίζειν EN65. The first variation occurred as early as the creation story. On the other hand, it is true to say that this Greek word, like the Hebrew, indicates the direction of biblical thinking in this matter. In both cases we are pointed to the transcendent and therefore unique character, to the mystery, of the divine action described as creation. We cannot lay too strong an emphasis on this mystery. According to Heb. 11³ creation is coming into being which no φαινόμενα EN66 either precede or underlie. According to Rom. 4¹⁷ it is an act of God which can be linked only with the resur-rection of the dead—creation and resurrection being distinctive marks of the God to whom Abraham yielded the faith which was imputed to him for righteousness. A number of pas-sages in the New Testament deal with the καταβολὴ κόσμου EN67 beyond which nothing exists or is even conceivable (according to Eph. 1⁴) apart from our election in Jesus Christ as the eternal decree of the will of God, and therefore apart from God Himself. And if more is needed, we are taught by the declaration of Ps. 73²⁵: "Whom have I in heaven but thee? and there is none upon the earth that I desire beside thee" by Mk. 13³¹, that heaven and earth will pass away, but the words of Jesus will not pass away; and by the definite expectation of a new heaven and a new earth in Rev. 21¹ and 2 Pet. 3¹³, how immeasurably transcendent in the sense of the biblical witness is the act denoted when we say that God created the present heaven and earth. How can this act, and the relationship based upon it, be really known except in Jesus Christ, and therefore in the faith of the New Testament witnesses? And how can it be confessed, therefore, except in the form of an article of the Christian creed?

EN54 craftsman
EN55 disorder
EN56 cosmos
EN57 to create
EN58 to make, to fashion
EN59 to establish
EN60 to create
EN61 to craft
EN62 to create
EN63 city-state
EN64 creator
EN65 to create
EN66 phenomena
EN67 foundation of the world

(*d*) The object to which the statement about creation refers is "heaven and earth." Whatever these two terms may denote both individually and in concert, there can be no doubt that in the sense of the biblical witness from Genesis to the Revelation of John, they denote the sum of the reality which is distinct from God. They tell us that within the one reality which is distinct from God [018] there is this distinction of heaven and earth. This distinction is relative in view of their common distinction from God. It is relative to the extent that it does not exclude but includes an association and even a unity of both. But it is a distinction which is definitely posited and cannot be dissolved in any association or unity of the two. Heaven is not earth and earth is not heaven. Yet they do not stand in a relationship of equilibrium and symmetry. Heaven undoubtedly has a definite superiority over earth. This certainly does not approach the primacy of God in relation to the whole, but it is still a real and ineffaceable superiority. It is the higher creation within the whole, distinguished both outwardly and inwardly. Earth for its part is not without God. But it is also not without heaven. It is under it, and in this way it participates in its distinction. But it has its own dignity, which in relationship to God is not less, but which is determined and ordered by God through its inner creaturely relationship with heaven. Heaven and earth in this differentiation form a totality. They are one in the fact they are not God, but are distinct from God, and yet willed and posited by God. In this way they are the totality of the reality distinct from God. What is not divine, what is not God Himself, is heaven and earth in this difference and homogeneity. The statement that God created heaven and earth tells us, therefore, that God created the whole, i.e., everything that is not God Himself, from the very highest within this sphere to the very lowest. It also tells us that there is nothing in this sphere which did not require His creation in order to be; and also nothing which He did not consider worthy for His creation, i.e., nothing which does not have both the lowliness and the glory of the creature; which is not absolutely dependent on the Creator and absolutely upheld by Him. And since the reference is to the totality of creation, to heaven and earth, it is also to man. All that the Bible and the creed say about creation as a whole points to man—and most impressively because they do not name him. They do not need to name him because in him heaven and earth are together in this fixed order; because man is and represents the secret of the creature. They do not wish to name him because it is by this solemn refusal to do so that they say the decisive thing about him—that he is on earth and under heaven, and therefore between these two worlds, which for all their distinction are still the one world created by God. The reason why God created this world of heaven and earth, and why the future world will be a new heaven and a new earth, is that God's eternal Son and Logos did not will to be an angel or animal but a man, and that this and this alone was the content of the eternal divine election of grace. He it is for whose sake God loved man from eternity and for whose sake He willed and as the Creator gave reality to the existence and being of man as this creature on earth and under heaven. His words—as the seed and

[019] pledge of a new heaven and a new earth—will not pass away, even if this heaven and earth pass away as they have come into being. He (in His humanity) is the centre of all creation, of the whole reality of which the creed says that God created it, that it has duration and existence through God alone. From this side too, then, the statement of the creed is a statement of faith. Nor is it a subsidiary and incidental statement—a mere prolegomenon of faith. But in its own manner and form it is the one and only statement of the confession. We believe in Jesus Christ when we believe in God the Father Almighty, Maker of heaven and earth. These words of the first article do not make sense if for all the particularity of their meaning they do not anticipate the confession of the second and also the third articles.

The particular nature of heaven and earth, their inter-relationship and their unity in man, require many exegetical and terminological elucidations for which we have no space in the present context.

The following points are, however, incontestable and of great significance for our purpose. The Old and New Testament Scriptures, when they speak of God's creation, actually do so in such a way that they repeatedly and most emphatically describe it as twofold, and then just as emphatically comprehend the two elements in a single totality, and understand this totality as the creation willed and created by God. Rather significantly, the Old Testament has no word for this uniform conception of the "world." It occasionally uses (Ps. 8⁶, Is. 44²⁴) the expression "the whole" (*hak-kol*), but as a rule it can only enumerate the various elements. To some extent "heaven and earth" form the backbone of this enumeration, although the order may be reversed according to the standpoint of the passage concerned, and sometimes (as in Ex. 20¹¹ and Neh. 9⁶) the sea may be added (to which there is a special relationship!). Everything that goes by the name of and is occasionally referred to as creature (in great detail in passages like Job 38 f.)—the sun and moon and stars in the one case and earthly creatures in the other—is what is "therein" (Ex. 20¹¹), comprehended in heaven and earth, the inhabitants of heaven and earth. The same usage persists for the most part in the New Testament. According to the solemn exposition of Ex. 20¹¹ in Rev. 10⁶, God is He "who created the heaven καὶ τὰ ἐν αὐτῷ EN68, and the earth καὶ τὰ ἐν αὐτῇ EN69, and the sea καὶ τὰ ἐν αὐτῇ EN70" (cf. also Rev. 5¹³, Ac. 4²⁴, 14¹⁵). According to Col. 1¹⁶, He created τὰ πάντα ἐν τοῖς οὐρανοῖς καὶ ἐπὶ τῆς γῆς, τὰ ὁρατὰ καὶ τὰ ἀόρατα EN71, and according to Hebrews (1², 11³) the αἰῶνες EN72. In Jn. 1¹⁰, Rom. 1²⁰ and Ac. 17²⁴, and in connexion with the concept of the καταβολή EN73, there is mention of the κόσμος EN74 as the object of creation.

This double kingdom is the totality (τὰ πάντα EN75 in Col. 1¹⁶, Eph. 3⁹ and Rev. 4¹¹) of that which is created. In order to understand the biblical witness we must bear in mind the three-fold content of the statement. That this kingdom is double characterises it—more precise elucidation will be required—as one in which there is an upper and a lower, and therefore an orientation even within creaturely life, i.e., the possibility and necessity of a definite,

---

EN68 the whole
EN69 and all that is in it
EN70 and all that is in it
EN71 all things that are in heaven, and that are in earth, visible and invisible
EN72 ages
EN73 foundation
EN74 world
EN75 all things

irreversible direction. Augustine's interpretation may be quoted in this connexion (*Conf.* XII, 7, 7): *De nihilo fecisti coelum et terram, magnum quiddam et parvum quiddam ... unum prope te, alterum prope nihil, unum quo superior tu esses, alterum quo inferius nihil esset*[EN76]. And Col. 1[16] gives us the direction for further thinking on this matter. There is in this sphere of creation both a lower, smaller and visible and also an upper, larger and invisible reality. The two spheres have been repeatedly understood in this sense since the time of Irenaeus (*Adv. o.h.* II, 30, 9), especially by Augustine, but also in the later confession of the Church since the *Nicaenum*[EN77]. This double sphere is, however, the totality of creation, which as such is homo-   [020] geneous and united, and in this homogeneity and unity the only creature. This is true even though, according to the witness of both Testaments, it is as such immensely rich and varied, deep and incomprehensible. No matter what God has created, it is to be found in this double sphere of reality. It may take thousands of forms unknown to us. It may be infinite in itself. But there is no reality outside this sphere apart from that of God Himself. In heaven and earth and man as their unity, we have to do with the work of the whole, undivided love of God. As the creature in whom these two are one, we are the object of His whole, undivided attention. And the fact that this double sphere is created as a totality by God—$\dot{\epsilon}\xi$ $o\tilde{v}$ $\tau\grave{a}$ $\pi\acute{a}\nu\tau a$[EN78] (1 Cor. 8[6], Rom. 11[36]) and: *ex omnibus nihil subtractum est*[EN79] (Irenaeus, *Adv. o. h.* I, 22, 1)—means that there may be pretended but no genuine gods and lords, either here below on earth in the sphere of our observation of accessible natural elements and forces, or up above in heaven in the higher, hidden regions of the spirit and spirits. There can be no greater secularisation of that which on its highest as on its lowest rung belongs to *saeculum*[EN80] than the recognition that God really created heaven as well as earth. For according to this insight even the most powerful dominion in the former sphere is no less really in His hand than the most obvious impotence. That the totality has been created by God also means that there can be many pretended but no genuine things that are not within this totality; nothing wholly contemptible either in heaven or on earth, either in the realm of the spirit or in that of matter. And there can be no greater honour for the secular reality of that which is not God than the recognition that God really created earth as well as heaven. For according to this insight even that which is most miserable in the sphere of earth is no less really in His hand than that which most obviously is glorious in the courts of heaven. *Ecce sunt coelum et terra; clamant quod facta sint; mutantur enim atque variantur .... Clamant etiam, quod se ipsa non fecerint: Ideo sumus, quia facta sumus; non ergo eramus antequam essemus, ut fieri possemus a nobis*[EN81] (Augustine, *Conf.* XI, 4, 6).

And in the centre between heaven and earth as their unity is man, who, according to Gen. 2[7], was formed from the dust of the ground, had breathed into him the breath of life, so that he was made this special "living soul" (*nephesh ḥayyah*). Is. 45[12] thinks of him in the same way: "I have made the earth, and created man upon it: I, even with my hands, have stretched out the heavens." And it is obvious that Ps. 8 envisages him similarly. He is a "babe and suckling" in comparison with heaven as the firmament established by God, and yet "only a little less

---

EN76 From nothing You made heaven and earth, one great and the other small ... one near to You, the other near to nothingness, so that you might be higher than the one and that nothing might be lower than the other

EN77 Nicene Creed

EN78 from whom are all things

EN79 there is nothing excepted from all this

EN80 the present age

EN81 Consider the heavens and the earth: they cry out that they were made; they are subject to change and variation .... And they cry out that they did not make themselves: So also we are only because we were made; therefore we were not before we were made, as though we could have been the agents of our own creation.

than the angels," appointed to have dominion over all living creatures: "What is man that thou art mindful of him? and the son of man that thou visitest him?" (v. 4). It is surprising that man is not seen more frequently and emphatically in this context, although it is undoubtedly as the climax and goal of the divine work that he appears in the two creation narratives in Gen. 1 and 2. In the great creation Psalm 104 he is mentioned only incidentally: "When the sun ariseth," and the young lions return to their dens, "man goeth forth unto his work and to his labour until the evening" (v. 23). In the rest of the Psalm he is then completely lost in a host of other creatures. Similarly, in the great speech of God "out of the whirlwind" in Job 38 f., there is no mention of him among the other wonderful created figures. Unforgettable things are said about the earth, the sea and the stars, the foolish ostrich and the spirited horse, and finally the hippopotamus and the crocodile; but man seems to be ignored, except that it is he, in the person of the murmuring Job, who must constantly allow himself to be led *ad absurdum*[EN82] by the question whether he had conceived, elected, determined and posited all these things. We certainly cannot ignore Ps. 139$^{14f.}$: "I will praise thee; for I am fearfully and wonderfully made; marvellous are thy works; and that my soul knoweth right well. My substance was not hid from thee, when I was made in secret, and curiously wrought in the lowest parts of the earth. Thine eyes did see my

[021]

substance, yet being unperfect; and in thy book all my members were written, which in continuance were fashioned, when as yet there was none of them." To this we may add allusions like those in Ps. 119^{73} and Job 10^8, but it is not often that the creation of man is magnified in this way. Was Luther right or wrong, then, when in the *Smaller Catechism* he reversed this relationship, and opened the explanation of the first article with the words: "I believe that God has created me and all creatures, and that He has given me and maintains a body and soul, eyes, ears and all members, reason and every sense … "? It is certainly not for nothing that the Bible does not speak in a way which is so explicitly anthropocentric. For it is no help to the knowledge of God as Creator and man as His creature, and therefore the knowledge of the difference and true relation between them both, if man thinks of himself as the central point in creation otherwise than in fidelity to the divinely posited upper and lower levels as in Ps. 8. Yet Luther was also right in his own way. As compared with Gen. 1–2 the pictures in Ps. 104 and Job 38 f. are undoubtedly like picture puzzles in which the true object is as such incorporated into many others and thus concealed. In them man has to be found, or to find himself, as the secret of heaven and earth. In Job. 38 f. it is to him that all these figures are brought forward as pertinent questioners, forcing him to withdraw his accusation, to regret his defiance, and to make his peace with God (42$^{1f.}$), and thus making possible and accomplishing his reinstatement (42$^{7f.}$). According to Ps. 104$^{14f.}$, it is to supply the needs of man that the earth brings forth its fruits: "That food may come forth from the earth; and wine that maketh glad the heart of man, and oil to make his face shine, and bread which strengtheneth man's heart." And it is man who in face of the marvels of God's creation addressed himself at the beginning and end of the 104th Psalm: "Bless the Lord, O my soul." Man was certainly not required to make the work of creation great and glorious. As Luther so profoundly emphasises, man is only the eye and ear, the reason and sense, to perceive the greatness and glory of it; and only the mouth appointed to praise this work. But for this very reason he is the more impressively accredited with his right and incomparable honour in the centre of the whole, and his existence and being are the more eloquently described, than is the case when he is made the object of special praise, as so often in the piety of the Enlightenment. But the knowledge of man's existence and being and right and honour in the centre of creation, and therefore the knowledge of the unity of everything created, is no small matter. There can certainly be no question of a more naive and direct

---

EN82 to absurdity

anthropocentricity. Who is this one for whom, as for God, heaven and earth are *hak-kol*, τὰ πάντα, a whole, the whole, the God-created whole, because he himself is a similar whole, i.e., soul and body, and as such the epitome of this greater whole? That it is only the New Testament which ventures to speak of the cosmos, and that it does so in a passage of such importance as the Prologue of John, can hardly be explained as a mere linguistic accommodation to Hellenism, but in the last resort only in theological terms. "Who is man that thou art mindful of him?": man for whom not only God is one, but also heaven and earth are one, because he himself is both, and as their unity one; man who in face of all creation does not call upon himself in vain: "Bless the Lord, O my soul!"—this soul which itself is simply the praise of the Lord of the creation. The New Testament knows of this man. But it does not know of him in the light of the discovery of man made in Hellenism. That would have long since led to something very different from: "Bless the Lord, O my soul." It knows of him in the light of the person of the Messiah of Israel, of the Son of Man, in whom the man of God, uniting heaven and earth in Himself, appeared as a reality among men. This man is the secret of heaven and earth, of the cosmos created by God. To know Him is to know heaven and earth in their diversity, unity and createdness, and to know God as their Creator. The Old Testament insight into this matter can thus be understood as meaningful and practicable only if it is understood as the promise, or prototype, of the knowledge of the Messiah. [022] And there is no other way to this knowledge than that indicated by the fact that it has this character.

To sum up, the statement concerning creation cannot be anything but an *articulus fidei*[EN83] because (1) its assertion of the reality of the world maintained in it and (2) its grounding of this reality in God are possible only as a statement of faith, and because (3) it is determined in all its elements (subject, predicate and object) by the linguistic usage of Holy Scripture and the content of the terms employed—which means again that it can be understood only as a statement of faith.

We now turn to the positive exposition of our first thesis that the doctrine of creation is a doctrine of faith, that it is knowledge and confession in the reception of the divine self-witness and response to it. The positive meaning of this thesis has necessarily emerged already in the apagogic proof which we have advanced, and especially in the analysis of the biblical witness regarding the individual elements of the creation dogma. But we will now set it in the forefront.

How do we know that God created heaven and earth and man, that they are therefore reality, and that they owe it to God that this is so? The question is not: How do we come to be justified in supposing this? What premonitions and feelings, what outward and inward probabilities, testify to us that it may be the case? Nor is it: What logical necessities support the view that it must be so, that there is no alternative but to postulate that it is so? Nor is it, of course: What good does it do us that it is so? What good and comforting and helpful convictions result?—convictions which are perhaps so good that even the wish to have them and to live with them might cause us to say that it is so. No, the question is: How do we arrive at the position where we can simply say that we

---

[EN83] article of faith

know that it is so? How is it that the Christian Church—whether or not it is illuminating and pleasing to itself and the world, and in spite of every objection and contrary opinion—can publicly confess this work of God the Father, the creation of heaven and earth, as truth and indeed as absolute and exclusive truth? That is to say, how can it make this confession side by side with its confession of Jesus Christ, the Son of God, our Lord, and of His way from the lowliness of His birth, suffering and dying to the majesty of His resurrection and session at the right hand of God the Father; and its confession of the Holy Ghost and His whole work of redemption which includes the whole deliverance and salvation of man? How can it make it in such a way that if the confession of the work of creation is false and impotent and impossible, so too is that of the work of reconciliation and redemption? How can it make it in such a way that the whole necessarily stands or falls with the dogma of creation as with every other constituent element? How can we confess this dogma with the definiteness and certainty which permits and commands the Christian Church and each individual Christian, in its proclamation and instruction, to accept responsibility for the fact that this confession is not the expression of a more or less well-founded human opinion or doctrine, but of the Word of God Himself? What is it that permits and commands us to regard the content of this confession, whether explicitly stated or not, as the truth of God which is infallible in all circumstances and therefore to be respected; to treat this truth as the presupposition which has to precede all other presuppositions, axioms and convictions, and the effectiveness of which can be counted on in every conceivable connexion?

[023]

The conditions for an acceptable and valid answer to the above question cannot be too strict at this point where we are apparently—but only apparently—in a sphere which is free from philosophical obligations. There has often been a tendency to laxity in this respect. And the result has been a lack of thoroughness and precision in the answer given, with a consequent failure to achieve the necessary definiteness and certainty at this point in the confession, and the diffusion of vagueness and uncertainty over the confession as a whole.

If a thorough and precise answer is to be given to the strict question concerning the basis of this statement, it is not enough to say that it occurs at the very beginning of the Bible, that it is developed in the form of a twofold creation narrative, and that it is plainly recalled and explained in many subsequent passages and texts in the Old and New Testaments. This is, of course, perfectly true, and has to be said. The impregnable basis of this statement is indeed the *fact* that it is in the Bible. And the *form* in which it is there will occupy us intensively in what follows. But the fact that the Bible gives us a reliable basis for our knowledge and confession, that it tells the truth on which we can rely, on which the Church can base its proclamation, and on which each individual Christian can confidently build his own conclusions, is itself true in and by reason of the fact that the Bible gives us God's own witness to

Himself, that it gives us the witness to Jesus Christ. Its word in all words is this Word. And it is this Word, its witness to Jesus Christ, which makes all its words the infallible Word of God. As the organ of the Spirit it helps us to this knowledge of the Father through the Son. In what it says about creation it also helps us to the knowledge of the Creator through the One in whom the Creator has reconciled the creature to Himself, in whom He has ordered the relationship of the creature to Himself, in whom He has given to the creature His eternal future, in accordance with the fact that in Him He loved and willed it from all eternity. The whole Bible speaks figuratively and prophetically of Him, of Jesus Christ, when it speaks of creation, the Creator and the creature. If, therefore, we are rightly to understand and estimate what it says about creation, we must first see that—like everything else it says—this refers and testifies first and last [024] to Him. At this point, too, He is the primary and ultimate object of its witness. We cannot afford to ignore this object. To the extent that we do, we expose ourselves to the danger of seeing nothing at all. What is said in prospect of Him can be understood only in retrospect of Him. That is, the whole circumference of the content of Scripture, including the truth and reality of the creation of the world by God, can be understood only from this centre. How can we respect Scripture as the organ of the Spirit if we want it otherwise? How else can Scripture prove and demonstrate that it is the organ of the Spirit? How else can it give us true and clear and certain knowledge of God the Creator? It is true enough that the statement about God the Creator has its infallible basis in the fact that it is in the Bible. But even on this basis it will be seen by us only if we halt before this centre of the Bible, directing the question of its basis to Jesus Christ and allowing Him to answer it.

Besides the right and necessary and central biblicism, there is a scattered and peripheral. This does not know that the Bible is a totality and that it is meant to be read in all its parts in the light of its unity, i.e., of the One of whom it everywhere speaks. On the contrary, it regards Jesus Christ merely as one object of its witness among others. It regards the Bible as a repository of all sorts and degrees of pious knowledge. It knows nothing of the triunity of the God whose revelation and work are attested. It may also confess a belief in the triunity of God in isolated connexions, but it does not take it seriously. It thinks it can talk about God the Father and Creator on the basis of Scripture, i.e., in the light of this or that passage of Scripture, without allowing itself to be taught by Scripture, i.e., the whole of Scripture, to know the Father through the Son, the Creator through the Redeemer. It may persuade itself—with or without the lame hypothesis of the 17th century doctrine of inspiration—that the peripheral knowledge which it takes from the Bible is God's true and clear and certain Word, but it cannot possibly be obedient to the Spirit of Scripture in this way (because the Spirit of Scripture is the Spirit of God the Father and the Son). The result is that it cannot possibly see the immovable basis of the statement that God is the Creator. No insistence on the letter of Scripture can give the one intrinsically necessary and convincing answer to the question how we may know this truth. Here, too, a word of warning is required against this type of biblicism.

It is hard to see how we can safely proceed in relation to the creation dogma except from the point which the Bible indicates from the very first and on every hand and the radiance of which gives from the very outset brightness and clarity to each individual reference. This point is the Messiah, the Lord of the Church, who was expected by Israel and who really came according to the promise given to it: the Head of the whole integrated community of the Old and the New Testaments; the man who according to Is. 7^{14} is called Emmanuel—God with us. His revelation and faith in Him help us in this matter of creation to the one true, clear and certain knowledge besides which there may [025] be other assumptions, hypotheses and postulates and even pious philosophies, but no other knowledge: i.e., none which is worth making the object of the confession; none on which the Church can rely; none with which one can live and die. It has the decisive advantage over all assumptions, hypotheses and postulates that it has reference to, and can therefore be considered only in connexion with, the divine self-witness. This being the case, it has also the formal advantage that it is obvious and simple, and can be attained at any time. What is entailed is the simple exegesis of the fact indicated in the name Emmanuel, namely, that God has accepted man in Jesus Christ, that in Him He has become man and that He is revealed in His unity with this man. It will not be an exhaustive exegesis, for this fact contains very much more than what it has to say about the problem of creation. But even in this respect it has something definite to teach us. And the instruction which it gives is reliable. In this it stands in sharp contrast to all other supposed instruction. For, strictly speaking, what else do we know of God, the world and man in their mutual inter-relationship? Does not all thought and discussion concerning them become confused myth and wild metaphysic as soon as we wander away from the text of this fact attested at the heart of the Bible? Indeed, what is the value of the rest of the biblical witness to creation without the centre? Can we really gather from it a clear and certain knowledge in this matter? It is here that God Himself has revealed the relationship between Creator and creature—its basis, norm and meaning. At this point we are secured on all sides. And everything else that is to be learned from the Bible may be learned *in nuce*[EN84] here.

From this revealed fact of the unity of God with man effected in Jesus Christ, the first truth that we learn is the simple one that God is not alone. He does not live His divine life only in His own space. There is a world-space in which He is the Lord of a being distinct from Himself, i.e., of man, thus giving proof of its reality. Because He is not only God in Himself, but also outside Himself, God has in this other being an opposite, a partner, who is completely subject to His lordship and under His control, but who has his own existence and his own nature; with whom He was not one but became one according to His eternal will and in a free, contingent act. The person of Jesus Christ proves that there is a sphere in which God acts and reveals Himself apart from His own sphere; and that there is someone upon whom and with whom He acts, and to whom and through whom He reveals Himself, apart from Himself. The person of

---

[EN84] in a nutshell

Jesus Christ is the proof that although the creature is not a second God beside the One, although it is not of the nature of God and therefore self-existent, it does exist after its own fashion by the will of God. It is the proof that the creature is not excluded and denied, but established and determined by Him. In view of the person of Jesus Christ we definitely cannot maintain or even suspect that there is nothing outside God, that the existence and being of the creature is only an appearance, and that God has not created heaven and earth. It is just as certain that God created them as that His eternal Word, without ceasing to be God, became something else, namely, flesh—and therefore not nothing. But His Word became flesh for the sake of His community, i.e., as the Messiah of Israel and the Head of the Church: to be the Representative of each believer before God; to take on life and form in each believer; to suffer and die for the sins of the whole world; in His resurrection to put on eternal life as light for the whole world; and in the function of Prophet, Priest and King to be the Lord over all powers and dominions in heaven and earth. That was why the Word became flesh. In Him, therefore, we do not merely find His own humanity affirmed and taken seriously in His existence, and acknowledged in the distinction and purposefulness of His special created being. We cannot see Him without also seeing His Israel, and His Church, and all who believe in Him, and among them ourselves, the whole world of men for which He died and rose again, and finally the ambiguous, enigmatical and mysterious outlines of the created reality of heaven and earth whose lordship is in His hands. He stands security that it is reality, distinct from God, but also distinct from nothing; that it is and is not appearance; that we ourselves are and are not not. No one and nothing else can guarantee this, but He does so with absolute authority.

[026]

From the same revealed fact of the unity of God with man effected in His person, we also learn that man is not alone, and that the sphere in which he lives is not the only one. In contrast to God, however, man and his world are not absolute, self-grounded or self-reposing. For it does not belong to man's nature to be actual in and through himself. In the person of Jesus Christ there is ascribed to him no other honour than that of the creature which is actual by the grace of God. For the fact that this man is, and what he is, are the work of God's grace. This man is as and because God's eternal Word has received and adopted him to unity with Himself. Men did not seek out God for common life in this unity, but God sought out man. And God did not need this unity, but man was wholly and utterly in need of it. He lives, because God lives, because God lives for him, and it is God's free will to live for him. So man lives as God's creature. That God makes the existence and being of the other reality His own is clearly seen at this point where between God and the reality distinct from God there takes place this absolutely once-for-all and unique relationship; where His eternal Son becomes a creature, and as a creature calls Him Father. Here, then, God confronts the creature as Creator. Here this other reality can only exist before God as it is thankful to Him. Here thankfulness is shown to be

25

[027] the essence of the creature, of the reality distinct from God. In face of the person of Jesus Christ we certainly cannot assign to either the creature or to God any other place. In face of the person of Jesus Christ we certainly cannot assert, or even suppose, that man is alone, that he is his own master and lord, that God has not created heaven and earth. It is just as certain that God has created them as that His Word is eternal even in time; that His Son is the Lord even as He becomes man; that in the authority of the eternal Lord He is also the Messiah of Israel and the Head of the Church; that He intercedes omnipotently for all those who believe in Him; that He dies and rises again from the dead; that He is King of heaven and earth in every sphere of reality. In all these things He confronts the One who deals with His creature as Creator. We cannot know Jesus Christ and His community and kingdom without an immediate awareness of this confrontation, i.e., of God's existence and essence as the being of the Almighty, the Father, to whom all things great and small, in the height and in the depth, are absolutely indebted, owing Him absolute thanks without any reciprocity. As Jesus Christ stands security for the reality of the creature in His person and work, so too He stands security for the reality of the Creator. He alone does this with authority. But His authority is absolute authority.

And it is again in Jesus Christ that we finally find all the individual elements in the biblical witness which go to make up the creation dogma united in such a way that their unity even as expressed in the dogma is seen to be necessary and is found to be illuminating as such.

In Him we learn to know the Subject "God" as His eternal Father, who, as He posits and grounds Himself in eternity in His Son, in the free expression of His grace ordains Himself the Creator, and heaven and earth His creatures. We learn to know Him as the Holy One of Israel, the Ruler of the history which reaches its goal in the appearance, death and resurrection of the Messiah Jesus. Where can we know this Subject except in the light of this goal? But at this point we can know it with clarity and certainty.

But the same is also true of the predicate "Creator" in so far as it designates a perfect, a contingently historical divine will and achievement from which the being and the whole history of heaven and earth derive. As in Jesus Christ God and man, eternity and time, converge and overlap in a temporal and time-transcending perfect willed and achieved by God, so it is in the act of creation. As God *has* accepted man in His Son, He *has* created him once for all with heaven and earth. The fact and the way that God has acted historically cannot be mistaken in creation when we have learned to know it, as we must, in the light of the atonement, and therefore of the person and work of Jesus Christ.

[028] It is at the same place that we learn that this predicate "Creator" speaks of an act whose content as the free positing of reality by the omnipotence of divine love is incomprehensible, indeducible and therefore unique. God acts in this way—as He alone can act—as He has reconciled the world to Himself in Jesus

Christ, i.e., as the One who in His death reveals the end of all creatures, and at the same time their new beginning in His resurrection. The way in which He acts as Creator cannot be mistaken when we see how He has acted here.

Here, too, we may see the curiously named object of creation—"heaven and earth" and man in their centre. *Ecce homo!*[EN85] is true in this respect. Here is the Son of Man. Here is humanity at the heart of the cosmos: with its upper and lower aspects; with its whence and its whither; over the earth but destined to come under the earth and itself to become earth; under heaven but destined to be above all heavens; and in both respects limited by the creative will of God and ordered with reference to a new heaven and a new earth. When we have discovered man as God's creature at this point, in Jesus Christ, we have made direct discovery of heaven and earth as the object of the divine act of creation.

It is thus from this point that we look, and we apprehend, recognise and know that the confession, the creation dogma, speaks the truth. From this point we confess with it, not in the form of a postulate or hypothesis, but with the absolute certainty with which one may confess, and with which alone one may confess, that "in the beginning God created the heaven and the earth."

But this is not by a long way the whole of what is to be seen with regard to the relation between Jesus Christ and creation. Indeed, we have spoken only of the noetic connexion; of the fact that the reality of creation is and can only be known with clarity and certainty in the person of Jesus Christ. But where there is a genuine noetic connexion, we can always count on the fact that it has an ontic basis. This is the case here. Jesus Christ is the Word by which the knowledge of creation is mediated to us because He is the Word by which God has fulfilled creation and continually maintains and rules it. As is required by a number of passages in the New Testament, we shall have to discuss this thoroughly at a later stage. Our present concern, however, is with the noetic connexion. We have established that from every angle Jesus Christ is the key to the secret of creation. It is thus clear that the knowledge of creation, of the Creator and of the creature, is a knowledge of faith, and that here too the Christian doctrine is a doctrine of faith. In all our previous deliberations we have presupposed that we do not have an unknown but a known quantity in Jesus Christ as the revelation and fulfilment of the eternal decree of God, as very God and very man; in His work as the Reconciler of the world with God; in His existence as the Messiah of Israel and the Lord of the Church; and in His majesty over every creature in heaven and earth. It is with the help of this known quantity that we have proved what had to be proved. All deliberations stand or fall with the fact that it is a known quantity. But Jesus Christ is a known quantity in the [029] comprehensive sense presupposed only at the point where He has called upon

---

[EN85] Behold the man

men to believe in Him and found men to believe in Him, i.e., by the work of the Holy Spirit of the Father and the Son in the sphere of His community. We have presupposed that He is actually this known quantity for us as His own, as members of His body, as adherents of His Church. And in the light of this known quantity we have perceived and understood the truth and necessity of the statement that God created heaven and earth. But this being the case, it obviously follows that this perception and understanding are those of faith. Our first task was to show that here, too, it is the case: *Credo, ut intelligam*[EN86]. In the present instance this means: I believe in Jesus Christ, God's Son our Lord, in order to perceive and to understand that God the Almighty, the Father, is the Creator of heaven and earth. If I did not believe the former, I could not perceive and understand the latter. If I perceive and understand the latter, my perception and understanding are completely established, sustained and impelled by my believing the former. Thus the confession of God the Creator belongs integrally to the rest of the confession. It does not constitute a foreign body in the confession—a mere prolegomenon. It is not for nothing that the word *credo*[EN87] stands before this first statement of the faith. Nor is it merely because it has to stand at the head of the whole confession. But it is used here with its full Christian content.

With our reference to the noetic connexion between Jesus Christ and creation we emphasise something which has been strangely overlooked and neglected, or at any rate not developed in any detail, either in more recent or even in earlier theology. It is curious that this should be the case, for at least the older theology had a clear awareness of, and tried to do justice to, the ontic connexion about which we shall have to speak later, i.e., the great truth of Jn. 1^3, etc. that God created all things "in Him," in Jesus Christ. From this point it surely ought not to have been difficult to proceed to a consideration of the significance of Jesus Christ for our knowledge of creation.

There was one point at which one might have supposed the deduction to be quite unavoidable. The insight that even the work of creation has to be understood as an act of the pure and free goodness of God is to be found as early as Origen ($\pi\epsilon\rho\grave{\iota}\ \mathring{a}\rho\chi\hat{\omega}\nu$, II, 9, 6), John Dam. ($\mathring{o}\rho\theta.\ \pi\acute{\iota}\sigma\tau.$, II, 2) and Gregory of Naz. (Or 38, 9). But it is encountered especially in Augustine: *Ex plenitudine bonitatis tuae creatura tua subsistit, ut bonum, quod tibi nihil prodesset nec de te aequale tibi esset, tamen quia ex te fieri potuit, non deesset. Quid enim te promeruit coelum et terra, quae fecisti in principio? ... Quid te promeruerunt ut essent saltem informia, quae neque hoc essent, nisi ex te?*[EN88] (*Conf.* XIII, 2, 2). Indeed, he can put it even more strongly: *Quadam non improbanda ratione dicitur gratia Dei qua creati sumus, ut nonnihil essemus nec ita essemus aliquid ut cadaver, quod non vivit, aut arbor, qui non sentit, aut pecus, quod non intelligit, sed homines ... et de hoc tanto beneficio creatori nostro gratias agere valeamus, unde merito et ista gratia dici potest quia non*

[EN86] I believe in order to understand

[EN87] I believe

[EN88] Your creature subsists out of the fullness of Your goodness, so that its goodness, which was neither of benefit to You nor equal to You, yet because it was able to be made by You, might not lack anything. For what did the earth and heaven, which You made in the beginning, profit You? ... What did they gain for You, that they should be anything but unformed matter - though they could not be even this, except through You

praecedentium aliquorum operum meritis, sed gratuita Dei bonitate donata est[EN89]. (Ep. 177, 7). Anselm of Canterbury also knew this proposition, for he tells us that besides that which is grace in the strict sense (the grace of reconciliation), it is also true that *omnis creatura gratia existit, quia gratia facta est*[EN90] (*De conc.*, qu. in, 2). And: *Creasti me, cum non essem; redemisti me, cum perditus essem. Sed conditionis quidem meae et redemptionis causa sola fuit dilectio tua*[EN91]. [030] (*Medit.* 12). So, too, did Thomas Aquinas: *Sua bonitas est ratio quare vult alia, quae sunt diversa ab ipso*[EN92]. (*S. c. Gent.* I, 86). Luther (in the *Smaller Catechism*) concludes his recitation of the blessings of the Creator with the words: " ... and all this out of pure fatherly divine goodness and mercy without any merit or worth of mine, so that for it all I owe Him thanks and praise, and service and obedience; this is certainly true." And Calvin writes that there is no creature, *in quam non effusa sit eius misericordia*[EN93], according to Ps. 145⁹: "The Lord is good to all: and his tender mercies are over all his works" (*Instit.*, I, 5, 6). And Polanus: *Creatio est lata significatione gratia, i.e., beneficium gratuitum .... Nam quod Deus nos et alia creavit et gubernat conservatque, non ex debito fecit et facit, sed ex mera gratia*[EN94]. (*Synt. Theol. chr.*, 1609, *col.* 1646). In all these passages it is clear that what was known of God's love, goodness, grace and mercy was used as a key to the understanding of creation; the doctrine of justification, according to which man is undeservedly accepted by God in grace, being made at least an analogy and explanatory principle of creation. We do not overlook the certain hesitation: *quadam non improbanda ratione ... dici potest ... lata significatione*[EN95]. But the line is actually drawn. And the explanation of Luther in the *Smaller Catechism* sounds far too categorical for us not to assume that he very definitely wanted this analogy to be seen, and the explanation advanced and recognised that it too is already "pure, fatherly, divine goodness and mercy." In a way which is almost too impressive, even Luther has so formulated his main statement on creation that it is characterised wholly and utterly as a favour evinced by God to man. On what ground does he make this venture, claiming that "this is certainly true," not in a theological treatise, but in this simplest exposition of his teaching for children and the common man? In the light of what *analogans* is he so sure of this *analogatum*[EN96]? The same question must also be addressed to Augustine, Anselm and Calvin: On what grounds do they venture the equation of *creatio*[EN97] and *gratia*[EN98]? Can they do it on any other basis than the centre of Christian doctrine? Augustine, Anselm, Luther and (at this point) even Calvin do not give us an explicit answer. But the answer has to be given and it is as follows. If the analogy is not merely to be an edifying game, it cannot be ventured except from the knowledge of Jesus Christ. But on this ground it must be ventured, and there should be no hesitation. Creation,

---

[EN89] It is not without good reason that we are said to have been created by the grace of God, so that we might be what we are and not something else, like a corpse, which is lifeless, or a tree, which is without feeling, or a sheep, which is without understanding, but rather human beings ... so that we should have the power to give thanks to our Creator for this great kindness; for it is rightly said that this grace was given not because of any preceding works of merit, but by the gratuitous goodness of God

[EN90] every creature exists by grace, because each was made by grace

[EN91] You created me, although I did not exist; you redeemed me, although I was lost. And truly the only cause of my existence and redemption was your love

[EN92] His goodness is the reason why He wishes other beings that are different from Himself

[EN93] on which His grace has not been poured out

[EN94] Broadly speaking, creation is simply grace, that is, gratuitous kindness .... For that God should have created us and all things, and that He governs and preserves us, He neither has done nor now does by reason of obligation, but by sheer grace

[EN95] not without good reason ... it can be said ... broadly speaking

[EN96] analogy drawn

[EN97] creation

[EN98] grace

too, is already the work of the free, fatherly grace and mercy of God. We have only to follow the argument of Jn. 1^3, etc., holding to the fact that Jesus Christ is indeed the real ground of creation, to realise that this equation must be ventured in full seriousness and without any hesitation, as in the categorical assertion of Luther. The advance in this direction in *Question* and *Answer* 26 of the *Heidelberg Catechism* is stronger than anything that has been mentioned up to now. To the question: "What believest thou when thou sayest: I believe in God the Father Almighty, Maker of heaven and earth?", the answer in the main clause is: "That the eternal Father of our Lord Jesus Christ ... for the sake of His Son is my God and Father." To the subject "the eternal Father of our Lord Jesus Christ," there is related an intervening clause: "who created from nothing, and governs and sustains by His eternal counsel and providence, heaven and earth and all that therein is." And to the predicate "for the sake of Christ my God and Father," there is attached a second subsidiary clause describing the practical trust, arising out of this recognition, in the loving care of God the Father for which He is able by reason of His omnipotence and ready by reason of His faithfulness. This takes us a decisive step farther than the statements of the previous fathers to the extent that it clarifies the relationship between the second and first articles of the creed. That God is our God and Father emerges as the substance of the first article and of the doctrine of creation in particular. And that He is this is based on the fact that He is the Father of Jesus Christ, and that for His sake (because Jesus Christ is our Brother) He is also our Father. Because He is the Father of Jesus Christ, He is also the Creator, Sustainer and Ruler of heaven and earth. And because, as the Father of Jesus Christ, He is also our God and Father, we may put our complete trust in His loving care. There is thus a full inter-relationship, and we can understand why the words "I believe" must also stand before the statement on creation, and also why it cannot have here a weaker and less Christian significance than in relation to the second and third articles. Our own attempt to make it clear that the content of the subsidiary clause, the work of creation as such, is itself the object of faith and therefore of the knowledge of Jesus Christ, does not involve more than a very small step from the standpoint of this deep and comprehensive exposition of the *Heidelberg Catechism*. For if the Father of Jesus Christ is the Creator of heaven and earth, and if we know the Father of Jesus Christ as such, and Him again as our God and Father because we believe in His Son, it is difficult to see how we can know the Creator of heaven and earth other than in the same faith in the Son and therefore in Jesus Christ.

[031]

To my knowledge, the strongest testimony of theological tradition in this direction is Calvin's foreword to his *Commentary on the Book of Genesis* (1554). In this work he recalls 1 Cor. 1^{21}: "For after that in the wisdom of God the world by wisdom knew not God, it pleased God by the foolishness of preaching to save them that believe." What Paul obviously means is: *frustra Deum quaeri rerum visibilium ductu, nec vero aliud restare nisi ut recta nos ad Christum conferamus. Non igitur ab dementis mundi huius, sed ab evangelio faciendum est exordium, quod unum Christum proponit cum sua cruce, et in eo nos detinet*[EN99]. In view of this, Calvin's conviction is also: *frustra quidem in mundi opificio philosophari, nisi qui evangelii praedicatione iam humiliati, totam mentis suae perspicaciam crucis stultitiae subiicere didicerint. Sursum, inquam, et deorsum nihil reperiemus, quod nos ad Deum usque attollat, donec in sua schola nos Christus erudierit. Id porro fieri non potest nisi ex profundis inferis emersi crucis eius vehiculo supra coelos omnes tollamur, ut illic fide comprehendamus, quae oculus nunquam vidit, auris nunquam audivit, et quae longe corda mentesque nostras superant. Neque enim illic terra nobis obiicitur, quae fruges velut in diurnum alimentum*

[EN99] it is vain for God to be sought by reference to visible things, and indeed that anything should remain, except so that we should be brought straight to Christ. Therefore we should make our beginning not with the things of this world, but with the gospel, which puts forth one Christ with his cross and holds us in him

suppeditet, sed Christus ipse in vitam aeternam se nobis offert, nec coelum solis ac stellarum fulgore oculos corporales illustrat, sed idem Christus, lux mundi et sol iustitiae, in animis nostris refulget, nec aer inane spatium nobis ac spirandum porrigit, sed ipse Dei spiritus nos vegetat et vivificat. Denique illic invisibile Christi regnum omnia occupat, et spiritualis eius gratia per omnia diffusa est[EN100]. To be sure, this ought not to prevent us from looking to heaven and earth as well and in this way fortifying ourselves in the true knowledge of God. *Christus enim imago est, in qua non modo pectus suum nobis Deus conspicuum reddit, sed manus quoque et pedes. Pectus appello arcanum ilium amorem, quo nos in Christo complexus est; per manus autem et pedes, quae oculis nostris exposita sunt opera, intelligo*[EN101]. But: *A Christo simulatque discessimus, nihil est tam crassum vel minutum, in quo non hallucinari necesse sit*[EN102]. (*C.R.* 23, 10 f.). We do not find in Calvin any more detailed explanation or exposition of this programmatical assertion either in the *Commentary on Genesis* or in the relevant passages in the *Institutio*. Yet there can be no doubt that he has given us a stimulus to further thinking in this direction. The step which we ourselves have attempted along the lines he so impressively indicated is only a logical conclusion which is as it were set on our lips by the statements of the fathers, although they did not draw it for themselves.

We cannot conclude this whole discussion, however, without some indication at least of what kind of faith it is that, as faith in Jesus Christ, contains within itself the knowledge of the secret of creation, the Creator and the creature. Just because we have simply taken faith for granted in this connexion, reckoning with Jesus Christ as with a known quantity and on this basis assuring [032] ourselves of the reality of creation, we must consider what happens and what is really involved at the point where this presupposition is valid, where it is really believed, where the knowledge of creation in Jesus Christ is not therefore a structure which cannot stand any strain or stress, where it is itself sustained, where it is living and activated, where it can be allowed at any time and by anyone in the simplicity which we have applauded. The faith in Jesus Christ which contains within itself faith in and therefore the knowledge of God the Creator, and which is therefore capable of giving life and strength to this structure, is a very definite attitude and decision. It consists in the fact that the man

---

[EN100] indeed it is vain for any to philosophize in the manner of the world, unless they have first been humbled by the preaching of the gospel, and have instructed the whole compass of their intellect to submit to the foolishness of the cross. I say that we will find out nothing above or below that will lift us to God, until Christ has educated us in his school. Nothing further can be done, if we are not raised up from the lowest depths and carried aboard his cross above all the heavens, so that there by faith we might comprehend what no eye has ever seen, nor ear ever heard, and which far surpasses our hearts and minds. For the earth is not before us there, nor its fruits supplied for daily food, but Christ himself offers himself to us unto eternal life; nor do the heavens illuminate our bodily eyes with the splendor of the sun and stars, but the same Christ, the light of the world and the sun of righteousness, shines forth in our souls; nor does the empty air spread its ebb and flow around us, but the very Spirit of God quickens and enlivens us. And so there the invisible kingdom of Christ fills all things, and his spiritual grace is diffused through all things

[EN101] For Christ is the image, in which God not only allows his breast to be seen, but also His hands and feet. By 'breast' I mean that secret love, by which we are enfolded in Christ; by 'hands' and 'feet' I understand those works which are set before our eyes

[EN102] As soon as we have departed from Christ, there is nothing is so gross or trivial that we can avoid being mistaken as to its true nature

who has and confesses this faith takes seriously the truth that God is the Creator of all the reality distinct from Himself. It consists in the personal recognition that this reality is at the disposal of God as the theatre, instrument and object of His activity. It consists, therefore, in a recognition of the fact that God has controlled and does and will control it. Faith in Jesus Christ is more and other than this. Necessarily, however, it is this too, i.e., a serious acceptance of God as Creator, a recognition of His right and power to control, a genuine reckoning with His control over past, present and future. We obviously do not believe in the Son of God and Son of Man, in the Messiah of Israel who is also Lord of the Church, in the power of His death and resurrection, in His lordship over all the world, if we try to evade this attitude and decision, not accepting them in and with this faith. And to the extent that faith in Jesus Christ has this side too, containing within itself knowledge of the truth of the Creator, it is the presupposition on which Jesus Christ becomes the known quantity in face of which the reality and relationship of Creator and creature cannot remain hidden from us.

Faith in Jesus Christ is a life in the presence of the Creator. No matter who or whatever else is there for the believer in Him, there can be no doubt that Jesus Christ is there for him as the Creator: an absolute new beginning brought about by God; an absolute new beginning of his existence; an absolute new beginning of all things; an authority which is posited basically and decisively before all others; a power which has not only illumined and altered and improved his whole reality but completely transformed it. How he regards it, what attitude he adopts towards it, what justice he does it, is another matter. But it cannot conceal the fact that for those who believe in Jesus Christ the Creator has entered in in His person. For a mere creature cannot be so absolutely revolutionary in relation to another. The authority which posits itself in this way before all others, this transforming and renewing power, cannot of itself place itself before us as is actually the case in Jesus Christ. In Him we are confronted with our Creator, the Creator of all reality. He and He alone acts in this way. And acceptance of His presence and action—no matter what it may

[033] involve or what he may make of it—is the attitude and decision of the man who believes in Jesus Christ. And because he accepts it, because his *Credo*[EN103] thus contains this attitude within itself, it comes to pass that he is able to participate in the knowledge of the secret of creation.

We cannot do better at this point than turn to the passionate closing words of the Epistle to the Galatians. Paul has just made a final outburst against the Judaisers ("they desire to have you circumcised, that they may glory in your flesh"). He then continues in $6^{14f.}$: "But God forbid that I should glory, save in the cross of our Lord Jesus Christ, by whom the world is crucified unto me, and I unto the world. For in Christ Jesus neither circumcision availeth any thing, nor uncircumcision, but καινὴ κτίσις[EN104]. And as many as walk according to this

---

[EN103] I believe
[EN104] a new creation

rule (τῷ κανόνι τούτῳ), peace be on them, and mercy, and upon the Israel of God." Paul's attitude and position in relation to the whole problem of Jewish and Gentile existence have been so radically changed by his relationship to Jesus Christ that, looking back on them, he can only understand them as his creation to a new existence. Nor does he in any sense regard this as an experience which affects only himself. The "Israel of God" as such, Christians from both Jews and Gentiles, find themselves in the same changed position and attitude. As certainly as Jesus Christ is their common Lord, they all walk according to this "canon," on this new ground. That is to say, they are, like Himself, a "new creation," and as such they participate in the peace and mercy of God. Paul speaks along the same lines and in the same sense in 2 Cor. 5¹⁴. The love of Christ is the track on which he runs (συνέχει ἡμᾶς) EN105. A crisis has broken over him to which he must adjust himself and the justice of which he must acknowledge in his own judgment. This one death for all means the death of all, i.e., it happened in order that they should no longer have their life for themselves, but for Him who died and rose again for them (v. 15). He no longer knows himself and others and even Jesus Christ Himself κατὰ σάρκα EN106, i.e., in the way that he knew things and people and relationships before the crisis came upon him, and before he acknowledged it to be just (v. 16). It is thus the case—in a further general conclusion—that if a man is "in Christ" (not only he the apostle, but every Christian as such), he is καινὴ κτίσις EN107, a new creature in and with this being in Christ: τὰ ἀρχαῖα παρῆλθεν, ἰδοὺ γέγονεν καινά EN108. In other words, the passing of one whole order of reality and the coming of another is the meaning of the change which took place for all with the death of Christ for all (v. 17). Paul continues in v. 18: τὰ δὲ πάντα ἐκ τοῦ θεοῦ EN109—a slightly different version of the saying in Rom. 11³⁶ which is an obvious reference to creation: ἐξ αὐτοῦ ... τὰ πάντα EN110. It is this, the Creator-God, who through Jesus Christ reconciles us to Himself, and who has committed the apostolic work of reconciliation to Paul. Paul has already made the same point in 2 Cor. 4⁵. He does not preach himself, but Christ Jesus the Lord, and himself as their, the community's, slave for the sake of this Jesus (v. 5). What is the reason for this divestment of personality, which still contains within itself the unprecedented claim of his apostolic function? The answer is given in v. 6: "For God, who commanded the light to shine out of darkness, hath shined in our hearts, to give the light (ἔλαμψεν ... εἰς φωτισμόν) of the knowledge of the glory of God in the face of Jesus Christ." The express reference here to "our hearts" indicates much more than the apostolic plural and therefore a general application of what is said to all Christians. As those who like the apostle are in their own way used in the service of Christ, they are enlightened in such a way that only the "Let there be light" of Gen. 1³ can be the analogy, and only the Creator who uttered this "Let there be light" the ground of their enlightenment. The general reference is quite unequivocal in Eph. 2⁸ᶠ: "By grace are ye saved through faith; and that not of yourselves (οὐκ ἐξ ὑμῶν): it is the gift of God: not of works, lest any man should boast." "For (note that what follows does not disprove, but substantiates) we are his workmanship, created in Christ Jesus unto good works, which God hath before ordained that we should walk in them.'" The saving grace which falls to Christians excludes all self-boasting, or boasting in works, because those to whom it is imparted are as such its work, or creature, by it alone being made what they are and qualified to do what they do. We have to do with God the Creator no less in our pardon than in our creatureliness. Indeed it is only in our pardon that we really have to do with Him. The same

[034]

EN105 compets us
EN106 according to the flesh
EN107 a new creation
EN108 old things are passed away; behold, all things are become new
EN109 and all things are of God
EN110 from Him ... are all things

conclusion recurs in Eph. 4^{24}, this time in the form of an exhortation to put on like a new and awaiting garment the new man "which after God (κατὰ θεόν) is created in righteousness and true holiness." The parallel passage in Col. 3^{10} says that Christians should put on the new man, i.e. (in close approximation to 2 Cor. $4^{5f.}$ and Gal. $6^{15f.}$), the man who is renewed in knowledge after the image of his Creator, where the distinctions between Greek and Jew, circumcision and uncircumcision, barbarian, Scythian, bond and free are without substance and of no account, but Christ is all in all. In Eph. 2^{15} too the realisation of Christian existence beyond the enmity of Jew and Gentile is described (in full accord with Gal. 6^{15}) as a κτίζειν[EN111] of two into one new man; and the making of peace (the breaking down of the middle wall, v. 14) between the two as a ποιεῖν[EN112], which in this case is expressly the ποιεῖν[EN113] of Jesus Christ Himself. In conclusion we may also mention Jas. $1^{16f.}$, where Christians are warned against the supposition that anything but good gifts can be expected from the "Father of lights." "Of his own will begat he us with the word of truth, that we should be a kind of firstfruits of his creatures" (v. 18). In view of this we certainly cannot regard it as merely the language of liturgical rhetoric when, according to Mt. 11^{25}, Jesus addresses God as "Father, Lord of heaven and earth," and praises Him as such, "because thou hast hid these things from the wise and prudent and hast revealed them unto babes. Even so Father: for so it seemed good in thy sight." It is the act of the good-pleasure of the Lord and therefore the Creator of heaven and earth that there is this concealment on the one side and disclosure on the other. And reference to the need for a point of contact in natural theology is not enough to explain why, in his speech on Mars' hill, Paul described the God whom the Athenians worshipped but did not know as supremely the One who created the world and all that is therein, and then went on to say that this "the Lord of heaven and earth dwelleth not in temples made with hands; neither is worshipped with men's hands, as though he needed anything, seeing he giveth to all life and breath and all things." An address which is to close (v. 31) with the proclamation of the resurrection of Jesus Christ from the dead must obviously begin with the creation, and there is no natural theology either in the one case or the other. In the New Testament to meet the Messiah Jesus is always implicitly or explicitly to meet the secret of God the Creator, and faith in Him always means acceptance of the secret of His presence. If we are not prepared to take account of this relationship it is difficult or impossible to realise either the fact or extent that faith in Him really contains within itself the knowledge of creation.

This leads us to certain concrete determinations of this faith.

If it is a life in the presence of the Creator, it is a life in the actual experience and recognition of His power over all things and situations. Whatever other powers the believer in Jesus Christ knows, and rightly or wrongly thinks that in their way he ought to respect, Jesus Christ has intervened for him as the Bearer of this power over all powers—the power which is qualified and distinguished from all other powers, not only because it is greater and has dominion over them, but decisively because it is itself their origin, and that without it they would not be powers at all, this being the reason why they are subject to it. [035] Jesus Christ is the Bearer of the power of the Creator. It may be an open question how far this is visible to the believer, how far Jesus Christ Himself will make it visible even to the believer. If, as believer and therefore not as onlooker, he

---

[EN111] creation
[EN112] making
[EN113] making

sees something of it in this life, it will always be a sign, and it will always be grace that this sign of it is given him, and that he may see it as such. But this does not alter the fact. With or without signs, those who believe in Jesus Christ have to do *ipso facto*[EN114] with the Lord of heaven and earth, i.e., with the One who can dispose in the whole realm of reality distinct from God, and who does actually dispose always and everywhere, whether secretly or (in signs) openly. The attitude and decision of those who believe in Jesus Christ is that they take into basic account this possible and actual power of disposal, and that they are ready to be summoned always and everywhere to take it into account. When they adopt this attitude and decision, the secret of creation cannot and will not be concealed from them.

The faith which (according to Mt. 8[5f.]) Jesus did not find in Israel, but in the Gentile centurion of Capernaum, is that confidence in Him in which the centurion begs Him to speak only a word and his servant will be healed, just as he himself says to one of his soldiers, Go, and he goeth; and to another, Come, and he cometh; and to his servant, Do this, and he doeth it. But at this point we should really refer to all the accounts in the Gospels which show us that Jesus really possessed this power and freely exercised it; that He found faith, i.e., this trust in His power, in all kinds of hopeless sufferers, and that these people simply counted on the fact that He could help them if He were willing to do so. Again, we should quote all the occasions when He rebuked His disciples—it is noticeable that this time it is always the disciples—for their "little faith" ($\mathpartial\lambda\iota\gamma o\pi\iota\sigma\tau\iota\alpha$) because they had failed in practice, in a given instance, basically to count on His power over nature and therefore to live always as these who expect His control over all things and situations. It is as and because Jesus has the $\mathexists\xi o\upsilon\sigma\iota\alpha$[EN115] of the Word, of doctrine, of revelation (unlike the scribes, Mt. 5[29]), the $\mathexists\xi o\upsilon\sigma\iota\alpha$[EN116] to forgive sins on earth (Mk. 2[10]), that as a sign—in order "that ye may know"—He says to the sick of the palsy: "I say unto thee. Arise, and take up thy bed, and go thy way into thine house." And it is in virtue of this $\mathexists\xi o\upsilon\sigma\iota\alpha$[EN117] that this is exactly what takes place. What would the Four Gospels be without this constant reference to the possession and exercise of power by Jesus, and without the constant appeal to believe in Him as the Bearer of this power? It is as such that He is the Messiah. "What manner of man is this that even the wind and the sea obey him?" Who is He indeed? He is the fulfilment of the promise: "Behold, I create a new heaven and a new earth: and the former shall not be remembered, nor come into mind. But be ye glad and rejoice for ever in that which I create" (Is. 65[17f.]). This creation of a new heaven and a new earth will take place and will be revealed in the exercise by Jesus of the power of the One who has already created this heaven and this earth. And therefore faith in Him, however small, must have the quality that it corresponds on its side to this divine creating, that it removes mountains and trees and that nothing is impossible to it (Mk. 11[23] and par.). If it does not have this quality, it is not faith in Him, the promised and manifested Messiah. To Him it belongs essentially that He should act with creative power, and therefore this quality is not an unimportant or dispensable determination of faith in Him. Without it the assertion that faith involves a knowledge of creation is without foundation, and any attempt to construct this knowledge is a worthless fabrication.

[EN114] for that very reason
[EN115] authority
[EN116] authority
[EN117] authority

[036]   But faith as life in the presence of the Creator is just as necessarily a life in the experience and recognition of His right over His creature. There may intervene, of course, all kinds of creaturely rights and attacks and encroachments on the divine right on the part of the creature, so that believers give the lie to their own faith. But in so far as they believe, it is still true for them that not merely supreme power but with it supreme right has entered in in Jesus Christ, as an authority which not only rules but which is worthy to rule, which in this worthiness demands respect, so that we not only must but should and finally may subject ourselves to it because there is no real reason for us not to do so; as an authority the contemplation of which gives rise to reverence as well as amazement. The right of the Creator in respect of the creature is based on the simple fact that the latter belongs to Him, not by subsequent acquisition, but as an original possession, in and with the very existence which it owes to Him. There is thus no conceivable aspect under which it is not indebted to its Creator. Jesus Christ has established this right of the Creator by reconciling the world with God. It is inevitable, then, that believers in Him will encounter this right and submit to it. That they are prepared to do this is the attitude and decision of the Christian faith to which the secret of creation is perceptible.

This right of the Creator is particularly brought out in the Gospels by a distinctive and dominating figure of speech which constantly recurs in all kinds of different forms. We refer to the "lord" who according to Lk. $17^{7f.}$ demands of his servant, to whom he owes nothing for what he has done, that he serve him until he has eaten and drunken (it is to be noted that this hard parable in Luke is Jesus' answer to the disciples' request for more faith (v. 5), and at the same time an explanation of the saying regarding the omnipotent power of faith even to remove trees). This lord is obviously the same as that of Mt. $25^{14f.}$ who distributed talents to his servants as he himself saw fit, giving five to one, two to another and one to a third, and then returning to demand an account and make appropriate recompense. It is also the lord of Mt. $18^{24f.}$ who when he reckoned with his servants as their king had compassion on his greatest debtor, loosing him and remitting the debt, but later, because this servant dealt so very differently with his fellow-servant, revoked his decision with the same sovereign power, "and delivered him to the tormentors, till he should pay all that was due unto him." It is the lord who in Mt. $20^{1f.}$ called the unemployed to work in his vineyard, first in the morning, then at the third, the sixth and eleventh hours, and finally gave the first the same wages as the last: "My friend, I do thee no wrong: didst not thou agree with me for a penny? Take that thine is and go thy way: I will give unto this last, even as unto thee. Is it not lawful for me to do what I will with mine own? Is thine eye evil, because I am good?" It is also the father of the two very different sons of Lk. $15^{11f.}$, especially in the second half of the parable, in the splendid reception of the younger son who was lost, and the answer to the elder son who was so much better. It is also the owner of the field of Mt. $13^{24f.}$ who when he saw that an enemy had sown tares among the wheat commanded that both should be allowed to grow together until the harvest and that the tares should then be burned and the wheat gathered into his barns. It is also that owner of the vineyard of Mt. $21^{33f.}$ whose ser-

[037]   vants and son the husbandmen so shamefully maltreat in the hope of seizing the property for themselves, and who will not hesitate to punish them for it, to restore order and to put other husbandmen in their place. It is also the king who in Mt. $22^{1f.}$ prepares a wedding feast for his son and when the officially invited guests prove so ungrateful gathers in unofficial guests from the streets, but when he finds amongst them a man who has come without a

wedding garment has him expelled into the darkness from which he has come. It is the bridegroom of Mt. 25[1f.] who comes to the feast at his own time, and the virgins who are ready go in with him, but those whose lamps are short of oil have to be told by him: "Verily I say unto you, I know you not." It is the man who, according to Lk. 13[6f.], has planted a fig tree in his vineyard and for three years running finds no fruit when he comes to inspect it: "Cut it down; why cumbereth it the ground?"—and yet who still accedes to the gardener's request that it should be allowed to remain another year. And the same figure stands behind the caricatures of the unjust steward of Lk. 16[1f.] and the unjust judge of Lk. 18[1f.] In every case it is that of the exacting, insistent lord who lays unconditional claim to his inheritance, position and majesty, who maintains his established rights in relation to all around, and against whose decree there can be no effective opposition because a denial of its legitimacy is impossible. This is the right of the Creator with which we have to do when we encounter Jesus. It is by His right as Creator that according to the dominant conception of the New Testament God comes to be the Judge of men. He does not have to become or to make Himself the Judge. He is it from the very outset. He is it as God the Creator, who as such can claim that the creature should be responsible to Him; who has the authority to decide whether it justifies its existence, i.e., whether it satisfies the right of the One to whom it owes its existence. If He answers this question in the affirmative, it is justified. If He answers it in the negative, it has no justification at all. It is wholly dependent, therefore, upon an affirmative answer. Hence it is not at all the case that the witness of the Old Testament to the majesty in which God rules and decrees according to His pleasure as the measure and sum of all right has altered in the very slightest in the proclamation of the New. In the well known description of Jeremiah's visit to the house of the potter we are told in Jer. 18[6f.]: "Cannot I do with you as this potter? saith the Lord. Behold as the clay is in the potter's hand, so are ye in mine hand, O house of Israel. At what instant I shall speak concerning a nation, and concerning a kingdom, to pluck up, and to pull down, and to destroy it. If the nation, against whom I have pronounced, turn from their evil, I will repent of the evil that I thought to do unto them. And at what instant I shall speak concerning a nation, and concerning a kingdom, to build and to plant it; if it do evil in my sight, that it obey not my voice, then I will repent of the good, wherewith I said I would benefit them." Is this caprice? We are given the answer in Jer. 27[5]: "I have made the earth, the man and the beast that are on the ground, by my great power and by my outstretched arm, and have given it to whom it seemed meet unto me." Or in Is. 45[9f.]: "Woe unto him that striveth with his maker! Let the potter strive with the potsherds of the earth. Shall the clay say unto him that fashioneth it, what makest thou? or thy work, He hath no hands? Woe unto him that saith to his father, what begettest thou? or to the woman what has thou brought forth? Thus saith the Lord, the Holy One of Israel, and his Maker, Ask me of things to come concerning my sons, and concerning the work of my hands command ye me. I have made the earth and created man upon it: I, even my hands, have stretched out the heavens, and all their host have I commanded." Or in Ps. 89[11f.] (cf. 24[1]): "The heavens are thine, the earth also is thine: as for the world and the fulness thereof, thou hast founded them. The north and the south thou has created them." Or again in Ps. 95[4f.]: "In his hand are the deep places of the earth: the strength of the hills is his also. The sea is his, and he made it: and his hands formed the dry land." Because as the Creator He is the [038] owner and as the owner He has the right of control (v. 6 f.): "O come let us worship and bow down: let us kneel before the Lord our maker. For he is our God; and we are the people of his pasture, and the sheep of his hand." It is because of this that according to Jer. 10[11f.] the God of Israel distinguishes Himself from the gods of the heathen, and His claim on man is qualified as theirs can never be: "Thus shall ye say unto them, the gods that have not made the heavens and the earth, even they shall perish from the earth, and from under these heavens. He hath made the earth by his power, he hath established the world by his wisdom, and hath stretched out the heavens by his discretion. When he uttereth his voice, there is a multitude of waters in the heavens, and he causeth the vapours to ascend from the ends of the earth; he maketh lightnings with rain, and bringeth forth the wind out of his treasures." What, then, is man with his graven images? "They are vanity, and the work of errors: in the time of their visitation they shall perish. The portion of Jacob is not like them: for he is the former of all things (*hakkol*): and Israel is the rod of his inheritance: The Lord of hosts is his name." Or in the brief and annihilating words of Ps. 96[5]: "For all the gods of the nations are idols: but the Lord made the heavens." What else is the proclamation of Jesus and the New Testament but the establishment, revelation and execution of this long-attested right of the Creator to His creature? It is in this way, in the fulness of power accredited to God in these Old Testament passages, that the lord or king or landowner of the parables deals with his possession, defends his dignity and position, guards his honour and thus encounters the men around him. The figure is not, therefore, that of a despot. It is always right because it is always free to do as it likes; because it is obviously the figure of the Creator who as such is also Law and Judge and therefore legitimate Ruler. It is with this legitimate Ruler that we are confronted when we are confronted with Jesus Christ. And when we are called and awakened to believe, it is a question of recognising His legitimacy. It is the faith which makes this recognition that is the power and root of the knowledge that God created heaven and earth.

Finally, if faith is a life in the presence of the Creator, it is necessarily a life in the recognition and experience of His benevolence. It is not self-evident that the reality which surrounds man, even his existence, is a reflection of the benevolence of the One to whom it owes its reality. In and for itself it is certainly not this. Menacing evil, or a polluted source of no less evil than good or menace than promise, might equally well underlie it as the benevolence of the Creator. But be that as it may, for those who believe in Him, there has entered in in Jesus Christ the Bearer and Proclaimer of the benevolence of the One who willed and created the world and themselves. Just because there can be no question here of a glorification of the ethical, aesthetic or any other excellence of the creature as such, just because the creature is here regarded and addressed at every point as in need of reconciliation, peace and redemption, it is all the more clear that He who as Creator has all power and all right over it, has always desired its good, that He has honoured and loved it from the very first, that He has always willed to procure its right, that He has always willed to be helpful, that He has always been friendly disposed towards it. It is not His fault if it does not realise this or accept the fact. And what really emerges in [039] Jesus Christ, even in the concealment in which it is enwrapped for our perception, is the unmistakeable fact that the omnipotence and righteousness of the Creator is that of His mercy. How can that be otherwise when He is the Mediator between God and man, the Executor of the eternal covenant which God in His love concluded between Himself and man? Those who believe in Him necessarily grasp and understand also this mercy of the Creator, the love of the Creator, who willed to call them as men His own dear sons. It is another matter how far and how seriously they really believe in this respect too, and therefore realise what is true and evident for them in Jesus Christ. But there is no faith in Jesus Christ which does not count on the mercy and therefore the benevolence of the Creator as well as on His omnipotence and righteousness; which does not have also this quality. Those who believe in Jesus Christ have adopted an attitude and made a decision in this respect also (and supremely). God the Creator has become worthy of their confidence, and they have admitted that they really owe Him this confidence of which He is worthy. In this decision their faith is also a true and certain knowledge of the secret of creation.

It was not really arbitrary, therefore, but right and necessary from the Christian standpoint that those fathers from Augustine onwards wanted creation to be understood as the grace of God. And the *Heidelberg Catechism* gives us a most profound insight when (*qu.* 26) to its description of faith in the Creator who is the eternal Father of our Lord Jesus Christ, and for His sake my God and Father too, it adds the words: "In whom I therefore trust, not doubting but He will care for my every need of body and soul, and turn to good all the evil that He sends me in this vale of woe, seeing that He can do this as an almighty God, and therefore will do it as a faithful Father." This is the true reference of the divine title Father. In the New Testament this title is not really a sentimental expression for the human experience of the goodness to man of the supreme being who rules in and over the world. It is as Jesus is the Son of God that God is His Father and He calls Him by this name. And it is as He calls us to fellowship with Himself and to His discipleship, as He summons us to pray with Him, that He invites us too to know and address God as our Father. It is as we know this Father that we know the Creator, and not *vice versa*. But as we know the Creator in the Father, we know His goodness in action. Fatherliness in the anthropomorphic sense is not the benevolence of the Creator, but it is very much so in the true and theological sense of the New Testament. And so faith in Jesus Christ as admission to fellowship with Him and His discipleship and therefore relationship with the Creator is undoubtedly complete trust in Him as such. It is He who feeds the birds of the air, who neither sow nor reap, nor gather into barns. It is He who causes the lilies of the field to grow and clothes them, even though they neither toil nor spin, and are only grass, which to-day is, and to-morrow is cast into the oven (Mt. $6^{26f.}$). Without Him not one sparrow falls to the ground, and by Him also all the hairs of our head are numbered (Mt. $10^{29f.}$). He wills that we should pray with the same confidence for our daily bread as for forgiveness of sins, or the revelation of His own name, or the coming of His kingdom, or the doing of His will on earth as it is done in heaven (Mt. $6^{9f.}$), and He will certainly hear and answer. If earthly fathers, being evil, know how to give their children the good things they ask for, how much more does the Father in heaven know how to do this (Mt. 7^{11})! For this reason faith in Jesus Christ, if it is true faith, cannot contain any elements of worry and fear; it is pure and wholehearted confidence in the One who is Lord over all. "And shall God not avenge his own elect, which cry day and night unto him, though he bear long with them? I tell you that he will avenge them speedily" (Lk. 18^7). "Nevertheless when the Son of man cometh—this is how the passage continues—shall he find faith on the earth?" (v. 8). It is obviously a question of the particular faith, i.e., the faith which in His discipleship is genuinely confident of the fatherliness and therefore the benevolence of God, and therefore excludes all care and fear. The Old Testament parallels echoed in all these passages show at once that this faith is not self-evident and that it is a pertinent question whether we have this faith or not. The prayer of Hezekiah in face of Sennacherib's arrogant messenger is one which those who have known the true God, the God of the covenant whose fulfilment has been made manifest in Jesus Christ, must and may also pray: "O Lord God of Israel, which dwelleth between the cherubims, thou art the God, even thou alone, of all the kingdoms of the earth; thou has made heaven and earth. Lord, bow down thine ear, and hear: open, Lord, thine eyes, and see: and hear the words of Sennacherib, which hath sent him to reproach the living God ... save thou us out of his hand, that all the

[040]

kingdoms of the earth may know that thou art the Lord God, even thou only." So, too, is the prayer of Is. 64[8f.]: "But now, O Lord, thou art our father; we are the clay, and thou our potter; and we all are the work of thy hand. Be not wroth very sore, O Lord, neither remember iniquity for ever: behold, see, we beseech thee, we are all thy people." And the answer to this kind of prayer is immediately at hand in Is. 43[1f.]: "But now thus saith the Lord that created thee, O Jacob, and he hath formed thee, O Israel, Fear not: for I have redeemed thee, I have called thee by thy name; thou art mine. When thou passeth through the waters, I will be with thee; and through the rivers, they shall not overflow thee: when thou walkest through the fire, thou shalt not be burned; neither shall the flame kindle upon thee. For I am the Lord thy God, the Holy One of Israel, thy Saviour." And again in Is. 44[1f.]: "Yet now hear, O Jacob my servant; and Israel, whom I have chosen. Thus saith the Lord that made thee, and formed thee from the womb, which will help thee; Fear not, O Jacob, my servant; and thou, Jesurun, whom I have chosen. For I will pour water upon him that is thirsty, and floods upon the dry ground: I will pour my spirit upon thy seed, and my blessing upon thine offspring: And they shall spring up as among the grass, as willows by the water courses." It may be seen how divine election, creation, mercy and superabundant help are all related at this point and form a single whole. When Jesus summons His own not to be anxious or to fear the obvious reference is to this whole. But this call must be heard; this whole of divine readiness and help understood and grasped in faith. The enemy of this faith, which robs man of the divine answer and the confidence based upon it, is man's faith in himself, which always forgets and denies the Creator. It is described in the Song of Moses in Deut. 32[15]: "But Jeshurun waxed fat, and kicked: thou art waxen fat, thou art grown thick, thou art covered with fatness; then he forsook God which made him, and lightly esteemed the rock of his salvation." Or again in Hos. 8[14]: "For Israel hath forgotten his maker, and buildeth temples; and hath multiplied fenced cities: but I will send a fire upon his cities, and it shall devour the palaces thereof." Or again in Is. 22[9f.]: "Ye have seen also the breaches of the city of David, that they are many: and ye gathered together the waters of the lower pool. And ye have numbered the houses of Jerusalem, and the houses have ye broken down to fortify the wall. Ye made also a ditch between the two walls for the water of the old pool: but ye have not looked unto the maker thereof, neither had respect unto him that fashioned it long ago .... Surely this iniquity shall not be purged from you till ye die, saith the Lord God of hosts."

[041] How can the grace of creation be recognised, or man live by this grace, when, trusting in himself, he forgets and denies that creation is grace? Creation is understood and apprehended as grace in faith in Jesus Christ. That is why this faith is life in trust and confidence in the Creator, in unchangeable and never failing hope in His benevolence. "Thy hands have made me and fashioned me: give me understanding, that I may learn thy commandments" (Ps. 119[73]). Without this understanding the benevolence of the Creator cannot and will not be perceived. But faith in Jesus Christ is this understanding, and as such it is a powerful instrument for the knowledge of the mystery of God the Creator.

CREATION AND COVENANT

Creation comes first in the series of works of the triune God, and is thus the beginning of all the things distinct from God Himself. Since it contains in itself the beginning of time, its historical reality eludes all historical observation and account, and can be expressed in the biblical creation narratives only in the form of pure saga.* But according to this witness the purpose and therefore the meaning of creation is to make possible the history of God's covenant with man which has its beginning, its centre and its culmination in Jesus Christ. The history of this covenant is as much the goal of creation as creation itself is the beginning of this history.

1. CREATION, HISTORY AND CREATION HISTORY

When the Bible and the Church's confession speak of creation they mean by it a specific work, or a specific element in the one divine work, in which, by reason of His own inner will and determination, God turns *ad extra*[EN1]. Creation as such is not reconciliation or redemption, although both reconciliation and redemption have their presupposition in creation, and to that extent already begin with it. To say that the whole revelation of His glory, willed and determined by God, already becomes an event in creation, does not mean that we reverse the statement and say that it is limited to creation, or that all the further content of this revelation can be understood only as a continuation and unfolding of creation. On the other hand, it is not as if creation had only a temporary and dependent meaning alongside the other works, or alongside the other elements of the one divine work, and were thus not equally worthy of independent consideration. God's Word and work, attested by Holy Scripture and the confession of the Church, is articulated and demands to be heard and considered with special attention in each of its articles, and therefore here too, as the self-revelation of God the Creator.

The distinctive element in creation consists in the fact that it comes first among God's works. The Bible begins with it and so does the creed. All the [043] things distinct from God begin with it. If the eternal and determinate will of

---

* A more natural rendering of *Sage*, which is from the same root as *sagen* (to say or tell), would perhaps be tale or story. If saga is retained as a closer equivalent, it is in the precise sense given on pp. 81 ff., and in indication of the distinctive *genre* there perceived.—Ed.

[EN1] outside of God

God is the source of their inner beginning, creation is the source of their external beginning. And herein lies the peculiar dignity of the creation, that as the external beginning of all things it stands in certain respects in direct confrontation with its inner beginning, its eternal source in God's decision and plan. It has no external presupposition; it follows immediately the eternal will of God. Beyond it we can think only of God's triune being in all its perfections, of the depth of the holiness and grace of His decree. It is emphatically the work of God's freedom, and therefore also emphatically God's miracle. If everything is free and glorious in God's other works, it is because in them too God acts and is revealed as Creator. Creation as such is the immediate correlate and realisation of the divine purpose to begin with the revelation of His glory. It begins with the fact that the recipient, the scene and the handiwork of this revelation receive existence through Himself. When this takes place, everything commences—everything, that is, which is not the eternal God Himself and His purpose. Excluding God Himself and His purpose, anything prior to this beginning, to the putting into operation of the divine purpose whose goal was this beginning, cannot even be imagined. In all space outside God, creation is the first thing; everything conies from it, is maintained and conditioned, determined and shaped by it. Only God Himself is and remains the First prior to this first. Only God Himself is and remains free and glorious in relation to it. Only God Himself can and will preserve and condition, determine and shape all things in the course of His works otherwise than in the work of creation. But even God Himself, and especially God Himself, will act in such a way in the continuation of His creation, in each new miracle of His freedom, that He remains faithful to this first work of His. He will transform the reality of the creature, in a transformation which includes death, dissolution and new creation, but He will not destroy it; He will not take it away again. He will never be alone again as He was before creation. Nor will the creature be again as it was prior to creation. In all that He will do, God will not cease to be the One who has done this first thing.

But as God's first work, again according to the witness of Scripture and the confession, creation stands in a series, in an indissolubly real connexion, with God's further works. And these works, excluding for the moment the work of redemption and consummation, have in view the institution, preservation and execution of the covenant of grace, for partnership in which He has predestined and called man. The history of these divine works which follow creation is itself the execution of the eternal decision of God's will and decree to which it corresponds. But in view of the biblical economy and emphasis, it has to be [044] said at once that the history of this covenant of grace, though its actualisation follows creation, has in God's intention and purpose a dignity which, although different from that of creation, is not inferior but equal. It follows creation, but does not derive from it. Even as it follows it, it constitutes the scope of creation. It would be truer to say that creation follows the covenant of grace since it is its indispensable basis and presupposition. As God's first work, it is in the nature of a pattern or veil of the second, and therefore in outline already the form of the second. Creation sets the stage for the story of the covenant of grace. The story requires a stage corresponding to it; the existence of man and his whole world. Creation provides this. If, according to Rom. 11[36], all things are "through God" (this is the content of God's deeds for the institution, preservation and execution of the covenant of grace), and finally and lastly (in redemption and consummation) "for God," then, to begin with, all must be "from God." How could things be, and in this existence be "through God" and "for God," if they had not received their specific existence for this purpose "from God"? That this be given to them is in the totality of God's works the function of creation.

Creation must not be separated from this context. It is for this reason that the concept of creation is not in any sense identical with the general concept of a first cause or the final contingency of all things. Of course it includes this concept also. Where else can we look for the first cause or the final contingency of all things if not in creation? But in the Christian concept of the creation of all things the question is concretely one of man and his whole universe as the theatre of the history of the covenant of grace; of the totality of earthly and heavenly things as they are to be comprehended in Christ (Eph. 1[10]). On the Christian view nothing has come into being or exists in itself and as such, but only in this way and for this purpose. On this view there is no such thing as a self-existent first cause or final contingency of all things. To say that they are "of God" is to say at once, and conclusively, that they were called into being and exist in this concrete connexion, that they are of the God who is Lord and Ruler of this history. On the other hand, the absolute authority and power of the divine lordship and rule in this history rest on the fact that it does not take place on soil that is originally foreign to it, but in a sphere ordained and prepared for it and for it alone from the very beginning; in the humanity and universe which are God's creation and therefore His property, and as such the object, scene and instrument of His acts.

Hence on the one side it may be said with Augustine: *Ipse est autem creator eius (hominis) qui salvator eius. Non ergo debemus sic laudare creatorem, ut cogamur, imo vero convincamur dicere superfluum salvatorem*[EN2]. (*De nat. et gratia*, 34, 39); and on the other with Gregory of Nyssa: Τῷ γὰρ ἐξ ἀρχῆς τὴν ζωὴν δεδωκότι μόνῳ δυνατὸν ἦν καὶ πρέπον ἅμα καὶ ἀπολομένην ἀνακαλέσεσθαι[EN3]. (*Or. cat.* 8).

In relation to the dogma of creation, F. C. Baur has ventured the statement "that such [045] doctrines do not at all have the meaning for Christian consciousness which it was once believed had to be read into them, since, as soon as the essential element of the world's dependence on God is affirmed, the definite form of it has no further claim on Christian interest" (*Lehrb. d. Dogmengesch.*, 1847, 268). In answer, it must be said that the affirmation of

---

[EN2] For He who is its (humankind's) creator is also its saviour. Therefore we ought not so to praise the creator, that we are compelled, still less constrained to say that the saviour is unnecessary

[EN3] For Him alone who gave life in the beginning was it possible and proper to recall life from destruction

the world's dependence on God is an "essential element" in the Christian confession, identical with the Christian doctrine of creation, only if it speaks of an absolutely definite God—who is also recognised as the Lord and Ruler of that history—and of the world's dependence on this God. The general conception of a common, supreme and final Whence of all things, and therefore of the general conception of its ground and its dependence, do not suffice at this point. For example, Kant has given us the definition that creation is "the cause of the existence of a world or of things," that it is the *actuatio substantiae*[EN4] (*Kritik. d. Urteilskraft*, ed. Vorländer, 335). But from the standpoint of the Christian confession, while this is not untrue, it is completely meaningless. For the question of the Creator is deliberately left open according to Kant's express elucidation of this definition. But at this point everything depends upon the fact that the One from whom the world comes and on whom it depends should not be "God" in the sense of this or that conception, but He who in the process of history reconciles the world to Himself in order to give to it, as its Redeemer, its new and eternal form. If He is not this, He does not in any sense deserve to be called God from the Christian standpoint. And if the world is not founded by and dependent on this God, then according to the Christian confession its foundation and dependence have nothing whatever to do with its relationship to God. The general concept of the world's dependence on God may conceal all kinds of speculations which are of no interest to the Church's confession, or of myths which contradict it.

But conversely we have also to consider in what serious sense God can be Lord and Ruler of this history, or what can be meant by His grace and the covenant made with man for the sake of His grace, if, as King of this covenant, He is not at the same time the Creator of all things? The Christian doctrine of creation, according to which the Creator and Deliverer are one and the same, teaches that I do not first exist and then deal with this history from my own particular standpoint, but that my own standpoint, my existence, has been given to me by the One who in this history has already dealt with me, so that even as I exist I find myself at the centre of this history. I always come from God the Creator when I am confronted by God the Deliverer. Moreover, the Christian doctrine of creation, equating the Creator with the Deliverer, tells us that the world too, the whole nexus of being and movement in which I exist, has no prior existence; that there is absolutely nothing which can take precedence of the history of the divine covenant of grace, nothing from which either claim or influence can be expected, nothing which can effectually limit or cross this history; but that the whole world and I with it—everything that is actual—must serve the work of God the Deliverer because it owes its existence solely to the work of God the Creator.

Thus from both standpoints it is hard to deny that in relation to the dogma of creation it will repay us not to confine ourselves to generalities but to seek after Christian truth. But the basic condition of such precision is that we should remember the concrete connexion between the first and second articles of the creed—between creation and covenant.

[046] When the Christian doctrine of creation speaks of God as the sum total of the first cause and the final contingency of all things, it does so in recognition of the God who is the Father of the Son and who, together with the Son, is the source of the Holy Spirit, and who, as such, is the divinely free and loving person—the Almighty. It tells us that God's first work, the positing of the distinct reality of man and his world, is indelibly marked off from every other source or beginning by the fact that it precedes and prepares for the second work, God's gracious dealing within the sphere of this reality. It tells us that the

---

[EN4] realisation of substance

44

world and man are real only as they proceed from the hand of God and are kept by Him; only as they are bound and pledged and committed to the God who, as Father, Son and Holy Spirit, wills to manifest in them the glory of His grace within the context of all His works. It tells us that the creature as such is predestined to participate in the history which has its ground and direction in the will of God; that while it *is* and is *what* it is, it is from the very first the bearer of the promise that is unveiled in this history. Conversely, it tells us that the grace of God toward His creature as seen in this history is no less highly and deeply and firmly founded than the ground of its own existence. It shifts God's covenant, and man's part in this covenant, and the destiny of the world, to the point where this covenant is to be concluded, preserved and executed, viz. from the sphere of contingency to the beginning of all things. It forbids us to think meanly of Jesus Christ, His kingdom and His Church, as if the work of our salvation and redemption were a kind of afterthought which we might ignore in view of creation as God's first and principal work. It is precisely in view of creation that we cannot possibly ignore Jesus Christ. And the Christian doctrine of creation tells us all this in the full certainty of the knowledge that God the Father, Son and Holy Spirit is One, and that this One cannot be untrue but is true to Himself.

Later Jewish doctrine (cf. W. Foerster, *TWzNT*, III, 1019 f.) obviously accepted this connexion. It spoke of seven things that are pre-existent, i.e., created before creation: the Torah, God's throne, the fathers, the people of Israel, the tabernacle, i.e., the temple, the name of the Messiah, and repentance. And it did not think that the world could have received or maintained its existence without the Torah. God created the world for the sake of Abraham, the Fathers, Israel, Moses and the righteous. But He did so decisively in the foreknowledge that Israel would accept the Torah. "The meaning of creation is to prepare a place in which the will of God will be done." There was also another and, at first sight, less nomistic tradition, according to which this aeon with its temporality was created that man might recognise his time, count his life and think of his sins. The characteristic Jewish perversion of this insight had still not been overcome by Lactantius (*Div. instit.* VII, 6, 1–2), whose attitude to this matter can be perceived from the following words: *Idcirco mundus factus est, ut nascamur; ideo nascimur, ut agnoscamus factorem mundi ac nostri Deum; ideo agnoscimus, ut colamus; ideo colimus, ut immortalitatem pro laborum mercede capiamus ...; ideo praemio immortalitatis afficimur, ut similes angelis effecti summo Patri ac Domino in perpetuum serviamus et simus Deo regnum. Haec summa rerum est, hoc arcanum Dei, hoc mysterium mundi*[EN5]. And judged by the better insight gained in the meantime, Kant's view (*Kr. d. Urteilskraft*, ed. Vorländer, 336) that the ultimate purpose of the world's existence lay in the "existence of rational beings under moral laws" was a retrogression into Judaism. The same can be said of I. A. Dorner's position (*Syst. d. chr. Gl. Lehre²* Vol. I, 1886, 458), according to which the "glance of

---

[EN5] For this reason the world was made, that we might be born; and for this reason we are born, that we might come to know the maker of the world and our God; and for this reason we know, that we might worship; and for this reason we worship, that we might receive immortality as the reward of our labours ...; and for this reason we are brought to the prize of immortality, that, having been made like the angels, we might serve the supreme Father and Lord forever and be in the kingdom of God. This is the goal of things, this is the secret plan of God, this is the mystery of the world

[047]　creative love" was originally directed on "a world of free agents destined for fellowship with God"—free agents who through the original love are to become living and real images of God. It is also true of A. E. Biedermann, according to whom (*Chr. Dogm.*, 1869, 638) the ultimate purpose of the world-process lies in spiritual being, i.e., the spiritual being which has this process as its presupposition and means—that of the eternal Spirit; or, according to another passage (p. 756), "in the realisation of the divine determination of creaturely life in the Spirit in the uniform multiplicity of individual finite spirits expressing the will of the absolute Spirit." Similarly, it is true of R. A. Lipsius, according to whom (*Lehrb. d. ev. prot. Dogm.²*, 1879, 285 f.) the world of nature is the divinely appointed basis of man's world, its purpose is God's revelation in the life of the human spirit, or the self-disclosure of the infinite spiritual foundation of the world in the finite spirit evolving on the basis of natural life, and the purpose of the human world is the realisation of the spiritual determination of humanity for freedom over nature in fellowship with God, or the realisation of the kingdom of God." It is true again of A. Ritschl, according to whom (*Unterricht i. d. chr. Rel.*, 1875, § 12) "the world was created for the purpose of the kingdom of God, i.e., in order that a kingdom of created spirits might mutually exist in a perfect spiritual union with God." It is also true of R. Seeberg, according to whom (*Chr. Dogm.*, Vol. I, 1924, 472) the absolute Spirit "creates the material world in order that a multiplicity of created spirits might exist, and that they might develop their spirituality in the midst of the material world." It is true finally of E. Troeltsch, according to whom (*Gl. Lehre*, 1925, 384) the divine purpose of the world is "the training of divinely filled personality." The Jewish element in all these statements is that when stripped of all flowery language they all tell us that the divine purpose of creation is simply ideal man and the process of his spiritualisation or deification. What the Bible describes as the covenant of the grace of God with man can scarcely be recognised, or at the most only very indistinctly, in the above statements concerning the purpose of creation. But even if this is possible on a more careful interpretation of the language of these writers, there still remains the noticeable difference that according to the biblical insight this covenant and its history as such are not in any sense the purpose of creation but the content, made possible by creation, of the divine work of reconciliation. It may be said that creation aims at this other work. It may also be said that this other work already begins in and with creation. The biblical stories of creation say this, and in view of this we shall have to develop this connexion between creation and the covenant. But it cannot be said that the work of creation is the cause of this other work, and that this other work is thus the purpose of creation. All that can be said is that creation consists in the establishment of the ground and sphere and object and instrument of this other work.

　　The better declarations of theological tradition differ from others in two respects: (1) they do not put man and his elevation to humanity into the centre of the quest for the meaning of creation, but God's dealings with man in the history of the covenant; and (2) they make it plain in some way that in the purpose of creation as such we are concerned only with the making possible and not the actualisation of this other divine work. This is the position of the Didache (10, 1): ἔκτισας τὰ πάντα ἕνεκεν τοῦ ὀνόματός σου[EN6], i.e., "in order that in and through all this Thy name might be revealed and praised." It is also that of Irenaeus (*Adv. o. h.* IV, 14, 1): *Deus plasmavit Adam, ut haberet in quem collocaret sua beneficia*[EN7]. It is also that of Tertullian (*Apol.* 17): God created the world *in ornamentum maiestatis suae*[EN8]. It is also that of Calvin (*De aet. praed. Dei*, 1552, *C.R.* 8, 294): *Hoc axioma retinendum: Sic Deo fuisse curae salutem nostram ut sui non oblitus, gloriam suam primo loco haberet adeoque totum mundum hoc fine*

[EN6] Thou didst create all things for Thy name's sake
[EN7] God formed Adam so that He might have someone on whom to bestow his benevolence
[EN8] for an ornament of His majesty

1. Creation, History and Creation History

condidisse, ut gloriae suae theatrum foret[EN9]. (cf. Instit., I, 5, 5: mundus in spectaculum gloriae Dei conditus) [EN10]. It is also that of Melanchthon (Enarr. Symb. Nic., 1550, C.R. 22, 239): the causa finalis[EN11] of the divine positing of all creatures is ut se in eis patefaceret et eis suam sapientiam et bonitatem communicaret. Nam essentia optima voluit habere opera, in qua rivulos suae sapientiae et bonitatis spargeret et a quibus vicissim agnosceretur et celebraretur[EN12]. It is also that of Polanus (Synt. Theol. chr., 1609, col. 1706) who tells us that it consists in the gloria seu celebratio Dei in omnem aeternitatem[EN13]. It is also that of Quenstedt (Theol. did. pol., 1685, I, c. 10, § 1, th. 12), for whom it consists in solius Dei ... ex libertate voluntatis se communicantis beneplacitum[EN14]. The superiority of these explanations to the later Jewish, or that of Lactantius, Kant and the modern theologians quoted, is obviously that they do not turn with undue haste and urgency to man and his relation to a divine law, his elevation from the state of nature to that of spirit; to the kingdom of God to be embodied in man (it is to be noted how Lactantius, R. A. Lipsius and A. Ritschl agree at this point with the old Jewish doctrine); to the fellowship with God and His angels ordained for him—as if there were any sense in directing creation so abstractedly to man. Instead—evidently with the conviction that in this way the cause and destiny and future of man are best preserved—they look on the name and benefits and majesty and honour and revelation of God; in short, on the Word of God as the goal of that first work of His. Room is thus made for a continuation worthy of that beginning. In this way what is seen on the farther side of creation is not just ideals which may perhaps be very wonderful but which, when they are set up as ends in themselves, may prove to be illusions and lead to bitter disappointment—neither the ancient Jews nor modern Idealists have been spared this—but again and in the full and true sense the cause of God, His purposes and actions in the world and among men. And just because it is recognised that on the farther side of creation too God leads the host without needing to be relieved by man as the sum total of the purpose of His creation, and thus without surrendering into man's doubtful hands the purpose of creation, for this very reason the continuation of that beginning can be the more confidently seen in its particularity and distinguished from that beginning, and the more plainly it can be shown that with the revelation and praise of the divine name, with the collocare[EN15] of the divine beneficia[EN16], there is introduced something which is quite new and transcends creation, and that the ornamentum[EN17] and the divine majesty, the theatrum[EN18] and the gloria Dei[EN19], the opera[EN20] of the Creator and the rivuli sapientiae et bonitatis[EN21] which are to overflow them, are and always will be two very different things. On the one side we have a blatantly or more subtly imaginative, on the other a sober and for that reason all the more powerful conception of the great truth that creation and covenant

[048]

EN 9 This principle must be held firmly: God's concern for our welfare was not such that he forgot himself, but He held His own glory so very much in the first place that He founded the whole world to this end, that He might establish a theater of His glory

EN10 the world was established for the display of God's glory

EN11 final cause

EN12 so that He might reveal himself in them and communicate to them His wisdom and goodness. For the supreme essence wished to have works in which to make flow streams of His wisdom and goodness, and by which, in turn, He might be known and magnified

EN13 the glory or magnifying of God into all eternity

EN14 the only God...in the freedom of His will communicating His own good pleasure

EN15 bestowing

EN16 benefits

EN17 ornament

EN18 theater

EN19 God's glory

EN20 works

EN21 streams of wisdom and goodness

belong together. It is along the second line that a doctrine of creation which is attentive to the witness of Scripture must undoubtedly move.

The decisive anchorage of the recognition that creation and covenant belong to each other is the recognition that God the Creator is the triune God, Father, Son and Holy Spirit. Where this is and remains clear, the idea of creation will itself receive the necessary concretely Christian form and meaning. It will show itself inflexible in the face of all reinterpretations as a common concept of origin and dependence. By proving itself as its presupposition and backbone, it will also prevent the isolation and therefore the enervation of the idea of reconciliation. But it will also remain within its limits. It will not expand into the sum total of the divine works, nor give occasion for a legalistic or idealistic interpretation of the notion of the covenant. The recognition of the unity of the divine being and its particularity as Father, Son and Holy Spirit will [049] prove effective in all these directions for the recognition not only of the interconnexions but also of the variations in the relation between creation and covenant.

When the older Protestant dogmaticians (cf. Melanchthon's *Enarr. Symb. Nic.*, 1550, *C.R.* 22, 238; Bucanus, *Instit. theol.*, 1605, *L.*, V, 2; Polanus, *Synt. Theol. chr.*, 1609, *col.* 1650; J. Gerhard, *Loci*, 1610 f., *L.*, V, 2, 8 f.) expressly described creation as the work of the whole Trinity, they made a statement which has material as well as formal significance.

The creed speaks of God the *Father* as the Creator of heaven and earth. This is meaningful and right because between the particular character of the first divine mode of existence ("person") and the work of creation as the first of the divine works there exists a definite correspondence and likeness. As the Father, God is in Himself the origin which has no other (not even an eternal and divine) origin, the source of the other eternal modes of existence of the divine essence; and as the Creator, in virtue of His originative activity *ad extra*[EN22], He is the absolutely sovereign Lord of all that exists and is distinct from Himself. As the Father, God procreates Himself from eternity in His Son, and with His Son He is also from eternity the origin of Himself in the Holy Spirit; and as the Creator He posits the reality to all the things that are distinct from Himself. The two things are not identical. Neither the Son nor the Holy Spirit is the world; each is God as the Father Himself is God. But between the two, i.e., between the relationship in God Himself and God's relationship to the world, there is an obvious proportion. In view of this it is meaningful and right to designate God the Father in particular (*per appropriationem*[EN23]) as Creator, and God the Creator in particular (*per appropriationem*[EN24]) as the Father.

As concerns Holy Scripture, it is to be noted that, as far as I can see, there is nowhere any

---

[EN22] outside of God
[EN23] by appropriation
[EN24] by appropriation

direct or explicit juxtaposition of the concepts "Father" and "Creator." This does not, of course, mean that it is excluded. But it is a warning not to overestimate its importance.

The affirmation that exclusively God the Father is the Creator, or God the Creator the Father, and all the corresponding departmental divisions, would make of the triune God a triad of gods. No serious theology of the Trinity can accept responsibility for this. *Opera trinitatis ad extra sunt indivisa*[EN25]. Hence the proposition that God the Father is the Creator and God the Creator the Father can be defended only when we mean by "Father" the "Father with the Son and the Holy Spirit." It is not without His Son but as the Father of Jesus Christ that God bears the name of Father in Scripture and the creed. Again, it is not without the Son but in Jesus Christ that according to Scripture and the creed He makes Himself known as the sovereign Lord of all things and the Creator. And again, the Holy Spirit of God is the self-communication of His fatherhood as well as His lordship as Creator, so that without Him God could not partake of the name of Father and Creator. How else can the proposition   [050] that God the Father is the Creator be understood except in the sense that by appropriation, but also by implication, its true reference is to the triune God? But as, rightly understood, it has this reference to the triune God, it attests the connexion between creation and covenant. It is in *this* God, and strictly speaking in each of His three separate modes of existence, that this connexion is grounded.

This emerges at once when we try to understand what it means that God the Father is the Creator of all things in or by His Son or Word. That this is so follows from the only possible implied understanding of the first proposition. But what does it mean that this is the case?

It is legitimate and imperative that by the expression "Son" or "Word of God" we should here understand the second mode of existence ("person") of the inner divine reality in itself and as such. There exists between it and creation the following connexion. In the same freedom and love in which God is not alone in Himself but is the eternal begetter of the Son, who is the eternally begotten of the Father, He also turns as Creator *ad extra*[EN26] in order that absolutely and outwardly He may not be alone but the One who loves in freedom. In other words, as God in Himself is neither deaf nor dumb but speaks and hears His Word from all eternity, so outside His eternity He does not wish to be without hearing or echo, that is, without the ears and voices of the creature. The eternal fellowship between Father and Son, or between God and His Word, thus finds a correspondence in the very different but not dissimilar fellowship between God and His creature. It is in keeping with the Father of the eternal Son, the One who speaks the eternal Word as such; it is wholly worthy of Him, that in His dealings *ad extra*[EN27] He should be the Creator. This

---

[EN25] The works of the Trinity outside of God are undivided
[EN26] outside of God
[EN27] outside of God

is one understanding of the function of the Son or Word of God in this matter.

But this understanding alone is inadequate. For undoubtedly the expression Son or Word of God also indicates the One who in the divine decree and will humbled Himself already from eternity and therefore before the creation of all things; who manifested and exercised His deity when He willed to become the Son of Man, flesh, in order that in His person He should bear and bear away the curse of sin for all men; and who, because of His obedience even to the cross, was to be exalted by God and thus to become, again in His person, the Bearer of the divine image for all men. The connexion between Him and creation is obviously even closer and more significant. In respect of His Son who was to become man and the Bearer of human sin, God loved man and man's whole world from all eternity, even before it was created, and in and in spite of its absolute lowliness and non-godliness, indeed its anti-godliness. He created it because He loved it in His Son who because of its transgressions [051] stood before Him eternally as the Rejected and Crucified. And again, in respect of His Son who was to become man and the Bearer of the divine image, God attributed to man and his entire world from all eternity, even before He created it, enough glory, as a likeness of future glory, to cover and indeed obliterate its misery, because He thought of it in His own Son who, for its justification, stood eternally before Him as the Elected and Resurrected. If by the Son or the Word of God we understand concretely Jesus, the Christ, and therefore very God and very man, as He existed in the counsel of God from all eternity and before creation, we can see how far it was not only appropriate and worthy but necessary that God should be the Creator. If this was God's eternal counsel in the freedom of His love, the counsel actualised in the manger of Bethlehem, the cross of Calvary and the tomb of Joseph of Arimathea, it was not merely possible but essential for God to be the Creator. The fact that God has regard to His Son—the Son of Man, the Word made flesh—is the true and genuine basis of creation. To be sure there was no other necessity than that of His own free love. But a genuine necessity is constituted by the fact from all eternity He willed so to love the world, and did so love it, that He gave His only begotten Son (Jn. 3^{16}).

We have had in mind, of course, the well-known series of New Testament texts which speak of the ontological connexion between Christ and creation; and we have been attempting an exegesis of these passages. In Col. 1^{17} it is said of the Son of God: αὐτός ἐστιν πρὸ πάντων^{EN28}; in Jn. 1^{1} of the Word of God: ἐν ἀρχῇ ἦν ὁ λόγος^{EN29}; in 1 Jn. 1^{1} (without any direct description) of the object of the Christian proclamation: ὁ ἦν ἀπ' ἀρχῆς^{EN30}; and in 1 Jn. 2^{13c}: ἐγνώκατε τὸν ἀπ' ἀρχῆς^{EN31} (an indisputable masculine). To the same group there also belongs Col. 1^{15} which tells us that the Son of God is the πρωτότοκος πάσης

---

^{EN28} he is before all things
^{EN29} In the beginning was the Word
^{EN30} that which was from the beginning
^{EN31} ye have known Him that is from the beginning

κτίσεως EN32 (not as the first of creatures but as the image of the invisible God, as the One "through" whom all was created). The meaning of all these passages can only be that Christ stands as God and with God before and above the beginning of all things brought into being at the creation; He is the beginning as God Himself is the beginning. Jn. 1¹ adds expressly that the Word was with God and was God. It is also said of God's Son in Col. 1¹⁷: τὰ πάντα ἐν αὐτῷ συνέστηκεν EN33; again of the Son in Heb. 1³: φέρων τε τὰ πάντα τῷ ῥήματι τῆς δυνάμεως αὐτοῦ EN34; of the Word of God in Jn. 1¹¹: εἰς τὰ ἴδια ἦλθεν EN35; of Christ in Col. 2¹⁰: ὅς ἐστιν ἡ κεφαλὴ πάσης ἀρχῆς καὶ ἐξουσίας EN36; and of Christ again in 1 Cor. 8⁶: δι' οὗ τὰ πάντα EN37. Mt. 28¹⁸ records Christ's own words: ἐδόθη μοι πᾶσα ἐξουσία ἐν οὐρανῷ καὶ ἐπὶ γῆς EN38; and so too does Jn. 5¹⁷: πατήρ μου ἕως ἄρτι ἐργάζεται, κἀγὼ ἐργάζομαι EN39. In Jn. 5¹⁹ we read: ἃ γὰρ ἂν ἐκεῖνος ποιῇ, ταῦτα καὶ ὁ υἱὸς ὁμοίως ποιεῖ EN40; in Jn. 16¹⁵: πάντα ὅσα ἔχει ὁ πατὴρ ἐμά ἐστιν EN41; and in Jn. 17²: ἔδωκας αὐτῷ ἐξουσίαν πάσης σαρκός EN42. It should not be overlooked that in all these passages the position, dignity and power of the Creator—the exercise of unlimited lordship over against His creatures—are unquestionably ascribed to Christ. But we read distinctly in Rev. 3¹⁴ that He is Himself: ἡ ἀρχὴ τῆς κτίσεως τοῦ θεοῦ EN43; in Heb. 1²: δι' οὗ καὶ ἐποίησεν τοὺς αἰῶνας EN44; and in Heb. 1¹⁰: σὺ κατ' ἀρχάς, κύριε, τὴν γῆν ἐθεμελίωσας καὶ ἔργα τῶν χειρῶν σού εἰσιν οἱ οὐρανοί EN45. In Jn. 1³ we read of the Word of God: πάντα δι' αὐτοῦ ἐγένετο EN46, and καὶ χωρὶς αὐτοῦ ἐγένετο οὐδὲ ἓν ὃ γέγονεν EN47, a negative expression which confirms the positive. Of the same Word we read in Jn. 1¹⁰: ὁ κόσμος δι' αὐτοῦ ἐγένετο EN48; and Col. 1¹⁶ tells us of the Son of God: ἐν αὐτῷ ἐκτίσθη τὰ πάντα ἐν τοῖς οὐρανοῖς καὶ ἐπὶ γῆς, τὰ ὁρατὰ καὶ τὰ ἀόρατα ... τὰ πάντα δι' αὐτοῦ καὶ εἰς αὐτὸν ἔκτισται EN49. The above passages make it clear that the Son or Word of God, or concretely Jesus Christ, does not just become but is Lord of all things, for He is as God and with God, instituted as such by God, and Himself in full divine dignity and power the Creator of all things. *Omnia per ipsum fecit Pater*EN50. (Irenaeus, *Adv. o. h.* I, 22, 1). Polanus (*Synt. Theol. chr.*, 1609, *col.* 1653) rightly interpreted not only Irenaeus but also the διά and the ἐν EN51 of the New Testament when he paraphrased this sentence: *ipsius propria vi et efficacia et potentia omnia esse creata*EN52, thus desiring the Son or the Word to be understood not merely as *causa*

[052]

EN32 the firstborn of every creature
EN33 by Him all things consist
EN34 upholding all things by the word of His power
EN35 He came unto His own
EN36 which is the head of all principality and power
EN37 through whom are all things
EN38 All power is given unto me in heaven and in earth
EN39 My Father worketh hitherto, and I work
EN40 for what things soever He doeth, these also doeth the Son likewise
EN41 All things that the Father hath are mine
EN42 thou hast given Him power over all flesh
EN43 the beginning of the creation of God
EN44 through whom also He made the worlds
EN45 Thou, Lord, in the beginning hast laid the foundation of the earth; and the heavens are the works of thine hands
EN46 All things were made through Him
EN47 and without Him was not anything made that was made
EN48 the world was made through Him
EN49 in Him were all things created, that are in heaven, and that are in earth, visible and invisible ... all things were created through him, and for Him
EN50 The Father made all things through Him
EN51 through ... in
EN52 all things were created by His own proper strength and efficacy and power

instrumentalis seu administra[EN53], but as *causa* αὐτουργός [EN54], as *causa efficiens, socia Patris in creando*[EN55]. It should be observed in this connexion that even the διά [EN56], which seems to be particularly well brought out by the thought of a *causa instrumentalis*[EN57], is applied also to the activities of the Father (Rom. 6⁴, 1 Cor. 1⁹, Eph. 2⁴).

It is now known that in this respect the writers of the New Testament found themselves on prepared ground inasmuch as the notion of a second divine being assisting in the work of creation had become general in their day. What they ascribe to Jesus Christ in all the above passages was not only ascribed by Philo to the Logos but also by the syncretistic theosophy and cosmology of the time to Hermes, to death, to Athene, to the Wohu-Manu, to the Mithra of Zoroastrianism and to the Mandaean Hibil-Ziva. The bearer of revelation who was to bring the low, dark world into contact with the exalted, pure God was generally thought of as the one by whom the relation between God and the world is established, i.e., by whom creation is accomplished. So great is God, and so great is the riddle of the universe, that a mediator of this kind is required. And so great is the bearer of revelation that he is the instrument of the original mediation which lays the foundation. There can be no doubt that in the passages under consideration the New Testament writers were referring to this element in the religious world of their day. The shattering of the consciousness of God and the world was revealed in the invention of this intermediate being, in the proclamation of all kinds of bearers of revelation and finally in the identification of the bearers of revelation previously recognised with this intermediate being. But to say that the apostles were referring to this element in the religious inheritance of their environment does not mean that what they said was borrowed from it. This was not the case. They had no need to take over from their contemporaries even the form of their statements about Jesus Christ. They could be quite content merely to refer to what they heard their contemporaries say. For, quite apart from questions of substance, the third part of the Old Testament Canon offered them an older literary model in Prov. 2 and 8 and Job 28 with their portrayal of the "wisdom" which is inaccessible to man, or accessible only by its self-revelation—a wisdom which is nothing other than God's holiness and righteousness addressing and instructing and directing and sustaining man for the sake of His patience, and the beginning of which must always be for us men the fear of the Lord. Of this wisdom they read in Prov. 8²²ᶠ that God had possessed it from eternity, before the beginning or origin of the world; that it was present with Him as His favourite (or as His overseer) when He made the heavens and laid the foundations of the earth, after the separation of the waters below and above the firmament. They read quite expressly in Ps. 136⁵ and Prov. 3¹⁹ that God had created the heavens and the earth by this "wisdom." If the foregoing New Testament quotations are to be traced to any literary source it is certainly this one, which even later Judaism had pertinently utilised and diligently exploited. But in this "wisdom" of the Old Testament which had participated in creation—and this brings us to the material difference—we do not have (1) any metaphysical principle to unite the God-concept with the riddle of the universe. We have to realise that these passages do not in any sense deal with the problems of the doctrine of God and an understanding of the world; that this "wisdom" is in reality very simply and profoundly the divine revelation addressing and directing the man covenanted with God as practical wisdom; and that it is undoubtedly understood in this sense in the one New Testament passage which deals with it expressly, i.e., 1 Cor. 1 and 2 (and also in Mt. 11¹⁶⁻¹⁹; Col. 1⁹ ²⁵ᶠ, 4⁵; Eph.

[053]

[EN53] instrumental or administrative cause
[EN54] self-sustaining cause
[EN55] efficient cause, equal with the Father in creating
[EN56] through
[EN57] instrumental cause

$1^{7f.\ 17f.}$, 5^{15}; and Jas. $1^{5f.}$ and $3^{13f.}$). There is thus no trace in any of the New Testament passages quoted of the suggestion that the participation of Jesus Christ in creation is significant for these writers because they too had been affected by the general shattering of the consciousness of God and the world, or because they had been seeking an intermediate principle and had given to this postulate the name of Jesus Christ. Not they but their contemporaries had been shaken and were therefore looking for such principles. They, the apostles, on the other hand, were the bearers of the objective, shattering message of the kingdom of God drawn near, and the consequent end of all mediating philosophy, theosophy and cosmology. As against the views of their contemporaries, which seemed to be so similar, they could not have spoken more critically than they did when they described Jesus Christ as the One "through whom" or "in whom" God had created all things. In so doing they were actually extending to every doctrine of God and view of the world an invitation to faith, i.e., to practical participation in God's covenant of grace and its history. And so the "wisdom" of the Old Testament is not in any sense (2) an intermediate being—a kind of third existence— between God and the world. It had certainly become something of this kind in the interpretation of later Judaism. But in the canonical passages it is never more than God's revelation to man; it has no third aspect but only that of God and man—of the One who gives it and the one who receives it. It is only in this way, and not as a "hypostasis," that according to these verses it is in the beginning, and is indeed itself the beginning, the Creator of all things. What these passages say is that this divine activity with man had already begun in and with creation as its meaning and basis. But this is also the case when the New Testament passages speak of Christ in the same connexion. It is clear (1 Tim. 2^5) that He is for them "the Mediator between God and man," but that He is not for this reason an intermediate being, a third between the two. Between God and man there is the world of angels. But even angels are not "intermediate beings"; they belong by nature to the creaturely sphere. The New Testament does not ascribe this function to any angel. The passage cited from Heb. 1^{10} stands in a context whose point is precisely to distinguish Christ from the angels, as is also done expressly in 1 Cor. 8^6 and Col. 1^{16}. He to whom the New Testament ascribes participation in creation has only divine and human form, like the "wisdom" of the Old Testament. He is not an "intermediate being." He is the divine person who acts, suffers and triumphs as man; the Humiliated and Exalted, the Crucified and Resurrected. And in this way, and just because He is not a "hypostasis," He is the Mediator between God and man, like the "wisdom" of the Old Testament. What interest would the writers of the New Testament have had in interpreting Him as a "hypostasis," and from what standpoint could they have done so? He meant something much more and far better to them than that. And again, they could not have been more critical of the views of their contemporaries than when with undoubted reference to them they said of this person—that God had created all things by Him. In so doing they summoned man to faith in God. And in this way they did not add another to the plethora of supposed "intermediate beings."

Far more important than the question of religious history is the factual question how the writers of the New Testament for their part understood the important δι' αὐτοῦ or ἐν αὐτῷ [EN58]; what they meant by associating with God the Father His Son or Word or Jesus Christ in creation. It is clear from all the passages quoted—we have only to think of the most important, Jn. $1^{3f.}$, Heb. $1^{2f.}$ and Col. $1^{15f.}$—that we are dealing with a special emphasising and distinction of the person of Jesus Christ. It is not God or the world and their relation which is the problem of these passages but the lordship of Jesus Christ. The starting point is [054] not that deity is so exalted and holy or that the world is so dark; nor is it the affirmation that there is something like a mediation between the two which bears the name of Jesus Christ.

EN58 through him ... in him

What they have in view is the kingdom of God drawn near; the turning point of the times, revealed in the name of Jesus Christ, as the fulfilment of all the promises of the covenant of grace. To give to the Bearer of this name the honour due to Him, or rather to bear witness to the honour which He has, they venture the tremendous assertion that the world was created through Him and in Him as through God, and in God, in God's eternal will and purpose. And so we have to see first the simple fact that in so doing they thought concretely of the ineffable and inclusive reality of Jesus Christ as the κύριος EN59; that their aim was to give a comprehensive description of His κυριότης EN60; and that they therefore found it necessary to describe it in this way, setting it at the beginning of all things.

But now we may and must ask further whether it was the eternal Son (or eternal Word) of God as such in His pure deity that they had in mind; or whether, more inclusively and more concretely, it was the Son of God as the Son of Man, the Word made flesh. If it was only the former, the λόγος ἄσαρκος EN61, the "second person" in the Trinity in itself and as such, to whom they referred with their δι' αὐτοῦ and ἐν αὐτῷ EN62, one can only be astonished at the force with which these expressions so unmistakeably point to a specific creative causality. It is certainly true that the wisdom and power of the Creator are also those of the eternal Son or Word of God. But this would not explain the particularity of the divine causality of which these expressions appear to speak. As we have seen, the only possible connexion between the eternal Son or Word of God on the one hand and creation on the other is that it is commensurate with and worthy of the Father of the eternal Son, the Speaker of the eternal Word as such, that He should be the Creator in His dealings *ad extra* EN63. Perhaps the writers of the New Testament wished to say this too. Indeed, there can be no doubt that they did. But was this all they wished to say? If so, they could not have described Jesus Christ as the actual divine ground of creation, as the peculiar creative causality, to which those expressions seem to point. It has to be kept in mind that the whole conception of the λόγος ἄσαρκος EN64, the "second person" of the Trinity as such, is an abstraction. It is true that it has shown itself necessary to the Christological and trinitarian reflections of the Church. Even to-day it is indispensable for dogmatic enquiry and presentation, and it is often touched upon in the New Testament, though nowhere expounded directly. The New Testament speaks plainly enough about the Jesus Christ who existed before the world was, but always was with a view to the concrete content of the eternal divine will and decree. For this reason it does not speak expressly of the eternal Son or Word as such, but of the Mediator, the One who in the eternal sight of God has already taken upon Himself our human nature, i.e., not of a formless Christ who might well be a Christ-principle or something of that kind, but of Jesus the Christ. The One who according to Heb. 1³ upholds all things by the Word of His power is also the One who according to the following verse, when He had purged our sins, sat down on the right hand of majesty on high. According to Col. 1¹⁵, He is "the first-born of every creature," and, according to v. 14, the One in whom we have ἀπολύτρωσις EN65, i.e., the forgiveness of sins. According to verse 18, He is the "firstborn from the dead; that in all things he might have the preeminence." How could this be said of the λόγος ἄσαρκος EN66? We shall misunderstand the whole Johannine Prologue if we fail to

---

EN59 Lord
EN60 lordship
EN61 Word without flesh
EN62 through Him ... in Him
EN63 outside of God
EN64 Word without flesh
EN65 redemption
EN66 Word without flesh

see that the sentence οὗτος ἦν ἐν ἀρχῇ πρὸς τὸν θεόν [EN67]. (Jn. 1²)—which would other-wise be a wholly unnecessary repetition—points to the person who is the theme of the whole ensuing Gospel, and of whom it is said in v. 14: "the Word became flesh and tabernacled among us." And in just the same way in this event it became historical reality, as the Word incarnate—how else?—this Word was in the beginning, i.e., in the divinely determined counsel with God before the world was. The real basis of creation, permitted and even demanded by the unprecedented continuation in v. 3, that "all things were made by him, and without him was not anything made that was made," is that the Word was with God, existing before the world was, and that from all eternity God wanted to see and know and love His only begotten Son as the Mediator—His Word incarnate. It is not difficult to prove that no other meaning can be read into the passages adduced than that they refer to Jesus the Christ, who is certainly very God, but who is also very man. Irenaeus has correctly assessed the meaning of the New Testament (in this respect no other assessment is really possible): *Mundi factor vere verbum Dei est: hic autem est Dominus noster, qui in novissimis temporibus homo factus est, in hoc mundo existens, et secundum invisibilitatem continet quae facta sunt omnia et in universa conditione infixus, quoniam verbum Dei gubernans et disponens omnia; et propter hoc in sua venit* [EN68]. (*Adv. o. h.* V, 18, 3). Coccejus, too, has rightly assessed the meaning of the New Testament: *Fundatio mundi subordinatur decreto electionis et ad id respectum habet* [EN69]. (*S. Theol.*, 1669, 37, 29). *Ille qui ab initio coelum terramque condidit, est is, qui Deus Israelis nuncupari voluit, et quum ea creavit, iam tum vidit se facere mundum theatrum gloriae gratiae suae* [EN70] (note the quiet but very definite improvement of the expression of Calvin) *qua velut praecipua laude triumpharet* (*ib.*, 33, 1). So, too, has H. Witsius: *Ipsa terrae fundatio sine intuitu mortis Christi facta non est. Nam quum manifestatio gloriosae suae gratiae in homine per Christum summus Dei hominem creantis finis fuerit, fundatio terrae, ut bonis habitaculum esset, medii ad finem istum rationem obtinet. Neque conveniens Deo fuisset terram condere in habitaculum hominis peccatoris, nisi eadem illa terra lustranda aliquando fuisset sanguine Christi, sanctificantis et glorificantis electos suos. Propter omnes has rationes mactatio Christi* (Rev. 13⁸) *et fundatio mundi non incommode iunguntur* [EN71]. (*Oecon. foed.*, 1693, III, 4, 16). Also J. Wichelhaus (*Die Lehre d. hl. Schrift,* ³ 1892, 349 f.): "How could God call into existence what is not-God ... what is in itself dead, obscure and transitory? He could not have done so had there not been something in God which in His eternal love He posited outside and before Himself, had there not existed in Him an eternal decree (on p. 352 a divine counsel and covenant of peace which had been formed between Father and Son before the foundation of the world) in which all His perfec-tions were to be revealed (Eph. 1¹⁰, Col. 1¹⁵ᶠ·). God could not have created a world which He

[055]

[EN67] The same was in the beginning with God

[EN68] Truly the maker of the world is the Word of God: and this is our Lord, who in the last times was made a human being, living in this world, who in His invisible power contains everything that was made and penetrates the whole creation, because the Word of God governs and directs of all things: and for this reason He came to His own

[EN69] The foundation of the world is subordinate to the decree of election and must be referred to it

[EN70] He who in the beginning established the heavens and the earth is He who wished to be called the God of Israel, and when He created them, He saw to it that He made the world a theater of the glory of His grace ... by which He might triumph as by excellent praise

[EN71] The creation of the earth was not accomplished without a view to the death of Christ. For since the showing forth of God's glorious grace in humanity through Christ was God's chief end in creating humankind, the creation of the earth is reckoned a means to that end, so that the good might have a dwelling-place. For it was not suitable for God to establish the earth as a habitation for sinful humanity, unless that same world were at some time purified by the blood of Christ, who sanctifies and glorifies his elect. For all these reasons it is not inappropri-ate that the execution of Christ and the creation of the world are linked together

could have loved for its own sake and which could have had life in itself. ... What God had in view at creation was His Son, the Son of His love, and a Church elected in Him by eternal decree. ... What God has created in Christ Jesus is a dark world which He willed to enlighten and to fructify, and a poor son of man whom He willed to save." Or on p. 351: "It was the will and good-pleasure of inexplicable kindness and mercy, the free movement of grace and love, that in His Son, in Christ, God willed to impart His glory to a creature which in itself is dust and ashes; that He willed to exalt the most needy and most helpless creature above all the works of His hands (Ps. 8, Heb. 2). And it was thus that His eternal love willed to create for itself an object of its compassion and kindness." "The glorification of God's name in Jesus Christ is accordingly the final goal of creation, so that everything is ordered for this purpose, and everything, be it light or darkness, good or evil, must serve this purpose" (p. 355).

To sum up, the New Testament passages in question say that the creative wisdom and power of God were in the beginning specifically the wisdom and power of Jesus Christ. For in the first place He was the eternal Son and the Word of God, the whole of divine being revealed and active in creation being His own eternal being. Second, His existence as the Son of God the Father was in some sense the inner divine analogy and justification of creation. Finally and supremely, He was already in the eternal decree of God the Mediator; the Bearer of our human nature; the Humiliated and Exalted as the Bearer of our flesh; a creature and precisely as such loved by God; and in this way the motivating basis of creation. If God willed to give His eternal Son this form and function, and if the Son of God willed to obey His Father in this form and function, this meant that God had to begin to act as Creator, for there could be no restraining His will. Hence, as these passages of the New Testament declare, it is not only God the Father, but in particular the Son Jesus Christ, who is *propria vi et efficacia et potentia*[EN72] the Creator of all things.

[056]

Here as elsewhere what is true of the Father and the Son is also true of the Holy Spirit of the Father and the Son. The Holy Spirit is with the Father and the Son the true, eternal God in so far as, like the begetting Father and the begotten Son, He is the communion and self-impartation realised and consisting between both from all eternity; the principle of their mutual love proceeding from both and equal in essence; the eternal reality of their separateness, mutuality and convolution, of their distinctness and interconnexion. To this extent it may well be said that it is in the Holy Spirit that the mystery of God's trinitarian essence attains its full profundity and clarity. He is at once the innermost secret of God, and in God's relationship with man the great, bright and incontrovertible revelation of the unity and diversity of the Father and the Son. It is in the Holy Spirit that the commission of the Father and the obedience of the Son, the good-pleasure of the Father and the glory of the Son, obviously coincide in the decree which is the intra-divine beginning of all things.

In this respect we may and must describe Him in His eternal, intra-divine reality as the "Spirit of the Lord," who is the "Spirit of wisdom and understanding, the Spirit of counsel and might, the Spirit of knowledge and of the fear of the Lord" (Is. 11$^{2f.}$).

There pre-exists in Him (since He is the Spirit of the Father and the Son,

---

[EN72] by His own proper strength and efficacy and power

and since the Father and the Son meet in Him in relation to the world and man), the whole reality of the fatherly compassion of God, His self-expression, His own glorification in His Son, the whole truth of the promise, the whole power of the Gospel, and therefore the whole order of the relation between God the Creator and His creatures. Because God is also the Holy Spirit in His will and activity toward and with the world and man, God becomes possible and supportable for the creature and the creature for God: God for the creature, so that it no longer entails its immediate destruction to be without and before God; and the creature for God, so that He can find in it something more and better than revolt and blasphemy and the violation of His glory. We may say in a word that it is in God the Holy Spirit that the creature as such pre-exists. That is to say, it is God the Holy Spirit who makes the existence of the creature as such possible, permitting it to exist, maintaining it in its existence, and forming the point of reference of its existence. For it is He who in that counsel anticipates and guarantees its reconciliation with God and redemption by Him in the union of the Father and the Son. It could not of course exist if, in relation to it, God had not been One with Himself from all eternity, if He [057] had not been from all eternity the Holy Spirit of love, who in that agreement has willed its existence and assumed it on His own responsibility. For that reason it is only in the Holy Spirit that the creature can be sure that it can and may exist. For it is only in the Holy Spirit that there can be revealed to it that unity and agreement between the Father and the Son as that which makes it possible and legitimate. That this agreement exists and is valid is the work of the Holy Spirit in creation. As may be seen, this too is from a particular angle the *opus indivisum totius trinitatis*[EN73].

We possess no series of direct New Testament attestations of the relationship between the Holy Spirit and creation similar to those which occupied us in connexion with the Son or Word of God. When the *Symb. Nic.-Const.* calls the Holy Spirit τὸ ζωοποιοῦν[EN74], it is, of course, quoting directly from Jn. 6⁶³: τὸ πνεῦμά ἐστις τὸ ζωοποιοῦν[EN75]; and there is also an allusion to 1 Cor. 15⁴⁵: ὁ ἔσχατος Ἀδὰμ εἰς πεῦμα ζωοποιοῦν[EN76], and to 2 Cor. 3⁶: τὸ δὲ πνεῦμα ζωοποιεῖ[EN77]. But we have to remember that in all these references ζωοποιεῖν[EN78] is primarily a soterio-eschatological term, describing the quickening and animation effected by the work of Jesus Christ, or by faith in Him, in those who without Him are the victims of death, and that it was certainly adopted in this sense in the *Nic.-Const.* All the same this deliverance effected by the Holy Spirit is itself the confirmation of creation when God first gave to man the life which he then lost. That the New Testament writers had this connexion in mind is obvious from the fact that in the three references (and particularly 1 Cor. 15⁴⁵) there is a clear allusion to Gen. 2⁷, where through God's inbreathing of the "breath of life" (πνοὴ ζωῆς) man becomes a "living soul" (ψυχὴ ζῶσα). And this certainly means that it is by the communication and impartation of that in which God exists as God

---

EN73 undivided work of the entire Trinity
EN74 the giver of life
EN75 It is the spirit that quickeneth
EN76 the last Adam was made a quickening spirit
EN77 but the spirit giveth life
EN78 to give life

that it comes about that man can exist as man. Gen. 7^{15} describes not only the human but also the animal world as ἄρσεν καὶ θῆλυ ἀπὸ πάσης σαρκός, ἐν ᾧ ἐστι πνεῦμα ζωῆς[EN79]. Ps. 33^6 says that even the host of heaven is made by the breath of God's mouth (πνεύματι τοῦ στόματος αὐτοῦ). Ps. 139^7 asks even more inclusively: ποῦ πορευθῶ ἀπὸ τοῦ πνεύματός σου[EN80]. And finally in Ps. $104^{29f.}$ we have the remarkable antithesis : "Thou takest away their breath (τὸ πνεῦμα αὐτῶν), they die, and return to their dust. Thou sendest forth thy spirit (τὸ πνεῦμά σου) they are created: and thou renewest the face of the earth." We are thus confronted with the remarkable fact that the Old Testament statement under consideration undoubtedly refers to the first creation and the preservation of the world and of man. It does not say anything concerning the breath or Spirit of God corresponding to what is said of "wisdom" in Prov. 3 and 8. That is, it does not say (nor is this the meaning of Ps. 33^6) that the world was created "by" the Spirit. But it describes Him (this is especially clear in Ps. $104^{29f.}$) as the divine *conditio sine qua non*[EN81] of the creation and preservation of the creature. It says that it is only through Him that the creature has its indispensable life; only through Him that it has continued enjoyment and exercise of the existence loaned to it in creation; and that without Him it cannot possibly be what on the basis of its creation it was destined to be. But this very statement, which was no doubt intended cosmologically, is the one which in those New Testament passages is suddenly adopted and understood soterio-eschatologically. We are told in Jn. 6^{63} how in a final allusion to His return to the Father Jesus adds to the "hard saying" about the eating and drinking of His flesh and blood as the true meat and the true drink the explanation: "It is the spirit that quickeneth; the flesh profiteth nothing: the words which I speak to you, they are spirit and they are life." In 1 Cor. 15^{45} the distinction and sequence of the present existence of the creature and its future spiritual existence to be realised in the resurrection is emphasised by an antithesis which expressly points back to Gen. 2^7: "The first man, Adam, was made a living soul; the last Adam was made a quickening spirit." And in 2 Cor. 3^6 the "new covenant" of Jer. 31^{31}, which is not of the letter but of the Spirit, is explained by the statement: "For the letter killeth, but the spirit giveth life." Thus the Spirit of Jesus (His words spoken to His disciples which, as such, carry the Spirit and bring life) makes His flesh and blood—impotent in themselves for this pur-pose—the true meat and the true drink. The last Adam (in virtue of His resurrection from the dead) is Spirit, and therefore that which makes the first a "living soul"; and again, it is the Spirit who is the distinctive essence of the apostolic ministry. What does this mean? It surely means that the writers of the New Testament look into a dimension which is still hidden in the Old Testament sayings about the "breath of God." But it also means that they too, look-ing into this new dimension, describe the Spirit as the *conditio sine qua non*[EN82] of creaturely existence, i.e., of its glorification, its hope, its adaptability for its appointed existence and activity. Like the Old Testament, they are answering the question: How exactly can the crea-ture as creature not only become but be? The answer is necessarily indirect. For them there is no ζωή[EN83] and therefore no ζωοποίησις[EN84] of the creature apart from that already initiated in the resurrection of Jesus Christ and to be expected from Him. And it is in this ζωοποιεῖν[EN85] that they see the work of the Spirit. In this indirect way, by expecting life—life in the new aeon which is true life for them—from the work of the Spirit, and from Him alone, they also bear witness that there could be no creature, nor any creation, if God were

[058]

[EN79] male and female of all flesh, wherein is the breath of life
[EN80] Whither shall I go from thy spirit?
[EN81] necessary condition
[EN82] necessary condition
[EN83] life
[EN84] giving of life
[EN85] act of giving life

not also the Holy Spirit and active as such, just as He is also the Father and the Son and active as such.

This being so, we obviously cannot say that theological tradition moved along unscriptural lines when it referred the ζωοποιοῦν EN86 of the *Nic.-Const.* to the presence and the activity of the Holy Spirit in the first creation. The lines of the Whitsun hymn *Veni creator Spiritus:*

> *Imple superna gratia*
> *Quae tu creasti pectora,*

show that in so doing it followed much the same line of exegesis as that which we have just propounded. Among the Reformers Calvin especially took up the position that the Holy Spirit is to be understood as the divine *virtus*EN87 poured out on all things and supporting, sustaining and quickening all things (*Cat. Gen.,* 1542, qu. 19; *Instit.* I, 13, 14), although unfortunately he did not give any more detailed explanation of the relationship. This should not be too difficult if we keep in mind that the Holy Spirit is in some sense the necessary divine justification and sanctification of the creature as such, and therefore, if not the ground, at least the fundamental condition of its existence. The ground of creation and of the creature is, as we have seen, the incarnate Word of God as the content and object of the eternal divine decree of grace—the pre-existent Jesus Christ. It is for His sake that God wills the creature and accomplishes creation. But this decree of grace, and the creative will of God founded on it, has its necessary inner presupposition in the fact that the unity, love and peace between God the Father and Son are not unsettled or disturbed but transcendently glorified by the fact that the Word of God becomes flesh, that in His Son God takes to Himself man's misery and undertakes his redemption, thus addressing His love to another than Himself, i.e., the creature, and willing and bringing about the existence of another than Himself, i.e., that of the creature. That in His very humility and exaltation in human nature, in Jesus Christ crucified and risen and for His sake in the existence of the creature, the being of God should radiate and triumph—bigger and stronger than if He had kept His glory to Himself—is obviously the inner presupposition of the divine decree of grace and of the divine creative will founded upon it. In some sense it is a matter of the self-justification [059] and self-sanctification of God without which He could not have loved the creature nor willed or actualised its existence. The fulfilment of this presupposition, the eternal accomplishment of this divine self-justification and self-sanctification, is the Holy Spirit of the Father and the Son *qui procedit ex Patre Filioque*EN88, who in His common origin in the Father and the Son not only does not hinder their fellowship but glorifies it; in whom God does not restrict His deity but causes it to overflow even in the decree of grace and His creative will. In this way the Holy Spirit is the inner divine guarantee of the creature. If its existence were intolerable to God, how could it be loved and willed and made by Him? How could it emerge and be? That its existence should not be intolerable to God but destined to serve His greater glory—the creation of this essential condition of its existence is the peculiar work of the Holy Spirit in creation. In view of this work of His, He can indeed be called with Calvin God's *vertu et puissance, laquelle est espandue sur toutes créatures: et neantmoins reside tousiours en luy*EN89. If, then, in the New Testament especially His activity in the historical execution of the covenant of grace is described as the ζωοποίησις EN90 of the creature subjected to death, as the

---

EN86 giver of life
EN87 power
EN88 who proceeds from the Father and the Son
EN89 strength and power, which is spread over all creatures: but which nevertheless remains always in Him
EN90 making alive

divine power of the work and witness of Jesus Christ, and therefore as the power of the new birth and faith, of salvation and hope, we do not find it difficult to recognise in this activity the character which is already peculiar to Him in that first work of His.

The aim of creation is history. This follows decisively from the fact that God the Creator is the triune God who acts and who reveals Himself in history. God wills and God creates the creature for the sake of His Son or Word and therefore in harmony with Himself; and for His own supreme glory and therefore in the Holy Spirit. He wills and creates it for the sake of that which in His grace He wills to do to it and with it by His Son or Word in the Holy Spirit. The execution of this activity is history. What is meant is the history of the covenant of grace instituted by God between Himself and man; the sequence of the events in which God concludes and executes this covenant with man, carrying it to its goal, and thus validating in the sphere of the creature that which from all eternity He has determined in Himself; the sequence of the events for the sake of which God has patience with the creature and with its creation gives it time—time which acquires content through these events and which is finally to be "fulfilled" and made ripe for its end by their conclusion. This history is from the theological standpoint *the* history.

To distinguish it from world history, national history, the history of civilisation and even Church history, the conservative theology of the 19th century called it the history of salvation. The expression is materially correct and important. In the sequence of these events—from creation to the dawn of the last time (our own) with the birth, death and resurrection of Jesus Christ—we have to do indeed with the provision and revelation of salvation, or, to be more precise, of man's indispensable deliverance by his reconciliation with God as a presupposition of his eternal redemption and fulfilment. But this history of salvation is not just one history or element among others. It is not just a kind of red thread in the texture of all other history, of real history. Those who use the expression "history of salvation" must take good care that it is not transformed in their hands into the secular concept of "history of religion," i.e., the history of the religious spirit, which as such can only be one history among many [060] others in the context of history generally. The history of salvation is *the* history, the true history which encloses all other history and to which in some way all other history belongs to the extent that it reflects and illustrates the history of salvation; to the extent that it accompanies it with signs and intimations and imitations and examples and object-lessons. No other history can have any independent theme in relation to this history, let alone be a general and true history in the context of which the history of salvation can only be one among others. The covenant of grace is *the* theme of history. The history of salvation is *the* history.

Since the covenant of grace, and therefore history, is the aim of creation, creation itself belongs to history and therefore to the sequence of events which fulfils time. It occupies a highly unique position and significance as the first of all God's works, and by reason of this it is clearly distinct from all the rest. But it belongs to all the rest, for it is itself a sequence of events fulfilling time, historical actuality, in just the same way as the consummation and redemption as the conclusion of God's works will be an event fulfilling time, historical actuality. There is no μετάβασις εἰς ἄλλο γένος [EN91] between creation and what follows it. Nor does creation itself break off or cease when the history of the covenant begins and continues. What we shall have to understand specifically as God's providence, as the preservation and government of man and the world by Him, is also creation, continuing creation, *creatio continua*. But true as this is, the converse is also true that history for its part begins with creation; that creation itself has as such a historical character and is an event fulfilling time. This must not be minimised or obscured. Creation is not a timeless truth, even though time begins with it, and it extends to all times, and God is the Creator at every point in time. According to Scripture there are no timeless truths, but all truths according to Scripture are specific acts of God in which He unveils Himself; acts which as such have an eternal character embracing all times, but also a concretely temporal character. As Jesus Christ Himself is eternal as God and stands as Lord above all times, but is also concretely temporal and in this way the real Lord of the world and His community, so it is with creation. Those who regard God's creation as an eternal but timeless relation of the creature and its existence can certainly boast of a very deep and pious conviction, but they cannot believe it in the Christian and biblical sense. For this timeless relation has nothing whatever to do with God's decree of grace in which God from all eternity has condescended to His creature in His Son in order to exalt it in His Son; nor with the acts in which God has accomplished this decree according to the revelation of Himself. It does not exclude the possibility that God may not yet or no longer be gracious to man and the world. In this timeless relation there is not yet or no longer to be seen anything of His will to condescend to His creature in order to exalt it to Himself. We could only in some sense persuade ourselves on our own responsibility that this relation exists, and then give it a positive meaning, again on our [061] responsibility. That we can understand our creaturely existence as such as the gift of divine grace depends—if "grace" is not to be just a pious word—on the fact that its creation and preservation is a concrete act of God and therefore a historical reality fulfilling time. Then and only then does our creaturely existence as such already stand in connexion with the organising centre of all God's acts, with the reality of Jesus Christ; then and only then can we understand our existence and nature as God's grace; then and only then can we believe in our existence and nature as we believe in Jesus Christ, as we believe in the triune God.

From this standpoint it is no mere coincidence but of supreme and basic importance that the biblical witness mediates to us not only the history of the covenant of grace in itself and as such, but first and supremely, although in indissoluble connexion with the former, the history of creation in various forms. In relation to the first pages of the Old Testament two views have to be taken into account. On the one hand they may be regarded as meaningless.

[EN91] change of categories

On the other they may be supposed to embody a revealed cosmosophy of a metaphysical or scientific or mixed character which is merely followed by the account of the commencement of the intercourse and covenant between God and man.

The first of these views means that to answer the obvious and by no means indifferent question concerning the ground and being of man and his world, we are referred to our own metaphysical or scientific genius, or to our own powers in the construction of myth or saga. In this case, every age and in the last analysis every individual has to answer the question according to the light of his own mental abilities and powers. The understanding of the beginning and progress of the intercourse and covenant between God and man will necessarily fall victim to a corresponding variety. It is an open secret what usually happens to the knowledge of God's works when the first pages of the Bible are treated as if they were in fact meaningless.

The other view means that in these pages we do have actual instruction about the ground and being of man and his world, and that because it is revealed we have good cause to appropriate it and a duty to do so. Let us suppose that we seriously try to do this and that up to a point we succeed. We are then confronted by the difficulty that between the beginning of the Bible and its continuation there yawns the abyss that on the one side we have to do with a non-historical and on the other with a historical reality of God. In what sense, then, can we really believe in both cases when according to all that follows in the Bible "believing" signifies a relationship to the specific historical acts and attitudes of God? How can we really answer the question concerning the relationship between the two different realities of God? In the last resort, is [062] it not we ourselves who will necessarily determine this relationship on our own responsibility, and with it the interpretation of the whole? Nor is this question theoretical. It is again no secret what happens to the knowledge of all God's works when quite apart from and against the text itself what is written on the first pages of the Old Testament is treated as a kind of revealed cosmosophy.

Both these views mean that the historical narrative of Scripture (beginning with the fall) refers from the very outset to the acts of God in a foreign sphere: a sphere in which something other than God's acts had previously been authoritative; a sphere in which we have to orientate and direct ourselves by a different knowledge than that of God's acts; a sphere in which we need a different relation to God than that of faith. We may believe in God's acts, and in Jesus Christ, but even with this faith and even with Jesus Christ we will necessarily feel isolated and threatened in this sphere. And it is common knowledge that there is much sincere and profound Christianity which has not rid itself of this feeling of isolation and threat in a sphere ultimately foreign, and that this is the reason why there is so much Christianity which behaves as if the first pages of the Bible were meaningless, or as if what is written there were not the history of creation but a philosophy of creation which one cannot believe and to which we are forced to seek a different attitude. But what is written there is the history of creation, and therefore, in a unique sense which we shall have to discuss later, it is no less history, the history of the covenant, than the continuation which obviously bears this character.

By beginning with the history of creation the Bible sets the ground and being of man and his world in the light of the grace which later reveals itself as God's meaning and purpose in that which in the fulfilment of time takes place between God and man. This means that the question about the origin, existence and nature of things cannot be withdrawn from the sphere of grace; that we cannot call for any independent answers foreign to this sphere or develop an independent system of thought in opposition to the revelation of God or His rule in the reconciliation of the world to Himself, as if there were a corresponding natural system of reality where the grace of God does not yet have, or no longer has, the final word. There is, of course, a realm of nature which as such is different from the realm of grace. But for all its distinctiveness there is in it nothing which does not point to grace and therefore already come from grace; nothing which can enjoy independent life or exercise independent dominion. And conversely, for all the newness and particularity of the realm of grace, there is no place in it for anything unnatural, but from the creation everything is also nature. By beginning with the story of creation the Bible protects the faith in God to which it invites and summons from being regarded as a special function related to a special sphere of reality. On the contrary, it relates everything to faith, showing that even faith's presupposition, i.e., the [063] existence of the creature, is the object of faith and therefore belongs to faith and cannot be recognised except by faith. It also shows on the other hand that faith is related to the whole of reality, and thus prevents the feeling of isolation and threat which is unavoidable when creation forms a distinct sphere from that of revelation, nature from that of grace and existence from that of faith. These are the inner reasons why we have cause to be grateful that the biblical witness begins neither with silence about creation nor with a philosophy of creation but with the history of creation.

The two forms of the creation story in Gen. 1 and 2 do not constitute a foreign element in this witness. They are an integral element in the pre-history of the people of Israel which commences with the history of the first man, and are thus indissolubly linked with this history in the strict sense as it begins in Gen. 12¹. The technical term for the "history of creation," according to a saying in the Priestly Code which may well have been the original title (Gen. 2⁴ᵃ), is "the *toledoth*^EN92 a new creation of the heavens and the earth," i.e., the "genealogy" of the universe revealed in the sequence of the divine works of creation. The unaptness of the expression gives a particular significance to its use. Later on (cf. Gen. 5¹, 6⁹, 10¹ᶠᶠ·) *toledoth* are real genealogies, i.e., they indicate the sequence of human generations and thus constitute the nerve of the pre-history and history of Israel which is to be represented as the history of the divine covenant of grace. The reference to the *toledoth* of the heavens and of the earth is a clear indication that creation and covenant, creation and history, belong together. As there is subsequently a history of Israel, there is previously a history of creation.

EN92 generation

63

It is also to be noted that in the Yahwistic account (Gen. 2^4-3^{24}) the story of creation and the subsequent story of the fall almost merge into one another without transition, so that the comprehensive title "the story of Paradise" which H. Gunkel (Genesis 3, *Aufl.*, 1910) has given to the whole is at least worth considering. That in and with his existence man is already the object of the electing grace of God is shown by the context of both accounts, as is also the fact that the heavens and the earth were not only ordained to be the scene of the operations of this gracious God, but were originally created for this purpose. It shows that the Lord who will later converse and deal with Abraham and all his people is the true Lord, because heaven and earth, because the world in its totality, are in the very strictest sense His, because He is their Creator. But it also declares in advance the fact and reason why the utterances and dealings of the Lord of this history will always be creative utterances and dealings, always positing new beginnings, or in the strict sense always positing new beginnings of the world, always accomplishing the laying of new foundations. The connexion between creation and history as it emerges in the fact that the history of creation and the rest of the Pentateuch and therefore the rest of the Old Testament belong together, illuminates on the one hand the meaning and purpose of creation, and therefore of the existence of man and the universe. It shows us that God desires the general for the sake of the specific, the most specific; that He desires the creature because He desires Israel. And it illuminates on the other hand the meaning and the purpose of the history of Israel. It shows us that God desires this specific, this most specific, for the sake of the most general, for the sake of man and his universe created by Him; that He desires Israel as and because He desires the creature. His cosmos is thus wholly related to His Church, but His Church is also wholly related to His cosmos. According to the witness of the Old Testament this is necessary, and it is actually the case. To

the question why it is so, the Old Testament witness as such does not give any answer except to refer to the factual will and act of God. The Head of the Church who (according to Col. 1^{16-18}) is also the Head of the cosmos, the ground of the covenant who is also the ground of creation—who unites both in Himself, and who relates and achieves them mutually—cannot as yet be designated and named by the Old Testament witness as such. It has to be content merely to promise His existence, and with this promise to summon to obedience and hope.

The New Testament not only knows and says that there is this connexion, but it also knows and says why this is the case. It finds the centre and unity between creation and covenant, between cosmos and the Church, in the person of Jesus Christ; and it calls it by His name. In this respect, then, it is the answer to the question of the Old Testament. But in this respect the Old Testament is also the indispensable material presupposition of the New. The remarkable juxtaposition, sequence and relationship of the histories of creation and the covenant in the Old Testament shows us what question is answered in the name and person of Jesus Christ. If the Church of Jesus Christ wants to recognise its Lord as such; if it wants not merely to affirm the connexion between nature and grace, existence and faith, cosmos and community, not merely to conclude and postulate it on inner grounds, but to practise it as the truth of God's Word; if it wants to live consciously and peacefully in this truth, it cannot possibly overestimate the witness of the Old Testament. It will not be afraid, but rejoice, to allow the Old Testament history of creation to speak as a true and timefulfilling history of the acts of God the Creator and in its connexion with the history of the covenant; to give it the freedom to say what it has to say.

The exegesis of these passages has thus to be on its guard against two errors to which easy access is far too often conceded.

First, it must not overlook or explain away the fact that these texts deal with genuine events and not with timeless, metaphysical, or physical explanations of the world. It is true, of course, that God is the only actively operative Subject of these events, and that they include the beginning of time in which they also take place. This clearly distinguishes them from the later biblical histories. They are very definitely pre-historical. But this does not alter the fact that here too we have narratives, that no timeless truth is presented or proclaimed, but that accounts are given of once-for-all words and acts. If we will not accept this fact, then in respect of these passages we may well become entangled in the dilemma in which Augustine obviously found himself towards the end of his *Confessions* (XI, 3; XII, 18, 23, 31), so that he finally had to assume that these passages have many different senses, one of which may well be identical with that which according to his Neo-Platonic metaphysics he regarded as a true description of the timeless relationship of God to His creature. And if we take the same view, but like Basil and Ambrose (in their *Hexaemera*), and many modern apologists we are more interested in physics than metaphysics, we shall think it necessary to help the narratives by clothing what we think are the far too naive and scanty words of the Bible by the fulness of our own natural science with which we seek to harmonise them, as is also the case in *qu.* 65–74 of the *S. theol.* I of Thomas Aquinas. But either way the biblical history of creation, which claims to be concrete history, is quite unable to say what it wants to say and thus to mediate any profitable perception.

The other mistake which has to be avoided is that of a lack of attention to the connexion between the biblical histories of creation and what follows in the Pentateuch and the rest of the Old Testament. Apart from some isolated references, the exegesis of the Early Church fails at this point too. At any rate, it is certainly not guilty of the preoccupation with New Testament Christology of which it has so often been accused. If only it had looked a little more in this direction! But on the whole it paid far too little attention to the rest of Genesis and the rest of the Old Testament, and the result was that it made too little rather than too [065] much of these accounts. What the accounts offer is not in any sense a preface or prolegomenon, but the pre-history or, if we will, the primal pre-history of the people of Israel. They do not speak of the work of any creator of the world, but—like all that follows—of the words and acts of the very One who later made Himself known and attached Himself to the people of Israel as *Yahweh-Elohim*EN93. As Creator He is already the same as He becomes later as the God of Sinai and of Zion. And He will later reveal Himself on Sinai and in Zion as the same as has spoken and acted here. The decisive commentary on the biblical histories of creation is the rest of the Old Testament. This will have to be consulted in all its details. And for their part the details of the biblical creation histories call for this commentary. Since the close of the 17th century there has been a lamentable lack of attention in this direction on the part of the "modern" investigation and appraisal of these passages. In contrast to the exposition of the early Church, it boasted, and as is well known still boasts, of its lack of historical presuppositions, its impartiality and open-mindedness. But a confusing presupposition is again made if, instead of seeking the decisive commentary on these pages where it is really to be found as indicated by the texts themselves, we seek it in the presuppositions of the general history of religion, in the mysterious feeling of the total dependence and determination of man's existence, and in the primitively human reflection, achieved in this feeling, on the mysteries of the alternation of day and night, the succession of winter and summer, the relation between becoming and perishing, the connexion between begetting, life and death—as if the distinctive thing represented in the biblical history of creation were the product of this feeling and of the reflection achieved in this feeling. It should be plain enough that even under this aspect the passages cannot clearly convey what they intend to convey; that in a new form a timeless meaning is foisted upon them in exactly the same way as with Augustine, and at the very point where the real context demands that regard should be had to their temporal meaning.

EN93 the LORD God

According to the biblical witness there is a history of creation and creation itself is thus a historical reality. But this means that creation is characterised as that which makes possible and prepares and lays the foundation for the divine being and attitude which forms the object of all the rest of the Bible. This divine being, however, is not that of a supreme being which is present always and never, everywhere and nowhere, but the being of a divine person who always and everywhere speaks and acts only once. And its divine attitude is not an ordinary operation in which the distinctive element is only a particular but fundamentally casual, transitory and irrelevant form of the general and not its true and proper essence. On the contrary, its true and proper essence is always and everywhere the particular element in His words and acts, the single events and persons adduced by Him, the concrete reality of definite histories in their relationship, His works in their particularity and sequence. The God of all holy Scripture is the Lord who reveals Himself and acts in these historical works. His Word is not therefore an unutterable or inaudible Logos beside which there might be all kinds of other inaccessible human words, but an utterance which is always and everywhere spoken and heard, being addressed to men in all their humanity and put on the lips of men in all their humanity. His Gospel, then, is not the general truth that He is the gracious Father, but the specific and concrete truth that in His own Son He has taken our place in order to put right by His death and resurrection the wrong that we have done. In this way His Law is not at all a general rule of the "good," but the concrete instruction given to every man in the fact that in virtue of His death and resurrection the Son of God who has taken his place is also his Lord. Thus the whole relationship between God and man, proclaimed in the witness of the Bible as the reality of grace willed, created and revealed by God, is a historical relationship, which does not mean, of course, one which is incidental, external or merely apparent, but genuinely historical. The covenant of grace has its origin, takes place and is accomplished in histories; not alongside, behind or above these histories in the form of ideas, but really in them. These histories are really attested and summarised and illustrated as the proper object of the biblical witness even by the apparently general conclusions about those who are united in this covenant, i.e., about God and man, or about the world as the setting of this covenant; and by the apparently general directions and commandments for the formation of human life in this covenant. In these biblical histories everything has its natural place and from these histories it has its light, meaning and authority. If we reverse the relationship and read the Bible histories as mere illustrations of general truths and regulations, we dissolve them, robbing them of their character as truth and regulation, so that, however highly they may be valued, they are no longer the Word of God.

[066]

According to the witness of the Bible, creation—i.e., creation understood as a history according to the same biblical witness—is that which makes possible, prepares and lays the foundation for the work and Word of God. It is the preface in so far as in it God steps out of the state in which He is for Himself in

66

order to become the Lord and Partner of all these histories, and the Saviour dealing in grace. But it is a preface to these biblical histories and for this reason it is itself a pre-history and not a non-historical pre-truth. Even the basis of creation in God's eternal decree is not a non-historical pre-truth, for this eternal pre-truth itself obviously has a historical character in the bosom of eternity. Not even the pure, eternal being of God as such is non-historical pre-truth, for being triune it is not non-historical but historical even in its eternity. How, then, can creation be a non-historical pre-truth? If it were, how could the continuation harmonise with the beginning? In that case, the continuation of this beginning would undoubtedly have to consist in the depiction of a non-historical truth, basis and regulation of the relationship between God and man. This is contradicted by the continuation as it actually worked out according to the witness of the Bible. But this actual continuation corresponds to what the witness of the Bible designates as the beginning, i.e., to creation as history. It is in this particular form, and this form alone, that it aims at what follows, and what follows is already contained in it as the beginning. Creation as history fashions in every sense and dimension the pre-form (as yet concealed) of the work and Word of God which is to consist in the accomplishment of a series of histories of the revelation, representation and communication of God's grace to man. Creation as history fashions the world as a sphere for man who is to be a participant in this grace. And it fashions man as the being who precisely in this sphere is to become grateful to God for this grace and to correspond to it. As creation is itself history, the Lord of the subsequent history of the covenant will not really enter a strange land which does not belong to Him from the very outset, but in the words of Jn. 1[11] will come to His own possession, so that even if His own people will not receive Him, they will have no excuse on the score that they were not His from the very outset. They are this originally and from the very outset. They are pledged and committed to Him from the very first. They have no real possibility not to accept Him. They are already historical when this history commences. They have no natural existence behind them in which they might have been ordained and prepared for something other than the grace of God. They find themselves on no natural heights from which, in relation to the grace of God, they might legitimately have chosen any relationship, i.e., something other than the grace of God. They are what they are for the grace of God. And the whole cosmos was precisely created that in it there might be this event and revelation—that man might be what he is by the grace of God and for the grace of God. The grace and therefore the history or histories in which there take place this event and revelation are rooted in creation itself and as such. Is it not inevitable, then, that creation should itself be a history, the supremely distinctive pre-history, clearly distinguished from all that follows, but bearing throughout the character of a history? Is it not inevitable that we should find it attested and presented as such on the first pages of the Bible?

[067]

But if God's creation is a history, this means that it takes place in time. Time, in contradistinction to eternity, is the form of existence of the creature. For its part, of course, eternity is not merely the negation of time. It is not in any way timeless. On the contrary, as the source of time it is supreme and absolute time, i.e., the immediate unity of present, past and future; of now, once and then; of the centre, beginning and end; of movement, origin and goal. In this way it is the essence of God Himself; in this way God is Himself eternity. Thus God Himself is temporal, precisely in so far as He is eternal, and His eternity is the prototype of time, and as the Eternal He is simultaneously before time, above time, and after time. But time as such, i.e., our time, relative time, itself created, is the form of existence of the creature; it is, in contradistinction to eternity, the one-way sequence and therefore the succession and division of [068] past, present and future; of once, now and then; of the beginning, middle and end; of origin, movement and goal. When God creates and therefore gives reality to another alongside and outside Himself, time begins as the form of existence of this other. It is itself, of course, the creation of God (or more correctly, the creation of His eternity). But it actually begins together with His creation, so that we have to say that His creation is the ground and basis of time. But we must also say that His creation takes place in time and therefore has a genuine history. It is undoubtedly true that God in His eternity is the beginning of time. There is thus no sense in talking of a divine creation which was only eternal, which did not carry with it time, our time, relative time, as the form of existence of the creature, and which to that extent did not already take place in time. If we are not prepared to venture this statement, we will have to take back all that has been said about the historicity of creation.

The concept of a creation which does not take place in time is one which can be legitimately applied only to God's decree of grace and creation as it was taken in the bosom of His eternity. Our present concern, however, is with its execution and actualisation; with creation itself and as such, with which time is at once actualised as well, which with the creature posits time as its form of existence, and which to that extent does not take place before but in time. For the rest, the concept of a creation not taking place in time can only be used illegitimately to describe God's eternal original relation to an eternal world exactly like Himself. But the doctrine is obviously false which tells us that there is really no creation, denying both the reality of God and that of the creature, both of eternity and time, and affirming both the isolation of God and that of the creature. That it is not in time is something which can be said only of God's eternal being as such, i.e., God in His pure, divine form of existence. Even in this sense God is not non-historical and therefore non-temporal. He is not non-historical because as the Triune He is in His inner life the basic type and ground of all history. And He is not non-temporal because His eternity is not merely the negation of time, but an inner readiness to create time, because it is supreme and absolute time, and therefore the source of our time, relative time. But it is true that in this sense, in His pure, divine form of existence, God is not in time but before, above and after all time, so that time is really in Him. According to His Word and work, God was not satisfied merely with His pure, divine form of existence. His inner glory overflowed outwards. He speaks His Word and acts in His work with and for "another " than Himself. This "other" is His creature.

The creature, however, is not eternal but temporal, i.e., in time, in that one-way sequence, in that succession and separation, on the way from the once through the now to the then. To be a creature means to be on this way. But how can there be any possibility or actuality of the intercourse between God [069] and the creature, and of the establishment and commencement of this intercourse, if not by God's graciousness to His creature, by His condescension to it, by His entrance into its form of existence, by His acceptance of its way, by the utterance of His Word and the accomplishment of His work in time? The converse, i.e., that the creature for its part exalted itself to God, entered His form of existence, trod His unsearchable way and thus fitted itself for this intercourse, does not arise for obvious reasons—and least of all in connexion with the establishment and commencement of this intercourse. If God is not gracious to the creature—and that means concretely if He does not accept it in such a way that He gives Himself to its level, entering into its form of existence, communing with and working for it in this form of existence—then its creation cannot take place at all. In this case, there cannot be any intercourse at all between Creator and creature. In this case, God cannot become the Creator, and the creature for its part cannot come into being or exist before Him. In this case, God's being remains in His eternal triune essence, in His entirely different form of existence, on His own unsearchable way. There is no overflow of His inner glory. No less than everything depends upon the truth of the statement that God's creation takes place as history in time. If this is false, God is not the gracious Creator, and there is no creature to whom God can be gracious. In this case all God's words and acts are intrinsic to Him and can concern nobody and nothing except Himself. God could have willed this. He could have remained satisfied with the fulness of His own being. If He had willed and decided in this way, He would not have suffered any lack. He would still be eternal love and freedom. But according to His Word and work which we have been summoned to attest He has willed and decided otherwise. He has had compassion on His creature and accepted it. But if this cannot be gainsaid, we cannot and must not deny or even question the further fact that in giving the creature its existence and form of existence, He Himself stooped down to it, appropriated to Himself and His Word and work the form of the existence of the creature, and therefore as the Creator and Lord of time addressed and dealt with it in time: in time from the very basis and beginning; in the time which itself commenced because as the Creator He gave to the creature its basis and beginning. If this were not the case He would not have had compassion on the creature or accepted it. He could not have begun to take it to Himself. If His utterance and operation had been merely eternal, this would inevitably have meant that it would not have been a creative utterance and operation, the beginning of intercourse with another than Himself.

In this respect we have tacitly joined issue with an opinion of Augustine which has played a prominent and important role in the history of dogma. To the puzzling question: What did God do before the creation of the world? he gave an answer which is undoubtedly right. He
[070] would not say (*Conf.* XI, 12): *Alta scrutantibus gehennas parabat*[EN94]!—for: *Aliud videre, aliud ridere*[EN95]! But he would say: *Non faciebat aliquid; si enim faciebat, quid nisi creaturas faciebat*[EN96]? Any divine operation *ad extra*[EN97] prior to creation would itself have been creation. And (*op. cit.*, XI, 13, 15) creation includes the creation of time; *Id ipsum tempus tu feceras*[EN98]. There was thus no time prior to creation, and therefore no past to which it might look back. *Non enim erat Tunc, ubi non erat tempus*[EN99] Again (*op. cit.*, XI, 13, 16). *Nec tu tempore tempora praecedis, alioquin non omnia tempora praecederes. Sed praecedis omnia praeterita celsitudine semper praesentis aeternitatis et superas omnia futura quia illa futura sunt; et cum venerint, praeterita erunt; tu autem idem ipse es*[EN100]. So far so good. Only the Creator is prior to the creature; only the eternity which transcends and includes all time is prior to time. It is another matter, however, when Augustine (*op. cit.*, XI, 30) denies not only a time prior to creation but also the temporality of creation itself; when he even adopts the proposition that God has "never" created (*nunquam fecisse*) at least in the sense that God has never created in time (*nullo tempore fecisse*), but that God has to be recognised as before all time the Creator of all time (*te ante omnia tempora aeternum creatorem omnium temporum*[EN101]). In *De Civ. Dei*, XI, 6, again rightly repudiating the notion of a time prior to creation, but again, and even more plainly, in a more dubious extension of this repudiation to creation itself, he has reduced this view to the formula: *Procul dubio non est mundus factus in tempore, sed cum tempore*[EN102]. His meaning is that if creation happened in time, this would mean that it took place after a past and prior to a future time. But a time preceding creation and therefore a past time in this sense is unthinkable, because prior to it there was no creature whose time this past time could have been. Thus the world could be created with time but not in it. But this proof is not as such conclusive. It is not the case that in the divine creation and the coming into being of the creature and the commencement of time, God first created and then the creature emerged and in this way time commenced. For does not Augustine himself reckon with a kind of time prior to time when he tries to ascribe to the divine creation as such this kind of—what else can one call it?—temporal priority over the emergence of the creature and the beginning of time? As he describes it, an effect follows a cause within the nexus of the universe and therefore in time. But the divine creation by which this whole nexus of causes and effects as such, and with it time as a form, is first posited, has a different and higher priority over the being of the creature and time. As God begins to speak and to act as Creator, His eternity unfolds not only its pre-temporal but also its supra-temporal (more accurately, co-temporal) and post-

---

EN 94 He was preparing hell for those inquiring after matters too deep for them
EN 95 It is one thing to see, another to laugh
EN 96 He did not do anything; for what could have been the object of His action, if there were no creatures on which to act
EN 97 outside of God
EN 98 Thou didst make time itself
EN 99 For there was no 'then' when there was no time
EN100 And Thou didst not posit a time before time, otherwise Thou wouldst not precede all times. But Thou precedest all things that are past in the loftiness of Thine ever-present eternity, and all future events precisely because they are yet to come; and when they will have come, they will be past; but Thou art Thyself ever the same
EN101 Thou before all times art the eternal creator of all times
EN102 I have absolutely no doubt that the world was not created in time, but with time

temporal essence. Precisely as and because He is always eternal, exercising and revealing as Creator the whole glory of His eternity, His creation is simultaneous with the emergence of that which He creates, and therefore simultaneous with the time which begins with it, and therefore not outwith but in this time. What is the meaning of *cum tempore*[EN103] if it does not mean *in tempore*[EN104]? If there is no creature and therefore no time prior to creation, it is no less true that there is no creation prior to the creature and time. Prior to the creature there is only God's pure being at rest and at movement in itself; and prior to time there is only His eternity. But His eternity is itself revealed in the act of creation as His readiness for time, as pre-temporal, supra-temporal (or co-temporal) and post-temporal, and therefore as the source of time, of superior and absolute time. And therefore His revelation, the act of creation, is simultaneous with the emergence of the creature and the commencement of time; it does not take place outwith but within the new sphere which is posited by it. In other words, creation no longer takes place in the sphere of God's pure, inner being, where it finds its basis and possibility and (as an *opus ad extra internum*[EN105]) is willed and planned in the divine decree of salvation and peace. But (as an *opus ad extra externum*[EN106]) it now takes place outside this sphere, where over against and distinct from it the creature comes into being in the new sphere posited by it and arising from the fact that it takes place. For all the material priority of the one and secondariness of the other, the history of creation is at one and the same time both the originating divine activity and the originated creaturely occurrence. And in it the two are not only coincident but (for all their difference in dignity and power) co-inherent. Thus Augustine's question concerning the past which precedes the time of creation is quite pointless. He is right when he says that this is unthinkable. But the statement that creation took place in time does not maintain this unthinkable notion. As creaturely being, emerging by God's creation, is both something that has been and something that is coming into being, the same is true of its time. Beginning as present, it is as such both past and future. It would not be real, i.e., our relative time, with its succession and separation of now, once and then, if, beginning as present, it did not at once have its past in its future. In contradistinction from eternity time is just this division into present, past and future; this flux of that which is from the past, through the present, and into the future. It would not be really created, it would not be really time in contrast to eternity, if it were not immediately this flux. Thus in its very beginning, as it is created, it is not only present and future but also past. There is thus no need to reckon with a past preceding it and the divine creation. And so there is no reason on this score not to assert against Augustine—for all the correctness of his original purpose—the following formulation of the temporality of the creation: *mundus factus cum tempore, ergo in tempore*[EN107]. "The commencing time-process is the correlative of the concept of the creation of the world" (A. v. Oettingen, *Luth. Dogm.* II, 1, 1900, 302).

[071]

And that is precisely what the first creation narrative expressly says when it describes creation as an articulated sequence of individual words and acts of God and a consequent emergence of the creature, and when it makes the completion of each divine work and the essence of each creaturely being coincide with the passage of a day, and the completion of the whole with that of a week. According to this account time undoubtedly begins with the first divine "Let there be" and the first creaturely "It was." As God spoke His "Let there be,"

EN103 with time
EN104 in time
EN105 internal work directed outward
EN106 external work directed outward
EN107 the world was created with time, and therefore in time

and the corresponding emergence of the creature took place; as God named the first created thing "light" and its uncreated counterpart "darkness," it was "evening and morning, the first day" and the second and third day followed accordingly. And if it is only God's fourth work—the creation of the constellations (Gen. 1^{16-18})—that gives us the measure of time which man finds so useful and which forms an objective basis for the knowledge of time (although not, of course, its real basis, not time as such, but the clock and calendar to establish it, not for God the Creator but for man) this does not overthrow the preceding truth that time had actually commenced with the divine creation and the emergence of the creature, time being from the very first the form in which creatures began to exist and even the underlying divine speech and action of the Creator proceeded.

If we accept this as valid, the connexion between creation and covenant appears in a new light. The temporality of creation is not only the necessary correspondence to the grace of the Creator in so far as this is indeed divine and eternal and yet condescends to another than God, namely, the creature, in order to take up intercourse with it, with that which is non-divine and non-eternal, in a manner appropriate to it. The time of the history of creature has also two counterparts in the time of the history of the covenant and salvation which follow it. It cannot seriously be contended that the sphere of the latter is time, although here, too, we have to do with the speech and action of the eternal God. To attack its temporality would be to attack its reality. For if we [072] have here to do only with the being, speech and action of the eternal God, and not also with man existing in time, with the covenant which God made with him, and the salvation which He allotted him, it has certainly never taken place. And in this case it may well be God's eternal plan and purpose, but this would not be executed. And how can we possibly envisage an unfulfilled divine plan and purpose? In the divine plan and purpose actually executed, in the history of the covenant and salvation as it has actually taken place and does take place, we have to do with man as he exists in time. Time is undoubtedly the sphere of this history. Since this is the case, and since the covenant and its history are the ratification and renewal of creation on the one hand, and creation is the presupposition of the covenant on the other, it follows from this that the temporality of creation and its history is a necessity.

The first counterpart of the time of the history of creation in the time of the subsequent history of the covenant is "our" time in the stricter sense of the concept, i.e., the time of man as isolated from God and fallen into sin. It is the time whose flux has become a flight. It is the time in which there is no real present and therefore no real past and future, no centre and therefore no beginning and no end, or a beginning and end only as the appearance of a centre which is in reality the one and only thing and in one respect or another is not true and proper time. It is the time which, like an insoluble riddle, seems as though it must necessarily be finite as well as infinite, but no less necessarily cannot be either the one or the other. It is the time of which—although it is our only time—it can unfortunately be maintained only as a hypothesis that it is even related to a real absolute time as its origin or goal or secret content, thus having the character of reality. It is time without any recognisable ground or meaning in eternity. This is how time appears and must appear when it is no longer an order established by God and to be appropriated and acknowledged by man, but a human work and institution. This is the form it must take in the imagination and for the existence of the man who is not content to enjoy and treat it as something loaned to him, but tries to possess and use it as his very own, as the predicate of his thinking, willing and existence. As the time of lost man it can only be lost time. And it is with this lost man, who has only this lost time, who in reality has no time at all, that God in His time—at the beginning of His time of grace—has concluded His covenant. The history of this covenant is for his salvation. In the light of this history, in the light of the commencement of the divine time of grace, it has to be said that even this, our lost time, problematical and unreal though it is, is not completely empty, since as a distortion and caricature it does at least seem to point to something real, i.e., to a flux that is not just a flight, to a genuine present with a genuine past and future, to a finite beginning and a finite goal in the midst of the infinity of an [073] absolute time, and, therefore, to a real relation to it to the extent that for all its reluctance and inconsistency it bears witness even in its totally confused structure to a time which is different from itself and which as God's time loaned to His creatures can be a real form of the actual life of the creature instead of lost time. Without God's grace and revelation this prototype of "our" time cannot attain a form. Without faith in God's grace and revelation this prototype of "our" time has never even been envisaged. But the grace and revelation of God are in vain and faith in them are void unless they have this result. If, then, in connexion with the history of the covenant of grace and as its presupposition, the biblical witness to God's grace and revelation tell us that there is a history of creation, the history of the creation of unfallen man and his world, then we are forced to say that the time of this history in which God spoke and acted with man prior to the covenant but with a view to it as the Creator, was the pure prototype of "our" distorted and caricatured time, and that "our" time, distorted and caricatured as it is, is in reality the counterpart of this time. Indeed, our lost time could not be at all without that first and genuine time, just as man could not have been lost had he not first been created in that first time with a true and proper nature which he afterwards lost.

But the second counterpart of the time of creation in the sphere of the covenant of grace is far more important. This is the time of grace itself and as such, i.e., the time in which the covenant takes place. Within "our" time, i.e., the time of the man who has fallen into sin and is isolated from God, there is initiated with God's acceptance of man in grace the new time which God has for us and which, now that we have lost the time loaned to us, He wills to give to us again as the time of grace. With the commencement of this time, our lost time as such is both condemned to perish but also transformed and renewed. This time is constituted by God's own presence in Jesus Christ in the world created by Him. As the time of the Creator, whose concept cannot be confused by any blunder on the part of the creature, it is a genuine temporal present with a genuine temporal past and future. If the Word of God had not become temporal it would not have become flesh. Becoming flesh, it clothed itself with time, the time of a man's life, together with the pre-time and post-time which belong to the life-time of a man as the equally genuine past and future of that genuine present. In this necessary clothing of the true humanity of His Son; in this present, past and future, God creates from our lost time His time of grace—the time of His covenant with man. In this, our own time, entered and mastered and appropriated by God, was condemned to perish as lost time but was also exalted as a new and true and fulfilled time, i e , a time ruled by God. The incarnate Word of God *is.* But this means that it was and will be. But again

[074] it was never "not yet," and it will never be "no more." On the contrary, it is "now" even as it is "once" (and to that extent "no more"); and it is also "now" even as it is "then" (and to that extent "not yet"). It is a perfect temporal present, and for that very reason a perfect temporal past and future. It enters fully into the succession and separation of the times which together constitute time, and transforms this succession and separation into full contemporaneity. In the death of Jesus Christ the old has passed, but only in such a way that He Himself and His death and the whole witness of the Old Testament concerning Himself and His death are not just past but are still present and future. And in the resurrection of the same Jesus Christ something new has appeared, but in such a way that He Himself and His resurrection and the whole witness of the New Testament concerning Himself as the Resurrected are not only future but are also present and past. He does not extinguish time; He is "the first and the last and (so) he that liveth" (Rev. 1^{17}). He normalises time. He heals its wounds. He fulfils and makes it real. And so He returns it to us in order that we might have it again as "our time," the time of the grace addressed to us, even when we had lost it as "our" time, the time of the sin committed by us. He thus invites us in faith in Him to become contemporaries of genuine time, so that in Him and by Him we, too, have real time. Really to have time is to live in Him and with Him, in virtue of His death and resurrection in the present which is the turning point in which the sin and servitude and condemnation and death of man (and with it also "our" lost time) lie behind us as the past, in which they can be present only in Him, i.e., as the burden borne by Him for our sakes, and in which man's innocence and obedience and justification and sanctification and felicity lie before us, but are already present in Him, i.e., as His work and triumph. Really to have time is to be in Him and with Him, in virtue of our participation in His present, on the road from this past into this future. Really to have time is—*simul peccator et iustus*^{EN108}—to live in this transition (*transitus*), and to go with Him from the one to the other. This real time which we are privileged to have in and with Jesus Christ is God's time of grace—the time of the old and new covenants.

---

^{EN108} at once a sinner and righteous

And this time is the true counterpart of the time of creation. This time—and the same cannot be said of "our" lost time—is the true continuation and sequel of the days, the week, in which God in His goodness created all things and finally man. For the time of creation is also a turning point, a time of transition, a time of decision by God's gracious volition and execution. Already in creation it is the direct Word and work of God Himself which constitute time by fashioning the creature as such and causing it to live, i.e., by bringing it out of non-existence and giving it existence, thus giving it both present and future and therefore past. For the creature to have time is even in creation to participate in the present of God, to be on the road from a yesterday when [075] God said No to its non-existence to a to-morrow when He will say Yes to its existence. Even in creation the creature really acquires and has time; the time which God allots and lends it from the unsearchable riches of His eternity; which at its divinely ordained centre stands in a clear, definite relation to God's own, absolute time; which from this centre has also reality and stability; which is guaranteed and preserved even as past and future; which does not flee but flows; which is now, but which always is already even when it is not yet, and which is still even when it is no more. In this way the time of grace, the time of Jesus Christ, is the clear and perfect counterpart of the time of creation. Like it, and in contrast to "our" empty time, it is fulfilled time.

But according to the Scriptures of the Old and New Testament it is not the case that "our" empty time was able to squeeze in between the two fulfilled times and in some sense constitute a vacuum between them. Of course "our" empty time was and is. Yet it is not as if there had ever been only this empty time. But when this empty time commenced after the time of the divine creation, God's time of grace commenced simultaneously with it as the true and proper sequence and continuation of the time of creation. The empty time of a sinful man which opened at that point was also the fulfilled time of Jesus Christ which has its centre in His life-time, i.e., the pre-time which was His life-time when this had even not yet commenced as such. When man lost the time loaned to him, he received it back again in Jesus Christ, i.e., in the history, commencing immediately after creation, of the covenant of grace which was fulfilled in His death and resurrection. From the beginning his lost time was surrounded and enclosed by the time of the divine covenant of grace directly continuing the time of creation. Thus God Himself sees to it that from the very first, in accordance with His promise and in the offer made with His promise, time is fulfilled time, like that of creation, for all its human emptiness.

Are we to say of the time of grace that it is itself nothing more than a continuation of the time of creation in defiance of human sin? We can certainly say that its nature as time in contrast to our time is at least the same as that of the time of creation; and that creation and its time has not ceased but its duration extends to the time succeeding it, and therefore to the time of grace. Conversely, are we to say of the time of creation that is was nothing more than the commencement of the time of grace? We can certainly say this, since the two times are undoubtedly identical in nature, and the meaning and content of the time of grace are unquestionably those of the preparatory time of creation. But we are well advised to make a distinction as well. In the lost time of sinful man the time of grace has an opponent which the time of creation did not encounter; and the time of creation is as such commencing time, which is not the case with the time of grace.

[076]   Another question demands a less equivocal answer. We have called the time of grace the counterpart of that of creation. But it can and must be asked whether in the last analysis the time of creation is not on the contrary to be understood as the counterpart of that of grace, and therefore the time of grace as the true prototype of all time. In the last resort, we cannot evade this elucidation. If it is true that the world and man are created in Jesus Christ, i.e., for His sake and for Him, in actualisation of the compassion in which from all eternity God turned to the creature in the person of His Son bearing and representing it, then creation does not precede reconciliation but, follows it. In this case it is not in creation but in reconciliation that this compassion reaches the goal towards which God had looked from all eternity. In this case, too, the first and genuine time which is the prototype of time is not the time of creation but that of the reconciliation for which the world and man were created in the will and by the operation of God. Real time, in this case, is primarily the lifetime of Jesus Christ, the turning point, the transition, the decision which were accomplished in His death and resurrection; together with the time preceding and following this event in the history of Israel and the existence of the Christian Church. It was in correspondence with this real time, and as the necessary and adequate form of this event, that time was originally created—in and with creation and at the same time also as the form of the history of creation itself. We say originally, because it was the beginning of all time. But it was created as a reflection and counterpart when we consider it in relation to its material origin and ground. Here too, then, we see that there is occasion to separate and distinguish creation and covenant and therefore their times, even though we recognise and acknowledge their indissoluble connexion and mutual relationship. And, finally, we again see how necessary it is to understand creation too as a genuine history fulfilling time. If the time of creation is ultimately a reflection and counterpart of the time of grace, then as the beginning of all time it is necessarily real time in the supreme sense.

But at this point a further aspect is disclosed which demands our attention if we are to gain a true understanding of the story of creation, and especially of the Bible witness to this story. As we have seen, the fact that creation encloses in itself the commencement of all time does not alter in the very slightest the fact that it is itself real history and that as such takes its place in time. But it cannot be overlooked that this fact gives this history a supremely distinctive and exceptional character in relation to all others. Its distinction obviously consists objectively in the fact that it has no pre-history with which to stand in a retrospective connexion or relationship, but that it consists in an absolutely new event which seen from the standpoint of the creature commences with itself. Prior to the emergence of the creature there is only the Creator, and prior to commencing time there is only God's eternity. We may also put it in this way. Since creation is the beginning of all things and does not cease but continues as such; and since the whole existence and nature of the creature rests on God's continuing creation, all history is in fact characterised by the distinction that it stands in this immediacy to God. But the history which follows the beginning of creation is also characterised by the fact that it is at the same time mediate to God, i.e., that it takes place simultaneously with a pre-history, in connexion and relationship with another than God, and in a time already begun. Even of the miracles of the time of grace which most plainly reveal that God's creation actually continues; even of the miracle of all miracles, the resurrection of Jesus Christ, it has to be said that in the above sense it takes place in a relationship of mediacy to God as well as immediacy. But we cannot say this of the history of creation as such, i.e., of the history of the beginning of the divine operation. Its content is the pure emergence of the creature as such, beyond which there is from the standpoint of the creature either nothing at all or, as it learns by revelation and in faith, only God and His will and act. This is what makes it objectively a singular and unique history in relation to all others. But this objective peculiarity is reflected—and this is the important thing for an estimation of its biblical attestation—in an appropriate peculiarity in its perception. From what source and in what way can man know this history and be able to recount it? The obvious difficulty of this question has often led to a denial of the historicity and temporality of creation and the reinterpretation of the biblical witness as a declaration which really aims at an unhistorical and timeless relationship between the Creator and the creature. But the biblical witness opposes this reinterpretation. In the provisional enquiry into the relationship between creation and covenant we have seen that this is not an accident which can be brushed aside. The biblical witness must oppose such a reinterpretation. Even here it can only recount history and it can be understood and evaluated as historical narration. It has to say what it does in fact say—that creation was the commencement of time but that it has also taken place in this commencing time (the commencement of which it encloses in itself). If this were not the case, it would not be what it is according to the same witness—the presupposition and preparation of the whole history which follows it. But although this is necessary *in se*[EN109], it does not mean that the difficulty of understanding it can be overlooked. It is perfectly understandable that there should be an attempt to avoid the difficulty by reinterpretation. How can this history be related? How can this history be an object of human knowledge at all? How can anyone know and say what took place there where all occurrence had its origin? How can anyone have seen and comprehended this event?

[077]

[EN109] in itself

[078] A. Schlatter is obviously right when he says: "As we cannot of ourselves observe the point at which nature and spirit merge, we are denied any conception of how nature proceeds from God .... We never see nature in any other way than that in which it unveils itself to our perception, and on its Godward side it will always be for us an inaccessible sphere" (*D. chr. Dogma*², 1923, 60). "As the concept of creation is given to us, we stand at the frontier of our power of vision. The apprehension of how things began and came into existence is everywhere denied us. We know only that which has come into being, only the results of the operation. Even in ourselves the processes of coming into being are completely veiled from us .... Because we are not the Creator we cannot see or understand any creative act" (*op. cit.*, 36). "The narrative of creation seeks to tell in a visible manner about the wholly invisible operations of God. That something comes out of nothing is utterly indescribable" (W. Zimmerli, *Gen. 1–11*, 1943, 27).

But history which we cannot see and comprehend is not history in the historicist sense. This history, i.e., the history which is accessible to man because it is visible and perceptible to him and can be comprehended as history, is from the objective standpoint creaturely history in the content of other creaturely history, as an event prior to which and side by side with which there are other events of the same basic type with which it can be compared and integrated. And from the subjective standpoint it is the picture of this creaturely occurrence in its creaturely context. But it is just this content that the history of creation lacks. Its only content is God the Creator. For this reason it is not history in the historicist sense, and there can be no history of it. For this reason it is a "non-historical" history, and it can be the subject only of a "non-historical" history. We must add at once that this is true of all history to the extent that God's creation continues in it and in all its movements, relationships and forms there is an element in which it is immediate to God and immediately posited by Him. And we cannot overlook the fact that all history is properly and finally important and noteworthy only to the extent that it has this element and is thus not only historical but "non-historical" in the historicist sense. We cannot overlook the fact that all historical writings become soulless and intolerable to the extent that they try to be just historical and nothing more. But the rest of history is mediate to God as well as immediate, and therefore historical as well as non-historical. The rest of history subsequent to creation has a creaturely element, i.e., a similarity and relationship with other creaturely occurrences. This relationship may be anything but obvious. It may be easily and almost completely obscured. This is particularly the case where history assumes the character of miracle. It is most apparent at the centre of the history of the covenant of grace—in the resurrection of Jesus Christ. What does it really mean to see and grasp a real miracle? What does it mean to perceive and establish a resurrection from the dead? In this case the historical element in the event seems almost to have disappeared and the "non-historical" to have taken the upper hand. Even the human account of it, the description of the event, seems necessarily to have to burst through the frame-
[079] work of historical relation. And this is what actually takes place. This history, the history of the covenant of grace, is undoubtedly at its decisive centre more

78

than mere history. If in the case of other histories we can at a pinch overlook or reinterpret the "non-historical" element (to the detriment of a true appreciation), it is not very easy to do so at this point or in the proximity of this point. Hence in relation to this whole context the only alternative is openly to admit that it is only in part that we have to do with "history" and "historical" accounts. Yet we do have to do so in part. For even here there is always a certain relationship and similarity with other creaturely and to that extent visible history. Even here the "historical" element is not wholly extinguished. There is a deep "historical" twilight but not absolute obscurity. The latter is the case, however, when we consider the history of creation in itself and as such: the history in which only the creating God and the creature which comes into being by His creation confront one another as partners; the history in which time begins with the creature without any prior time, the history which cannot be compared with or supported by any other history. For what *could* actually be perceptible and comprehensible and therefore "historical" in this story? If the history of the covenant of grace with its miracles, and especially its great central miracle, is not only undoubtedly historical but also (to the extent to which it is itself a continuation of the history of creation) highly "non-historical," we can only say of the history of creation in itself and as such that it is by nature wholly "non-historical," and that the biblical accounts of it are also by nature wholly "non-historical" and can only be read and understood as such.

By nature! When we say this, we make *no* concessions. We are not adopting the verdict of an alien and non-theological "historical criticism," but espousing a theological proposition. We say that the history of creation is "non-historical, " ie., that it is a history which cannot be "historically" perceived and understood, but has in face of all "history" its own historical reality. If this is not the case, it is not the history of creation. Hence the account of it cannot possibly be understood as a "historical" relation.

When we say this, we take seriously the fact that the Bible tells the story of creation as one which (apart altogether from its content) had no human witnesses. "Where wast thou when I laid the foundation of the earth? Declare, if thou hast understanding" (Job 38⁴). If man cannot declare where he was, then obviously he cannot declare "historically," from personal observation and understanding, what took place when God laid the foundation of the earth, or how it took place. If there is no historian, even for this reason (accepting his ability to perceive and understand what took place), there can obviously be no "history."

But secondly we maintain the fact that the content of the biblical creation stories as such has a definite pre-historical character; obviously in the sense of being prior to natural history. They naturally deal with an occurrence which took place in time, but this occurrence is that of the emergence of the natural presuppositions of all other history. There can be no historical account where heaven and earth and sea, plants and beasts and finally man make their first appearance, i.e., where they do not yet exist but are to do so as portrayed in broad outlines in Gen. 1 and also more briefly in Gen. 2. Only occurrences within the existent reality of nature can be historical. But at this point we have to do with occurrences on the frontier of the non-existence and existence of nature. If there can be any accounts of such occurrences at all, they certainly cannot be "historical." [080]

And thirdly we take into consideration the fact that on the first pages of the Bible we do not have only one but two different accounts of creation, and that these are expanded but also partially contradicted by isolated references to the theme in the rest of the Canon. When we come to the exegetical appraisal of these passages, and the attempt to understand them in the setting in which they confront us in Genesis, it is to be noted that they not only describe the events with greatly varying interests but also in very different ways. Seen from the point of view of the other, each of these accounts reveals painful omissions and irreconcilable contradictions. The suspicion becomes strong that they derive from different sources, originating at different times, against different backgrounds, and from a different intellectual approach. A thoughtful consideration will certainly hold itself aloof from the evaluation and disparagement (Gunkel) often associated with the familiar hypothesis of different sources, because these have really nothing to do with exposition. Yet even if that is done, even if we do not fail to see the common denominator of both narratives, even if we establish that the common denominator is undoubtedly the decisive element in both, we cannot fail to see again that what might be considered "historical" in either—if not contradicted on other grounds—does not come under this common denominator, so that even if it were intrinsically possible to construct a "historical" picture from the narratives we cannot actually do so without doing violence to one or the other or both. The older expositors who attempted a "historical" harmonisation of the two accounts did not adhere too closely to what is actually written. What is written—and this may be said independently of all source-hypotheses—is ill-adapted in its juxtaposition of two different accounts to mediate a "historical" sub-stratum. We can only do violence to it if we read and interpret it in this way.

The history of creation is "non-historical" or, to be more precise, pre-historical history. We must be careful not to fall back into the equally impossible exegetical and dogmatic proposition that it is not history but the disguise of an unhistorical and timeless reality. But again we have to insist on dogmatic and exegetical grounds that it is not a "historical" history. Not all history is "historical." We repeat that in its immediacy to God every history is in fact "non-historical," i.e., it cannot be deduced and compared and therefore perceived and comprehended. But this does not mean that it ceases to be genuine history. In its decisive elements or dimensions, in the direction in which alone it is ultimately important and interesting, all history—as genuine history—is "non-historical." And this the more so, and the more palpably, the more this element predominates, the more this dimension—the immediacy of history to God—emerges. The history of creation has *only* this element. In it Creator and creature confront each other only in immediacy. In this supreme sense it is genuine history, but also in this supreme sense it is "non-historical," prehistorical history. And for this very reason it can be the object only of a "non-historical," pre-historical depiction and narration.

[081]   We must dismiss and resist to the very last any idea of the inferiority or untrustworthiness or even worthlessness of a "non-historical" depiction and narration of history. This is in fact only a ridiculous and middle-class habit of the modern Western mind which is supremely phantastic in its chronic lack of imaginative phantasy, and hopes to rid itself of its complexes through suppression. This habit has really no claim to the dignity and validity which it pretends. It acts as if only "historical" history were genuine history, and "non-historical" false. The obvious result is to banish from the portrayal and understanding of history all immediacy of history to God on the pretext of its non-historicity, dissolving it into a bare idea! When this is done, the horizon of history necessarily becomes what it is desired to be—a highly unreal history, a more or less explicit myth, in the poor light of which the historical, what is

supposed to be the only genuine history, can only seem to be an ocean of tedious inconsequence and therefore demoniac chaos. We must not on any account take this course. In no way is it necessary or obligatory to maintain this rigid attitude to the "non-historical" reality, conception and description of history. On the contrary, it is necessary and obligatory to realise the fact and manner that in genuine history the "historical" and "non-historical" accompany each other and belong together.

In addition to the "historical" there has always been a legitimate "non-historical" and pre-historical view of history, and its "non-historical " and pre-historical depiction in the form of saga.

As far as I can see and understand (cf. the competent articles in *RGG²* by H. Gunkel, W. Baumgartner, O. Rühle, P. Tillich and R. Bultmann), modern ethnology and religious science cannot give us any illuminating and acknowledged clarification, distinction and co-ordination of the terms myth, saga, fable, legend and anecdote, let alone any useful definition of their relationship to history and historical scholarship. The non-specialist must try to find his own bearings in this sphere.

In what follows I am using saga in the sense of an intuitive and poetic picture of a pre-historical reality of history which is enacted once and for all within the confines of time and space. Legend and anecdote are to be regarded as a degenerate form of saga: legend as the depiction in saga form of a concrete individual personality; and anecdote as the sudden illumination in saga form either of a personality of this kind or of a concretely historical situation.

If the concept of myth proves inadequate—as is still to be shown—it is obvious that the only concept to describe the biblical history of creation is that of saga.

That it does actually contain a good deal of saga (and even legend and anecdote) is due to the nature and theme of the biblical witness. It also contains "history," but usually with a more or less strong wrapping of saga. This is inevitable where the immediacy of history to God is prominent, as in the histories which the Bible relates. On the other hand, it also contains a good deal of saga with historical wrappings, and this again is not surprising when by far the greater part of the events related by it takes place in the sphere where "history" and "historical accounts" are at least possible in principle. To put it cautiously, it contains little pure "history" and little pure saga, and little of both that can be unequivocally recognised as the one or the other. The two elements are [082] usually mixed. In the Bible we usually have to reckon with both history and saga.

It is to be noted at this point that the idea that the Bible declares the Word of God only when it speaks historically is one which must be abandoned, especially in the Christian Church. One consequence of this misunderstanding was the great uncertainty of faith which resulted from an inability wholly to escape the impression that many elements in the Bible have the nature of saga, and an ignorance where and how to draw the line which marks off what is finally historical and therefore the true Word of God. But in other cases it led to a rigid affirmation that in the Bible, as the Word of God, we have only "historical" accounts and no saga at all—an affirmation which can be sustained only if we either close our eyes or violently reinterpret what we see. In other cases again it resulted in an attempt to penetrate to a "historical" kernel which is supposed to give us the true, i.e., "historical" Word of God— the only trouble being that in the process it was unfortunately found that with the discarding of saga we do not lose only a subsidiary theme but the main point at issue, i.e., the biblical witness. We have to realise that in all three cases the presumed equation of the Word of God with a "historical" record is an inadmissable postulate which does not itself originate in the Bible at all but in the unfortunate habit of Western thought which assumes that the reality of a history stands or falls by whether it is "history." It was when this habit emerged and asserted itself (at the close of the 17th century) that developing theological Liberalism began to be preoccupied with the thought of a "historically" purified Bible, and declining theological orthodoxy took its stand on the theory that the Bible contains nothing but "history" and is therefore in its entirety the Word of God. Both Liberalism and orthodoxy are children of the same insipid spirit, and it is useless to follow them. For after all, there seems no good reason why the Bible as the true witness of the Word of God should always have to speak "historically" and not be allowed also to speak in the form of saga. On the contrary, we have to recognise that as holy and inspired Scripture, as the true witness of God's true Word, the Bible is forced to speak also in the form of saga precisely because its object and origin are what they are, i.e., not just "historical" but also frankly "non-historical." It would not be the Bible if it did not do this, and if it did not usually do it by mingling the two elements—and that in such a way that a dividing line can only be drawn with the greatest difficulty. Undoubtedly it is not by this dividing line that it can be decided that it is God's revelation and must be believed. The decision about its nature as revelation, the confirmation of its reality as the Word of God, is reached by the fact that in its "historical" parts and also particularly and precisely in its "non-historical" (or sagas)—although always in connexion with the former— it attests the history of the great acts of God as genuine history, and that this witness is received and accepted through the power of the Holy Spirit.

In accordance, however, with the unique nature of its theme, the biblical history of creation is pure saga, just as in other places in the Bible—also as an exception to the rule—we have pure and more or less incontestable "history." The standpoint, presentation and depiction of the history of creation rest on a very different possibility from the account which rests on perception and concept, and which in the region of perception and concept deduces, compares, co-ordinates, and in this way demonstrates. This other possibility, in virtue of which "non-historical" and "pre-historical" history can also be recognised and [083] presented, is that of the divinatory and poetical historical saga. Divination means the vision of the historical emergence which precedes "historical" events and which can be guessed from that which has emerged and in which "historical" history takes place. And poetry means the articulated form of this divining vision and therefore of the historical emergence seen in this way. In this kind of divination and poetry narrative saga arises distinct from history and in connexion with it—and woe to the history which lacks this connexion. For the most part, it has to do with the constitutive events of history, with its origins and roots. It looks to the point where from the standpoint of "history" everything is dark, although in fact it is only from this point that "history" can emerge and be clear. It looks to the basic and impelling occurrence behind the everyday aspect of history, where the latter is not only no less history than on this everyday aspect but has indeed its source and is to that extent history in a higher sense. It looks to the hidden depth of time where time is already time, and indeed genuine time. It looks in a most literal sense to the "radical" time of history. Where divinatory and poetical saga is not allowed to speak, no true picture of history, i.e., no picture of true history, can ever emerge. It is just as necessary as pure "historical" perception and expression. Of course there is also empty, false, worthless and dangerous saga. But this is not because it is saga. It is because it is bad saga; the bad poetry of a vain divination, of a misunderstanding of the genuinely historical origins and roots. The form of saga is as little discredited on this account as the form of history by the fact that there is plenty of utterly empty, false, worthless and indeed dangerous history. Side by side with a good deal of bad saga there is also much that is good. If the biblical creation stories agree in content and character with the rest of the biblical witness, we ought not to be offended because they are sagas. We are no less truly summoned to listen to what the Bible has to say here in the form of saga than to what it has to say in other places in the form of history, and elsewhere in the form of address, doctrine, meditation, law, epigram, epic and lyric.

Cf. in this connexion W. Vischer's *Das Christuszeugnis des Alten Testaments* Vol. I, 1934, 47f. and the quotations (to be used with caution) which he adduces from J. G. Hamann, J. J. Bachofen and N. Berdyaev. A. Schlatter has fully described not only the "historical" but also the divinatory and poetical activity of the biblical historian in the following words: "With all the uncertainties of his historical retrospect and prophetical prospect, the biblical narrator is the servant of God who quickens a remembrance of Him and makes known His will. If he does not do it as one who knows, he does it as one who dreams. If his eye fails, his imagination steps in and fills the gaps. In so doing he conducts further the divine gift which had entered in the course of history, making it fruitful for those who follow. That he must serve God not only as one who knows and thinks but also as one who writes and dreams, lies in the fact that he is a man and that we human beings cannot arrest the transition of thought into poetry. This demand fights against the measure of life given to us" (*op. cit.*, p. 377).

But the concept of saga has to be marked off from that of myth as well as "history." [084]

The customary definition that myth is the story of the gods is only superficial. In myth both the gods and the story are not the real point at issue, but only point to it. The real object and content of myth are the essential principles of the general realities and relationships of the natural and spiritual cosmos which, in distinction from concrete history, are not confined to definite times and places. The clothing of their dialectic and cyclical movement in stories of the gods is the form of myth. The fairy tale, which is more interested in details than in the whole (as are legend and anecdote in relation to saga), and which inclines not to concrete history but to all kinds of general phenomena, truths or even riddles of existence, is a degenerate form of myth as are legend and anecdote of saga.

The creation stories of the Bible are neither myths nor fairy tales. This is not to deny that there are myths, and perhaps in part fairy tales, in the materials of which they are constructed.

It is obvious that in the two principal passages in Gen. 1 and 2 we have the introductory narratives in a connected history which is later continued in the same manner. The first account moves from the creation of light, through that of other creatures to the creation of the first human pair, and then on to the divine rest on the Sabbath day. The second account begins with the creation of man, deals with a restricted realm of creatures and leads up to the creation of woman. Both accounts, like those which follow, are portrayals of concrete events important to them as such. These events are pre-historical. They deal with the emergence of creation as such. Thus both accounts are pure saga. But there is nothing to show that they are not meant to be pure narration without any afterthoughts, just like the passages which follow. They are not a historical cover for non-historical speculation. All their utterances should be taken literally: not in a shallow but a deep sense; not in a narrow but an inclusive sense; yet in such a way that the obvious meaning of the direct narration should always be given its proper weight; in such a way, too, that the account as such does not give rise to a picture of all kinds of timeless connexions and relationships which cannot be recounted; but in such a way that the narrative has also and primarily to be taken in all seriousness; in such a way that even the deeper and more inclusive literal sense is sought only on the plane of the historical and therefore of that which can be recounted and is in fact recounted in what follows. What the biblical accounts offer is creation saga. But this means creation history and not creation myth.

The concept "creation myth" has often been applied unthinkingly to the creation sagas of Israel as well as to the myths of other nations. On a careful examination, it surely contains a *contradictio in adiecto*[EN110]. Real myth has never really had creation as its theme and object. Myth does, of course, take narrative form, and it is often far more dramatic and lyrical than the biblical creation sagas. But its tales and their events and figures are obviously pictures and embodiments of what happens always and everywhere and to that extent does not happen "anywhere or at any time." Not without a nod and a wink, ironically, condescendingly, by way of accommodation, myth tells a story "for children and those who love children." It chooses and uses the form of a story, but in the case of all intelligent persons it makes the demand that they should look through this story, that they should not cling to it as such, but that in all the enjoyment of its events and forms, spurred on by its cheerful play, they should press on to its true non-historical, timeless and abstract sense, to a perception of the eternal truth presented in the play. How can we understand myth if we ignore this demand and do not try to meet it? Myth has always arisen and still arises from the higher recognition, divination and poetic understanding of this kind of eternal truth. It has always been a worthy *alter ego* of philosophy. It can and will be genuinely understood only when the way of its origin is in some sense retraced by the hearer or reader; only when the web of its narrative is again thoughtfully and yet imaginatively and feelingly analysed and reduced to its non-historical and timeless and abstract sense. Genuine myth makes use of the form of creation saga. But it only makes use of it. Even in the form of creation saga it can never have the real creation for its object.

[085]

EN110 contradiction in terms

The gods and their acts, the creators and creations of which it also tells, are figures and scenes in its imaginative plays, words and names in its figurative language, but never that which its dedicated inventors and poets intended and its dedicated hearers and readers are to receive. Genuine myth never means a genuinely pre-historical emergence, a beginning of the reality of man and his cosmos in encounter with distinct divine reality. However dualistically or trialistically the imaginative play of its narration may seem to be in intention, in the actual meaning given to it and to be gathered from it, myth is always monistic. It knows only the one reality of man and his cosmos—their predicates and their inner movement. It thinks to know their depth, but only the proper depth of this reality. It speaks of creators and creations, but it understands the process of emergence with which it is concerned only as an element in this one reality. It understands even God or the gods and divinities only as figure-heads, as personified agents in the economy of this one reality. It only appears to tell of creation, but in reality it speaks of a particular view or solution of the enigma of the world; of a combination of real or supposed world-elements by which a man or an era think that they can explain the existence of these elements in their cyclical aspects. Never is man more himself and at home in his world, never does he have in his own strength a better understanding of himself and his world, than as an inventor and author or an intelligent hearer and reader of myth. On the remarkable road of myth, away from the reality of an everyday view of things, he ascends to the heights of a significant world of images, returning to the final depth of a vision of reality, of the One in All, which is to be seen in the contemplation of that world of images, but only as in a well-polished mirror, while in reality it is a third thing which belongs neither to this world, nor to the reality of an everyday view. In myth man understands that in the last resort he and his world in their identity with this One and All have no history, no Creator and no Master, but that in the secret of their emergence they are moved in themselves and rest in themselves. Thus the concept of "creation myth" rests on a misunderstanding. No real myth is creation myth. If we understand it as such, believing that it does seriously speak about creation, we act as novices who have not yet caught sight of an esoteric meaning which lies beyond all history and therefore beyond all creative history. [086]

For the same reason it again rests on a misunderstanding if we apply the concept of myth to the creation saga of the Israelites and the Bible. Since myth as such can never be creation myth, the genuine creation saga with which we have to do in Gen. 1 and 2 is not as such a myth. If it points beyond itself, it is to the historical saga and "history" which follow it and in union with which it forms a whole, but not to an non-historical meaning. What is fundamental to myth, namely, the contemplation of man and his cosmos as self-moved and self-resting, the contemplation of his emergence as one of his own functions, is not only not essential to it but is declared by it to be groundless in every respect. And what is unessential to myth, namely, God and His activity, the

85

distinction and confrontation between the Creator and the creature, the liberty of another divine reality which encounters man and his world and sovereignly decrees without reference to them, is not only fundamental to the biblical creation saga but the one and only thing that it seeks to exhibit. It does not speak only improperly or exoterically of the Creator and creation, but properly and in a way which is for all. It does not unfold a mere imaginary world when it speaks of the divine Subject who is so different from man and his world, and from His words and acts. It does not originate in any esoteric knowledge, nor does it wait for any esoteric interpretation. It does not leave the hearer and reader to guess and interpret what lies behind or stands above the historical picture as such: a truth in face of which the historical picture is only a covering which can and must be abandoned. Its truth is identical with the historical picture which is presented by it and the depth of which is to be sought only in the fact that it is the first in a whole series of further historical pictures, not portraying or signifying a "non-historical" reality but being itself eternal truth only in its historicity and its connexion with what follows. The biblical creation saga speaks in this way without any nods or winks, without irony, without condescension, without accommodation. Its divination and [087] poetry are intended to say exactly what it says in itself and in this connexion. It does not merely use narrative as an accepted form. It is itself a narrative through and through. It has no philosophical system as an accompanying *alter ego* whose language can express abstractly what it says concretely. What it says can be said only in the form of its own narrative and what follows. Putting it in this way, and only in this way, it really speaks of God's creation and it really speaks pre-historically, attesting that the reality of man and of his cosmos is not infinite, that it is not the One and All of reality, but that it has a genuine horizon which cannot be transcended and which cannot be absorbed in the immanence of that reality, that this horizon—decisively important for all that is and takes place within it—is the divine will and utterance and activity; that for this very reason man is not isolated as he would like to be as the inventor and author or hearer and reader of myth; that in his existence he is confronted by his Maker; that he takes part in the history founded by the divine will and utterance and activity; and that in his position and function he is a part of the creation which is subject and responsible to the divine sovereignty. But this means that even in manner and form the biblical creation saga, as a genuine narration of creation as history, is the direct opposite of myth. That it does not do this without betraying its familiarity with myth, and occasional polemical references to it, is anything but a serious reason why it should be brought under the concept of myth, especially under the intrinsically untenable concept of creation myth.

This comes out very clearly when we compare the biblical creation saga with the genuinely mythical texts of the Babylonian epic *Enuma elish* (*c.* 2000 B.C.) which calls at once for historical consideration in this context; and also with the cosmogony of Berosus (3rd century B.C.), etc. (H. Gressmann, *Altorientalische Texte zum A.T.*[2], 1926, 108f.). The researches of experts appear to agree (cf. F. Delitzsch, *Genesis*, 1887, 40 f., and Gunkel, *op. cit.*, p. 119f.), that there can be no question of a direct dependent relationship between these passages and Gen. 1 and 2, but only of a common relationship to still older traditions from which Gen. 1 and 2 and these Babylonian texts may perhaps derive. But it also seems to be generally accepted that the material agreement of Gen. 1 and 2 is only in "certain parts" (Gunkel, p. 129) or "isolated relics" (p. 128); and that the mythical tradition in Gen. 1–2 has been "very much deflated" (p. 122), or "muffled," or even "reduced to a mere fragment" (p. 130), having been "amalgamated" (p. 129) with the religion of Israel. In relation to the other biblical passages which touch on creation, it has been said that in Israel myth has been "historicised" and rendered "impotent" as myth; that it has no autonomy but remains only in individual cases as a "poetic ornament" (W. Eichrodt, *Theol. d. A.T.*[1] Vol. II, 1935, 56). But "historicised" myth is not myth but a saga which, although it may work with mythical materials, differs sharply from myth in the fact that it does seriously and without any afterthought try to say how things actually were. In these circumstances, it is hard to see why there has been no agreement that the kind of saga which is found in the biblical creation narratives of creation is as such different from myth, and that the theme of the Babylonian myth—irrespective of textual relationships—is different from that of the biblical saga, so that the latter cannot be called myth in virtue of its theme.

The epic *Enuma elish* is not a history of creation, nor "pre-history," but a portrayal of the constantly recurrent change of relationships which is exactly the same in pre-historical time as any other within the cosmos as it has come into being and now exists. The unity, totality and singularity of the cosmos are not altered by the fact that there are in it the dreadful contradictions, changes and convulsions, bases and emanations, causes and consequences, births and deaths, conflicts, victories and defeats, divisions, reconciliations and fresh divisions, which are the theme of myth. But all this is merely the inner rhythm of the cosmos and has nothing to do with its creation. Tiamat, the mother of the gods, the gods who originate in her, and her youngest and most successful scion the hero and later demiurge Marduk, who by his final victory over the original power which is both friendly and hostile comes to the aid of the other more or less impotent divinities—all these are of one species and kind. And if heaven and earth arise because Marduk (who according to Berosus is identical with Bel and the Greek Zeus) literally attacks the arch-mother of all the gods and all beings, cleaving and dismembering her and turning her into heaven and earth this decides the fact that everything outwith the Godhead is in fact only a transformed but genuine element of the divine being, and that conversely we have to recognise in this the original form of all being. In these forms and events we nowhere see a genuine horizon of this One and All as it is found in the concept of creation. There is no qualitative difference between divine and every other reality. What kind of a deity is it in whose very bosom there is so much darkness and such a dialectic of good and evil, in whom conflict, victory and defeat, life and death, reign side by side? It cannot possibly be the Creator of the cosmos but only its first cause, partly struggling and partly suffering, dividing itself in a dreadful self-contradiction, in an unnatural but necessary tumult. It is no modern supposition that in all this we have an allegorical presentation of natural processes, but one which was declared as a self-evident truth by Berosus, a priest of Marduk's temple. The same relationship is to be found as between the Godhead and man. This is prefigured already in Marduk hastening to the aid of the older gods as a champion against Tiamat, and it is fulfilled in the event which follows. The gods themselves need completion; indeed, according to tablet 6 of the epic, they need a redemption which must be accomplished in the form of service rendered to them. For this purpose man, i.e., Babylonian man, is necessary, and therefore the city of Babylon is necessary as the seat of the gods who would otherwise be homeless. And so according to the supremely laudable decree of Marduk one of the other gods is sacrificed, and from his blood there is formed the man who will build Babylon and there render true service to the gods. But it is obvious that this cannot and obviously will not be understood as true creation and a true history of creation. The *Enuma elish* also formed the textbook of an annual dramatic liturgy enacted on New Year's day (at the close of the rainy season) when the reigning monarch had to act the role of Marduk. We may ask whether it is possible to imagine a similar application of Gen. 1 and 2 and the personification of the Creator God of Israel by a David in Jerusalem. But it corresponds only too well to the nature of myth. Marduk's role, the person of the mythical "creator," can indeed be acted by the creature, for properly and originally it is his own role and person. Nor is mythical "creation" anything but the timelessly valid connexion, confirmed in constant repetition, between emergence and existence, dissolution and rebirth, in the world of created things. Nor has mythical creation anything to do with a pre historical positing of the world of created things. The fact that it is accomplished in the actions of gods and god-like figures does not in any sense make them real founders and lords of this world, either individually or collectively. It is not they who have produced the world. On the contrary, they have emerged from the same basic cause and are to that extent of the

[089]   same nature. They, too, are in their way weak and helpless. They, too, are condemned to suffer. They, too, are an embodiment of its dualism. They are not this out of free and superior participation and compassion, but because they have no option, because the same destiny that rules the world rules them, because they themselves are the first who must endure the dualism, the schism and the need which are evidently distinctive of that basic cause. And if the creaturely world is nothing but the sum of the transformed and fashioned members of their own half-friendly and half-hostile arch-mother, it is clear that they are not really over the world. They do not really control it. They have in their relation to it no claim to a greater or indeed to any real honour. On the contrary, they are bound and under obligation to it. And finally and supremely they depend no less on man, who is himself formed of divine blood, than he depends on them. The position of man is that he has to exist, that he has to be created, that Babylon has to come into being, for the sake of the gods, because the gods need the worship of a human shrine. And man is made out of divine blood which is given under compulsion. Thus he is surely as much the lord of the gods as the gods lords over him. We may calmly ask indeed if there is any true or final distinction between him and these gods; between these gods and gigantic but shadowy projections of human experiences and needs, struggles and sufferings, hopes and possibilities; between the Babylonian deity and the Babylonian king and Babylonian man. In the figure of Marduk the three are in fact indistinguishable. There can be no question in this epic of any prehistory, of any genuine history of creation. On the contrary, we have only the transparent apparel of a deep insight into the already existing reality of the world and of man. This reality and its inner problem have here no boundary, no beginning and no end, no given determination enabling it to escape the caprice or fate of its own movement.

What we read in Gen. 1 and 2 are genuine histories of creation. If there is a connexion with the Babylonian myth or its older sources, it is a critical connexion. Everything is so different that the only choice is either to see in the Jewish rendering a complete caricature of the Babylonian, or in the Babylonian a complete caricature of the Jewish, according to the standpoint adopted. In Gen. 1 and 2 no less than everything obviously depends on the uniqueness and sovereignty of the Creator and the creative act—so much so that a reciprocity of creaturely speech or activity is not even mentioned in the first account, and only incidentally at the end of the second (in the naming of the animals and the saying about the woman brought to man). Gunkel is not wrong when, with reference to the "development of the action" in Gen. 1, he almost complains that "there is no real plot and no opponent. The whole narration consists of related words and acts of God" (p. 117). What the two accounts of Genesis offer is cosmogony in the strict and exclusive sense of the term. This means in the first instance that they really visualise the emergence of the world by the Word and work of God to the exclusion of the notion of a world-basis presupposed in this act. And it means secondly that they are not in any sense a theogony: they visualise the origin of the world to the exclusion of the notion of a preceding or simultaneous genesis of the Deity. For this reason there can be no question in either account of a monistic or dualistic speculation and systematisation. A monistic is excluded because God the Creator is always different in essence from His work; because there is no transition and mediation between Him and the creature; and because no secret identity between God and the world is possible. And a dualistic is excluded because the possibility and reality of a world contradicting the will and the act of God are excluded in and with the act of creation and can come into consideration only in this exclusion, while in the world as it is willed and actually created by God there is as little duality and schism as there is in God Himself. Creation, according to Gen. 1 and 2, is not in any sense a proper predicate of the creature, or identical with the self-propelled "wheel of emergence" (τροχὸς τῆς γενέσεως, Jas. 3⁶). Creation includes this motion of the creature in [090] itself only in so far as it first gives rise to it, and indeed gives to the propelling and propelled creature its existence and nature. Creation, then, does not aim at the kingdom, the power and the glory of man. It does not aim at the government, the building of cities, the wars and lion hunting of any hero or potentate. Its aim is the history of the acts of God in the world created and controlled by Him and in relation to the man created and guided by Him. In this way it is an original and typical reflection of the purpose and plan and triumph of God, and not of the ambiguities of man's experiences and possibilities of the advent of his kingdom, of the glorification of his name, and of the successes and adventures to which he looks forward when the storms subside. Here, then, we have a record of genuine history, unique of its kind; and not just a textbook which can be consulted with the same zest as each New Year day comes with its retrospect and prospect. Here the concept of pre-history is fulfilled, as is also the concept of pure saga. The reference is not to a timeless primal state but to a genuine primal time and its events as the hidden beginning of our time and its events. And it is this historical source of actual history which here forms the object of divination and poetry. This may also be seen in the fact that there is here no necessity to people the pre-historical era, as is done particularly in the cosmogony of Berosus, with all kinds of obviously meaningless and artificial mythological creatures (like two or four-winged, two-headed and bi-sexual men, or crosses between men and animals, or fishes and dogs or horses, and other monstrosities), but that the world and its inhabitants emerge in the state in which they will later exist as the theatre and bearer of the historicity which follows creation. No particular events or figures need here be invented to depict pre-time. These are needed only in play or acting, where the narrative is used only under the proviso of esoteric interpretation and at bottom there is only timeless speculation. They are not needed in these histories because God the Creator is quite enough on the one hand and the actual creature as it always has been and will be on the other. And as the content of these histories, as the event which takes place between these two, the speech and operation of God is quite enough on the one hand and the emergence of the creature on the other. For this reason there can be full and clear continuity between primal time and that which follows, primal history and the "historical" history which succeeds it. This is the originality of the biblical creation saga. This is its relationship to myth. And even though we recognise material elements, this may be rightly assessed only as a critico-polemical relationship.

The biblical history of creation is pure saga, and as such it is distinguished from "history" on the one side and myth on the other. Precisely in this form it is a constituent part of the biblical witness and therefore itself a witness to God's self-revelation.

It is to be noted that for all the obvious peculiarity the problem of the theological estimation and interpretation of the biblical texts is basically the same in this case as in all others.
To be sure, "history" is in this case wholly replaced by saga and has become pure pre-history.
But in this respect there is a formal similarity between these passages and others in which it is
evident that "history" is replaced by prophecy and therefore by post-history, and sometimes
quite explicitly by pure post-history. In other places too, sometimes in whole sections, the
historical narrative is interrupted by reflection and poetry. "History" is not *the* biblical form
of presentation, but is only one among others. The question, always and everywhere, is that
of the actuality of the historical self-revelation of God. This has also a "historical" aspect, and
to that extent its witnesses must observe and think and speak "historically." It has, too, a
[091]   deeper, metaphysical or ethical aspect and to that extent its witnesses must place at its disposal their reflections and meditation. It has a personal aspect, and to that extent the witness
must be lyrical in nature. In a strict (or less strict) sense it has a post-historical aspect, and to
that extent the witness will necessarily take the form of prophecy. Similarly it has a "non-
historical" aspect, and in the creation history a wholly "non-historical" or pre-historical, and
to that extent the witness must become saga, its authors being summoned, claimed and
committed to exploit the possibilities of historical divination and poetry. In principle, of
course, these are general possibilities, although not equally accessible to all. If the pre-
historical sphere as such belongs to the world of created things, the relation between it and
other spheres is not basically closed, nor its recognition impossible. It is inaccessible only to
our perceptive experience and to the concepts of our understanding which connect these
experiences. But the human possibility of knowing is not exhausted by the ability to perceive
and comprehend. Imagination, too, belongs no less legitimately in its way to the human
possibility of knowing. A man without imagination is more of an invalid than one who lacks a
leg. But fortunately each of us is gifted somewhere and somehow with imagination, however
starved this gift may be in some or misused by others. In principle each of us is capable of
divination and poetry, or at least capable of receiving their products. In principle each of us
can be open to the actualities of pre- and post-history; each of us can produce saga and
prophecy or at least perceive them when they come from others. Thus the biblical writers are
not witnesses of the Word of God, of His historical self-revelation and faith in it, merely
because we perceive in them this openness and see them producing saga and prophecy.
From time immemorial this has been done by those who did not share their function. It is no
great commendation that in their special function they are also seen to use the possibility of
divination and poetry. In itself, this has nothing to do with their inspiration, with their distinctiveness as witnesses of revelation, or with their credibility. On the other hand, it is not in
any sense a disqualification, and spiritual invalids are merely guilty of self-contradiction if
they use these formal grounds as an argument against the authority and trustworthiness of
the biblical writers. To such we must confidently answer with the ancient wisdom that there
are more things in heaven and earth—and even in the human capacity of perception and
presentation—than are dreamed of in their philosophy.

The true mystery and miracle of the biblical creation history (and the same
is true in principle of the whole Bible) consists in the fact that—under this
peculiar aspect—we now see man in one of his possibilities of perception and
presentation confronted with this particular object and occupied with this particular realisation. According to the contents of this saga, the Israelite man,
shall we say, who has conceived these sagas and given them their present form
(although not without a connexion between his view and that of the rest of the
ancient Orient), has been encountered by God, The Lord, the Creator of

heaven and earth, and this encounter has taken place in His speech and operation in the sphere of pre-history, so that from an unknown quantity God has
become a known. In the histories of creation man gives an account of this
encounter and bears witness to it. He can do this only in the form of saga;
otherwise, how could it be God the Creator who had encountered him? How
could it be a history of creation which he has to narrate and attest? It was only
by means of his imagination that he was fit for that encounter, and these presentations could be given only in a divinatory and poetical form. How else
could he have perceived and presented a history of creation if not imagina-   [092]
tively? Yet the relevant and important thing in this process is not that it has this
form, but that the imagination of this people—unlike that of other people—
had this object. Why did not the imagination of the Israelites turn like others
to the wide field of myth? Why did it not arrive at very different conceptions
and presentations even in this field? Why is it that we have here a palpable
criticism of myth? Why is it that there emerges here, and only here, what might
intrinsically have been the object of Babylonian or Egyptian imagination—a
real Creator and a real creation? To these questions there is no answer. We can
only affirm that it is a fact. And this fact alone is the distinctive characteristic of
the biblical creation histories. It is because they are in fact imaginative in this
different way that they are inspired, that they bear witness to God's self-
revelation, and that they demand faith and can lay claim to faith. This decision
is not formal but material. As and because they have this content, attesting the
God who has already spoken and acted in pre-history, or, more concretely,
attesting His words and acts in this sphere, they are true witnesses to this God.
And therefore if He is the true God they are true witnesses to the true God.
And this is not in spite of the fact but as and because they give their imagination free rein under the guidance and discipline of its object, and what they
produce is genuine saga, but saga of this event. It is sacred saga, because it
speaks of God and because it speaks of Him—this is its peculiar feature—as the
Creator. Myth does not do this, nor do other sagas which may formally seem to
be similar, or to have a similar origin. In this respect the distinction of biblical
saga from corresponding productions is absolute, whereas in all other respects
it is only relative.

It is obvious that we can realise this distinction—and especially its absolute
character—only if we keep in mind and do not lose sight of the connexion
between the creation sagas or the history of creation on the one hand and the
succeeding saga and history or the history of the covenant on the other. We
can clearly do so only if we ourselves as covenant-partners consciously take part
in this history of the covenant. If we do not know the God of Israel, the Father
of Jesus Christ, who is Himself Jesus Christ in concealment, how can we possibly understand the speaking and acting Subject of the biblical creation saga?
How can we realise what it means that the reference here is to a real Creator
and real creation? How can we differentiate between myth and saga, or
between this saga and others? But to know this God, and in this way to realise

91

the absolute uniqueness of the saga which speaks of Him, is to know Him as one's own God and as a covenant-partner consciously take part in the history of the covenant which succeeds the history of creation. If the Spirit Himself who has spoken to the biblical writers does not also speak to their hearers and [093] readers, and the inspiration of these writers is not revealed and known in the inspiration of their readers and hearers, we may perhaps see a deep phenomenological and therefore a relative distinction between the biblical witnesses and all kinds of other witness, but here, too, no essential and therefore absolute distinction may be perceived.

> We say "here too" because the history of creation does not differ from the other biblical witnesses in respect of the fact that the object alone can reveal and make Himself known in His divinity to the reader and hearer of these testimonies, or else He will not be revealed and known at all in His divinity. This is no less true when the Bible speaks in a different form from what it does here. It is no less true when it speaks "historically." How can God's self-revelation be guaranteed just because the Bible speaks "historically"? The biblical writers are never more than ministering witnesses, and for the confirmation of their witness the self-witness of the divine reality by the *testimonium Spiritus sancti*[EN111] is everywhere indispensable. And this is the case here too where they speak non-historically or pre-historically.

Here, too, the biblical witnesses speak as men and not as angels or gods. Thus we have to reckon on their part with all kinds of human factors, with their individual and general capacities of perception and expression, with their personal views and style, as determined by age and environment, and of course with the limitations and deficiencies of these conditioning factors—in this case with the limitations of their imagination. The same holds good of passages in which the Bible speaks in a historical or reflective or ethical or lyrical manner. It would not be a concrete historical document if it did not possess a concrete historical form and therefore the unavoidable weakness of such a form. It is also true in this case. The biblical creation-histories are not heaven-sent declarations of the truth itself dropped from the sky but human attestations of the revelation which has taken place in the creaturely sphere. It is in this way, and only in this way, that they declare the truth. They do this in relation to what God has given to certain men to apprehend concerning Himself, and they do it through the imagination and lips and writings of these men who in themselves are as fallible as others. They are not, then, an adequate but a very inadequate medium. In respect of their content and credibility, they live wholly by their object, i.e., by the self-witness of the Holy Spirit to whom alone they owe their origin and power. This is the determination and limitation which we must not overlook in our appreciation and interpretation of them. Their relationship to their object is the very unequal one of a heavenly treasure to the earthly vessels to which it has been entrusted for preservation and impartation. But this relationship is their mystery and miracle. It is in this relationship, and only in this relationship, that they are inspired and speak the

---

EN111 witness of the Holy Spirit

Word of God. We deny their mystery and miracle, their inspiration, if we describe this relationship in any other way, i.e., in a way less contradictory. If and because the task of interpretation is to bring to light the reality of the historical self-revelation of God to which they bear witness, the human side of their witness as such must not be overlooked or expunged, but introduced even in its humanity and therefore its fraility and problematic character, although with no shame that it has so concrete a form; with no desire, in the face of this concrete form, to be better informed by the imported presuppositions of the interpreter; with no haste to amend or improve it, or to cover its indisputable nakedness, or to abandon it where its human limitation seems too palpable and disturbing to the expositor. How do we know whether the self-witness of its object is not loudest and most important precisely where its historical and linguistic determination, the fallibility of the writers and the limitation and deficiency of their imagination, seem to strike us most forcibly? A thoughtful interpretation will be all the more careful and reverent with the biblical witness when its humanity is most clearly recognised: not for its own sake; not out of any magical respect for the letter, which as such is a letter like others; but out of respect for the object which has not been ashamed to raise up these human witnesses with their limitations and to make use of this letter, and which we can know, if at all, only through this witness, and through the letter of this witness. [094]

What we have just said means that our attempted presentation of creation itself and as such must consist materially in the demonstration of the relationship between creation and covenant, and formally in the interpretation of the two biblical stories of creation. It has also fixed the attitude and expectation with which we must approach the basic task of the section of Church dogmatics upon which we have now embarked.

2. CREATION AS THE EXTERNAL BASIS OF THE COVENANT

The creature is not self-existent. It has not assumed its nature and existence of itself or given it to itself. It did not come into being by itself. It does not consist by itself. It cannot sustain itself. It has to thank its creation and therefore its Creator for the fact that it came into being and is and will be. Nor does the creature exist for itself. It is not the creature itself but its Creator who exists and thinks and speaks and cares for the creature. The creature is no more its own goal and purpose than it is its own ground and beginning. There is no inherent reason for the creature's existence and nature, no independent teleology of the creature introduced with its creation and made its own. Its destiny lies entirely in the purpose of its Creator as the One Who speaks and cares for it. The creature's right and meaning and goal and purpose and dignity lie—

[095] only—in the fact that God as the Creator has turned toward it with His purpose. Any other attitude than that of God's free acceptance of this turning towards it and therefore of this advocacy and care; any claim to a right inherent in its being and nature, to a meaning which has not first been received, to a goal which it has fixed for itself, to a purpose which it has in and for itself, to a dignity independent of the free will of its Creator—all this is just as meaningless as the illusion that it came into being of itself, that it consists in itself and that it can sustain itself. By its very creation, and therefore its being as a creature, all such views are shown, like this illusion, to be basically impossible, and thus disclosed as falsehoods.

But this means that the divine creation in itself and as such did not and does not take place for its own sake. Creation is the freely willed and executed positing of a reality distinct from God. The question thus arises: What was and is the will of God in doing this? We may reply that He does not will to be alone in His glory; that He desires something else beside Him. But this answer cannot mean that God either willed and did it for no purpose, or that He did so to satisfy a need. Nor does it mean that He did not will to be and remain alone because He could not do so. And the idea of something beside Him which would be what it is independently of Him is quite inconsistent with His freedom. In constituting this reality He cannot have set a limit to His glory, will and power. As the divine Creator He cannot have created a remote and alien sphere abandoned to itself or to its own teleology. If, then, this positing is not an accident, if it corresponds to no divine necessity and does not in any sense signify a limitation of His own glory, there remains only the recollection that God is the One who is free in His love. In this case we can understand the positing of this reality—which otherwise is incomprehensible—only as the work of His love. He wills and posits the creature neither out of caprice nor necessity, but because He has loved it from eternity, because He wills to demonstrate His love for it, and because He wills, not to limit His glory by its existence and being, but to reveal and manifest it in His own co-existence with it. As the Creator He wills really to exist for His creature. That is why He gives it its own existence and being. That is also why there cannot follow from the creature's own existence and being an immanent determination of its goal or purpose, or a claim to any right, meaning or dignity of its existence and nature accruing to it except as a gift. That is why even the very existence and nature of the creature are the work of the grace of God. It would be a strange love that was satisfied with the mere existence and nature of the other, then withdrawing, leaving it to its own devices. Love wills to love. Love wills something with and for that which it loves. Because God loves the creature, its creation and continuance and preservation point beyond themselves to an exercise and fulfilment of His love which do not take place merely with the fact that the crea-

[096] ture is posited as such and receives its existence and being alongside and outside the being and existence of od, but to which creation in all its glory looks and moves, and of which creation is the presupposition.

This, then, is a first aspect of creation which Scripture directs us to consider. It is the presupposition of the realisation of the divine purpose of love in relation to the creature. Creation is the indispensable presupposition because it is a question of the realisation of the *divine* intention of love. The case is different where it is a question of mutual love in the creaturely sphere. Here the one who is loved has its existence and being independent of the one who loves. Here the one comes upon the other and loves it for the sake of its being and nature. But divine love is perfect love, the inaccessible prototype and true basis of all creaturely love, because it does not rest on a presupposition of this kind, but creates the presupposition. God loves the being which could not exist without Him, but only does so by Him. God loves His own creature. This is the absolutely unique feature of the covenant in which His love is exercised and fulfilled. Its external basis, i.e., the existence and being of the creature with which He is covenanted, is the work of His own will and achievement. His creation is the external basis of this covenant. So firmly is this covenant established! So trustworthy is its presupposition not only on God's part but also on the part of the creature! So great is the faithfulness and constancy which it can as such expect from God in this covenant! And so transcendent is also the authority of the Founder of this covenant! There is absolutely no external basis that this covenant can have which was not posited by the God who here enters into covenant with man. There is no existence of the creature in which it can originally belong elsewhere than to this compact. It has no attributes, no conditions of existence, no substantial or accidental predicates of any kind, in virtue of which it can or may or must be alien to the Founder of this covenant. Nor, of course, are there any claims which it can raise or adduce to a right or dignity which can be asserted in contrast and opposition to the will of the Founder of this covenant. It has no ground on which it can deal with Him on an equal footing. In this covenant God gives to it what He undertook to give to it when He first gave it its being and nature. And God wills from it as a partner in this covenant only that for which He prepared and bound and pledged it when He first gave it its being and nature. The creature to whom He has bound Himself belongs to Him. It is only God's free love that makes Him bind Himself to it. In so doing, He does not in any sense discharge a debt. How can He be impelled by anything but Himself, in perfect freedom, really to love the creature which owes its existence and nature to Him alone, to enter with it into this relation and therefore to provide this sequel to His creation? But as He does this, as His love is so incomprehensibly high and deep that He is not ashamed to will and do it, His activity has its solid external basis in the fact that [097] what He loves belongs to Him. In the partner of His covenant He does not have to do with the subject of another nor a lord in his own right, but with His own property, with the work of His will and achievement. The external dynamic of this covenant is that it rests on creation. In virtue of its being and nature, the creature is destined, prepared and equipped to be a partner of this covenant. This covenant cannot be seriously threatened or attacked by the

95

nature of the creature or its surroundings, nor by any attribute of man and the world. By its whole nature the creature is destined and disposed for this covenant. There is no peculiarity in man and the world which does not as such aim at this covenant. As a partner of this covenant, the creature will always have to do exclusively with its Creator on God's side, and exclusively with its own God-given nature on its own.

We have to make a self-evident restriction. Creation is not itself the covenant. The existence and being of the one loved are not identical with the fact that it is loved. This can be said only in respect of the love with which God loves Himself—the Father the Son and the Son the Father in the Holy Spirit. It cannot be said of God's relationship to the creature posited in distinction from Himself. The existence and being of the creature willed and constituted by God are the object and to that extent the presupposition of His love. Thus the covenant is the goal of creation and creation the way to the covenant. Nor is creation the inner basis of the covenant. (At a later point we shall have to state conversely that the covenant is the inner basis of creation; but this relationship is not reversible.) The inner basis of the covenant is simply the free love of God, or more precisely the eternal covenant which God has decreed in Himself as the covenant of the Father with His Son as the Lord and Bearer of human nature, and to that extent the Representative of all creation. Creation is the external—and only the external—basis of the covenant. It can be said that it makes it technically possible; that it prepares and establishes the sphere in which the institution and history of the covenant take place; that it makes possible the subject which is to be God's partner in this history, in short the nature which the grace of God is to adopt and to which it is to turn in this history. As the love of God could not be satisfied with the eternal covenant as such; as it willed to execute it and give it form outside the divine sphere, it made itself this external ground of the covenant, i.e., it made necessary the existence and being of the creature and therefore of creation. It is, however, only its external basis. If it has taken place for its sake and may be called grace in view of this goal, it is so only as it points to grace itself and prepares for it. But what does "only" signify in this connexion? As that which genuinely points to grace, as its necessary preparation, it is itself already grace, but only in this sense and context and not without it. This is the first aspect under which we have now to consider it.

[098]   The first biblical creation story (Gen. 1^1-2^{4a}) develops this particular aspect for us in contrast to the second. It describes creation as it were externally as the work of powerful but thoroughly planned and thought-out and perfectly supervised preparation, comparable to the building of a temple, the arrangement and construction of which is determined both in detail and as a whole by the liturgy which it is to serve. But the beginning of the peculiar occurrence to which creation points is touched upon only towards the end, and therefore on the fringes of the account: clearly enough to make the teleology of creation apparent; but with sufficient reticence not to allow us to forget that creation is

one thing and its continuation in the history of the covenant of grace quite another. What is here to be presented is how "heaven and the earth and all the host of them" (Gen. 2^1) are created with a definite purpose, i.e., with a view to the history of the covenant.

What will finally take place according to the account (Gen. 1^{26}-2^3), is the appearance of man at the summit of creation, man and woman created in and after the image of God. With reference to this creature, with which the whole creation will be completed on the sixth day, God will see the totality of created things and find it very good. And God will then rest on the seventh day. It is not man entering upon the work appointed at his creation who is to be the hero of the seventh and last day of creation, although everything now seems to be ready for him to commence to multiply and spread abroad on the earth, ruling over the rest of the animal creation and finding the food which he is specially allotted. The very man commissioned for this task is now to witness a very different occurrence. It is not man who brings the history of creation to an end, nor is it he who ushers in the subsequent history. It is God's rest which is the conclusion of the one and the beginning of the other, i.e., God's free, solemn, and joyful satisfaction with that which has taken place and has been completed as creation, and His invitation to man to rest with Him, i.e., with Him to be satisfied with that which has taken place through Him. The goal of creation, and at the same time the beginning of all that follows, is the event of God's Sabbath freedom, Sabbath rest and Sabbath joy, in which man, too, has been summoned to participate. It is the event of divine rest in face of the cosmos completed with the creation of man—a rest which takes precedence over all man's eagerness and zeal to enter upon his task. Man is created to participate in this rest. It is the covenant of the grace of God which in this event, at the supreme and final point of the first creation story, is revealed as the starting-point for all that follows. Everything that precedes is the road to this supreme point. The connexion and sequence of the individual events in the history of creation, and these individual events themselves—each in its own place and manner—all point to this last event, to this positive and yet limiting relation of God's Sabbath rest to the man striding forward to the work [099] for which he is prepared. Rightly to understand this passage, it is necessary to read it backwards. There has to be an awareness of where it seems to lead us— out of the pre-historical and into the historical sphere. It leads to the point where God rested on the seventh day after the creation of man and prior to any human activity. It leads into a sphere where it cannot be overlooked that whatever may happen the truth of the relationship between God and man will be the divinely instituted covenant of the wholly sufficient and wholly sovereign grace of God. This is what we have to bear in mind from the very outset in the first creation saga.

(Gen. 1^1.) It is the divine will and accomplishment in relation to man—and nothing else—which really stands at the beginning of all things. It was in this way—and no other—that heaven and earth originated. Not man and not a wisdom or folly, a power or impotence, immanent in the world of man, willed and accomplished the creature, but God—the God who rejoiced in man as in His own image. This, and nothing else, took place at the beginning, for anything else that might have taken place had already passed in virtue of the fact that this had taken place. The present and future of this beginning of all things, even of the beginning of time, and therefore of all genuine present and future, was this divine volition and accomplishment. Thus the work of this beginning was not an accidental thing, either self-formed or formed by a strange idea and force, but a cosmos, *the* cosmos, the divinely ordered world in which heaven and earth—a picture of the relationship between God and man in the covenant of grace—confronted one another in mutual separation and inter-connexion as an upper sphere and a lower: the one essentially invisible to man, the other essentially visible; the one transcending him in unknown heights, the other his own and entrusted to him. This is the creation chosen, willed, and posited by God; the creation which, for this reason, is "good," indeed "very good," in His sight. It is so because, in virtue of this typical superiority and subordination, it is adapted to be a theatre of the covenant which is the purpose of the divine volition and accomplishment; and because, in virtue of its nature, it is radically incapable of serving any other purpose, but placed from the very first at the disposal of His grace.

(Cf. for what follows, not only the commentaries by F. Delitzsch, H. Gunkel and W. Zimmerli to which we have already referred, but also Alfred Jeremias's *Das A.T. im Lichte des alten Orients*[4], 1930, and B. Jacob's, *Das erste Buch der Thora*, 1934.)

The *b'reshith*[EN112] of v. 1 has a twofold implication. It tells us first that this history, and with it the existence and being of the world, had a beginning, i.e., that unlike God Himself it was not without a beginning, but that with this beginning it also looks to an end. "If anything has a temporal beginning, doubt not its end" (Basil, *Hex.* 1, 3). And it tells us secondly that this and this alone was its beginning—the creative act of God. As the *subject Elohim* points to the sum and Lord of all divine powers, so the predicate *bara*'[EN113] points to the creative act whose subject can only be this Elohim and whose nature that which corresponds to this Elohim, i.e., a pure act of creativity, unhindered by any opposition, unlimited by any presupposition, not requiring the co-operation of any other agent and excluding any idea either of the co-operation of a pre-existent reality or of conflict against it.

There is an indisputable literary connexion between 1[1] and 2[4a]: "These are the generations (*tol'doth*) of the heaven and of the earth." Opinion varies whether the latter verse is a signature, i.e., a recapitulatory postscript to the whole account (Delitzsch), or whether it originally stood at the head and thus formed the beginning of the passage (A. Jeremias, Gunkel). What is certain is that the summary in 2[4a]; is subjected by 1[1] to a distinctively critical refinement. It is the works of the divine *bara*'which are the *tol'doth*, the "generations" of the heaven and of the earth, as the word is rightly ascribed in the rest of Genesis to all kinds of people, but wrongly ascribed in myths to the reality of the world as such. This is how it really was in the beginning where myths would again like to see a generation, a primeval generation of *Tiamat*, and in the last resort a kind of eternal self-generation of the world-reality. What really happened was God's free positing of this world-reality. The unique thing

[100]

[EN112] in the beginning
[EN113] to create

about the "generation" of the heaven and of the earth is that it cannot be comprehended with the aid of natural analogies, but it can be described only by the word "creation" (Zimmerli). Thus the history of the great acts of God replaces and supplants myth even at the first stroke of this account with its purely general reference. In respect of Gen. 1¹. even Gunkel can praise the Priestly Code. "A great word! Simply but effectively the author at once establishes the dogma that God has created the world. There is no word in the cosmogonies of other nations that can compare with this first word of the Bible."

The expression "heaven and earth" refers comprehensively to the decisive thing, namely, the existence, the distinction and the being of that which is above and that which is below. It is thus used in the rest of the Bible to denote the ordered and fashioned universe. We do violence to the text if with Augustine (who was followed at this point by Thomas Aquinas, by Luther and Calvin, by Protestant as well as Catholic orthodoxy and even by Wellhausen) we equate "heaven and earth" with the *informis materia quam ex nihilo Deus fecit*[EN114] mentioned in 1², explaining that this *materia informis*[EN115] is here called "heaven and earth" *non quia iam hoc erat, sed quia hoc esse poterat*[EN116] (*De Gen. c. Man*, I, 7, 11; cf. *Conf.* XII, 4, 4, etc.). This *opinio communis* must be resisted. Certainly according to 1² there is a chaos, and a very definite divine relationship to chaos. But the view that God first created chaos, that He accomplished "a positing of the formless and unordered universe" (so also B. Jacob), and only then called out of this *rudis indigestaque moles*[EN117] the reality of heaven and earth potentially existing in it, is not only entirely foreign to the rest of the Bible but also to these first verses of Genesis. "The thought of a creation of chaos is in itself contradictory and amazing; chaos is the world prior to creation" (Gunkel). The truth is that Gen. 1¹ is an anticipatory formulation of "the fact of creation in a general expression" (Delitzsch). Gen. 1¹, then, does not stand in any positive relation to 1², but is a superscription referring in advance to what is developed from v. 3 onwards as the form of this fact of creation.

The concept "earth" in Gen. 1¹ and 1² means "earth" in contradistinction to "heaven." But this does not exhaust its meaning. It is more comprehensive than our concept "earth," and refers (A. Jeremias) to the threefold earthly ("tellural") totality of the sky (the "atmosphere" and "stratosphere"), the earth as we understand it, and the sea, which includes the depth of the nether ocean which supports the earth. In this respect Augustine is quite right when he says: *Ad coelum coeli etiam terrae nostra coelum terra est*[EN118] (*Conf.* XII, 2, 2). Where, as in Ex. 20¹¹, Neh. 9⁶, Rev. 5¹³, 10⁶ and Ac. 4²⁴ and 14¹⁵, the triad is called heaven, earth and sea, there—*pars pro toto*—this earthly totality is meant. With the exception of the works of the first   [101] two days which touch on the broader and higher scope of what is created, Gen. 1 deals explicitly with the creation of this tellural totality. This alone is *in concreto*[EN119] the theatre of the history whose beginning is here narrated as creation. In v. 1, however, there is implicit witness—made explicit in the description of the work of the second day in v. 2—to the creation of heaven, i.e., the threefold heavenly totality, which consists of the highest heaven, the "celestial ocean," and the "celestial earth." Augustine over-simplifies the problem when he characterises the totality of this celestial heaven as *creatura intellectualis*[EN120] (*Conf.* XII, 9, 9). The characterisation is true enough, perhaps, of the angels who inhabit heaven (although not exclusively heaven), but not of heaven as such, not even of the highest heaven. From vv. 6–8, where a distinction is made between the firmament and the waters

---

[EN114] unformed matter which God first created from nothing
[EN115] unformed matter
[EN116] not because it was these things already, but because it was able to be made into them
[EN117] coarse and disordered mass
[EN118] Compared with the heaven of heavens, even the heaven of our earth is earth
[EN119] concretely
[EN120] intellectual creature

above the firmament which are separated by it from the waters of the earthly totality, we learn that here too there is a solid element (corresponding in this respect to the earth) and a fluid one (related to the terrestrial ocean). According to v. 17, the sun, moon and stars are attached to this firmament. From the rest of the Old Testament, however, it is clear that the concept "heaven" is not exhausted by this twofold meaning ("firmament" and "celestial ocean"), and that the inclusive and comparatively recent word of Gen. 1^1 necessarily indicates a third meaning. From Gen. 28^{12}, 1 K. 8^{12}, Pss. 2^4, 11^4 and Is. 66^1 we learn that heaven is the dwelling-place or palace or throne of God, and in this sense it can refer neither to the firmament nor to the celestial ocean above it. The fact that in the later histories of the Old Testament God is often called *Elohe hash-shamayim*[EN121] obviously points to a wider sphere. And so in Deut. 10^{14}, 1 K. 8^{27}, Neh. 9^6 and 2 Chron. 2^6 and 6^{18} there is a clear and formal distinction between "heaven" and the "heaven of heavens," which itself can contain God as little as any other place, and therefore evidently belongs to the sphere of that which is created. According to Ps. 68^{33} this is the highest and eternal heaven. In Ps. 14^{84} it is topographically located opposite the celestial ocean. In Is. 14^{13}, where the proud king of Babylon is pictured as himself aspiring to be God, it is designated as "the mount of God, in the extreme north," i.e., obviously the cosmic polar point. And Paul obviously has this in mind when he speaks in 2 Cor. 12^2 of his rapture to the "third heaven." This highest and proper heaven is also visualised in Gen. 1^1, although there is no further reference to it in what follows. Why not? With B. Jacob the answer is perhaps to be sought in Ps. 115^{16}: "The heavens are the heavens of the Lord, but the earth hath he given to the children of men." In relation of this highest heaven, God's heaven, we need only be told that this too is created, and that according to Ps. 73^{25} only God can be against us in heaven, but that in fact He is for us. The Babylonian idea that the tellural universe is somehow suspended in the upper or heavenly sphere (Job 26^7) does not appear to have had any interest for the author of this passage, nor is there any trace of the view that pillars support the sky (Job. 26^{11}), or that the earth rests on special foundations, as we are told in many other places (e.g., Ps. 104^5). These things do not seem to have any constitutive significance for the concept of creation and the permanency of the world founded on it. The point of Gen. 1^1 is that God has created the totality of everything above and below, of the invisible and the visible universe, and that there is nothing either in the one or the other that does not stand under the sign of the *bara' Elohim*[EN122]. It may be said, then, that too much has not been read into it in the creed, which also refers to this inclusive twofold reality of the world-order, but that the interpretation there given is essentially correct.

(Gen. 1^2.) Everything else, i.e., everything neutral or hostile to God's purpose, ceased to be when time commenced with this divine volition and accomplishment, and the world was fashioned and ordered by God in time. It is that [102] which, denied by God's will and act, belongs only to the non-recurring past of commencing time. It is that which is excluded from all present and future existence, i.e., chaos, the world fashioned otherwise than according to the divine purpose, and therefore formless and intrinsically impossible. If even the world willed and posited by God as His creation is not itself divine in virtue of its creation, it is at least preserved from the necessity or possibility of being ungodly or anti-godly. That which is ungodly and anti-godly can have reality only as that which by God's decision and operation has been rejected and has

---

[EN121] the God of heaven
[EN122] God created

disappeared, and therefore only as a frontier of that which is and will be according to God's decision and action. The power to keep itself from the curse and misery of that which is ungodly and anti-godly—even the power to be good in God's sight and judgment and to prepare itself for the sphere of the fulfilment of the divine purpose—this power which the creature did not possess in itself and of itself, God had and used in the place and on behalf of the creature. He saw the threatening curse and the threatening misery. He rejected the reality of a creation that might be neutral or hostile to Him. He pushed it back and outside the limit of the world willed and determined by Him. He thus had pity on His creation. Although He did not create it divine, He did not create it ungodly or anti-godly, but in harmony and at peace with Himself, and therefore, according to His plan, as the theatre and instrument of His acts, an object of His joy and for participation in this joy.

Gen. 1² reads: "And the earth was waste and void; and darkness was upon the face of the deep; and the Spirit of God moved upon the face of the waters." This verse has always constituted a particular *crux interpretum*[EN123]—one of the most difficult in the whole Bible—and it is small comfort to learn from Gunkel that it is a "veritable mythological treasure chamber." Already Augustine (*Conf.* XII, 21) enumerated five different ways in which the notorious *tohu wa-bohu* of this verse might be understood. Does it mean the material, especially of things terrestrial and corporeal, as created by God but so far without form, order or light? Or does it mean the formless material created by God from which the physical heaven and earth and everything in them were later to be created and were created? Or does it mean the formless material created by God from which the higher heaven as well as the earth and the physical heaven were later made? Or does it mean a formless material which was already there prior to the creation of the upper universe and the lower, and was used in their creation? Or finally does it mean the formless material which was there already prior to the creation of the lower universe and particularly used in its creation?

The first and basic question is obviously this: Does v. 2 (with or without reference to v. 1) speak of *tohu wa-bohu*, of darkness and flood, as a primeval condition which preceded creation, and therefore a primeval reality independent of creation and distinct from God? Or does it affirm that creation commenced with the fundamental positing of *tohu wa-bohu*, of darkness and flood, as the primeval state—a positing not included in the work of the six days, but promisingly accompanied by the Spirit of God brooding over this dark and disorderly totality. The first explanation must surely be rejected. I am not sure whether Gunkel really takes it that there is a reference to the "primeval condition of the world which preceded creation," or whether he means only that such an idea is not altogether foreign to the text. On this point we may say that in so far as the author worked with the Babylonian myth the idea could not be strange to him, but that he definitely could not and would not appropriate or reproduce it. It would clash too much with the decisive concepts of v. 1, with the *b⁴reshith*, with the *bara'*[EN124], and above all with the concept of *Elohim* in this later source. It is clear enough that there is a chaos; that creation is "somehow" related to it; that it plays its part even in the later history which begins with creation; and that there too there are definite encounters between it and God. But there is no such thing as a "reality of chaos" independently confronting the Creator and His works, and able in its own power as matter or a hostile principle to oppose His operations. It may well be that the concept of a *creatio ex*

[103]

[EN123] interpretative challenge
[EN124] in the beginning with the created

nihilo[EN125], of which there is no actual hint in Gen. 1–2, is the construct of later attempts at more precise formulation. But its antithesis—the mythological acceptance of a primeval reality independent of God—is excluded in practice by the general tenor of the passage as well as its position within the biblical context.

But in our consideration of v. 1 we have already decided against the second explanation, i.e., the *opinio communis*[EN126] that in v. 2 we have a description of the *informitas materiae, quam sine specie feceras, unde speciosum mundum faceres*[EN127] (Augustine, *Conf.* XII, 4). This exposition could not be more briefly or finely stated. Ambrose, who was also of this opinion, believed that God had first created the creature in such weakness (*infirmitas*) *ne ἄναρχον, ne increatam et divinae consortem substantiae crederemus*[EN128] (*Hex.* I, 3, 8). According to Luther's exposition, v. 2 (in its accepted connexion with v. 1) is to be explained as follows: "What does it mean when it says ' God created heaven and earth, and the earth was waste and void '? Just what I have said before, namely, that the Almighty God has not created the world in a day but taken time for this purpose, as when He now creates a child. He first creates the rudiments of heaven and earth, but these as yet unfashioned, and waste and void, with no life or growth or shape or form. We must not think here as the philosophers Plato and Aristotle have done with their ideas, but in the simplest way recognise that there was a real heaven and earth, as the verse itself says; and therefore a first creation, although nothing was so far fashioned as it was to be. Just as originally the infant, although it is not nothing in its mother's womb, is not yet formed as a perfect child is to be; and just as smoke is not nothing, but has neither light nor radiance, so the earth was as yet unfashioned and had no dimensions either of breadth or length, neither was there any seed or trees or grass on it, but poor and barren earth like an uninhabited land or desert where nothing grows. And similarly heaven was without form, although it was not nothing" (*Sermon on Genesis*, 1527, *W.A.* 24, 25, 24). The decisive objection against this exposition, which Zimmerli rightly calls "a desperate expedient," is as follows. In view of the emphasised expression "the heaven and the earth," the presupposed connexion between v. 1 and v. 2 is inadmissible. Apart from this connexion, there is nothing in the passage about a prior creation of the world in a raw or rudimentary state. If the author had really had this in mind, it is inconceivable that he should have remained silent about it; that he should not have included this fundamental act in the work of the six days, and therefore in his presentation of the creation of the world by the Word of God. Such a silence could only spread great confusion not only over v. 1 but also everything that follows; the confusion into which we do actually stumble if we imagine that he is referring to this prior creation in v. 2 (either with or without any reference to v. 1). For in this case he would not really have questioned and denied the primal reality postulated by the Babylonian myth— and it is to this that v. 2 refers—but would actually have described it as the beginning of the true work of creation willed and posited by the God of Israel prior to His creative Word. In Is. 45[16] we read the very opposite: "For thus saith the Lord that created the heavens; he is God (*Elohim*) that formed the earth and made it; he established it, he created it not a waste (*lo-tohu beraah*): he formed it to be inhabited. I am the Lord and there is none else."

[104]

The dilemma in which we find ourselves by refusing both interpretations is not inconsiderable. The choice between the two appears to be unavoidable. If the raw and rudimentary state of the world depicted in v. 2 is not a reality independent of God and His work, what else can it be but God's creation? And if it is not God's creation, what else can it be but a reality

---

[EN125] creation from nothing

[EN126] common opinion

[EN127] the primeval state of matter, which Thou hadst made without form, but from which Thou wouldst make the well-formed world

[EN128] lest we should believe that this counterpart of the divine substance was itself without a lord or uncreated

independent of God and His work? But the real question is whether v. 2 does actually speak of the *informitas materiae*[EN129], of the *rudis indigestaque moles*[EN130], of a raw and rudimentary state of the world (either self-founded or willed and posited by God) which is genuine in the sense of the things created from v. 3 onwards. The dilemma remains only if this is the case. If it is not the case, the dilemma is only apparent. For in this case there is a third possibility.

Before we take up this point, let us be clear what is actually stated. In distinction from v. 1, v. 2 speaks directly only of the earth, i.e., of the lower, visible part of the universe. That the expression could also refer indirectly or synecdochically to the upper part of the world cannot actually be excluded. But neither can it be established that this was the meaning of the author. The whole problem of v. 2, according to the history which follows, is the problem which afflicts man and which therefore afflicts his world, i.e., the lower world. That, as the author sees it, it oppresses and in some sense compromises the celestial sphere is an imminent deduction but it is not openly drawn. What v. 2 offers, as Gunkel has rightly felt, is in contradiction (we can only say, in glaring opposition) to the created reality of heaven and earth summarily described in v. 1, and in glaring opposition to what is later described as God's "good" creation. It is a caricature of the tellural universe. In v. 2 there is absolutely nothing as God willed and created and ordained it according to v. 1 and the continuation. There is only "chaos." This Greek word, rightly used at this point, does not primarily denote confusion but a gulf, the ἄβυσσος[EN131]—a term which the LXX was right to introduce at least on material if not exegetical grounds—that which is absolutely without basis or future, utter darkness. And such is the earth according to v. 2—in supreme antithesis to v. 1 and especially to what follows. All expositions which overlook or weaken this antithesis, trying to find in it more friendly images like those of a world-egg or a mother-womb which bears the future, forget that the author undoubtedly knew this mythical conception but that his only possible object—and the later we put P the more sure we can be of this—is to contest it, to interpret and illumine it *in malam partem*[EN132].

"And the earth was *tohu* and *bohu*." According to this phrase the situation in which the earth finds itself is the very opposite of promising. It is quite hopeless. *Tohu*—according to A. Jeremias this term is definitely related to the Babylonian arch-mother *Tiamat*—is frequently used in the Hebrew language to describe a wilderness, a deserted city, etc. It is also used, however, to describe an empty assertion. In general it means that which is waste and void and empty. According to 1 Sam. 12²¹ it is applied to idols of heathen nations, and in Is. 41²⁹ and 44⁹ to those who fashion and worship them. The word *bohu* occurs in the Old Testament only in connexion with *tohu*. Possibly there is a connexion with the Phoenician and Babylonian goddess Bau who is for the Phoenicians a personification of night as the arch-mother of man, and simply means a "vacuum." The two terms thus bring us to the heart of the mythical world whose figures did not and could not have any precise or positive meaning for the thought and language of Israel-Judah but were simply personifications of that which is abhorrent. What *tohu* and *bohu* mean in practice can be gathered from the two prophetical passages where they are mentioned together as in Gen. 1². All the horrors of the approaching final judgment are summed up in the vision of Jer. 4²³: "I beheld the earth, and, lo, Wʰhinneh tohu ma-bohu, and the heavens, and they had no light." And, according to Is. 34¹¹, in the prophecy about Zion:"And he shall stretch over it the line of *tohu* (confusion) and the plummet of *bohu* (emptiness)." Thus the condition of the earth depicted in v. 2 is identical with the whole horror of the final judgment. If in face of this horror there is deliverance on [105]

[EN129] the primeval state of matter
[EN130] coarse and disordered mass
[EN131] abyss
[EN132] in a bad sense

103

the one hand and creation on the other—in both cases as God's act in contradiction to the threats of *tohu wa-bohu*—there can never be any question of a positive qualification of this utterly abhorrent thing as such. The earth as *tohu wa-bohu* is the earth which is nothing as such, which mocks its Creator and which can only be an offence to the heaven above it, threatening it with the same nothingness.

The same is even more true of the content of the second sentence: "And darkness (*ḥoshek*) was upon the face of the deep" (*tᵉhom*). Gunkel may be right when he says that a second and different view of this desolate state of the world is immediately set alongside the first (without any attempt at co-ordination). The various efforts of older expositors to combine the two systematically have all had to be abandoned. What emerges is not just one picture of a mythological world view, but several different and to some extent superimposed pictures. We again find ourselves in this sphere in the second sentence. *Tᵉhom* in the rest of the Old Testament is any great mass of water, or the depths of the sea, or the sea as such, including the ocean under the earth. But here (as also in Ps. 33⁷ and 104⁶) it means the primeval flood, which is a new and more striking expression for chaos, for the abyss of that which is intrinsically impossible. Used indeterminately as a proper noun, the term *tᵉhom* reminds us here, as elsewhere, that it originally designated a mythologically personified magnitude, probably again the Babylonian *Tiamat* presented as a divine she-monster and the personification of the primeval sea. It is one of the distinctive features of the first biblical creation story in formal attachment to the Babylonian tradition that it treats the element of water as the principle which in its abundance and power is absolutely opposed to God's creation. Gunkel has rightly perhaps pointed out that the tradition to which the Priestly Code makes particular reference had its origin in Mesopotamia and therefore in a "part of the world given to alluvial inundations." This is the precise opposite of the arid background of the Yahwist, who not only does not accept the negative qualification of water in this passage but emphatically takes the opposite view. That water, the celestial and terrestrial ocean, and with the latter the *tᵉhom*, later belong to the cosmic elements which are created by God and are as such His property and sphere, is another matter which does not alter in the slightest the fact that water (including the "celestial" as well as the "terrestrial") is something equivocal and dangerous which has always to be held back from man for his preservation, and even something evil when it is directly equated with *tehom*, as in the present passage. Nothing good can or will emerge from this primeval flood. Already in the *Tiamat* myth it is the evil mother, the enemy of all life who must first be killed so that from her members the world may be constructed. The Old Testament and the present text know absolutely nothing of any such "Die and become" with reference to *tᵉhom*. Nor do they know anything of a motherhood of *tᵉhom*. They give it no such chance. The only predicate given to it is that darkness lay upon it; the same darkness perhaps as that indicated by the *bohu* of the first sentence; the darkness in which there is no knowledge and therefore no objectivity; the darkness in which man cannot be man or can be only sleeping, intoxicated, dreaming man; the darkness of which it cannot later be said that God created it, but that God separated from it the light which He had created and which He found to be good. That the world was made out of darkness; that darkness was the primeval thing and light was in some sense born of it, has of course been the metaphysico-religious belief of many nations. And Novalis proclaimed in inspired language that night is the special friend of man: "Hast thou too, Dark night, A human heart?

[106] What dost thou wrap, Beneath thy mantle, That stirs my soul, With a mighty power unseen? Thine aspect only daunts—Yet from thine hand Drops precious balm. And from thy bundle poppies, In sweet intoxication Unfoldest thou the heavy wings of feeling. And grantest joys, Dark and ineffable, And secret like thyself, That give us thoughts of heaven .... More heavenly than the twinkling stars, In vast immensities, Shine out the endless eyes, Which night Hath opened in us." This is certainly not the view of the biblical saga. The obscurity in which

its God dwells is "the light which no man can approach unto" (1 Tim. 6¹⁶), and not darkness. "Yea, the darkness hideth not from thee; but the night shineth as the day: the darkness and the light are both alike to thee" (Ps. 139¹²). God's relation to this magnitude is one of victory over darkness. Hence darkness—even in its connexion with *t'hom* in v. 2, to which it is obviously related as heaven is related to earth in the world created by God—cannot possibly be regarded even as a potentially positive magnitude. Just as nothing that is good can come out of *t'hom*, nothing that is good can come out of darkness. Even the intransigeant statement of Is. 45⁷ cannot be adduced to prove the opposite: "I am the Lord, and there is none else. I form the light and create darkness; I make peace and create evil: I am the Lord that doeth all these things." This verse speaks of Cyrus whom—although he did not know it—*Yahweh* had made an instrument for Israel's sake. In opposition to the dualistic conception according to which darkness and evil (here the night of paganism from which Cyrus comes) might escape the sphere of *Yahweh's* power and control, the lordship and sway of *Yahweh* the Creator are also asserted over these spheres and powers. They are not what they are without Him but through Him, and can therefore be used according to His will. Had He not been the Creator of light, there would have been no darkness. As He is the Creator of light, darkness, too, is not without but through Him. The same truth is taught in Am. 3⁶: "Shall evil befall a city, and the Lord hath not done it?" Or again in Am. 4¹³: "He maketh the morning darkness." And in Lam. 3³⁸: "Out of the mouth of the Most High cometh there not evil and good?" But these passages do not say that God positively willed, created and posited darkness in the same positive way as light or evil as peace, as an independent goal and event of His plan. *Post tenebras lux*EN133—that is true, and in this *post* it is shown that God is Lord also over the *tenebrae*EN134, indeed that they are not what they are without Him, but only in opposition and therefore relationship to Him. *E tenebris lux*EN135, on the contrary, would be the untruth of myth which fails to recognise God's decree and act. Because the biblical story of creation is necessarily a witness to the truth in opposition to myth, because it too has in some sense to apprehend the Word *post tenebras*EN136 and therefore against the background of myth, it has to mention the primeval flood and the darkness which was upon it. It does not do this for its own sake, to present it as a reality or to certify and glorify it as such, and even less to refer back God's creation to it and deduce it from it, but in order to confront it with God's creation as a revelation of God, and thus to bring out the true reality of the world.

But there is a third statement in Gen. 1². According to Gunkel it is "a third and obviously again an originally allogenic theory" concerning the problematical state of the world prior to creation. "And the Spirit of God moved upon the face of the water." The visualised state of the world is again characterised by the fluid element. It is the world in which there is to be seen *nihil stabile aut solidum*EN137 (Calvin): the basic impasse which confronted Israel after its exodus from Egypt when its way was blocked by the Red Sea; the final monstrosity by which the disciples saw themselves threatened on the lake of Gennesareth; the underlying evil depicted by water, by an abundance of water, in the story of the Flood in Gen. 7¹⁰ᶠ. The third statement has this in common with the first two. Yet this time it is not darkness which is upon the face of the deep but "the Spirit of *Elohim*" who broods over it. For the first time there is revealed the relation of the God of Israel to this monstrous realm. But what kind of relation [107] is it? The reference is to the Spirit of God, and therefore, according to the usage of the Old Testament, to the divine power and operation particularly declared and represented in the

---

EN133 After the darkness light
EN134 darkness
EN135 Out of the darkness light
EN136 after the darkness
EN137 nothing stable or solid

equipment and experience of the prophets, but also manifested in Ps. $104^{29f.}$ as the quickening principle in the existence of the creature. It is therefore difficult to regard it (with B. Jacob) as a mere wind which vertically agitates the water from above like the beating of a bird's wings over its nest—a wind which as a *spiritus lenis*[EN138] precedes the divine *'amar* of v. 3, and is called the "wind of God" because it is itself created by God. Nor is it possible to interpret the function of the divine wind in analogy to Gen. 8^1, Ex. 15^8. 10, 2 Sam. 22^{16} and Job 26^{13}, thus connecting Gen. 1^{22} materially with v. 3: "And the Spirit of God moved upon the face of the water. And God said, Let there be light." For in v. 2 there is no reference to the moving and blowing of a wind of God, but the Spirit is depicted as a bird moving its wings in a hovering attitude (cf. Deut. 32^{11} which speaks of an eagle hovering over its young), as expressed in the verb *raḥaph*. This brings us close to the further idea, known already to the apostolic fathers, that this hovering and fluttering bird is "brooding," and therefore to the ancient and widespread myth of a world-egg from which heaven and earth originally emerged by cleavage. Did the author really wish to present this doctrine or a reminiscence of it? Did he really wish to convey that this brooding of the Spirit of God was a kind of preparation for the actual divine act of creation portrayed in v. 3? It has been said so again and again, but without any good reasons. For if we regard it as conceivable that this curious function is indeed positively ascribed to the God of Israel, how meaningless and confusing it is in relation to what follows! The egg whose existence would in some respects make intelligible the dark occurrence is not actually mentioned in our text, nor is any effect of the hovering and brooding on the waters over which it takes place. What can result from the hovering of a bird over such waters may be gathered from what we are told concerning Noah's raven and dove in Gen. $8^{6f.}$ And it is obviously impossible to gain any clear conception of the effects of brooding over a brood of this kind. And even if these difficulties are overcome, we still have to say that this whole conception presupposes the view that by reason of God's faithfulness chaos has the opportunity and capacity to develop from within into the cosmos which it has not so far become. But this view is openly contradicted by what follows in v. 3 f. For here the existence of the cosmos is not in any sense effected by a development from within, but by the will and deed of a God who disposes and acts without any presuppositions. Here, too, Gunkel is materially right when he says that v. 3 introduces a new creation-principle. "The God who creates and the Spirit which broods have really no inner relation but actually exclude one another …. The reason for the obscuring of this feature is obvious: supernaturalism has pushed the idea of an evolution into the background." But if this is so, we can understand the third clause of v. 3 only as a reproduction of the caricature presented to the author by the state of the world prior to creation—or more precisely apart from God's creation, and apart from the light spread by the revelation of the real Creator over real creation. In that monstrous sphere even the Spirit of *Elohim* would have been as depicted in this clause, for it belongs to the very nature and essence of such a sphere that in it even the Spirit of *Elohim* is condemned to the complete impotence of a bird hovering or brooding over shoreless or sterile waters. This would have to be and would be the appearance of God's relation to the world. This God who for His part has become a caricature would be the God of this world. How could this be the God who is seen to speak and act in v. 3 ff.? How could we recognise in Him, even vaguely, the God of the rest of Genesis and the rest of the Old and New Testaments? Where in the Bible is there any suggestion that this passive-contemplative role and function is ascribed to God? But if what is characterised at the start is the utter [108] irrelevance and untrustworthiness of the god of myth, in conscious and cutting contrast to the real God of creation and His work and in a picture of devastating irony, at once everything becomes clear. Full justice is done to this god and his spirit, i.e., to the god who is not

---

[EN138] gentle breeze

known as the God of Israel in this ignorance as such, who is as little the God of Israel, and therefore the only true God, as this monstrous world is the world created by Him. All the questions which necessarily arise in connexion with the bird brooding over the waters are rightly addressed to this god. This god will as little create a cosmos out of chaos as chaos is inherently capable of becoming a cosmos.

And now we can turn again with fuller understanding to the dilemma whether the subject of v. 2—the primal and rudimentary state of the world—is self-originated or willed and posited by God. Our answer is that it is neither the one nor the other. For the question of a primal and rudimentary state does not arise at all. The only primal and rudimentary state which calls for consideration is that of evil, of sin, of the fall and all its consequences. What is at issue is the possibility which God in His creative decision has ignored and despised, like a human builder when he chooses one specific work and rejects and ignores another, or it may be many others, leaving them unexecuted. It is to be noted that it is when God utters His Word that we see which is the real work chosen by Him and what are the heaven and earth to which anticipatory reference is made in v. 1. The theme of v. 2, however, is a world-state over which the Word of God had not been uttered. It is the world in a state in which it lacks the Word of God which according to what follows is the ground and measure of its reality. It speaks of the "nothing" (Zimmerli) which is destroyed by God's creative act. The "Spirit of God" who, according to the third clause of v. 2, hovers or broods over it—a divine power which is not that of the creative Word—cannot make good this lack but can only reveal it more sharply. What is desperately needed by this world without the Word of God is no less the existence than the reality and goodness of the creature which is later described as the creature of the Word of God and therefore a real creature. Our only option is to consider v. 2 as a portrait, deliberately taken from myth, of the world which according to His revelation was negated, rejected, ignored and left behind in His actual creation, i.e., in the utterance of His Word; and to which there necessarily belongs also the "Spirit of *Elohim*" who is not known in His reality and therefore hovers and broods over it impotently because wordlessly. Because this sphere is also real in its absurd way, very differently from the world willed and created by God, as a sphere of that which has no existence or essence or goodness, reference is here made to it (*hay'thah*) EN139, for it is only too well known to the author and all the biblical witness as the shadow which actually lies over the world willed and created by God. This ugly realm did exist. Seen from the standpoint of God's creation as outlined in v. 1, it is the epitome of that which *was*. The state of chaos portrayed in v. 2 is not that of the primal or rudimentary state but of the past of the real cosmos created by the Word of God. As v. 2 portrays it, in so far as God the Creator of heaven and earth passed by this lower sphere without a halt, it was originally and definitively superseded and declared to be obsolete by what He chose and accomplished by His Word. Only the shadow of this *hay'thah* can still lie over the real cosmos created by God. And this shadow can appear only when God's Word, and therefore the real choice, and the true work of God and therefore the reality of the cosmos itself are forgotten and disregarded. It is only behind God's back that the sphere of chaos can assume this distinctive and self-contradictory character of reality. This can, of course, happen. The creature can be so foolish. It can become guilty of the inconceivable rebellion of looking past the Word of God and the ground and measure of its own reality, and therefore of looking back and returning to its essential past, to this *hay'thah* and therefore to this state of chaos; loving what God hated in His love as the Creator, and thus drawing upon itself the wrath instead of the love of God the Creator. The primeval waters and dark-   [109] ness, the *tohu wa-bohu*, can become to it an acute and enticing danger. The cosmos chosen,

---

EN139 it was

created and decreed by God, can become to it a pathless, barren, monstrous and evil cosmos, which, of course, by reason of the Word of God it is not. And according to Gen. 6[5f.], God for His part can repent of creating man and his whole world. All this can happen because in its distinction from God the creature as such, while it is not ungodly, is non-divine, so that to posit it at all is undoubtedly a risk, since it is to posit a freedom which is distinct from the freedom of God. The fact that it is a risk is revealed particularly in the attitude of human creation. It is not by the use but the misuse of this freedom that man can look back and return to that past and conjure up the shadow of Gen. 1[2], thus enabling that past to defy its own nature and to become present and future. This is the undeniable risk which God took upon Himself in the venture of creation—but a risk for which He was more than a match and thus did not need to fear. That He can repent of His work does not in the least prevent Him from repenting of His repentance. That His creative Word can be forgotten and despised by man in the world created by Him—with all the consequences which this must bring—cannot prevent Him from remaining bound to this world by His Word. That chaos can also become present and future cannot alter the fact that it is essentially the past, the possibility negated and rejected by God. And the Genesis story which begins with creation bears witness to the fact that God actually repented of His repentance. It bears witness to the grace, compassion, patience and faithfulness of God toward His creature. He will not permit Himself to be obstructed by man's misuse of his freedom from actually making use of His own holy freedom in such a way that, through every judgment and catastrophe (for all the similarity to Gen. 1[2]), He will not cease to be the Creator of Gen. 1[1], and to abide by His Word as spoken in Gen. 1[3ff.] Compared with the story of the Flood (Gen. 6[5f.]), Gen. 1[2] shows that it is in fact the freedom of God which makes Him act in this way and not another, remaining faithful to His cosmos. In itself and as such, without the freely uttered and freely repeated Word of the grace of God, the cosmos has no real guarantee against precipitation into chaos, i.e., into a state in which it has neither existence, essence nor goodness. But it has this guarantee by the Word of God freely spoken and freely repeated. As this Word is spoken and repeated in the history of the covenant which begins immediately after the fall of man, it is thereby constantly decided that, in spite of all appearances to the contrary, the *hay'thah* of chaos is final—this world *was*. God will not allow the cosmos to be definitively bewitched and demonised or His creation totally destroyed, nor will He permit the actual realisation of the dark possibility of Gen. 1[2]. He will not allow the myth to become a reality. In face of the threat to His work from this direction He will always show Himself the God who originally and finally has passed by this monstrous world. This monstrous world will always show itself to be the possibility which He has originally and finally passed by and excluded. He will naturally take seriously the alienation from His Word of which man has become guilty and by which He has compromised the whole divinely created cosmos. But He will do so in a way commensurate with His faithfulness and the despised Word as such. If in Gen. 1[2] judgment upon a world alienated from Him is indicated as at least a possibility, it can actually be executed only at one point in the cosmos created by Him and in one creature. And at this one point and in this one creature God is Himself the One who is judged and suffers in the place and for the salvation and preservation of the rest of creation. This—the moment of darkness in which His own creative Word, His only begotten Son, will cry on the cross of Calvary: "My God, my God, why hast thou forsaken me?"—will be "the small moment" of His wrath (Is. 54[7]) in which all that is indicated in Gen. 1[2] will become real. For all the analogy of other kinds of darkness, there is no other moment such as this. In this way, and in no other, God will allow men and their world to reap the fruits of wrath which they have brought upon themselves. And as God's creative Word itself becomes a creature in the cosmos, suffering for the cosmos what it should itself have suffered on account of the misuse of its free will, it is by this Word that God will reconcile it to Himself, as by His Word He has created it for

[110]

Himself. He will exalt this one creature, the man Jesus Christ, as a sign of the promise given to the cosmos, so that His end in this vulnerable form will be the beginning of a new form in which He is no longer assaulted by this sinister possibility. In this one creature, at this one point in the cosmos. He will manifest Himself as the Light of the whole cosmos; as the One who according to Gen. 1³ᶠ· has already acted as the Creator; as the sovereign Lord even over the primal floods, over darkness and *tohu wa-bohu*; as the One who really can and does leave behind this sphere; as the One who has the will and power to make of the evening and morning a new day, i.e., a transition from that past which is essential because posited by Him to the future which He has also posited. Without this final aspect it would scarcely be possible to give a satisfactory answer to the enigma of Gen. 1². Gen. 1² speaks of the "old things" which according to 2 Cor. 5¹⁷ have radically passed away in the death and resurrection of Jesus Christ. It tells us that even from the standpoint of the first creation, let alone the new, chaos is really "old things," the past and superseded essence of this world.

(Gen. 1³.) Creation means the irruption and revelation of the divine compassion. Once and for all the Word of God went out against the rejected and vanished reality of an alien and hostile creature. Creation, the appearance of heaven and earth, the content of commencing time, was that God spoke and spoke again; that He thus did what was later to constitute in ever new faithfulness the covenant between Himself and man. The Subject and the Lord of this later history, the Lord speaking in a living voice to His own, was the Creator—not a dumb destiny, or irrational life-energy, or involuntary natural impulse. The Creator is the divine Person who as such will later act as the Lord, Advocate, and Guardian of His people and all peoples. That God will create man in His image implies that it is not man but God who is first a living Person as One who knows and wills and speaks. It was as such that He was the Creator, that He revealed Himself and acted in commencing time. Thus the creature in its totality was allied to this living, divine Person, being wholly referred to it for its existence and essence, its survival and sustenance. It came into being as the work of the Word of God corresponding to His utterance. So originally and intimately was it disposed for the grace of God! So little did it acquire a place from which it might legitimately withdraw itself from the grace of God! Encountered by this Word of grace, it encounters just the wisdom, kindness and power without which it could not be at all. Encountering the creature, this Word really comes to its own. That God created by speaking implies no less that the creature has come into being *by* God as posited and effected by a free, divine declaration and not merely *from* God as an emanation of the divine essence, than it does that there was no object, no material, from which God formed the creature but to which there may be ascribed a will and law independent of the will and purpose of God. What comes into being in consequence of the fact that God speaks in time is not God Himself but something which can do so only on the presupposition of the divine utterance. God's Word as God's creative act is the disposition of the creature. In the Word of God the creature becomes more than a kind of incidental or accidental accompaniment of its own course and work. On the contrary, it has in it its secret Lord who can never be wholly overlooked or forgotten, and will finally

[111]

be definitively revealed and self-declared as such. Only in error and falsehood, and to its own hurt, can it become untrue to its origin in the Word of God. One way or another, it will finally and at the last have to satisfy Him. Only in obedience to the Word of God will it be free, and remain free, and again become free. And when it becomes unfaithful and forfeits its freedom by disobedience, God will remain faithful to His Word and therefore to the creature, and will see to it that what belongs to Him does not perish. Whatever may result from the creature's own course and work, as it has become and is and will be by the Word of God, God has allied Himself with it. That "God is with us" is indeed God's revelation in the history of the covenant which begins with Israel and is fulfilled in Jesus Christ. But this is because man with his whole cosmos exists in no other way than by the Word of God, which is already the secret of his creation, existence and nature. He may deny this Word, but by no denial can he remove or abrogate it.

The *way-yo'mer Elohim*[EN140] which first emerges in Gen. 1³, and is put to constant and pregnant use in the ensuing picture of the work of the six days, is not of course the only description of the divine activity in this passage. It also speaks of a "creating," "doing" and "positing"; of a "naming"; in relation to the animal creation, including man, of a "blessing"; and, finally, of a divine "beholding"—the beholding of His good-pleasure with which all the six days conclude (with the significant exception of the second). But it is clear that when the author uses the words *bara'*, *'asah* and *nathan*, he is not describing actions which have to be distinguished from *'amar*, but paraphrasing *'amar* in the efficacy proper to it only at this point. *Qara'* (to name) is again only a continuation and completion of *'amar*. It is to the Word of God that the basic phenomena of the first three days—light, darkness, the firmament between the waters, land and sea, existence and essence—all owe their names. And the divine blessing and beholding of the creature are obviously a confirmation of the fact that it is created by the Word of God. All the sentences and expressions which here speak of a being and activity of the creature, e.g., when it says in Gen. 1³ that there was light, and that the evening and the morning were the first and then succeeding days, or when it says in Gen. 1¹² that the earth brought forth fresh verdure, and in Gen. 2¹ that the heavens and the earth were finished, refer only to the work of the divine Word as such. They are all bracketed by the *wa-yᵉhi-ken* "and it was so," which first occurs in 1⁷. What took place was not an autonomous movement of the creature but a movement in which the creature first received its being according to the divine utterance. "Nowhere is the real power of a master so fully apparent as in his commandment which is obeyed" (Zimmerli). It is also to be noted that it is no accident that the creative utterance at the creation of man in Gen. 1²⁶ is described as a divine soliloquy: "Let us make man ...." What emerges characteristically at this point is the connexion between the *opus ad extra*[EN141] and the *opus ad intra*[EN142] which precedes it; i.e., that God remains in Himself at the very time when in His utterance He proceeds out of Himself; or *vice versa* that the utterance of His Word signifies the execution of His inner decree. And the meaning, then, of the author of this first account might well be that even the divine soliloquy, which as such can and actually does take place before and outwith time, now takes place in the act of the creation of time and to that extent in time itself, and that in and with this divine soliloquy there has taken place that which is later described in the words:

[112]

[EN140] and God said
[EN141] work outside of God
[EN142] work inside God

2. Creation as the External Basis of the Covenant

"And God created man ...." With the special emphasis on the creation of man in the image of God, and the emphasis on the seventh day in its relation to the rest, this emphasis on the creative Word of God is a distinctive feature of the P account which has acquired a significance for the whole biblical conception of creation.

Naturally there can be no talk of an absolute originality of this view. Here, too, the biblical author drew on mythical tradition, in which there is more than one trace that the utterance of the creative deity has at least been taken into account in different ways. But if we compare the most important witnesses usually summoned in this connexion with the record in Gen. 1 we shall soon be convinced that tradition has been given a form which is so different as to be almost unrecognisable. On the one hand we have to consider an Egyptian source, the so-called book of *Apophis* found at Thebes. This is a magical papyrus, given to the deceased to take with them into the after-world as a protection against the dragon *Apophis* (H. Gressmann, *Altoriental. Texte z. A.T.*, 2nd imp., 1926, 1 f.). Here the "lord of all" (presumably the sun-god and chief of the gods, Thot) boasts that the "numerous forms" which came after him emerged from his mouth, the first thing to appear. Standing in the middle of the celestial ocean he commanded them: "I cast a spell in my heart; I created a new thing. I created all forms when I was alone ... when no other had yet appeared who might have co-operated with me in creation." But it now appears that what this creator first does with his mouth when he brings forth his children *Shu* and *Tefene* is something very different from creative utterance, namely: "I spat (something) out as *Shu*; I spat (something) out as *Tefene*." Following close upon this we read of an auto-procreation accomplished with his own shadow, and of an even more primitive sexual process. And as this god weeps over his children, "men were formed from the tears which came from my eyes." This is really all, and if we assume that the biblical author knew of this or a similar view, we have to add at once that, by making the divine utterance as such the sole agent of the whole process, he turns into its opposite the thinly veiled or blatant naturalism of this "creation myth." The thought of the distinct existence of a supreme (though originated) being prior to all others, the pre-existence of all things in him and his role as the Creator of these things, are the only points which the Egyptian story has in common with the biblical narrative, and they do not include the main essentials of the role and significance of the Word of God in the latter account. Another source which calls for consideration is the fourth tablet of the Babylonian epic *Enuma elish* (Gressmann, p. 117). In the council of the gods, preceding the struggle with the dragon and the creation of the world (and according to the conclusion of the third tablet accompanied by generous libations of alcohol), Marduk is appointed warrior, creator and later lord of heaven, and he has to prove his qualifications for this office and inaugurate his lordship. This takes place in the following manner: "They brought into the circle a garment And said to Marduk their firstborn: 'Your decree, O lord, transcends that of the gods; Command to destroy and to make, and it shall be done: Open your mouth and the garment shall perish; Command again and the garment will be unharmed.' Then he commanded with his mouth, and the garment was destroyed. Again he commanded, and the garment was created anew. When his fathers, the gods, saw what proceeded from his mouth They rejoiced and paid homage (saying): ' Marduk is king.'" Even if we could agree that this account reaches the high level of the Old Testament to the extent that the Word is obviously the instrument of the depicted activity, it is all the more doubtful what this activity has to do with creation. If A. Jeremias (*op. cit.*, p. 42) is correct in his view that this garment is the "world-cloak," the "cosmic garment which the lord of the universe wears at the decree of destiny," then according to the context this is merely a kind of preliminary and probationary witchcraft preceding Marduk's appointment as creator. In the actual story of the conflict with the dragon and creation there is no trace of a mighty utterance by Marduk. On the other hand the mighty utterance of *Elohim* in Gen. 1 has absolutely nothing in common with this type of magic, and

[113]

111

it does not seem to have any interest for the author merely as a miraculous achievement—which is the essential point in the Babylonian epic.

But however that may be, the emphasis on the divine utterance as the unique instrument of creation is of all the distinctive features of the creation story the point which has been most keenly noted and adopted in the rest of the biblical tradition. Its strongest parallel in this respect is Ps. 33[6f.]: "By the word of the Lord were the heavens made, and all the host of them by the breath of his mouth. He gathereth the waters of the sea together as an heap: he layeth up the depths in storehouses. Let all the earth fear the Lord; let all the inhabitants of the world stand in awe of him." We may also quote Ps. 148[5] (referring to the heaven of heavens and of the waters above the firmament): "He commanded, and they were created"; Am. 9[6]: "He that calleth for the waters of the sea, and poureth them out upon the face of the earth: the Lord is his name"; Is. 48[18f.]: "Mine hand hath laid the foundation of the earth, and mine right hand hath spread out the heavens: when I call unto them, they stand up together. Assemble yourselves, all ye, and hear; which among them (presumably among the gods) hath declared these things?"; and Is. 41[4f.]: "Who hath wrought and done it, calling the generations from the beginning? I the Lord, the first, and with the last, I am he. The isles saw and feared; the ends of the earth trembled; they drew near and came." It is also to be noted that in Deutero-Isaiah there is an exact parallel in 44[26f.] where God is called "He that saith to Jerusalem, Thou shalt be inhabited; and to the cities of Judah, Ye shall be built, and I will raise up the decayed places thereof; that saith to the deep, Be dry, and I will dry up thy rivers: that saith of Cyrus, He is my shepherd, and shall perform all my pleasure: even saying to Jerusalem, Thou shalt be built; and to the temple, Thy foundation shall be laid." The same view is to be found in the New Testament as well. According to 2 Cor. 4[6], "the God who commanded the light to shine out of darkness" is He who "hath shined in our hearts to give the light of the knowledge of the glory of God in the face of Jesus Christ." According to Rom. 4[17], Abraham believed on this God who calls things that are not as though they were. In Jn. 1[1] we read that in the beginning was the Word; in Heb. 11[3] that Christ upholds all things by the Word of His power. It is neither by accident nor caprice that from the very first Christian theology has given so much thought to this particular element in Gen. 1[3]. What threads of biblical knowledge meet and are to be seen together at this point? We may calmly admit that we have only a general and not a detailed knowledge of the view of divine utterance held by the author of Gen. 1[3f.] and the underlying tradition. We may also take into consideration the fact that its emergence and original singularity permit of all kinds of pragmatical explanations. If, for example, we turn to the relevant saying in Job 37[5]: "God thunders marvellously with his voice; great things doeth he which we cannot comprehend," in view of the context we cannot fail to see that behind this view there may simply be the experience of "real" thunder and of the storm which follows with all its accompanying phenomena. In the Old [114] Testament the voice of God is not infrequently set in relation to natural phenomena to which the oriental man is particularly susceptible, or at any rate described in terms of these phenomena. But what does this matter compared with the fact that a voice was always thought to be heard, i.e., the voice of God, and this as the creative origin of all reality? What counts is that we are actually told by saga—whatever may have been the circle and shape of its vision at the time when it was written down or in the underlying form—that God's utterance is for everything and all things distinct from God the absolutely first thing, the whence, behind and above which there is nothing else. In saying this, and not saying it in a vacuum but in the context and at the head of the whole witness of the Old and New Testament, it does in fact attest something which may be wrongly interpreted but can hardly be over-interpreted because—irrespective of its particular meaning either here or in Job, the Psalms, or Deutero-Isaiah—it does actually represent something which is imponderable if not unlimited.

2. Creation as the External Basis of the Covenant

In this place we can merely indicate a few things by way of anticipation. B. Jacob is certainly right when he derives from the *way-yo'mer Elohim* the negative suggestion that the world is not created *from* God, as is assumed in myth, but *by* God. All explanations of the origin of the world in terms of divine conception and birth are superseded when the "And God said" is put at the beginning. Gunkel has something similar in mind when he calls the comparison between the divine operation and the divine utterance "the classical expression of supernaturalism." "God impinges upon the world through His will; He does not merge with it ... but remains above and outside it, and commands what shall be. He speaks and it comes to pass." Ambrose was also right when he pointed to the unity between the creative utterance and its creaturely correspondence :*Non ideo dixit, ut sequeretur operatio, sed dicto absolvit negotium*EN143. So, too, is W. Foerster when he emphasises the utter incomprehensibility of the process described: "We can name only that which already exists, but God names that which does not yet exist and commands it, and in obedience to this fiat creation is accomplished .... The fiat in its concrete terms is the creative Word .... Creation means the operation of absolute power" (*TWzNT*, III. 1009 f.). But all this points only to the critical sense which this view undoubtedly has as well, but which can hardly explain the extraordinary importance attached to it by Clement of Rome, Justin, Irenaeus, Tertullian, Theophilus of Antioch and at a later date Athanasius. Augustine, too, seems to have had greater depths in view when at the thought of God's Word as the beginning of all things he exclaimed: *Quis comprehendet? quis enarrabit? quid est illud, quod interlucet mihi et percutit cor meum sine laesione; et inhorresco, et inardesco? Inhorresco in quantum dissimilis ei sum, inardesco in quantum similis ei sum. Sapientia ipsa est, quae interlucet mihi, discindens nubilum meum, quod me rursus cooperit deficientem ab ea, caligine atque aggere poenarum mearum*EN144. (*Conf.* XI, 9).

We do not go beyond the straightforward meaning of the passage if we say first that the *way-yo'mer Elohim* of Gen. 1 sets the creation in relation and connexion with all the divine utterances which will later on constitute the nerve and substance of the whole biblical history. As *Elohim's* utterance in Gen. 1[3f.] fixes the boundary from which the monstrous world of Gen. 1[2] can be seen and understood only as past, so *Yahweh* fixes a boundary—is it not ultimately the same boundary?—when He says to Abraham: "Get thee out of thy country and from thy kindred, and from thy father's house, unto a land that I will shew thee" (Gen. 12[1]). The relative chaos of the common history of the nations lies behind, and can no longer play a decisive role; the relative cosmos of Israel's history has begun. But within this history this boundary will be continually drawn afresh by the divine utterance; the old will be declared to have passed and the new come. When the "Thus saith the Lord" re-echoes from the lips of Moses and the prophets, history is made, i.e., something old is again and again shown to be old, and something new to be new. The one is shown to be that which has the accent of [115] judgment upon it, the other that which has the accent of the grace of God. The two together are continually revealed as evening and morning, as a movement of the hand of the divine clock which is as such the confirmation of the Word with which all time commenced and was created. They are together a token of the faithfulness and patience with which God does not cease to acknowledge His work. But clearly this divine utterance has everywhere a provisional and preparatory character. Its purpose is to guide and keep the people of Israel. To what end and for what purpose? The Old Testament witness as such does not give any

---

EN143 Therefore God did not speak, so that the work of creation might follow; rather, by the act of speech was the deed accomplished

EN144 Who can comprehend it? Who will describe it? What is it, that shines through me and strikes my heart without injury, so that I both tremble with fear and burn with love? I tremble, inasmuch as I am unlike Him; and I burn, inasmuch as I am like Him. It is Wisdom itself that shines through me by tearing away my gloom, which time and again covers me, and separating me from the dark mass of my punishments

answer. It only attests that it is so; that time has a continuation just as it has a beginning, and is constituted as such and comes into existence by the Word of God which is never dumb. It only attests that the history which fills this time has also a goal; and that the Israelite cosmos has a future transcending itself. And for this reason time flows on. For this reason a boundary is fixed even for this relative cosmos of Israel's history, which in the light of this frontier itself acquires the character of a relative chaos, of something old which has now passed. And again it is by God's utterance that this boundary is fixed. But this time it is *the* new thing which appears and antiquates everything that has gone before. This time there takes place something which had not happened even in God's utterance in Gen. 1. God's Word itself, the Word by which everything was created, becomes a creature among others, i.e., Abraham's seed, David's Son, Israel's Messiah, the man Jesus of Nazareth. In this way, in this voluntary humiliation, but also in this saving proximity and fellowship, the rest of creation is now addressed. In this way it makes the world created by it its own—its liability to temptation, its actual temptation, its corruption and need. In this way, too, the world for its part is made a partaker of the Word of God by which it was created; a partaker of its triumphant vitality, of its holiness and glory. Did Israel's whole history, or rather did the whole operation of the Word of God in and with the relative cosmos of Israel's history, move towards this goal, towards this definitive and perfect action? The witnesses of the New Testament affirm this. This is how they understand the witness of the Old Testament. If we think we know better we must show it by giving a clearer exposition of the Old Testament than that provided by its conclusion. If the New Testament is correct in its exposition of the Old, then the history attested by the latter was the week at the close of which the Sabbath dawned as the announcement of a new era and a new calculation of time. It dawned because God, who in time past (πάλαι) spoke at sundry times and in divers manners to the fathers by the prophets, has in the last days (ἐπ᾽ ἐσχάτου τῶν ἡμερῶν τούτων) spoken to us by His Son (Heb. 1¹). Hence this Sabbath, too, came in the full sense by the Word of God, which was now revealed as the divine utterance secretly addressed to all nations—to the whole world—even in the seclusion of Israel, and as such perceptible as the principle which actually governs the common world of nations. Until the end of all time, when it will again affect all heaven and earth, the same Word will declare the old to have passed and the new come, and with this declaration it will itself effect the passing of the one and the coming of the other. This is the context in which the *way-yo'mer Elohim* of Gen. 1³ᶠ· has also to be read (without detriment to its obvious and specific meaning) if we are really to grasp its obvious and specific meaning. When God speaks He reveals Himself as the Creator who by His activity, as this takes place by His Word, unfolds the history which according to the witness of the whole Bible is directed toward the reconciliation and finally toward the redemption of the world, and will reach its goal in the incarnation, crucifixion and resurrection of this Word of His. It is by His Word, by which He is the Creator, that in this history He also becomes the Reconciler, and at the culmination of this history, declared as such, will finally be the Redeemer. This is one dimension which we have to consider at this point.

[116]   But we do not go beyond the simple meaning of the text if we advance the further consideration that as God speaks, and in His speaking becomes the Creator, there takes place from the very outset a participation of God Himself in the existence of the creature. This is not an essential participation. At this point the critical understanding of the *way-yo'mer Elohim* is quite correct. All ideas of creation as divine emanation or creature as deity are forcefully and completely excluded by Gen. 1³ᶠ· We are not told that the world *is* the Word of God, but that it is by the Word of God. But as the world how could it be more closely bound to God than by the fact that it is by His Word? The Word of God is not less than God Himself. With Him it is eternal, holy, almighty and gracious. The fathers were right when they saw glimpses of the whole mystery of the Trinity in the *way-yo'mer Elohim* of Gen. 1³ᶠ· Describing God's utterance

as His creation, the biblical author—whatever he may have thought of it in detail—has equated the utterance of God, which is as such His "expression," with God Himself. *Uno eodemque Verbo dicit seipsum et quaecumque fecit*[EN145]. (Anselm of Canterbury, *Monol.*, 33). God alone creates. To describe His Word as "creating" is to say that His Word is God Himself—the one God. Before He uttered and therefore spoke it, it was in Him, and what is in Him is not less or other than Himself. But even as He utters and speaks it, and in speaking becomes the Creator, His spoken Word becoming the instrument of His creation, it remains His equal. Whether He is and remains in Himself, or whether in speaking and creating He posits something that is outside Himself, and speaks and acts in the thing that is outside Himself, God cannot cease to be God and therefore Himself. Thus in the *way-yo'mer Elohim*—whether we express it in the terminology of the doctrine of the Trinity or not—there is actually expressed the mystery of grace which is in every respect incomprehensible to our thought, to wit, that creation as such, taking place by the Word of God and therefore by God Himself, includes in itself the most exact and most perfect connexion between God and ourselves declared by that Word as it is revealed and told us and as we may hear it—gives us information. The Word of God continually spoken in the history of Israel and finally incarnate, tells us the truth when it says "God is with us" because heaven and earth and we ourselves are only by this same Word, and because as the creative Word by which we exist and from which we come it has basically actualised this "God with us." Although the world did not know the Word, in coming to the world it came unto its own (Jn. 1[10]), i.e., to a place where contradiction of its truth is objectively impossible because the world was made by it and is therefore in reality the first witness of its truth. In the course of this whole history, and finally in its incarnation, it tells us reliably and effectively that nothing less or other than God Himself is with us. In the one case as in the other it is nothing less or other than the acting God Himself in His *opus ad extra*[EN146], which, according to v. 26 of our passage, stands in direct relation to His *opus ad intra*[EN147]. This is because it is already God's Word as Creator. That according to His Word God wills to draw us to Himself, to reconcile us to Himself, and finally to redeem us (making a new heaven and a new earth and ourselves its inhabitants), is something which He has already promised in creating heaven and earth and ourselves by His Word. Revealing and speaking this Word to us, He tells us only that He will stand by the promise of His Word as Creator, and fulfil it. Luther's exposition of $\pi\acute{a}\nu\tau a$ $\delta\iota'$ $a\mathring{v}\tau o\mathring{v}$ $\mathring{e}\gamma\acute{e}\nu\epsilon\tau o$[EN148] (Jn. 1[3]) has to be considered if we are fully to understand the inner scope of Gen. 1[3f.]: "In this way St. John indicates and proves forcefully that the Son of God who is here the image of the invisible God is not created or made. Before the world, all creatures and even angels were created, and before all things commenced, the Word or Speech was with God; and it follows that all things were created by this divine Word or Speech, and that without it nothing was made that was made. This Word or Speech is from the creation of the world, over four thousand years before Christ was born and man made; yea, it was in the bosom of the Father from all eternity. If this is the case, then the Word must be higher and greater than all created things, i.e., it must be God Himself, for apart from God the Creator everything was created—all creatures, angels, heaven, earth, man, and every living thing. But John says that when in the beginning God created all things, the Word was already and had its being. He does not say that God created the Word, or that the Word became, but that the Word was already. From this it follows that the Word was neither created nor made. It is not a creature, but all things were made by it, as is made clear in the passage, and therefore it must be God if the principle

[117]

[EN145] By one and the same Word He speaks both Himself and whatever He has made
[EN146] work outside of God
[EN147] work within God
[EN148] all things were made through him

is established that the Word was before all creatures. It is a very lofty way of speaking of the divine nature and majesty of our Lord and Saviour Jesus Christ to say that in His divine essence He is the Word of the eternal Father. There is, therefore, no doubt, and reason can conclude, that if the Word was from the beginning, before all things commenced to be, it follows that the same Word is God. Reason can clearly distinguish that if anything exists and has its being before the world and the creation of all creatures, it must be God, for apart from the creature we can speak only of the Creator. All that exists is either the Creator Himself or else His creature—God or creation. But the Holy Spirit speaks through St. John and testifies: 'In the beginning was the Word,' and again: 'All things were made through him,' etc. The Word therefore cannot be counted among the creatures, but has its eternal being in the Godhead, and from this it follows invincibly and incontrovertibly that the same Word is God, as St. John also concludes" (*Exposition of John*, chs. 1–2, 1537–38, W.A. 46, 547, 29).

(Gen. 1$^{3-5}$.) The first creation of God, and therefore the first work of His Word, was light in its separation from darkness. Only in its separation from light is darkness also created, and therefore the creature of God. The subject is natural light and natural darkness: natural darkness as that which declares the reality which was rejected by God and has therefore vanished; and natural light as that which proclaims the will of God opposed to it. It is natural light as such which is the irresistible and irrevocable declaration of life, and therefore negatively of the conquest, separation, displacement and banishment of the alternative reality which God neither wills nor creates. Having this function, and constituting this declaration, it is called by God "day." The first day comes, and time and the cosmos in time commence, as light comes into being by the Word of God and this declaration is made. And it is in the same way that time will continue. All God's works take place during the day, and therefore in light and not in darkness. "In darkness" would mean under the sign of the proclamation of the present and future of that rejected and vanished reality, i.e., under the sign of untruth. This sign, too, was created by God in all its unimportance, and also in its immediate distinction from light, i.e., in its total inferiority to it. But no work of God takes place under this sign. After the creation of light, in spite of darkness and falsehood that reality never is to-day or will be to-morrow but always has been yesterday. For light will never again cease to shine. It was God's first work; and there thus dawned and passed the first day which other days can follow as days of the same light and therefore as days separating light from darkness and opposing darkness by light. The commencement of time took [118] place in such a way that its content as God's creation can consist only in the works of light, in a repetition of this proclamation, in confirmations of this clear distinction of the present and future cosmos from the past cosmos, in constant indication of this turn of the ages. None of God's works will lead behind this distinction. From none of these works can there be deduced the necessity or the right to turn again to the reality from which God in His compassion toward His creature has turned away. None of them will declare that the proclamation of darkness is right; none will be anything but an actual proof that this proclamation is wrong. And none of the days succeeding the first day when light was created may or must become a day of ungodly or anti-godly content, a day of apostasy and disaster. From creation every creature, and from the first day of the week of creation all time, takes part in the separation of light from darkness as it has taken place once and for all; in the refutation of darkness by light as it has been inaugurated once and for all and cannot be reversed but only continued. The cosmos created by God exists as such in light. When sun, moon, and stars are once created their necessary purpose will be to mediate light to creaturely eyes. And when creaturely eyes are created and opened they will see light and the cosmos in light. And light will declare to them that old things have passed away. Darkness cannot alter this, not even under the name of night under which it is the frontier of every day by the will and decree of God. The God who created the light has given it this name and position. Hence it follows that its proclamation can have no authority or results, can gain no power, can establish no opposing day or different time or second world. We observe that the Word of God creates light. Thus light is not itself God but a creature, dependent, threatened and corruptible like all others. Hence it has no power of its own. It lives by the Word of God alone. It needs the faithfulness with which God will acknowledge His Word. Thus even the separation of the cosmos from chaos by light depends on the Word of God. The incursion of darkness, the dawn of a dreadful counter-day, the day of falsehood, would be quite unavoidable if light were not again and again light and victorious truth by the same power in which it came to be. We notice further that it was God who saw that light was good. Thus it has no dignity or holiness of its own. It has both only in God's sight and by God's judgment. Day is day, the true time of salvation and not of perdition, only because God gives to light the name of day. Not every announcement of victory, separation, displacement and expulsion which takes place in the world makes the world a cosmos in genuine distinction from chaos. Only light does this—the light created by God through His Word, and not only created but found and pronounced to be good. Everything depends upon the fact that it is this. But as such it is the sign—established in and above the whole creaturely world—of the divine covenant of grace, of the faithfulness which God will maintain and acknowledge [119] to His creature in face of its sin and apostasy, in face of the death to which it has sold itself, in face of hell which opens up in consequence. As a principle of created nature the light which shines in darkness and overcomes the darkness is as such the promise that nature is not left to itself, but that it moves toward an encounter with the grace of God. In the heart of nature light is the symbol of the revelation of grace. With its creation there has been disclosed the decision of the good-will of God previously concealed. As this first work of His takes place, and in it God bears witness to Himself, He says Yes to the creature. Proclaiming His own glory as the Creator of light, God gives most eloquent proof of His concern for the creature. As yet there is no eye nor ear nor heart to perceive this gratefully. As yet there is no time to be enlightened and gladdened and summoned to faith by it. As yet there is no witness to whom it may be said and who can become its herald. We cannot find here more than a prototype of His revelation. But we can find a prototype. Revelation may be new when it comes, but it will not be absolutely new. When its time comes, it will fulfil that which must be fulfilled because creation commences and culminates in light, and for which all creation is prepared and destined because the first created thing is light. It will establish the knowledge of the Lord. From the very first light has been the prototype and sign and declaration of this event—of the knowledge of the Lord.

Our starting point in exposition of Gen. 1³⁻⁵ must be the insight of B. Jacob that the first work of creation is in every respect different from all the rest. It has been noted from a very early period that what Scripture means by creation is portrayed in these verses in a way which does not apply in any of those that follow. Only here do we see how God is quite alone prior to His creative utterance, and then never alone again, but always having before and beside and beneath Him this one other thing, light, as a sign of all the rest, of creation. Only here does the fiat so pregnantly confront the execution and the execution the fiat: "Let there be light, and there was light." Only here can we learn what the utter singularity of this coming into being means. Only of light can there be said—without violating the limitation of the creature, but honouring that which distinguishes the being and nature of this creature from all others—what is said in the parallel passage in Ps. 104¹ᶠ (and again at the head of the account): "O Lord my God, thou art very great: thou art clothed with honour and majesty. Thou coverest thyself with light as with a garment." If this leads us to think of the familiar role which light plays in Persian and especially Zoroastrian religion and mythology, we must not overlook the fact that there is here no mention at all of any deity or divine function of light, or of any conflict between light and darkness. The uncreated light which is God Himself and His Word is one thing; the light whose creation is spoken of here is quite another. The formula: "Let there be ... and it was so," clearly distinguishes between what takes place here and an emanation; between that which confronts God on the ground of this event and a God-like being. According to *Nic.-Constant.*, φῶς ἐκ φωτός EN149 is the Son of God. But in all its sublimity as God's first and most outstanding work the light referred to here is quite unlike the Son of God and non-divine. Between it and God there stands as the Word of power the uttered fiat to which it owes its existence and being. With all its distinction, its [120] glory rests exclusively on the fact that God saw that it was good. If it stands and acts in antithesis to darkness, we must remember that the true and original antithesis is not between light and darkness but between God and darkness, i.e., between His will as Creator and that which He has rejected. Light merely enters into this antithesis and serves it in correspondence with the divine will of the Creator. It is not that light in and of itself distinguishes itself from darkness, but that God Himself and of Himself distinguishes it from darkness. Giving it its nature, He sets it with this nature in that antithesis. Again, its significance as a constitutive principle of the day spoken of in v. 5 is not in any sense immanent. God is the One who knows and pronounces its name "day"; who gives it this name; and with this name gives it also its special nature as a principle of day. Thus point by point the confusion of this light with a light-god is made radically impossible. Within these limits, however, we cannot overemphasise the glory of this first creature. It does indeed dwell with God as His nearest confidant (Dan. 2²²). We remember, too, that in the Prologue to John's Gospel (which in other respects too is fully related to Gen. 1), and in the other Johannine writings

---

EN149 Light from Light

2. Creation as the External Basis of the Covenant

the concept of light forms the *signum*[EN150] for that of the divine revelation. It must also be said of 2 Cor. 4[6] that the comparison between the light of Gen. 1[3] and the apostolic "light of the knowledge of the glory of God in the face of Jesus Christ" reveals and mediates a most authentic understanding of this Old Testament passage. For the light created by God is implicitly what the apostolic office is explicitly—the sign and witness of God Himself at the heart of the cosmos. When He creates light God erects this sign and ordains this witness. To mention only a few things, when the Word of God (Ps. 119[105]), the Law (Prov. 6[23]), Israel (Is. 42[6]), John the Baptist (Jn. 5[35]) and the Gospel (2 Cor. 4[4]) are called light; when Jesus calls Himself (Jn. 8[12], 9[5]) and His disciples (Mt. 5[14]) "the light of the world"; when the call of Christians is described (in 1 Pet. 2[9]) as the call "out of darkness into his marvellous light"; when in 1 Thess. 5[5], Eph. 5[9] and Jn. 12[36] Christians are called "children of light," i.e., lightbearers and lightbringers; when Ps. 36[9] says: "In thy light we see light"—these are not just pictorial utterances or analogies but highly exact representations of the meaning already given to the creation, existence and function of light in Gen. 1[3]. As the creative will of God commences to be done with the creation of light, it at once begins to be revealed. As He does what this verse says He does, He at once tells us what He wills in this and all His other actions. The scope of the creation of light is disclosed in the distinction of light from darkness, in the assignation of light as day, in the constitution of day as a unit of time and therefore in the constitution of time as such. What is constituted once and for all with the creation of light is the law of the history willed by God. Where this law is proclaimed and recognised by the creature; where there is revelation in an objective and subjective sense of the concept, there we have the ministry of the light created by God according to Gen. 1[3], so that we may speak of light and its work, not pictorially and hyperbolically, but with supreme strictness and realism.

According to the first creation narrative, light was created prior to all luminaries and heavenly bodies. The offence which modern science is the first to take is very obvious. Indeed, it is almost too obvious to be taken too seriously, although whether it has the same weight for more recent physics as that previously ascribed to it is another matter. We certainly cannot attribute this circumstance merely to the naivety of ancient science which regarded light as an independent thing, as a material which is transparent but can be localised and weighed (thus Gunkel). The witness who here speaks the language of tradition knows very well what he means theologically, whether with or without natural science, in contradiction to or agreement with it. His presentation is at this point an open protest against all and every kind of sun-worship, or the worship of other heavenly bodies. We have only to be able to read it with the ears of an ancient Egyptian, with his deep-rooted tradition [121] of the inestimable glory and majesty and divinity of the sun, to gauge how profound is the change undertaken in this verse—that light is put before the sun and all the constellations! Which of the religions of the ancient Orient is not hereby contradicted? Why is it that they did not make use of that naive—or by modern ideas not quite so naive—view of light if it was really the general view? Why did Israel alone obviously do this? It is quite explicable if we note that the view and concept of light is intensively distinguished in this case by the fact that it is the sign and witness of the divine revelation, the first and most original correspondence to the divine Word. That which stands in primary and fundamental relation to the Word of God because it was not only created by it but because it was also created at once for its service, to be its sign and witness, cannot be dependent on the existence of sun, moon and stars; it must precede their creation. Sun, moon and stars can render it help only as they receive of it fulness, becoming its bearers and representatives, and therefore witnesses and signs of a second order. As they have to bow down before Joseph in his dream (Gen. 37[9f.]), so

---

[EN150] sign

119

they are related from the very first to the firstborn of all created things—light. But there is an extensive as well as an intensive distinction. When the Bible speaks of light it means an occurrence which embraces and includes the shining of the sun and constellations, but which is not in any sense exhausted by their shining, or tied to their existence and function. According to Mk. 13^{24} the sun and moon will one day lose their lustre, and the stars will fall from heaven. What then? Will there be no more light after that? Will the darkness of Gen. 1^2 have the last word? No; we must take note of Is. 60, where in a portrayal of its future glory, in which Zion is summoned to arise and shine—"for thy light is come, and the glory of the Lord is risen upon thee" (v. 1)—we are finally told in v. 19: "The sun shall no more be thy light by day, neither for brightness shall the moon give light unto thee: but the Lord shall be unto thee an everlasting light, and thy God thy glory .... I the Lord will hasten it in its time." This is the view taken up in Rev. 21$^{23f.}$ and 22^5 in the picture of that city which "had no need of the sun, neither of the moon, to shine upon it, for the glory of God did lighten it, and the lamp thereof is the Lamb. And the nations shall walk amidst the light thereof .... And the gates thereof shall in no wise be shut by day ... for there shall be no night there ... and they need no light of lamp, neither light of the sun, for the Lord God shall give them light." What we are told by this view is not that there will be no created light at all, but that God with His own light takes the place and function of all the created lights known to us, so that He will be His own witness, His own sign and to that extent created light itself, even as and though He dwells in light inaccessible. Hence from this standpoint, too, light is made independent of the existence of all the luminaries known to us. There is really "more light" than that which all the sun-worshippers of all ages have considered to be *the* light!

It is now said of light that God saw that it was good. This is followed at once by a reference to the existence of darkness. But just as it does not say that God created darkness, so it does not say that He saw that it was good. This can be said of light and of light alone—of the light which according to what follows was separated from darkness. And if the same will later be said of God's other works, they will all be characterised by this first work as works of light and not of darkness, of the day and not of the night; their goodness necessarily corresponding to the goodness which God found and saw in this first work. But what does it mean when it says that God "saw the light, that it was good"? Gunkel gives the following exposition of this expression and its later parallels: "Like an artificer who critically passes in review his work when the bustle of activity has passed, so God subsequently proves each created thing and sees what has come of it, and He finds each to be good and beautiful. His work has suc-
[122] ceeded .... The verdict of the narrator is naturally the same as God's verdict on the world: the world is good. In this Song of Triumph the ancient Israelites celebrate the wisdom and goodness of the Creator of the world. The thought of later Judaism is altogether different; to it the world was in the hands of the evil one." With all due respect we can only say that this exposition is at every point quite inapposite. It is obviously foolish to speak of a coming and passing hustle and bustle of activity in a process which consisted solely in God's *way-yo'mer.* And surely the fact that God saw it does not imply that He passed it critically in review. What it does say is rather that "God saw the light, that it was good," i.e. (as B. Jacob correctly paraphrases it) how good it was. That it was good because it was created by the Word of God is self-evident. But it is not at all self-evident that God should see and accept as good this good thing which is so different from His own goodness; that He should recognise as good this good thing outside His own goodness; that it could be the object of His good-pleasure. Nothing outside God Himself, and nothing that He Himself has created and created good, has any claim and right in and by itself to His good-pleasure and therefore to be called good with genuine and final truth. "Why callest thou me good; there is none good but God alone" (Mk. 10^{18}). Except, of course, when someone or something is found to be good by God Himself! But when this is the case it is always God's discovery, and His freedom is not surren-

dered or lessened because He has created the thing in question good. That it was good when He created it does not mean the impartation and appropriation of an inherent goodness which no longer needs the divine discovery. As its becoming good is a matter of divine creation, so its being good is a matter of divine seeing. But this seeing is grace. There is no need of created light for God to see at all. Again, it is not as He sees it in its own goodness and in the power of its truth that He sees how good it is. It is in the freedom of undeserved and unmerited favour that God grants to it—and later grants to all His other works—His good-pleasure; that in its distinction from Himself He finds in it a correspondence to the goodness of His creative will and acts. In this connexion only that can be called "good" which corresponds to God's will and act as Creator, and for this reason and in this way in a positive relation to Himself. The recognition of this correspondence is the grace of the Creator, His seeing of the goodness of the creature. This divine "seeing," and what the biblical author desires to attest by this expression, has nothing to do with a divine optimism, or an ancient Hebrew optimism whose triumphant song could later give way to pessimism (like that of the followers of Leibnitz after the Lisbon earthquake). For "good" does not just mean "good and beautiful," but is obviously related to the separation of light from darkness which is mentioned immediately afterwards. In finding light worthy of this separation—and this is not self-evident, for it is only a created thing and not God—God sees how the light is good, i.e., that it is good for something, to wit, to be His witness and sign. The other qualities and advantages of light, e.g., that it enables us to see, that it is usually accompanied by heat, that it is one of the necessities of animal life, have all claimed the attention of various exegetes, but they do not seem to be of any interest to the biblical author. The good thing about light as it is graciously seen by God is that according to the phrase which follows He plans to establish it as a landmark against darkness, and therefore against chaos.

The fact that the divine fiat is: "Let there be light," and not: "Let there be darkness," means that the possibility of the latter creation and creature is rejected by God. In this way He supersedes the sphere of Gen. 1^2 and reveals His wisdom and the sum of all wisdom. His righteousness and the sum of all righteousness, and His truth and the sum of all truth in contrast to all folly, unrighteousness, and falsehood, whose negativity was decided by the fact that He created light and not darkness, and saw how and why light was good and not darkness. Here and in the second act of creation, and clearly enough even in the first part of the third, to create is to separate. What is entailed by this separation emerges clearly in vv. 3–5. It is not merely that light is the appointed boundary of two spheres like the firmament of vv. 6–8, or that there are two spheres in their variety as in vv. 9–10, but that as the boundary light is also itself that which bounds or is bounded. Between light and darkness there is no third element like the firmament between the waters above and below (vv. 6–8). Nor are light and darkness peacefully co-existent like the terrestrial ocean and the mainland (vv. 9, 10). They are mutually exclusive. The one confronts the other; light darkness, and darkness light. Nor is there any question here of symmetry or equilibrium between the two. They confront one another in such a way that God separates the light, which He acknowledges to be good, from the darkness. "In darkness and night remnants of that primal state intrude into the ordered world" (Zimmerli). The reference can be only to the darkness mentioned in v. 2 as the predicate of chaos, for otherwise it would mean that darkness was also created by God and found good in its own way. Since this is not the case, it is obvious that the antithesis to light, and therefore to the good creation of God, is chaos. And it belongs necessarily and integrally to the creation which begins with the creation of light that God rejects chaos, that He has for it no creative will or act or grace, but has these for light and light alone. Commencing in this way, creation is also a clear revelation of His will and way. Whatever may become a reality from and for chaos, by the commencement of the divine creation it is separated as darkness from light, as that which God did not will from that which He did, as the sphere of non-grace

[123]

from that of His grace. Only from the majesty and supreme lordship of God is it not separated. Since darkness cannot offer any resistance to the emergence of light; since it has to acquiesce in the fact that light is separated from it; since it is later given a name as well as light, and has assigned to it a somewhat anonymous place in the domain of day, it is clear enough that it is not exempt from the sway of God, but has to serve Him in its own way, so that there can be no question of an absolute dualism. Here, then, and at root in the processes depicted in v. 6 f. and v. 9 f., to "divide" does not mean only to "distinguish" and "separate" but to "create order." At the same time it is to set up an impassable barrier. Whatever else may take place between light and darkness, light will never be darkness and darkness will never be light. It is also to establish an inviolable hierarchy. However small and weak it may be, light will always be the power which banishes darkness; and however great and mighty it may be, darkness will always be the impotence which yields before light. It is light that *is*. Of darkness it can be said only that, as long as light is, it is also, but separated from it, marked and condemned by it as darkness, in opposition to it, as its antithesis, and at the same time serving light as its background. Darkness has no reality in itself; it is a by-product. It would like to be something in itself. Again and again it claims to be this. But it cannot make good its claim. It necessarily serves that which it tries to oppose. It is obviously in view of the place and role assigned to them in the hierarchy of creation that the existence of light and darkness are described in Job 38[19] as the secret of God, and that Is. 45[7] can and must say of darkness that God has "created" it. In this striking application of the verb *bara'* there is revealed the reverse side, the negative power, of the divine activity, which we cannot, of course, deny to the divine will. The best analogy to the relationship between light and darkness is that which exists between the elect and the rejected in the history of the Bible: between Jacob and Esau; between David and Saul; between Judas and the other apostles. But even this analogy is improper and defective. For even the rejected, even Satan and the demons, are the creation of God—not, of course, in their corruption, but in the true and original essence which has been corrupted. But darkness and the chaos which it represents are not the creation of God any more than the corruption of the corrupt and the sin of the rejected. Thus a true and strict analogy to the relationship between light and darkness is to be found only in the relationship between the divine election and rejection, in the eternal Yes and No spoken by God Himself when, instead of remaining in and by Himself, He marches on to the *opus ad extra*[EN151] of His free love. When God fulfils what we recognise in Jesus Christ to be His original and basic will, the beginning of all His ways and works in Himself, He also accomplishes this separation, draws this boundary and inaugurates this hierarchy. This is what is attested by the story of creation in its account of the work of the first three days, and particularly in its account of the work of the first day.

[124]

But so far we have not given independent consideration to the final element of the first act. This consists in the fact that God gives a name to light and darkness, calling light "day" and darkness "night"; and that this naming has creative power. It is by reason of this naming that we have evening and morning—one day, day number one, the first day. The first point which calls for notice, in retrospect of what precedes, is the order of this naming. The obvious purpose of the creation of light and its separation from darkness is still maintained. The first thing to receive its name is not darkness—as though it were either there first or first created as in the misunderstanding of v. 2—but light. Nor should we miss the unmistakeable nuance in the presentation of the creative effect of this act. It does not say that as a result of this naming the first day and the first night come into being, but only the first day. Even here there is no simple parallelism. If God speaks and acts and rules in the one no less than the other, it is plain enough that He does so very differently in the two cases, and that the

---

[EN151] work outside of God

separation, order and hierarchy remain in force. In the Bible the name of a person or thing is not an accidental appendix or a sign of recognition, but is something that designates the nature and function of the person or thing in question, thus corresponding to it. Israel is not called Israel without reason. Jesus is not called Jesus without reason. Judas is not called Judas without reason. Every person or thing is what its name implies. Namelessness and anonymity mean unreality. For this reason the naming of a thing is never an incidental act in the Bible. It is always a decisive act, as is presupposed even where it is not expressly mentioned. To give a thing a name is thus an act of lordship (cf. 2 K. 23^{34} and 24^{17}), and originally and properly an act of divine worship (Zimmerli). When man names a thing (as when he has the task of naming the animals in the second creation story in Gen. 2^{19}), he does so in some sense as the delegate and plenipotentiary of God and not on his own authority. This is shown by the fact that the naming of heaven (v. 8) and earth and sea (v. 10), and therefore of the cosmos in its totality, is described as an act of right and might executed only by God. The naming of light and darkness is supremely the affair of God and of God alone. It is God who decides what this created and that non-created thing is to be called, i.e., what are to be its being, states and function. No one can take His place in this matter. At this point He alone is Judge and Ruler. For this name-giving involves both an act of judgment and an act of lordship, both a verdict and a decree.

"God called the light day." Literally, He determined and appointed the light to be day. What we have here is a continuation and effect of the fact that He "saw." We can now see how and why He found it good. In His grace He found it worthy and adapted to be day and to be called day. That this is His judgment, and that this judgment has the character of a valid decree, is now described as the further content of the creative Word of God. According to the biblical author we are still in the sphere of creation. There was no day before God called the light day and assigned it the property of being day. It was solely due to this divine ascription that day came into being; that the light became day.

Here again an exegetical note by Gunkel is worth mentioning. In relation to the *way-yiqra' Elohim* he writes: "It is naturally presumed that God speaks in Hebrew. Hebrew is the true language. Other nations do not really ' speak ' but only ' stutter.' Such is the naive pride of every ancient nation." We may comment that it is quite self-evident that God should be presumed to have spoken in Hebrew. Otherwise how could the Hebrew author have understood Him? What other presupposition was possible in a true saga? And if the existence and name of Israel as the nation of the covenant, of revelation and of the Messiah are not arbitrary or accidental, the same is true of its language, and of the fact God did not call the day ἡμέρα or *dies* but *yom*, which, although it is related to the Assyrian *ûmu*, is Hebrew and not Assyrian. We have thus to accept the fact, without any ironical condescension, that in this matter God did not speak and was not understood in Chinese but in Hebrew, and that the Hebrew language is in fact the "true" language. And if in this respect and in connexion with the choice of Israel there was obviously a particular pride of the Israelites which perhaps seemed only too similar to that of all ancient (and modern) nations, we must not overlook the fact that when two people do the same thing it is not necessarily the same even when it is perverted in both instances. Thus phenomenologically at least the pride of the chosen people is to be distinguished from ordinary national pride. [125]

But what is meant by day? There is obviously meant the same thing as that whose emergence is later described in the words: "And it was evening and it was morning." Whatever else this may mean, it certainly means that which is limited and designated by evening and morning. We must not evade—and here we side with Gunkel against Delitzsch and A. Jeremias—this plain and simple meaning. It is true that according to Ps. 90^4 a thousand years are as one day for God, but this does not alter the fact that, according to Gen. 1^5, God has made and given to us a day which is not of a thousand years' duration but of twenty-four hours. It is certainly as such that the biblical authors understand the ensuing days of creation up to the seventh day, the day of God's rest. We only cloud the picture, involving it in dreadful and not very helpful confusion, if for the clear concept day we try to substitute an indeterminate and immense period of time under cover of which astronomical light-years and geological periods can be introduced for apologetic purposes. Even Delitzsch's argument that there can be no such day prior to v. 14, because the measure of time, the sun, has not yet been created, is not really convincing. For as our passage allows light to be created prior to the sun, in the same sovereign denial of all solar cults it allows light to be named and evening and morning to become day. According to these verses, God creates day quite irrespective of what we know or think we know to be the cause of evening and morning, and therefore the cause of the reality of day. It is true enough, as Delitzsch further claims, that our time is incommensurable with its prototype, i.e., with the divine temporality. But when the question is an *opus Dei ad extra*[EN152] which has already commenced and is actually in progress, and when it is a question of the unity of time in this context, what authority have we to retranslate this concept into that of the divine reality? It is thus unfortunate that Delitzsch too—laughing after the manner of Sarah—thinks it necessary to discredit and possible to reject a literal understanding of this concept as "childish and wholly absurd." Why cannot we allow the saga quietly to finish what it has to say on this point before we consider what we are going to make of it? For it has something very remarkable to say on this point, namely, that God created time: not just time in general, but our time, the actual time in which each creature actually lives; or concretely time as a unit, i.e., the day, and time as a sequence, i.e., the week; and that He created it by giving to light the name day. Given this name by God, light is day: in the first instance day number one, the first day; but also each succeeding day, accompanying and succeeding the first. The same formula: "There was evening and there was morning," is used to denote the creation of all the other days (with the remarkable exception of the seventh). This obviously means that the divine activity of all these other days implicitly signifies a repetition of the activity of the first day, and therefore the activity of a further unit of time, of a new day, until the number is completed.

[126]

The fact that God calls the light day means formally that the day as our unit of time is not an arbitrary human invention or convention, but a divine work and institution. The day is thus given to the creature as the sphere of its existence. It is not originally and naturally its property but God's property, and therefore it is not originally and naturally at the disposal of the creature but at the disposal of God. Day is light adopted and consecrated by God in His gracious good-pleasure—dedicated and ordained for His special service and therefore for the declaration of His will. No one and nothing, not even the sun or any constellation, let alone man, has the right to withdraw from day the purpose assigned to it by the consecration of light, and therefore to withdraw himself from participation in this ministry of light.

And the fact that God calls the light day means materially that it is not darkness but light that God has exalted and ordained to be the unit of time and therefore the measure of our life-span. As time is granted to the creature, it has been decided concerning it that as such, existing in time, it should belong to the side which God affirms as the possibility chosen by Him; to which He turns His gracious good-pleasure; which He has completely separated from the other side, from chaos; and which He has fundamentally and definitively exalted above it. To have time is to be allowed to exist as and with light under and by the divine Yes; it is not to be overtaken by God's No; it is to be preserved and sheltered before Him. The first day was a day of light, and each succeeding day, being day and not night, must be the same. This is what we are told by the saga, and this is the teaching which we evade if we are not prepared to take it literally. For everything depends on the fact that what is in question in

---

[EN152] work of God outside of God

this passage is concretely our time, and not just indefinite periods of times but measured and limited time and therefore real days. Both the formal fact that we in our time belong to God, i.e., to the same service of God which is also that of light, and the material fact that we in our time can exist like and with light under God's Yes, are decided only when there is between light as the creature affirmed and applied to God's service on the one hand, and our actual time on the other, the relationship which necessarily results from a literal understanding of the present passage. The interpretation constantly given by Augustine (e.g., *De Gen. ad litt.*, IV, 27, 44; *De Civ. Dei*, XI, 9, and *passim*), that the six or seven days of Genesis are in reality a single day described six or seven times over, and that even this one day is not really more than a single moment (cf. Anselm of Canterbury, *Cur Deus homo?* I, 18)—this interpretation no less than that of modern exegetes with apologetic interests destroys all the teaching about *our* time which is to be gained at this point. Our time consists neither in millions of years nor in a single instant but is made up of real days. If we filch from Gen. 1 the relationship of light to a real day, the relationship of light to our time is destroyed, and Gen. 1³ᶠ· ceases to be a proclamation of the meaning of history and becomes a more or less interesting, credible and binding scientific or philosophical theory. If it is more likely that the purpose of the story of creation in Genesis—of the beginning of the history of the covenant and salvation developed in the Old Testament—is to instruct us in the sense of this proclamation rather than of such a theory, it follows that we must take the "days" of which it speaks, and especially the "day" of Gen. 1³ᶠ·, in the literal sense of the term.

But we are told in the first clause of v. 5 that God has given a name to darkness as well; that He has called it "night." Like the separation of light from darkness this obviously means in the first instance that the Creator of light is also the Lord of darkness. The fact that darkness, and the chaos which it represents, is not His creation does not mean that it has escaped and evaded Him. Even in the negation proper to it, it can only be what He will make of it and accomplish that for which He will use it. It is not darkness itself, nor Satan, nor man, but God who gives it its name, assigning it a place and giving it a role to play and a duty to perform. And when He does this after He has given a name to light, when He calls darkness "night" and sets it alongside light, He numbers it with His creation. This implies two things: first, that having separated it from light He continues to reckon with it, willing to have and uphold the cosmos as it is assailed and threatened by chaos and assigning even to the threat a certain right and a specific function, corresponding to the relationship between the Yes and No of His eternal will; and secondly, that, corresponding to its character, He reckons with darkness in this particular way, not permitting to chaos more than the nature of a threat at the edge of the cosmos, giving darkness a name which describes it as such, i.e., its nature which is wholly different from that of light and by which it is always to be distinguished from the latter according to His act as Creator. In Job 17¹² we read the indignant words: "They change the night into day; the light, they say, is near unto darkness." Job is quite right with his protest, for this is the very thing which cannot and must not take place. Light and darkness cannot and must not be confused or mixed as if they had not been separated by God's will and Word. "Woe unto them that call evil good, and good evil; that put darkness for light and light for darkness" (Is. 5²⁰). The dreadful misunderstanding against which the voice of the prophets is raised (Am. 5¹⁸ and Zeph. 1¹⁵) is that Israel expects "a day of the Lord" but that in this expectation it is really on the way to darkness because its knowledge of *Yahweh* and therefore its expectation is false. The New Testament has the same confusion in view in Lk. 11³⁵ (cf. Mt. 6²³): "Take heed therefore that the light which is in thee be not darkness." This confusion is possible because of the "powers of darkness" (Lk. 22⁵³, Col. 1¹³). It is confronted by the divine naming as both a warning and a promise. According to the divine decision, the essence of darkness is very different from that of light. "Shall thy wonders be known in the dark?" asks Ps. 88¹², and the answer which appears to be in the writer's mind is that this is

[127]

impossible. There is, of course, decision and a wonderful transition between light and darkness, but there is no fusion of essence. Light "excels" darkness, as is significantly stated in Eccl. 2^{13}. It is thus possible to speak of the two only as adversaries: "Darkness passeth, and the true light now shineth" (1 Jn. 2^8). "What communion has light with darkness?" (2 Cor. 6^{14}). For this reason: "Ye are not in darkness. ... Ye are all the children of light, and the children of the day" (1 Thess. 5$^{4f.}$). Or even more pregnantly: "For ye were sometimes darkness, but now are ye light in the Lord; walk as children of light" (Eph. 5^8). Calling and conversion from darkness to light (1 Pet. 2^9) is the only possibility in this relationship: the miracle of the eyes of the blind seeing out of darkness (Is. 29^{18}); of God Himself making darkness light before them (Is. 42^{16}). This is how God ordered the relation between cosmos and chaos, between light and darkness, when He gave darkness its name. This is how He fitted darkness into the realm of His lordship, and ordered its relationship to light. This is how He granted it its right. It is the right of one who is set absolutely in the wrong. When darkness is called night and not day—not even a part of day—it is decided that it has thus no constitutive significance for the reality of day and therefore for time. Darkness gives way to light; it accompanies and limits it. Between it and light, decision and change continually take place. Even those who walk in the light are never quite free from its danger and threat. The light which God created and called day is distinguished from God Himself as the uncreated, eternal light by the fact that it is never unchanging like God (Jas. 1^{17}), or without the opposition and threat of darkness. So great is the power of darkness. But its power is not so great that it can be a constitutive part of the reality of day and therefore of time. That is why in Gen. 1$^{3f.}$ night is in no way presented as a second concept of time beside day, but only as its negation and limita-

[128]

tion. It is in this sense, and not in the sense of a peaceful juxtaposition of two spheres of time, that we must interpret Ps. 74^{16}: "Thine is the day, thine also is the night." Again, it is in this sense, and in this sense alone, that Jer. 33^{19} speaks of God's covenant with the day and with the night. That God has made a covenant with the night too implies that it is under His control; that He cares for it; that while it limits the day it has on its part its own limits; that after every night a new day commences with the dawn of the morning; that after a serious danger and threat our time is given us again in the form of a new day of light. It is not for nothing that Jer. 33 speaks so expressly of a twofold covenant. The one is entirely different from the other, although the God who has made both is one and the same. If, as the One who has given night and day their names, He is "the God of days and the God of nights" (Lavater), He is the one in very different ways and with very different intentions from the other. The numerous biblical passages where the expression "day and night" apparently describes the uninterrupted duration of an activity or state must never be taken as a simple equivalent of "uninterrupted." The relationship between day and light, night and darkness, remains. Where the two terms are used, it is always with the same antithesis—an antithesis which is not accidental but basic, and therefore demands our attention. This is what confronts us and is overcome when life proceeds in one of its forms "day and night." It is not self-evident that this should be the case. The fact remains that it was light, and light alone, that God saw to be good, and that it was light, and light alone, that He called day. The fact remains that night as such is terror (Ps. 91^5, Song of Songs, 3^8). It is not self-evident that dawn should bring release from this terror. It might be otherwise. To the question from Seir: "Watchman, what of the night?" (Is. 21^{11}) the prophet has to answer: "The morning cometh, and also the night," and we seem to have here the hint of a very different possibility. "Day and night" does not simply mean twenty-four full hours in irresistible progression, but day with the gracious inclusion of night; time with the gracious sum of what is not time. Sometimes, of course, the emphasis is reversed: there is the dreadful encroachment of night upon day; an inundation of time by what is not time. It is certainly consoling that—from whatever angle we see Him—God is above this antithesis and gives to both sides of the antithesis their names. But what is really consoling is that it is He who causes it to be day and night. In itself the fact that night exists alongside day means that as long as we live in our time we find ourselves in a danger zone. It is as well, therefore, that all true morning and evening hymns of the Church protest against the banalising of the concept of "night" and therefore against that of the concept of "day," and therefore against that of the whole concept of time, and therefore against the emptying of that consolation, by reminding us expressly—in the evening:

> "O sun, where is thy light?
> Descended hath the night.
> The enemy of day"   (P. Gerhardt);

or:

> "Gone is the sun's declining ray.
> And darkness stealeth over day;
> Grant us, O Christ, Thy living light.
> May we not stumble in the night"   (N. Herman);

or:

> "Lord Jesus Christ, with us abide.
> Around us falls the eventide.
> On our dark souls may there still shine,
> The radiance of Thy Word divine"   (N. Selnecker);

and in the morning: [129]

> "Where darkness was before me.
> Shades of night closed o'er me,
> Satan sought to take me.
> God did not forsake me"   (P. Gerhardt);

or:

> "Heartfelt praise, O Lord, to Thee,
> That through the watches of the night,
> From grief and pain and danger free,
> I journied safely to the light.
> Upheld in every gloomy hour,
> Against the tempter's glistening power"   (H. Albert);

or:

> "Thanks be to God who through this night
> Hath kept me from the devil's might"   (N. Herman).

It is of a piece with this description of the character of night and its relationship to day that in Rev. 21[25] and 22[5] we are told expressly that there will be no night in the heavenly Jerusalem. That day is accompanied by night and time by what is not time, that darkness still has this power, is one of the marks of the provisional nature of the creation of heaven and earth recorded in the Bible. This juxtaposition will be eliminated in the new creation. Neither darkness nor night will then be allowed to play its dangerous and menacing role. So much for the clause about the naming of darkness.

The second statement in v. 5: "And the evening and the morning were the first day," records the emergence of the day corresponding to the divine Word. It may be compared with the "and it was light" of v. 3. It tells us that when God called the light "day," day came into being as a reality, and that it did so in such a way that it was evening and morning.

We note first concerning the material content of v. 5b that the creation of day and therefore of the unit of time is actually the work of the divine name-giving. It was not automatically, but by the Word of God which summoned light and called and made it day, that day and time came into being. There is no day or time without the Word of God—the Word which summoned light and called and made it day. Day—each day succeeding the first day—is able to exist by and for the Word of God, i.e., for the Word which creates light. This is confirmed by the creation of the other days, and therefore of the whole week as the sequence of time. These other days too will be works of the Word of God, and the Word of God which created them too will attest itself as that which created the light. For all the works of these other days, and finally the works of the whole week, will continually add to the first creature—light— fresh witnesses of the glory of God and servants of His self-revelation. Time is the natural predicate of light, and therefore of the divine self-revelation. It is as such that day is created first. And as such it is a creature. It serves light, but in the common service of God. Any other service to which it might be subjected could consist only in the dangerous and ultimately futile attempt to exchange and confuse light with darkness, and thus to rob time of its reality. The nature given to time at creation will always resist this attempt. No creature really has time for anything but participation in the service of light; for attestation of the divine self-declaration. It is to be noted further (concerning the first material content of v. 5b) that no corresponding creation follows the prior naming of night. Only at the creation of the heavenly bodies (v. 14 f.) is the distinctive existence of night side by side with day expressly recalled. What is described as the accomplished work of God is simply the fact that day came into being. This does not deny but confirms and characterises even on that other side God's whole act of lordship, which is quite clearly attested in these verses. But whatever may be the reality of night, however close may be its relationship to day, however strictly it may be divinely co-ordinated with it, it cannot be said that like day it was made by the Word of God and is therefore ranked with day as God's creation. This is denied to it by the very fact that it has only the name and nature of darkness.

The second and more difficult aspect of v. 5b consists in the actual statement that it was evening and morning and therefore a day in the full sense of the term, and indeed the first day. The curious order, evening-morning, obviously corresponds to the Jewish way of calculating a day and especially the Sabbath. But this does not explain it, because for its part the Jewish calculation (as it may be seen in Neh. 13[19] and Dan. 8[14] in the Old Testament and in 2 Cor. 11[25] in the New) may be traced back to our text or to the tradition which lies behind or runs parallel with it. What, then, is the calculation of our passage and tradition? Luther's translation "And so the first day was made of evening and morning," is perhaps more penetrating than might appear at first sight. But it is better to divide the statement into two clearly distinguished clauses: "It was evening," and "It was morning"—a parallelism which rightly and even necessarily reminds us of the twofold covenant of Jer. 33. "It was evening." In this way a *terminus ad quem*[EN153], a final point of time, is rather strangely mentioned as the first constitutive element of day. The word *ereb*[EN154] seems also to include the concept of fulfilment. But however that may be, if we read this clause in connexion with the preceding statement, it necessarily means that the Creator has executed and completed His first work. He had spoken and His Word was followed by a fulfilment: there was light, and it was separated from darkness. The *opus Dei ad extra*[EN155] had for the first time become a finished event.

[130]

[EN153] ending point
[EN154] evening
[EN155] work of God outside of God

2. Creation as the External Basis of the Covenant

A reality that is different from God had taken on form and existence. And then finally God had called the light day. Did this also have a fulfilment and correspondence? The text answers: "Yes, it was evening." But this means that with this crowning naming of light God's accomplished work received the form of time. Time as such came into being, and was at once made a day, the first day. It is the naming which characterised God's accomplished work as an historical act, as the first in the series of all God's other historical acts. It was not in the instant of an eternal moment, nor in an indefinite time, but in a day limited by an evening that the *opus Dei ad extra*^{EN156} became an event. It is in such a day that it obviously wills to become and will again become an event. It is this fundamental act of the divine compassion and condescension which becomes apparent in the fact that God not only has eternity but also time, and that now He also gives time to His creatures as the living-space appropriate to them; that He not only wills to act uninterruptedly, in accordance with the constancy of His own nature, but that He also wills, as He is able, to do so interruptedly in individual, concrete and, of course, finite acts, in accordance with the finitude of the created reality distinct from Himself. It is in this manner that He wills to speak and act, and will do so, as the Lord of His creation. He will have time for it. He will be Lord of its history. And here in particular, when it becomes evening after God has created light and separated it from darkness, in His condescension from eternity to the finite being of the creature, God makes Himself the Lord of its history. Here it is revealed that He has time for it. Here He gives it time as its living-space, corresponding to its finitude. It would obviously have been impossible to say this with greater emphasis than when the saga calls the evening the first constitutive element and therefore the goal and end of the day. Once we realise that it is a matter of the end and goal, the *terminus ad quem*^{EN157}, of the divine activity, and thus of the end and therefore the completion of the day and therefore of creaturely time, it is clear that what takes place in the morning and up to the evening is God's work. But what is present in the evening—in certain respects as the by-product of the divine work. as the sphere which   **[131]** the *opus Dei ad extra*^{EN158} had created for itself but also for its creation—is day, i.e., finite time in distinction from, but obviously also in relation to, God's eternity. What the saga has to say positively about the creation of day, and with it of time, has all been said in the clause: "It was evening."

But what about night, and the darkness which according to v. 5a God has solemnly called night? It is clear that the author does not describe night the second constitutive element of day, and that according to his earlier statements he cannot possibly do so. It is the work of God that constitutes the day. But God's work consists in the creation of light and not of darkness. Even the darkness which God called night has no part in the constitution of day. As it is not created, no time is created with it. But we have seen that, according to the presentation of the biblical author, it is undoubtedly present in its peculiar way, and wholly within the majesty and lordship of God the Creator. It exists, of course, only in virtue of the denial implicitly made in His affirmation. But in this way it does exist. And existing in this way, how can it escape the sphere of His power and decision? Hence it, too, has been given its name. It, too, exists in the nature which He has assigned it. Its name and nature is night. And as light limits darkness, so day limits night. Thus with the creation and activity of day, night also comes within the sphere of day. It is not as if day consisted of day and night. Such a statement is not only self-contradictory but constitutes a hopeless banalisation of the concept of time presented here. The truth is rather that, while as such it has as little to do with night as light

---

^{EN156} work of God outside of God
^{EN157} ending point
^{EN158} work of God outside of God

with darkness, day includes and encloses night, i.e., it surrounds it both before and behind, encircling it like a beleaguered fortress.

This encirclement of night by day comes out plainly in the second clause: "And it was morning." It is clear that a second constitutive element of day is now named. It is also clear that this second element is described in such a way that account is taken of the reality of night, which comes between evening and morning. But it is clear finally that this takes place in such a way that although night is passively included in the constitution of day, in view of the utter peculiarity of its reality it is obviously excluded from any active role in its constitution. To be sure, the word *boqer*[EN159] contains the thought of a penetration. But the matter is self-evident. The author takes into account the fact that night follows evening and therefore day. But where does it belong? Does it belong to the day which terminates with evening? This is out of the question, for day was created and came into being with the work of God and therefore with the work of light, and night is the name given to darkness. Yet it is still the case that night follows day; that it comes within the sphere of day. No reader or hearer who observes the sequence "evening-morning" can or should omit to think of the night that lies between. As B. Jacob has finely put it, it is "the shadow and dark train of day." But is it really only this? It is not self-evident that it should be only this. Might it not be the victorious shadow, the endless train of day? Might not darkness be stronger than light? If the latter is created and finite—and day with it—it cannot of itself assert and renew itself. How can night follow day, existing in the sphere of day as non-time in the midst of time, without becoming eternal night, and thus overwhelming day as it seeks to do as its enemy? Have we now serious and final grounds for alarm when we think of it? Who or what resists and limits it, co-ordinating it with day in such a way that the latter can assert and renew and thus repeat itself as a unit of time; that day can again follow night; that there can not only be a unit of time but also, in spite of the threats of non-time, a sequence and continuance of time? It is here that the clause about the emergence of morning comes in. It obviously describes in itself a *terminus a quo*[EN160], a beginning. There is no need to describe the end of the preceding day, for its constitution has already been denoted by its evening and therefore by its end. But to show how day is constituted when God creates it and causes it to come into being it is obviously necessary to say that beyond this end, because night follows it, there is a beginning, a new day; that the first is not the only day; that no darkness has the power to prevent the light from being called and actually being day again—true day. We have seen that day was constituted by an act of God. But now we can say further that it was constituted by an act of God which when it is performed is resumed and continued by God. We have seen that it was constituted by light. But now we have to add that it was constituted by the light which, as created light, is accompanied by darkness but cannot be and is not overcome by it. The fact that night naturally follows evening, and morning night, shows that created light is superior to darkness. For what takes place in the morning, what commences in the morning and will continue till the evening, will again be the work of God, the work of the second day, whereas the night has no such divine work to show. The fact that the morning of the second day follows night—and with it the new penetration of the positive will of God, its new event—shows that this and not night is the second constitutive element in the first day. In all its glory as the day of created light, this day does not exist for itself, as the one day completed by an act of God. For this reason it is only relatively and not absolutely that it can be made yesterday, the past day, by the threat and irruption of night. It has a promise which lights up the shadow of invading night: the promise of a new beginning beyond its end; the promise of morning chasing away the night; and therefore the promise of another day following it.

[132]

[EN159] morning
[EN160] starting point

Without this promise, and therefore without this hope, it would not be day at all—the day which has been created by God, and which has come into being by His Word as the name of light. Hence it is constituted not merely by the fact that God speaks and acts, but by the fact that He will again speak and act. It is thus a unit of time in the sequence of time, a week-day in the series of days which for their part end in the Sabbath and will recommence with it. As the living-space of the creature to-day, it is the promise and hope of further living-space still to be granted. That "seed-time and harvest, frost and heat, summer and winter, day and night" will not cease is stated again (in confirmation of this first constitution of time) in the parallel divine saying after the Flood (Gen. 9^{22}). Beyond this we must also add that there also emerges at this point the necessary connexion between creation and the new creation, between created time and the last time to which it moves. God has not created time without this reference to its own *eschaton*^{EN161}. In creating it He has made it a time of hope. It is for this reason that morning, the *terminus a quo*^{EN162} of the following day, emerges as a second and absolutely indispensable constitutive element in the first day. It would not have been day at all if at its close it had not become morning, and therefore day again. That which lies between its close and the commencement of this other day, the new Word and work of God, is night: this and only this. Night is no more than this. It is not eternal night. It is only a fleeting triumph of darkness. It is not a victorious shadow or endless train of day. And its power is taken from it as it grasps and uses it. According to the remarkable presentation in these verses it is only anonymously that it can remain in the sphere of day. This is true even though it is the name which God has given to denote the nature and essence of darkness. The meaning of this characterisation is thus revealed. Night is the name of the nameless and the nature of the natureless. It is only in this way that it follows and accompanies the day of light. It is enclosed and hemmed in by day and by the new day of light which really follows it as its true companion. In this way it, too, is always in the sphere of God's power and glory; in this way it, too, enjoys His sustaining patience and has its own right. But it can be given no other right than this. And if by reason of this right, which God for the moment does not refuse it, it can and actually does threaten the creature, it cannot and will not destroy it. For this it has no right or might. This *terminus ad quem*^{EN163} and the *terminus a quo*, and in both cases the Word and work of God the Creator, prevent it from doing this, forcing it indeed into the order of creation and compelling it in its own involuntary way to join in creation's praise. It is in this sense—to follow Luther—that "the first day was made of evening and morning." It was indeed made "of" evening and morning to the extent that evening and morning are together the elements out of which the first and every day is made. [133]

(Gen. 1$^{6-8}$.) Strictly speaking, the creation of light was a pointer to what was to take place in the separation of the chaos-reality which God rejected. So far this had taken place only in the form of this announcement. So far the rejected, uncreated world was still there in all seriousness. What was present as the sign of darkness when God spoke, being rejected and perishing by His creative utterance, is revealed only when the first step is taken towards the actual establishment of order proclaimed by the creation of light. Perishing with commencing time, in the light which was created by God, by the further fulfilment of God's Word, with the dawn and completion of the second day, the infinite waste of waters is revealed as the absolute antithesis of the ordered

---

^{EN161} last days
^{EN162} starting point
^{EN163} ending point

world of "heaven and earth," as an enemy of all life, as the death of every possibility of life. It is this power as such which is radically broken by the creative work of the second day. What is basically secured by this work is the theatre of life, and therefore of man. In precise correspondence to the announcement made in the creation of light, it consists in the establishment of a boundary. The delineation of this boundary will be continued in the work of the third day. Its commencement consists in the radical crushing of the sovereignty of the element of chaos; in the liquidation of its finality, form and structure; in a division into "waters above" and "waters below" in which it can no longer speak a final inimical and mortal word, but can only be a last threat which cannot make man and his world impossible and thus destroy them. It is separated. It can exist only in this separation. Hence it has completely ceased to be what it was. It is no longer the one and all. As the one and all it merely *was* in the past posited by God's creative Word. In its state of separation it is and will be in the present and future determined by God's creative Word. Hence in its separation it, too, is a creature. It is no longer an element of chaos but of the cosmos. In the cosmos it is a reminder of the past, of the mortal danger which the Word and act of God have removed. It threatens and will threaten. It is and will be a sign that creation could have been the catastrophe of the creature; that the creature had no power to avert this; and that it was God alone who averted it. Itself a creature, it cannot and will not be again a catastrophe to its fellow-creature. It cannot prevent the cosmos into which it is integrated from being the cosmos. It is subjected to, associated with, and incorporated into it. According to the saga, this took place with God's creation of the firmament— of the solid lowest part of heaven. This forms the unbreachable wall between the waters. It breaks their infinity. It prevents their conflux. It does not allow

[134] them to be the one and all. It ensures the existence of a lower cosmos, ensuring that its beginning is not its doom, nor its existence its extinction. It restrains and keeps back what would inevitably have taken place if God had willed to fashion the creature in His wrath. It is the proof that God did not will to do this and did not do it. Being heaven in the form of the firmament, it is the sum of that which is above, of that which is invisibly superior to what is below, and therefore to man. Thus the upper, hidden cosmos cannot be an object of real terror to man. He need not fear that chaos, death and destruction will crash down upon him from heaven. If it commands fear and trembling in respect of what might and must have happened without it, it commands even greater confidence in view of the fact that it prevents it from happening. The menacing waters of heaven are indeed invisibly above the lower cosmos and therefore man. But they are only intermediate. They are neither the last thing nor the first. The last thing which is expressly described by this saga is the highest heaven which is the creaturely dwelling-place of God. And as surely as there is also a first thing, this is the throne of His mercy, which does not will the death of a sinner but that he should be converted and live. The first thing—and it is on this that the saga lays all its emphasis—is the firma-

ment which restrains and limits the menacing intermediate waters. With its creation God has actually said No to a world in which man would at once be lost, and Yes to a world in which man can know that he is protected because he is actually protected. This stability of the firmament, of this boundary, of this Yes and No, of the fulfilled divine decision in favour of His cosmos and against the sovereignty, against the present and future reality, of the primal flood and the element of chaos, corresponds to the stability of the divine throne. As "day" is the name of that for which God has given man time by making light and thus indicating and promising His decision, so "heaven" is the name for the space which God has given to man in creating the firmament and thus executing His decision. In this work of the second day, with the creation of heaven, a definite beginning is made of the disarmament of chaos and the establishment of the cosmos. There can now be no going back. That which has become a thing of the past in this decision cannot return. Nor must we miss the typical character of this creative work. The creation of the firmament, with its comprehensive opposition of form to formlessness, of the possibility of life to the necessity of death, aims at a peaceful and meaningful existence of the creature before and with its Creator. It testifies that at all events He has not created it in His wrath, but for freedom. It testifies that it need not expect any unrestrained or destructive evil from above, from the world-reality which is invisibly superior to it. It testifies that no matter how weak or impotent the creature might be, no matter how great the burden imposed upon it, no matter how sinister the overhanging threat, it may at least breathe, since there is   [135] no last and therefore no first thing that can rob it of its confidence to exist before and with God, but every threat can only be intermediate, and therefore limited and restrained, being itself a creature of God and as such forced in its own way to praise the Lord and to work for good to those who love Him. The ground on which God in His revelation can meet the creature, and on which it can believe His revelation;, is laid and cannot be removed. The essential condition of man's existence before and with God is ordered by the fact that his life is lived under an upper cosmos and on a metaphysical horizon which is called "heaven" and which has in its ultimate and primary forms a comforting, and even in its intermediate a finally harmless, meaning and function. The world is created for the proclaiming and hearing of a lifegiving Gospel and not of a death-dealing Law. From the very beginning, from the foundation of the world, God has had good intentions toward man. If this is revealed in the institution and history of the covenant of grace, it is not an absolute novelty in the light of the basic condition of his existence posited on the second day, but corresponds to the preparation which took place in creation.

Gen. 1[6-8] presents an exegetical puzzle the answer to which we can anticipate at once. In the Hebrew text these verses lack the phrase which is consistently used elsewhere: "And God saw how good it was." An accidental omission of these words is almost inexplicable in a passage where every word counts. The translators of the LXX thought it necessary to supply them. But this was perhaps an attempt at harmonising which missed the intention of the verses. It is clear enough that there is a material connexion between the second and the third work of creation (or at least the first part of the third). In both cases we have to do with the limitation of water. In vv. 6–8, however, the problem of this limitation is solved from the more important aspect of its metaphysical rather than its physical side, and not so far as a decree with reference to the lower cosmos. *Nondum exstabat utilitas, donec aquae terrestres in proprium locum se reciperent*[EN164]. (Calvin). Both are obviously so closely related in the eyes of the author that he appends this concluding statement only to the account in vv. 9–10. There can be no doubt that in v. 10 he is looking back to vv. 6–8 as well.

The statement of v. 5b: "And it was morning," has to be taken into tacit account. Darkness, called "night," was present after the first day, but could not master the light. "It was morning"; a second and new day had commenced because God had spoken again, and had thus commenced to create and posit a new time, until towards the evening this second day had been completed, and was confirmed as a real day by the fact that in defiance of the second night it again became morning, thus having its future in a third day. And again God uttered His "Let there be." The repetition of this formula is not pedantic; it expressly recurs only in v. 14. For all its precision the passage uses the free language of saga and not that of a dogmatic treatise. We shall have to understand the other fiats of the Creator used in this passage in the strict sense of this "Let there be." All along, even where one creation refers to that which has already preceded, the question is one of the emergence of that which had not previously been. But the creation of vv. 6–8 does not look back to any such previous creation. To be sure, the expression *way-ya'as Elohim*[EN165] occurs for the first time in v. 7. But as v. 7 is only a paraphrase of v. 6, describing the intention and immediate effect of the divine Word, so this [136] "God made" is obviously a paraphrase of the decisive *wa-yomer Elohim*[EN166] of v. 6. In speaking, God created. B. Jacob's suggested translation and paraphrase of v. 7 is illuminating: "God made the firmament, and as He made it the firmament did what it had to do (in accordance with the function assigned to it); it divided the waters above and below the firmament." If we interpret it in this way, we can understand the otherwise difficult juxtaposition of vv. 6 and 7 and the otherwise inexplicable position of the words *wa-y'hi-ken*[EN167] at the end of v. 7. B. Jacob pertinently asks: "How else could God first say (v. 6) that the *raqiac*[EN168] was to separate and then (v. 7) do it Himself?" And what could be the meaning of "and it was so" in v. 7b when according to v. 7a God had just done the thing in question? These difficulties are all resolved if in meaning and intention the *way-ya'as*[EN169] of v. 7 is an alternative for the *way-yo'mer*[EN170] of v. 6.

The second thing created by this second Word, or by the Word of God continuing in this second fiat, is the *raqia' b'thok ham-mayim*[EN171]. This expression must be understood as a unity. We are not told that God created the firmament between the waters already created by Him. What we are told is that He created "the firmament in the midst of the waters" (v. 6a), and then, as an indication of its purpose, that He created it to "divide the waters from the waters" (v. 6b). Our text is so little interested in the world as such, but so much in the history, and its presuppositions, which takes place in the world, that the account of the creation of the waters above and below is wholly and utterly subordinated to, i.e., implied in that of the

---

[EN164] Usefulness was not yet established, since the terrestrial waters had not been gathered to their proper place
[EN165] and God made
[EN166] and God said
[EN167] and it was so
[EN168] firmament
[EN169] he said
[EN170] he said
[EN171] firmament in the midst of the waters

creation of the barrier established between the two. In willing and creating this barrier God wills and creates that which is divided by it. The waters created by God are the waters which are divided and bounded by the *raqia'*. We cannot abstract from this purpose. We cannot go beyond it to visualise what the author meant by the waters. The state of undivided and unbounded waters is seen only in retrospect. The reference can only be to the primal flood of chaos. But chaos lies behind as the world which God did not will or create, and so too does its water—the primal flood. The water created by the Word of God is a different water. Essential to it is something which the other lacks, namely that it is divided by the firmament, and is not therefore the totality, or without a master, or unreal. It is water limited by God and relegated to its place. For this reason, the three occasions on which it is mentioned in vv. 6–8 have no independent interest but refer only to this division. No matter how we explain v. 2, in vv. 6–8 the undivided and unseparated state of water is past when God speaks, and it is possible to think of water only as the water divided and separated by the work of the Word of God. If it is overbold to take it that according to the author the waters were created by God simultaneously with the creation of the firmament, there can be no doubt that as he sees it they do not have a prior or autonomous being and essence from God but only in and with the creation of the firmament. In the sphere of God's creation there is no water *in se*. There is only water that is separated by the Word of God.

What is this "firmament between the waters"? *Raqia'* means something firmly pounded together, and is rightly translated στερέωμα, *firmamentum.* The Babylonian word for it is *shupku* and signifies the heaped up mound or dam of the celestial earth which fences off the celestial ocean. Since vv. 14, 17 and 20 later refer expressly to the "celestial firmament," there is an obvious correspondence to the earth in this account too. According to Job 37[18] the firmament is "strong as a molten looking glass," and according to Job 26[11] it is supported by pillars like the earth. According to Ezek. 1[22f.] and 10[1] it is the platform which, resting on the four living creatures, forms the basis of the divine throne, i.e., of the throne-chariot, so that like the earth it is a massive and stable structure. When we are told in Is. 40[22] that God "stretcheth out the heavens as a curtain, and spreadeth them out as a tent to dwell in," and when Is. 42[5] and *passim* speak similarly of a "stretched out heaven," this is "poetical hyper-bole" (Eichrodt, *op. cit.*, p. 45), a comparison which desires to depict the superior lightness [137] of this divine creature, but is certainly not intended to throw doubt on the solidity of the structure. We are told in Ps. 19[1] that it is the work of God's hands, and Ps. 150[1] states the obvious truth that it belongs to God, and that God is to be praised on account of it. It is His purpose, revealed in the present passage, which demands the firmament. What it has to do is no less than to separate the terrestrial and celestial oceans whose conflux would signify the victory of chaos. There are doors or windows in this firmament (Ps. 78[23], 2 K. 7[2, 19]). Every-thing depends upon the fact that God as its Lord should keep these windows shut (Gen. 8[2]) and not open them, as once happened in the Flood (Gen. 7[11]). It is to be noted that even in this extreme case there is no question of a collapse or abolition of the *raqia'*. For "mercy shall be built for ever in the heavens; faithfulness was established by thy mouth" (Ps. 89[2]). The firmament is the creaturely guarantee of the continuance of the lower universe. A relation to the animal kingdom is evident in the Old Testament only to the extent that according to v. 14 f. the heavenly luminaries are suspended upon it. But this seems to be for the author only a subsequent determination of the firmament. It is itself prior and superior to the heavenly luminaries, and its true purpose is clearly to divide the waters above and below.

Now it is actually the case that with its emphatic mention of the creation of this celestial firmament the biblical witness expressly accepts the view of a celestial ocean. This is not merely the obvious presupposition of the story of the Flood, but also meets us explicitly in Ps. 104[3] and 148[4], and perhaps also in the image of a treasury of snow and hail in Job. 38[22]. Above all, it is the silent presupposition of the distinctive and almost always threatening character which the terrestrial waters, and especially the sea, are usually given in the Bible. Behind and above the physical danger there lurks the metaphysical danger of the upper sea held back by the *raqia'*. Hence we cannot accept the explanation of F. Delitzsch and many of the ancient fathers, that the "waters above the firmament" are "the mists and clouds which pass over us; the watery masses which are suspended on the vault of heaven and from which, breaking through the clouds, the rain descends ...." According to v. 14 f., the heavenly luminaries which our author surely perceived to be above and not below the clouds, are obviously fixed on the under side of the celestial firmament, which according to our text bars off these upper waters. And when Calvin, who also identifies the *aquae superiores*[EN172] with clouds, remarks brusquely that the idea of *aquae coelo superiores*[EN173] is *alienum a sensu communi*[EN174], he uses a rationalistic form of argument which is quite out of place in the exposition of Gen. 1[6f.] Luther was more imaginative and stuck exemplarily to the text. "We cannot know what kind of water was above the firmament. Therefore, as I have said, we must give place to the Holy Spirit and say that He knows better than we can understand. God can certainly contain water above the sky. I would construe the water above the firmament as the atmosphere except that this is still under the heaven. So we must admit that we are at a loss and accept the fact that heaven is placed between the waters" (*W.A.* 24, 33f., *Sermon on Genesis*, 1527).

Remarkably enough, this matter became a bone of contention between the Lutherans and the Calvinists, and A. Quenstedt, for instance, devoted to the subject (*Theol. did. pol.*, 1685, I, *cap.* 10, *sect.* 2, *qu.* 8) a full discussion: *An dentur aquae supra firmamentum coeli*[EN175]? On exegetical grounds, and finally also on dogmatical, we can only side with Quenstedt in his positive answer: *Dantur aquae supracoelestes, coelum undique ambientes*[EN176]. (In this *ambientes*[EN177] we can recognise the Ptolemaic understanding which in its improved mediaeval form was still authoritative for the Reformation and the 17th century. According to this view the earth is regarded as a fixed ball located at the centre of the universe and surrounded by a circular heaven which for its part is again surrounded by the *aquae supracoelestes*[EN178] as by an immense watery globe.) *Deus enim veras naturales aquas, subcoelestibus prorsus homogeneas, in primaeva creatione supra coclum, sideribus die quarto exornatum, reposuit, ut S. Scriptura asserit*[EN179]. It is instructive to observe one or two aspects of the proof advanced for this statement. In respect of these upper waters we have to do with something which we cannot know by experience and reason but *ex scriptura sola et quod sint et quid sint intelligimus*[EN180]. Yet they are not *aquae allegoricae vel phantasticae*[EN181] but *aquae vere et proprie sic dictae*[EN182], although their particular purpose is unknown to us. Quenstedt does, of course, mention the possibility that they may serve to cool the heavenly bodies and also to form a massive external buffer between the vault of heaven and violent upthrusts of wind from below. But their *finis ultimus et universalis*[EN183] emerges from Ps. 148[4] and the Song of the Three Children in the fiery furnace (v. 37). Their office is to praise the Lord, and they

[138]

EN172 upper waters
EN173 upper waters in heaven
EN174 alien to common sense
EN175 Whether there are waters above the firmament of heaven
EN176 There are heavenly waters surrounding us on all sides
EN177 surrounding
EN178 heavenly waters
EN179 When God in the original creation arranged the true, natural waters in the sublunar regions, He at the same time set others like them above that heaven that was decorated with stars on the fourth day, as Holy Scripture affirms
EN180 from Scripture alone we understand both that they are and what they are
EN181 allegorical or imaginary waters
EN182 are truly and properly called waters
EN183 final and universal end

are thus an integral part of the universe. *Deus enim et natura nihil faciunt frustra*[EN184]. If their πῶς καὶ διότι[EN185] are hidden from us, we must remember that their on is manifest. The *me'al*[EN186] of v. 7 signifies *supra*[EN187] and the *raqia'* (*firmamentum*[EN188]) the starry sky. Since the clouds are below the sky, the water *supra firmamentum*[EN189] cannot be identical with clouds. To the objection that there is no natural place for water above the sky it may be observed: *Illud naturale est, quod cuique assignavit Deus in prima creatione*[EN190]. The God who can keep the earth within the universe can also in some way keep the waters above. *Quoque modo ibi sint, ibi easdem esse non dubitandum*[EN191]. Both the strength and weakness of 17th century orthodoxy emerge at once and plainly from this presentation. Its strength consists in the fact that (in contradistinction from much earlier and later theology) it could read what is actually written in the Bible, even though this entailed obvious difficulties in view of its other presuppositions. It would keep to historical exegesis even in these difficult cases, accepting the offence involved. And in face of other explanations and objections which did not rest on biblical views, it was bold to assert that this is what is written and that it must be maintained at all costs. Its weakness, however, lay in the fact that—like a modern historicism such as that of Gunkel—it was strangely rigid and inflexible when it ought to have estimated and understood theologically individual data which it had correctly established and maintained exegetically. In the present instance, for example, it failed to advance from the palpably miraculous character of these supra-celestial waters to their open secret. How curious it is that Quenstedt should ignore the diacritical character of the *raqia'* which is so strongly emphasised in the text; that he should rigidly fix his eyes on the *aquae superiores*[EN192] and have no other interest but to maintain their existence attested by the Scriptures ; and that in so doing he should snatch at hypotheses which at best were illuminating only to the natural science of his day, instead of stopping to ask what function is ascribed by Gen. 1 and the rest of the Bible to these waters *supra firmamentum*[EN193] which are separated by the *raqia'* from the terrestrial ocean. It is not enough merely to say that the author of this passage, and the rest of the Old Testament, accepted the view of a celestial ocean. It is not enough merely to say that in so doing, as we now know, he drew on Babylonian myth, which in this respect conforms to that of the Egyptians, Persians, Chinese and other nations. The point is that he knew what he was doing when he did this, for he obviously did it in his own distinctive way. His interest did not lie in the upper waters in themselves and as such as an integral part of the universe. He certainly knows them as such, and he would certainly have agreed with the general explanation of Ps. 148[4] that they too must and may praise the Lord. But in his account of creation they are mentioned, like x with y, only in conjunction with the other waters, from which they are separated by the divinely created firmament. His particular interest in the upper waters is the fact that it is by the firmament that their threat is removed: the threat of a power breaking in from above, i.e., from the sphere of a cosmos equally created by God but invisible and unaccessible to man; a power which would completely destroy the lower cosmos as the dwelling-place of man; a power whose victory—against the Creator-will of God—would change the cosmos into chaos. According to the Old Testament

[139]

[EN184] For God and nature make nothing without a purpose
[EN185] how and why
[EN186] that
[EN187] above
[EN188] firmament
[EN189] above the firmament
[EN190] That is natural which God assigned to each creature in the original creation
[EN191] Even if we do not know how they are there, we must not doubt that they are there
[EN192] upper waters
[EN193] above the firmament

it is the function of the *raqia'* to prevent this evil. And in the Old Testament the *aquae superiores*[EN194] are the sum of this evil. It is self-evident that the author was not thinking of "allegorical or metaphysical water," but of real water, as in the myth and indeed the natural science of his day, which in this respect was that of the 17th century as well. And it is equally self-evident that he regarded the solid *raqia'* as a roof made of an unknown hard material—to the amusement of Gunkel, since, "as we know," the vault of heaven is only an optical illusion. But with its account of the *raqia'* and the waters divided by it, the saga is telling us that the life of man and the existence and survival of his whole known and accessible world is not merely threatened in itself, by the demons of its own natural force (associated in the Old Testament with the terrestrial sea), but that it is also radically threatened by a power of a much higher and more dangerous order, whose triumph would inevitably mean the end of all things, with no possibility of a new beginning as after every natural catastrophe. Knowing of this power, and wanting to speak of it, the saga turns—not this time in rejection but in acceptance and affirmation—to the material presented by the view of myth, or of ancient natural science, and speaks of the upper waters. With all antiquity, it really means a genuine sea, but with this genuine celestial sea it has in mind that "higher power"—in the strictest sense of the term—which indicates the metaphysical danger under which human life is lived. To be precise, however, the saga is not interested in this metaphysical danger as such, but in its repulsion by God's creative Word, and therefore in the fact that man and his lower cosmos are protected and guarded against it. It proclaims the good news that God willed, created and established the *raqia' b'thok ham-mayim*[EN195] in order that there might be no conflux of the upper and nether waters; in order that man and his world should be exposed to both a finite and an infinite threat but not to both at once; in order that in every finite threat—through the waves and billows of the earthly ocean passing over him and seeking to swallow him up—he should find comfort and absolute security in the fact that there is no infinite threat, but that even if the terrestrial sea does actually swallow him for a time, as the whale swallowed Jonah, it must surrender him again, because it is not the mortally dangerous celestial ocean, the latter being restrained by the barrier of the *raqia'*[EN196]. What a pity that 17th century orthodoxy, with its defiant "It is written," does not seem to have found the courage, the time or the desire for considerations such as these, which are demanded by both the context and the detailed wording of Scripture!

In the story of creation everything depends upon the fact that this boundary is set by the Word of God, as in the prior case of light when, as God's creaturely self-attestation, it separated itself from darkness. The firmament, too, is God's witness. It proclaims (Ps. 8³, 19¹ and 102²⁵) "the works of his hands," i.e., by its existence and durability it proclaims its creation by God, and therefore its origin in His wisdom and omnipotence, and therefore His refusal to will chaos and His protest against it, and His decision and capacity to uphold the cosmos. "A firmament hast thou ordained because of thine enemies, that thou mightest still the enemy and the avenger" (Ps. 8²). The apparent superfluity of words in v. 7 is not for nothing if in contrast to vv. 3–5 the intention of God's Word and work, the concrete service of His second work, are to be made plain. God said (v. 6), and in this way it came to pass that "God made the firmament, and divided the waters which were under the firmament from the waters which were above the firmament" (v. 7). It must not be overlooked at this point that the different waters above and below are only in a sense predicates of the one firmament, and above all that the firmament is not an end in itself, as may in some degree be said of light, but has to divide these waters and keep them divided. We are indebted to B. Jacob for an

---

[EN194] upper waters
[EN195] firmament in the midst of the waters
[EN196] firmament

illuminating comment on v. 7. As he points out, it seems as if two things are demanded of the   [140]
raqia' by the creative Word of God: first, that it should come into being, and secondly, that it
should divide. "But the two are really identical. For the function corresponding to the aim
arises simultaneously with its coming into being. The firmament is not formed somewhere
outside and then brought into its place and position; it comes into being at the very point
where it is to function: *b'thok ham-mayim*[EN197]." The expression "And it was so," refers to the
fact that it both is and functions.

According to v. 8, it is this firmament which is called "heaven" by God and therefore
authentically and authoritatively. It makes no odds if we take this to mean the firmament and
(from the standpoint of earth) the whole upper cosmos behind and above the firmament.
The whole upper cosmos, as the great counterpart of that which is below, as a witness and
participant in its history, bears the image and character of the *raqia'*; and it is not for nothing
that the latter (as *pars pro toto*)[EN198] is described as "heaven." As "day" is the name for the
time which God gave to man when He created light, so "heaven" is the name for the space
which God gave to man when He created the firmament. Wherever the name "heaven"
appears we have first to think of this firmament, and therefore of the limitation and assurance given by the construction of this firmament; of the fact that man has the basic possibility of this living-space. It is the fact that heaven is identical with this technical, fundamental
presupposition of all history which makes it so "high" in relation to the earth. It is compared
in Ps. 103^{11} with the mercy of God which is high above those that fear Him, and in Is. 55^9
with the ways and thoughts of God which are high above those of Israel. God's Word is
settled in heaven (Ps. 119^{89}). And according to Ps. 36^5, 57^{10} and 108^5, God's goodness is as
high as heaven. Heaven is therefore unfathomable and inaccessible (Jer. 31^{37} and Is. 40^{12}).
"Who hath ascended into heaven, or descended?" (Prov. 30^4). The attempt of the nations
(Gen. 11^4) to build a tower whose top was to reach heaven is therefore both impertinent and
ridiculous. And it can be said of the ungodly in Job $20^{6f.}$: "Though his excellency mount up
to the heavens, and his head reach unto the clouds, yet he shall perish for ever as his own
dung; they which have seen him shall say, Where is he?"; of Babylon in Jer. 51^{53}: "Though she
should ascend up to heaven, and though she should fortify the heights of her strength, yet
from me shall spoilers come unto her, saith the Lord"; and of Israel in Am. 9^2: "Though they
climb up to heaven, thence will I bring them down." This is just what happened to the
Babylonian usurper, the "son of the morning," who said to himself: "I will ascend into
heaven, I will exalt my throne above the stars of God; I will also sit upon the mount of the
congregation in the sides of the north" (Is. $14^{14f.}$). As we are told in Deut. 1^{28} and 9^2, no
earthly cities are "walled up to heaven," as some of the terrified Israelites feared. The only
ladder whose top reaches heaven is that on which angels ascended and descended (Gen.
28^{12}). It was only the fire of God on the mountain of revelation which "burned with fire unto
the midst of heaven, with darkness, clouds, and thick darkness" (Deut. 4^{11}). And "no man
hath ascended up to heaven, but he that came down from heaven, even the Son of man
which is in heaven" (Jn. 3^{13}). To have His throne in heaven (Pss. 11^4, 103^{19}, Is. 66^1, etc.), or
in the words of the New Testament to be the "Father in heaven," and yet to be "higher than
the heaven" (Job 11^8, Ps. 57^5, 113^4, 148^{13}), is God's prerogative. The publican of Lk. 18^{13}
was quite right when he would not even so much as lift up his eyes to heaven. We see, then,
how the character of the *raqia'* as a boundary opposes all human pride and tumult. "God is
in heaven, and thou upon earth" (Eccl. 5^2). That this is the case; that in so far as He lives in
the cosmos God has in some sense His residence in heaven, so that in later parts of the
Canon He can be called "the God of heaven" (Jon. 1^9, Dan. $2^{18f.}$); that He sees from heaven

---

[EN197] in the midst of the waters
[EN198] the part for the whole

(Ps. 14², 33¹³, etc.); that He hears (1 K. 8³²ᶠ·); that He hears and answers (Ps. 20⁶, Neh. 9²⁷); that He sends help (Ps. 57³); and above all that He speaks, according to many Old and New Testament passages—all this is in any case to be understood with reference to the *raison d'être*[EN199] of heaven as the technically indispensable condition of earthly existence. To live "under heaven," as Deuteronomy and Ecclesiastes like to put it, means originally and properly to live under the conditions fixed by God, and therefore under His protection and lordship, but also His jurisdiction. According to the beautiful passage in Ps. 85¹¹, righteousness looks down from heaven upon the earth; yea, the heavens themselves declare this righteousness (Ps. 50⁶, 97⁶). According to Dan. 12³, the brightness of heaven is also the type and source of all earthly wisdom. But, according to Jer. 4²⁸ and Is. 50³, the heavens can also mourn because of the judgments which God has decreed to execute on the earth. And according to Rom. 1¹⁸ the wrath of God can also be revealed from heaven. From heaven comes the blessing of God (Gen. 49²⁵, Mal. 3¹⁰); the dew (Gen. 27²⁸ᶠ·, Deut. 33²⁸); the rain (Deut. 11¹¹ᶠ·); and with the rain bread (Ex.16⁴, Jn. 6³³). But it can also remain shut (1 K. 8³⁵, etc.). It can be like iron (Lev. 26¹⁹) or brass (Deut. 28²³). The holy fire, the sign of the divine acceptance of man's sacrifice (1 K. 18³⁸, Lev. 9²⁴), but also the consuming and destroying fire of the divine judgment (Gen. 19²⁴, Rev. 13¹³, etc.), may fall from heaven upon the earth. In this way heaven forms in many respects a kind of divine horizon of all life on the earthly cosmos. That it is not rigid as such, but has a door as well as windows, the opening of which means good and not evil (Gen. 28¹⁷); that it can be opened in the sense of a divine revelation (Ezek. 1¹)—is a view which we occasionally find in the Old Testament and frequently in the New. It was from heaven as the divine horizon of earthly life that Jesus came (Jn. 3³¹), returns (Lk. 24⁵¹, etc.), and is finally to come again (1 Thess. 1¹⁰, etc.). Sent by Jesus, the Holy Spirit has also descended upon the Church from heaven (Ac. 2² and 1 Pet. 1¹²). From this standpoint it can be said of heaven that it is open (Jn. 1⁵¹ and Ac. 7⁵⁵). By this is meant that it is opened from the inside outwards, so that between the upper and the nether world, and therefore between God and man—the initiative being wholly from above, from God— there is the possibility and actuality of a direct relationship without the threat which is warded off by the creation of heaven. Thus when heaven was opened in the person of Jesus and for the outpouriug of the Holy Spirit, it was impossible for the *raqia'* to intervene between God and man either to divide or even to estrange. When this particular opening of heaven took place, the metaphysical danger from above was obviously rendered innocuous quite apart from the continuance of the *raqia'*. We can thus understand that even the Old Testament can speak of a moment in which the heavens shall vanish like smoke (Is. 51⁶), or be rolled together as a scroll (Is. 34⁴); and that the New Testament especially speaks of the dispersion (Rev. 20¹¹) and even the dissolution of the heavens (Mt. 5¹⁸, 24²⁹, Rev. 21¹, ², 2 Pet. 3¹⁰). That this carries a message of salvation and not of perdition is possible, in terms of Gen. 1, only on the assumption that in and with this moment the metaphysical danger which exists in the upper cosmos and threatens the lower, but has so far been restrained by the *raqia'*, will be completely removed, i.e., transformed, the upper sea becoming a sea of crystal in a new heaven, and therefore firm and transparent (Rev. 4⁶. 15²). With this transformation the *raqia'* will obviously become superfluous as a barrier and boundary. It can thus be removed without involving the end of all things for the lower cosmos. And it will no longer be a hindrance, as it now is, to the direct vision of God. But everything obviously depends on the fact that it is opened as has actually taken place in the person of Jesus and the work of the Holy Spirit. Everything depends on the fact that this unique opening of heaven means its final removal, its replacement by a new heaven.

[EN199] reason of being

Once the living-space of man has been made possible, its actualisation follows with the creation of the earth (Gen. 1^{9-13}). There is again an exact correspondence to the declaration made at the creation of light, and therefore a [142] separation and the demarcation of a frontier in face of the element of chaos. As heaven was created by the separation of water from water, so the earth is created by its separation from the water under heaven. Again therefore, this time in the form of the terrestrial sea, that which is past is revealed, rejected, displaced and banished, being subordinated to the cosmos and co-ordinated and associated with it. Again, and least of all at this point where it is a question of the life of man, it cannot be the sovereign one and all. It is only in this second separation that we see how full and incontestable is the goodness of the first. Even under the protecting sky there was direct danger from the terrestrial ocean—an immanent threat to that which was basically sheltered by the existence of heaven. Its direct and practical protection had not yet been attained. It was attained with the creation of the earth in the form of a separation of land from sea. In this way the earth becomes for the first time the living-space which it is enabled to be by what has gone before. It has no more made itself this than was the case with heaven. But God acts again by His Word, and He does so by commanding the water of the lower cosmos to retreat and to be gathered in its special place, so that the dry land might be seen as a habitable place on the one side, and the sea in its separation on the other. As this takes place they are both created. As they are land and sea in their separation, they are both creatures of God. It is in this way, and only in this way, that they have a present and a future. It is in this way, and in this way alone, that they correspond to the proclamation made at the creation of the light. And in their relationship there is now repeated that of light and darkness, or day and night, but also of the cosmos protected below and the threatening celestial ocean above. In other words, the firm and habitable land is that which is properly and positively willed and intended by God. But the land has beside it the sea—assigned by the creation of the earth to its own place—as a creaturely sign (this time a near, direct and visible sign) of the existent but averted threat of the reality which by the wrath of God might reign yet by His goodness cannot reign but only threaten, being forced in its own way to praise God and work for the good of those that love Him. This gracious No must be continually heard, and therefore it must be expressed in the creaturely world if God's Yes is to be understood and in the revelation of God there is some day to be in this world a knowledge of the Lord. Its expression in the lower cosmos is guaranteed by the existence of the ocean in its affinity to the divinely rejected and past reality of chaos as a power which, although it exists, does not reign, but is averted and restrained as a threat at the edge of the creaturely world. It was for this purpose that the ocean was created by God. Because the divine covenant of grace is the meaning of this world, and God's free mercy, His superior help and deliverance and emancipation are what He purposes for His creation, the creaturely

[143]   world has to have this periphery. From the standpoint of this periphery, it may be seen how threatened creation is, and how much it has need of mercy, help, deliverance and emancipation. But even more important is the fact that already with creation mercy, help, deliverance and emancipation are promised and assured to a threatened creation by the Creator. This is what is brought out unmistakeably by the creation of the earth and the separation of the land from the sea. But in itself this is not what makes the earth habitable, a place of life. It is that which is dry and fruitful by the Word of God. And because it is dry and fruitful man can live *on* the earth and *of* the earth. Future creation will be the furnishing of this house. But the twofold work of the third day is its construction. On the third day as on the sixth we have to do with two special works which belong together. In both cases we have an end and a new beginning which together constitute a whole. So far the question of life has only been implied, to the extent that the creation of light, the construction of the firmament and the foundation of the dry land have made possible a providential preservation from death. But there is now a new beginning. According to the explanation now given, a creature is alive when through its seed it can continue in the existence of similar creatures, and in addition can bear fruit. This could not be said of light (with darkness), of day (with night), of the firmament (with the waters above and below), of land (with sea). These all have a distinctive glory, but they are not alive. Life commences after these works of separation, and on the basis of the final work. Hence there is an end which belongs to this new beginning. The vegetable kingdom which grows out of the dry land in obedience to the Word of God will not be the only living creature. But it is the first, and the presupposition of all the rest. Every living creature is alive because of that which it has in common with the vegetable kingdom, and it remains alive because it finds its food, its spread table, in the vegetable kingdom. This spread table belongs necessarily to the centre of the house built by God. But this relationship is not seen immediately. The plant is undoubtedly created for its own sake as well. Only in its superabundance will it later serve that purpose. When man finally appears at the centre of all the older circle of creation, and when it is shown in fact that everything must serve him, it must not be overlooked that man is thus revealed to be the most necessitous of all creatures. Will his sovereignty over plants and beasts consist in anything but the fact that he has more to be grateful for than these other earthly creatures, not only for his own existence, but for that of the whole earthly sphere which is the indispensable presupposition of his own? Will he be able to exercise and preserve his sovereignty otherwise than by expressing thanks both in his own name and at the same time in the name of all other earthly creatures? In this way, as the "highest" of the living creatures among which the plants now

[144]   appear as the "lowest," he will really have to be and remain the lowest. It is in this way, and in this way alone, that we can understand the work of the third day as the establishment of a sphere for human life, and especially the creation of the vegetable kingdom as the erection of a table in the midst of this house

which is finally and supremely for man. What is proclaimed in this teleology of creation is not the glory of man but the glory of the God who has turned to him in His mercy. What is prepared is the table of the Lord to which man is invited and admitted. What is prefigured in nature is the covenant of grace— the order in which only the last can be first, but the first must be, and remain, and continually become the very last.

The striking fact that in the account of the third day of creation in Gen. 1$^{9-13}$, as in that of the sixth, there is reference to two divine works, clearly distinguished by the two formulas: "And it was so," and then: "And God saw ... ", has given rise to the conjecture that in the P narrative of creation a formal arrangement into six days of creation is intercrossed by a material which gives us eight (or perhaps even ten) actual works. Gunkel passionately bewails the fact that the latter has been "completely destroyed" by the former, which is designed by the author to establish the sanctity of the Sabbath. If plausible attempts have been made by the methods of critical analysis to arrange the narrative under eight or ten works—and this is not intrinsically impossible—it is to be noted that certain things are "completely destroyed in the process." The first is the very impressive correspondence between the third and sixth days, where in each case the second work ascribed to these days (vegetation on the one hand and man on the other) reveals the transition to a new stage of divine creation. The second is the inner reciprocal connexion between each of the two works of these two days. (How the works of the third day are linked together we have seen already, but we shall do so fully only with those of the sixth day.) Again there is the important relationship of the whole concept of creation here presented to that of time—a relationship which cannot finally be restricted to the demonstration of the divine and therefore the first Sabbath, but is no less significantly revealed as the constitution of the day as a unit of time and the week as its sequence. Finally and supremely, we should destroy the remarkable nuance, emphasised by B. Jacob, that although the author counts the days he does not count the works of God because they are innumerable, and because the sober enumeration in which modern criticism sets before him the suspected original order that he is supposed to have destroyed would probably have seemed to him a minor form of blasphemy. And even if he did have before him an order by works instead of days, however well it might have been selected, it certainly could not have formed the meaningful introduction to the biblical history which the text of our author must be recognised to be. At any rate, the latter had very obvious reasons—and concern for the Sabbath is not the most important—not to follow this other order. And we have not to forget that its existence is in any case only a conjecture, and that it is not supported by any important parallels.

The creation of the earth, according to v. 9, is accomplished in such a way that it becomes visible, i.e., to God, for as yet there are no other agents or spectators, as dry ground, *terra firma*[EN200]; as something different from the waters below, so that according to v. 10 it and the waters can receive their different names from God, and God can actually see it and them in their diversity and separation, and see how good they are. Prior to that the earth had no history. Its history begins with the fact that in consequence of the withdrawal and concentration of the lower waters it is visible to God and therefore to every other eye. This does not   [145] happen because it makes itself visible, revealing itself in some sense as a reality, but because God removes the terrestrial waters which covered it, gathering them and assigning them to their place. This removal, concentration and localisation of water is the proper creative act of vv. 9–10, and again it is accomplished solely by the Word and command of God. *Yiqqawu* like *tera'eh* is in the passive mood and is not therefore to be translated by "they are to gather

---

[EN200] dry ground

themselves" but by "let them be gathered." In the same way the waters are not said to move of themselves but to be moved. It does not say, as B. Jacob maintains, that the divine "wind" (Spirit) of v. 2 was the active element in this process, for if it did it would destroy the uniformity with which our account describes the Word of God as this active element, and its commanding force as the power behind creation. The waters are, then, gathered and removed, i.e., to a place left and ordained for them in the sphere of the earth. That is here the work of the Word of God. There is no question of a complete liberation of the earth from the sea, just as created light was not completely liberated from darkness, or day from night, or the lower cosmos from the danger threatening it from above. This is a matter for the new creation which does not form the commencement but the culmination of earth's history. For the time being the sea, too, has a divinely ordained and allotted place, and therefore in creation the earth receives this limitation, and in this way and to this extent comes at once under the sign of the threat which takes place with this limitation. This is the divine fiat, and what becomes a reality in accordance with this fiat in v. 9. And this is what is confirmed in v. 10 by a further (twofold) name-giving and which, as it exists and continues under the divinely given names, is both seen, and seen to be good. Calvin was rightly interpreting the sense of the passage when he wrote of this process: *Quod in tumulos reducta maria locum hominibus concedunt, hoc est quasi praeter naturam .... Sciamus ergo nos in sicco habit are, quia Deus mandato suo aquas submovit, ne totam terram submergant*[EN201]. Luther expressed himself even more forcefully: "See how easy it would have been for God to drown the world, for it is the nature of water that it should go right round and over it. But by God's Word and command it is kept against its nature, for otherwise it would not be restrained but overflow everything" (*Serm. on Genesis*, 1527, W.A. 24, 38).

To understand the saga we have to realise that what we have here is no less a miracle than the subduing of the celestial ocean. It may be noted that both are mentioned in one breath in the famous exaltation of wisdom in Prov. 8[27f.]: "When he prepared the heavens, I was there: when he set a compass upon the face of the depth: when he established the clouds above: when he strengthened the fountains of the deep: when he gave the sea his decree, that the waters should not pass his commandment: when he appointed the foundations of the earth: then I was by him, as one brought up with him ...." And in Jer. 5[22] there is a presentation of the same process which comes closer to what is in our view its natural content than the description in Gen. 1[9-10]: "Fear ye not me? saith the Lord: will ye not tremble at my presence, who have placed the sand for the bound of the sea by a perpetual decree that it cannot pass it: and though the waves thereof toss themselves, yet can they not prevail; though they roar, yet can they not pass over it?" Even in this understanding it serves no less a purpose than to present the immutability and sovereignty of God. The simple assertion of Ps. 95[5]: "The sea is his, and he made it, and his hands formed the dry land," is sufficient to evoke the enthusiastic call which immediately follows: "O come, let us worship and bow down; let us kneel before the Lord our Maker, for he is our God; and we are the people of his pasture, and the sheep of his hand." But by the very nature of the case the miracle of this process should admit of much more dramatic depiction in this passage. We may refer to Ps. 33[7], where we are told: "He gathereth the waters of the sea together as an heap; he layeth up the depth in storehouses"; or to Ps. 139[9], where the view emerges that the sea forms as it were the outer rim of the whole of the lower cosmos; or to Gen. 7[11], 49[25], Ps. 24[2], 136[6], where the sea surrounds the earth from below so that the latter is "founded upon it"; or, on

[146]

[EN201] That the seas should have drawn back into heaps and left a place for human beings, this is almost contrary to nature ... And so we should acknowledge that we inhabit dry land only because God drained away the waters by His command, so that they should not flood the whole earth

the other hand, to Ps. 90², which speaks of the origin of the mountains; or to a presentation such as that of Ps. 104⁵ᶠ·: "Who layeth the foundation of the earth, that it should not be removed for ever. Thou coverest it with the deep as with a garment: the waters stood above the mountains. At thy rebuke they fled; at the voice of thy thunder they hasted away. They go up by the mountains; they go down by the valleys unto the place which thou hast founded for them. Thou hast set a bound that they may not pass over; that they turn not again to cover the earth"; or to Job 38⁶ᶠ·: "Whereupon are the foundations thereof fastened? or who laid the corner-stone thereof; when the morning stars sang together, and all the sons of God shouted for joy? Or who shut up the sea with doors, when it brake forth, as if it had issued out of the womb? When I made the cloud the garment thereof, and thick darkness a swaddlingband for it, and brake up for it my decreed place, and set bars and doors, and said. Hitherto shalt thou come, but no further: and here shall thy proud waves be stayed?" It is obvious that the latter passages, which are the most detailed parallels to our present text, partially presuppose and express rather different conceptions, this being due to the fact that they obviously depend to some extent on other mythical traditions. Yet the important thing is that these two passages are both decisively interested, like Gen. 1, in the concept of a limit, and that they obviously resort to mythical conceptions because the process of the separation of the earth from the sea, and therefore the constitution of both, is in their view no less, and perhaps even more, a divine miracle than it is to the author of Gen. 1. In both Ps. 104 and Job 38 the true theme which gives occasion for the handling of this matter is wonder at the immeasurable greatness of God. But here as elsewhere the miracle of God to which the biblical witness refers in the language of myth is itself only a sign of God's mystery. While the passage undoubtedly looks upon the real processes and relationships of nature as such, it sees in them, and attests in their presentation, the being and work of the God of Israel, the basic act of the history of salvation which takes place in Israel. The "sea" of which it speaks is, of course, literally and concretely the fluid element in all its earthly fulness, gathered and maintained in its place in relation to the earth, and forming the natural western boundary of Palestine. But as such it is much more. Hence the miracle of its encirclement and limita- tion, great as it is, is not merely an end in itself, but as this concrete miracle it is a sign which points beyond itself. This is inevitable, seeing that the terrestrial ocean is of the same nature as the celestial—a physical repetition and disclosure of the metaphysical danger, a concrete presentation of the endless and nameless threat under which man's life is lived but from which it is now protected. Similarly, "earth" is literally and concretely the *terra firma*ᴱᴺ²⁰² on which, protected from the onslaught of the sea, man may and will have his being. But while it is this, it is much more. The miracle of its existence as such is also a sign, since by nature it is akin to the celestial firmament by which the upper waters are restrained, and therefore, like the latter—but visibly and palpably—it is a presentation of the grace in virtue of which God sustains and protects man for Himself and His purposes for him, and of the patience of God by which man is constantly upheld. If the processes and relationships of nature are to all appearance the primary things considered in this and the other passages, it must be added at once that the primary things which they really have in view are not the billows of the Mediterranean Sea, nor the frequently mentioned "sand" of the Palestinian shore which forms its boundary, but the miraculous passage of Israel through the Red Sea as depicted in Ex. 14 and frequently extolled in later writings (cf. Is. 43⁶ᶠ·, Ps. 106⁹, etc.), and its repetition at Israel's entrance into the land promised to their forefathers. What the account of the creation of land and sea has in view (beyond the general processes and natural events por- trayed) is the fact that at the Red Sea "the Israelites passed through the midst of the sea on dry ground while the waters on their right and on their left stood like a wall," to flow back [147]

ᴱᴺ²⁰² dry ground

and to swallow up their persecutors, and that according to Josh. 3[15f.] (cf. Ps. 114[3, 5]) the same thing happened again at Jordan at the very time when it overflows its banks, the waters which came down from above standing still and rising up "upon an heap very far from the city Adam that is beside Zaretan: and those that came down toward the sea of the plain, even the salt sea, failed." Note should be taken of passages like Ps. 66[6] and 77[17f.], where the description of the general divine order of the relationship between land and water is so interlocked with that of the events at the Red Sea that it is almost impossible to say which is really in view, since the obvious reference is to both.

But the fact that water, and the apotropaic act of God against it, plays this outstanding role in both of the decisive events for the constitution and preservation of the people of Israel leads us to the further point that for a very powerful strand of Old Testament thinking, which we cannot afford to ignore in our exposition of Gen. 1[9–10], it is a representative of all the evil powers which oppose and resist the salvation intended for the people of Israel, thus trying to resist God Himself, but finding themselves unable to do so because God who is also their transcendent Lord Himself fights against them, checking their arrogance and confining them to their place. The suspicion cannot be avoided that in this presentation and equation use was made of the common oriental conception of a struggle between the deity and the chaos-monster represented particularly by the sea. Even the most concrete form of this idea—the picture of the triumphant struggle of the deity with a serpent or dragon—is not altogether alien to the Old Testament. We may refer to Am. 9[3]: "Though they be hid from my sight in the bottom of the sea, thence will I command the serpent, and he shall bite them"; to Is. 27[1]: "In that day the Lord with his sore and great and strong sword shall punish leviathan the piercing serpent, even leviathan that crooked serpent; and he shall slay the dragon that is in the sea"; to Ps. 74[13–14]: "Thou didst divide the sea by thy strength: thou brakest the heads of the dragons in the waters. Thou brakest the heads of leviathan in pieces, and gavest him to be meat to the people inhabiting the wilderness"; to Ps. 89[9–10]: "Thou rulest the raging of the sea: when the waves thereof arise, thou stillest them. Thou hast broken Rahab in pieces, as one that is slain; thou hast scattered thine enemies with thy strong arm"; to the no less aggressive saying in Hab. 3[8]: "Was the Lord displeased against the rivers? was thine anger against the rivers? was thy wrath against the sea, that thou didst ride upon thine horses and thy chariots of salvation?"; to Nah. 1[3], Is. 50[2] and Ps. 18[15], where we are told that the sea was rebuked and dried up; and the similar passage in Ps. 77[16]: "The waters saw thee, O God, the waters saw thee; they were afraid; the depths also were troubled." The acceptance of all these ideas is neither accidental and superficial nor meaningless, neither does their employment signify an excess of poetic license. But while it is all meant and to be understood in a most realistic way, in its realism it is a representation of the dangers which continuously threaten the externally and internally small and impotent people of the covenant in a hostile world, and of the help and salvation granted to them again and again by the power of their God. "The sorrows of death compassed me, and the floods of ungodly men made me afraid" (Ps. 18[4]). "Save me, O God, for the waters are come in unto my soul. I sink in deep mire, where there is no standing: I am come into deep waters, where the floods overflow me" (Ps. 69[1–2]). "Let not the waterflood overflow me, neither let the deep swallow me up, and let not the pit shut her mouth upon me" (Ps. 69[15]). "For thou hadst cast me into the deep, in the midst of the seas; and the floods compassed me about: all thy billows and thy waves passed over me" (Jon. 2[3]). For all its realism the conception is not exhausted by a naturalistic interpretation. We read in Is 8[6–8]: "Forasmuch as this people refuseth the waters of Shiloah that go softly, and rejoice in Rezin and Remaliah's son; now therefore, behold, the Lord bringeth up upon them the waters of the river, strong and many, even the king of Assyria, and all his glory; and he shall come up over all his channels and go over all his banks: and he shall pass through Judah; he shall overflow and go over, he shall reach even to the

[148]

neck; and the stretching out of his wings shall fill the breadth of thy land, O Immanuel." It is the king of Assyria who is this water, and his victorious march through Palestine the coming flood. Is. 17$^{12f.}$ uses the same threat against Assyria: "Woe to the multitude of many people, which make a noise like the noise of the seas; and to the rushing of nations, that make a rushing like the rushing of mighty waters! The nations shall rush like the rushing of many waters." The Babylonian threat against Jerusalem is the same in Jer. 6^{23}: "Their voice roareth like the sea; and they ride upon horses, set in array as men for war against thee, O daughter of Zion." And the prayer of Ps. 144$^{7-8}$ is in the same terms: "Send thine hand from above; rid me, and deliver me out of great waters, from the hand of strange children; whose mouth speaketh vanity and their right hand is a hand of falsehood." So, too, is the invocation of Ps. 65^7: "Which stilleth the noise of the seas, the noise of their waves, and the tumult of the people"; and the grateful cry of the emancipated man of Ps. 124$^{2-5}$: "If it had not been the Lord who was on our side, when men rose up against us, then they had swallowed us up quick, when their wrath was kindled against us: then the waters had overwhelmed us, the stream had gone over our soul: then the proud waters had gone over our soul." According to Is. 57^{20} (cf. Jude 13), the wicked are like the troubled sea which "cannot rest, whose waters cast up mire and dirt." Thus whenever we read of God's lordship and victory over the sea or water, of His help and salvation from its threat, we must see through the appearance to the real point at issue. "When thou passest through the waters, I will be with thee; and through the rivers, they shall not overflow thee" (Is. 43^2). "Thy throne is established of old: thou art from everlasting. The floods have lifted up, O Lord, the floods have lifted up their voice; the floods lift up their waves. The Lord on high is mightier than the noise of many waters, yea, than the mighty waves of the sea" (Ps. 93$^{2-4}$). Or the first strophe of Ps. 46 (vv. 1–4): "God is our refuge and strength, a very present help in trouble. Therefore will not we fear, though the earth be removed, and though the mountains be carried into the midst of the sea; though the waters thereof roar and be troubled, though the mountains shake with swelling thereof. The Lord of hosts is with us; the God of Jacob is our refuge." What is really meant by water and sea and their submission and limitation in all these passages? Are they a mere image? Certainly not: for as an image and representation of this reality—the real course of the divine history of salvation—they fully participate as an image in the actuality of a higher order which is the theme of the history of Israel. Water has a part in all the force of the human world which is hostile to Israel and therefore opposes the interests and glory of Israel's God, but which is nevertheless ruled and guided and used by Him. And the subduing of the waters has a part in God's triumph over this opposition to His decree and its revelation. But in the light of this participation of the image in the reality itself, how can we overlook the thing itself, this actuality of a higher order, this course of the divine history of salvation which expresses itself (in the reality of the sign instituted by God) in the waves of the sea and their limitation? Water, in the form of the sea and its subjugation, has always the character which is decisively given it by those events at the outset of Israel's history.

It is self-evident that in this submission and limitation the roaring of the sea must also have a part in the triumphant song: "The Lord reigneth" (1 Chron. 16^{32}). On the other hand, it is certainly no coincidence that according to the Old Testament the Israelites were not a sea-faring people like the Phœnicians, although the tribes of Zebulun, Asher and Dan had lived by the seashore and in havens for ships (Jud. 5^{17}, Gen. 49^{13}, cf. Deut. 33^{18}). Of an expedition such as that ascribed to Solomon in 1 K. 9$^{28f.}$, we can say only that (like his new and positive attitude to the horse) it is one of the extraordinary and even—we must say—Messianic features of this immediate son of David. We are told in 1 K. 22$^{49f.}$ that a similar venture on the part of Jehoshaphat immediately came to grief. And in view of its starting point and disastrous end, Jonah's voyage is no exception to the rule. The Old Testament ranks a sea voyage (Ps. 107$^{22f.}$) with desert-wandering, captivity and sickness as one of the forms of extreme

[149]

human misery; of the misery from which it is the gracious and mighty will of God, which we cannot extol too highly, to redeem us. It is thus the more noteworthy that the most striking Messianic deeds of Jesus are His walking on the sea in royal freedom, and His commanding the waves and storm to be still by His Word. And when we are finally given in Ac. 27–28 an accurate description, down to the last nautical details, of Paul's stormy but ultimately successful voyage from Caesarea through Crete and Malta to Puteoli, it is certainly not done merely for the sake of historical completeness or out of curiosity, but because the New Testament author, too, knows the sign of the sea and sees in this occurrence an emulation of Solomon, Jehoshophat and Jonah, a confirmation of the hymn of praise of Ps. 107[13f.], and finally, in connexion with the miracles of Jesus Himself on the sea, the fulfilment of all Old Testament prophecy concerning God's lordship over the dangerous sea, and therefore a confirmation of Gen. 1[9–10]. In the new heaven and the new earth, as we learn from Rev. 21[1], there will be no more sea, i.e., man will be fully and finally freed from each and every threat to his salvation, and God from each and every threat to His glory.

The enclosure and limitation of the sea is, however, only the negative side of the miracle and secret of the third day of creation. Where in virtue of the Word of God there can be no presence and power of water or sea, there we have the earth. The secure establishment of the earth by the removal and the gathering of the waters is the positive meaning of this Word of God on the third day. That this work has the character of a conflict lies in the fact that the waters of the upper as well as the lower cosmos constitute the sign of chaos which has been negated by God, i.e., of the cosmic possibility or impossibility which He has rejected. As this sign—and therefore displaced and removed, of lower rank and visibly signifying in their particular creatureliness that from which the Creator seeks to protect His creation—they are the boundary not only of the earth but also of the positive will of God. Their existence demonstrates that the will of God will be fulfilled in a history which takes place in the sphere of His creation, and that what God does with the waters is no more and no less than a preliminary indication, indeed an anticipation of this history in its character as a divine triumph. It is for the sake of this history that the waters exist, but because it will be a triumph they will cease to do so at its culmination. They do not belong to the positive content of the creative will of God, or to the cosmos which is the goal of creation, i.e., of the history purposed and initiated with it. They can only indicate this cosmos by the fact that they are subdued, by their retreat and finally by their complete disappearance. This cosmos consists entirely of heaven and earth. And therefore, seen in its positive sense, the work of the third day is the earth and the earth alone. As Luther and Calvin rightly perceived, the miracle is with reference to the earth, and it is a question of the earth in the mystery of this second horizontal division of the waters. On this side God says Yes while on the other He says No; on this side He founds and establishes and builds while on the other He divides. Gen. 9[13] deals with the ratification and renewal of the covenant between God and the earth. In virtue of this covenant it may be said in Ps. 93[1] and 96[10]: "The world also is stablished, that it cannot be moved"; or in Ps. 75[3]: "The earth and all the inhabitants thereof are dissolved: I bear up the pillars of it"; or again in Eccl. 1[4]: "One generation passeth away, and another cometh: but the earth abideth for ever." Thanks are due to God alone that it is so firmly established (Is. 44[24]). "He hangeth the earth upon nothing" (Job 26[7]). But He does do this, and in so doing He grounds and establishes and preserves it together with and no less than heaven, though in relation to the heaven earth is undoubtedly the lower and weaker and more threatened creation. If heaven is God's throne, the earth is His footstool (Is. 66[1], Mt. 5[35], Ac. 7[49]). And this is a sufficient honour. Its glory is that God sits "upon the circle of the earth so that its inhabitants are like grasshoppers" (Is. 40[22]). In this way the earth and everything in it (Ps. 24[1]) is full of the goodness of the Lord (Ps. 33[5]); full of His praise (Hab. 3[3]). God fills it with His presence as He fills heaven (Jer. 23[24]). What purpose does the earth serve? For what

[150]

purpose has He created and formed and made and established it? The answer is given in Is. 45^{18}: "He created it not in vain, he formed it to be inhabited." And in Is. 42^5: "He that giveth breath unto the people upon it, and spirit to them that walk therein." Also in Ps. 115^{16}: "The heaven, even the heavens, are the Lord's: but the earth hath he given to the children of men." And so in our account (v. 28) it is said that man is to fill the earth and subdue it. Between man—not the beasts, be it noted, but man—and the earth there exists, as we are told in the second creation narrative (Gen. 2^7), the most intimate connexion that man himself was formed by God out of earth, and only as an earthly creature of this kind received the divine breath. And as he has come from the earth, and is himself earth, he must return again to the earth (Gen. 3^{19}, Job 10^9). Conversely—and certainly not without connexion with the earthly character of man—the earth itself bears from the very outset a human character. It belongs *a parte potiori*[EN203] to man. It is inhabited by the human race and appointed for it. It is the home where he lives and dies. It is the place of his joy and sorrow, of his might and impotence, of his sin and worship—but all this in the course of the history with a view to which God has created the whole cosmos, both upper and lower. It is, of course, man who is the addressed and responsible partner in the covenant of Gen. 9^{13}. It is he who is referred to when it says that God speaks with the earth (Deut. 32^1, Ps. 147^{15}); or that God smites the earth with the rod of His mouth (Is. 11^4); or that God's voice will shake the earth (Heb. 12^{26}); or that the earth trembles when God beholds it (Ps. 104^{32}); or that the earth is terrified (Is. 2^{19}, Job 9^6); or that He works salvation in the midst of the earth (Ps. 74^{12}); or that the earth receives blessing from the Lord (Heb. 6^7); or that God is the confidence of all the ends of the earth (Ps. 65^5); or that God arose in judgment to save all the meek of the earth (Ps. 76^9). The reference is to man, and the control and meaning and goal of his history are described, when Jer. 9^{24} says of God that He exercises lovingkindness, judgment and righteousness in the earth, and when Is. 42^{3-4} says that He is the light which does not fail and the staff which does not break until He brings forth judgment unto truth. It is because of the fall and misery of man that especially in the New Testament (and here particularly in the Apocalypse) the term "earth" and ' earthly" acquire the very definite sense not merely of "imperfect" but of "opposed to God"; that Jesus necessarily encounters men as One who according to Jn. 3^{31} and 1 Cor. 15^{47} is not of the earth but from heaven; that Christians (Col. 3^2) are exhorted to seek those things which are above, and not things on the earth; that believers, as we are told in Heb. 11^{13} (and earlier in Ps. 119^{19}), are not citizens but pilgrims and strangers on earth; and that the earth itself (Is. 51^6) shall "wax old like a garment" (corresponding to the dissolution of the heavens). Thus the earth has every reason to fear and tremble before God. But we must not overlook the fact that this discrediting and threatening of the earth is only one element, indeed only a provisional stage, in the biblically attested history of the creature which is the specific meaning of its existence. The earth does not cease to belong to the Lord because it has so "earthly" a mien, and is in fact so "earthly,"and therefore moves with heaven toward a great dissolution. When the earth quakes in the hour of Jesus' death (Mt. 27^{52}), its sin is sealed and revealed, but also removed; its destruction is determined, but also averted. It is still the case—confirmed and revealed by what takes place in the death of Jesus—that the meek are called blessed as those who are to inherit the earth, the real earth (Mt. 5^5). Even the fire which Jesus declared He had come to bring upon the earth (Lk. 12^{49}) means peace on earth according to Lk. 2^{14}. "The earth shall be filled with the knowledge of the glory of the Lord, as the waters cover the sea"(Hab. 2^{14}). In spite of all the "earthly" nature of man and his earth, this and this alone is the will of God which according to Mt. 6^{10}

[151]

[EN203] chiefly

is to be done on earth as it is done in heaven. The history which commences with Abraham, or rather is revealed in Abraham as the history of God with man, as the execution of God's covenant with the earth, cannot be reversed or arrested. Of Abraham (Gen. 12³, etc.) it is said that his name is to become a blessing to all the nations of the earth. And this is the sum of the promises of which God cannot and will not repent (Rom. 11²⁹). When it speaks of the establishment of the earth, the creation saga looks back to these Abrahamic promises. It is for their sake that the whole of the Old Testament is so sure of itself when it knows and says of the waters of the seas that they are allowed to go "thus far and no further." It is for their sake that man in the Old Testament is so sure of his ground in spite of every strangeness, and for their sake that the possession of land—of the land of Palestine as epitomising the whole earth—is so dear to him. It is for their sake that, according to Ex. 20¹², he expects "long life in the land." It is always the land which the Lord his God will give to him. It is this land which the creation saga has in view when it speaks of the dry land separated by God's wisdom and power. And when it speaks of the land of the Israelite it speaks precisely of the whole earth which as such, by the ministry of Israel and in fulfilment of the promise given to Abraham, is to be revealed in its totality as the Lord's possession. Israel will be a blessing (*the* blessing) in the midst of the earth, between Assyria and Egypt (Is. 19²⁴). "If ye will obey my voice indeed, and keep my covenant, then ye shall be a peculiar treasure unto me above all people: for all the earth is mine" (Ex. 19⁵). This is what Pharaoh (Ex. 9²⁹) ought to have learned from the judgments which overtook him, but what he failed to learn. As Israel is the bearer of this promise, there is indeed no nation upon the earth as the people of Israel (2 Sam. 7²³).

And at this point, both in observation and in substance, we have to remember that there are mountains on the earth as a kind of supreme manifestation of earth. It is striking that in many passages these are used to illustrate the fact that the earth does not owe its stability and continuity to itself, and that as the place of man's fall and misery it moves towards the great dissolution which nothing can escape, not even that which is highest and most enduring. "The mountains saw thee, and they trembled" (Hab. 3¹⁰). "The hills melted like wax at the presence of the Lord (Ps. 97⁵)." Every mountain and hill shall be made low, and the crooked shall be made straight, "when the glory of the Lord will be revealed (Is. 40⁴). Mountains may depart and hills may be removed in contrast to the grace of God which shall not depart, or the covenant of peace which shall not be removed (Is. 54¹⁰). There are, of course, other mountains to which this does not apply: "the mountains of God," which like His righteousness endure (Ps. 36⁶); the mountains to which I lift up my eyes as to those from which help comes (Ps. 121¹); the mountains on which God Himself desires to dwell (Ps. 68¹⁶); above all, mount Horeb; or even more explicitly and definitively mount Zion, where God has His dwelling-place (Is. 8¹⁸), where God is King (Is. 24²³, Mic. 4⁷), from which He fights (Is. 31⁴), where salvation is to be found (Joel 3⁵), to which many nations shall flow in the latter day: "And many nations shall go and say, Come ye, and let us go up to the mountain of the Lord, to the house of the God of Jacob; and he will teach us of his ways, and we will walk in his paths: for out of Zion shall go forth the law, and the word of the Lord from Jerusalem" (Is. 2³), and on which the Lamb will finally stand, "and with him an 144,000, having his Father's name written in their foreheads" (Rev. 14¹). Of a removal of these mountains, of this mountain, there can, of course, be no question. These mountains of God are not only on the earth; they are themselves, and particularly mount Zion, the earth in its assured stability as envisaged in Gen. 1⁹ᶠ, the place where God's honour dwells, and where man can and will therefore dwell. And as mount Zion is for its part the Abrahamic promise given to Israel, we can differentiate here too between the sign and the reality, but we must not separate them.

And now, in the middle of the third day of creation, we are told for the second time (v. 10b) that God saw how good His work was. The expression has reference not only to vv. 9 and 10 but also to vv. 6 and 8, for it is obvious that there is for the author an inner connexion between these events. God sees the two accomplished acts, and the two divisions. And He sees that these divisions, and in virtue of these divisions the things divided, are in both cases good, i.e., that they correspond to His will and purpose and Word. God acknowledges this work of His—even the waters above and below as the sign of what He does not will—as in v. 3 He acknowledges the light created by Him. No complaint or grievance which might arise in the sphere of the cosmos can be levelled against Him, and no final or absolute fear can continue in face of these signs.

But this inner connexion of the two great divisions does not mean that they are bound together as the work of a single day. It would have been simple to present the matter in this way. The saga sees it in a different light. The third day is the day of the earth as a dwelling-place and sphere of life; the day of that which is indispensable, of that which is required of the earth, in fulfilment of its destiny. For this reason the separation of land from sea in the lower cosmos belongs to the work of the third day, and the creation of the vegetable king-dom belongs also to the work of this day. The termination of the work of the sixth day, and therefore the culmination of the whole, will be the creation of man after that of the land animals. And it is to man and the land animals, and with them to the whole animal kingdom, that according to v. 29 God has given vegetation for food. The question at stake in the second half of the third day is this presupposition, and with it the material foundation of the history of which the earth is destined to be the theatre. Only where there is life can there be history. But life presupposes life. Vv. 11–13 deal with this life which must be presupposed for the life of man and beast. They say that this life too—the plants and trees by which man and beast are to be fed—is created by the Word of God. God provided for this need before it existed. The fact that creation takes place in this order at once removes any cause for human care. Man has no need to look round anxiously with the question: "What shall we eat? or, What shall we drink? or, Wherewithal shall we be clothed?" (Mt. 6[31]), for before he can ask, before he is there at all, everything is already to hand. God provided for him before He created him. It is to be observed, of course, that according to v. 29 man will not be in a position to meet his requirements of himself. It is a special gift from God that this provision is made for him. "These all wait upon thee; that thou mayest give them their meat in due season. That thou givest them they gather: thou openest thine hand, they are filled with good" (Ps. 104[27f.]). Since creation takes place in this sequence, any proud or arrogant usurp-ation on the part of man is rendered impossible at the very root. The plants and trees were there without him and before him. They also had and have their own dignity and justifi-cation. Only at a later stage did man appear to enjoy their superfluity by the will and Word of God. Only in this way were they placed at his disposal. Thus man lives from the very first by God's grace as he lives from this table prepared for him prior to his creation. Every morsel of which he partakes is not only a sign of grace but the grace itself without which he cannot and would not live.   [153]

The question how the vegetable kingdom could exist without the primary condition of sunlight is as little discerning as the similar question with reference to light in v. 3. It is obvious, as Basil has rightly perceived (*Hex.* V, 1), that, with or without a knowledge of the relevant physical laws, the author is maintaining this against every solar cult, and especially the Egyptian: *Antequam solis fiat luminare, herba nascantur: antiquior sit civs praerogativa, quam solis. Ne error hontinum convalescat, germinet prius terra, quam fotus solis accipiat. Sciani omnes, sotem auctorem non esse nascenliunt. Dei dementia terras relaxat; Dei indulgentia praerumpere facit fructus*[EN204]. (Ambrose, *Hex.* 6, 27). Like man the usufructuary, the sun which is the condition of all earthly vegetation appears on the scene only after its creation, *ut discamus, Deum per creaturas agere, non tamquam alienae opis indigum, sed quia sic illi placeat*[EN205]. (Calvin). God Himself, and God alone, is the Creator both of light and life, and God alone is the point of contact between the two. This makes it perfectly clear that the commandment addressed to the earth in v. 11: "Let the earth bring forth grass, the herb yielding seed, and the fruit tree yielding fruit after his kind, whose seed is in itself upon the earth," is not addressed to any inherent capacity of the earth as such. What is the origin of growth and fertility, or life as its presupposition, in a place which was previously dry ground and barren earth? There is only one explanation: *Quia semel loculus est Deus, hoc est, aeternum suum decretum protulit: terra autem et quae ex ea proveniunt, Dei mandato, quod semper exaudiunt, praebent obsequium*[EN206]. (Calvin). The fact is that the earth now becomes and is an active subject, bringing forth plants and trees as commanded. But it does not do this in its own creative power, nor as an agent side by side with the divine Word and work, but because it was made worthy to hear God's fiat, and receiving it as such was enabled to do what it certainly could not have done of and by itself. It may well be said that we have here an archetype of the capacity for obedience (*potentia oboedentialis*) on the part of the creature as the Bible understands it. In genuine *potentia*[EN207] there is genuine *oboedire*[EN208], which corresponds to the *audire*[EN209] granted to the creature, and takes place wholly and utterly in virtue of what is said to the creature. *Deshe*, vegetation, is now the epitome of all that the earth was to bring forth (v. 11), and did bring forth (v. 12), in this capacity for obedience and act of obedience. We may note the difference both in activity and results as compared with vv. 3, 6 and 9. Light has only to become and be what it is. The firmament has only to divide. The waters have only to gather. The results of the activity of the action of these creatures do not extend beyond themselves to the existence of other creatures. But the earth—and this is the turning point in the second half of the third day of creation—"yields herbs"; its activity does not consist in the bare fact that it is; it has a transitive character. It produces things that are different from itself; things that are now new and different "on the earth." Corresponding to the special Word of God, corresponding to earth's special obedience, we have that which is new and different—vegetation, or literally fresh vegetation. But this means that what was produced by the Word of God is itself something that produces. As the dead earth becomes green in the power of God's Word it produces life. For the common feature of this new production—of plants and trees—is to bear seed: either plain seed, as in the case of plants; or fruits which carry seed, as in the case of trees—and each "after his kind," i.e., individually, but in definite species. This is life, the living creature, itself produced by God and, without being untrue to its nature, able to reproduce itself in the form of seed, which without being untrue to itself can again be productive. It is a creature which can reproduce itself in new forms, but still be itself in each reproduction, in each individual example: "a stamped form which is alive and develops"

[EN204] Before the sun was made to shine, the plants were brought into being: its privilege is older than the sun's. Lest human error should gain strength, the earth sprouted before it received the sun's warmth. Let everyone know that the sun is not the source of living things. The mercy of God opens the earth; the favour of God makes its fruits burst forth

[EN205] that we might learn that God acts through creatures, not because He has need of another's help, but because it pleases Him to do so

[EN206] Because as soon as God has said, 'This is to be,' He has put forth His eternal decree: and the earth and what comes forth from it show their compliance to God's command, which they always obey

[EN207] capacity

[EN208] obedience

[EN209] hearing

(Goethe). "Fresh vegetation" is the first and typical form of this creature, and one which is indispensable for all that follow. Beasts and men will also be creatures which bear seed and are therefore alive, and what is here called "fresh vegetation" will serve to sustain their life. The second miracle of the third day of creation consists in the fact that, although the earth itself is not a living creature (and does not become this even when it becomes green at the command of God and in the power of this command), it brings forth this "fresh vegetation." And this miracle ratifies and explains the first to the extent that the vegetation shows why it was that the dry land had to appear with the gathering of the waters to one place—not in order that it should be dry, but that this other might appear "on earth," the living creature. By the fact that there is life on earth through the Word of God, this day—the third day of creation (v. 13)—is not merely given the formal promise that it will be followed by a morning, but also a filled and meaningful future. But its new and future day is the day of ripening and harvest: the day on which the product of the earth, the living creature, will itself "bring forth," when the plants will bear seed and the trees their seed-bearing fruits; the day which in its fulness can also look forward to another day, to a fresh harvest, and to an unlimited series of days and harvests. *Prima enim illa vox Dei singulis creaturis impertita gignendis, lex naturae est, quae terris in omne aevutn remansit, futurae successionis datum praescriptutn. quemadmodum vel generandi vel fructificandi in reliquum usum adolesceret*[EN210]. (Ambrose, *Hex.* III, 6, 26). The creation of plants and trees—and we could not say this of the earlier creations—involves the beginning of natural history, which is both a precursory type and also a substratum of the history of the covenant of grace. As the earth is here commanded to be green, so on the sixth day (and again in the second half of the work, v. 28) the man who is created in the image of God will be charged to "be fruitful, and to multiply, and replenish the earth, and subdue it." What the first command signifies and intends, what is already prefigured by it, emerges in this commission which constitutes the Messiah the beginning and the goal of human history. Thus natural history begins in vv. 11–12 as a type determined by this future prototype.

The passage emphasises that natural history commenced along two lines. The green things which now form "on earth" the future of the earth consist of plants and trees. Gunkel can put in a word of praise at this point: "Considered as a rudimentary attempt at botany, this classification is not bad." But this classification is definitely not to be regarded botanically. Its significance is brought out clearly by v. 29 f., where we see that the reference is to the animals and men who are to find their food, the former in plants and grasses, the latter in-fruits and vegetables. We are reminded of the story of Nebuchadnezzar (Dan. 4), whose glory is first compared to a tall and strong tree in the midst of the earth (v. 7 f.) and reaching unto heaven, and whose deep humiliation is then compared to this tree as it is cut down to the stump of the roots (v. 14). His deep humiliation consists in the fact that at the very moment when he tries to boast of this great Babylon which he has built by the might of his power and for the honour of his majesty, his human heart is taken from him and he is given the heart of a beast (v. 13), and "he was driven from men, and did eat grass as oxen, and his body was wet with the dew of heaven, till his hairs were grown like eagles' feathers, and his nails like birds' claws" (v. 33). What we have here is no less than an abrogation or reversal of the classification of Gen. 1$^{11-12}$. What is announced in the divinely willed and created form of the vegetation ordained to be the food of man and beast is the dignity of man—which only human pride can seriously jeopardise—as compared with the rank of the animal realm which he has to rule but not to imitate. The destiny of grass and plants is to produce seed

[EN210] For that primeval voice of God which summoned all creatures individually into being is nature's law, which has remained on the earth through every age, the given form of future succession, with respect to how creatures should multiply in the future, whether by procreation or bearing seed and then to wither and to be cut down and burned, or in some way to perish. In this respect they resemble the beasts. If all flesh and the people is as grass; if it has to be said of man: "The grass withereth, the flower fadeth" (Is. 40[7]), this presupposes a terrible perversion and cor-

[155] ruption. It can and should be quite otherwise. The righteous man is compared to "a tree planted by the rivers of water, that bringeth forth his fruit in his season; his leaf also shall not wither" (Ps. 1[3], cf. Jer. 17[8]). Again, "the righteous shall flourish like the palm tree: he shall grow like a cedar in Lebanon. Those that be planted in the house of the Lord shall flourish in the courts of our God. They shall still bring forth fruit in old old age; they shall be fat and flourishing; to shew that the Lord is upright: he is my rock, and there is no unrighteousness in Him" (Ps. 92[12]). The destiny of a tree is to stand upright, to bear fruit, and to endure. And in affinity to it, man is ordained to bear fruit like a good tree (Mt. 7[17]). That is why wisdom is called (Prov. 3[18]) "a tree of life to them that lay hold upon her." That is why it can sometimes be said generally: "Let the field be joyful, and all that is therein" (Ps. 96[12])—for to this sphere there usually belong the trees which are summoned (Is. 44[23], Ps. 148[8], 1 Chron. 16[33]) to join in creation's universal praise of God, and once even (Is. 55[12]) to "clap their hands." It is another matter that—particularly because of its height—a tree can become unfruitful, like Pharaoh (Ezek. 31[3]), or Nebuchadnezzar (Dan. 4), or the fig tree (Mt. 21[19]), and that it will then wither (Joel 1[12]) and perhaps fall a victim to the fire (Ezek. 21[3]) or the axe (Mt. 3[16]). But even this only serves indirectly to confirm the more exalted nature of this creature. Grass and plants are not capable of guilt and humiliation like a tree. Thus, while the classification is botanical in form, its true significance is typical, like everything else in the account. We do not have here the same kind of division as in the first half of this day, but there is an emphatic distinction of which it must perhaps be said that, like a punctuated line, it does in a sense continue that division.

At any rate, there can be no doubt that the future history of Israel is distinctively prefigured in it. This is true irrespective of the classification. It must not be forgotten that the green earth as such is to Old Testament man as much an antithesis of the destroying sea as of the barren desert. The transition from vv. 9–10 to vv. 11–12 is the passage of a danger point which is not without an inner relationship to Israel's march through the desert. When the dry ground is freed from the sea, will it be only dry ground? This would be like a man escaping one monster and falling into the clutches of another. The desert is a "terrible land." Is. 21[1f.] shows what is to be expected there. The miseries of desert wandering may be gathered from Ps. 107[1f.] According to their frequent and intrinsically not unjustifiable complaint (Ex. 14[11], Num. 14[12], 16[13]), the Israelites thought that they would perish in the desert. That the fair land of Palestine, with its fields and cities, should again become a desert is one of the most impressive threats uttered by the prophets in Is. 24[1] and many other passages. On the other hand, their most impressive promise is of a time when "the voice of joy and the voice of gladness, the voice of the bridegroom, and the voice of the bride" will be in what is now a wilderness, and there will be pastures for shepherds causing their flocks to lie down (Jer. 33[11f.]). "Be not afraid, ye beasts of the field: for the pastures of the wilderness do spring" (Joel 2[22]). "The wilderness and the solitary place shall be glad for them; and the desert shall rejoice, and blossom as the rose. It shall blossom abundantly, and rejoice even with joy and singing; the glory of Lebanon shall be given unto it, the excellency of Carmel and Sharon, they shall see the glory of the Lord, and the excellency of our God" (Is. 35[1-2]). "I will plant in the wilderness the cedar, the shittah tree, and the myrtle, and the oil tree; I will set in the desert the fir tree, and the pine, and the box tree together: that they shall see, and know, and consider, and understand together, that the hand of the Lord hath done this, and the Holy One of Israel hath created it" (Is. 41[19-20]). It was in the wilderness that God found Israel (Hos. 9[10], Deut. 32[10]) and adopted it (Hos. 13[5]), never to leave it again (Neh. 9[19]), but to lead it (Deut. 8[2]) and in spite of its unbelief to furnish a table for it (Ps. 78[19]). This is what

makes the wilderness for Israel a passage and a transition, signifying the removal of the   [156]
danger which the dry land might have had for it. And this is the historical view which as an
antitype has in the creation account of Gen. 1$^{11-12}$ its prototype. We have to realise this when
the second half of the third day's work (v. 13) closes with the divine pronouncement that it
was good. Good is the earthly life which has its beginning; good is the earth which is the
scene of this life; good is the twofold form of life in which further living creatures are envisaged; good is God's presence in the wilderness, and His deliverance from the wilderness,
and His transformation of the wilderness into a garden. It is all good because, with the
separation of land from water, it all prepares and prefigures the history which is to take place
on earth, and because as this preparation and prefiguration it corresponds to the will and
Word of God.

(Gen. 1$^{14-19}$.) With the work of the fourth day there begins the furnishing of
the cosmos. The question now is not of its persistence but its wealth—which it
owes to the will and Word of God. Even man, whose relationship is increasingly
revealed as the ultimate goal, belongs to this sequence. Coming after the sun
and moon and stars, after the fowls of the air and the fishes of the sea, he is,
with the beasts of the earth, the last drop of the overflowing glory of God in
creation, the last miracle of His wisdom and goodness. The first in this
sequence are the sun and moon and stars. We have here an obvious correspondence to the work of the first day and there can clearly be no question of
competition. Light was there prior to the luminaries. The luminaries are the
centres, or bearers, or mediators of light for creaturely eyes. It does not follow
of itself that light, the firstborn of all God's creatures, is recognisable as well as
existent. It does not follow of itself that for the creature as well as for God day is
distinguishable as day and night as night, with all the alternation and progress
of time. It does not follow of itself that the creature which has time knows
about time. That this may be possible is the work of the fourth day with its
creation of bodies to carry and mediate light. They are not themselves light,
but they participate in light. This makes it clear that a new order of creation
has commenced. The creation of light, of the heavenly firmament to which
they are assigned and of the earth for which they shine, is the indispensable
presupposition of these lights. Though they are above, they belong to the
lower and visible cosmos. They are in fact the practical principle of its differentiation from the upper cosmos, and its visibility. They show to the creature
(which is not the Creator) that it is not heavenly but earthly, but that even
though it is earthly it is created in the sign of light and that it possesses time,
namely, the divinely created time of light. In this way they mediate the objective message of the will of God—light, the first of all God's creatures—to these
other creatures, and finally and supremely to man, for whom this message is
not only to be present in force but who is to hear and obey it, who is not only to
possess time but who is to have knowledge of it and to fill it. This and nothing
else is the status, role and significance of the heavenly bodies in the cosmos.   [157]
For this function they exist and are indispensable. God has as little need of
them as He has of any other creature. There can be no question of regarding
them as divine or ascribing to them God-like power. Even divinely created light

as such does not need them: it would be light and would shine even if they did not exist. Even heaven or earth, and, as the saga sees it, the vegetable kingdom, do not need them. All these would be there and would exist in light—the immediate light of the first day of creation—without this mediation. But there is another—shall we say higher or shall we say lower?—creature, stronger than these because it can live in the light with open eyes, but weaker because it can live with open eyes only in mediated but not in unmediated light. It is this stronger and weaker creature, the beast, and finally and supremely man, which needs the heavenly bodies and their mediation of light. This is not in order that light may shine for man, but in order that by his senses and reason he may participate in it, and himself become light. For this purpose light has to shine for him through heavenly bodies, and therefore in a concrete form and in concrete distinction from darkness. There could be time, there could be natural history and human history, even without these luminaries. But without them there could not be the time and history in which man, surrounded by the animal kingdom, can play a conscious and active part as a partner of the Creator. It is for this that light must enlighten him; for this that he must be able to have awareness of it; for this that he must be put in a position to know time as the time of light. If man in the midst of the animal kingdom can become an interested partner of the Creator, he owes it to the work of the fourth day of creation. To that extent there commences here the sequence of relatively if not absolutely indispensable works of creation. The preceding works all aimed generally at man, or rather at God's relationship with man. But from this point onwards everything aims particularly at man's interested partnership in his relationship with God. The wisdom and goodness of the Creator abound in the fact that, following the creation, establishment and securing of a sphere of human life, He wills to fashion and does fashion it as a dwelling-place for the man who can recognise God and himself and his fellow-creatures, and who in the recognition of what is and occurs can be grateful and express his gratitude. He would be blinded without the lights which according to his strength and weakness permit him to recognise this; and this would leave him blind in the midst of light, timeless in the midst of time, and without history in the midst of history's course. The office of these lights, the heavenly bodies, is to summon him in relation to his Maker to sight, consciousness and activity. If he lived in a world which lacked this presupposition, he could not have been created in the image of God nor called to be a partner in the divine covenant of grace. In [158] creation this cannot be more than a presupposition. The heavenly bodies cannot be more than servants. Not the sun, moon or stars, but God Himself creates man in His own image. Not they, but God alone grants him this interesting partnership, gives him sight, consciousness and activity in his relation to Himself, and makes him a real participant in His covenant. They serve the purpose of orientation. They show how a day is formed out of evening and morning, i.e., how after every divine Word and work, which as such takes place in light, darkness may appear under the name of night as a threatening but already circumscribed reminder of God's rejected No; how with the dawn of a new morning, and therefore a new divine Word and work, it has limits which it dare not overstep; how it cannot exist and rule except as a frontier of light. They give man and the animal kingdom around him indications both for the necessary course and also for the free formation of their life. They offer them guidance in time and space. They show them the boundaries within which the natural life proceeds and according to which man for his part can order his life and direct his undertakings. They make it possible for him to see his history as history, to take up a position in relation to it, and therefore to be not merely its object but its subject, albeit a creaturely and earthly subject. In this way they give light to the lower cosmos. In this way they make possible the determination of man within the cosmos. They cannot see to it that he actually has this determination and is summoned to the fulfilment of it. Here, too, creation and covenant are two different things. But by creating these heavenly bodies God sees to it that man can possess this determination. It is an idle question whether this presupposition might be lacking. God and man would not be what they are if the covenant lacked or could lack this presupposition in creation. Because God is the merciful Lord, because man is the covenant-partner who shares but also needs this divine mercy, and because God is at the same time the Creator of this man, it belongs to creation that man should be given this objective direction to distinguish for his part that which God distinguishes and wills should be distinguished. That is why man's cosmos should not merely be orientated by God but orientating for man. According to our passage, it becomes and is this with the creation of the constellations. We abstract from the reality of the covenant of grace if we suspect extravagance at this point in the abundance of creation. The biblical witness has not incurred the guilt of this abstraction.

The work of the fourth day too (vv. 14–19) shows the familiar correspondence between the fiat (vv. 14, 15) and the execution (vv. 16–19). Again, it is to be observed that the "And God said" with which the fiat and the "And God made" with which the execution are introduced do not signify two different actions, but that God's fiat is His distinctive creation. It is to be noted, however, that the differentiation between the heavenly bodies (the great light, the lesser light and the stars) is not mentioned until the description of the execution of the work in v. 16. And it is particularly to be noted that in this case—and from now on right up to the sixth day, not excluding the creation of man—there is no divine naming of what is created. In this respect there is an obvious demarcation of these three works from the first three. We read in Ps. 147[4] that God "telleth the number of the stars; he calleth them all by their names." But to give them their names is a matter for man. Hence the terms "sun" and "moon" and the names of stars do not occur in this passage. Already the heavenly bodies belong to the sphere which is particularly created as the sphere of human knowledge and power.

It is to be noted further that for this reason they belong to the sphere of "living" creatures, those which have a "soul" in the Old Testament sense of the word. Gunkel's verdict that "the constellations are only things" can hardly be accepted in this unequivocal sense, nor can his extolling of the passage on the ground that it prepared the way for modern natural philosophy by despiritualising the universe. Can we overlook the fact that the constellations

[159]

appear in close conjunction with plants, birds, fish, land-animals and man? Are we merely to understand symbolically the function of "ruling" ascribed to them in vv. 16 and 18, or the reference to a heavenly "host" in 2¹? And when we come across the common Old Testament terms "the Lord of hosts," and "the hosts of the Lord," can we fail to think of the constellations? Did Joshua (10¹²) merely address a "thing" when he commanded the sun to stand still? Are the sun and moon and stars understood as "things" in Joseph's dream (Gen. 37⁹)? Is the sun a "thing" in Ps. 19⁵ ("as a bridegroom coming out of his chamber, and rejoicing as a strong man to run a race")? What is meant in Jud. 5²⁰ when it says that the stars fought against Sisera? Or how are we to understand Is. 24²¹ᶠ·: "And it shall come to pass in that day, that the Lord shall punish the host of the high ones that are on high, and the kings of the earth upon the earth. And they shall be gathered together, as prisoners are gathered in the pit, and shall be shut up in the prison, and after many days shall they be visited. Then the moon shall be confounded, and the sun ashamed ...." That the heavenly bodies do not live in the sense in which plants, animals and men live is of course decided by the fact that their place is the firmament of heaven and not earth. But again, it does not appear to be excluded that the Old Testament, although it does not over-emphasise the fact or draw dangerous inferences, does ascribe to them a kind of personal being and activity. Of course, the other ancient oriental religions obviously did this too, and it cannot be regarded as improbable that the Old Testament has appropriated this traditional material and set it to its own use, especially in the creation narrative.

The distinction between ordinary Eastern myth and the biblical saga is in respect of the divinity of the heavenly bodies rather than their personality. This emerges at once in the fact that the heavenly bodies are obviously given a subordinate place and role even within the creaturely world. They are not just lights but *meʾoroth*, φωστῆρες, light-bearers, candlesticks, lamps. And they are lights *birʿqiaʾ hash-shamayim*, i.e., they exist on this, the earthward side of the celestial firmament, and are presumably attached in some way to it. They thus belong to the cosmos, namely, the lower cosmos. No matter how great their glory, it is less than that of the celestial firmament to which they are so manifestly subordinated; and very much less than that of light in which they can only participate; less, too, than that of the earth and its inhabitants, with a view to which they were created. How then can divinity be ascribed to them? B. Jacob is not exaggerating when he says that what happens to the heavenly bodies in Gen. 1 as compared with their position in oriental myth amounts to a degradation. This appears very plainly in the unmistakeable stress laid in Gen. 1 upon their purposiveness. It is to be observed that with the exception of the very last creation—that of man himself—this does not occur in any other creation in so blatant a way as it does at this point where it gives [160] great offence not merely to our modern conceptions but also to those of antiquity. The modern view of the sidereal world, with its reckoning in terms of millions of sun systems and thousands of light-years, and the ancient view which found instead very powerful ruling deities, are comparable in the sense that they both seem to exclude, with a kind of magical respect, the question of any purpose in this cosmic system, and especially of its relationship to the earth and its inhabitants, i.e., the view that man is the purpose of this world. But the present passage says nothing concerning the sidereal world which is not relative to its purpose for the earth, and properly and finally for man. In the last analysis the nature of the heavenly bodies may be stated in terms of their purpose. Shining from the celestial firmament upon earth, in their diversity and alternation they have to divide day from night and light from darkness. They are given to be signs, to indicate time, to mark off days and years, and therefore to rule day and night. God institutes them for this purpose. He thus makes them His servants, officials or functionaries, although only indirectly for His own service, and directly (according to this whole teleology) for the service of the earth and its inhabitants, and particularly for the inhabitant of the earth who is able to observe and to receive these signs not only in fact but freely and in full understanding, not only unconsciously but consciously. In this way the heavenly bodies are no longer deities and lords to whom man owes and shows respect, worship and service, nor, according to modern interpretation, representatives of the infinite universe which absolutely determines man. On the contrary, they are helps given by God to man. Gunkel is right: "Faith in *Yahweh* has triumphed over the worship of heavenly bodies." But do we realise what this means? A more radical *volte-face*[EN211] cannot be imagined. The author accomplished this in the framework of a pre-Copernican conception of the world. But even the Copernican discovery only means a readjustment within the view which is here questioned not only in its pre-Copernican but also in its Copernican form. What is it that this passage dares to maintain? And what are the implications if what it says is true? The question is raised as early as Ps. 8[3f.]: "When I consider thy heavens, the work of thy fingers, the moon and the stars which thou hast ordained; what is man, that thou art mindful of him? and the son of man, that thou visitest him? For thou hast made him a little lower than the angels, and hast crowned him with glory and honour." We cannot easily attain a sufficient loftiness or depth in our understanding and interpretation of the author's view of man expressed in v. 26 f., if it is to correspond to the *volte-face*[EN212] accomplished at this point in favour of man, and if we are not to dismiss this passage (in its opposition to modern no less than ancient views of the matter) as so much anthropocentric nonsense.

Yet the degradation of the heavenly bodies, and with it the polemic against a myth which is not restricted to its ancient form, is only a side issue in the present passage. In its development of this teleology its primary and decisive message is positive. It gives to the heavenly bodies the honour which is their proper due because it ascribes to them this purpose which is so alien from both ancient and modern standpoints. What would the cosmos lack without the heavenly bodies? What does it receive when the heavenly bodies are created on the fourth day? These are the questions which the passage answers. It tells us first that when God commands them to be, and they are made by His Word and come into existence, they assume the function of separation. Hence the recurrence of the verb *badal*[EN213] which was used of God in v. 4 and of the firmament in vv. 6, 7. Now it is the lights that are to separate day from night (v. 14), and in accordance with these names light from darkness (v. 18). This is surprising, for according to v. 4 this separation has already taken place once and for all. By it God revealed His will and set it in opposition to that which He did not will, creating the first day and dividing it from the night. If the same is to take place again and again through the service and work of the heavenly bodies, it is clear that it can be rendered by the heavenly bodies only in imitation of the divine example. They cannot do this on their own initiative, for God has already done it, so that they can only follow Him. Nor can there be any repetition of the divine work. It does not need to be and cannot be repeated, for it was done perfectly once and for all. There can only be an imitation of the divine work in the creation of light. But what is the purpose of this imitation and representation, of this secondary separation of light from darkness, of day from night, which is to be rendered by the heavenly bodies, and for the accomplishment of which they were created? In this respect a second point emerges. In the form of this imitation and representation, there is to be given to someone a sign of what God did on the first day. Someone for whom the constellations shine as an imitation and representation of the divine work is to be instructed by this work, i.e., by the introduction of the service and work of the stars: someone whom God holds worthy not only to be in the cosmos first established by the separation of light from darkness, but also to

[161]

[EN211] about face
[EN212] about face
[EN213] to separate

know about this separation with the God who has spoken this separating and creative Word; someone who is to exist with God in this consciousness (συνείδησις, conscientia); but someone who cannot of himself raise himself to this consciousness; someone who is not like God, and therefore unable to know about this separation, and therefore about the victory of God's will over that which He does not will, in the same way as God Himself does according to His Word; someone who cannot immediately recognise the light as light, or day as day, or time as time; someone who, because he is himself a creature, must be helped by the service of creatures if he is to be enlightened by light, the first of all created things, and if day is to dawn for him too, and he too is to have time. It is this someone who is in view when there is this imitation and representation of the creation of light in the creation of the heavenly bodies. It looks forward to this someone for whom the heavenly bodies will be signs, and by whom these signs will be seen and recognised and understood as signs that day is day and night night, that light is light and darkness darkness. It is the endowment of the cosmos with an objective criterion which will stand continually before the eyes of this someone and from the existence of which he will be able to read continually that he finds himself in a world created by God, and therefore in a world in which light is separated from darkness, in which there are genuine days and genuine time, and in which his own destiny is to experience genuine history. The existence of this someone who is so linked to God and yet so unlike Him is not, of course, the work of the fourth day. All that we can and must say is that this points to him. Nor, indeed, does the work of the fourth day decide whether this someone will be able for his part to see and understand and accept this sign; whether the language of the heavenly bodies will be intelligible to him; or whether his capacity will be matched by the event in which God actually allies Himself with him in such a way that he knows as God does; that he really understands what he is capable of understanding and accepts what he is capable of accepting; that he is really accepted and enters into the relationship to the creation of light as is made possible for him through its imitation and representation by the heavenly bodies created by God. Neither the capacity nor the event is a work of the heavenly bodies.

Shining partly by day and partly by night, they divide day from night for man, i.e., as a presupposition of his recognition of day and night, of his participation in the history ordained for him by God. It is to be noted at this point—and this is not an accident—that not only is day characterised by its light, the great light of the sun, but night is also characterised by lights, the lesser light of the moon and those of the stars. There is thus no special sign for night and therefore for darkness as such. If darkness were a special, positive work of God, how could it fail to have a special sign to mark it as such? But it does not have this. Its signs, too, are lights, and therefore in their way signs of day, i.e., signs of the evening from which [162] night proceeds and of the morning to which it moves. In both cases light-bearers constitute the material for divine instruction, and there are no sources of darkness. In both cases light-bearers, and light-bearers alone, constitute the presupposition of man's recognition. It is their diversity and alternation alone which give to man an awareness of day and night as such, making it possible for him to distinguish the one from the other. And so it is they which are to him in this basic function of dividing day and night signs or signals as they are described in v. 14. In this connexion we can think of the weather, and the four points of the compass, and the "seasons" for agriculture and navigation (whose objective meaning has a recognisable correspondence in the life of nature, plants and beasts), and the possibilities of demarcation for "days and years," and therefore the means of fixing and reckoning time. The service which they render is to make it possible for man—assuming that he for his part can and does realise this—to live a life which is not merely dreamy and vegetative, but which is marked by a wakeful consciousness of time and of history. This is what they can and should and will do. As a repetition and representation of the divine creation of light, they prepare the cosmos not merely for the presence of man but for his activity as the earthly subject of the history appointed for him by God. They make it possible for him to be a participant and responsible witness and not merely a spectator of the process by which day is continually formed out of evening and morning. They make it possible for each day which dawns for him to be his day; for all the time given to him to be his time; for his history really to be his history. They are in fact the formal presupposition of his recognition of day and night, and therefore of the divine creation of light; the formal presupposition of his participation in the "Let there be light," and in the "It was so." They cannot be other or more than this. Where they are other or more than this to man, he mistakes their nature, refuses their service and must not be surprised if he necessarily misses the very thing they offer him. All that they are and do is summed up in this service, and is to be gratefully understood and accepted in connexion with this service. It cannot, of course, escape us that much that the heavenly bodies actually or potentially render is not expressly stated in this passage. It says nothing about the most obvious fact that the heavenly bodies diffuse by day and night the brightness and warmth which man needs for his life, nor does it say anything about the influence of these operations on the life of the vegetable kingdom and animals and men. It says absolutely nothing about the relationship, affirmed by ancient and modern astrology, between the heavenly bodies and the concrete chances and opportunities given to man by reason of his special structure. It is clear that the author consciously avoids anything which transcends the comprehensive but very sober assertion that the heavenly bodies are the objective measure of time and space; the objective clock and objective compass with the help of which man can orientate himself and thus be capable of history. Similarly, the passage does not say more than that they are luminaries in the firmament and shine upon the earth. Even the fact that, according to vv. 16–18 and the exact parallel in Ps. 136^{8f} (cf. also Job 38^{33}), they are to "rule" or govern day and night does not make the sun and moon into deities and kings, but is only a reminiscence of the dethroned Babylonian and Egyptian conception of their role. For one thing, this "ruling" takes place on the basis of a divine commission, and therefore only with the authority and power of a subordinate. But again, the context makes it plain that this ruling consists in the separation of day from night, in the giving of the sign by which they make visible and known to man the divine creation of light, the revelation of God's will. And finally, whatever the other activities not mentioned here, they may rule over day and night but they do not rule over man. In any case, the external determination of human life by the stars, as asserted by astrology, is quite out of the question in this passage, for it expressly ascribes this rule (v. 16) to the sun and the moon but not to the stars. Naturally, we have to reckon with the fact that although this rule of the stars is irrelevant in this context, and is not   [163] therefore mentioned, it may well have been familiar to the author. But what he can say comprehensively about all the heavenly bodies, whatever their nature, is that, created by God, they have their place in heaven and shine upon earth; and that, whatever their influence, their diversity and alternation make it possible for a being capable of receiving this sign to orientate himself in time and space, and therefore to participate in the divine creation of light when this participation is really granted to him. In this function they too praise the Lord (Ps. 148^3). That they do not recognise them in this their function is the reproach made against the Pharisees (Mt. 16^2) when they are reminded of their ability to read the appearance of the sky but not the "signs of the times." So immeasurably great and important are these functions to the author that, quite unconcerned about natural history and held by the prospect of the coming history of salvation, he prefers to say nothing at all about other possible functions of the heavenly bodies in order to say this one thing and therefore everything. Their whole diffusion of brightness and warmth, and all the other determinations which may emanate from them, are all summed up in the fact that they dispense the objective possibility of a human awareness of time and place; thus making it possible for man as a creature to have a history with God. Shining from above, they are the signs of this history as it was commenced by God Himself at the creation of light. Thus to understand Gen. 1$^{14f.}$, we must not abstract from the concept of terrestrial history. When the creation of the heavenly bodies is described in the Persian *Bundahish* as the institution of twelve signs of the zodiac, twenty-eight moon-houses, 486,000 zodiac stars, etc., and when the planets are called leaders of the fixed stars, it is obvious that we have to do with a scientific attempt to explain the world quite foreign to the intention of the biblical saga. Similarly, the Egyptian tradition, which tells us that the sun-god Re appoints Tot to be the moon-god and as such his representative during the time of his absence in the underworld, is describing a transaction within that inner hierarchy of the gods which cannot even exist according to this passage.

Nor must we abstract from Gen. 1$^{14f.}$ the fact that the history which it has in view, the content of the time which sun, moon and stars are created to measure, is not something indefinite, but the specific history of salvation which commences with the creation of light and receives its direction and purpose from the God of Israel. The relation of the creation of the heavenly bodies to chronology, and to that extent to history, is not unknown to the.Babylonian myth, according to the fifth tablet of the *Enuma elish*. But it is to be noted that in this case a metaphysical problem seems to be set in the forefront with the creation of the heavenly bodies. The sidereal world is supremely the abode of the great deities Anu, Enlil and Ea. And because the fundamental idea of Genesis is completely lacking, i.e., the separation of day from night as the action of sun and moon constituting time as day, all the emphasis falls, again with the precision of natural science, upon the phases of the moon dividing time into months—something which is not even mentioned in the present passage (note the complete absence of "month" in v. 14). It is obvious that in the two accounts there is not merely a different chronology but a different conception of time. And it is to be noted that the specific biblical concept of time breaks through even where it is emphasised, as in Ps. 104^{19}, that God made the moon to divide the year. The day and time and history envisaged in Gen. 1$^{14f.}$, and the reason why the luminaries shine from the firmament upon the earth to give signs and seasons and days and years, is made clear in v. 18, where day and night are again expressly interpreted as light and darkness. The signs of the sky are of no value for the man who is merely concerned at random to orientate himself with the help of compass, clock or calendar, and to become the subject of any earthly history. They are of value only for the man whose day, season and history are to consist in his participation in the separation of

[164]

light from darkness, because the God who separated light from darkness has created him in and as His own image, and because he was born and is called to be God's partner in this covenant. From this standpoint the curious correlation of the two parts of Ps. 19—even if it is due to later compilation—is not a literary accident but well considered and very impressive. The description of the sun in v. 6 with its conclusion: "His going forth is from the ends of the heaven, and his circuit unto the ends of it: and there is nothing hid from the heat thereof," could not possibly have had a more impressive continuation, from the standpoint of Gen. 1^{14}, than that of v. 7 f.: "The law of the Lord is perfect, converting the soul: the testimony of the Lord is sure, making wise the simple. The statutes of the Lord are right, rejoicing the heart: the commandment of the Lord is pure, enlightening the eyes. The fear of the Lord is clean, enduring for ever: the judgments of the Lord are true and righteous altogether. More to be desired are they than gold, yea, than much fine gold: sweeter also than honey and the honeycomb. Moreover by them is thy servant warned, and in keeping of them there is great reward. Who can understand his errors? cleanse thou me from secret faults. Keep back thy servant also from presumptuous sins; let them not have dominion over me: then shall I be upright, and I shall be innocent from the great transgression. Let the words of my mouth, and the meditation of my heart, be acceptable in thy sight, O Lord, my strength and my redeemer." This is the aspect of day as it is set under the "rule" of "light." It is the day on which the Word of God, which cannot be too highly praised, is spoken to man, and judges him, and becomes his radically saving and preserving promise, and summons him to pray for the grace of God. The day continually dawns for man, and the sun, moon and stars which indicate the separation of day from night shine for him, in order that he may know that he has time and place for this. We observe the same pregnant concept of time in Jer. 31[35f.]: "Thus saith the Lord, which giveth the sun for a light by day, and the ordinances of the moon and of the stars for a light by night, which divideth the sea when the waves thereof roar; the Lord of hosts is his name. If those ordinances depart from before me, saith the Lord, then the seed of Israel also shall cease from being a nation before me for ever"; and again in Ps. 72[5] where it is said of Israel's king: "They shall fear thee as long as the sun and moon endure, throughout all generations," and in v. 17: "His name shall endure for ever; His name shall endure as long as the sun"; and again in Am. 5[8-9]: "That maketh the seven stars and Orion, and turneth the shadow of death into the morning, and maketh the day dark with night: that calleth for the waters of the sea and poureth them out upon the face of the earth: the Lord is his name: that strengthened the spoiled against the strong, so that the spoiled shall come against the fortress"; or, conversely, in Mt. 5[45], where it is said that the heavenly Father makes the sun to rise on the good and the bad. We must not be too quick to dismiss these as mere comparisons. Of course they are comparisons. But the remarkable thing here as elsewhere is that God's creation of the heavenly bodies and their work may be compared in this way with the work of His Word and His grace and judgments in Israel. This is possible because the cognitive relationship obviously present in the Old Testament corresponds to an ontological and factual disclosed in Gen. 1[14f.] in connexion with Gen. 1[26f.] We have always to remember this when the two terms of the comparisons are brought even closer together than in these passages. We may quote as an example the closing words of the Song of Deborah (Jud. 5[31]): "Let them that love him be as the sun when he goeth forth in his might"; or again Ps. 37[6]: "He shall bring forth thy righteousness as the light, and thy judgment as the noonday"; or Mal. 4[2]: "But unto you that fear my name shall the Sun of righteousness arise with healing in his wings"; or Mt. 13[43]: Then shall the righteous shine forth as the sun in the kingdom of their Father." We may also refer to Messianic passages like Num. 24[17]: "I shall see him, but not now: I shall behold him, but not now: there shall come a Star out of Jacob and a Sceptre [165] shall rise out of Israel"; or Is. 30[26]: "Moreover the light of the moon shall be as the light of the sun, and the light of the sun shall be sevenfold, as the light of seven days, in the day that the Lord bindeth up the breach of his people, and healeth the stroke of their wound"; or Lk. 1[77f.], where the subject is the tender mercy whereby the ἀνατολὴ ἐξ ὕψους will visit us; or the verse which says of Jesus (Mt. 17[2], cf. Rev. 1[16]), or of the angel with the Book (Rev. 10[1]), that his countenance shone as the sun. And above all we may quote the description of the "wife" of Rev. 12[1]—undoubtedly the Christian Church in its great tribulation—as" clothed with the sun, and the moon under her feet, and upon her head a crown of twelve stars." Of course all these are images, but it is not due to accident or caprice that these particular images are used. For light is the revelation of the will of God, and the heavenly bodies, above all the sun, are His servants in the sense that they indicate to man the seasons given him for the recognition of this revelation—his day as a day of revelation, his time as a time of revelation, and his history as a history of revelation. Thus if they are used as images of the righteousness of God and the life of the righteous, of Israel's Messiah, Jesus, and the Christian Church, it is because on the biblical view they are originally and properly, by reason of their creation, the image of these very things, i.e., the imitation and representation of the divine creation of light, and because from the very outset they are ordained to serve this purpose. There can be no question, therefore, of poetical or any other license in the use of these images.

Once we grasp this, we can begin to understand the reason why the Old and New Testament are so unequivocally opposed to the cult of the heavenly bodies, as in the warning of Deut. 4[19] (cf. 17[3]): "And lest thou lift up thine eyes unto heaven, and when thou seest the sun, and the moon, and the stars, even all the host of heaven, shouldest be driven to worship them, and serve them." We read as early as Amos (5^{26}) of the reverence bestowed upon Chiun, i.e., the planet Saturn. According to Jer. 8^2, 9^{13}; Zeph. 1^5; 2 K. 17^{16}, $21^{3f.\ 5\ 12}$, there existed in Jerusalem in the days of the later kings a cult of the "heavenly host" on house-top altars. And we are even told in Ezek. 8^{16}: "And he brought me into the inner court of the Lord's house, and, behold, at the door of the temple of the Lord, between the porch and the altar, were about five and twenty men with their backs toward the temple of the Lord, and their faces toward the east; and they worshipped the sun toward the east." It sounds almost incredible that these things should have taken place in Israel. "If I beheld the sun when it shined, or the moon walking in brightness; and my heart hath been secretly enticed, or my mouth hath kissed my hand: this also were an iniquity to be punished by the judge: for I should have denied the God that is above" (Job 31^{26-28}) It is of a piece with this that astrology is almost universally condemned in the Bible. The only exception which calls for notice is the remarkable one of the story of the wise men from the East (Mt. $2^{1f.}$), of whom it is said uncritically that they had seen in their country the star of the new born king of Israel and had come to worship Him, and that this star had in some way led them until finally it stood still over the place where the little child was. It can hardly be denied that the Evangelist presupposes a given reality of this occurrence and therefore of the whole possibility of astrology, and that he draws upon it as such in his presentation of the miraculous birth of Jesus Christ. But this does not mean that he justifies the action of the Magi or gives an invitation or even permission to imitate it and thus to make use of what is acknowledged to be a real possibility. The fact that some pagans are chosen, like the Magi, is not a vindication or commendation of their paganism. And when this story tells us that in the form of a comet, or (as it was later assumed) a conjunction of Jupiter and Saturn, there appeared a kind of holy star with this extraordinary function, the exception to the rule only confirms that it is not the

[166] normal function of stars to give such signs. That is why "seeking alter" the heavenly bodies is classified with their reprehensible worship in Jer. 8^2. In Jer. 10^2 we are told explicitly: "Learn not the way of the heathen, and be not dismayed at the sign of heaven; for the heathen are dismayed at them. For the customs of the people are vain." And Is. $47^{13f.}$ says of Babylon: "Thou art wearied in the multitude of thy counsels. Let now the astrologers, the stargazers (Luther: 'the masters in the course of the heavens'), the monthly prognosticators, stand up, and save thee from these things that shall come upon thee. Behold, they shall be as stubble; the fire shall burn them; they shall not deliver themselves from the power of the flame." Soothsaying (Luther: "the choice of days") is grouped with fortune-telling, snake-charming, witchcraft, necromancy and spiritism (cf. Deut. $18^{10f.}$) as one of the possibilities which may be real—and the Old Testament unquestionably reckons with their reality—but which are not to be used by the people of God. According to Is. 2^6, the Philistines were soothsayers, and the inhabitants of Jerusalem ought never to have become the same. According to Jer. 27^9, it is soothsayers who with all kinds of false prophets, fortune-tellers, witches, etc., are responsible for the false confidence of the Jerusalemites that they will not have to serve the king of Babylon. Similarly, the apostasy of the Galatian Church from Christ to the Law is shamefully connected (Gal. $4^{9f.}$) with a re-enslavement to the weak and beggarly στοιχεῖα τοῦ κόσμου[EN214] which found expression in their observance of "days, and moons, and times, and years." The spread of error in Colossae seems to have had the same result according to Col. 2^{16}. Why is it that this biblical rejection of astrology and star-worship is so necessary and so powerful? The answer is not to be sought merely in the monotheistic character of Israelite and Christian worship. The specific reason is obviously to be found in the fact that

---

[EN214] worldly elements

we have here a *corruptio optimi*[EN215] which as such is *pessima*[EN216]. The decisive fact is that the heavenly bodies are to "rule" in a way corresponding to the destiny given them in their creation, and that this is not the case when they are worshipped or even consulted by man. In both cases an objective order of God's creation is disturbed when man erroneously alienates the heavenly bodies from their specific destiny as images of the divine creation of light: ostensibly in their own favour, by exalting them to be lords and deities or at least teachers and counsellors; but in reality to the detriment of their real function, and for that reason to God's dishonour and man's destruction. They then cease to be signs and *media* of instruction for the history of the divine covenant. They lose their proper dignity when in their own fulness they take precedence of what they should depict, of what they should reveal in their transparency; or when what they should depict is not sought in the grace and judgment of the Word of God but in a supposed disclosure of other, arbitrarily invented necessities of human life.

Finally, it belongs to their created function that in a series of eschatological passages the Bible speaks of a cessation of their function and therefore of their shining. That it can come to this is due to the fact that like the rest of the world the sun, moon and stars were created by God, and that as a finite reality. As God can remove the mountains and shake the earth, so, according to Job 9⁷, He "commandeth the sun, and it riseth not; and sealeth up the stars." That God will do this is indeed one of the most characteristic threats of Old Testament prophecy. It is found in Am. 8⁹: "And it shall come to pass in that day, saith the Lord God, that I will cause the sun to go down at noon, and I will darken the earth in the clear day." The experience of the "land" during the plague of locusts (Joel 2¹⁰), which mounts in an ever-increasing crescendo to the great and dreadful day of the Lord, will be repeated in the "valley of decision" over the assembled nations: "The sun and the moon shall be darkened, and the stars shall withdraw their shining" (Joel. 3¹⁵). It shall come to pass that over Babylon "the stars of heaven and the constellations thereof shall not give their light: the sun shall be darkened in his going forth, and the moon shall not cause her light to shine"(Is. 13¹⁰). And God says of Egypt: "And when I shall put thee out, I will cover the heaven, and make the stars thereof dark; I will cover the sun with a cloud, and the moon shall not give her light. And all the bright lights of heaven will I make dark over thee, and set darkness upon thy land, saith the Lord God" (Ezek. 32⁷⁻⁸). According to Mk. 13²⁴ and Mt. 24²⁰ the sign which will immediately precede the end of the age and the return of Christ is that the sun will become dark, the moon will cease to give light, the stars will fall from heaven and the powers of heaven will shake. In the same connexion, Luke (21²⁵) has merely a general reference to signs which are to appear in the sun, moon and the stars. Luke's reticence at this point can perhaps be explained by the fact that when he mentions the darkness which occurred at the death of Jesus (23⁴⁵) he expressly adds that "the sun was darkened," his obvious purpose being to indicate that in this event he sees a central and typical fulfilment of prophecy. There can be no doubt that the other Evangelists held the same view of the darkness although they did not express it. As all promising beginnings point to the beginning of the coming new age which took place typically in the resurrection of Jesus; and as all judgments point to the divine judgment and the end of the age which took place in His death on the cross, so the darkness, i.e., the darkening of all created lights in the hour of His death, is the darkness of all darkness to which we must refer even the recurrent repetitions of the Old Testament prophecies in different parts of the Apocalypse (6¹², 8¹⁰, 9¹). It is to be noted, however, that the New Testament (probably in conjunction with the saying about the morning star in Is. 14¹²) refers several times to the "falling" of stars but not to the passing away of the sun, moon and

[167]

[EN215] corruption of the best
[EN216] the worst

stars (corresponding to that of heaven and earth). It is clear that even the Old Testament consciously avoided this expression. The only content of prophecy is that the sun and moon are to cease to shine, and this is all that we are told in the account of the death of Jesus. Nor does Is. 60[19f.] say that when God Himself is the eternal light, the sun and moon will cease to be, but merely that they will cease to shine, i.e., that their light will be completely eclipsed by God Himself as the eternal light. In Rev. 20[23] and 22[5] we seem to have a true interpretation—that the light of the sun and moon will no longer be necessary. The very fact that their light will be replaced by the light of God Himself is indeed a specific guarantee that "thy sun shall no more go down; neither shall thy moon withdraw itself" (Is. 60[20]). We have thus to reckon with the fact that on the biblical view the end of the world will consist in a passing away of heaven and earth, in the cessation of the function of the heavenly bodies and in the extinction of their particular light, but that the heavenly bodies themselves and as such—like the throne of God and the celestial sea and the angels—will not pass away but will be preserved and given a new function. What is actually meant by the extinction of the heavenly luminaries as such we learn from Job 3[3f.], where Job curses the day of his birth with the words: "Let the day perish wherein I was born, and the night in which it was said, There is a man child conceived. Let that day be darkness; let not God regard it from above, neither let the light shine upon it. Let darkness and the shadow of death stain it; let a cloud dwell upon it; let the blackness of the day terrify it. As for that night, let darkness seize upon it; let it not be joined unto the days of the year, let it not come into the number of the months. Lo, let that night be solitary, let no joyful voice come therein. Let them curse it that curse the day, who are ready to raise up their mourning. Let the stars of the twilight thereof be dark; let it look for light, but have none; neither let it see the dawning of the day: because it shut not up the doors of my mother's womb, nor hid sorrow from mine eyes." It could not be more clearly stated that light and therefore the ministry of the heavenly bodies constitutes day, time and history. If, like Job, we want to curse a day as such, i.e., in some sense to strike it out as a day, we can only wish that the light of the heavenly bodies should be withdrawn from

[168] it. Hence Job's wish that the day of his birth might never have been is equivalent to the wish that the light of the heavenly bodies might never have shone upon it. It is when there is no light of the heavenly bodies that there is no day, time or history. This then is the actual content of the threat of judgment but also of the corresponding promise of Is. 60 and Rev. 20–21. The wisdom and patience of God which has founded human history has a definite goal, and the finite time granted to man in relation to this history has actually an end. As the death of Jesus is the goal of that history, it is also the end of time. As all prophecies point to Him, they necessarily speak of the last time this side of His resurrection and return, of the end of time this side of the dawn of the new creation. And they do so by uttering their terrifying warnings but also their friendly promises, not about the end and dissolution of the constellations, but about the end and dissolution of their shining and therefore of their ministry. This ministry of theirs reaches its boundary with the personal entry of God on behalf of His creation, with His own shining as the eternal light, with the resurrection and return of Jesus. Thus the meaning of the work of the fourth day, the meaning of the fact that God found it good (v. 18b), emerges clearly on this side too, and we can only say that in this case, as in that of the first day, the concluding assertion in v. 19—that the evening and the morning were this fourth day—has a particular significance. For here again, but this time subjectively, we have to do with the material point at issue—the creation of day, time and history.

(Gen. 1[20-23].) The fifth work, which deals with the creation of fish and birds, corresponds to the second work in the same way as the fourth corresponds to the first. If the second work saw the basic securing of the lower cosmos by the establishment of a firmament between the waters above and below, the fifth sees the completion of an entirely new creation under the protection of this firmament, although in the sea on the one side, and therefore at the heart of the hostile territory which borders the dry land, and above the earth on the other, and therefore in close proximity to that other hostile frontier. This entirely new creation is clearly distinguished from the first creation of life in the form of the vegetable kingdom; it is the creation of the first autonomous living creatures. There can be no doubt that we are now approaching with immense strides the climax of the narrative. Two points are to be noted: the peculiar nature of this creation; and its spheres of operation. The former is to be found in the fact that what God creates on the fifth day, in contrast not only to light, heaven, earth and the luminaries, but also to the vegetable kingdom, consists of creatures which live in autonomous motion, abounding and flying. Not by a long way do we see as yet the free decision and action which will make man man and for which man is ordained as created in the image of God; but we certainly have a first intimation of it. And if we do not have as yet living creatures which form the immediate companions and friends of man in his particular exaltation, we can at least see that as a living creature of this kind man will not be alone, but in similarity and dissimilarity he will stand at the centre and head of a whole world of such creatures. When the Word of God creates fish and birds by the fact that His fiat sets them in independent motion in their own elements; when the sphere of life previously established receives inhabitants for the first time and in a first form, we catch a first glimpse, in [169] strange, almost bizarre, but very definite outline, of the being which will be God's partner in this sphere, of the animal creation, of a divinely created race of creatures endowed with independent life. It is as part of the order now inaugurated, of the animal creation, that man will finally appear; a final innovation within this order, but inseparable from it; not to be confused with fish and birds, but prefigured by and associated with them as a being with independent life. But we must also note the two spheres of the fifth work of creation. These are the sea and the air. That is to say, they are the spheres of the lower cosmos which are by nature more distant and alien to man, in which he cannot live or move at all, or can do so only artificially and temporarily, and which are dangerous because of their proximity or even original relationship to the element of chaos. It is in these spheres—surely the least expected—that the life of autonomous creatures begins by God's creative fiat. It is here that the first creatures with independent life emerge. It is here that there come into existence these whole races of self-propelled beings. It is here that God has first prepared for Himself the praise of such beings. In the depths below and the heights above He begins His work on and with such beings. So great is His mercy! So much is He the Lord and Master of all things, including these regions! So thoroughly did He see to it that even these regions cannot be more than threatening signs of His wrath; that chaos is controlled, and life is made possible in its immediate vicinity! Where man imagines he can see the open jaws of death, God causes things to swarm and to fly, and things stir and move which are living creatures like himself, sharing his own animal nature. The spectacle offered in these spheres is one to inspire confidence. For what are fish and fowl compared with him? How favoured he is by comparison! In what a safe stronghold he is privileged to live when we consider their native spheres! Where there are open eyes to see this spectacle; where the witness of fish and of birds is perceived, there need be no fear of the immensity of creaturely space, but vital energy for the venture of existence within it. If these imperilled races already live and move here, "each after its kind," surely man, who is so much more protected, can confidently do the same after his kind. If there are no monstrosities there, no chaos-monsters, but only animals of the same species to which man belongs; if when he looks in this direction he finds himself among very distant friends and relatives, what has he to fear in the safe place, on the firm ground, where God has created him? What can terrify him here when there is nothing to terrify there? God saw that what He created on the fifth day in these inhospitable regions was also good. But that is not the end of the story. For we now have for the first time the reference to a blessing which God bestowed on creation. We are told of the fecundity, multiplication and expansion of these aquatic and aerial denizens. At the creation of light, the

[170]   firmament, the earth, vegetation and the luminaries, there was no question of any such blessing, nor was it demanded. These things seem to be blessed by being what they are. But, in addition to the special capacity for movement, it appears that the need of divine blessing belongs necessarily to the animal creation, especially if it is to continue and multiply in new individuals. A thing is blessed when it is authorised and empowered, with a definite promise of success, for one particular action as distinct from another which is also a possibility. The procreation of posterity, and therefore the existence of nature in the form of natural history, of a sequence of generations, is a definite venture where it has the form of a spontaneous act of a creature qualified for the purpose. And it is a venture for which, by reason of its similarity with the divine activity, it requires divine permission and the divine promise if it is not to be arrogant and purposeless. Already the living creatures which are created on the fifth day and belong to the outermost circle need and actually receive this blessing. It is to be observed that for the first time (still within the history of creation) there now appears the problem of history proper as a continuation of creation, and that it appears in the form of the problem of the sequence of procreation, of fatherhood and sonship, which is later so characteristic of the biblical history of the covenant. In God's blessing of the fish and birds we really transcend the concept of creation and enter the sphere of God's dealings with His creation. What we have here is the beginning of its history, or at least an introductory prologue which announces the theme of this history, i.e., the establishment of a covenant between God and His creation which moves independently like Himself and renews itself by procreation after its kind. What is here revealed, still as an element in the history of creation but already

as an element in the history of the covenant, is that there is to be a God-like creature ordained for fatherhood and sonship and continuing its existence in the relationship of fatherhood and sonship. It is not to strive against Him but to be at peace with Him; not to live in impotence but in power; not in its own arrogance and strength but in the strength of His blessing, authorisation and promise, living and active in fruitful begetting. Again, what is revealed is that God will turn in kindness and faithfulness to this creature as this creature has always been the goal of His creation. What is revealed is the grace which does not will that the fashioning of creaturely nature, for all its difference from the divine, should be futile or unfruitful; the goodness of the Creator which does not allow this creaturely nature to exist in its relative independence and self-propulsion without permission and hope, but wills in all friendliness to bear and surround and rule it in the exercise of the freedom granted to it. It merely throws into relief the inner significance of this process that this is first revealed in these distant and dangerous realms of the created universe, and in this outer circle of the animal kingdom. The prologue and prefiguration of the covenant of grace begin in fact at the very point where we should least expect [171] them. Even these inhospitable regions, even the sign of God's wrath directly visible in the earthly ocean, must not be without this countersign. And the most remote and strange circle of the animal creation whose bright centre will be occupied by man, must also bear witness to this covenant. It is obvious that with the record of this blessing—that God created even this circle good, and that man may therefore live, not in fear but in trust and confidence—the account and admonition of the saga acquire specific content and overwhelming force.

Gunkel was surely ill advised when he commented on vv. 20–22: "According to their kind fish and birds hardly belong together; here too it is obvious that the six-day schema does not fit the material. The writer has had to combine two different works in order not to exceed the number six." The "combination" of fish and fowls has nothing whatever to do with zoological questions, but rests on the fact that the creation of the *raqia'* on the second day implied that of the earthly heaven which borders on the upper world, and that the creation of the ocean was explicitly accomplished on the third, so that the earth was surrounded by two bordering spheres which are properly inaccessible to man, or at least uninhabitable as far as he is concerned. And now the purpose is to show that when he looks at these spheres man has every reason to feel at home on earth. For they, too, have denizens, and their denizens are of the same kind as the inhabitants of the earth, and therefore for all their peculiar characteristics they are of the same kind as himself. There is nothing in these spheres which does not also owe its existence and nature to the will and Word of God; nothing which is fundamentally strange to the nexus within which man himself is created and has his determination. From this theological standpoint, fish and fowl belong together. That both are caught with a net (B. Jacob) is a *tertium comparationis*[EN217] which can hardly have had any particular interest for the saga. The fact that fish are mentioned first is in accordance with the regular linguistic practice of the Old Testament. In every summary enumeration of the animal kingdom fish are placed first, except, of course, when the order is

---

[EN217] basis of comparison

reversed to begin with man (e.g., Deut. 4^{18}, 1 K. 5^{13}), and then they come second. The present passage (like Ezek. 38^{20}) is working up to man, and therefore fish are given the priority; in the creation saga the sea is the most distant possible place.

The Septuagint and Vulgate versions take it that according to the fiat of the Creator in v. 20 the sea is to produce animals as the earth did herbs in v. 11, and their renderings imply that even the origin of birds is to be traced back to the same element. Calvin, too, understood the passage in this way, and found in this astonishing origin of birds one of the special *documenta divinae potentiae quae nos in stuporem cogerent*[EN218]. In reality water produces neither birds nor fish. That which is proper to the earth in vv. 11 and 24 is not in any sense proper to water as the present passage sees it. And what is worthy of vegetation in v. 11 is not worthy even of this first example of the creature now to be called into being. It is no accident that (for the first time since v. 1) the verb *bara'*[EN219] is used in v. 21. In the description of man's creation in v. 27 it will reappear three times in close succession. The animal kingdom with man at its summit is in a very definite sense a direct creation. Thus the divine command is *yishrtsu*[EN220] (20): not προσαγαγέτω or *producant*[EN221] but "Let it stir" (Luther), or "Let it abound" (Zurich Bible). The water merely indicates the place or element in which this is to take place. Correspondingly it says later that birds are to fly above the earth and under the firmament. In both cases, as in vv. 3, 6 and 14, we have creative fiats which, in contrast to v. 11, do not take account of any magnitude already created. It is to be noted how distin-

[172] guished are the denizens of these spheres in this respect. Like vegetation, the land animals proceed from the earth (v. 24). Fish and birds, on the other hand, are called into existence because they are commanded to do what is characteristic of their nature, viz. to abound in water and fly in the air. Here where there is no "Let there be" the existence and function of the creature are more intimately related than at the creation of the firmament and lights. Because the "Let there be" is absent, the corresponding "And it was so" is absent also. The LXX, and with it the Zurich Bible, thought it necessary to supply these. The Vulgate and Luther rightly kept to the original. The concept of "coming into being" is naturally present, but in relation both to the command and its execution it is contained wholly in that of the beings to be created and actually created: they are the *nephesh hayyah*[EN222], i.e., physical beings existing in a relatively autonomous individuality *vis à vis* the rest of creation. The earth is not this, for in itself it is dead. Neither is vegetation, although it is alive. This is true for the first time of the "animal" creature. For that reason its coming into being by the Word of God consists immediately in the fact that God commands it to live in its own peculiar manner, i.e., to "abound" in water and fly between heaven and earth. Calvin was thus right when he was forced to understand creation at this point as a particular miracle. The only point to notice is that the miracle of the fifth day does not consist in the fact that water produced fish and birds, but that life in its higher and individual form, the animal form (which is also man's), commenced independently by reason of the fiat of God's Word; and in the fact that this took place in the most remote regions, the hostile regions of water and air, and therefore in places where it was least to be expected. The secret of the fifth day lies in the fact that this particular thing took place in this particular sphere. We must also note its correspondence to the work of the second day. If on that day the basic securing of the lower cosmos was accomplished by the establishment of the firmament between the waters above and below, the existence of corporeal beings now becomes possible and actual under the

---

[EN218] signs of divine power which drive us to astonishment
[EN219] to create
[EN220] let it swarm
[EN221] let them produce
[EN222] living begins

protection of this firmament, although in the immediate vicinity of the repelled forces of chaos both above and below. In creating fish and birds God in some sense certifies that the firmament is a genuine firmament: the invasion of the celestial ocean is prevented, and in the last analysis the nether ocean with all its terrors cannot be a metaphysical danger. It is a matter to inspire confidence that fish and birds move about so cheerfully in these elements which hold such dread for man. In the sure stronghold in which he finds himself man may venture in some measure to do the same. Fish and birds teach him that as a free corporeal being like themselves, but on much firmer ground, and so much more favoured than they by nature, he may really be bold to do this.

That we really have to think of the frontiers of the human sphere of existence, and there-fore to remember the second work of creation, is shown by the striking fact (v. 21) that, contrary to the usual practice of the text, express mention is suddenly made of one of the species of abounding aquatic creatures as the first object of the divine *bara*: "God created great whales." The upshot of the matter is indeed that the *tanninim*[EN223] are great whales or similar aquatic animals created by God. But behind this result there stands a whole history. The *tanninim*[EN224] are not introduced because by reason of their size they are special wit-nesses of the divine creative power, but because it is not self-evident that they too, and espe-cially, are living creatures created by God akin to man, and in their way inspiring confidence; and that according to Ps. 148[7] they too must join in the praise of God. For according to the general linguistic usage of the Old Testament the *tanninim*[EN225] are intrinsically sinister and threatening creatures. They are the wounded, swallowing monster, the serpent or dragon which is in some respects the representative of the restless and dangerous sea with its threat of destruction; the enemy which God has fought and conquered in primeval time (Is. 27[1], 51[9]; Job 7[12]; Ps. 74[13]). By mentioning the *tanninim*[EN226] first and foremost as if they were   [173] merely a specially noteworthy species among other aquatic animals, the creation saga has in some sense taken the bull by the horns. That the *tanninim*[EN227] were also created by God, not merely as the first among aquatic animals but among all creatures with independent life; and that they are introduced merely as a type of whale (shark? cuttle-fish?), denotes in the con-text of Old Testament thinking an act of demythologisation the importance of which we cannot overlook. It means precisely that the sinister sea hides no monsters of chaos. Such monsters are the possibility or perverse reality which is at once ruled out by the divine cre-ative Word that rules even over the sea. The monsters which myth makes so dreadful are indeed great and dangerous signs—like the sea which they inhabit—of the frontiers which God Himself has set for His creation. They are indeed signs of the frontiers of humanity and of God's own will. But they are signs which have been set up by God Himself. And in them-selves, like man himself at the far end of the series which begins at this point, they are only living beings, of the same nature as all other swimming creatures, or all creatures gen-erally.

No other species is mentioned. Indeed, no species of birds is mentioned at all. That spe-cies are indeed willed and posited by God is established by the fact that here again, as in the case of vegetation, we are told that God created the inhabitants of water and air "after their kind," i.e., after their different kinds. The special mention of the *tanninim*[EN228] makes it certain that there is no species in these spheres that is not created by God; no species that, far from questioning, does not confirm the habitable condition of the earth for man. There

---

[EN223] great whales
[EN224] great whales
[EN225] great whales
[EN226] great whales
[EN227] great whales
[EN228] great whales

is as little zoological interest in this account as there is botanical in v. 11 f. or astronomical in v. 14 f. For instance, the question whether what we call amphibians are to be classed with fish, or whether insects are to be classed with birds, is quite irrelevant from the standpoint of this passage. It would thus be childish to press against the saga the question whether birds ought not to be classified with land animals in view of the fact that they too are warm-blooded creatures, and build their nests and brood and find nourishment on the earth. At this point, as at others, the Church fathers can only obscure what the passage is really trying to say when in their commentaries and sermons they try on the one hand to make use of all the natural science of their day, and on the other to attach to its constituent parts the most diverse edifying and naturalistic allegorisings: a greedy man being typified by the predatory fish; ideal nuptial love and fidelity by the viper and muraena; cunning by the cuttle-fish and crab; the ideal state of primeval man by the community life of the crane; love for children by the piety of storks; mother love by the swallow and her nest-building; chaste widowhood by the turtle-dove; the possibility and credibility of the Virgin Birth by the vulture and other birds; the godlessness of worldly wisdom, etc., by the owl with its fear of light, etc. (Ambrose, *Hex.* V). If we are to understand the passage we must turn our backs resolutely on all scientific or pious considerations and look only in the two directions which it indicates, namely, the depth of the ocean and the height of the atmosphere, to learn that in these spheres too God has creatures and witnesses to His Word, so that when we look in these directions we need not feel strange or frightened, for here too and particularly God has creatures and witnesses to His Word in the form of independent living beings which are very unlike and yet very like man himself, who has been called to live in obedience to the same Word.

God saw that the inhabitants of these external regions were good, and with this the account of this act of creation closes. But the unity of the special creation of the *nephesh ḥayyah* which begins here and ends with man may be seen by the fact that from v. 22 onwards an element in the divine utterance and activity is disclosed which had previously been invisible. God blessed them—the creatures that swim and that fly—and said: "Be fruitful and [174] multiply, and fill the waters in the seas, and let fowl multiply in the earth." There was no question of blessing the light, the firmament, the earth, vegetation or the heavenly bodies. Blessing is the Word of God to the extent that this ascribes—and because it is the Word of God actually gives—to a creature some power or benefit which will be of value to it in its future autonomous movements as a creature. Light, the firmament, the earth, vegetation and the heavenly bodies do not need any blessing because they are not *nephesh ḥayyah* and do not perform any independent creaturely movements, but perform their function by being what they are. In certain respects they are blessed from the very start. The command that the earth should be green (v. 11) cannot be interpreted as a special blessing because the earth is not in a position to do this of itself but only by reason of the divine creative fiat. Strictly speaking, only the things created from the fifth day onward can be considered as objects of the divine blessing. The creatures which by reason of their creation can live in independent movement as *nephesh ḥayyah* need God's blessing if their movement is not to mean alienation from God and their own destruction but abundance according to the will of God. But what is in question here is the most slender and inclusive form of this abundance, namely, that the creature is to procreate and multiply itself and therefore really to occupy the spheres assigned to it—in this case water and air. In the case of vegetation this takes place in connexion with the earth without having to fulfil an independent movement, to be a *nephesh ḥayyah*EN229: αὐτομάτη ἡ γῆ καρποφορεῖ (Mk. 4²⁸). For its procreation vegetation does not need any special blessing by the Word of God because it already possesses it by reason of its nature. The animal which requires for its procreation "the spontaneous association of two

---

EN229 living begins

mutually adapted beings" (B. Jacob) needs this blessing, i.e., it needs the Word of God even in respect of the living acts which it spontaneously accomplishes. It needs not only the presence but also the accompaniment of the powerful Word of God. This accompaniment of the creature by the Creator by whom it is continually enabled to accomplish its own living acts—not in its own power, but by the power of God which is indispensable to a creaturely act—is the blessing of which v. 22 speaks. This blessing points forward to the fact that with the history of man, and the natural history which underlies it, a history of the preservation and renewal of created life as such is to take its course. When the Word of God blesses the creatures which need it, from fish and fowl to man himself, it provides in this higher order for the possibility and reality of natural history. It provides for the preservation as well as the creation of the earth as a dwelling-place for man. And therefore it provides especially for the preservation of the associates of man in the form of the *nephesh ḥayyah*. Only His Word as His blessing can do this. Only His Word as His blessing does in fact do it.

Calvin stops at this point to ask whether when He blessed them God really addressed the fish and birds as must obviously happen in a blessing. He answers in the affirmative. As he sees it, the *experimentum ipsum*[EN230] shows that the Word of God has taken root in the nature of these creatures, and this actually proves that God has spoken to them. It is to be noted (B. Jacob) that the address in question is only indirect and not direct, as later in the case of man ("God blessed them, and God said unto them … "). Animals, too, could actually be the objects of direct address. In Gen. 3[14] we are told that God condemned the serpent to crawl on its belly and to eat dust; in 1 K. 17[4] that He commanded the raven to provide for Elijah; in Jon. 2[11], that He commanded the fish to spew out Jonah on the land; in Rev. 19[17], that an angel standing in the sun cries "with a loud voice, saying to all the fowls that fly in the midst of heaven. Come and gather yourselves together for the supper of the great God"; and in Ps. 148[10] that beasts and all cattle, creeping things, and flying fowl, are also summoned to praise God. But this is obviously a different address from that which man experiences. It has advantages over the latter which must not be overlooked. It is addressed directly to the being of the animal: *vis verbi concepta in eorum natura radices edit*[EN231]. (Calvin). It does not first summon the animal to a decision, but accomplishes this by its utterance. It thus takes place in such a way that there can be no question of disobedience on the part of the animal. In short, it takes place with the immediacy with which light, the firmament, the waters on the earth, the earth itself and finally the luminaries were addressed according to this passage. "He spake and it was done; he commanded and it stood fast" (Ps. 33[9]). To that extent the goal and final triumph of the divine Word are much clearer in the address to beast than to man. But these are advantages which for the being thus addressed are so many disadvantages. That man hears the Word of God mediately, reflectively and deliberately is due to the fact that he is ordained to meet the divine reason with reason, something that is not granted to the beast. There can be no biblical support for sermons such as those which St. Anthony addressed to fish or St. Francis to birds. That man is summoned to decision by the divine address means that the fulfilment of God's will becomes a revelation of the freedom which is the secret of the grace offered to the creature; a revelation which can be present in the animal only as a passive and not an actively participating witness. That man can be disobedient is the dark converse of the immeasurable distinction that he is ordained to obedience, whereas the beast properly speaking can only be submissive. It is in this direction that we must look for the actual difference between the blessing of man and that of fish and birds recounted in v. 22. Yet with all its advantages and disadvantages this is significant as the first special dealing of God with His creature. He might almost describe it as the prologue to the history which is

[175]

[EN230] experience itself
[EN231] when the power of God's word is received in their natures, it puts forth roots

grounded in creation as a whole. It is the act in which God for the first time engages Himself to His creature as a faithful God.

The material significance of the process is actually emphasised by the fact that this happens to the fish and birds; that it is with them that at least the prelude to this history opens. Even from the standpoint of this blessing we can see how much more is the creation and blessing of man. "Are ye not much more than they?" (Mt. 6²⁶). Yes "ye are of more value than many sparrows." and because this is so, therefore, "fear ye not" (Mt. 10³¹). What happens here to fish and fowl prefigures the divine promise to Abraham which initiates the whole history of salvation, namely, that through a son God will make of him a great nation, as numerous as the stars of heaven and as the sand by the sea-shore, "and thy seed shall possess the gate of thy enemies" (Gen. 12¹, 15¹, 22¹⁵). This involves the multiplication and replenishment of the earth, and therefore the fulfilment of the blessing pronounced on fish and birds as well as man, as it takes place in the ensuing history of salvation whose meaning and goal are revealed in the kingdom of Jesus the Messiah. Even in these distant and strange regions of water and air the first dealings of God already point in this direction. We have to see this relationship if we are to understand the position of Ps. 50¹⁰ᶠ·: "For every beast of the forest is mine, and the cattle upon a thousand hills. I know all the fowls of the mountains: and the wild beasts of the field are mine. If I were hungry, I would not tell thee: for the world is mine, and the fulness thereof." It is the God of Israel who can say this *de jure*[EN232], for He has really blessed the beasts as a prelude and prefiguration of His special dealings among men, and in this His activity He is its original and legitimate Lord, and therefore does not need the offerings and sacrifices of men.

We may conclude with some specific observations concerning fish and birds. Even in relation to them and their particularity within the whole animal kingdom it may be said that God saw creation in its goodness. This creation, too, forms the content of a full and separate day. While it is a prelude, like all the creations of the first five days, it has its peculiar significance and dignity in the fact that it is the creation and also the blessing of the *nephesh ḥayyah* in these strange and distant regions, filling these regions too with witnesses to the divine goodness and faithfulness. It is one of the differences between the Old Testament and the New— within the context of different attitudes to water and the sea—that it is only the latter, but in these very prominently, that much interest is really displayed in the fish. To be sure, we have a noteworthy parallel to Gen. 1²⁰ᶠᶠ· in Ezek. 47⁸ᶠ·, which tells us that the waters of the Dead Sea are to be healed by the stream of living water proceeding from the temple, and that as a result it will swarm with living creatures like the waters of the Great Sea. The negative point may also be made that aquatic animals never actually take the form of monsters in the Old Testament, as they might well have done in certain cases, for even the fish of Jon. 2¹ᶠ· is a creature subjected and obedient to the command of God, and after three days it has to disgorge its prey as it had previously swallowed it up. Yet it is only in the New Testament that fish take their place with bread as the food of man (Mt. 7⁹ᶠ·, 14¹⁷ᶠ·; Lk. 24⁴²). But here fishing (Mk. 1¹⁶) is the earthly calling from which the disciples are called away to follow Jesus and in which they are later confirmed by Him. And the miraculous draught of fishes (Lk. 5⁴ᶠ·, Jn. 21¹ᶠ·) epitomises the Messianic blessing of man and at the same time represents the origin of the Church. So trustworthy has the strange and distant region of the sea now become that the sacrament of calling and reconciliation can now be baptism in which man is taken out of the water—perhaps there is an allusion to this in the phrase "fishers of men." Indeed, it has become so familiar that according to inscriptions found in catacombs early Christians used the fish with the lamb and baptism as a special symbol of their faith and as a diagramme

[176]

[EN232] by right

ΙΧΘΥΣ[EN233] of the name Jesus. It is of a piece with this that in another instance a bird, the dove, is also associated with the land animal, the lamb, in this respect. Strictly speaking, it is only in the New Testament that the bird—in the form of the dove—becomes the familiar creature which it was meant to be according to Gen. 1$^{20f.}$ In the Old Testament—we think of the bird "alone upon the house-top," the pelican of the wilderness and the owl of the desert (Ps. 102$^{6f.}$)—it is for the most part the creature which is lost and forsaken; which is threatened by the hunter and must flee (Hos. 11^{11}, Ps. 11^1); which can certainly fly away and escape (Ps. 124^7); but which, in the form of the dove especially, looks anxiously for a rest for the sole of its foot until it finds one (Gen. 8$^{6f.}$). Even in the form of a bird of prey, it never becomes a dangerous monster, but it is frequently mentioned (e.g., I K. 14^{11}) in the form of the vulture, and as such it is a sign of the prophetic threats and one of the instruments of their execution. Properly speaking, there is among the living creatures which fly between heaven and earth only one proud and undaunted aviator, the eagle, whose ascent forms a subject of comparison both for those who wait upon the Lord (Is. 40^{31}) and also for a hostile race hastening from the ends of the earth (Jer. 4^{13}, Deut. 28^{49}). But just as it is not the lion but the lamb, not the horse but the ass, so in this sphere it is not the ascending eagle but the descending dove alighting on the earth, which is singled out by the New Testament. Is it because ancient science thought it to be without gall that it is called *ἀκέραιος*[EN234] (Mt. 10^{16}), and in the account of the baptism of Jesus (Mk. 1^{10} and par.) represented as the form of the Holy Spirit? We are perhaps nearer the mark if we find the explanation in the fact that, unlike the eagle, it is not a bird of prey, and its homeward flight to rest is more characteristic than its upward. But however that may be, in this unequivocally positive form the avifauna have their own share in the understanding and proclamation of the New Testament, and are thus confirmed in their creation and blessing by God.

(Gen. 1$^{24-31}$.) The termination of creation is not its completion. That is to say, it is not completed because it is concluded, but because on the presupposition of this conclusion God rested on the seventh day. The completion of creation is the joyful readiness in which the Creator and creature, the Master and the work which He has set before Him, are now conjoined, and together [177] anticipate the common history which now commences. But the sixth day of creation marks the point in the created order to which God in His rest looks back after His creative work is done; or, from the standpoint of the created order itself, the final form in which it anticipates the further resolve and action of its Creator and Lord.

The sixth day of creation reveals the same correspondence to the third as does the fourth to the first and the fifth to the second. Externally this is revealed already by the fact that we are again dealing with a twofold and obviously related work. The protection of the land against the sea is matched by the creation of land animals which first inhabit this protected dwelling-place of man, and are themselves akin to man. Then the planting of the ground and therefore the first appearance of living creatures is matched by the appearance of man—the final and proper form. The juxtaposition and differentiation are again significant. We again have to do with a termination and a new beginning which together constitute a unity.

[EN233] fish (a Greek anagram for Jesus Christ, Son of God, Savior)
[EN234] without blemish

The biblical creation saga views man in all his individuality: yet not in isolation but in this environment and company; in association with the various tame and creeping and wild beasts of the land which like himself, and like the fish and fowls before them, but now immediately and unavoidably, as his inseparable companions, are living creatures, i.e., living in independent movement and multiplying themselves by free acts of generation. If it is true that creation finds its conclusion in man, it is equally true that his Creator has given him precedence not only over light, the firmament, the protected and fruitful earth, the constellations, the creatures of sea and air, but also over his immediate but very different fellow-animals within the one dwelling-place. If it is true that man is more noble than these creatures, it is also true that he has just as much need of them as of all that went before, whereas they for their part have no need of him whatever. If it is true that man, created with the beasts by the will and Word of God, may freely hear and obey this Word, it is also true that he will constantly have before him in the animal world immediately around him the spectacle of a submission to this Word which, if it is not free, is in its own way real and complete. The creature precedes man in a self-evident praise of its Creator, in the natural fulfilment of the destiny given to it at its creation, in the actual humble recognition and confirmation of its creatureliness. It also precedes him in the fact that it does not forget but maintains its animal nature, with its dignity and also its limitation, and thus asks man whether and to what extent the same can be said of him. The fact that with him it depends on the same objective guarantee of its dwelling-place and the same light by day and by night, and has been assigned to the same table spread by God, is a living reminder to man of his own needs. The fact that it is subjected to his dominion

[178] is a living reminder of the responsibility which is laid upon him with his own dignity. As the first to be blessed, as the first to receive both permission and promise for the exercise of its power of procreation, in its enjoyment of this blessing and constant use of this power and consequent fruitfulness in multiplying and replenishing the earth, it is a dumb but eloquent type, not in the distant spheres of sea and sky but in close proximity on earth, of that which, as the mystery of fatherhood and sonship, will constitute the theme of human history. Thus at every point it is inferior to man and yet his companion and even forerunner. It is inferior, for man alone is created in the image of God. He alone will hear and obey the Creator. He alone is honoured to be God's partner in the covenant of grace. With him alone will there be an independent history. But in all these things the beast will be a constant companion. Everything which will take place between God and himself is to be significantly accompanied by what takes place, by life and death, in the animal kingdom; and in these events it will have witnesses which cannot be silenced even where human witnesses fail, and which will often speak more forcefully and impressively than all human witnesses. Man's salvation and perdition, his joy and sorrow, will be reflected in the weal and woe of this animal environment and company. Not as an independent partner of the covenant, but as an attendant,

the animal will participate with man (the independent partner) in the covenant, sharing both the promise and the curse which shadows the promise. Full
of forebodings, but also full of confidence, it will wait with man for its fulfilment, breathing freely again when this has taken place provisionally and will
take place definitively. And this companion is also his forerunner. In the first
instance, this is true only in so far as man continually meets it as he did only the
sixth day of creation, in all its inferiority but also in its prefigurative character.
Then, it is true because in all its unfreedom it brings before him the perfect
essence of uncreated being long before he in his freedom is aware of it and
decides to recognise it. And finally it is true—but here we anticipate—because
precisely in its lowest humiliation, as the animal slain and sacrificed, it will
bring before him the final mystery of his own history, i.e., that of his own
fatherhood and sonship; the indispensable but saving offering of the promised
Son of Man as the proper content of the permission and promise given to him.
For in all its animal limitation and impotence, the beast could hardly have
been a more important precursor of man than by giving him this picture
which he has good reason to try to escape and which he himself is quite unable
to fulfil.

Significantly, the creation of man and of these living beings is the work of
one and the same day. The earth is to produce them; they are to proceed from
the earth, i.e., their existence and nature belong to the earth, to its destiny and
preparation as the dwelling-place of man. According to the Word of the Creator—as on the third day, at the creation of the flora—they belong indissolubly to the man who lives on the earth. But its execution—which is now more   [179]
clearly separated from the command—consists in the fact that God made
them as He made the heavenly firmament, the lights, the fish and fowls, the
land animals, and later man. They are His creatures and not those of the earth.
Again, the difference between this creation and that of man is quite unmistakeable. This may be seen already in the correspondence between the twofold work of the sixth day and that of the third, where beast and man are
related as the dry earth as such is there related to its qualification as the sphere
and possibility of living creatures. From this it follows that there is no mention
in this first saga of a real connexion between the earth and man as between the
earth and beast. But it also follows that the creation of land animals is simply a
continuation of the creation of fish and birds on the fifth day. To the grouping
of aquatic and aerial animals there now corresponds that of domestic animals,
creeping things and wild beasts. There is also repeated the emphasis upon the
variety of the God-created species within these groups, and it is obvious that
what was said about the blessing of the first living creatures in respect of their
procreation and expansion also applies tacitly when we reach this inner circle.
Nothing is said about groups and species (i.e., races, nations, etc.) in the
account of man's creation, but an eloquent silence is maintained. And if no
express mention is made of the blessing of land animals, this is certainly not

because the saga disputed it, but because it aimed to make a clear-cut distinction between the blessing of man, in all its similarity with that of the first creatures with independent life, and the blessing of his immediate environment and company, characterising it as something new.

When the creative fiat of v. 24 says of the land animals that the earth is to "bring them forth," the case is the same as with that of v. 9: "Let the waters be gathered," or that of v. 11: "Let the earth bring forth," or that of v. 20: "Let the waters bring forth abundantly the creature that hath life." In its execution, the earth ceases to be the subject and God "makes" the beasts (B. Jacob). We are spared the thought of a bearing "mother earth" as the principle of the world (Gunkel). What is meant (F. Delitzsch)—parallel to the emergence of dry land on the third day—is that we have to do with living creatures which by nature of their corporeality and mode of existence belong and are confined to the earth. "They live of the earth and the earth will be their grave; it must therefore be their origin." "They are in some sense the moving ground, as fish (v. 21) are animated water" (B. Jacob). In the second creation saga we shall be dealing with a more intimate and real connexion between earth, beast and man. But the first saga certainly does not envisage it in the sense of a literal "bringing forth."

It is obvious that in v. 25 there is no express mention of a blessing of land animals similar to that of fish and birds in v. 22 and of man in v. 28. Is this omitted "in order not to overload the work of the sixth day which had already become very long?" Or is it merely due to a scribal error? (Gunkel). Or may it be explained by the simple fact that it is self-evident in view of v. 21? (Delitzsch). It certainly ought to be supplied, since there is no serious reason [180] why it should have been intentionally left out. For there is no solid basis for the view of B. Jacob: "The land animals are not blessed because the Torah could not say that they should multiply without restriction and replenish the earth, since this would be disastrous to man."

The linking of man and beast in the account of the sixth day of creation corresponds to a familiar thought in the Old and New Testaments. Attention may be drawn in this respect to Is. 43[20–21]: "The beast of the field shall honour me, the dragons and the owls: because I give waters in the wilderness, and rivers in the desert, to give drink to my people, my chosen. This people have I formed for myself; they shall shew forth my praise." When God deals with man, there is necessarily a prefigurative presence of man in greater or lesser proximity. The reason why Noah's ark has to be so huge a structure is because, in addition to eight souls, it has to carry a pair of each animal species, "to keep them alive" (Gen. 6[19]); "to keep seed alive upon the face of all the earth" (Gen. 7[3]). This has to be remembered in 1 Pet. 3[20] where the ark is used as a type of the Church. When the flood prevailed, God remembered not only Noah but "every living thing, and all the cattle that was with him in the ark" (Gen. 8[1]) And in the covenant made with Noah after the Flood there are included not only his sons and their posterity, but also expressly "every living creature that is with you, of the fowl, of the cattle, and of every beast of the earth with you" (Gen. 9[10]). Similarly the new covenant of peace and grace in the latter days is expressly described by Hosea (2[18]) as first and foremost a covenant for the benefit of Israel "with the beasts of the field, and with the fowls of heaven, and with the creeping things of the ground"; and it is impressively portrayed in similar terms in the well-known passage in Is. 11[6f.]: "The wolf also shall dwell with the lamb. ... " In Is. 11 and Ezek. 34[25], [28] this is taken to mean that the wild beasts will no longer be a threat to the tame beasts and man, but in Joel 2[22] it is given the rather different sense that the beasts of the field for their part will have nothing to fear. To the same line of thinking there also belongs the commandment concerning the Sabbath rest (Ex. 20[12], 23[12]), which expressly protects not only the slave and the stranger but also the ox and the ass of the Israelite. And we remember that when, unlike His impatient prophet, God has pity on the great city of Nineveh (Jon. 4^{11}) it is described as a city of "over 120,000 souls which cannot distinguish between right and wrong, and also much cattle." Again, in Prov. 12^{10} we are told that "a righteous man regardeth the life of his beast." Again, we are told in Mk. 1^{13} that when Jesus the Messiah commenced His ministry He was "with the wild beasts; and the angels ministered unto him." And if, according to the prophecy of Zech. 9^{9} and in the fulfilment of Mt. 21^{1}, the ass is given the peculiar honour of carrying the Son of David into Jerusalem, it does not owe this merely to the fact that it is the reverse of the proud war-horse of a worldly conqueror, but also to the fact that precisely at this moment and in this situation the beast as man's forerunner and companion must not fail to be present, with babes and sucklings, amongst the bearers and proclaimers of the divine blessing now in process of fulfilment. It is a remarkable fact that (according to Lev. 20^{25} and many other places) a distinction has to be made not only between clean and unclean people, or between clean and unclean conditions and things, but also between clean and unclean beasts; that among the first-born which specially belong to God and are to sanctify Him (Ex. 34^{19}, Num. 18^{15}) we must also reckon the first-born among the beasts, as if something like the problematical sequence Adam-Cain were also to be taken into account in this sphere; and that when a hostile city is captured (Deut. 13^{15}, 1 Sam. 15^{3}) even the cattle is to fall under the curse of death. But the beast will also fall under the judgment which is to overtake Israel itself: "Therefore (because there is no fear, no judgment, and no knowledge of God in the land) the land shall mourn, and every one that dwelleth therein shall languish, with the beasts of the field, and with the fowls of heaven; yea, the fishes of the sea also shall be taken away" (Hos. 4^{3}). "Behold, mine anger and my fury [181] shall be poured out upon this place, upon man, and upon beast" (Jer. 7^{20}). "For the wickedness of them that dwell therein the beasts are consumed, and the birds" (Jer. 12^{4}). "Behold, at my rebuke I dry up the sea, I make the rivers a wilderness: their fish stinketh, because there is no water, and dieth for thirst" (Is. 50^{2}). Also in the description of the day of Gog and Magog: "So that the fishes of the sea, and the fowls of the heaven, and the beasts of the field, and all creeping things that creep upon the earth, and all the men that are upon the face of the earth, shall shake at my presence" (Ezek. 38^{20}). That neither man nor beast will continue; that they are to be destroyed together—this is one of the constant elements in the prophetic threat. Hence we can understand even the strange command of the king of Nineveh (Jon. 3^{8}) that man and beast should be clothed in sackcloth as a sign of their common repentance. Paul's well-known statement in Rom. 8^{20} about the ἀποκαραδοκία of the κτίσις^{EN235}, which involuntarily, for man's sake, and therefore not without hope, has been subjected to vanity, and thus groans and travails with us for the day of the Messiah, certainly applies to the beast. It is not for nothing that, in its totally different nature and form of existence, it is so near to the innermost circle of creation. It is not for nothing that it is blessed with the same blessing with which man is also blessed. This means that it is also burdened with the curse which man has to carry. It also shares in the confusion of his existence and his world. It must suffer and die with him. But (in its own way) it will also be freed from the bondage of φθορά^{EN236} into the glorious liberty of the sons of God. "O Lord, thou preservest man and beast" (Ps. 36^{6}), is a thread which runs through the whole of the Bible; and it first emerges in a way which is quite unmistakeable when the creation of man is classified in Gen. 1$^{24f.}$ with that of the land animals.

For all its relation to the second part, the first part of the work of the sixth day also has the appearance of a conclusion—the conclusion of everything

---

^{EN235} earnest expectation of the creation
^{EN236} destruction, decay

that has preceded from the creation of light onwards. To that extent its function seems to be that of an accentuating prologue to that which constitutes the true content of the work of this day (which is the preparation for the Sabbath), i.e., the creation of man. Only with the positing of this new beginning is the whole of the work of creation concluded and made ready for its completion on the day of the divine rest. With all its manifold presuppositions, consequences and reservations, this whole has aimed and moved towards man as the true occupant of the house founded and prepared by God, the central creature on the ground and in space and in the midst of all others, the one being capable of and participating in light. It is only when man is created that it can be said that God saw all that He had created, and that it was "very good." It must be clearly understood that the fact that God ended or "completed" His work is expressly described as the work of His rest on the seventh day and not as the work of creation on the sixth. Even man is not an end in himself. It is only with reservation that he can be described as "the crown of creation." Strictly speaking, creation is crowned only when God in His joyful Sabbath rest looks back upon it and down on what He has created. But it is the work concluded and terminated on the sixth day with the creation of man that is the object of this completing divine rest and joy. At this point the decision is made which reveals

[182] this work as the act and fulfilment of His will in respect of the existence of a theatre, instrument and object of His love distinct from Himself and His own sphere and powers; in respect of the existence of a partner with whom He willed to ally Himself. Everything that precedes only prefigures this decision and prepares for it. By its very nature it is preliminary. It points beyond itself to God's further decisions in His dealings in this theatre, with this instrument, in relation to this object and in fulfilment of the covenant with this partner. But if this is the case the preliminary thing really presupposed in these further decisions is man as the central creature on the ground and in space. The completion of God's creation as the work of His rest on the seventh day, the establishment of the covenant of which creation is the external basis, has reference to this termination. Only now is the external basis truly laid, and no more is to be expected, or necessary, for the laying of this external basis of creation. Creation as such, although it is not completed, is ready and finished with the work of the sixth day to the extent that this includes the creation of man. If God does not cease to be the Creator and therefore does not cease to work, He will not create anything new or different from what He has previously created, i.e., from the creation of light up to and including the creation of man. In every new creation it will be partly a question of the gracious preservation and confirmation, and partly of the gracious renewal, of the creation which in itself is ready and finished. In one way or another, the whole of the divine goodpleasure applies to it as such.

For this reason, with a new solemnity and content as compared with what precedes, the introductory formula to this final creation record is "God said," not "Let there be," nor "Let the earth bring forth," nor "Let there be fish to abound and fowl to fly," but "Let us make man." There takes place a divine soliloquy, a consultation as though between several divine counsellors, and a divine decision resting upon it. It is the first creation record which is either sufficiently naive or instructed to regard God as capable of the soliloquy expressly narrated in the plural. It is this which thinks it relevant to introduce it at this point. However it may be understood, there can be no doubt that, notwithstanding the singularity of the divine being and uniqueness of the divine work, it certainly did not represent the Creator as alone, and felt it important to say so at this particular point in the creation of man. In the first instance the creative fiat is not directed outwards towards the creature to be created, but inwards in the form of the "Let us"; it is a summons to intra-divine unanimity of intention and decision. We can hardly avoid the conclusion that the execution of this decision, which is recounted in the customary phrase "God created"(emphasised by threefold repetition), is not pictured by the biblical witness in such a way that the "Let us" does not find any genuine correspondence but the actual creation of man is the act of a lonely God. He is obviously [183] thinking of a divine creation which takes place in the intra-divine unanimity corresponding to this summons. Naturally, his meaning with reference to the command as well as its execution is not that this unanimity has first to be achieved, as though it were lacking in the earlier works of God. He only brings out at this point, where the totality of creation reaches its terminus and goal, the meaning and presupposition of all God's creative utterances and actions from the very outset. But at this point he thinks it necessary to bring out expressly the non-solitariness of God on the one hand and His free agreement with Himself on the other; a confrontation in the divine being and sphere but also peace, unity and common determination in this confrontation. The divine sphere, God Himself, does not exist in a vacuum, outside space and time. God is not dead but alive. He is One, but He is not for that reason one thing. But this being the case, He can become the Creator and therefore have a counterpart outside Himself without any contradiction with His own inner essence, but in confirmation and glorification of His inner essence. Creation is something entirely new and free and non-obligatory in relation to His life in Himself, but far from being a denial, betrayal or surrender it is a revelation of His deity. Thus the "Let us" might well have been the formula for all God's creative utterances and actions. Indeed, it is necessary to apply this formula retrospectively as a commentary on all the other formulæ used. At this point, however, it has obviously forced itself irresistibly upon the witness. When man was to be the subject, it had to be said that the creative basis of His existence was and is a history which took place in the divine sphere and essence; a divine movement to and from a divine Other; a divine conversation and summons and a divine correspondence to it. A genuine counterpart in God Himself leading to unanimous decision is the secret prototype which is the basis of an obvious copy, a secret image and an obvious reflection in the co-existence of God and man, and also of the existence of man himself.

But this brings us to the concept which is used by the first creation saga to denote the purpose and fulfilment of the divine creative will. The summons is as follows: "Let us make man in our image, after our likeness." "In our image" means to be created as a being which has its ground and possibility in the fact that in "us," i.e., in God's own sphere and being, there exists a divine and therefore self-grounded prototype to which this being can correspond; which can therefore legitimate it for all that it is a heterogeneous imitation; which can justify its existence; and by which, when existence is given to it, it will in fact be legitimated and justified. That it is created in this image proves that it has in it its ground of justification. The phrase "in our image" is obviously the decisive insight of the saga, for it is repeated twice. The other phrase: "In our likeness," means to be created as a being whose nature is decisively character-[184] ised by the fact that although it is created by God it is not a new nature to the extent that it has a pattern in the nature of God Himself; to the extent that it is created as a likeness of this divine image, i.e., in the likeness of this image. The being created in the likeness of this image is man. The rest of creation has this character of a copy or image only in so far as it has found its conclusion and climax in the creation and existence of man. We can thus see that the witness had a reason for keeping back this "Let us" until now, and for producing it only at this point. It is in the co-existence of God and man on the one hand, and man's independent existence on the other, that the real and yet not discord-ant counterpart in God Himself finds creaturely form and is revealed to the creature.

If we think of the rest of creation without man, we can think in terms of something other than God, but only in the sense of something distinct from God and not of a counterpart. Only with the first creatures with independent life do we begin to glimpse a true counterpart alongside and before God in the sphere of the rest of creation. But not until the creation of man does it find a genuine and clearly visible form. Only in him does a real other, a true counter-part to God, enter the creaturely sphere.

This innovation is repeated in the distinctive existence of man as such. What is created without and alongside man exists in juxtaposition and even in a certain full-scale co-existence, but not in the true confrontation and reci-procity which are actualised in the reality of an "I" and a "Thou." Neither heaven nor earth, water nor land, nor living creatures from plants upward to land animals, are a "Thou" whom God can confront as an "I," nor do they stand in an "I-Thou" relationship to one another, nor can they enter into such a relationship. According to the first creation saga, however, man as such exists in this relationship from the very outset.

"He created them male and female." This is the interpretation immediately given to the sentence "God created man." As in this sense man is the first and only one to be created in genuine confrontation with God and as a genuine counterpart to his fellows, it is he first and alone who is created "in the image" and "after the likeness" of God. For an understanding of the general biblical use of this concept, it is advisable to keep as close as possible to the simple sense of "God-likeness" given in this passage. It is not a quality of man. Hence there is no point in asking in which of man's peculiar attributes and attitudes it consists. It does not consist in anything that man is or does. It consists as man himself consists as the creature of God. He would not be man if he were not the image of God. He is the image of God in the fact that he is man. For the meaning and purpose of God at his creation were as follows. He willed the existence of a being which in all its non-deity and therefore its differentiation can be a real partner; which is capable of action and responsibility in relation [185] to Him; to which His own divine form of life is not alien; which in a creaturely repetition, as a copy and imitation, can be a bearer of this form of life. Man was created as this being. But the divine form of life, repeated in the man created by Him, consists in that which is the obvious aim of the "Let us." In God's own being and sphere there is a counterpart: a genuine but harmonious self-encounter and self-discovery; a free co-existence and co-operation; an open confrontation and reciprocity. Man is the repetition of this divine form of life; its copy and reflection. He is this first in the fact that he is the counterpart of God, the encounter and discovery in God Himself being copied and imitated in God's relation to man. But he is it also in the fact that he is himself the counterpart of his fellows and has in them a counterpart, the co-existence and co-operation in God Himself being repeated in the relation of man to man. Thus the *tertium comparationis*[EN237], the analogy between God and man, is simply the existence of the I and the Thou in confrontation. This is first constitutive for God, and then for man created by God. To remove it is tantamount to removing the divine from God as well as the human from man. On neither side can it be thought away. That it is God's divine and man's human form of life is revealed in the creation of man. God wills and creates man when He wills and creates the being between which and Himself there exists this *tertium comparationis*[EN238], this analogy; the analogy of free differentiation and relation. In this way He wills and creates man as a partner who is capable of entering into covenant-relationship with Himself—for all the disparity in and therefore the differentiation between man as a creature and his Creator. The grace of man's creation—in which all creation is now revealed as an act of God's creation—consists not only in the fact that He sets man in fellowship with Himself as a being existing in free differentiation and relationship, but in the fact that He has actually created him in fellowship with Himself in order that in this natural fellowship He may further speak and act with him.

It is striking, but incontestable, that in his description of the grace of God in this final and supreme act of creation, the biblical witness makes no reference at all to the peculiar intellectual and moral talents and possibilities of man, to his reason and its determination and exercise. It is not in something which

---

[EN237] basis of comparison
[EN238] basis of comparison

183

distinguishes him from the beasts, but in that which formally he has in common with them, viz. that God has created him male and female, that he is this being in differentiation and relationship, and therefore in natural fellowship with God. The only thing that we are told about the creation of man, apart from the fact that it was accomplished by the Word of God in and after the image of God, is that "God created them male and female." Everything else that is said about man, namely, that he is to have dominion over the animal kingdom and the earth, that he is blessed in the exercise of the powers of his [186] species and the exercise of his lordship, and that he is to draw nourishment from the plants and trees, has reference to this plural: he is male and female. And this plurality, the differentiation of sex, is something which formally he has in common with the beasts. What distinguishes him from the beasts? According to Gen. 1, it is the fact that in the case of man the differentiation of sex is the only differentiation. Man is not said to be created or to exist in groups and species, in races and peoples, etc. The only real differentiation and relationship is that of man to man, and in its original and most concrete form of man to woman and woman to man. Man is no more solitary than God. But as God is One, and He alone is God, so man as man is one and alone, and two only in the duality of his kind, i.e., in the duality of man and woman. In this way he is a copy and imitation of God. In this way he repeats in his confrontation of God and himself the confrontation in God. In this way he is the special creature of God's special grace. It is obviously the incomprehensible special grace of God that His singularity finds correspondence in a, created singularity. That the grace of God has this particular form; that it is in the differentiation and relationship of man and woman, the relation of sex, that there is this repetition, is an indication of the creatureliness of man—for this is something which he has in common with the beasts. But this creaturely differentiation and relationship is shown to be distinct and free, to reflect God's image and to prove His special grace, by the fact that in this particular duality (i.e., to the exclusion of all others) he is alone among the beasts and in the rest of creation, and that it is in this form of life and this alone, as man and woman, that he will continually stand before God, and in the form of his fellow that he will continually stand before himself. Men are simply male and female. Whatever else they may be, it is only in this differentiation and relationship. This is the particular dignity ascribed to the sex relationship. It is wholly creaturely, and common to man and beast. But as the only real principle of differentiation and relationship, as the original form not only of man's confrontation of God but also of all intercourse between man and man, it is the true *humanum*EN239 and therefore the true creaturely image of God. Man can and will always be man before God and among his fellows only as he is man in relationship to woman and woman in relationship to man. And as he is one or the other he *is* man. And since it is this and nothing else that makes him man, he is distin-

---

EN239 human essence

guished from the beast and every other creature, existing in the free differentiation and relationship in which God has chosen, willed and created him as His
partner. The fact that he was created man and woman will be the great para-
digm of everything that is to take place between him and God, and also of
everything that is to take place between him and his fellows. The fact that he
was created and exists as male and female will also prove to be not only a copy
and imitation of his Creator as such, but at the same time a type of the history
of the covenant and salvation which will take place between him and his Cre-   [187]
ator. In all His future utterances and actions God will acknowledge that He has
created man male and female, and in this way in His own image and likeness.
But these are matters which are more explicitly treated by the second biblical
witness, and we will not anticipate their development at this point. The first
witness, in the obvious context of his account of the divine likeness of man, is
simply content to mention the fact and to give it a central position. God created them male and female, in this true plurality but in this alone. All else
refers to men in this plurality. Men are all that this differentiation and relationship includes in its whole dialectic (not developed in this context) of gift and
task, of need and satisfaction, of lack and fulfilment, of antithesis and union,
of superiority and subjection. In every other differentiation and agreement
they will always be male and female. Every other differentiation and agreement will continually prove to be preliminary or supplementary as compared
with the fact that they are male and female. And this strictly natural and creaturely factor, which is held in common with the beasts, is not in any sense an
animal element in man but the distinctively human element—not in itself but
because it has pleased God to make man in this form of life an image and
likeness, a witness, of His own form of life.

Of men who repeat the divine form of life in their creaturely being it is now
said that God has assigned to them an exalted position of lordship within the
surrounding animal kingdom of land, air and water. But it is not in this that
the divine likeness consists. It is in consequence of their divine likeness that
men are distinguished from all other creatures, and in the first instance from
all other creatures with autonomous life, by a superior position, by a higher
dignity and might, by a greater power of disposal and control. It is only in this
relationship, in dependent connexion with man, that the animal kingdom can
and will participate in the mystery of all creation as it is revealed in man, and in
the promise of this mystery. The ascription of this position and function to
man does not mean that the rest of creation is excluded from this mystery; it
describes the manner of its inclusion. In this way, in basic subordination to
man, and as his comradely followers and environment, they too are witnesses
and to that extent partakers of the divine image and the history promised to
him with his special creation. More than this must not be read into man's
dominion over the beasts. Man is not their Creator; hence he cannot be their
absolute lord, a second God. In his dignity and position he can only be God's
creaturely witness and representative to them. He can be a *primus inter*

pares[EN240] among those over whom he rules. He can carry out a commission. But he does not possess the power of life and death; the right of capital punishment. Man's lordship over the animals is a lordship with internal and external limitations. His dignity and power over them is accompanied by a natural inferiority in the things which he has in common with them. Nor is any mention made in this connexion of his rationality as a feature which distinguishes him from them. As the Creator God is no less over him than He is over the animals. What distinguishes him and gives him authority and power is the fact that, although he is not radically different from the other creatures with independent life, he has been honoured by the grace of God to be the image of God in the uniqueness of his plurality as male and female. The animals in their multiplicity are not confronted by different groups and species of men, but, for all the provisional and subsequent differentiations in every individual, by the one man—male and female. This is what gives and maintains his superiority. But this, of course, is grace, and it can be brought out and asserted only as the superiority of grace. In the last analysis, therefore, it cannot be an end in itself. The distinction, responsibility and promise ascribed to man in the biblical witness which follows are undeniably more and other than the possession and exercise of this lordship. This is not the essence but the accessory of his true determination. The latter will include—but properly only as a negative determination—the fact that within the animal world of land, air and water he is distinct and superior, and that it has been placed under his control. His divine likeness does not depend upon this, but his power and position depend on his divine likeness.

[188]

That the saga has to be understood in this way may be proved by the fact that even after his creation man needs the special blessing of God for the exercise of his lordship. Like the procreation of his kind, his multiplication and expansion, this lordship is a matter of his own activity as this special creature with independent life. Like them, it takes place in spontaneous acts for whose legitimate and successful execution he has as much need of the Creator's authorisation, enabling and promise as he has of His creative Word for his existence. As God's image and likeness man exists as male and female, and no further blessing is needed for this presupposition of all his actions. This is not in any sense a matter of his spontaneous action. It is given and assured by the fact that in virtue of the divine creation man can actually be what he is. It consists in the fact that God chose and willed man in the utterance of that "Let us" and in the fact that it was actualised. But man needs God's blessing when (animal-like in this respect) he moves forward as male and female to the procreation of new individuals, to the multiplication and expansion of his kind; and when (Godlike in this respect) he again moves forward as male and female to the exercise of this lordship. At the latter point his activity—in clear differentiation from that of the beast—assumes a dangerous proximity to God's activity as Creator

---

[EN240] first among equals

in which it may be both supremely insolent and wholly ineffective. Here there commences the post-creation history in which not only the beast but also man would be lost if creation had not been accompanied at once by God's permission and promise for his activity, and if God had not stood behind him from the very first with His blessing. It is, therefore, still an element in the history of creation and already an element in the history of the covenant that man, male and female, created as God's reflection and image, needed and was actually granted the divine blessing for his future activity. From this we learn that the divine likeness of man does not affect in the slightest the creatureliness which he has in common with all other beings and in which, with all other beings, he is dependent on God's aid. In itself it would have preserved his actions neither from insolence nor ineffectiveness. It is a copy and not an original; a reflection and not a prototype. In virtue of the divine likeness, man—even more than the beast over whom he is given dominion—is directed in all his acts to hear this friendly Word of God. Furthermore, and supremely, we learn that he does actually hear this friendly Word of God; that he does actually receive the blessing of God for his propagation as well as for his actualisation as a being in the divine image. When his propagation takes place, and his power and position are actualised, his actions will take place under the blessing of God and therefore with His permission and promise. And when the first man and the first woman continue to live in their children and therefore in new individuals; when they multiply and populate the earth and have dominion over it, these new individuals will also be blessed with the blessing addressed to the first man in and with his creation. God will acknowledge them as He acknowledged the creaturely partner whom He chose and willed, and created at the very outset in His image and after His likeness. God will not retract His permission and promise either from the first man or his posterity, just as He will not cease to be their Creator, or to govern and sustain them as their Creator. Whatever the threats and dangers that may arise, they can only be temporary breaks in the line which commenced with God's blessing. Everything that takes place on this line must and will essentially and properly be salvation history. Only incidentally—even in its most dreadful form—will it be the reverse. Because it rests on this divine blessing, at bottom it must always be a history of peace and covenant, not of enmity, conflict and wrath. The blessing may well be turned into a curse (i.e., the permission may take on the character of an abandonment and the promise of a burden), but the curse can only be a reversal of the blessing. Even the wrath and judgment of God which may overtake man do not indicate any retraction, but only a special form, and in the last analysis the most glorious confirmation, of the permission and promise given to him. It will indeed be shown that man, male and female, created in the image and likeness of God, does not owe his divine likeness to himself, and that he is unable of himself to maintain his existence. It will be shown that the repetition of his being in this image and after this likeness cannot be his own concern, but only that

[189]

187

[190]   of a divine restoration and renewal. It will be shown that the divine likeness cannot actually exist for him in the continuance or even the progressive development of a deposited quality, but can only be the object of his hope in God his Creator; that as man he can look only for the man who is not only created in this image and after this likeness, but in accordance with it will actually be God's image. There will be the episode of the fall of man and woman—an arresting and disturbing intervention between their creation and corresponding being. And this will entail also the wrath and judgment of God, the turning of the blessing into a curse. It will be plainly revealed that the man who does not accomplish or merit either his creation or his blessing, but has brought this perversion upon himself, is in no position to endure, let alone to reverse it. And it will then be seen that, as God's image and likeness, he is wholly directed to set all his hope on God. But it will also be made plain that he may grasp and hold this hope because he is God's image and likeness, and because he was originally blessed, and is still blessed in spite of the fact that the blessing has been turned into a curse. It will be revealed also that God is faithful to Himself and work and Word; that the creation of man as male and female, and therefore in the image and likeness of God, is not overthrown by the episode of the fall, but remains even in face of the total contradiction between it and the being of man. It will be shown that man has reason to look for the man who will be different from him, but who for this reason will be real man for him, in the image and likeness of God male and female in his place and on his behalf, namely, Jesus Christ and His community. The history of the covenant whose beginning, centre and goal will be this man—this man and this woman—will confirm the history of creation, and thus confirm and fulfil the blessing given to man in relation to the act of his propagation and in relation to the assumption of his position of power and dignity as compared with other creatures. For both these he has the divine permission and promise, and these will not be abrogated by any episode or fall for the simple reason that they have reference to the man who will be the open mystery of the covenant history which begins after the completion of the history of creation. He has the divine permission and promise just because his own existence, willed and created by God, is only the external basis of the existence of this other man, but as the external basis of the existence of this other man may really be an existence in genuine hope on God which cannot be affected even by his own sin, even by the whole conflict between God and himself, even by all the menace of God's wrath and judgment. When man and woman beget and bear children by the divine permission and promise; when in the indestructible unity of the human race they are more than all the beasts and the rightful lords of the earth, they continually realise in themselves the sign of this hope. This human activity is the sign

[191]   of the genuine creaturely confrontation in open differentiation and joyful relationship which is the image and likeness of the divine form of life. In itself and as such their activity is no doubt a denial of their divine image and likeness, and laden with all the mortal sickness which is a consequence of this

denial, but this does not in any way alter the fact that this activity as such is the sign of the hope given to man; the sign of the Son of Man and of His community. And if man, if male and female necessarily point beyond themselves in this activity; if their activity has meaning only in the fact that it is the realisation of this sign, this again does not alter in the very least the fact that in realising this sign they participate in that to which they themselves point—in Jesus Christ and His Church, in the being of this man corresponding to His creation— even before they know Him, even before they believe in Jesus Christ, even before they are called to His Church. It does not alter the fact that in all their humanity, willingly and wittingly or not, they may have their hope in the divine will and plan which has this man as its goal, and may live in the strength of the truth and certainty of this hope. This is what has to be said of the power of the blessing given to man; of the range of the friendly Word of God which is spoken to him at the beginning of his way as the special creature with independent life that he is. This friendly Word affirms that the natural being and activity of man, irrespective of individual vagaries, is fundamentally and finally destined to be a sign of the fact that the One of whom he is the image and likeness, God Himself, has in and with his creation constituted Himself his pledge and hope.

What are we to make of the divine plural in v. 26? The question is important because it not only says "Let us make man," but then goes on to say expressly: "in our image, after our likeness," so that what we mean by this "image" depends on our decision concerning the subject envisaged by the saga. Expositors are unanimous that the use of this striking plural is connected with the peculiar significance of the creation of man now under discussion: *magnum se quiddam et singulare aggredi testatur* .... *Est homo eximium quoddam inter alias creaturas divinae sapientiae, iustitiae et bonitatis specimen*EN241. (Calvin). "This supreme creature could be created only by the common activity of the whole divine council" (Gunkel). "A special self-determination of God indicates the extraordinary event which is to follow" (G. von Rad, *TWzNT*, II, 388). Expositors are also unanimous that it cannot be interpreted merely as a formal expression of dignity. We are reminded of the so-called *Plur. maiestat.*EN242, which is usually traced back to a Persian origin, but this is quite foreign to the linguistic usage of the Old Testament. We cannot escape the conclusion that the saga thought in terms of a genuine plurality in the divine essence, and that the priestly redaction within which it is presented in Gen. 1 did not see fit to expunge this element. "Behold, the man is become as one of us, to know good and evil," is a parallel in Gen. 3^{22} (based on the J source). And again in Gen. 11^7 (in the story of the Tower of Babel) we find: "Go to, let us go down, and there confound their language." We may also refer to Is. 6^8: "Whom shall I send, and who will go for us?" And dramatic pictures of God's celestial entourage are given in such passages as Ps. 89^5. ^{7}, 1 K. 22^{19}, Job 1^6, Dan. 4^{14}, 7^{10} and particularly in relation to creation in Job 38^7. But Gen. 1^{26} does not speak of a mere entourage, of a divine court or council which later disappears behind the king who alone acts. Those addressed here are not merely consulted by the one who speaks but are summoned to an act (like the "going down" of Gen. 11^7), i.e., an act of

[192]

EN241 it is evidence that we are approaching something marvelous and singular... Among all the other creatures, humanity is an extraordinary example of divine wisdom, justice and goodness
EN242 royal plural

creation, the creation of man, in concert with the One who speaks. There is no reason why we should assume with F. Delitzsch and B. Jacob that they did not actually participate in the work in question but were merely present as interested spectators. The truth is rather that the saga wishes the creation of man to be understood in the true sense as a concerted act on the part of the speaker and those addressed by Him. Further, it is to be noted that in the "Let us make man" we have to do with a concert of mind and act and action in the divine being itself and not merely between God and non-divine beings. How could non-divine beings even assist in an advisory capacity in an act of creation, let alone have an active part in the creation of man, as we are expressly told? And the image which in v. 26 is called "our" image is immediately afterwards (v. 27) expressly described as "His," God's image. The explanation of F. Delitzsch, that man was created "in the image of angels as well as God," has no support in the text, is alien to the purpose of the saga, and can hardly be regarded as biblical in view of Ps. 8^5 ("Thou hast made him a little lower than the angels"). If we take the passage as it stands, there are indeed serious difficulties against the view of F. Delitzsch and B. Jacob that we can at once refer the "we" with whom God associates Himself to a heavenly council or court of angels, spirits and Elohim in the improper sense. For if we wish to speak of a plurality of Elohim in this connexion, we cannot dispute the fact that in ascribing to them an active part in creation, and calling their image the image of God, we give to the term its most proper sense, and thus endow them with the attribute of true deity. The well-known decision of early exegesis was that we have in Gen. 1^{26} a reference to the divine triunity. It may be objected that this statement is rather too explicit. The saga undoubtedly speaks of a genuine plurality in the divine being, but it does not actually say that it is a Trinity. On the other hand, it may be stated that an approximation to the Christian doctrine of the Trinity—the picture of a God who is the one and only God, yet who is not for that reason solitary, but includes in Himself the differentiation and relationship of I and Thou—is both nearer to the text and does it more justice than the alternative suggested by modern exegesis in its arrogant rejection of the exegesis of the Early Church (cf. for instance, Gunkel). If we think that what is here said about the Creator can finally and properly be understood only against the background of the Christian doctrine of the Trinity, we have at least the advantage of being able to accept everything that is said quite literally and without attenuation in this or that respect. We can take seriously not only plurality in the being of God, but also the "Let us" as a summons to a real divine act of creation, and the "our" image as the true image of God as in the equivalent in v. 27. Those who are not prepared to think of God's triunity must ask themselves whether they can really do the same.

If we agree that we must keep close to the wording and context of the passage if we are to understand the divine likeness of man as expressed in vv. 26–27, then—not without genuine astonishment at the diversity of man's inventive genius—we shall have to reject a good deal that has been said in supposed exposition, and decide for a path which is more direct.

The exegesis of the Early Church (cf. Ambrose, *Hexaem.*, VI, 7) maintained at once that since the divine likeness is not to be found directly in the body of man it is to be identified with the soul. It can thus be found either with reference to the divine Logos in the intellect (Athanasius, *De incarn.*, 3), with reference to the Trinity in the three spiritual powers of *memoria, intellectus* and *amor*EN243 (so St. Augustine and his followers), or with reference to the Law of God (the view of the Reformers and their followers), in the moral integrity, purity, justice and holiness which were originally proper to man, corresponded to the law, and as Luther saw it were linked with definite physical characteristics. An age more bold to draw conclusions could then say of the human soul: "It is the image of the Godhead and seeks to stamp this image upon everything around it; it makes the manifold one, seeks truth

[193]

EN243 memory, understanding ... love

in falsehood, radiant activity and operation in unstable peace, and is always present and wills and rules as though it looks at itself and says: 'Let us,' with the exalted feeling of being the daughter and image of God. We cannot conceive of any more inward activity than that of which a human soul is capable; it retires into itself, rests on itself, and can turn and overcome a universe" (Herder, *Vom Erkennen und Empfinden d. meschl. Seele*, 1778, ed. Suphan, Vol. 8, 195). Hegel explains that the divine likeness in man means that the genuine being of man in himself, the idea of man in his truth, is an element of God Himself in His eternal being, so that the nature of man is divine (*Phil. d. Rel.*, Part 3, ed. Lasson, 102). According to A. E. Biedermann it means that man "has the potency and determination, posited within him as an animal soul by the absolute spirit, to actualise a spiritual life which in form and content is in harmony with the absolute spirituality of God and rooted in it, but which must exist independently in the element of the world outside God and therefore in a finite existence, thus reflecting as its own goal and end the eternal basis of the world process" (*Chr. Dogm.*, 1869, 665). According to R. A. Lipsius it means formally man's spirituality and materially his freedom (*Lehrb. d. ev. prot. Dogm.*[2], 1879, 331); according to J. A. Dorner his determination "for living fellowship with God, or for religion" (*Syst. d. chr. Glaubensl.*, Vol. I, 1886, 515); according to R. Seeberg "his volition and freedom of action" (*Chr. Dogma*, Vol. I, 1924, 499); and according to E. Troeltsch, not an original state which has been lost, but, on the supposition of the soul's affinity with God, "a yearning for completion and therefore the principle of historical development" in emergence and conflict (*Glaubensl.*, 1925, 295). We might easily discuss which of these and the many other similar explanations is the finest or deepest or most serious. What we cannot discuss is which of them is the true explanation of Gen. 1[26f.]. For it is obvious that their authors merely found the concept in the text and then proceeded to pure invention in accordance with the requirements of contemporary anthropology, so that it is only by the standard of our own anthropology, and not according to the measure of its own anthropology and on exegetical grounds, that we can decide for or against them. Indeed, is it not almost refreshing to observe that in the end Troeltsch quite obviously makes no attempt whatever to expound Gen. 1[26f.] but decides for an independent reconstruction of the concept? The procedure is characteristic of the tendency in much that has been said at this point by other writers both ancient and modern.

There are, of course, other explanations which do keep closer to the text. In sharp contrast to the exposition of the Early Church, Gunkel tried to argue that, although the spiritual element is not excluded, the primary reference of the divine likeness is physical. As he sees it, the Old Testament always speaks with great naivety about the form of God, His ears and hands and feet; His mouth and back; His walking in the Garden of Eden, etc. And when it says in Gen. 5[3] that Adam begat a son (Seth) in and after his image, the obvious meaning is that the son resembles the father, and resembles him in form and appearance. It is along these lines that we must interpret Gen. 5[1]: "In the day that God created man, in the likeness of God made he him," and similarly Gen. 1[26f.] In reply, it must be pointed out that if God's creating and Adam's begetting are two different things, so too are the likeness of Adam to God and the likeness of Seth to Adam. Again, neither in Gen. 5 nor in Gen. 1 is there any obvious mention of form or appearance as the *tertium comparationis*[EN244] between original and copy. Again, the realism of what the Old Testament says about the quasi-human members of God is only meant, like the references to His knowledge, will, speech and activity, to give concrete attestation to the fact that He is genuinely and supremely the living God. But nowhere is there any independent interest in this realism, and it nowhere claims to give a concept or picture of God as a magnified and more terrible man. Finally, the passage Gen.

[194]

[EN244] basis of comparison

1$^{26-31}$ does not seem to pay any more attention to the body of man than it does to his soul or intellectual and spiritual nature.

A connexion has been found by some—and there is a good deal in its favour—between the dominion which man is given over the beasts and his divine likeness. Delitzsch thinks that the *imago Dei*^{EN245} consists in the fact "that he is a self-controlled being (self-conscious and self-determinative), and therefore superior to all creatures." B. Jacob believes that the point of comparison between God and man, and therefore the divine likeness, is to be found in his animation, or vitality, especially in its supreme forms and manifestations; in the fact that he possesses "spiritual capacities and an innate nobility of rule" which enable him in his dominion over the earth and the animal kingdom to be the divine viceroy as the heavenly bodies are appointed to rule over day and night. But on this view it is too readily assumed that the saga affirms a technical connexion between the divine likeness and the *dominium terrae*^{EN246}, the latter being explicable in terms of the former, and the former in terms of the latter. There can be little doubt that the two are brought together and that the *dominium terrae*^{EN247} is portrayed as a consequence of the *imago Dei*^{EN248}, but the question remains whether a technical connexion is intended. If this were the case, would it not have had to be expressed? Are not expositors who follow this clue really more interested in a Greek and modern concept of humanity than an Old Testament? And is not the pragmatics which they assert in trying to exploit it foreign both to the more immediate and the wider context? Is not the whole point of the saga simply to show that man is the being who is allotted this distinguished position *vis à vis* the rest of creation, whereas when it speaks of the presupposition of this, describing him as created in the image of God, it has in mind something quite different and of a very different order?

We certainly come closer to the text, and decisively so at the most important point, if with W. Vischer (*Das Christuszeugnis des A.T.* Vol. I, 1934, 59 f.) we take Gen. 1$^{26f.}$ to mean that in man God created the real counterpart to whom He could reveal Himself; "that man is the eye of the whole body of creation which God will cause to see His glory; that all creation aims at the confrontation of God and man and the inconvertible I-Thou relationship between Creator and creature, ... which is the true and sole motive of the cosmic process." It cannot be contested that the wider literary context, of which the biblical creation history is the first part, is not interested in man *in abstracto*^{EN249}, in his soul or spirituality, in his body or even in the superiority which he certainly enjoys over all other creatures, but in the future partner of the covenant, the kingdom and the glory of God, in the true counterpart of God, in the earthly subject, addressed and treated by God as a "Thou," of a history which begins with the creation and continues right up to the end of time. In what other sense than this is man in the Bible an *eximium divinae iustitiae et bonitatis specimen?*^{EN250} Can it be otherwise at this point? Is there any justification for the extraordinary apparatus set in motion for the creation of man: "Let us make man in our image, after our likeness," if, in harmony with all that follows, the aim is not already this confrontation, this differentiation and relationship in a particular historical relation between God and man, if the point at issue is not the making possible of this relation? If we are to get to the root of the primary interest of the passage, we shall have to think further along the lines already indicated by W. Vischer.

Dietrich Bonhoeffer (*Schöpfung und Fall*, 1933, 29 f.) offers us important help in this respect. He asks how God can see, recognise and discover Himself in His work. Obviously

---

^{EN245} image of God
^{EN246} dominion over the earth
^{EN247} dominion over the earth
^{EN248} image of God
^{EN249} in the abstract
^{EN250} an extraordinary example of divine wisdom, justice and goodness

only if and to the extent that the thing created by Him resembles Him and is therefore free: not free in itself; not possessing a freedom which (as in a vacuum) is its own quality, activity, disposition and nature; but free for Him who as the Creator willed and always does will to be free for His creature. That God makes man free in this sense, and causes him to be free, is expressed in the fact that He created him as an earthly image of Himself. "Man is distinguished from other creatures by the fact that God Himself is in him, that he is the image of God in which the free Creator sees Himself reflected. ... It is in the free creature that the Holy Spirit calls upon the Creator; uncreated freedom is worshipped by created freedom." But this created freedom finds expression in the fact "that that which is created is related to something else created; that man is free for man." It is expressed in a confrontation, conjunction and inter-relatedness of man as male and female which cannot be defined as an existing quality or intrinsic capacity, possibility or structure of his being, but which simply occur. In this relationship which is absolutely given and posited there is revealed freedom and therefore the divine likeness. As God is free for man, so man is free for man; but only inasmuch as God is for him, so that the *analogia relationis*[EN251] as the meaning of the divine likeness cannot be equated with an *analogia entis*[EN252].

[195]

Bonhoeffer comes closer to the text than Vischer, for obviously he not only takes seriously and exploits the concept, inseparable from the idea of a prototype and copy, of a counterpart realised in free differentiation and relationship, but also emphasises the content of v. 27, where (with the threefold application of *bara'*[EN253]) it is stated in a way that cannot be overlooked: "And God created man in his image, in the image of God created he him; male and female created he them." Is it not astonishing that again and again expositors have ignored the definitive explanation given by the text itself, and instead of reflecting on it pursued all kinds of arbitrarily invented interpretations of the *imago Dei*?[EN254]—the more so when we remember that there is a detailed repetition of the biblical explanation in Gen. 5¹: "In the day that God created man, in the likeness of God made he him; male and female created he them." Could anything be more obvious than to conclude from this clear indication that the image and likeness of the being created by God signifies existence in confrontation, i.e., in this confrontation, in the juxtaposition and conjunction of man and man which is that of male and female, and then to go on to ask against this background in what the original and prototype of the divine existence of the Creator consists? "These two, male and female, are to Him 'man' because they are one before Him. Both are created in this divine image, so that the enjoyment of the divine felicity—to the extent that a creature was made capable of receiving it—was communicated to man as a married couple, filled by God and in God with mutual divine love, from which we may understand and conclude the high dignity of marriage" (H. F. Kohlbrügge, *Schriftauslegungen* Vol. I, 14). Is it that expositors were too tied to an anthropology which expected the description of a being in the divine likeness to take the form of a full description of the being of man, its structure, disposition, capacities, etc., and found it impossible to think that it could consist only in this differentiation and relationship? But the text itself says that it consists in a differentiation and relationship between man and man, and they ought to have kept to this point. Or did they perhaps find it too paltry, too banal, too simple, or even morally suspect, that the divine likeness of man should consist merely in his existence as man and woman? But when it is twice there in almost definitive form, why did they not let themselves be constrained to consider it instead of speculating at large, and especially to make sure that the differentiation and relationship

---

[EN251] analogy of relation
[EN252] analogy of being
[EN253] he created
[EN254] image of God

between man and woman is really so unimportant or even disreputable as they were obviously inclined to accept? Why did they not allow such passages as Hos. 1$^{2f.}$, 2$^{2f. 16}$, 3$^{1f.}$; Is. 54$^{5f.}$, 62^5; Jer. 3$^{1f. 6}$, 4^{30}, etc.; Ezek. 16^1. 23^1; 2 Cor. 11^2; Eph. 5$^{23f.}$; Rev. 12^1, 21^2 to put to them the question whether this differentiation and relationship, as distinct from whatever may be said about man's spirituality and corporeality, might not actually have the constitutive meaning

[196]   for the being of biblical man here ascribed to it (and even more expressly in the second creation saga)? There is indeed no good reason why we should continue to neglect this aspect of the matter, loitering at the distance where one explanation may indeed be more attractive but is also more arbitrary than another.

But if we proceed on the assumption that the saga really finds the being and therefore the divine image and likeness of man in the confrontation and conjunction of man and woman, and if it is against this background that we enquire concerning the original and prototype in the being of God, we are not driven to a pragmatical construction like exegetes who jump from the *dominium terrae*[EN255] to the *imago Dei*[EN256]. In this way we can also emphasise, with the text itself, a fact which has not been taken into account either by Vischer or by Bonhoeffer, i.e., the "Let us" as the distinctive form of the creative fiat in v. 26, and therefore the plurality in the divine being plainly attested in this passage, the differentiation and relationship, the loving co-existence and co-operation, the I and Thou, which first take place in God Himself. Is there no significance in the fact that this matter is expressed in this connexion? It is not palpable that we have to do with a clear and simple correspondence, an *analogia relationis*[EN257], between this mark of the divine being, namely, that it includes an I and a Thou, and the being of man, male and female. The relationship between the summoning I in God's being and the summoned divine Thou is reflected both in the relationship of God to the man whom He has created, and also in the relationship between the I and the Thou, between male and female, in human existence itself. There can be no question of anything more than an analogy. The differentiation and relationship between the I and the Thou in the divine being, in the sphere of the *Elohim*, are not identical with the differentiation and relationship between male and female. That it takes this form in man, corresponding to the bisexuality of animals too, belongs to the creatureliness of man rather than the divine likeness. It also belongs to his creatureliness that the relationship between the I and the Thou in man takes place only in the form of the differentiation and relationship between two different individuals, whereas in the case of God they are included in the one individual. Analogy, even as the analogy of relation, does not entail likeness but the correspondence of the unlike. This correspondence of the unlike is what takes place in the fact that the being of man represents, in the form of the co-existence of the different individuals of male and female, a creaturely and therefore a dissimilar repetition of the fact that the one God is in Himself not only I but also I and Thou, i.e., I only in relation to Himself who is also Thou, and Thou only in relation to Himself who is also I. This is the God who as Creator is free for man, and the corresponding being is the man who as a creature is free for God. This God can see, recognise and discover Himself in man; and for his part the man who corresponds to Him can know God and be the seeing eye at which all creation aims and which is "the true and sole motive of the cosmic process." This God can and will say to man "Thou," and the man who corresponds to Him can also be responsible before Him as an "I." But between this God and the man who thus corresponds to Him there exists—and we have to emphasise this point by way of supplement to Vischer and Bonhoeffer—a unique relationship in organic creation to the extent that among plants and the different animals of land, air and water, as

---

[EN255] dominion over the earth
[EN256] image of God
[EN257] analogy of relation

is continually underlined, there are different groups and species, but that this is not the case among men, so that in relation to other organic creatures man is an *ens sui generis*[EN258], and the distinction of sexes found in man too is the only genuine distinction between man and man, in correspondence to the fact that the I-Thou relationship is the only genuine distinction in the one divine being. Hence it may be seen that the distinction has not only a special but a unique connexion with the divine likeness, and from this standpoint it may be appreciated that the dominion of man over the beasts already has its inner basis in his divine likeness, but that there is no compulsion pragmatically to deduce the one from the other. Supplemented and focused in this way, the thesis of Vischer and Bonhoeffer is surely the [197] explanation of Gen. 1[26f.] which comes closest to the actual text of the narrative.

The concept of "image" used in vv. 26–27 needs a special word of explanation. We venture to translate: "Let us make man in our original, according to our prototype." The venture of this translation is not so much in the nouns as in the prepositions.

It is not the case that *tselem* and *d*e*muth* are simply synonyms, or that the difference between them is so colourless as in the usual translations "image" and "likeness" (Kohlbrügge: "identity," Delitzsch: "equality") or "image" and "similitude" (LXX: εἰκών and ὁμοίωσις; Vul.: *imago* and *similitudo*). In the concept of "image," and therefore in that of a repetition and correspondence to an original (adapted to suggest the idea of this original), the two nouns do certainly coincide, and this should have been even more apparent in the translations than is the case in all these suggestions. But *tselem*, which is used to describe plastic or painted representations and even idols, emphasises more the character of the image as a completed work (in contrast to its subject), whereas *d*e*muth* in some sense analyses the concept and origination of the image and means a "copy" or "duplicate" or "imitation" (in contrast to an original). Thus *tselem* should be rendered "representation" and *d*e*muth* "imitation." In fact, however (cf. Delitzsch), both words admit of a double usage, so that *tselem* can describe not only the representation but also the original reflected in it, its subject; and *d*e*muth* not only the imitation, the copy, but also the prototype which lies behind it. The question poses itself whether in this case the text is not deliberately ambiguous. In itself the "image of *Elohim*" might just as well mean the image which *Elohim*[EN259] has of Himself to the extent that He has cognisance of Himself and knows Himself—in which case it is the copy and imitation—as the image which *Elohim* Himself is to the extent that He is the subject and the original of all existing images of Himself—in which case it is the model and prototype. But this is perhaps to ascribe to the saga far too complex a consideration. If it is necessary to choose, the second possibility and therefore the translation "model" and "prototype" is to be preferred because it is clear from the prepositions k^e and b^e that both nouns refer to the image of *Elohim* and not to that of the man formed in the image of *Elohim*, so that the translation of the Vulgate *ad imaginem et similitudinem nostrum*[EN260] (v. 26) and *ad imaginem*[EN261] (twice in v. 27) must be rejected. Man is not created to be the image of God but—as is said in vv. 26 and 27, but also in Gen. 5[1] (and again in the command not to shed human blood. Gen. 9[6])—he is created in correspondence with the image of God. His divine likeness is never his possession, but consists wholly in the intention and deed of his Creator, whose will concerning him is this correspondence. Even if we were to translate *tselem* and *d*e*muth* by "copy" and "imitation," we should immediately have to interpret them as the "copy" and the "imitation" which God has in His knowledge of Himself. But this is more simply expressed if we go back immediately to the object of this copy and pattern of this

---

[EN258] unique form of being
[EN259] God
[EN260] toward our image and likeness
[EN261] toward the image

imitation, to God Himself, and therefore translate *tselem* as "original" and *d'muth* as "proto-type." At any rate, the point of the text is that God willed to create man as a being corres-ponding to His own being—in such a way that He Himself (even if in His knowledge of Himself) is the original and prototype, and man the copy and imitation.

The question of a correct translation of the prepositions is more difficult. The preposition *b'* has the intrinsic meaning of "in," and in contexts like the present it suggests *in hunc modum*[EN262], so that the noun which follows (the *tselem* of vv. 26–27 and also Gen. 9⁶) is indicated (cf. Delitzsch) as the original mould in which the copy receives its form as such. On the other hand, the preposition *k'* always has the significance of "after" (*instar*[EN263]), and thus points to the noun which follows (the *d'muth* of v. 26) as the model which precedes the imitation, as the norm or ideal which the artificer has before him. This seems to be clear enough and agrees with our interpretation of *tselem* and of *d'muth*. But the question is com-plicated because the conjunction of the two prepositions with the two nouns is not constant. For instance, in Gen. 5¹ it is said that God made man *bid'muth Elohim*[EN264], and afterwards (5³) that Adam begat Seth *bid'muth k'tsalmo*[EN265]. If we leave the particular problem of the second passage, it still follows from the *bid'muth* of 5¹ that *d'muth* can be interpreted other-wise than in Gen. 1²⁶⁻²⁷ as the prototype in which the decision concerning the form of the imitation is taken. Are we to think here of the direct meaning of *d'muth*, and therefore of the fact that in God's self-knowledge there exists a supreme copy of Himself? Undoubtedly it can also be said that man was created in correspondence to this copy (i.e., as Jacob suggests, in imitation of this divine copy). Nor can there be any exclusive opposition between *tselem* and *d'muth* or *be* and *ke* in vv. 26–27. Here too *d'muth* is in some sense a more precise definition of *tselem* and *k'* of *b'*. It may well be that the *bid'muth* of 5¹ is an abbreviation in which the *b'tselem* (which also recurs in 9⁶) is silently retained. In any case the *bid'muth Elohim* of 5¹ must also be translated "in the image of God," and if doubt is thereby thrown on our rendering of 1²⁶⁻²⁷ (as on all others) there can be no question of its impossibility.

But what is the original in which, or the prototype according to which, man was created? We have argued already that it is the relationship and differentiation between the I and the Thou in God Himself. Man is created by God in correspondence with this relationship and differentiation in God Himself: created as a Thou that can be addressed by God but also as an I responsible to God; in the relationship of man and woman in which man is a Thou to his fellow and therefore himself an I in responsibility to this claim.

Very little is said directly about the divine likeness in the rest of the Old Testament. We shall have to refer to Ps. 8⁶ᶠ· when we return to the problem of the *dominium terrae*[EN266]. Gen. 5¹ is merely a repetition of 1²⁷ at the head of the first genealogical table from Adam to Noah. The prohibition of homicide in Gen. 9⁵ is grounded in the fact that God has made man in His image, and has thus declared that control over human life—as opposed to that of the beasts and even after the fall—is reserved exclusively to Himself. What the murderer touches is not a dignity of divine likeness inherent in man—for here again the only reason adduced is the divine creation and no reference is made to any essential predicate of man—but by robbing another man of life he affronts the dignity of God, namely, His intention and action in the creation of man. Care is also demanded when we expound the begetting of Seth by Adam *bid'muto* and *k'tsalmo* (Gen. 5³). It does not really say that Adam begat Seth "after and in" the image of God, but that he begat him—and this is quite different—"after and in" his

---

EN262 in this form
EN263 after
EN264 in the likeness
EN265 in his own likeness, after his image
EN266 dominion over the earth

[198]

own image, i.e., that of Adam. For the purpose of distinction it is also important that according to v. 1 God creates man male and female, but according to v. 3 Adam only begets a son. The change of sequence of the nouns (as compared with Gen. 1²⁶) and the interchange of prepositions, if it is not pure coincidence, is perhaps a pointer to the fact that the text does not see this process in the same light as that of Gen. 1²⁶. It is not at all the case that God's activity now finds as it were renewal and continuation in Adam's procreation. If we are to relate this to Gen. 1, our first reference must not be to what is said about the divine likeness, but to what is said there about the blessing of man, of which there is an explicit remininiscence in 5²: "Be fruitful and multiply." Like the plants, and in the same spontaneous way as the beasts, man has the capacity to procreate himself in other individuals of his kind. That he has not lost the power to do this by the fall; that the blessing which gives him this permission and promise is not extinguished, is first proved in P by the genealogical table of Gen. 5, and in the first instance by Adam's begetting of Seth. It is a drastic oversimplification to deduce from v. 3 of this chapter "that the divine likeness is thought of as passed on in the physical sequence of the generations and therefore in a bodily sense," and [199] that this guarantees "the theological actuality of the witness of the divine likeness to all generation" (G. von Rad, *TWzNT*, Vol. II, p. 389). What can be "passed on" through Adam's procreation of Seth, and then in the physical sequence of the generations and therefore in bodily form, is in the first instance only the existence of the human race as such. It is shown that Adam—in accordance with the blessing which he has received with the beasts—is able to copy, confirm and repeat himself in another individual of his kind. He can become a father and have a son whom he can call by a name distinct from his own. This in itself is a great thing, for nothing less than the possibility of a history of the human race is thereby secured. By reason of that divine blessing, the guarantee of this possibility is actually entrusted to man's free determination and action. But it is in the same way that the possibility of a natural history of the animal kingdom is assured. The particular feature in the history of the human race is not given or actualised merely in the fact that it can renew and preserve itself by a continuous procreation of its kind. This history is a peculiar history in relation to that of all the other creatures because it is the history of a fellowship and intercourse between man and God. But the possibility and continuity of this history as such is not assured by the fact Adam can be reflected in Seth; that man can become a father and have a son. Nor is it the human father who can transmit to his son that which will make him not only a living being but the subject and bearer of this history. Nor is he this himself in virtue of his existence as man, but solely in virtue of the fact that God has created him in and after His image. The special feature of human existence in virtue of which man is capable of action in relation to God; his nature as a Thou which can be addressed by God and an I which is responsible to Him; his character as an I and Thou in the co-existence of man and man, of male and female—all this, and therefore the divine likeness, cannot be transmitted by the father to the son merely because he is the cause of his physical life. The father can, of course, hope that God the Creator will so acknowledge the new creature to whom he as father has been able to mediate life that the son whom he has begotten may like himself be created in and after the image of God. But the realisation of this hope has not been left to his decision and action. How can he hope to be able to pass on what does not in any sense belong to him, but is his only because when He created him God willed to have mercy on him among all His creatures and to acknowledge him in this particular way? The actuality of the witness repeated in Gen. 5¹ is not guaranteed to all succeeding generations merely because there will be these generations. If God acknowledges Seth in the same way as He acknowledged Adam; if the latter is also a Thou to God and an I confronting Him; if the relationship between himself and his kind is repeated; if he find a partner in woman (who is not mentioned in Gen. 5³, in the table which follows, or—significantly—in any of the genealogical tables of the Bible), this is not by inheritance, but is the realisation of a hope which can be fulfilled only in a direct decision and action on the part of God Himself. It can and must be said that this hope is connected with human procreation and birth, with the whole nexus of filiation, with the physical sequence of the generations, with the genealogical tables. The latter play a leading role in the Bible, and we are forced to regard it as the place where divine decision and action are continually realised, as a sign of the patience in which God fulfils His blessing of the human race and makes possible its history (as a natural history within all other natural history). But we cannot say that filiation, the sequence of the physical gener-ations and the genealogical tables include in themselves as such the continuity of the divine likeness. There is no genealogical table of beings in the divine likeness, but from generation to generation the genealogical table aims at divine likeness. This divine likeness is the pledge and promise with which God accompanies the physical sequence of the generations and gives it meaning, thus giving meaning to the patience of God which makes it possible. The difference between likeness to God and likeness to Adam emerges clearly enough in the text and context of Gen. 5³.

[200]

But this is the sum of what the Old Testament has to say directly about the divine likeness. We certainly cannot deduce from this that man has lost it through the fall, either partially or completely, formally or materially. The Reformation thesis concerning the loss of the *imago Dei*[EN267] through the fall is understandable and necessary against the background of the Reformation understanding of the *imago*[EN268] as a *rectitudo animae*[EN269], or *status integritatis*[EN270], which man had originally possessed but immediately forfeited by reason of his guilt and as its consequence and punishment. But there is no basis for this conception of the *imago*[EN271] in Gen. 1. The biblical saga knows nothing of an original ideal man either in Gen. 1, Gen. 2 or elsewhere. Hence it is not surprising that neither in the rest of the Old Testament nor the New is there any trace of the abrogation of this ideal state, or of the partial or complete destruction of the *imago Dei*[EN272]. What man does not possess he can neither bequeath nor forfeit. And on the other hand the divine intention at the creation of man, and the consequent promise and pledge given with it, cannot be lost or subjected to partial or complete destruction. This is proved by the fact that the history of God's fellow-ship and intercourse with man is not abrogated with the fall as the actualisation of man's rejection of this relationship. On the contrary, it really begins with the fall. For although it involves for man a complete reversal of the divine intention and therefore shame and judg-ment, it is at this point that God acknowledges His intention, addressing man as a Thou and making him responsible as an I, and that men themselves must stand and fall together as I and Thou, as man and woman. The divine likeness which the two accounts of creation ascribe to man, the free and gracious will of the Creator by which man is to be one with whom He can deal as with an equal, has not been lost according to the saga of the fall or the rest of the Old Testament. On the contrary, the Old Testament as a whole counts on it that this free and gracious will of the Creator is continually fulfilled in man: not in the course of any natural compulsion, and therefore not merely in and with generation; but in the divine decisions and actions which are always the hope by which the generations are accom-panied.

In this indirect way, then, the whole of the Old Testament confirms the witness of the creation saga. It speaks uninterruptedly of the fact that, without being tied to the sequence

---

EN267 image of God
EN268 image
EN269 original righteousness
EN270 state of innocence
EN271 image
EN272 image of God

of generations, God in His free choice, as this may be seen in the genealogical table of Gen. 5, accompanies a definite sequence of generations with His special decisions and actions, so that for all its sinfulness the divine likeness of the whole race is continually renewed as hope at this particular place and in this particular history. Speaking of this fact of the covenant-history, the rest of the Old Testament agrees with what is said in the creation sagas about what makes this fact basically possible. The prohibition of images in the Old Testament is also an indirect confirmation of this witness. Even if the reasons for this prohibition vary, they undoubtedly include the argument that it is absurd to try to portray God when the fashioning of His image is not only His supreme work of creation at the very first but is continually repeated and confirmed by Him and therefore in principle can never be 'the work of man. The image of God, and therefore the divine likeness of man, is revealed in God's dealings with Israel and therefore in the history of Israel. But it is revealed only as the hope which accompanies and supports all the events of this history, as the goal towards which it moves in all its multiplicity, so that it can never take a single concrete form as an object of imitation by man." I shall be satisfied, when I awake, with thy likeness "—this is the thought and language of the righteous man in the Old Testament (Ps. 17^{15}). From Gen. 1 we learn that originally the image of man no less than the image of God was prohibited. It was only in later Judaism—and only at certain periods and in certain places—that the synagogues were decorated with representations from biblical history. And even there the Jewish element emerges palpably (cf. G. Kittel, *TWzNT* Vol II, 380 f.) in the fact that, in contradistinction to the contemporary religious art of Hellenism, the portrayal is of man in his dealings with God (e.g., Ezekiel apprehended by God, or Moses at the burning bush, or the Israelites protected by God and the Egyptians smitten by Him), and not of the historical hero or the contemporary saint in his piety, in short, not of man for his own sake or as such. If the image of God is such that, as the *analogia relationis*^{EN273}, it can never cease to be God's work and gift or become a human possession; if it is indeed the hope which accompanies and continually precedes the history of Israel, we can understand the prohibition of images and the various attempts to respect it, even though to some degree it was later superseded.

[201]

It is now possible and necessary to say something about the New Testament use of the phrase "the image of God" and its relationship to Gen. 1. It is of a piece with what we have just said that the first New Testament community has no images either of God, of Jesus, of the apostles or of the events recorded in the Gospels. "The cultic image of Mithras is an essential part of the religion of Mithras. The image of Serapis dates from the origin of this religion. There is no Caesar-worship without a statue of Caesar. But in the Christian religion there is no question of an image to be worshipped or a holy myth represented by it, but solely of the Word to be heard" (G. Kittel, *op. cit.*, p. 384). It was only with the second and third centuries that things began to change. As opposed to Israel, the original absence of all images is so self-evident that there is no trace of any prohibition in the New Testament. Only in conflict with the later change of practice did fresh prohibitions and controversies arise in the Church. In the Church of the New Testament there seems to have been an astonishingly direct assurance of something much better than all man-made images of God and man could offer. The decisive linguistic point (cf. G. Kittel, *op. cit.*, p. 393) is the fact that in the New Testament the reference of εἰκών^{EN274}—in contrast to the double meaning of *tselem* and *d*r*muth* in the Old Testament, but in a way which is obviously important for their understanding—is always to the prototype itself, to the form which is copied and essentially revealed in the image. There can be no question of this image being "only" an image—a

---

^{EN273} analogy of relation
^{EN274} image

secondary and therefore perhaps a deflated and displaced form of its object. On the contrary, the object itself is introduced with the image. A supreme Platonism can suddenly become the (apparently unavoidable and in this sense adequate) medium of expression when we are told in Heb. 10¹ that the Law has only the shadow of things to come, οὐκ αὐτὴν τὴν εἰκόνα τῶν πραγμάτων EN275, i.e., that it does not have the things which are actually present in the image. The things themselves in the image! And as εἰκών EN276 here is supremely more than σκία EN277, so in Rom. 1²³ it is more than ὁμοίωμα EN278. The εἰκών EN279 of corruptible man and birds and beasts and creeping things referred to in this passage is the reality which the heathen change into ὁμοίωμα EN280, i.e., into the image of an idol, just as in Heb. 10¹ the εἰκών EN281 of things to come finds its shadow in the Law. It is to be observed that the beast which ascends from the sea (Rev. 13¹ᶠ·) and also the εἰκών EN282 of this beast (13¹⁴ᶠ·) are both worshipped by the lost (Rev. 14⁹, ¹¹); that they are both overcome (Rev. 15²); and that they are mentioned together in not a few places (e.g., 16², 19²⁰). We may even ask whether the εἰκών Καίσαρος EN283 on the Roman dinar (Mk. 12¹⁶ and par.) does not prove that what is Caesar's should be given to Caesar because Caesar himself is present in all his power in and with the coin which bears his image.

It is in the same realistic way that we must understand Paul's description of Jesus Christ as the εἰκὼν τοῦ θεοῦ EN284 (2 Cor. 4⁴) or the εἰκὼν τοῦ θεοῦ ἀοράτου EN285 (Col. 1¹⁵). Or rather, it is because Paul and Christians generally saw and thought of the εἰκών EN286 so realistically in Christ that they had to do this in other directions as well. And it is because they had in this image the reality itself that in contrast with the pagans around them they did not need any other images, nor, in contrast with Israel, did they need any prohibition of images.

[202] Jesus Christ makes both images (of God and man) and also the prohibition of images superfluous. Where images are made, and have to be prohibited, it is clearly attested, in spite of every assertion to the contrary, that there is no assurance concerning that which is copied and that the need to introduce it, although it cannot be avoided, must at least be suppressed. Jesus Christ abolishes this need. If we have seen Him we have seen the Father (Jn. 14⁹, cf. 12⁴⁵). The invisible God Himself has become visible in Him. In Him we have *the* image in face of which the question of the original is finally answered. The connexion with Gen. 1²⁶ᶠ· is unmistakeable even in passages which merely express the simple equation. πρωτότοκος πάσης κτίσεως EN287 is indeed the predicate which in Col. 1¹⁵ is immediately linked with the εἰκὼν τοῦ θεοῦ τοῦ ἀοράτου EN288.

A bold step has been taken from the standpoint of Gen. 1²⁶ᶠ· and the rest of the Old Testament. The creation saga is careful not to say of Adam that he either was or in some way possessed the image of God. In this record the image of God is exclusively the affair of God Himself in His disposing of man in incomprehensible mercy. Similarly the rest of the Old Testament, even when it refers back to this passage, refrains even in its supreme depictions

---

EN275 not the very image of the things
EN276 image
EN277 shadow
EN278 likeness
EN279 image
EN280 likeness
EN281 image
EN282 image
EN283 image of Caesar
EN284 image of God
EN285 image of the invisible God
EN286 image
EN287 the firstborn of every creature
EN288 image of the invisible God

or in respect of any of its figures from claiming that the image of God is revealed in a man or in human events. The Old Testament hopes for the image of God, and for that reason it is not seen, and there are no direct equations. Plato was bold (Timaeus 92c) to describe the cosmos as the visible image of the invisible God. Plutarch *inter alia*[EN289] tried to find an image of God in the sun. In Hellenistic Egypt the same thought was even incorporated into the style of rulers, who were only too ready to receive adulation—"Epiphanes," i.e., manifested deity. But in the sphere of Israel and a Judaism which in some measure was still faithful to the canonical tradition these possibilities were all excluded by Gen. 1[26]. If the rabbis made mention of the concept of God's image, they used it—even at this distance we can still recognise the Old Testament view—as a kind of moral ideal which each individual either keeps or loses according to his faithfulness or unfaithfulness to the Law, according to his moral or immoral conduct. To be God-like is to be worthy (cf. Kittel, *op. cit.*, p. 392). In contrast, Philo completely abandons the sphere of the Old Testament when, anticipating the Church fathers, he tries to find the image of God in the number seven, in the *Monas*[EN290], in the heavenly *sophia*[EN291] or the heavenly *nous*[EN292], in the *Logos*[EN293], and finally in the human soul as the image of the *Logos*[EN294].

In face of these pagan and true or false Jewish conceptions, Paul's daring equation of the man Jesus, who is the Messiah of Israel and the Son of God, directly with the divine image, is an unprecedented and radical innovation. A man who was crucified and who died in Jerusalem is the Messiah, the Son of God, and the image of God. The last of these three predicates was certainly not inferior to the first two, nor was it less strange. Was it an innovation even in relation to the Old Testament, to Gen. 1[26f.]? We must admit that formally the Pauline equation is even more distant from the Old Testament than from pagan and later Jewish doctrines and modes of expression. The distinctness and concreteness with which Paul spoke is foreign to all of them. But may it not be that the greater formal difference betrays the greatest material agreement? Here, too, we can only say that, if the hope of the Old Testament was not meaningless, if its covenant-history really had a supremely definite and concrete goal, if Jesus Christ really was Israel's Messiah, the Son of God and therefore the fulfilment of Israel's own existence, the meaning and goal of its whole course, and therefore the answer to the enigma of Gen. 1[26f.], Paul did not represent any innovation in relation to the Old Testament but pointed to its fulfilment. The decision whether this is the case is not an exegetical question. Then and always it is answered only in the form of faith or unbelief, by proclamation or denial.

If with Paul we take it that it is to be answered positively, with Paul we have to add to our exposition of Gen. 1[26f.] that the question of the divine likeness is not just a matter of the divine control of man, and therefore of the divine promise and pledge, but also passes into man's possession and becomes a human reality. In the light of the fulfilment of the Old Testament as it took place in Jesus Christ, Gen. 1[26f.] certainly seems to have this meaning. If the Old Testament is seen together with Jesus Christ—and the revelation and discovery which is the basis of the whole of the New Testament Church, and Paul as its most skilful advocate, is that the Old Testament must be seen in conjunction with Jesus Christ—it will be realised that although the Vulgate (*ad imaginem*[EN295]) is wrong linguistically it is right in substance. For in and with the creation of Adam God created man not only in and after His

[203]

EN289 among other things
EN290 Monad
EN291 wisdom
EN292 mind
EN293 Word
EN294 Word
EN295 toward the image

original and prototype, but also, in fulfilment of this "in and after," as a copy and imitation. According to 1 Cor. 11⁷ there is a man who actually *is* the εἰκὼν καὶ δόξα θεοῦ EN296, and from this standpoint the same can be said of every man. And side by side with this man there is a woman who is His δόξα as He (the Head of the woman but not without her) is the δόξα of God, and from the standpoint of this woman, or rather of her Husband, the same can be said of every woman. This man together with this woman is the man who is the image of God, who *is* it and does not merely indicate it or establish its physical possibility, like Adam and Seth and all the subsequent members of the genealogical tree. This man (with this woman) is, according to Paul (1 Cor. 15⁴⁵), the "last Adam," and (v. 47) the "second man from heaven," i.e., the man for whose sake, with whom in view, towards whom and therefore in and after whom, God created the first man. Adam (with his wife) was created a "living soul" and as such the first member of the physical sequence of the generations whose last member was to be this man (with this woman). Adam was "of the earth, earthy," but since he was created such by God he was also the promise and guarantee and even presupposition of the "man from heaven" who was to come according to the divine disposing and promise. According to Rom. 5¹⁴, Adam, as the firstborn and archetype of sinful mankind, was even the τύπος τοῦ μέλλοντος EN297, i.e., of the man (and His wife) who was to be the First-born and Archetype of the gift of grace addressed to the same sinful human race. Therefore he himself (with his wife) was also the last as the first, the heavenly as the earthy, the righteous as the sinner. The "Let us make man in our image, after our likeness" was no meaningless word even for Adam. Neither he himself, nor his son Seth, nor his posterity, lives with an empty hope. A hope which is finally fulfilled is no empty hope; nor can it leave empty those who are not yet witnesses of its fulfilment. Conversely, the last Adam who is its fulfilment is already the first who is only prophecy if He is really the πρωτότοκος πάσης κτίσεως EN298, as Paul expressly states in Col. 1¹⁵. Thus the heavenly man is also the earthy, the righteous man the sinner. In other words, Adam is already Jesus Christ and Jesus Christ is already Adam. In the relationship of prophecy and fulfilment in which Paul conjoined the Old Testament with Jesus Christ, this identification is valid for all the self-evident differences. In this way Paul regarded the man Jesus as the real image of God, and therefore as the real man created by God. Both images and the prohibition of images were thus superfluous. For the need for both had disappeared. The just had now awakened and was satisfied with the image of God.

If we are to understand this, we must not overlook the fact that according to 1 Cor. 11⁷ Paul always thought of the man who is God's εἰκὼν καὶ δόξα EN299 (even in passages where there is not immediately obvious) in conjunction with his wife, and therefore of Jesus, not as an isolated figure, but as Israel's Christ, the Head of His community. This will not surprise us if we read Gen. 1²⁶ (not to speak of Gen. 2) with open eyes. Paul did not find there an isolated male, but man and his wife. If Jesus Christ is the image of God, and therefore man, to say "Jesus Christ" is necessarily to speak also of the other—pneumatically, of course, and not physically—who was divinely created with man, who with him is addressed by God as a [204] Thou and made responsible to God as an I, the other who confronts him as a Thou and whom he himself confronts as an I. It is in this way that Paul actually speaks of Jesus Christ when he describes Him as the image of God and therefore man.

It is not in an exclusive but an inclusive sense that Paul conceives the divine likeness of man, of the one man Jesus. Continuing the contrast between Adam and Christ, he writes in I

EN296 image and glory of God
EN297 the figure of him that was to come
EN298 the firstborn of every creature
EN299 image and glory

Cor. 15⁴⁹ as if it were self-evident that we are to bear the image of the heavenly man as we have borne that of the earthy. Who are the "we" who in full assurance evidently expect to have a share in the divine likeness of Jesus Christ? Who is to attain to this? Who is to be included in this identification of Adam with Jesus Christ?

We read in 2 Cor. 3¹⁸ that we all with open face, i.e., wholly revealed as those we are, reflect the glory of the Lord. And therefore we ourselves are a mirror in whom the Lord sees Himself and in whom He discovers His own image, so that, confronting us, He takes and uses us as a mirror, and we are actually "changed into His image"—$\tau\dot{\eta}\nu$ $a\dot{v}\tau\dot{\eta}\nu$ $\epsilon\dot{\iota}\kappa\acute{o}\nu a$ $\mu\epsilon\tau a\mu o\rho\phi o\acute{v}\mu\epsilon\theta a$ $\dot{a}\pi\dot{o}$ $\delta\acute{o}\xi\eta s$ $\epsilon\dot{\iota}s$ $\delta\acute{o}\xi a\nu$ EN300. His glory becomes our glory, and His image our image. Is it of ourselves, in virtue of our decision and action, by reason of our suitability, that we are this mirror? No, but $\kappa a\theta\acute{a}\pi\epsilon\rho$ $\dot{a}\pi\dot{o}$ $\kappa\nu\rho\acute{\iota}o\nu$ $\pi\nu\epsilon\acute{v}\mu a\tau os$ EN301. This object—the Lord and His glory—makes us mirrors in this way, bringing about the change in which His image becomes ours and by reason of which we become bearers of the image of the heavenly (1 Cor. 15⁴⁵). He can and does it because according to I Cor. 15⁴⁵ He is the $\pi\nu\epsilon\hat{v}\mu a$ $\zeta\omega o\pi o\iota o\hat{v}\nu$ EN302, and as the quickening Spirit He is our Lord. But who are the "we" to whom this happens, who without any concealment, without any ideological transfiguration of our reality, can be with Him in glory through Jesus Christ?

We read in Rom. 8²⁹: "Whom he (God) did foreknow, he also did predestinate to be conformed to the image of his Son ($\pi\rho o\acute{\omega}\rho\iota\sigma\epsilon\nu$ $\sigma\nu\mu\mu\acute{o}\rho\phi o\nu s$ $\tau\hat{\eta}s$ $\epsilon\dot{\iota}\kappa\acute{o}\nu as$ $\tau o\hat{v}$ $\nu\acute{\iota}o\hat{v}$ $a\dot{v}\tau o\hat{v}$ EN303), that he might be the firstborn among many brethren." Again, it is He, the Son of God, who is first of all the bearer of the image in and after which God created man according to Gen. 1²⁶ᶠ. But in this passage we are told expressly that God has also predestined others, namely, those whom He foreknew, to be made conformable to His image, to be partakers of Him. What He is in Himself He is not to be for Himself alone. He is to be the Firstborn among many brethren, among many who are like Him. God's will for Him is from the very outset, as the will of Him who had created Him in His image, aimed also at these His future brethren. Who are these brethren of whom God thought simultaneously with His Son, who for His sake are as precious to Him as the latter Himself, whom He wills to liken to His Son without detriment to His uniqueness?

And finally we read in Col. 3¹⁰ that we are not to lie, that we are to put off the old man with his deeds "and put on the new, which is renewed in knowledge after the image of him that created him ($\kappa a\tau'$ $\epsilon\dot{\iota}\kappa\acute{o}\nu a$ $\tau o\hat{v}$ $\kappa\tau\acute{\iota}\sigma a\nu\tau os$ $a\dot{v}\tau\acute{o}\nu$ EN304): where … Christ is all, and in all." This passage is important because it shows that for Paul "our" participation in the divine likeness of Christ does not rest on our decision and action but on a transformation which has happened to us, on God's decision concerning us and therefore on Jesus Christ Himself who is the quickening Spirit, so that it is no less than our own decision and action as well, our decisive putting off of the old man and putting on of the new. To the "image of him that created him," i.e., to God's image revealed and reigning where Christ is all and in all, there corresponds in those who see it, in those who are subject to His dominion, the resolute recognition which leaves lying and the whole world of falsehood behind. But who are the people who have this image before them, before whose eyes Jesus Christ has been evidently set forth (Gal. 3¹), to whom this resolute knowledge can and must be entrusted? Who is it that can here be directly summoned to this divine likeness which is wholly and utterly the divine likeness of Jesus Christ?

EN300 we are changed into the same image from glory to glory
EN301 even as by the Spirit of the Lord
EN302 quickening spirit
EN303 predestinated to be conformed to the image of his Son
EN304 after the image of him that created him

[205]   The answer which is so illuminating for Gen. $1^{26f.}$ is given in Col. 1^{15}, which begins with the simple equation: "The Son of God is the image of God," but ends with the statement: καὶ αὐτός ἐστιν ἡ κεφαλὴ τοῦ σώματος τῆς ἐκκλησίας^{EN305}. The body of which Jesus Christ is Head, the community of which He is Lord, is obviously the clearly distinguished "we" and "they" of the other passages. It is with them that Jesus Christ is God's image. It is from among them, representing the basis of their own existence, that Paul makes this equation. He has no abstract christological interest in this equation. Or rather, this christological equation has at the root an inclusive character, so that it is also an ecclesiological and therefore even an anthropological equation.

It is from this standpoint that the realism of the Pauline doctrine of the image of God is to be understood—the realism of the whole primitive Christian conception, for which the image and the reality are not two different things but the reality is present in the image. The community, Christians, are also present in all that Jesus Christ is, and therefore in the fact that He is the image of God. As they are present, their knowledge of the matter is not indirect but direct, not theoretical but practical, and therefore realistic. The man is certainly not without the woman. He is the head of the woman, and the woman is his δόξα^{EN306} as he himself is the δόξα^{EN307} of God. In this relationship all that is said about Him is also said about her. In this relation she too is the image of God. There is no need for us to pursue at this point the anthropological equation in respect of this relationship between man and wife as Paul develops it in 1 Cor. 11 and Eph. 3. It is obvious that all that he had to say about man and woman was seen from this angle, in the light of the relationship between Jesus Christ and His community, and therefore of His divine likeness, and that it is only in this way that it is presented as an "order of creation." We must be content merely to assert that the agreement of Paul's teaching with Gen. $1^{26f.}$ must not be underestimated in this respect (where it is often overlooked).

In the divine fiat in v. 26 and the blessing of man in v. 28 we read of his empowering and summons to lordship over the earth, or more precisely over the animal kingdom of land, air and water. The reference is to the distinction, exaltation and dominion of man. Like man himself, the beasts have a *proprius nutus: minus videntur alieno imperio subesse*^{EN308} (Calvin). But in contrast to man they have no independent dignity and function even within the creaturely world. They belong to man. This is expressed in the second creation narrative (Gen. 2^{19}) in the fact that God brings them to man in order that he might name them. To this extent it may be said that the relationship between man and beast is in the creaturely world a very unequal repetition of the relationship between God and all the creatures. Man is God's earthly representative (B. Jacob). The expressions used in v. 26 and in v. 28 are strong. *Radhah*^{EN309} is the commanding power which exacts work and tribute; *ḥabhah* means to trample down, to step on something with the consciousness of a ruler, to force a way through (B. Jacob). It is to be observed that these refer expressly and primarily to the creatures of sea and air. The point in question is that of solid and undoubted sovereignty within its limits. Its limits, and therefore the inequality between the divine and human lordship, are self-evident. The latter cannot be an absolute lordship. It is not said, and cannot be said, that the beasts belong to man, for "the earth is the Lord's and the fulness thereof, the world and they that dwell therein" (Ps. 24^1). Nor does the saga wish to say anything about an expansion of human lordship beyond the animal kingdom. Even the important parallel in Ps. $8^{6f.}$

---

^{EN305} and he is the head of the body, the church
^{EN306} glory
^{EN307} glory
^{EN308} distinctive form of life: by no means should they be seen to be subject to hostile rule
^{EN309} to have dominion

describes it expressly with this limitation: "Thou madest him to have dominion over the works of thy hands; thou hast put all things under his feet: all sheep and oxen, yea, and the beasts of the field; the fowl of the air, and the fish of the sea, and whatsoever passeth through the paths of the seas." It is thus foreign to the passage when Gunkel discerns here "the whole programme of the cultural history of the human race," or when B. Jacob links man's "unlim- ited lordship over the earth" with the view that such things as the tunnelling and levelling of [206] mountains, or the drying up or diversion of rivers, cannot be described as a blasphemous assault. Even hypothetically the Old Testament has surely no interest in questions such as these. And the statement in Ps. 115^{16}: "The heaven, even the heavens, are the Lord's: but the earth hath he given to the children of men," refers to the dwelling place of man in earth (in contrast to God's throne in heaven), and not to a lordship over the earth. As we can gather from the vision of Dan. $7^{1f.}$, man's only possible rival is the beast. But this passage tells us that the beast is no true rival, that God has not given the earth to animals but to man, and that man stands in royal superiority over the animal. No technical proof is given of this superior- ity, either by reference to man's form or by reference to his rationality as the instrument of his sovereignty. Indeed, no such proof can be given if we are to be loyal to the spirit of the passage. Of course the asserted sovereignty has its basis, but this is to be sought only in the divine likeness of man, and therefore in the creation of man as male and female to the exclusion of all other differentiations, and therefore in the unity and uniqueness of the human race. The fact which draws from Gunkel a rather patronising comment—that the variety of races has not yet entered the author's field of vision—is the starting-point for further reflection in this respect. But the basis which emerges when this fact is joined with the words about man's divine likeness is not a technical basis. By reason of the fact that man is created in and after the image of God, and therefore in this uniqueness, no means are put at his disposal for the exercise of this lordship over the animals. What is given to him—and it is to this that the passage refers—is the divine destiny and promise of this lordship. Among all the living creatures of land, air and water, man is to have and will have the pre-eminence. For all his similarities and links with animals, he is not to be one animal with others, but is to have them all under himself—in correspondence with God's relationship to all creatures. He and he alone, male and female, is to be the one "animal" to whom God will reveal and entrust His own honour within creation, with whom, in the course of a special history which will not be that of any beast, He will make common cause, and from whose activity He will expect a definite recognition of Himself, the praise of His might and of His right. Obviously this lordship, this distinction, cannot give man a technical superiority over the beast. It rests exclusively on the divine destiny and promise of his divine likeness. It is the immediate consequence of this, and must not be separated from it. Only in this way is it the answer to the question of Ps. 8^4: "What is man, that thou art mindful of him? and the son of man, that thou visitest him?" Only in this way does the answer which follows (v. 6) have meaning: "Thou madest him to have dominion over the works of thy hands; thou hast put all things under his feet." Where is the fulfilment of this destiny and promise? According to Ps. 8^2 the Old Testament answers again: "Out of the mouth of babes and sucklings hast thou ordained strength." It tells us (in the story of the fall in Gen. 3^1) how in antithesis to the destiny and promise given to him man was deceived by the most cunning of the creatures over which he was to have dominion, and yet how in spite of this the destiny and promise (Gen. 3^{14}) were again renewed and preserved. It thus recounts the history of the covenant between God and man as it was fashioned in God's relationship with Israel. In the history of this covenant it becomes true that man was created, not to be the lord of creation, but to be a lord in cre- ation and in token of this to be lord over the beasts. And the New Testament (Heb. $2^{5f.}$) has given this answer a final and true elucidation by referring the whole of Ps. 8 directly to the man Jesus who, for the suffering of death, was crowned with glory and honour. A thoughtful exposition of Gen. 1²⁶ᶠ· will certainly have to move along the line which leads to this point. The biblical creation saga had no occasion to speak of any other lordship of man over animals than the one actualised along this line.

[207]   That man is directed absolutely to set his hope on God alone has its solid and undeniable counterpart in the fact that he is completely dependent on the cosmos surrounding him. And it is an incontestable and unshakeable sign of the real grace of God addressed to him that the cosmos is a home prepared to satisfy his own and his fellow-creatures' needs, to nourish him and them, and in this way, when existence has been given to them, to assure their continuation as the presupposition of the activity assigned to them.

The first point to notice is that the establishment of this relationship, namely, that men and animals can and should be nourished by the vegetable kingdom, is not self-evident, nor does it in any sense rest on an arbitrary choice or appropriation on the part of men and animals, but on a formal and in some sense juridical declaration by God: "Behold, I have given you," and again: "And to every beast of the earth I have given." Just as it is not the case that men and beasts possess the divine blessing as a matter of course, without needing to receive it for their continuation, and in the case of man for the exercise of his power and dignity among the beasts, so they do not have any right of themselves, or in virtue of their necessity, to make use in a way which they think good and necessary of the produce of the vegetable world around them. The fact that plants and trees are there, and are there for them, i.e., as suitable food, is a free divine decision to which neither men nor beasts have any natural right. This relationship between creature and creature, to which men and beasts owe their continued existence, is no less grace than their creation and that of plants. The petition: "Give us this day our daily bread," corresponds to the unalterable order of creation, in which it might well be understood as a special, final work that this declaration was uttered, that between the cosmos in the form of the vegetable kingdom on the one hand and men and beasts on the other this relationship was established. To the particularity of the blessing granted first to beasts and then to men there corresponds the whole particularity of the fact that it is now possible for both to make use of this permission and promise. Provision is made for the practicability of their activity, but only in this way: "Behold, I have given you." As He gives man everything—light, the firmament, dry land, animal companions and finally existence—so now He gives the necessary food. He and His gift will never fail when man is in need. God's table will always be abundantly spread for all.

The second point is that in this respect the saga has obviously classified man with the beasts—just after differentiating him from them. It is no accident, however, that the order is now reversed. Man is the first to be invited and admitted to this table, and only then the beasts. This order makes it plain that in the creation of man all creation is shown to be the external basis of the covenant of grace; that the cosmos is prepared to make possible the existence and continuance of man as God's partner in this covenant; that even the ani- [208] mal kingdom which precedes the creation of man points to man, not as an end in himself, but as the theatre, instrument and object of the realisation of the divine end. But man too, and above all, needs the divine invitation and admission. And the table to which he is invited is the same as that to which animals are also invited. Like his sexuality, the fact that he must and may eat when he is given to eat signifies his intimate relationship to all other creatures with autonomous life, and in this way to the whole created cosmos. His exaltation above the cosmos, or the exaltation of the whole cosmos which takes place in him, does not take place without vindicating and maintaining the similarity between him and the cosmos. His divine likeness does nothing to alter the fact that he has his original and prototype in the beast as well. In this way the fact is continually brought before him that his humanity rests on God's free compassion.

The third point—and although it is not the only one it must not be overlooked—is that God is said to have appointed plants to be the food of men and animals, and not animals themselves. The fact that no mention is made of the latter is a clear indication of the fact that God the Creator did not intend them for food. Whether or not we find it practicable and desirable, the diet assigned to men and beasts by God the Creator is vegetarian. This makes it clear that the supremacy given to man over animals is not one of life and death. Man does not enjoy any capital jurisdiction. Nor has God the Creator given this power to animals themselves or among themselves. Where this power is used by men and animals it is used illegitimately from the standpoint of their creation. Special legitimation will be needed in connexion with a very different order. Another point which strikingly emerges is that the creation saga is speaking of relationships and connexions which precede history and even natural history. In the field of natural history there do not appear to be many spheres where nourishment does not involve the enjoyment of flesh, i.e., where life does not involve the death of another life. But the biblical witness looks beyond the field of natural history. Hence we must not be scandalised if we find it difficult or impossible to imagine the execution of this decree given to men and beasts. The only important thing is to ask in what sense the saga speaks of this decree. There are two aspects to be considered in this connexion. The first is that the sphere to which the saga looks and which it portrays is that of the emergence of the creature as effected by God. But this means the sphere of life which includes dissolution, since it is temporal, but not death, destruction or annihilation, so that there can be no question of taking life. It is the sphere of the existence given and limited by God, and therefore not of a struggle for existence to be waged by creatures among themselves. It is the sphere of the need which is met by God, and therefore not of a need which arbitrarily and violently snatches at fulfilment. Creation means peace—peace between the Cre- [209] ator and creatures, and peace among creatures themselves. The fact that according to the order recounted by the saga man is nourished by the seeds of vegetables and fruits, and that animals are nourished by grass and plants, does not disturb this peace. On the contrary, it confirms it. For they do not in this way destroy vegetation; they partake and enjoy the superfluity assigned to them in common. Carnivorousness, however, presupposes the killing of animals, and this, as the irrevocable annihilation of beings which have independent life as opposed to plants, is a breach of this peace. The biblical witness does not lose himself in the depiction of a "golden age," but he knows and says—and this is the one meaning of the decree—that the creation of the cosmos by God does not envisage this breach. He describes the relationship between creature and creature in terms of sustenance, but not as a destruction of one creature by another. In eloquent silence he tells us how God protected the beasts from attacks either by man or by one other by referring both to the products of the vegetable kingdom. It is only under the very different order of the being of the creature which follows creation and is under active or passive threat, only in the sphere of history which will become that of the intervening incident of the fall, that things will turn out differently, and an order of creaturely relationship will be set up which will be commensurate with the breach of peace between God and man, which will have regard to this breach, and in which the killing of animals will be permitted and even commanded. Even then the prohibition of homicide and eating the blood of animals will be a reminder that the life of another being does not belong to other living beings but to God alone. It will be impossible to overlook the fact that this new order lies under the shadow of the divine abandonment and the oppression of man and therefore of animals involved in the fall, and that every use made of this new order, and all the consequent suffering of the creature, takes place under this shadow. The first order of peace between man and beast and therefore among beasts—an order corresponding to and instituted at the creation—is thus in the first instance a reminder that in the beginning it was not so, and that the nourishment of one creature at the expense of another, although it corresponds to God's order, does not correspond to an original order and will not therefore correspond to a final. The other aspect of the matter is that the post-creation period of the being of the creature under active and passive threat will as such also be the period of the divine covenant of grace. The new order of relationship commencing with the dawn of this period, the introduction of capital jurisdiction between creature and creature, will not in any sense signify a kind of divine submission to creaturely degeneration. It will receive at once a very definite, positive meaning. The content and supreme fulfilment of the covenant of grace will consist in the reconciliation of man by capital juris-

[210] diction. It is with a view to this that the animal is now sacrificed, i.e., that the surrender of its life is demanded and accepted by God as a substitutionary sign for the forfeited life of man, and therefore as a sign of his reconciliation accomplished by God; that the animal is smitten and slain; that the life—not of

208

beasts of prey but of "innocent" domestic animals which have no part in the mutual slaughter, and not of these indiscriminately but only of certain "clean" animals—is offered up by man for man at the command of God, and their flesh is then eaten in this context. A meal which includes meat is a sacrificial meal. It signifies a participation in the reconciling effect of the animal sacrifice commanded and accepted by God as a sign. It presupposes, therefore, that God demands and will accept the surrender of the life of the animal for that of man as a substitutionary sign, and man's participation in the reconciliation thereby signified. But it also presupposes the inviolate continuance of animal life except as arranged by God. It presupposes the sole right of disposal which God still enjoys over it even when in the form of this arrangement He transfers it to man. It thus presupposes an original order from which this divine arrangement stands out as an extraordinary new regulation of the relationship; a rule which is certainly broken but also confirmed by this arrangement. On this—but only this—presupposition sacrifice, the sacrificial meal and therefore carnivorousness is not a crime in the sphere of the covenant of grace, but is in positive agreement with the will of God. But this presupposition is the original order of the Creator in virtue of which, since man had not yet forfeited his life, he had no need of the provision of reconciliation or of the demand and acceptance of sacrifice as its sign, so that no need for the eating of flesh had to be met, and a vegetarian diet could satisfy both men and beasts. The creation story portrays the original, orderly state of affairs which corresponds to this arrangement and without which its later change would be meaningless. Hence it sets a limit to the diet of men and beasts. In this way—if we consider the twofold meaning of this limit—the narrative of the work of the sixth day constitutes a complete and harmonious whole.

Verses 29–30, which deal with the nourishment assigned to men and beasts, are not in this context to be expounded with a special concern for the negative fact that only a vegetarian diet is envisaged. To be sure, this has to be noted. But it is not the case that this is the reason why the verses are put in, and it is certainly not the case, as might appear from Gunkel's commentary, that there is presented at this point a kind of doctrine of a "golden age" of universal peace among the creatures. It is quite true that some such conception can be found between the lines, but it is to be noted that it can be found only between the lines.

In the first instance, the passage tells us positively that as creaturely life the life of man and beast stands in need of special support, and that for this purpose provision has already been made by the furnishing of the divinely created cosmos, but that it needs a special permission and command to make good use of it. Calvin was certainly right when he saw in these verses a modification of man's dominant position on earth. *Nunc demum iuris sui compos efficitur, quum* [211] *audit, quid sibi datum sit a Domino .... Magni enim referi nihil nos ex Dei bonis attingere, quod non sciamus nobis ab eo permissum: neque enim aliter bona conscientia ulla re fruimur, nisi quum eam suscipimus quasi ex Dei manu. Atque ideo docet Paulus (Rom. 14²³) edendo et bibendo nos semper peccare, nisi adsit fides. Ita a solo Deo petere docemur quidquid nobis necesse est: usu autem ipso donorum in meditanda eius bonitate paternaque cura exercemur. Huc enim spectant Dei verba: Ecce tibi paratum a me victum antequam faetus esses; me igitur patrem agnosce, qui tibi nondum creato tam diligenter prospexerim*[EN310]. It must not be overlooked that in these verses men and animals—irrespective of the dominant position of the former—are associated in the same necessity, the same support and the same permission and command. These are the points in which the passage is positively and primarily interested.

But, of course, we cannot overlook or attenuate the implied command not to eat flesh or to kill animals. Calvin does this. And Jacob's view—that the eating of flesh is not literally prohibited to the first men, so that the door to a later permission is left open—is more than contestable. We cannot avoid the conclusion that, with the permission and command which refer men and animals to the table of the vegetable kingdom prepared for both on the third day of creation, they are explicitly prohibited from preying the one on the other for the sake of food. There can be no doubt that in relation to what is said here a new factor is introduced with the permission given to Noah to eat flesh in Gen. 9[3f.] The killing of animals will have its place in the sphere of sinful man, and its right in that of the God who is gracious to sinful man. The killing of animals and the eating of flesh will be legitimated by the sacrifice ordered by God. In the sphere of creation as the emergent state of the creature this is lacking. Its later legitimation is an interim regulation which in all its relativity is necessary and significant for the history of the covenant between God and man. Creation as such is not itself this covenant, but the external basis of this covenant. In creation as such no sin takes place and no sin is envisaged. In it, therefore, there is no need of sacrifice, and therefore the killing of animals and the eating of flesh cannot be envisaged or even left open for "later permission." Attention must be paid to the emphasis on the demarcation indirectly made in this way between the origin and continuation of creaturely existence. But too much is read into it, and we are diverted from the declaration and intention of the passage, if we try to find in this prohibition—which after all is only indirect—the account of a "golden age" of universal peace on earth. To be sure, creation as such is peace. But it seems as if the biblical saga deliberately does not find a place for the Persian, Greek and Roman view of an original peaceful era of creaturely existence. Even in respect of this final element in the creation of man and creatures generally, the "it was so" means only that man and all creatures commenced to exist "in this way," i.e., as they received this permission and command and were thus set implicitly under this prohibition. The time or "era" of this commencement is the pre-historical era in which strictly speaking—and the saga confines itself to this—the question can only be that of God's permission and command and not of the corresponding activity and existence of the creature, so that it cannot be the object of a pictorial presentation. When the creature *is* which comes into being by God's creation; when its history as such commences; when its activity and existence can be depicted, the intervening regulation also begins, whereas that which precedes cannot be represented or can be so only in the form of a reminder of God's original will. It is different with the post-historical era which is the goal of the history of the same covenant whose external basis is the creation. This final era will bring redemption and perfection and also general peace, and it will thus include peace between man and beast in accordance with the commandment of the Creator. When

---

[EN310] Not until after the scope of his authority is established, does he hear what the Lord has given to him ... For it is of great importance that we touch nothing of God's good things, unless we know that God has permitted us to: neither may we enjoy anything with a good conscience, unless we receive it as from the hand of God. And therefore Paul teaches (Rom. 14:23) that we always sin in eating and drinking, unless we do it in faith. So we learn to seek from God alone whatever we need: moreover, as we use His gifts we should be active in contemplating his goodness and fatherly care. Indeed, God's words might be interpreted in this sense: 'Behold, before you were made I had prepared food for you; therefore know me as a father, who looked out for you so lovingly when you were not yet created.'

it looks to this goal the Old Testament, as we may see from Is. 11[6f.], Hos. 2[18] and Is. 65[25], will [212] give concrete depictions, although without expressly thinking of any cancellation of the interim regulation. "The wolf also shall dwell with the lamb, and the leopard shall lie down with the kid; and the calf and the young lion and the fatling together: and a little child shall lead them. And the cow and the bear shall feed; their young ones shall lie down together: and the lion shall eat straw like the ox. And the sucking child shall play on the hole of the asp, and the weaned child shall put his hand on the cockatrice' den. They shall not hurt nor destroy in all my holy mountain: for the earth shall be full of the knowledge of the Lord, as the waters cover the sea." In the final era we have to do specifically with the redemption and perfection of the creature, and therefore prophecy can and must give a clear portrayal. The present verses also refer, of course, to the peace of the last era. But we have to see that this is the reference, and that the Bible does not speak explicitly at this point but is content merely to draw this emphatic line of demarcation. It is obviously the intention of the Old Testament witness lightly to indicate the history of the final era as the hope set up with the covenant between the gracious God and sinful man. It is obviously not his intention to unfold the history of the creatures' original state of innocence and peace, thus moving the reader to homesickness instead of hope, and therefore to an optimistic view of human origins. The proper history of the Old Testament, i.e., the history of the covenant of grace between creation and perfection, will commence with a description of the conflict between God and man and with that of God's faithfulness in this conflict. The history of creation is obviously intended to give clear indication of this conflict, and of the faithfulness of God which outlasts it, by the contrasting reminder of God's original will for His creatures. But this does not mean that it intends to speak of an original excellence of the existence of the creature. Like the sayings about the divine likeness of man and his rule on earth, this permission and command with the involved prohibition, and therefore the prospect of creation as the kingdom of peace, will have to be understood decisively as a promise whose fulfilment is to be sought beyond the immediate horizon of the passage.

"And it was so." This statement looks back to the totality of man's creation, thus embracing his special blessing and the final order relating to the nourishment of man and beast, and it tells us that all this, as the conclusion of creation, took place as described; that by the Word and work of God man really became the being which, as male and female, exists in correspondence with the divine original and prototype, which has received from God permission and promise for his increase and special function among other creatures, and to which in fellowship and peace with these other creatures there has finally been granted the possibility of life corresponding to its creaturely necessity. All this took place. All this was God's creation of man. And it is added at once: "And God saw every thing that he had made, and, behold, it was very good." The retrospect to the creation of man is thus retrospect to the whole work of creation. All the earlier divine approvals from the first day onwards are now repeated and confirmed. What, then, was good, indeed very good, in the events of these first of all days preceding all history? The answer is unmistakeable. It was the establishment and construction of the cosmos, from the actualisation of light to the actualisation of man as the image and likeness of the Creator Himself, and therefore to the actualisation, as the proper inhabitant of the cosmos, of a partner who knows light as light and can have dealings with [213] God. All this, as such, was very good, as a divine act and work wholly corresponding to the divine will. "It was very good" means concretely that it was adapted to the purpose which God had in view; adapted to be the external basis of His covenant of grace. There was no place for grievance or complaint in face of this totality (for who could make it? who could be the critic?), but only for the praise and thanksgiving of all creatures in heaven and on earth. Again, this totality could only look forward to a very good future corresponding to this present. In face of this totality there was no reason whatever to expect anything else. In the light of this origin, as the history of the reality established in this way, everything else that might or did take place stood under the promise that finally it would have to be and would be, not bad or half-good, but, in accordance again with the ruling will of God, very good. Since God was the Creator and as such the absolute Lord of His creation, and since His will was and must be the measure and criterion of all that is good, it is necessary and compulsory to conclude from this present of the creature to its immediate and total future.

(Gen. 2^{1-3}.) Creation is finished, but the history of creation is not yet concluded.

It was not for nothing, but as a commentary worth noting, that a later age opened a new chapter with the depiction of what took place on the seventh day. Nor was it for nothing that in this way what took place on the seventh day was brought into the immediate vicinity of the second creation saga which is so very different in orientation. It is a fact that there is an inner connexion between the Sabbath rest of God recounted in the first saga and the history of the Garden of Eden which is the form of the second. To the Creator who keeps this rest in the first saga there corresponds in the second the human creature which is in that pre-eminent position, which is fed and maintained by God, and which attains its perfection as man and wife. Even in the first saga the divine rest stands in direct relationship with the creation of man. When creation ended with man, having found its climax and meaning in the actualisation of man, God rested on the seventh day from all the work that He had done. It was to this that He looked in the recognition that everything was very good and therefore did not need to be extended or supplemented; in the recognition that His will in respect of the existence and being of the creature had been done in heaven and on earth. What God saw and recognised there as a perfect creature which did not require to be supplemented, but only confirmed and preserved under His rule, is related in the second saga in the form of a different and special version of man's coming into being. The first saga is content merely to have introduced man, as male and female, and makes his creation the work of the day of preparation which preceded the divine Sabbath.

"Thus—namely, in the relationship of God to the creation concluded in man—the heavens and the earth were finished, and all the host of them." But this very completion is the special divine act of a seventh day of creation. To complete does not mean "merely to put the finishing touch." This is what God had done on the sixth day, and it was now superfluous. In relation to it the completion of His work was a new divine act, and consisted in the fact that He [214] confirmed the conclusion of His work, Himself confronting the work which was finished in itself. And this confirmation and confrontation consisted in the fact that "God rested from all his work."

It is not a question of recuperation after a toilsome and well-done job. Even the Sabbath rest of man corresponding to the divine rest does not have this sense in the Old Testament, but means negatively a simple cessation and abstention from further work. The freedom, rest and joy of the Sabbath consist in the fact that on this day man is released from his daily work. On the Sabbath he does not belong to his work. Nor is it merely a question of having to recuperate from the work that lies behind him and to fortify himself for the new tasks that are ahead. On the Sabbath he belongs to himself. Whether he be farmer, artisan, servant or maid, he is just the man who for six days had to be these things and to perform the corresponding tasks, but whose being and existence are more than all these things and his work, who in and with these things and his daily work seeks to be a man, this man, male and female, and as such to be before God. That he does not strive in vain towards this goal; that his work cannot devour him but consists of steps towards this goal, is confirmed at the end of each week by the proffered freedom, rest and joy of the workless Sabbath which he is granted. It is this which gives perspective and depth, meaning and lustre, to all his weeks, and therefore to his whole time, as well as to the work which he performs in his time. So expressly and directly has the biblical witness linked the divine activity of the seventh day of creation with the institution of the Sabbath which man is to observe, that it is impossible to understand it otherwise than from this angle. What man may do on the Sabbath is just what God Himself did on the seventh day: He rested, i.e., He ceased from further creative work. Though He did not cease to be the Creator, He was alone on the seventh day. He was no longer in the process of a new work of creation. He was neither tired of His previous work nor concerned about His future work. He was free from all activity, resting now that His work was finished and rejoicing that it was so good. For a moment one might be inclined to think that He had thus returned to the aseity of the inner glory of His being and existence before creation and without the world and man. But there was no need for God to return to His inner glory before creation, for He had never really lost it as the Creator. And obviously God could not and would not return to an existence without the world and man, since the rest, freedom and joy of this seventh day are described as the completion of His creation of the world and man.

The fact that God rested means quite simply, and significantly enough, that He did not continue His work of creation, i.e., that He was content with the creation of the world and man. He was satisfied to enter into *this* relationship with *this* reality distinct from Himself, to be the Creator of *this* creature, to find in *these* works of His Word the external sphere of His power and grace and the [215] place of His revealed glory. A limit was revealed. God Himself had fixed it for Himself and had now reached it. His creative will was divine from the very outset just because it was not infinite but had this specific content and no other. His creative work must now be discontinued because He did not will it. And He could cease to will it because He had not willed it from the very outset.

He could rest from all His works because from the very outset He had willed and planned these and no other works. It is precisely this rest which distinguishes God from a world-principle self-developing and self-evolving in infinite sequence.

The first feature of God revealed by His rest on the seventh day is His freedom. A world-principle without this limit to its creative activity would not be free like God, but would be tied to the infinite motion of its own development and evolution. In its unlimited creative activity it would not really belong to itself. It would not really be active but entangled in a process imposed upon it and subjected to its higher necessity. A being is free only when it can determine and limit its activity. And only the works of a being like this are acts. God is a being like this. His creative activity has its limit in the rest from His works determined by Himself, i.e. the rest of the seventh day. His freedom revealed in this rest is a first criterion of the true deity of the Creator in the biblical saga.

The second feature of God revealed in the rest of the seventh day is His love. A world-principle without this limit to its creative activity would not be loving like God, but would be a being without love, never ceasing, never finding time for any creature, never satisfied with any, always positing other beings in infinite sequence. Although it might seem to be an ocean of love, it would not really be love at all. Missing every possible object of love, at bottom it would be condemned to pursue its own shadow. Love has a definite, limited object. Love is a relationship which is itself limited and defined by this object. It is in this way that God loves. And the reason why He refrains from further activity on the seventh day is that He has found the object of His love and has no need of any further works. His love revealed in this rest is a second criterion of the true deity of the Creator.

When is He God more truly, or more perfectly Himself in the whole course of His work of creation, than in this rest on the seventh day? Here it is revealed unequivocally that His work cannot have any claim on Him or violate Him; that as the Creator He is always His own Lord, the One who is free and the One who loves, and in both cases God; that precisely as the Creator He has confirmed and revealed Himself as His own Lord, as the One who is free and the One who loves, as God. Here God is quite alone, no less but just as much as He [216] was and is prior to His creation in the aseity of His inner glory—the only difference being that He now willed to be and was this truly as the One who works *ad extra* EN311 and in relation to His work.

For it is to be noted that here too what the biblical witness has to say is not a contribution to an abstract concept of God but a narration. He tells us about a seventh day and about a definite divine attitude which fills it, just as earlier he told us about the first six days and their work. And there is no reason whatever why he should now be taken less literally and concretely than before. He tells

---

EN311 outside of God

us, then, that God finished His work in time as He had previously commenced and concluded it in time. Speaking of God's rest on the seventh day the biblical witness actually tells us that what God was in Himself, and had done from eternity, He had now in some sense repeated in time, in the form of an historical event, in His relationship to His creation, the world and man; and that the completion of all creation consisted in the historical event of this repetition.

What does this mean? In the first place, it obviously has the general meaning that God was not satisfied merely to create the world and man and set them before Him and then to leave them to their own being and purpose and course, to the development of an autonomous law, Himself retiring to the basically superfluous position of a supreme regent. On the contrary, He seriously accepted the world and man when He had created them, associating Himself with them in the fullest possible sense. To the reality of the creature there belongs constitutively not only the fact that it is created by God's grace and power, but also the fact that God willed to co-exist with it, and that when He had made it He constituted Himself its co-existing God in the historical event of the seventh day. In the light of this event—with all that follows right up to the incarnation of the Word and then the resurrection of the body and the new heaven and earth—it is meaningful to speak of God's immanence in the world. For in this work which completes creation—which, although it is not a work, is really the work of all works—God, when He had created the world and man, made Himself temporal and human, i.e., He linked Himself in a temporal act with the being and purpose and course of the world, with the history of man.

But this is only the general meaning. Its particular meaning is that the content of this event of the seventh day was the revelation of the true deity, the genuine freedom and love, of the Creator. In this self-revelation of His true deity He has thus united Himself with the world which He created. It completes and crowns all creation that, as the One He Himself was and is and will be, in His rest He associates Himself with it in the fullest possible way. In this historical event He repeats no less or other than His own perfect being, and declares Himself as such to belong to what He has created so entirely different from Himself. It is in this way—in the whole fulness of the freedom, rest and joy of His deity—that He is with His creation. And what He finally and supremely created was man. With the realisation of man all creation received its culmination and meaning. When man had been realised before Him, God ceased from His work of creation. He halted at this boundary. He was satisfied with what He had created and had found the object of His love. It was with man and his true humanity, as His direct and proper counterpart, that God now associated Himself in His true deity. Hence the history of the covenant was really established in the event of the seventh day. Hence it already commenced secretly on this day. Hence its whole range may be seen from this point. It will not be for God Himself an exotic or ephemeral incident demanding only casual attention. Having created the world and man. He has given [217]

Himself to this matter in person. He has made this last day and act of the history of creation an element in His own history. Now that He has given to the freedom, rest and joy of His deity this temporal form, the character of an historical event after and prior to the other historical events in the sphere of the creaturely reality, His honour is compromised and at stake. It will thus be to Him a matter of supreme and final importance what He will further do in this sphere after the day of rest. Having completed His creation in this way, He will do it for His own sake.

This is the meaning of the seventh day for God the Creator. We must not overlook the indirect meaning which it thus has for the creature as well. Not in itself, to be sure, but beyond itself, the creature finds its completion in the fact that God in His own person has given Himself to belong to it. Over and over again it will have to seek and find what God intends to undertake and do in this fellowship. But the seventh day has also a direct meaning for the creature. The biblical witnesses are obviously not suggesting that creation, with man at its head, went to work on this day of divine rest following the last working day. The clear inference is that creation, and supremely man, rested with God on the seventh day and shared His freedom, rest and joy, even though it had not as yet any work behind it from which to cease, and its Sabbath freedom, rest and joy could only look back to God's work and not its own. Its freedom, rest and joy could be grounded only in those of God and consist only in its response to the invitation to participate in them. The saga speaks expressly of this invitation: "God blessed the seventh day, and sanctified it," i.e., He gave it the power and special determination to have for the creature *mutatis mutandis*EN312 the same content and meaning, to be for it a day of the same conduct, as for Himself, i.e., a day free from work, a day wholly granted to it as opposed to other days. "Because that in it he had rested from all his work which God created and made." That God has done this is described by God Himself as the reason why the creature may and must do it. In this final act of the history of creation—which as such is obviously also the first act of a coven-
[218] ant history which commences between God and man—the divine likeness of man, created as male and female, finds its first confirmation in the fact that this invitation is given, that man's working week also reaches the goal of a seventh day, and that his whole working time is thus set once and for all under the sign of a future which is to be free from work and wholly granted to him. In this way the original acknowledges its copy and the prototype its reflection. In this way God has set a limit to the working time of His creation. In this way He has specifically revealed this limit in the shape of a genuinely special temporal day recurring after every six days and blessed and sanctified for this purpose. In this way God has fixed a goal, continually visible in the sign of this day, to the working time of creation—a goal of its existence which cannot be attained by toil and conflict but which is really granted to it and exists for it beyond toil

---

EN312 allowing for differences

and conflict, marking the end of the way of toil and conflict. The last day will be a Sabbath day, and man's final time will be a time of rest for him, and indeed of rest in fellowship with the rest of God Himself, of participation in the freedom, rest and joy of His true deity. That he for his part will be true man in this participation in God's final rest is the promise in the strength of which he can do his work. And it is in this—not then in anything he himself can achieve, but in what he receives as a fulfilment of this promise—that he himself and his work will be completed, just as God Himself completed the work of creation, not with another work, but with His rest after all His works. The divinely blessed and sanctified day attests this in its constant recurrence. It is the day which man for his part is to sanctify by hearing and accepting this witness in a special temporal act corresponding to the fact that God did not despise to take time on the seventh day of creation for the special act which is the ground and object of this witness. It is a day on which there is also given to man time to hear and accept this witness. What is concretely revealed in the first and divine observance of the Sabbath, and in the implied invitation to the creation to observe it as well, is no more and no less than the meaning and intention of the covenant between God and man.

It cannot be emphasised too strongly that this invitation comes at a time when creation, and particularly man, had nothing behind it except its creation by God, so that there can be no question whatever of a relationship between this Sabbath observance and any work completed by himself. Before and apart from all work and conflict, irrespective of any merits of his own, he is invited to cease from his own works, to rest, and therefore to enter into the freedom, rest and joy of God Himself. In his case, therefore, the Sabbath as the sign of the given promise does not stand at the end but at the beginning, i.e., at the beginning of his working week. And the promise itself, whose sign is the Sabbath, cannot be tied to his own volition, achievement or merit. What precedes it when it first occurs is wholly the work of God and not of man. God has taken it [219] upon Himself to do and accomplish what can now be for man as well as for Himself an occasion for freedom, rest and joy. As far as man is concerned, he has simply to recognise that God has really done all that is necessary, that He has invited him to participate in His rest, and that he may accept this invitation. In other words, he is left wholly and utterly with the grace of God. When this is addressed to him, there begins the history of man with God. Hence this really begins on Sunday and not on a weekday. It begins with the Gospel and not with the Law. It begins with the freedom of man and not his commitment; with a holiday and not an imposed task; with joy and not with toil and trouble. The latter will follow soon enough, but only in succession to the former. That God rested on the seventh day, and blessed and sanctified it, is the first divine action which man is privileged to witness; and that he himself may keep the Sabbath with God, completely free from work, is the first Word spoken to him, the first obligation laid on him. It is thus decided once and for all that the history of the covenant which begins here is to be the history of the divine covenant of grace. And with this decision creation is completed as the revelation of the will of God with regard to the existence and being of His creation. With it creation itself is also completed: "The heavens and the earth ... and all the host of them." Creation took place in order that man's history might commence and take place as the history of the covenant of grace established between God and himself. According to the first biblical witness it took place because God's love for man willed to be incomparably strong in the fact that man and his whole world and therefore the object of God's love should become God's creation and therefore belong from the very outset to God. Creatureliness, and therefore creation, is the external basis of the covenant of grace in which the love of God for man moves towards its fulfilment. It is in this teleology that it is presented in the first creation narrative of the Bible.

An understanding of the account of the seventh day depends very much on the exposition of the dominant concepts of the divine "completing" and "resting" and their context. We read: "Thus the heavens and the earth were finished, and all the host of them. And on the seventh day God ended his work which he had made." "Heaven" and "earth" do not here have the technical meaning of $1^{6f.}$ and $1^{9f.}$, but denote, as in 1^1 and 2^{4a}, the totality of creation in its basic structure as the upper and lower world, except that now the additional phrase "and all the host of them" describes it as a world which is fashioned and shaped and hierarchically ordered and integrated. To this "host" there evidently belongs everything described as creation, from light on the first day to man on the last. And as the saga clearly gives this account without any claim to scientific completeness, this is perhaps the point at which we may legitimately think of all the beings in the upper and lower world which the account does not expressly mention but the existence of which was certainly accepted by Old Testament Israel. This totality—heaven and earth and all their host—constitutes "the work which he has made." The expression $m^e la'khah$ (related to $mal'ak$, "messenger") describes "the work which realises a thought or decision or intention of the Creator. He breathes upon it and imparts to it something of His own being as a sender does to a messenger, so that it represents Him and speaks of Him" (B. Jacob). It is the work which praises its Master by the fact that it is ready for the use to which He will put it. And such was the work that God had made when He had made heaven and earth and all the host thereof. But it now says that God finished His work on the seventh day, that is, on the day immediately following the day of man's creation. The LXX wrongly took this to mean that God put the finishing touches to His work on this day, and since this is obviously an impossible statement in relation to what follows it amends it by turning the seventh into the sixth day. But the reference is obviously to the seventh day, and it is describing the completion (*kalah*) rather than the finishing, i.e., not the final stage of an action but the cessation which immediately follows and effectively closes this final stage; not the finishing off of a thing but the completion and ending of an action; the moment when the one who performs it ceases from his work and is satisfied with what he has done. This is what God did on the seventh day and not the sixth. B. Jacob has rightly drawn attention to the parallel in 2 Chron. 29^{17} where the cleansing of the temple under Hezekiah is described as follows. On the first day of the first month the priests commenced with the purification of the forecourt of the temple; on the eighth day they actually set to work on the porch of the temple and worked for eight days at the temple itself; and "on the sixteenth day of the first month (i.e., on the day after those seven and eight days) they made an end" (*killu*). This is the sense in which God finished His work on the seventh day. We cannot even accept the suggestive interpretation of Rabbi Raschi that on this day God created rest, for this presupposes the same misunderstanding. God did not in any sense

[220]

create anything further on the seventh day, but He confronted the last of His works, i.e., man, and therefore creation as a self-enclosed totality. He ceased from further works which would increase and improve this totality. The ground of this decision lay in the repeated judgment of Gen. 1³¹, to wit, that all that He had made was very good. And since His judgment was authoritative and His decision just; since He *a mundi creatione non prius cessavit, quam omni ex parte compleverit, ut nihil ad iusiam copiam deesset*EN313 (Calvin), this divine cessation was also the divine completion of creation. The expression, then, is not purely negative. God does not retire. As the Creator He now begins to confront the completed world-totality, and to be active towards it and in it. *Certum enim est, quatenus mundum sua virtute sustinet Deus et providentia gubernat, fovet creaturas omnes atque etiam propagat, esse in opere assiduum ... nec probe agnoscitur coeli et terrae creator, nisi dum perpetua illa vegetatio ei tribuitur*EN314. (Calvin). The divine action on this seventh day is to be understood as God's solemn enthronement in face of the world created by Him, as the inauguration of His lordship over it, of what was later described as the *creatio continua*EN315. But it is the world created in the first six days as depicted, and not another, which God now confronts as Ruler and in which He will now be active. This divine completion belongs integrally to the creation of the world as that which concludes and limits it. From this conclusion and limitation there later follows, in the course of many, many succeeding weeks, the history of the relationship between God and the world, i.e., between God and this world. Its completion denotes and defines the *status opificii qualem exstare voluit Deus*EN316 (Calvin). To that extent it belongs to the being and continuance, to the existence and therefore to the creation of the world.

The fathers thus betrayed a great obtuseness, and narrowed the horizon with serious consequences, when in their handling of creation they usually confined themselves to the *hexaemeron*EN317, although both externally and internally everything points to the fact that the story of creation is to be understood as a *heptaemeron*EN318, and that the record of the seventh day is quite indispensable. Similarly the concept "day" must not be reinterpreted or [221] expunged at this point, as if the saga were using the seventh day merely to denote all the time which follows (so Delitzsch and Jacob, and even Luther, *W.A.*, 24, 61), or even a time which lasts "always and eternally" (so Delitzsch). It is another matter that all that God does, including His action on the seventh day, takes place in His time, i.e., that as a divine activity it takes place originally in Himself, and therefore beyond all created time, and to that extent co-temporally with it. But we are mistaken if in view of this fact we suppress the truth that as the saga understands it this completing activity of God belonged also to the story of creation as such, and that it formed the content of an actual, definite and limited day. If we will quietly let it have its say, the saga tells us that the real world in which God was later to work did not come into being without being completed by the God who caused it to come into being; that the constitution of the world thus included from the very outset its completion. Without violating His own temporality, God has again taken time from our time for His action, and therefore really completed everything on a genuine last day of the first week. That even the history of God's lordship over the world moves towards a completion which

---

EN313 did not cease from creating the world until He had completed it in every part, lest anything should lack its proper fullness

EN314 For it is certain, insofar as God sustains the world by His power and governs it by His providence, that it is his constant work to nourish all creatures and also cause their increase ... so that He should not be rightly known as creator of heaven and earth, without that work of continual quickening being attributed to Him

EN315 continuing creation

EN316 the character of the work that God wished to display

EN317 six-day story

EN318 seven-day story

concludes time but to that extent is itself temporal, towards the dawn of a genuinely last day of redemption, has its definite correspondence in the history of creation. Why then is the saga not allowed to say this when it is quite obvious that it can have no other meaning unless alien concepts are introduced?

And now the second concept used in these verses, namely, that of God's rest, is at once equated with that of completion. "And God rested on the seventh day from all the works which he had made." It is not for nothing that in v. 2 this is a parallel to the statement about completion. *Shabhath*, too, means primarily to "cease," to "break off" and "leave off" an activity. It is, therefore, rightly translated in the Vulgate as *cessare ab omni opere suo*^{EN319}. The only point is that the reference is now less to the activity, i.e., to what has been done, and more to the active subject which, when it ceases from its work, is free from it and enters into its rest. That God completes the *mᵉla'khah* which He has made means for Him that He enters into His rest. Gunkel connects the ideas of tiredness and compensating recuperation with this divine rest. He concludes that it is a "strong anthropomorphism," and criticises those expositors who (like Delitzsch) appeal to Is. 40²⁸ ("God, the Lord, the Creator of the ends of the earth, fainteth not, neither is weary") in their anxiety to escape something which is offensive to the modern religious consciousness. But it is not our business to make concessions to the modern religious consciousness. In spite of Is. 40²⁸, anthropomorphism may be quite justifiable in this as in other passages. On the other hand, the real question is whether it is not a modern notion to interpret rest in the sense of recuperation after preceding exhaustion. It is true that in the parallel in Ex. 31¹⁷ God's resting after the completion of creation is connected with the concept of "refreshment" (*naphash*), and that in Ex. 23¹² this refreshment is also ascribed to the "son of thy handmaid" and the "stranger" who are also to keep the Sabbath. But as a comment on "resting" the term "refreshment" inclines us in the direction of "coming to oneself" or "reviving." And if (apart from the later laws of the Sabbath, cf. Ex. 20⁸ᶠ·, etc.) the decisive commentary is to be sought in the connexion, indicated in the passage itself (v. 3), with the day which is blessed and sanctified for man by divine precedent, it must be said that according to Ex. 16²⁹ the Sabbath is a divine gift to man. In bringing relief, it means positive blessedness, freedom, joy, rest and—it may be added—peace. According to Jewish consciousness still alive to-day, it brings man a "heightened sense of life" (B. Jacob). If in Gen. 2³ we have to reckon with a "strong anthropomorphism," it is because there is here ascribed to God the blessedness of the man who at the close of the week may come to himself [222] and belong to himself on the seventh day. In fact, however, the saga says and means the very opposite. It is a part of the history of creation that God completed His work and confronted it as a completed totality. The true and finished world in its actual constitution is heaven and earth and all the host of them, not without but with the God who willed and created them as the world, and who now confronts them in this being of theirs as the Lord. On the seventh day God was blessed as the One who had thus completed the world. And for this reason He has blessed and sanctified the seventh day to man as a day on which man may also be blessed and free and joyful, resting from his labours, belonging to himself in peace, breathing freely and being refreshed.

But it is to be noted that, in view of the express institution of the Sabbath (v. 3) with its invitation to man, God's rest on the seventh day cannot possibly mean that He has withdrawn from the world and lost interest in it. The close connexion between the concept of God's rest and that of completion shows that the reverse is the case. The day of God's rest is the very same day as that on which He finished His creative work and thus limited creation, calling a halt with the creation of man, and being content to have become the absolute Lord and King of this particular world. The question can be raised—and H. F. Kohlbrügge

---

^{EN319} ceased from all His works

2. Creation as the External Basis of the Covenant

(*Schriftauslegungen*) Vol. I, 1904, 23 f.) has raised it—how precisely God could rest after the creation of this world; on what grounds He could be satisfied with it, and particularly with man, as His final creation; and how, on the day on which He assumed dominion over it, He could enjoy the bliss of creation's Sabbath. This divine rest certainly cannot be explained or justified by what we learn from Scripture about the world and particularly about man, much less by what we know, or think we know, about the world and man from other sources. Ought not creation to have proceeded to the creation of much better and more satisfactory beings who would have been far more worthy of the divine completion and rest? But when we consider how all the decisive factors in the creation of man—his divine likeness, his position of lordship over the beast and peace among the living creatures on earth—have shown themselves to be elements in the promise, in the divinely determined future of man, we cannot escape the answer which Kohlbrügge gave: "Could God have rested if He had not done all these things with a view to Christ? Or did He not know that the devil would soon spoil all creation, including man? But as God created heaven and earth through Christ or in Christ, so He has created all things with a view to Christ. On the seventh day God was well pleased with His Son. He saw creation perfect through Christ; He saw it restored again through Christ; and He therefore declared it to be finished, and rested." There is no avoiding an eschatological explanation of this rest. God does not only look upon the present of His creation, nor does He only look back to that which He did in creating it. God knows its future. And He knows more, and more gladdening things, about the future of the work which is finished before Him, than is to be seen in the present state of the things themselves, or than the saga can indicate with a description of this coming into being. God rests when He completes, and celebrates when He has finished, because in relation to His work He knows what He has in view; because He looks forward to a completely different fulfilment and completion of its relationship to Him, and therefore of its own reality. God rests from His work at the completion of creation because He is quite sure of Himself and His intention and power in respect of it. If along these lines we look beyond the history of creation to the subsequent history of the relationship between God and His creation, to the history of Israel with all the contradictions and imperfections in which the creature confronts the Creator, and therefore again and again to a state of affairs which cannot possibly explain God's rest in face of His completed work (especially at the end of the first week), in the last resort we can think only of the goal of this history, of the intervention which God prepared in the history of Israel and finally actualised on behalf of man and the whole world, and therefore of Jesus Christ as the form of the creature in view of which God's rest on the seventh creative day is   [223] explained and justified. There can be no doubt that God's rest on that day involved a supremely positive relationship of God to the creaturely world and man as they now confronted Him. When He became the Creator, God did not need to have any regrets nor did He in any way violate His glory. He did not need a better world, nor, after the creation of man, did He need in this world any higher or more perfect beings, if even as the Creator He was to be worthy of His own deity. After the creation of this world, which reached its climax in man. He did not have to withdraw into Himself strained and tired and in need of recuperation (as man does after his imperfect labours and activities). By His work He had not lessened but confirmed His glory. As the Creator of this world He was not less but truly Himself in His pure deity. Resting on the seventh day, He does not separate Himself from the world but binds Himself the more closely to it. Since He is justified by His work, His celebration when it is finished is in reality the coronation of His work. We have already said that not man but the divine rest on the seventh day is the crown of creation. It is the radiance of this crown shining back on the totality of things (and primarily on man) which illumines and justifies this totality (and primarily man). When God celebrates the completion of His work, this totality becomes the festive hall and man His festive partner. His rest on the seventh day is the demonstration of His gracious turning to the world created by Him, of His gracious lordship over it and of His gracious presence and immanence in it.

For a proper estimate of the whole, the strange fact must be observed that the saga describes this divine rest as an independent event, as the content of a special and final day of creation in sequence with the other six. On this aspect, too, we suppress something important if we do not allow it to say what it actually says. It is tempting to ask whether what is here called the rest of God—His tarrying and being in His own glory—does not describe something which God, who is not confined to our creaturely time, is and has and does in Himself from eternity to eternity. Is it not an impossible limitation of God's being to interpret this divine rest as the special content of a created day? Should we not understand by this seventh day of the saga, with its ascription of rest to God, the totality of time instead of the limited period of one created day? But an answer which entails the dissolution of the concept "day" is far too obvious not to be suspicious. And it destroys too much to be acceptable. Of course God did not rest only on this seventh day. Of course He did and does so in Himself from eternity to eternity even apart from His relationship to the world which He has created. Of course He did not need its completion to be God, to be glorious in Himself, to be blessed and free and joyful. But the very fact that He does not keep this inner glory to Himself is the demonstration of His grace in the creation of this world. He crowns creation—without detriment to what He is and has and does without it—by actually taking upon Himself this limitation, and therefore by resting, by being glorious and blessed, within the world and its space and time. Nor does He do this only indirectly. He does do it indirectly by His activity as such. Indirectly the whole work of the six days, and therefore the whole cosmos, and each of its individual phenomena, is a demonstration of the inner glory which God did not will to keep to Himself, but which He caused to radiate and extend outwards in the form of a reality distinct from Himself, and to which He willed to give a witness, indeed a whole host of witnesses, in this reality. God's selflessness, His grace, the demonstration of His mercy, lordship and presence as Creator, and therefore His immanence in the world, are not exhausted by the indirect fact that He made the world as His *m'la'khah,* and that He is glorious in the fact of its being and existence. We are not merely directed by creation to see God in His works as such, although He has undoubtedly created a host of witnesses and is to be seen in His works as such. For apart from God's works His rest on the seventh day also belongs to creation. It is not merely without but also within His action as Creator, and therefore fulfilling time, that God is glorious and blessed and free and glad in Himself; the living God who did indeed work but who did not will to be absorbed and therefore to disappear in His work. It was not too small a thing for Him to reserve a special place in this sphere where He could be all by Himself and wholly Himself—but in this sphere, in the world created by Him which is our world. The "strong anthropomorphism" of this passage is that according to the saga God's all-completing rest from His works is not just an idea hovering over the whole but a concrete, definitive and historical element in the history of creation; that God's rest is brought into relationship with the totality of this history, so that for all its singularity it is in some sense integrated into the totality of the creaturely world. The world is not without the fact that from its beginning in creation the gracious address and lordship and presence of God are concretely true and actual even within its own constitution, not merely as the secret of all God's works and therefore of all creaturely phenomena as such, but also in an individual, special sphere of life and existence. That creation is really the external basis of the covenant finds its most pointed expression in this place if we will take it literally and not metaphorically, as a reality and not an ideal. Are we not forced to ask how in the framework of creation and the creaturely world, and without disturbing them, the whole history which follows can consist of more than world-events indirectly confessing God, of human acts and experiences under the incomprehensible because abstract sovereignty of a Creator and

[224]

2. Creation as the External Basis of the Covenant

Lord who is now distant and separated from the world and man? How is it that according to Holy Scripture this history is continually accompanied, supported and broken by supremely personal interventions, words and acts, by a constant element of the self-witness of God the Creator? By reason of what order can there be in the heart of the creaturely sphere a covenant of grace, accompanied by revelations, miracles and forces, by signs, insights and decisions which obviously cannot be deduced from or explained by the works of the first six days, nor from the constitution of the creaturely world, if this consists only of what God had created in the six days? From the standpoint of creation, to what order will it correspond if the history of the covenant of grace runs its course in the exceptional form of God's special relation to the one people Israel? And how is it to come to pass that in the end God Himself, without unfaithfulness to or contradiction of Himself as Creator, will become man in His Son, and indeed this one specific man Jesus, thus becoming in the most direct way His own witness? How can it happen, not in abrogation but in confirmation of creation, that certain temporal events as opposed to others, i.e., to the ordinary, temporal course of created things, can have the character of direct divine manifestations and dealings? All these are unanswerable questions if we try to understand creation only from the standpoint of a *hexaemeron*[EN320] arbitrarily considered for its own sake, and not of the *heptaemeron*[EN321] attested by the saga. The whole history of the covenant of grace is then left hanging in the air, and it is no wonder that the biblical proclamation is abbreviated either by approaching the history of the covenant of grace as if it had no basis in creation, and therefore in the natural being and existence of the world and man, with the result that it obviously seems to be only an accidental and capricious phantasy (although not a phantasy for which the Bible itself is responsible), or by an artificial attempt to reduce the history of the covenant of grace to the developments which can be interpreted as an evolution of the world created in six days, and therefore as a history of the world and man, thus necessarily denying, reinterpreting or juggling away, directly or indirectly, its most decisive elements, its character as a divine self-witness, and therefore as revelation and new creation. But these questions can be answered legitimately only if we keep to what is written, namely, that the Sabbath also belongs to creation: not as the ideal reality of the glory of God hovering high above the created world; nor as the (again ideal) reality of the whole time and history which follow creation; but genuinely as the actuality of the fact that God was not content merely to create the world but that when He had created it He associated Himself with it once for all and always as the Lord of glory that He is. From the very outset God has given Himself to it as its own, and therefore from the very outset He has made it His own. In a world created in this way, with the inclusion of the divine rest on the seventh day, the sphere of grace is not a foreign body; its history is in order; it is possible, without destroying the creaturely world, as a sequence of divine self-attestations with their revelations, miracles, signs and new creations. Is not this line of development obvious from the very outset? When He rested from His work, did not God from the very outset reserve this sphere for this further utterance and activity which transcends His work of creation as such? Did He completely enslave Himself? Did He limit His glory to that which He created? Did He enclose it in the reality of the creaturely world, and therefore pledge Himself to keep to its immanent evolution for the revelation of His glory? It is because He did not do this, because on the seventh day as the coronation of creation He was by Himself, Himself, the living God, because from the very outset He did not think it too mean a thing to be this with and for us, that He has established the future kingdom of grace as a kingdom of righteousness which is not exposed to the suspicion of any phantasy, and for this reason does not need any reinterpretation.

[225]

[EN320] six-day story
[EN321] seven-day story

223

In this light we can see the necessity and fundamental importance of the institution of the Sabbath in v. 3, i.e., of the invitation to man to participate in the divine rest on the seventh day. "And God blessed the seventh day and sanctified it: because that in it he had rested from all his work which God created and made." It is to be noted that, to the tacit annoyance of many readers and expositors, there is no corresponding invitation to action as participation in God's creative work. It is not in the latter but in the former that God calls man to follow and accompany Him. It is also to be noted that in the whole of the first account this is the only express, i.e., unambiguously expressed, reference to the history which follows creation. This invitation is the connexion between the freedom which in the act of creation God has reserved for Himself and that which is also promised to man; the freedom which declares itself "in the rest which commands itself to stop" (B. Jacob). Finally, it is to be noted how unmerited is this freedom offered to man. So far he has not done any work. In origin man's rest from labour can refer only to the rest of God and the creative work of God which it crowns. And it is in this relationship to God's activity that he is commanded to rest. For him, too, this day is to be a special action fulfilling time like his work, but in addition to and apart from his work it is to be the content of a day corresponding to the seventh day of creation. Calvin's exposition that God blessed and sanctified the seventh day *ut in eo celebraretur operum suorum praestantia et dignitas*[EN322] is surely correct. What is in question is the *solemnis consecratio, qua sibi Deus studia et occupationes hominum asserit die septimo*[EN323]. There should, of course, be a daily consideration of the *immensa Dei bonitas, iustitia, virtus, sapientia in hoc magnifico coeli terraeque theatro*[EN324]. But God has no illusions about man: *si forte minus sedulo, quam par esset ad eam intenti essent homines, ad supplendum quod assiduae meditationi deerat, Septimus quisque dies peculiariter delectus est*[EN325]. The point of the matter must be kept in view. It is not just a question of man having a holiday on this day, as if God had any particular pleasure in his inactivity. The point is *ut negotiis aliis omnibus soluti liberius mentes suas ad creatorem mundi applicent*[EN326]. It is a matter of the *sacra vocatio, quae homines mundi impedimentis eripit, ut totos Deo addicat*[EN327]. As may easily be seen, we have to do with a correspondence and repetition in the creaturely sphere of the divine day of rest. As God in His rest after His works reserves to Himself the freedom of direct action, the possibility of immediate self-witness, so man is [226] not to work incessantly, but is to cease working at regular intervals in order that he for his part may be free and open to God's immediate self-witness, in order "that ye may know that I am the Lord that doth sanctify you" (Ex. 31^{13}, Ezek. 20^{12}). What was demanded by Ritschl's theology is the very thing which must not happen. The life of man must not become just an ordinary day of "philosophy and morality." This ordinary day is bounded by the "day of the Lord," and it is significant for an understanding of this matter that this term can be used not only for the Sabbath but also for the day of *Yahweh's* appearance and judgment (the "last judgment") which will close this æon. Moreover, this "day of the Lord" is the real day which is given a name, whereas in the Old Testament the ordinary days of the week are not named

---

[EN322] so that in it the dignity and excellence of His works might be celebrated

[EN323] solemn consecration, by which God reserves human study and activity for Himself on the seventh day

[EN324] God's immense goodness, righteousness, power, and wisdom in this magnificent theatre of heaven and earth

[EN325] the seventh day was especially selected as a means of making good whatever might be lacking in diligent meditation, lest perhaps human beings were to attend to [to God's goodness] with less than proper zeal

[EN326] that having been released from all other business, they might more freely apply their minds to the creator of the world

[EN327] holy vocation, which snatches people from the distractions of the world, to bring them all to God

but only numbered (as in this account), and in the strict sense are only precursors of this one day. It is by the divine blessing and sanctification of the Sabbath that the week, and time, is concretely and teleologically constituted and ordered. On this day it receives its goal—a concrete goal which itself fulfils time. At this goal work terminates and the rest and freedom of man begin. Only when this proper day, this goal in time, is past, can a new week begin with its work, but a week which for its part can only move from the very outset towards another Sabbath as its true day, its goal in time. Here, too, the concrete aspect is quite essential—that in relation to the Sabbath we have to do with a proper temporal day and not merely with an idea of rest, joy and freedom hovering over all days. Here, too, we have to do with the foundation and preparation for the history of the covenant and salvation which follows the history of creation. From the standpoint of creation, this will not be identical with universal or cultural or intellectual or religious history as it takes place under the presupposition of the being and existence of the cosmos and of man. For all its relationships to ordinary history, it will also claim man in a special way. It will demand his concrete attention and participation. It will demand that he should give it the time which he must save from his time for other things, and which he cannot also apply to other things. As Thomas Aquinas (*S. theol.* II 2, *qu.* 122, *art.* 4, *ad.* 1) puts it, the commandment to keep the Sabbath holy is a *praeceptum morale quantum ad hoc, quod homo deputet aliquod tempus vitae suae ad vacandum divinis*[EN328]. As God is not satisfied merely to reveal Himself in the works of six days, but in addition to His indirect presence and lordship in the world is just Himself on the seventh day as the living God in His glory—and this in His relationship to His creatures—so the creature must not be satisfied with itself, nor man with man or the cosmos, but beyond this indirect relationship to the Creator he must be absolutely at the disposal of His Creator in a special movement and experience, and this in all his creatureliness. This is the positive reason for the cessation of his work on this day; and this the positive reason for his observance of this day. Calvin writes (*Instit.*, II, 8, 29): *Quiescendum omnino est, ut Deus in nobis operetur: cedendum voluntate nostra, resignandum cor, abdicendae cunctae carnis cupiditates, denique feriandum est ab omnibus proprii ingenii muniis, ut Deum habentes in nobis operantem, in ipso acquiescamus*[EN329]; and even more pointedly with reference to Gen. 2³: *Quies spiritualis est carnis mortificatio, ne amplius sibi vivant filii Dei, aut propriae voluntati indulgeant*[EN330]. The fact that this passage expressly bases the blessing and sanctification of this day on the example and pattern of God's rest on the seventh day of creation proves that the rest offered to man on this day must actually be brought into decisive connexion with the freedom which God has reserved for Himself in His relationship to the creature. What it signifies concretely in this connexion follows from the use which God has actually made of this freedom, and therefore from the history of the covenant of grace controlled by the divine self-revelation and continuing the history of creation. It is here that the *quies spiritualis*[EN331] will take place in imitation of God's rest on the seventh day. It is here, then, that the *operari Dei in nobis*[EN332] will take place. It is here that the commandment of *cedere, resignare, abdicere, feriari* and *mortificatio carnis*[EN333] will be kept. It is this which strictly speaking is inaugurated with this commencement according to the final   [227]

EN328 is a moral precept amounting to this, that the individual should set aside some of the time of his life to make space for divine matters

EN329 Above all, it is necessary to rest so that God may work within us: we must yield our will, surrender our heart, resign all desires of the flesh, and then free ourselves from all the duties of our own ability, so that, having God at work within us, we might rest in him

EN330 Spiritual quiet means the mortification of the flesh, so that the children of God should no longer live to themselves, nor indulge their own will

EN331 spiritual quiet

EN332 God's work within us

EN333 yield, surrender, resign, free oneself ... mortification of the flesh

sentence of the first creation narrative. When he commences to exist, man first receives this commandment, or rather this invitation. On the threshhold between the history of creation and its continuation, it makes clear that God has not created man and his cosmos to leave him to his own devices. Not for nothing has He created him in and after His image, or exalted him above the beast, or assigned him food for the preservation of his life with the promise of peace on earth. This invitation of the Creator to keep the Sabbath with Him sets him immediately above the common relationship of the creature to the Creator and in relationship with the God who even as the Creator is always the free and living God, and who as such will keep His promise. It tells him that in fulfilment of His promise God is disposed to accept him specially. It summons him to keep himself specially open to the God who is so disposed and purposed. It makes it clear that there is to be between the Creator and the creature not only an indirect but a direct connexion, not only a relationship but genuine intercourse. As a divine foundation and institution it makes it plain enough that this intercourse is initiated and maintained by God, and that it will rest throughout on God's free grace. As an invitation and commandment it also makes it plain, of course, that on man's part it will involve decision—obedience or disobedience. Will the human race keep the Sabbath or not? Will it enter into its promised rest or not? "We who have believed do enter into rest" (Heb. 4³), and "he that is entered into his (God's) rest, he also hath ceased from his own works" (Heb. 4¹⁰). Will we in fact realise our fellowship with the Creator and therefore believe? Are there not those concerning whom "God has sworn in his wrath that they shall not enter into his rest?" These are the questions which will continually demand an answer in the intercourse between God and man which follows the history of creation. There will always be a place for the exhortation and summons to be grateful for the grace of God, and to "labour to enter into that rest, lest any man fall after the same example of unbelief" (Heb. 4¹¹). But God's purpose, and His faithfulness to it, cannot be set in doubt by the necessity of such questions and exhortation. For from creation the immovable foundation on which God has not only taken His stand but also set man with the institution of the Sabbath is His own *requietio*^{EN334}, i.e., His own *regnum, in quo requiescens homo ille, qui perseveraverit Deo adsistere, participabit de mensa Dei*^{EN335} (Irenaeus, *Adv.o.h.*, IV, 16, 1). From creation—preceding and superseding every human decision of obedience or disobedience—there remains (ἀπολείπεται) for the people of God the Sabbath rest (σαββατισμός), the divinely willed and ordered fellowship, relationship and agreement between His own and human freedom as the goal and determination of the way to which this people continually have to be recalled, to which God never wearies to recall them, and to which, at the end and climax of that intercourse. He has definitively recalled them in His Son (Heb. 4⁹). That He *has* done this is the force of this ἀπολείπεται in face of a whole host of human Sabbath desecration and human enmity against the grace of God. All that has been imposed upon and is to be observed by us in the way of Sabbath observance is an *exercitium ... spiritualem quietem adumbrans, cuius in Christo apparuit veritas*^{EN336} (Calvin). The man in whom this *quies spiritualis*^{EN337} as the agreement between divine and human freedom, the *operari Dei in nobis*^{EN338}, the *cedere, resignare, abdicere, feriari*, and finally the

---

^{EN334} resting
^{EN335} kingdom, resting in which the person who has persevered in waiting on God will share in God's table
^{EN336} exercise ... of the spirit foreshadowing a restfulness, the truth of which has appeared in Christ
^{EN337} spiritual quiet
^{EN338} God's work within us

mortificatio carnis[EN339], finds actualisation according to the commandment of the Creator; the man who *perseveravit adsistere Deo*[EN340], is neither man in general, nor the Israelite, nor the Christian, but for every man, for the Jew first but also for the Gentile, for every one who believes on Him, this man, the one man Jesus Christ, who as He was and is God's image, as He achieved man's exaltation above all other creatures, as He founded the kingdom of peace on earth, also kept the commandment of the Sabbath, with the promulgation of which God completed the whole work of creation.

Here, too, an exposition of the first creation narrative can be concluded without a refer- [228] ence to the Christological content of the passage only if we artificially try to persuade our-selves that the truth and faithfulness of God in the blessing and sanctification of the seventh day are an open question. If the truth and faithfulness in this respect have been unequivo-cally revealed in the person and work of Jesus Christ, what else can we say but that in this respect too the creation saga refers prophetically to Him? Early Christianity undoubtedly meant and said this when according to I Cor. 16^2 and Ac. 20^7 it began to keep the first day of the week instead of the seventh as a day of rest, and this expressly as the κυριακὴ ἡμέρα[EN341] (Rev. 1^{10}). It ventured this apparent revolution against its divine order in creation, and it did not regard it as a revolution but as a debt of obedience, because according to Mk. 16^2, Mt. 28^1 and Lk. 24^1 the day of the resurrection of Jesus Christ was the day after the Jewish Sabbath, the first day of the week. Was this an innovation, or was it a true understanding and application of Gen. 2^3? If it is correct that the truth and faithfulness of God in the blessing and sanctification of the seventh day are revealed in the resurrection of Jesus Christ; if the history of the covenant and salvation between God and man inaugurated in the former is concluded in the latter; if in the latter life began in the new time of a new world, we have to admit that they were right; that this first day of this new time had to become literally as well as materially the day of rest which dominates life in this new time. And there is also a direct proof. If the Sabbath observed by God was the seventh day for Him, it was undoubtedly the first for man. Man's existence began with the fact that God kept this day, and that He ordained and blessed and sanctified it as a day to be kept by man. From this point of view man after this day was not set on the way to a Sabbath still to be sanctified, but on the way from a Sabbath already sanctified; from rest to work; from freedom to service; from joy to "seriousness" of life. Rest, freedom and joy were not just before him. He had no need to "enter" into them. He could already proceed from them, or commence with them. They had already taken place. He had already sat at the divine wedding-feast, and having eaten and drunk could now proceed to his daily work. The "Lord's Day" was really his first day. Hence it ought always to have been his first day and not his seventh and last. Each week, instead of being a trying ascent, ought to have been a glad descent from the high-point of the Sabbath. The teleology of each week—its direction towards the next Sabbath—ought to have derived its strength from the ἀπολείπεται of its commencement. In Christian chronology, the week has obviously gained this meaning. What took place was not an innovation but the discovery of the calculation which was already hidden in the calculation of Gen. 1^2. When God has planned and done everything well in the creation of man and his world, and when He has associated Himself with His creature as the free and living God, then man in free and living fellowship with God can begin his course. What is ostensibly his first day is really (thanks to the preceding grace of God) his second day, and his first real day was really the "Lord's Day."

[EN339] yield, surrender, resign, free oneself ... mortification of the flesh
[EN340] who has persevered in waiting on God
[EN341] Lord's Day

3. THE COVENANT AS THE INTERNAL BASIS OF CREATION

The Bible immediately compels us to consider the relationship between creation and covenant from a very different—indeed from the opposite angle. There can be no question of a material contradiction. We do not have to subtract from the insights already won nor do we need to add to them or correct [229] them. We are still dealing with the same theme. We can still call it by the same name, viz., creation as the presupposition of the history of the intercourse between God and man which rests upon it externally, which is made possible by it technically, which follows it externally and temporally, and which continues its history inwardly—creation as the way and means to the covenant. We must accept all that has been said about the subject under this head and from this angle—so far as we have seen it rightly. But the fact remains that it has another aspect; that it can and should also be seen from this new angle and therefore in a very different light; and that from this standpoint it must be given another name, and our view of it will assume a different form and move in a different dimension.

Let us frankly admit that if the remarkable fact of the juxtaposition of the P passage Gen. 1 and the J passage Gen. 2 did not show this other aspect of the same theme and force upon us the corresponding view and title, we should have no good reason not to regard the problem and theme as basically exhausted in the form in which they have already confronted us. It has often been the case, and particularly in expositions and evaluations of these first chapters of the Bible which are dogmatic in interest, that as far as possible the inviting and attractive outline of Gen. 1 has been observed and honoured as though this were the real biblical history of creation, whereas Gen. 2 has been regarded as a kind of interesting supplement on isolated points, especially in regard to the creation of man, i.e., man and woman, and therefore read and used only as a kind of dependent commentary on Gen. 1. But Gen. 2 is neither a supplement to Gen. 1 nor a commentary on it, but a new and different history of creation. It is true that it does not contradict the first and that it has the same pre-historical event in view; that it deals with the same God on the one hand and the same man and the world on the other; that the same relationship exists between the Creator and the creature in the act of creation, and the same connexion of this act with the purpose and work of God after creation. But it is also true that we have here to do with an independent saga in relation to this event, and that from first to last this second saga takes its own individual line *vis-à-vis* the first. And if, for all the differences in detail, there can be no doubt about the unity of the theme and therefore the material agreement of the two accounts, if there are indeed individual agreements or approximations, and if the second saga—particularly with reference to the creation of man—provides an elucidation of what we are given in the first, it is nevertheless the case that the two accounts can be generally brought into direct relationship, i.e., harmonised, only in an artificial way and by doing violence to the actual text. Our best course is to accept that each has its own harmony, and then to be content with the higher harmony which is achieved when we allow the one to speak after the other. Hence the second of the accounts must be read as if it were the only one. And superfluous though it may seem after reading the first account, the whole problem and theme must be reconsidered from a new angle.

Our first task is to give a general outline of the points raised.

The creature does not exist casually. It does not merely exist, but exists meaningfully. In its existence it realises a purpose and plan and order. It has not come into being by chance but by necessity, and therefore not as an accident but as a sign and witness of this necessity. This is already implied in the fact that it is a creature and therefore the work of the Creator, of God. As God Himself does not exist casually but in the power of His own divine meaning [230] and His own divine necessity, so also the creature exists by Him and is a revelation of His glory. The act of creation as such is the revelation of the glory of God by which He gives to the creature meaning and necessity. The creature could not assume these, nor could it have, possess or retain them, nor, having lost them, could it have regained them. But it does not need to do so. Creating it, God gives it meaning and necessity. Giving it being and existence, He makes it the exponent of His intention, plan and order. It could not exist if it were not, in virtue of its being, this exponent; if it were not, by reason of God's gift, the sign and witness of the divine meaning and the divine necessity. In and with this creation God makes it this exponent. This is the revelation of God's glory in the act of creation. The divine meaning and necessity which the creature reveals, which as such it denotes and attests, is God's free love, i.e., the love of God in which He wills and posits another by Himself and is Himself for it—the free love in which He accomplishes this willing and this positing in His own power and by His own independent resolve. It is in the same free love that He Himself is God, i.e., the Father in the Son and the Son in the Father by the Holy Spirit. Again, it is in the same free love that He has resolved in Himself from all eternity on His fellowship with man in the person of His own Son. As this free love is revealed, i.e., made visible outside His own being, His hidden glory is revealed. And this is creation to the extent that it makes the creature the exponent, sign and witness of the divine meaning and necessity. It is from here, from the free love of God, that the creature receives its meaning and necessity, and it is given to it to be the bearer of God's intention, plan and order. From this standpoint it may be said that it was not created other than to be the recipient of this gift, and that it does not exist otherwise than as the recipient of this gift. From this standpoint it may be said that, as it exists, it can only be grateful, and that it necessarily forgets and denies its existence if it is not prepared to be grateful. Its creation as such is its creation as a grateful being and for a grateful existence. It is and exists solely by reason and in accomplishment of the revelation of the glory of God's free love: the love which God has shown towards it without being under any obligation to do so; the love of the Father and the Son in the Holy Spirit; the love which already in the eternal decree of the giving of His Son for the sake of man did not will to be without a concrete extra-divine object. It was when this love began to be deed and event and therefore to be revealed that creation took place and the creature received its being and existence. The creature owes both the fact that it is, and what it is, to the revelation which has this content.

[231]   This is the other aspect of the matter. We have already considered the first aspect, to wit, that creation is the formal presupposition of the covenant in which God fulfils the will of His free love. God loves His creature and therefore a being which originally belongs to Him as the One who loves, to which nothing that happens from the side of God, the Lord of this covenant, can be foreign, and which in this respect cannot assert or maintain any divergent claims of its own. Creation is one long preparation, and therefore the being and existence of the creature one long readiness, for what God will intend and do with it in the history of the covenant. Its nature is simply its equipment for grace. Its creatureliness is pure promise, expectation and prophecy of that which in His grace, in the execution of the will of His eternal love, and finally and supremely in the consummation of the giving of His Son, God plans for man and will not delay to accomplish for his benefit. In this way creation is the road to the covenant, its external power and external basis, because for its fulfilment the latter depends wholly on the fact that the creature is in no position to act alone as the partner of God, that it is thrown back wholly and utterly on the care and intercession of God Himself, but that it does actually enjoy this divine care and intercession. What we now see is that the covenant is the internal basis of creation. It is certainly not its external basis. Its external basis is the wisdom and omnipotence of God, who is sure of Himself as Creator because He is God, who at the creation of the world and man, at the laying of the presupposition of the covenant, at the preparation of the creature for His grace, is never at a loss for the right ways and means, but whose Word is sufficient to give being and existence to the creature as the object of His love and as the partner of His covenant. But creation also has—and this is what we have now to consider—its internal basis. This consists in the fact that the wisdom and omnipotence of God the Creator was not just any wisdom and omnipotence but that of His free love. Hence what God has created was not just any reality—however perfect or wonderful—but that which is intrinsically determined as the exponent of His glory and for the corresponding service. What God created when He created the world and man was not just any place, but that which was foreordained for the establishment and the history of the covenant, nor just any subject, but that which was to become God's partner in this history, i.e., the nature which God in His grace willed to address and accept and the man predestined for His service. The fact that the covenant is the goal of creation is not something which is added later to the reality of the creature, as though the history of creation might equally have been succeeded by any other history. It already characterises creation itself and as such, and therefore the being and existence of the creature. The covenant whose history had still to commence was the covenant which, as the goal appointed for creation and the creature, made creation necessary and possible, and determined and limited the creature. If creation was the external basis of the covenant, the [232]   latter was the internal basis of the former. If creation was the formal presupposition of the covenant, the latter was the material presupposition of the for-

mer. If creation takes precedence historically, the covenant does so in substance. If the proclamation and foundation of the covenant is the beginning of the history which commences after creation, the history of creation already contains, as the history of the being of all creatures, all the elements which will subsequently meet and be unified in this event and the whole series of events which follow; in the history of Israel, and finally and supremely in the history of the incarnation of the Son of God.

From this outline of the new problem and theme it may be seen that the object in question is really the same. It may be seen that there are no factual contradictions; that nothing can be added to what has been said, or subtracted from it. The only change is in respect of the direction and dimension in which it is considered; of the concern and emphasis. The main interest now is not how creation promises, proclaims and prophesies the covenant, but how it prefigures and to that extent anticipates it without being identical with it; not how creation prepares the covenant, but how in so doing it is itself already a unique sign of the covenant and a true sacrament; not Jesus Christ as the goal, but Jesus Christ as the beginning (the beginning just because He is the goal) of creation. This is what we have now to maintain and appreciate. It must be conceded at once that without the existence of the second creation narrative we could hardly have the temerity to do this. But since the Bible offers us this second account we must and may attempt it.

In Gen. 2^{4b-25} we are dealing in some sense with a history of creation from inside. We have left the sphere of the Priestly witness with his architectonics and lucidity. It is no longer a question of building in a great nexus which will later reveal at a definite point the meaning and purpose of the whole. More than one expositor has at least raised the question whether the theme is really creation in any true sense. It is only on the periphery, as it were, that we discover that the second witness too is thinking of the foundation of "the heavens and earth, and all the host of them." His explicit statements concern only a tiny selection of the great cosmic happenings recorded in the first account. There can be no doubt that we are again in the sphere of the beginning and becoming of all things; it is again a question of historically explaining their being, and therefore the history of the covenant, by what has taken place prior to this history as the divine foundation of the creature. But in this case the explanation is limited to the narrowest possible sphere. And this sphere is as near as possible to that of the history which follows. What takes place is depicted wholly in the manner and with the colours of this later history. Only the fact that it has to do with a divine activity, and indeed a basic divine activity, shows us unmistakeably that here too we are in fact dealing with creation his- [233] tory. But the smallness of the sphere, the narrowness of the selection made, the consequent limitation of horizon, and the immediate proximity of the later history—all these features of the second narrative involve an essential foreshortening of the teleology of the first. There is no trace of the expectant and straining march from sphere to sphere up to the decisive centre. Without having first to look ahead, or to fill out what has gone before by what follows, we find ourselves from the very first *in mediis rebus*[EN342]. It is only in the great final act of the creation of woman, and here in contrast to the meagreness of the first account, that there is a striking teleological tension. Even here, however, the solution—"And the Lord God said, It is not good that the man should be alone; I will make him an help meet for him"—is formally anticipated in the opening words. And we certainly cannot say that this final item is itself the goal of creation as we have it in the accounts of the sixth and seventh days in the first record. The creation of woman as the helpmeet of man is a strongly emphasised aspect of the goal of the totality, but the creation of man in the concreteness here ascribed to him, the planting of the Garden of Eden, and the planting of the two special trees, are in their own way aspects of the same goal of creation. From the very outset we are already at the goal, and this not merely in the form of a forward prospect and reference, but in such a way that the end is already present and visible in the beginning itself and as such.

It does not seem to fit in with the normal characterisation of the two sources which must here be presupposed, but it is worth considering whether it would not help to characterise them more profoundly if it were agreed that in Gen. 1 we have a prophetical view of creation, whereas the view contained in Gen. 2 might usefully be described as sacramental.

It would be quite out of place, therefore, to apply the method used in relation to Gen. 1, selecting a certain point in the passage and using it as a criterion in our understanding of the rest. If we ask what the story is really leading up to, a general answer is given by its direct connexion with the ensuing account of the fall. It is palpable that it aims immediately at the commencement of the history of the covenant between God and man which takes place when the man created by God becomes disobedient and has to bear the consequences of this disobedience, but God for His part does not really cease but continues to be his God and faithful to him in this modification of the relationship between the Creator and the creature, as the One who controls the conflict which has broken out. The history of creation in Gen. 2 is the immediate presupposition of this event. It describes the coming into being of the world, and supremely of man as that of the being in whose nature and mode of existence there is prefigured the history which follows, and particularly this first event in this history, for all that it is so new and incomprehensible in relation to creation. It describes in the form of history the situation which forms the background to this event; the wall which gives rise to both the light and shadow of this event; the sphere within which this event will take place. It describes creation as the sign and witness of the event which will follow. To this extent it presupposes and prefigures it. Of course it does not say that man will sin against God, or that even if he does God will have to be faithful to him. It does not question the freedom which there will be on both sides in the history

[234]

[EN342] in the middle of things

which follows. But it describes the relationship, willed and ordered by God as the Creator of all that is, within which there will be these dealings on both sides. As a description of this relationship, and therefore in connexion with the aim of the whole, all the elements of the passage are equally important, and none of them can be picked out and used as a dominant exegetical motif for the understanding of the rest. On the contrary, we have to see that for all their historical succession they all stand together in the foreshortened and therefore impressive teleological connexion of the whole with what follows.

The first obvious sequence is to be found in Gen. 2^{4b-7}. And the first point to call for consideration—and it is decisive for all that follows—is that we now have to do with a new name for God. The God whose creative work is to be described is from the very outset called *Yahweh* Elohim: the God who reveals His name to Israel; who under this name has chosen and called Israel and has dealt with it as its Lord. So close are we here to the history of the covenant which commences after the completion of creation that even in the history of creation God must bear this name. So much is the story of creation to be considered as the presupposition of the history of the covenant, indeed as the visible prefiguration of its beginning! The Israelite who hears or reads about the Creator is to think at once of the One to whom he and his nation owe everything, against whom he and his people have sinned a thousand times, but who incomprehensibly has never failed to be faithful to him and his people. This God is the God of creation.

And this God made "the earth and the heavens." This striking inversion of the order is the second point to be noted. The fact that God is also the Creator of the heavens is true and familiar. But it is mentioned only once and incidentally and dependently and secondarily in the first sentence. The heavens are not overlooked or denied, but in this saga attention is focused on the earth. What interests the man who speaks here is the fact that God has made this lower earthly sphere visible and attainable to man, and that in it and from its elements He has made man himself. He praises the Creator because He is the Creator of the earth. This is natural enough in view of the fact that God has appointed the earth to be the sphere of man, and that He will accept the man who lives on earth and is himself taken from it, and that even in his creation He has already allied Himself so wonderfully with him. But from what follows it [235] is the earth itself which is important to him. Even man—this saga is not as anthropocentric as it is often made out to be—is first introduced only as the being who had to be created for the sake of the earth and to serve it. For we are told that the earth was originally barren because God had not yet sent rain and man was not there to till it. This twofold condition of a fruitful earth bearing trees and plants had still to be fulfilled in the onward course of creation: first, by a mist which went up from the earth and watered the whole face of the ground; and then—as part of the same perfecting of the earth—by the creation of man. That man has the concrete duty to cultivate and tend the things which God has planted will be emphasised later in the story of the Garden of

Eden. After the fall—although in very different circumstances—man is immediately sent to work on the land. Here, too, creation is really the creation of the
heavens and the earth (with an emphasis on the terrestrial sphere), and not
just that of man; indeed, it is the creation of the man who must work and serve
under the heavens and on earth, i.e., in relation to his fellow-creatures. It is to
be noted how different this is from the first account, which is far more anthropocentric at this point, suggesting that the world of vegetation was ordained
and created only to be the food of men and animals. For in this account it is a
kind of end in itself. The perfect earth is not a dry, barren or dead earth, but
one which bears shrubs and vegetation and is inhabited. God will plant it. But
to make that which has been planted thrive, God needs the farmer or gardener. This will be the role of man. He thus appears as the being which must
be able and ready to serve in order to give meaning and purpose to the planting of the earth. He has a gap to fill at this point. He is just as necessary as the
watering without which the earth cannot be brought to completion. In view of
his complete integration into the totality of the created world, there can be no
question of a superiority of man supported by appeals to his special dignity, or
of forgetfulness not merely of a general but of the very definite control of
Yahweh Elohim over man. In spite of all the particular things that God may
plan and do with him, in the first instance man can only serve the earth and
will continually have to do so.

What is said at the end of these verses—more concretely than in the first
saga—about the process of the special creation of man points in the same
direction of the indispensable humility of man's existence. In the first place,
we are told that God had formed him of "the dust of the ground." The verbal
connexion in the Hebrew is unmistakeable: man is a formation consisting of
detached and individual portions of the earth which is arid, barren and dead
in itself. Of course he is more than this. But he is this too. He is not a new
element planted by God like shrubs and vegetation. Seen even from this stand-
[236]   point, he has no independent position in the totality of creation. His nature is
that of the earth on which he lives and moves. He owes his existence wholly
and utterly to the fact that from a particular handful of the dust of the earth
God willed to make him. That God made him and that He made him of the
earth are both things which he has in common with the beast. The only difference between him and the beast is that he is dust formed into a human body.
But the human frame no less than the animal has a natural tendency to return
to the earth from which it was taken. Primarily, then, the distinctive election of
man is merely that he is formed from this dust as opposed to all other dust and
given this form which is distinct from that of the beasts. On the other hand,
what robs him of all claim is that while his nature is differentiated from the
earth and the beast it is still related to them, retaining its earthly and animal
character. He is not even distinguished from the beast—although from the
earth—by the fact that he became a "living soul," that he is a being which not
only possesses a body but also a soul, and finally that it is the breath of God

which makes him such a being. And if this is an exaltation and distinction which man as such a being shares with the beast, he also shares with it the problematical and threatened and transitory nature of his existence. God does not owe him the breath which, apart from his bodily existence, makes him a living soul, nor does it become his own in virtue of the fact that God made him for this purpose. If man is not renewed, the fact that he was once quickened will not prevent him from sharing the fate of the beast and becoming again what he was: arid, barren, dead, dust of dust, earth of earth; a soul without form or dwelling, assigned with the body to the depths of the earth, condemned without the Spirit of God to an impotent hopelessness. Thus from the beginning he stands under the law of humility and the fear of God. In what sense, then, does his election really distinguish him from the earth and the beast? According to the second creation narrative—and we have here a material parallel to what the first account called his divine likeness—only in one respect. The divine quickening is general, so that the animal kingdom too exists in virtue of it. But man becomes a living soul as God breathes the breath of life into his nostrils; in this most direct and personal and most special act. To no beast does God turn in this way, nor does any of the things which He has formed become a living soul in this way. It is to man, and to man alone, that God gives breath in this manner. It is man, and man alone, who becomes a living soul in this way. And this, and this alone, is the distinguishing feature of man—his humanity—according to this passage. And it is to be noted that this rests on the wholly free and special election and compassion of God, and that it stands or falls with it. As long as it stands, God, who can repeat this in-breathing even when man's frame of dust has returned to dust, is always the confidence of the one whom He has elected and addressed in this way. If it falls, man's only future and prospect is to return to dust. The fact that he is not [237] just earth moulded into a body, and not just a soul, but a soul quickened and established and sustained by God in a direct and personal and special encounter of His breath with this frame of dust, is the differentiating exaltation and distinction of man. In spite of his earthly and animal nature, indeed in this earthly and animal nature, God in his creation gave him cause to put his confidence in Him directly, personally and specifically, to hold to the One who already in his creation has covenanted with him. His nature is still problematical, threatened and transitory. He is set under the law of humility and the fear of God. But in all this, God is his refuge and hope. He is this because He willed to accept him of all His creatures. It was not by reason of any immediacy to God proper to himself, but only by reason of God's free immediacy in His attitude to him, that he triumphed over the aridity, barrenness and deadness of the dust to which he is still subjected. When we say this we must not lose sight here of the beginning of the passage. On the contrary, we have to understand the passage as a self-enclosed circle. It is just because man, with God as his refuge and hope, can triumph over the earthiness of earth from which he comes and to which he must return, that he is destined, within the totality of the creaturely world, to serve the earth as a husbandman and a gardener. The hope of the arid, barren and dead earth is that it will bear the vegetation planted by God. According to the second account of creation, we must add that this is the hope of the whole creaturely world. It proceeds from death to life. But the realisation of this hope waits for man as the being which, earthy by nature, will triumph over the aridity, barrenness and deadness of the earth because God is his refuge and hope, because God has constituted Himself as such. His existence will be the sign which will contradict the whole earthiness of earth. His act will be an act of release for the earth too, and for the whole creaturely world. And what he will take with him when he returns to earth will be the promise of life for everything terrestrial. Thus the existence of man within the whole is indeed the existence of one who is commissioned to serve and work. He must give himself to till and keep the earth in order that it may have meaning when God will bring it to perfection. In this function man is responsible to both God and the creature. And in this function he fulfils the meaning of his own existence. Yet it must not be forgotten that it is not he but God who will plant the earth and therefore fulfil its hope and bring about its perfection. And it is not he but God who will create the other condition for the fulfilment of this hope, who will provide a mist for the earth and therefore rain and the humidity without which the service and work of man would be in vain. Nor has man assumed this function which is the meaning of his existence; he has received it from God. Thus it is not he but God who is the ground which gives courage and confidence to all creation. But he is the sign of this courage and confidence—a sign which he is permitted to erect in his existence and work and service, and even in his necessary return to dust. The law of humility and the fear of God still remain even under this aspect. But the matter is also characterised by the fact that it is man whom God has chosen and created as a sign of the future which He has destined for all creation as such. We see, then, that properly understood, and taking into account all its aspects, it is full of prefigurative significance. From the very outset we are indeed *in mediis rebus*[EN343]. And it is not for nothing—even the first verses force us to say this—that this form of the creation saga gives to the Creator of the world the covenant name of *Yahweh* Elohim.

[238]

Self-evidently what we have here is in the first instance a childlike description of human existence, of the contradiction and unity of its visible corporality and invisible quickening or animation; and at the same time a description of the basis of the twofold reality of man in the direct will and activity of God. And again self-evidently we also have in the first instance and the same childlike form a magnifying of the state of the husbandman, his divine election and call.

It is inherently improbable, however, that these themes explain the origination or even the adoption of this account in the Old Testament sphere.

[EN343] in the middle of things

Behind these prefigurative pictures, which have their own meaning as such, there stands the whole of Old Testament anthropology. Like the beast, man is formed of dust, animated by God and destined to return to dust and non-existence. But in contrast to the beast, he is animated by God directly and personally. Of all creatures he is chosen and called by Him immediately. And he stands or falls by reason of the fact that God does not abrogate this relationship to him but maintains and continues it. And this man is set in the service of the ground from which he was taken, of which he has need and to which he will return. He is set in this service because, in that which it will bear and produce in the power and goodness of God, the ground also has a hope for the fulfilment of which man must be prepared with his existence and ability to work.

But it must not be overlooked that behind this anthropology as such there stands directly—conditioned and predestined by the will and act of *Yahweh Elohim*—the election and calling of Israel, its existence and position within the world of nations to which it belongs, its selection and special training from among these nations, its antithesis to them, but also its role as a mediator on their behalf, its being (subject to destruction) as light in their darkness, the responsibility of its mission, the exaltation and humility of its status as God's servant to them, and the insoluble connexion of its hope with the hope of the whole cosmos. In all the dialectic here ascribed to man, there did not first arise and live, as the Old Testament sees it, either individual man or man in general, but the people of Israel. And it is because the people of Israel lived out this [239] dialectic that this account of creation had to ascribe it to man.

It is difficult, however, for exposition merely to affirm that the riddle of Israel is the final subjective content of this passage, since throughout the Old Testament this riddle of Israel and therefore of man is a hard but also a hopeful eschatological riddle—a riddle which points beyond itself. And it is impossible for exposition to stop at this point if the hopeful riddle which might have confronted the writer as something final has not objectively pointed beyond itself in vain but found its fulfilment in Jesus as the Messiah of Israel. If we do not deny but believe this, we shall have to press forward to a final and deepest meaning of the content of the passage. He, Jesus Christ, is the man whose existence was necessary for the perfecting of the earth; for the redemption of its aridity, barrenness and death; for the meaningful fulfilment of its God-given hope; and especially for the realisation of the hope of Israel. He is the man who, taken from all creation, all humanity and all Israel, and yet belonging to them and a victim of their curse, was in that direct, personal and special immediacy of God to Him a creature, man, the seed of Abraham and the Son of David. He is the man whose confidence and hope was God alone but really God; who is what He is for all, for all Israel, all humanity, and even the whole world; who in the deepest humility and the fear of God gave up Himself wholly to the fate of the creature, man and Israel, and in this way was decisively exalted and reigns over all creatures, the King of Israel and Saviour of the world, triumphing over all their weakness. He is the man who did not return emptyhanded, but with the spoils of hope, to the earth from which He was taken but for which He was also given. The man of whom the saga spoke, objectively if not subjectively, is—in respect of the solution of the riddle of Israel and the fulfilment of its hope—this man Jesus. So near are we in this second creation history to the threshhold of the history of the covenant and salvation that, even though we continue to give due attention to the other strata of its content, we cannot interpret it finally, and therefore decisively, in any other way than this.

B. Jacob has questioned whether Gen. 2$^{4b\mathrm{ff}}$ is really a second story of creation at all. It is assumed that the earth, vegetation and even man are already created, "but they had not as yet met." The land was still forsaken. Vegetation was as yet in an "undeveloped state." Man had not yet commenced his work on the land and had not therefore attained his destiny. The passage speaks of the encounter of the earth, vegetation and man. In all this it is true, and in obvious agreement with the text, that the horizon of the narrative is indeed that of the husbandman and is therefore limited to the circle of the earth, vegetation and man. But within this limited horizon—and we cannot explain this away without doing violence to the text—it too is an account of creation, a history of the origins behind which no earlier ones are presupposed. It is difficult to see how in face of v. 7, which deals with the origin of man, and especially in face of the whole passage about the origin of woman, Jacob can make his
[240] derisive comment that Gen. 2 is a "story of creation in which nothing is created." The truth behind his contention is that the story of creation is here compressed into a story of the emergence of man, of the sphere of his activity, of his environment. There is only casual reference to the coming into being of earth and heaven in v. 4b. This passage, too, does of course think from a higher divine standpoint and not a lower, and it has in mind the totality of creation and not just man, whom it causes to enter this totality and assume an express function of service within it. Its concern, however, is with "a near world and a near Lord on earth" (D. Bonhoeffer). It is of a piece with this that it speaks of God far more anthropomorphically than the first saga. The importance of man in the creaturely world and the human likeness of the Creator as we have them in the first saga, are only the consequence and reflection of the proximity in which creation and the intercourse between God and man based on it are here seen together.

The key to the peculiar orientation of this creation saga is undoubtedly to be found in the obviously deliberate introduction of the twofold divine name which does not occur in Gen. 1—*Yahweh* Elohim. In the Pentateuch its only other occurrence is in Ex. 9^{30}, where Moses says to Pharaoh: "But as for thee and thy servants, I know that ye will not yet fear the Lord God" (*Yahweh* Elohim). But this means, you have not yet recognised that it is *Yahweh* who is really the God of Israel, and that as such He is to be feared. What the pagan world does not know but has still to learn is that *Yahweh* Elohim is God. But Israel—as is emphasised in Gen. 2—knows and has continually to learn that its God *Yahweh*, the God of Shem (Gen. 9^{26}), the God of Abraham, Isaac and Jacob, is Elohim, God the Almighty Creator. La Peyrère, the author of a book about the pre-Adamites which appeared in 1655 (cf. Delitzsch, p. 75), was thus basically on the right track when he propounded the theory that Gen. 1 tells the story of the natural, pagan man, and Gen. 2 that of the Jew, i.e., the man of the history of salvation. Reminders that in relation to creation the two divine names belong together are offered in the Book of Isaiah: "O Lord of hosts, God of Israel, that dwellest between the cherubims, thou art the God, even thou alone, of all the kingdoms of the earth: thou hast made heaven and earth" (Is. 37^{16}). "For thus saith the Lord that created the heavens; God himself that formed the earth and made it; he hath established it ... " (Is. 45¹⁸). The second creation saga embraces both the history of creation and that of the covenant, both the establishment of the law of God and the revelation of His mercy, both the foundation of the world and that of Israel, both man as such and man elected and called. This is the theological explanation of its peculiarity. It does not equate the two elements; it distinguishes them. But it tells us that already in the first of these elements we have a pattern of the second. It thus understands creation in the light of the covenant; the establishment of the law of God in that of the revelation of His mercy; the world in that of Israel; man in that of his election and calling. For this reason and to this extent it is anthropocentric, and for the same reason it is so anthropomorphic in what it says about God. With this theological peculiarity is also connected the fact that it does not put any particular stress on the temporal nature of creation. It undoubtedly presupposes this. It, too, is recounting history in the temporal sequence of events, and Jacob's attempt to explain this away is unconvincing. But it does not count any days. It is content to say expressly at the beginning: "In the day that the Lord God made the earth and the heavens (what follows in vv. 6–7 is a parenthesis) he formed man"; and then, without any indication of time, it goes on to portray how God planted the Garden in Eden, how He gave man the first commandment, and how in the beasts He gave him his provisional and improper, and in woman his true and proper companion. It is clear that in this way the history of creation is brought into proximity to the history which follows. To be sure, it has its own time, but this is also the beginning of the time in which the history of the covenant will later be realised, commencing with the fall. It is the time which from the very outset moves toward this event.

[241]

But it is also of a piece with the theological peculiarity of the second saga that according to v. 5 the *terminus a quo*^EN344—not of creation but of the present interest in creation—is the earth which is still arid, barren and dead. There were not as yet any plants on the earth, or herbs in the field, "for the Lord God had not caused it to rain upon the earth, and there was not a man to till the ground" (literally, "to serve it"). The unwatered, unplanted and uncultivated earth is a parallel here to the deep of Gen. 1², which, covered by darkness, represents the state which God in creation has negated and rejected. Gen. 2 does not go back quite so far. The saga is not thinking now of the terror of chaos, or of the celestial and terrestrial ocean as the menacing but guarded frontier of chaos integrated into the cosmos. It presupposes that this problem has been dealt with. It has, instead, a problem of its own which is only indicated in Gen. 1. The planting of the earth is for it not merely a decisive condition of its habitableness, as in Gen. 1⁹⁻¹³, but the sum of its future, the sign of the perfection without which it certainly will not be what God meant it to be. The earth now looks forward to its planting. Woe to it if its future is not actualised! Woe to it if God has not made it possible! Nor is God obliged to make it actual or even possible. There can be no doubt that in v. 5 we can sense a kind of subsequent anxiety: God might not have done it. But He has done it in His grace. In His grace He has made the future of the earth at least possible. How He made it actual finds expression in the ensuing account of the planting of the Garden of Eden. He made it possible, as we are told in v. 6, by the fact that "there went up a mist from the earth, and watered the whole face of the ground." The translation preferred by Gunkel and the Zürich Bible is "a stream" or "inundation," but this is hardly the true meaning of the passage. If we remember that this is the account of an agriculturalist, we can scarcely overlook the fact that an "inundation" is not what a farmer usually hopes for his land. And in v. 5 the God-given rain is expressly described as something which is expected but has not yet come to make vegetation possible. Gunkel's contention that a mist does not water but merely moistens the earth is a strange one. Surely we can see a reference here to something already well

---

^EN344 starting point

known to primitive man—the origin of rain from the clouds and of clouds from the moisture which rises from the earth. It is also a naive suspicion of Gunkel that the fact that Yah weh Elohim is not actually said to have created this *'edh* indicates the presence of "a very primitive idea" according to which it is a quantity which does not derive from *Yahweh*. The aim of this saga to derive the creaturely world wholly from God's creation is less strong than that of the first, and at this point it is hurrying on to the creation of man, and it tries to avoid any relativising of the significance of this event by equating it with the creation of the *'edh*, which is no less indispensable from the standpoint of the vegetable kingdom. But did it not say previously that God had not yet sent rain upon the earth? What else, then, are we to expect but that He now caused it to rain? If we take the rising of the *'edh* and its results as the fulfilment of the first unfulfilled condition, it is obvious that the divine establishment of this process too was self-evident to the saga. The remarkable point in all this is the attitude—so wholly different from that of the first saga—to the elements of water and earth. What in the former is earth's great adversary, held in check by God, is in the latter one of the conditions not only of its habitableness but of its divinely willed and executed future. What in the former is man's enemy on the heavenly and earthly horizon, the threatening if (for man's salvation) restrained sign of chaos and of the wrath of which God in His grace repents, is in the latter the companion and therefore the friend of man; the longed-for sign of the goodness of God and the coming perfection of the earth. Gunkel has a fine observation on this point: "These descriptions of P and J refer to very different climates. The one is that of an

[242] alluvial plain subject to inundation, the other of a land which in late summer languishes under drought until the deity sends the much-desired rain, and thus creates the whole world anew. The latter is the climate of the Syro-Arabian desert, of Northern Mesopotamia, Syria and Palestine." This is no doubt true, but is it enough? Can it be our final word on the matter? We shall return to this difference between the first and second sagas in relation to the story of the Garden of Eden and its rivers. But it may be noted already that, although there is certainly an inner connexion between the difference in climate and the difference in the material conception in which the two sagas originated and are to be understood, the alluvial flood-threatened land of Southern Mesopotamia of which Gunkel is thinking was not the land into which *Yahweh* Elohim had led His people and where He dwelt among them, but that from which He had brought forth Abraham. It was the past of the patriarch of God's people which had been lived under this threat. It was his past which could and had to be thought of in the framework of the universal conception of the first account. To forget this, to understand the Creator as the One who has given Israel, not the desert, but "the good land" upon which in His goodness He dispenses refreshing rain for its constant renewal, and therefore to think of water and earth in this very different way, is wholly in line with this second saga, because it has in view the fact that the Creator and Lord of the whole world is the Lord and King of Israel, and therefore of the seed of Abraham, who was taken out of Chaldea and to whom was given the land of Canaan. That the earth given to him should not remain arid; that it should constantly be a green earth and therefore first become moist, is the concern of man and the gift of God in this saga. When God turns to man, as happens in the history of the covenant whose proximity is announced in this second saga, the signs change. There is a more pressing concern than that God should repent of creating the earth and in His wrath allow chaos to return. The primary concern now is lest He should have created the earth in vain, denying it a future and hope. This is the thing that must obviously concern the man who lives by the grace of God when he rejoices in this grace but realises also that God does not owe it to him. This is the concern of the man who is elected and called. And it corresponds to this that the divine gift to man is also more intimate than that which consists in His commanding the threatening destruction to halt and setting it a limit. He does this too, but what commands our attention here is the more positive thing which

gives meaning to the negative, i.e., that He creates salvation and life, that He wills that the earth should be green, and therefore wills to make it a humid earth. The second part of the third creative work of the first saga assumes crucial importance at this point. God encounters positively the man who is allowed to live by His free grace. And the man who lives in salvation history clings to this positive purpose as to the opposing and overcoming of his intrinsically justifiable concern. The moment God and man enter into this relationship the signs change. And because it is this relationship which is prefigured in the second creation saga, water and earth take on a very different character in it. The change probably harmonises with the fact that the first saga follows a pattern with a Babylonian stamp, whereas the second is proportionately more original and may go back to Israelite or Canaanitish origins. But it is a necessary change even if the whole conjecture about the climatic conditions of the two accounts is only a conjecture.

The account of the origin of man is to be interpreted along the same lines: "And the Lord God formed man of the dust of the ground, and breathed into his nostrils the breath of life; and man became a living soul." After hearing and reading with bated breath what is said in between, including the account of the watering of the earth, we now come to the main clause introduced by the statement : "In the day that the Lord God made the earth and the heavens …." That man cannot be lord of the earth but can only serve it is decided already in the description of the *terminus a quo*[EN345] of creation in v. 5. It was not because man needed [243] vegetation that God had to plant it, but because God willed to plant the earth that He created man. But the fact that the sentence is placed at the climax of the whole passage indicates the extraordinary significance ascribed by the saga to this event—which cannot even be compared with the solution to the question of irrigation. The *terminus ad quem*[EN346] of creation as here understood has not yet been reached, of course. This comes only when the visualised totality is presented in all its elements: the Garden of Eden with its many trees (and two especially), its rivers and man as its inhabitant; the commandment given to man; man and the beasts; and finally man as husband and wife. But the *terminus ad quem*[EN347] of creation already begins to emerge even in the opening sentence of the account of creation. Three comparative observations are necessary for a true estimation.

1. The creation of man as it is described here is distinguished from the Babylonian and other pagan traditions by the strong emphasis on his creatureliness. On tablet six of the epic *Enuma Elis* there is a presentation of the same process which tells us that man is formed from the blood of a slaughtered deity in accordance with the needs of other gods. But in this saga there is no question of a similar, involuntary self-emptying of deity and consequent divinity or divine likeness of man. As far as his body is concerned, man is of the earth. He has been fashioned and shaped by God's fingers from the dust. Even as regards the life of the body, his soul, he is not at all "akin to God," or "an emanation of the divine breath" (Gunkel). He was quickened to his own existence by the breath of God. He breathes as God breathed into him. What is he, or has he, which he has not received, and in which, since he was created by Him, he is not distinct from Him?

2. In contrast to the Greek conception of man, the creation of man as it is described here does not signify that a divine or God-like being had found a prison in an inadequate physical organism, or a spiritual power a material veil, or a holy internal reality a less holy or unholy external. By the same hand and breath of God man is both earthy and alive, body and soul, visible and invisible, internal and external. If the soul given to man by God's inbreathing is the life of the body, the body formed by God's fingers cannot be a disgrace or a prison or a

---

[EN345] starting point
[EN346] ending point
[EN347] ending point

threat to the soul. Man is what he is as this divinely willed and posited totality. Because he has received all that he is and has; because as the creature of God he is distinct from God, it cannot in any sense be a humiliation for him to be what he is. Creatureliness can be regarded as humiliating only where the creature is thought to be in partial or total opposition to God. And it is because Jacob sees an opposition of this kind that he is forced to see in the statement: "And man became a living soul," the expression of man's "tragic loss," the "opposition between his sensual and divine natures which never ceases as long as he lives." It is remarkable that a rabbi should "platonise" in this way. According to the biblical saga and all biblical anthropology, opposition of this kind is definitely excluded. That is why there is a place in it for the true and genuine dignity of man.

3. As all the anthropogonies known to us correspond to the view of man held by the writers and thinkers, or the circles or peoples, responsible for them, so the present description of his creation corresponds to the Hebrew picture of man, or more precisely to the Old Testament picture indirectly but decisively determined by the prophets of Israel. At this point the comparison merges into a formal identity. The man who here comes into existence—earthy but breathed upon by God, breathed upon by God and yet earthy—is the man of Israel: most deeply humiliated but highly exalted, highly exalted and yet humiliated; the object of judgment and mercy, and of mercy and judgment (for we must always include them both)—as he stands and walks before his God, not as an individual but as a responsible member of his people, the people of Israel of every age and in all its members. This human picture postulates the material particularity of the present picture of man's creation. We must accept this Old Testament picture. We must see it in its individuality. We must not attempt to combine it with any other. This picture of man's creation will not necessarily follow from that of any other picture of man. Delitzsch has noted correctly that it is used here in a supralapsarian manner (the use of the word infralapsarian on pp. 67 and 78 is an obvious mistake). That is to say, the creation of man is understood and portrayed in the light of his later fall and its consequences. There is already present in his origin the possibility of death later actualised in connexion with his disobedience against God. But for the sake of completeness we must add at once that this picture of man's creation is used not only in a supralapsarian manner but in a suprafederal manner. That is to say, the creation of man is described in the light of the faithfulness of God confirmed on the far side of creation and the fall. Already in his creation God confronts man in a readiness to perfect that which is utterly unattainable and to give life to that which is intrinsically dead. On a serious estimation of this other aspect we may recall the saying of Job (19^{25}): "I know that my redeemer liveth, and that he shall stand at the latter day upon the earth." It is only when we keep in mind this human portrait, and this in all its dialectic, that we are in a position to appreciate why man's creation is here described in this and in no other way. The whole history of Israel prophetically understood, and ultimately the whole history of its fulfilment in Jesus Christ, lies behind this brief description which is so important from these two angles.

That *adam* is taken and formed from the dust of the *adamah*[EN348] testifies in the first instance that he belongs to it. *Adamah*[EN349] is the earth as cultivated land, the field. Adam thus means man of the earth or field or soil, the husbandman. In Latin, too, *homo* derives from *humus*[EN350]. According to v. 5, this name must primarily mean that man is destined for the earth, for its service, i.e., its cultivation. But there is also the more precise meaning that he is himself of the earth, that he is taken from it by God's creative act, that he is formed out of the earth, that he is distinguished from the rest of the earth. Hence he is not really *the*

[244]

[EN348] human being
[EN349] ground
[EN350] ground

creature but one creature in the totality of the creaturely world. He is not really a being of a higher order descended, as it were, from heaven to the nether world. He is neither a resplendent nor an uneasy guest, neither the bearer of a heavenly message nor banished hither or battered by a dreadful fate. Even Ps. 119^{19}: "I am a stranger in the earth," does not have this meaning. It is God alone, and not a higher origin, who makes him a guest and stranger where he is a citizen. But it is God who primarily and supremely has made him a citizen. He has not made him celestial but terrestrial. There is no place here, of course, for the idea of "mother earth." Gunkel's suggestion that it is given a "monotheistic turn" is quite inadmissible. It is quite impossible both in the sense and course of the saga and in the rest of the Old Testament. It is not the earth but God who produces man, and He does so according to His plan and decree, in the free choice of a lump of earth and in the sovereign formation of this lump. The Pauline association of creation with the resurrection of the dead (Rom. 4^{17}) is very much to the point in relation to Gen. 2^7, as is also the fact that creation is here called a καλεῖν τὰ μὴ ὄντα ὡς ὄντα EN351. For it does not say that from a lump of clay God formed a man, but that God formed man from a lump of clay. Even if we allow that the view that man and beast were formed of earth presupposes "that the cultural circle of the narrator is familiar with clay portraits of men and animals like those often found in excavations in Palestine" (Gunkel), there is no suggestion in the saga of the suitability of the earth for this purpose. Although it refers to an existing material for creation, it speaks of a new divine creation. Clay may be serviceable for the fashioning of images of men and animals, but it is not serviceable for the purpose which is here in question (and later in v. 19), namely, the formation of actual men and animals. A genuine *tertium comparationis* EN352 is necessarily lacking. For the sake of clarity it is best not to speak of a "deep sleep of creation" which man originally slept, "resting on virgin soil … in full surrender to the blessed earth," as D. Bonhoeffer wrote in commenting on the famous painting of Michelangelo. What existed prior to the event described here was not man, either in the womb of mother earth or sleeping on the earth. It was merely a lump of earth like others, but one out of which man was creatively fashioned by God. What was fashioned was undoubtedly the body of man as such. But it must not be forgotten that to the body (according to Ps. 22^{15}, 39^4; Prov. 14^{30}) there belongs also the heart, and therefore what we call the human personality. Man does not possess but is that which he is fashioned out of the earth. He is wholly and exclusively that which the hand of God formed and leaves him, in distinction from the earth, as an independent being, and the saga certainly has in mind all his special human capacities, including those which we call "spiritual." But it is from the dust of the earth that God forms him. In line with this Abraham says in Gen. 18^{27}: "Behold now, I have taken upon me to speak unto the Lord, which am but dust and ashes," and we are told in Ps. 103^{14}: "He knoweth our frame; he remembereth that we are dust." Apart from its basic sense of the fine, loose ingredients of the earth's surface, in which it can also denote an innumerable multitude (like the sand on the sea shore), '*aphar* EN353 signifies the lowly, threatened and even forfeited nature of creaturely and especially human existence in relation to God; it can even mean the grave. If dust is named as the material from which God formed man, attention must be paid to the fact. The whole goodness of human creatureliness consists in what God made of this material and what He has in mind for it. It does not, therefore, lie in the material. The material as such rather signifies the threat under which it stands if God does not confirm what He made of it by giving it life, or if He withdraws this confirmation: "Thine hands have made me and fashioned me together round about; yet thou dost destroy me. Remember, I beseech thee, that thou hast made me as the

[245]

EN351 calleth those things which be not as though they were
EN352 basis of comparison
EN353 dust

clay; and wilt thou bring me into dust again?" (Job 10⁸⁻⁹). Further reference is made to this threat, from which it is not protected by its formation from dust (however marvellous), in Job 34¹⁴⁻¹⁵: "If he set his heart upon man, if he gather unto himself his spirit and his breath; all flesh shall perish together, and man shall turn again unto dust"; and also in Ps. 104²⁷⁻²⁹: "These all wait upon thee .... Thou hidest thy face, they are troubled: thou takest away their breath, they die, and return to their dust." Ps. 90³ speaks of its actualisation : "Thou turnest man to destruction; and sayest, Return, ye children of men"; as does also Eccl. 12⁵ᵇ ⁷: "Man goeth to his long home, and the mourners go about the streets. Then shall the dust return to the earth as it was: and the spirit shall return unto God who gave it." That this threat was known also to the saga is evident from Gen. 3¹⁹, where God says to man that in the sweat of his face he must eat his bread "till thou return unto the ground, for out of it wast thou taken: for dust thou art, and unto dust shalt thou return." It is for this reason, because he is so much a citizen of the earth, that according to Ps. 119¹⁹ man is a "stranger," i.e., a pilgrim making a short journey across it. He depends on God and in Him alone has he hope—the hope that this pilgrimage will not be meaningless, that God has not created or formed him from the dust in vain, but that God wills and will effect this life.

The saga now portrays the creation of man as the fulfilment of this hope. God's breath gives to the man formed of dust that which he does not possess and cannot give himself as such: the stability and consistence which preserves him from disintegration into his constitutive elements; the substance and continuity of his being in his divinely given form and divinely effected distinction from the earth from which he is taken. This continuity and substance is the life, and in contrast to that of plants the peculiar life, of the "living soul." When God grants life to the man formed of dust he becomes this "living soul." He does so by [246] the communication of the *nishmath ḥayyim*, the πνοὴ ζωῆς ᴱᴺ³⁵⁴. By this we must understand "the breath which, creatively proceeding from God and entering into man, becomes the principle of his life expressed in breathing, namely, the creaturely spirit which finds a manifestation conformable to corporality in the soul" (Delitzsch). Immediately after the threatening words already cited, expression is given to this hope and its fulfilment in Ps. 104³⁰: "Thou sendest forth thy spirit, they are created: and thou renewest the face of the earth." There is reference to it also in Elihu's speech in Job 33⁴: "The Spirit of God hath made me, and the breath of the Almighty hath given me life." It is to be noted, however, that this is no more true of man than of the beast which is also formed of the earth according to v. 19. The latter also receives (as *principium principians*ᴱᴺ³⁵⁵) the πνοὴ ζωῆς ᴱᴺ³⁵⁶, and thus becomes (as *principium principiatum*ᴱᴺ³⁵⁷, ψυχὴ ζῶσα ᴱᴺ³⁵⁸) a "living creature." And on the basis of all the passages adduced, it is to be noted that this hope and its fulfilment, because it depends on God's free act and because God is the Lord of life and death, is itself the threat to man and beast. We recall how man and beast are linked in weal and woe in the story of the Flood (Gen. 7²¹ᶠ, 9¹⁰ ¹² ¹⁵). And the disquieting fact is that God can take away the life that He has given to man and beast. What is so painful is that man in his glory is "like the beasts that perish" (Ps. 49²⁰); that men are no more than the beasts: "For that which befalleth the sons of men befalleth beasts; even one thing befalleth them: as the one dieth so dieth the other; yea, they have all one breath; so that a man hath no preeminence above a beast: for all is vanity. All go unto one place; all are of the dust, and all turn to dust again. Who knoweth the spirit of man that goeth upward, and the spirit of the beast that goeth downward to the

---

ᴱᴺ³⁵⁴ breath of life
ᴱᴺ³⁵⁵ defining principle
ᴱᴺ³⁵⁶ breath of life
ᴱᴺ³⁵⁷ defined principle
ᴱᴺ³⁵⁸ living being

earth?" (Eccl. 3$^{19-21}$). In Job 14$^{7-12}$ we read that even a comparison between man and a tree is wholly to the disadvantage of the former, for "there is hope of a tree, if it be cut down, that it will sprout again, and that the tender branch thereof will not cease. Though the root thereof wax old in the earth, and the stock thereof die in the ground; yet through the scent of water it will bud, and bring forth boughs like a plant. But man dieth, and wasteth away: yea, man giveth up the ghost, and where is he? As the waters fail from the sea, and the flood decayeth and drieth up: so man lieth down, and riseth not: till the heavens be no more, they shall not awake, nor be raised out of their sleep." It is not man's material nature as such, nor the fact that he is formed from dust, which entails this equality with the beast and fatal inequality with the tree, threatening him so drastically with destruction and his body with dissolution and therefore with a return to the earth from which it is taken and to which his life or soul necessarily follows it, hopelessly and irresistibly caught up in its headlong plunge into the abyss. On the contrary—and this is what all the passages say—it is this hope and its fulfilment, the God who makes him a living being, that binds him to the beast in this way, bringing him down to a depth where he may well envy a tree, threatening him so utterly, without any hope of escape, resistance or salvation. Gen. 2^7 makes it very plain that the formation of man from dust is one thing and his animation by the communication of the *nishmath ḥayyim is* another. "The two acts did not coincide, although they were not far apart" (Delitzsch). God does not owe man the second act after He has honoured him with the first. And God can at all times terminate the second, and therefore the result of the first, by not repeating it, by allowing it to become the past. If He does this, the consequence is that the life of the body, the consistence of the frame of dust and therefore of the soul, life itself, immediately becomes the past, a shadow sinking into the earth and engulfed by it. Taken together, Gen. 2^7 and Gen. 2^{19} makes it very plain that the common fate of man and beast, their common dependence on the divine animation, and therefore the common problem of their being, are the will and decree and work of God, so that to the "Who knoweth?" of Eccl. 3^{21} the only answer which can be given even according to the creation saga is that God alone knows what is the special fate, being and pre-eminence of man, and whether his spirit, in distinction from that of the beast, does really go upward and not downward into the dust, the grave, the underworld. God alone knows whether this descent will not be the final fate of man. And it will depend on God's decision alone if, contrary to all appearances, there is for man an ascent above the dust. No immortality of the body or soul, no eternal destiny or expectation necessarily linked with man's existence as such, can guarantee it. God alone can give this guarantee. But the God who is the only hope is primarily the inescapable threat. Only in His free, unmerited grace (in defiance of this ineluctable threat) can God be this hope and give this guarantee. That this is actually the case is indicated in Gen. 2^7 only by the fact that in the second act of his creation, and therefore in his animation, there is a strikingly intimate and personal encounter between God and the man formed from dust. God remained in the direct proximity of man after He had created him from the dust of the earth. It was in this direct proximity that He created—this is the meaning of His inbreathing—the breath of life by which that which was fashioned of dust became a soul, alive. Hence in coming to life man became at once—Michelangelo expressed this very well—the immediate witness of the creation of his life; and God brought him to life, He created him as a soul, by breathing this breath of life into his nostrils. In this unique encounter man alone—as the saga obviously understands it—became, not merely something formed of dust, but a living creature assured of his continuance. That he became this only in this encounter is the hope and also the threat—the hope which defies and overcomes but also includes the threat—in which his existence commences. Man is the being which is literally dependent on the fact that God does not cease to re-encounter him, to draw near to him again, to make him again a witness of the creation of his own life, and to breathe again into his nostrils the breath of

[247]

life. Man would cease to be man if God were to cease to do this, to be a Creator in this way. Without the repetition of this second act of his creation his soul could not live; it could not guarantee continuance to the body; and with the dissolution of the mortal clay it would have to return to the place whence the latter is taken.

This is the way in which man was created according to Gen. 2^7. The history of salvation has not yet begun. Man has not yet proved by his deed how little he belongs to God and how much to the earth from which he is taken; how much he deserves, after eating his bread in the sweat of his brow, to go down like the beast to the place from which he was taken and derives. And God for His part has not yet spoken to man or dealt with him. It is not yet obvious how much God is justified in the creation of man described here. But the situation in which we see man created in these two distinct acts is already the situation corresponding to the history of salvation which begins later. The justification will come with this later history. Just as God forms man from a handful of dust taken from the rest, so He will choose Abraham and his seed from a multitude of nations, thus causing the body of Israel to come into being and fashioning it as a distinct and peculiar people, but one whose nature is like that of all peoples, so that God does not owe it anything in choosing and fashioning it in this way, but could at once cause it to sink and perish again in the mass from which it is taken. Yet He will again draw near to it in a second special act. He will ratify the choice of Abraham by entering into an immediate relationship with this people, by making a covenant with it, by giving it a prophetic Spirit. And by this Spirit from God, this people will receive a soul and will become, in contrast to all other nations, a living people. In virtue of this Spirit, all that was promised to Abraham will be confirmed at the Red Sea and Sinai and Jerusalem. But it will take place only in this way. *Yahweh*, who gives it His Spirit and makes it His people, is always free to take from Israel that which has been given it. The free grace of God, the expectation and realisation of new encounters with Him, is always its only hope, and there-

[248] fore—because its fulfilment is exclusively the affair of God—its threat. Israel for its part gives constant proof that, as a people taken from the midst of other peoples and only too obviously partaking of their nature; it is not different from them or better than they. It is disobedient like all other nations, as the first man of the saga was disobedient and therefore justified the necessity of his return to the earth. In its covenant relationship Israel cannot demonstrate or present any national soul corresponding to the Spirit or body corresponding to the covenant. If it is going to continue till its time is fulfilled, this will only be by reason of the fact that quite against its deserts *Yahweh* does not withdraw from it the living breath of the prophetic Spirit, but continually encounters it. For the sake of the earth which he is to serve, God renews His encounter with man. And for the sake of the nations to whom it is to be a sign, He also renews His encounter with Israel. But just as the man formed of the dust inevitably returns to the earth, so Israel as a nation is finally doomed to sink and perish in the mass of the nations, proving by its actual disappearance, towards which it moved in a sense from the very first, in fulfilment of the threat under which it stood from the very first, that it has no hope, that God alone is its hope, and that He alone is the hope of man and the hope of the whole world. "See now that I, even I, am he, and there is no god with me: I kill, and I make alive; I wound, and I heal: neither is there any that can deliver out of my hand" (Deut. 32^{39}).

Ezek. 37 is thus the most powerful commentary on Gen. 2^7. In this passage it has reached the climax of its history, and this climax is the end which always threatened and has now come. It shows us a valley full of dry bones (v. 1 f.), and the Israelites can only complain: "Our bones are dried, and our hope is lost" (11). To the question whether these bones can live, the prophet can only answer: "O Lord God, thou knowest" (3). But the prophet is commanded to prophesy over these bones: "Ye dry bones, hear the word of the Lord .... Behold, I will cause breath to enter into you, and ye shall live. And I will lay sinews upon you, and will bring up flesh upon you, and cover you with skin, and put breath in you, and ye shall live; and ye shall know that I am the Lord. So I prophesied as I was commanded: and as I prophesied, there was a noise, and behold a shaking, and the bones came together, bone to his bone" (4–7). And so it is: "And when I beheld, lo, the sinews and the flesh came up upon them, and the skin covered them above: but there was no breath in them. Then said he unto me, Prophesy unto the wind, prophesy, son of man, and say to the wind, Thus saith the Lord God; Come from the four winds, O breath, and breathe upon these slain that they may live. So I prophesied as he commanded me, and the breath came into them, and they lived, and stood up upon their feet, an exceeding great army" (8–10). One thing obviously was not killed and did not die when Israel became a valley of dry bones, and this was the prophetic Spirit by whom this people had become a nation. He might have shunned it, or withdrawn Himself, or scattered Himself to the four winds, thus giving up the body and soul of this people to vanity, as He had the right and freedom to do and as this people had deserved a hundredfold. But He for His part could not be destroyed. Thus the same Spirit who had once quickened it and kept it alive was now to quicken it afresh after its necessary and merited disappearance. It was of this return of the breath of life to an Israel already dead that Ezekiel spoke. If he really spoke of the fulfilment of its history as this took place in Jesus Christ on the far side of Israel's destruction, he did not prophesy in vain but in the name of God. For what took place in Jesus Christ is precisely the resurrection of Israel from the dead by the power of the prophetic breath of life which for the sake of the nations had created it as a nation, and which was not killed and did not die with Israel. That this God-given breath as the vital principle of the soul and body of man can and will be withdrawn; that in respect of both soul and body man is subject to death and has no immortality; but that even when this breath is taken from him it does not vanish, or cease to be the living and quickening Spirit; that by God's free disposal He can and will return and genuinely requicken man from the death to which he has fallen victim and in which he has actually perished—these are the lessons which we have to learn from Ezek. 37, as a commentary from salvation history, in our understanding of the anthropology of Gen. 2.

[249]

There can be no simple equation of the *nishmath ḥayyim* or *ruah*[EN359] of the Old Testament with the πνεῦμα ἅγιον[EN360] of the New. It is in deliberate emulation of Gen. 2^7 that Jn. 20^{22} tells us that Jesus breathed on His disciples with the words: "Receive ye the Holy Ghost." But as an anthropological concept "spirit" in the Old Testament does correspond to that which in the New Testament (1 Thess. 5^{23}) is distinguished as πνεῦμα ὑμῶν from ψυχή and σῶμα[EN361]. In other respects, neither in relation to the Old Testament nor the New can we speak without qualification of a trichotomy of the being of man. The being of man as such is in both cases body and soul, earthly form and earthly life. But that the body is not without the soul, that his earthly form is that of a being with earthly life, stands or falls with the fact that he receives and retains the Spirit. To die, as the A.V. (like Luther) inexactly but not incorrectly translated Ac 5^5, ^{10}, 12^{23}, is "to give up the ghost." When Jesus died, He commended (Lk. 23^{46}) His Spirit into the Father's hands. When Stephen died, he prayed Jesus to receive his spirit (Ac. 7^{59}). The spirit, then, continues beyond death, not as something belonging to man, but as the divine address and gift to man, which remains in readiness for him even when it is withdrawn, i.e., when it is surrendered by him. The question must be raised, therefore, whether the Redeemer (Advocate) or Guarantor (Job 19^{25}) who stands and is present above the dust is not concretely the *nishmath ḥayyim*[EN362], and whether the

---

EN359 breath of life or spirit
EN360 holy spirit
EN361 your spirit from soul and body
EN362 breath of life

$\pi\nu\epsilon\hat{\upsilon}\mu\alpha$ EN363 which Paul calls $\dot{\alpha}\pi\alpha\rho\chi\acute{\eta}$ EN364 (Rom. 8²³) or $\dot{\alpha}\rho\rho\alpha\beta\acute{\omega}\nu$ EN365 (2 Cor. 1²², 5⁵; Eph. 1¹⁴) is not also the breath of life which has to be distinguished from the Holy Spirit as the concrete form of the riches of the Christian hope.

The second passage of the second creation saga (Gen. 2⁸⁻¹⁷) deals with the planting of a Garden in Eden as the dwelling-place of man, with its trees and rivers, with the divine commission to man, with the permission and prohibition given to him.

A first impression as we come to this passage from the opening verses is one of a certain surprise. For everything is now transposed, as it were, into a higher key. The first concern of the Creator had been with the earth as such and its vegetation. To this end He had given it mist and rain, and man as a servant to cultivate it. The surprise is occasioned by the fact that there is now no further reference to the earth as such and as a whole. God's purposes for it have been executed. The future revealed and prepared for it has now become its present. It is planted by God. But the reality far transcends the intention. Where shrubs and herbs were envisaged we now have trees which God has made to grow out of the earth. The same is true in respect of the conditions to make this possible. The expectation had been rain, but the fulfilment—the mist has evidently not been ineffective or niggardly—is a whole river watering the Garden of Eden. So mighty is the river that contrary to the usual habit of rivers it later divides into four parts and fructifies other great areas outside of Eden. A final point is that it is man—the peculiarity of his creation now begins to appear— who is emphatically stated to have been set under these trees and on the banks

[250] of the still undivided river, and to whom there is assigned in this Garden his dwelling-place and duty. On the other hand, these new features are accompanied by the restriction of interest to a definite, limited place on earth, to the Garden in Eden, where all the fulfilments take place which so far exceed the initial expectations. We are not told expressly whether God caused shrubs and plants to grow elsewhere as the opening verses lead us to expect. The account obviously presupposes this, but it is clear that its interest in the whole earth, as in the heavens, is only indirect. It did not omit to say at the very beginning that God also made the heavens above the earth, but it turned at once to the earth and considered the totality of God's works in this one part. Similarly, it does not now forget the totality of the earth, as may be seen by the four branches into which the one river divides at the frontier of the Garden, and the naming of these branches. But as the first section has the earth in view, so the second has this definite place on earth, the region of the undivided river, the Garden of Eden. It is in this place that the totality is considered.

What kind of place is it? We must not be unduly influenced by certain necessary considerations. Eden means "delight." Hence the Garden of Eden was

---

EN363 spirit
EN364 first fruits
EN365 down payment, guarantee

undoubtedly a kind of "pleasure garden." And it is said of the trees of this Garden that their fruit was pleasant to the sight and good for food. Furthermore, the saga obviously means us to understand that the river which had its source in the Garden made it particularly fruitful. And in the midst of it stood the tree of life. But apart from this it has no claim to fame, for the land of Havilah where gold, bdellium and the onyx stone are found is outside the Garden of Eden. No mention is made of any other perfections of the Garden itself and delights to be expected there. The place is not described as an Elysium, an island of the blessed, a garden of Hesperides, or even a Lubberland. There are no particular attractions to entice us to it. In it man has to work, to serve the earth as such, as he was ordained to do at the beginning of the saga. And somewhere in this Garden, also planted by God, there is to be found the tree of knowledge of good and evil, with whose existence the divine permission and prohibition is linked. Thus from the very first this place is not without serious problems. The fact that in the Greek translation it is called "Paradise" must not mislead us. For while it is true that at a later date, and under Greek influence, Paradise became a kind of Elysium, in the Persian from which the term derives, and then in the Hebrew, it simply means a walled-in and therefore an enclosed and limited place, e.g., a royal park. What makes this Garden delightful is primarily and decisively the fact that it is specially planted by God and therefore specially belongs to Him. It is on this account that in later Old Testament reminiscence it is called the "Garden of Elohim" or the "Garden of *Yahweh.*" The only other thing to be said about it is that by reason of its fruitfulness and choice fruits it epitomises a good land desired by the husbandman or [251] gardener, a place on earth where it is clear that the earth which man is ordained to serve is also ordained to serve him. The outlook of the first account—that the earth and its vegetation are for the sake of man—emerges at this point. All the heightened features as compared with the first verses of the second account; all the supernatural aspects on which it appears that we have here a new creative act of God and the description of an incomparable pleasure garden, aim at something supremely natural—the man who finds on earth both his task and perfect satisfaction. Of course the supernatural elements in the description of the Garden must not be overlooked. There belong to it the tree of life at its heart and the tree of the knowledge of good and evil— each with its special purpose. There also belongs to it the peculiar river system in which one river becomes four—a process which can hardly be understood in terms of the familiar picture of the origin of a delta. Finally, we may recall the personal presence and action of God in the Garden. But all these elements have nothing whatever to do with a description of the Garden as an Elysium. It is not something abnormal but something normal, something corresponding to the harmony of the divine creation of earth, water, plant and man, which man is commanded and enabled to enjoy in Paradise, in the place specially planted by God, in the region of the one undivided river, once he has been put there, or, as we are told later, "taken" and "put" there. It is to be noted that just as this Garden did not exist in its place simply because God had created the earth, but was specially planted by God in a special and limited place, so the existence of man did not in any sense commence in the Garden, and it was not in any way self-evident that he should be appointed its inhabitant, husbandman and watchman, or find his way to it. His creation does not begin in the Garden but is completed in it. His creation commences by reason of the fact that elsewhere, in a place not indicated, he is formed from dust and quickened by the divine breath. And it is continued in the fact that when this has taken place he is put by God in the Garden and brought to rest there—the rest of his normal existence in relationship to his Creator and to the earth as the creaturely sphere. He has no home; nor does he seek or find one. It is prepared for him, and in a special third act of his creation he is brought home, and all this—it is to be noted—in the course of his creation, which has not yet been completed but is still on the way to completion. It also belongs to his creation that God prepares for him this pleasure garden—which is supremely delightful because it is God's Garden, but also delightful because it is a normal dwelling-place appropriate to him—and that God brings him to this part of the earth to fulfil his determination for the whole earth and therefore really to live. Obviously God's breath has made him a living being in order that he might live here under the special conditions of this special place on earth.

[252] Hence the creation of the Garden with its river and trees, and the transplanting of man into it, belongs to the creation of man as understood by this second account.

But where is this place? In answering this question we must avoid two errors, both of which are equally excluded by what the passage really says. For one thing, it is plain that the biblical witness is speaking of a definite place on earth, and not of the idea of a perfect country or Utopia. He localises the Garden terrestrially, for it lay "toward the East." Of the four branches of the river proceeding from the Garden he identifies at least two with rivers well-known to every hearer and reader, for Hiddekel is the Tigris and the fourth river is the Euphrates. He also gives definite territorial names in the description of the other two rivers—Havilah and Ethiopia. We repeat that the whole description of the Garden excludes any suspicion that we do not have here a concrete terrestrial region. But it is also clear, of course, that a geographical localisation of this region with the help of the indications of the passage is quite impossible and is obviously not intended by the saga. From the point of view of Palestine, the East is the Arabian desert, and then the mouth of the Euphrates and the Tigris and the Persian Gulf. But where is there even a hint of a region called Eden? And where is the one original river? Where are the other two branches of the river whose identification is still a matter of conjecture?—not to mention the fact that the Euphrates and the Tigris do not originate from the same source. Where was and is this river which divides into four? What is to be understood by Havilah and Cush? Who can say whether the description "toward the East" is not meant to point to more distant regions not unknown to antiquity? or whether its more immediate meaning—namely, that it points to the great desert but also beyond it to the coming light of day (*ex oriente lux*[EN366])—is not also its final and decisive meaning? By pointing to the desert, it certainly describes Paradise as inaccessible by human standards, and by pointing to the rising sun it identifies it with the future already present with the creation of man. It is of the very essence of such passages that while they are concrete in their mention of places they are only semi-concrete; that while they are geographical, their geography is indefinite and unpredictable. They are concrete and geographical because, as they speak in temporal terms, they aim to relate real history which has taken place on earth. But they are semi-concrete and geographically indefinite because as sagas they do not aim to present "history" but "pre-historical" history. Necessarily, therefore, we have to accept both the fact that Paradise was planted and existed somewhere and not just everywhere or nowhere but also the fact that there can be no actual investigation of this "somewhere." It is palpable that in these passages we have to do with a genuine consideration of real events, persons and things, but only with a consideration and therefore not with a historical review but with constructions which do not have their origin in observation but in imagination. It is, of course, highly characteristic of the whole nature of the second creation narrative, and most important for an understanding of it, that it brings its presentation so close to the "historical" and therefore the geographical sphere (as in the present instance) that the inquisitive question, Where was Paradise situated? is continually raised and can never be wholly silenced. But to be true to the passage, we must drop the question as soon as it is raised. [253]

More cannot be extracted from the passage, because more is not offered, than that it was a real place on earth, distant from and unique in relation to all other earthly places, yet belonging to the same plane, so that real man could be there on the real earth, and to this day cannot overlook or forget but must always remember that among all the known and accessible places on earth there was and is also that unknown and inaccessible place, that in addition to his own place there is also that which is lost to him, and that that place is his home. It was there that God originally put man and gave him rest when He had formed him. It was there that he could and should live. What he was there is his reality as the creature of God. And it is by that portion of the whole terrestrial space created by God that the totality has meaning and is to be understood. It is there that salvation, blessing, joy and peace originate for the whole earth because there is the first seat of the divinely willed life of the earth and plant and man, and a fulfilment already of His purpose in creation. There all the rivers of the earth have their common origin in a single river. With their division they bring fertility to the whole earth because first as the one river they watered Paradise and made it fruitful. They are the beams of that one light which shines in that unknown and inaccessible but earthly place. There would

---

[EN366] light from the east

be no rivers without that one river. There would be no plants if they did not have in the trees of Eden their prototype and pattern. There would be no earth if it were not for that Garden in its place. There would be no "here" if there were no "there"; no "without" if there were no "within." There would be no man if God had not first put man in Eden. It is of this First, without which there would be no Second or Third, that the biblical witness speaks. He does not speak about it in Greek, or he would have had to speak about an idea or mythologically of an Elysium. He speaks about it as a Semite, and that as a biblical Semite. For this reason he speaks of an earthly place created by God with earthly characteristics which even he himself could not have traced or indicated on any map. He speaks of God's Garden as a genuine and original place on earth, just as the first witness spoke of God's week as a genuine and original period of time on earth.

[254]   Attention may be directed to a series of individual features in the picture given. The general nature of Paradise is that of a sanctuary. Not man but God is the Possessor and Lord of this Garden. Man finds himself in a place appointed for this purpose by God and fenced off from the other earthly places. He is specially brought there and given rest—an indication that the establishment of Paradise is a distinctive spatial parallel to the institution of the Sabbath as a temporal sanctuary in the first saga. The duty of man in this place is to cultivate and keep it—literally, to serve and watch over it—and it is no fancy if we see here the functions of the priests and Levites in the temple united in the person of one man. And as the tabernacle and later the temple had their centre—not their geometrical but their virtual and functional centre—in the Holiest of Holies, so Eden had its centre in the two trees specially planted by God alongside all the other trees, namely, the tree of life and the tree of the knowledge of good and evil. The difference between this Garden and an Elysium is particularly striking in this respect. It is true enough that man finds here an appropriate dwelling-place, that the fruit of the trees of this place is in every way attractive and good for food, and that he finds here both nourishment and an activity commensurate with his creation; but all these things are subordinated to the fact that he is here in God's sanctuary.

It is for this reason that Paradise is emphatically described as an orchard or sacred grove, and therefore man's life and function in it as that of a fruit gardener. The fact that according to the beginning of the saga the earth was to produce shrubs and plants, and that man's determination was to cultivate the soil, recedes for the time being, being temporarily transcended by the account that God caused all kinds of trees to grow out of the earth in this place, just as He had previously taken man out of the earth and will later cause the river to issue forth from the earth; that with one exception man was permitted to eat of them all; that with another exception he obviously did eat of them all; and finally that he was ordained to tend and keep this orchard. What characterises this place according to the saga is the higher or highest vegetation. It is only in and with the later and true history of man, outside Eden, when it becomes inaccessible to him, that the field will again come into the picture and work on the field will really be necessary as on the original view. Here in the Garden man is really at rest in respect of nourishment, and his work—stated in terms of the first account—is the permitted minimum of the Sabbath which does not disturb the freedom, joy and rest of his existence.

It is not what man does and does not do, but the divine beneficence and order in favour of man and the whole earth, which dominates the present portrayal of this place. And it does so in such a way that what God has willed and done on behalf of the whole earth is particularly emphasised. Because it is so detailed, the most striking statement in the passage is that about the river which has its origin in the Garden and then divides outside the Garden into four branches which encircle other regions. The description makes it plain [255] that this watering is to be regarded as the sum of the divine favour which rules in Eden and from Eden over the rest of the earth. The great need of the earth, and primarily of God's chosen sanctuary on earth, is water, and it is this which it is actually given by God. Not for nothing did the mist ascend from the earth, for it returned to the earth as rain, and water collected to burst forth in Eden, thus bringing to the Garden the fertility it needed if God was not to cause the trees to grow in vain. These trees of Paradise are the first to be planted "by the rivers of water." They are the first to partake of the divine act of blessing executed in this springing forth of the river, and it is here that man first becomes a witness of this act of blessing and therefore realises what God has in mind for himself. But the reach of this blessing is to the whole earth. That the closed sanctuary with its trees has a symbolic or sacramental character is now revealed by the fact that the water which nourishes it does not take the form of a sea fed by a subterranean source and with subterranean exits, but that a whole river bursts forth which Eden is not to keep to itself but to take its own share and then to pass on to surrounding districts, and which is sufficiently powerful to divide into four parts—obviously indicating the four quarters of the compass—and to bring to these four quarters and therefore to the whole earth what it had brought to Eden. The meaning and assertion is undoubtedly that all the rivers of the earth and therefore all fertility, all possibility of vegetation, all life on earth, have their origin here in Paradise in the one river which springs forth in it. If man no longer lives in the Garden of Eden, if it has become inaccessible to him, he nevertheless lives by the streams and rivers of the earth; wherever there are fruit-bearing trees; wherever his labour on the land is not for nothing but serves the support of life; by the banks which in their final and supreme origin are those of the unknown and yet known, of the lost and yet real Paradise. Indeed, as the narrative sees it, all the precious things of the earth including its minerals, some of which are enumerated in the description of the land of Havilah, have their origin in the river of blessing which proceeds from Eden. Thus it is not just life itself, i.e., the possibility of the life given by God to the earth and man, but also all the glory and beauty of this life, which have their origin within it.

The contrast between the relatively sober description of Paradise itself and the fulness of the portrait of the river which flows out of it is surely intentional. It is certainly made clear that Paradise itself is the place of glory. Not in the fulness and beauty of its own life, however, can it be made known as the place of glory but only in the selflessness in which it gives back what it was first given, only in the external and distant fulness and beauty of the river which flows out of it and divides, and of the blessing of this river. It is made clear by this river [256] with its four branches that the one thing which God is and wills and does in His sanctuary contains and promises and releases the many things which He will be and do outside His sanctuary on His whole earth as such. And it is also made clear by it that all that He will be and do outside it goes back to the promise and revelation and gift which He first actualised in His sanctuary.

But all the distinctive features of this place are obviously focused on the fact that it has itself a centre, a Holiest of Holies. Among the many trees planted by God on the banks of the one river there stand two special trees. It is with reference to them that man is allotted his place and receives a permission and prohibition. These are the tree of life and the tree of the knowledge of good and evil. The lack of clarity which accompanies the statement that both are found in the midst of the Garden is probably intentional and necessary. At any rate, according to everything said about them both here and later, they are most closely related in significance. And like the other trees in the Garden, they both bear fruit which man may obviously enjoy.

A first point to notice is that man does not actually seem to have needed the fruit of the first tree. If he is not prevented from eating it, he does not appear to have done so. It is not taken into account until later that he might do so, and it is then made impossible by his expulsion from the Garden. Thus in relation to the many other trees in the Garden the "tree of life" seems in the first instance to be superfluous. Its purpose and use consist simply in the fact that it is visibly there with its adornment of fruit and that it constitutes the centre of the Garden. Its presence means that man is told where he is, to whom the place belongs, and what he may expect and be. It assures him of the benefit of life whose witness he is. For it obviously does not mediate this benefit. It simply indicates and represents it. Note that the later temptation is not a temptation to eat of this tree. Nor is the possibility that man might do this, when he has succumbed to the temptation in respect of the second tree, described as another temptation which actually overtakes him, but as a possibility which God realises may well overtake him as a temptation, and which He makes basically impossible in practice by his expulsion from the Garden. Nothing is said about any explicit promise in connexion with the existence of the first tree. The passage is content merely to name it, thus indicating its nature and maintaining its existence in the midst of the Garden. It is a sign which speaks for itself. The direct reality of the life of the earth and the Garden and its trees and man himself as the creatures of God is not in any sense a problem or question which requires an answer. Nor is the tree of life as a sign of the actuality of the creature. Its presence means that man lives in and with and by its promise without any need for the latter to find expression. He does not need to eat of its fruits. This first tree with its fruits is the divinely given sign of what he has to do with the earth and the trees which grow out of it. It is a confirmation of the fact that he may really live here where God has given him rest. [257] Hence there was no need for him to eat of the fruit of this tree. Certainly he could have done so. But if he had, he would have been neither the better nor the worse for it. He did not have to do so. He could leave this tree untouched. And he did leave it untouched.

Even when he became a transgressor he still left it untouched. If he had not done so, by an arrogant and wicked grasp at the direct reality of God, by an eating of the fruit of this tree, he would have increased the corruption resulting from his transgression, in some sense deifying his self-merited fate, giving to death itself, whose victim he had become as a transgressor, the meaning and character of eternal life, and thus delivering himself up to eternal death. It was from this potential danger that he was graciously withdrawn by his expulsion from Paradise. Otherwise the whole history of his salvation, of his reconciliation with God, could have had no object. No matter how deeply he fell, he was held and upheld even in his fall, and thus remained a possible object of future salvation in his actual acceptance of the restraint which had previously been quite voluntary and not compulsory. After doing what he did he had to die. But he did not do what would have entailed his sentence to eternal death with no possible hope of resurrection. God saw to it that he could not do this even if he wanted by taking from him the opportunity to do so.

And so the tree of life is really the centre of Paradise; the sign of life as God gave it to man at his creation and as he was permitted to live it as a divine favour; the sign of the home in which man was given rest by God because God Himself, and therefore the source of his life, was no problem to him, but present and near without his so much as having to stretch out his hand. In the beginning there was the joyful message of this life. In the beginning man stood under this sign. No continuation can alter or reverse this. On the contrary, the whole continuation can only confirm that this was man's beginning.

The second tree in the midst of Paradise is not by name or nature the sign, like the first, of a reality given to man by God, but the sign of a possibility presented to man by God. It, too, is planted by God and is called the "tree of the knowledge of good and evil." What the eating of its fruit involves is described as follows in the prohibition connected with it: "For in the day that thou eatest thereof thou shalt surely die." But intentionally it is not described as a "tree of death." Between the eating of its fruit and death as the outcome there is a third and intermediate stage from which the tree takes its name and nature; "the knowledge of good and evil." The explanation afterwards given by the serpent is therefore correct: "God doth know that in the day ye eat thereof, then your eyes shall be opened, and ye shall be as gods, knowing good and evil."

[258] To know good and evil, to be able to distinguish and therefore judge between what ought to be and ought not to be, between Yes and No, between salvation and perdition, between life and death, is to be like God, to be oneself the Creator and Lord of the creature. The one who can do this bears the supreme attribute and function of deity. The Creator distinguishes Himself from the creature by the fact that He exercises this power of distinction; whereas the creature is directed to accept and approve what God who is able and entitled to distinguish has done, does, and will do. If the creature could on its own judgment reject what on God's judgment it ought to accept, it would be like God, Creator as well as creature. And this is what the name means. This is the essence of the tree. By it God Himself reveals this possibility of an unheard of exaltation of the creature. Neither the tree as such nor its fruit constitutes or contains this possibility, but they show that it does exist. Nor is the eating of the fruit of this tree as such the realisation of this possibility, but when man eats of this fruit he shows and affirms that he is in process of realising this possibility.

The nature of this possibility is, of course, formally revealed already by the fact that God explains its meaning in words—the first that He addresses to man. In this case, unlike that of the first tree, we obviously have to do with a problem; something which man—the man who lives under the sign of the tree of life—cannot know of himself but which he must know and which has therefore to be told him, to be explained and interpreted to him. The reality of divinely given life speaks for itself. The possibility of divine likeness does not do so. It obviously does not do this positively; it does not commend itself. There is needed the encouragement of the serpent, and the first theological conversation connected with it, the debate with the woman, if this possibility is to be made clear and man prompted to participate in its realisation. On the other hand, the possibility does not contradict itself. The fruit of this tree is in itself at least as "pleasant to the eyes and good for food" as that of the other trees of Paradise. It could actually be eaten. Man has to be told specifically, and is in fact told, that it must not be eaten. But this is something other than the immediate self-revelation and presence of God in the sign of the tree of life. In the latter case it is enough that it is there. The divine Yes to human life which it pronounces can be heard and understood directly. But now a divine No is added to the divine Yes and therefore there has to be speech. Might not this be a positive possibility to be realised by man in accordance with the will and purpose of God for the completion of his creation? Of himself, man cannot know authentically whether this is the case or not. It is by what God says that he learns that it is not, and is shown the true and destructive nature of this possibility.

God does not will that man should eat of this tree. He does not, therefore, will that the possibility indicated by this tree should be realised. The prohib-
[259] ition stands out in strong relief from the permission: "Of every tree of the garden thou mayest eat." This is the exception to the general rule. As long as

the rule is valid, the exception is valid also: "But of the tree of the knowledge of good and evil, thou shalt not eat of it." If we eat with gratitude in the one case we are obliged not to eat with the same gratitude in the other. It is important to observe the abbreviated form of the reason given: "For in the day that thou eatest thereof thou shalt surely die." This points us to the final consequence of eating. If man eats he will perish. It will be as if he has taken poison and it is only a matter of minutes or hours before it takes effect. It is in view of this danger that the prohibition is made. The prohibition is thus revealed as an act of God's fatherly care. Fundamentally it is on the same plane as man's later expulsion from the Garden. The meaning is not, therefore, that God first prohibits and then adds a threat in order to give the prohibition weight, but that God prohibits because He wants to safeguard man against the threat connected with the doing of what is prohibited. As on the later occasion, it is clear that this threat is unavoidable and that God Himself is in some sense under constraint. If man eats of this tree, he must necessarily die. It is from this necessity that God seeks to restrain man when He forbids him to eat of this tree. We see here for the first time how He stretches out His protecting hand over the creature. He knows of a threat to its existence. He knows that we are dust. He has not formed man to let him dissolve into dust again. He has not given him a soul, a life, to take it from him again. He will keep what He has created. This prohibition is the first powerful promise with which God meets death. There is thus a plain connexion with the existence and function of the first tree, which had said silently and positively what in this prohibition is said openly and negatively—that man shall live by the will of God. The question of a grudging spirit on the part of God is not for nothing the question of the serpent. It is directed against the most valuable aspect of this prohibition—its character as grace. It would be sheer folly to burden our exposition with this question when it is so clearly excluded by the passage itself. But there are two other questions which cannot be evaded.

The first question concerns the threat which is so ineluctable that God Himself cannot arrest its fulfilment if man eats of the fruit of this tree. Why must he die the moment he eats of it? The answer is that he must do so because this tree is the tree of the knowledge of good and evil. If man transgresses His prohibition, God Himself cannot keep him from having his eyes opened to the knowledge of good and evil. In this knowledge he will necessarily die, i.e., the process of his life will be changed into a process of death, and his return to dust, the removal of the soul and life given to him, will be irrevocably introduced. The connexion is clear. The knowledge of good and evil is not a human but the supreme attribute and function which basically and radically distin- [260] guishes the Creator from the creature. It is the judicial wisdom of God to know, and His judicial freedom and office to decide, what He wills and does on the one hand and does not will or do on the other, and therefore what is good and evil, for salvation or perdition, for life or death. It is in this wisdom, freedom and competence of a sovereign Judge that God created heaven and earth,

Paradise and man. God knows what He created because He willed to create it, because He affirms it, because He found it good and salutary. He also knows what, in creating heaven and earth, Paradise and man, He did not create because He did not will to create it, because He negated and rejected it. In making this decision as the Creator He made use of His knowledge of good and evil. It is as this Judge, on the basis of this judicial knowledge and sentence, that He confronts man as the Lord. And the life proclaimed silently and positively by the first tree is life on the basis and under the natural presupposition of this judicial knowledge. The second tree is the express indication and revelation that a judicial knowledge of God does indeed constitute the presupposition of heaven and earth, of Paradise and finally of the being and life of man. Everything is what it is and how it is because God as the Judge has decided and ordered and willed it thus and not otherwise; because in His freedom, which is also His wisdom and power, His righteousness and goodness, He has chosen between good and evil, salvation and perdition, life and death; because He knew how to achieve that which is right and did achieve it. There is a knowledge of good and evil which is the basis of all things and the source of life, namely, that of God the Creator. The second tree in the Garden is the indication and revelation of this divine knowledge. Man is to know that his life originates and consists in the fact that God has affirmed and therefore denied, that He has chosen and therefore rejected, that He has willed one thing and therefore not willed another. Human life is to be lived in such a way that face to face with the second tree man takes his stand consciously and not unconsciously on the ground of this divine decision, that he accepts it as such, that he acknowledges and praises God as the One who in His sovereignty has willed and done this and not something else. This is what God wills with the existence of the second tree. Its function is to summon man to life in this knowledge and adoration. Otherwise how can it be life before and with God in distinction from the way in which plants and animals are also allowed to live their lives before and with God? The life of man is ordained to be lived in fellowship with God, i.e., in the acknowledgment of His deity and therefore of His judicial office in creation. But everything obviously hinges upon man's recognition and acceptance of the judicial office of God. And this raises the critical question whether he will do so. Will man acknowledge and praise God as the One who has found concerning good and evil, salvation and perdition, life and

[261] death, so that all that he has to do is to rejoice and be thankful—consciously thankful—on the earth which has been created? Or will he hold aloof from this offer of supreme fellowship between God and himself and lay down the impossible but tempting condition that he must first know evil as well as good, that he must first know what God has not willed and rejected as well as what He has willed and created, and then when he has achieved a certain competence, a knowledge of what God knows, he will accept His judicial sentence and place himself on the basis of it? Instead of recognising and praising God as the Judge, will he use the indication and revelation of the divine judicial office for

the purpose of standing alongside God in a perception of the depths of His wrath as well as His love, and in this divine likeness rejoicing in heaven and earth, in Paradise, and supremely in himself as the only percipient of the goodness of creation? Does man need to grasp after this possibility, to achieve this exaltation, and therefore to eat of the fruit of this tree? If he recognises as such the benefit of creation and the glory of the life which he is given; if he accepts them as self-evidently as they are given; if he recognises the verdict of God as such and cheerfully acquiesces in it because it is His; if he does not question His right, not claiming any right of his own and therefore not needing to test it; if it is enough for him that it is spoken and in force—he certainly does not need to grasp after this possibility. But what if he thinks otherwise? It is here that the prohibition comes in—a prohibition which at this turning-point demands no less attention than the tree itself, since without it the tree itself would not be there or call for consideration. If man thinks otherwise; if he grasps after the fruit of this tree and therefore attains this exaltation; if he really gains unnecessary possession of the divine knowledge of good and evil, it means that he will now have to share with God the whole responsibility of His judicial office, knowledge and sentence. He for his part will now have to choose and reject. He will have to know what is good and evil, salvation and perdition, life and death. By reason of his knowledge of things he will have to prefer the one to the other. Secondarily, at least, all things will depend on his verdict as primarily they depended on God's. But this is a responsibility which exceeds his capacity. He will necessarily collapse under this burden no less than if he were given the whole globe to carry. For the choice between good and evil, and the knowledge essential to this choice, is a responsibility which is absolute both in scope and difficulty. In face of it man will always, and necessarily, fail. He will not achieve that which is right but that which is not right. Unlike God's, man's decision will be a decision for evil, destruction and death: not because he is man, but because he is only man and not God; because the willing of good and salvation and life as such is a concern of God which cannot be transferred to any other being. Gazing into the abyss on the left hand— which the decision of God has graciously veiled—man can only give way to [262] dizziness and plunge into it. That is why he is graciously kept back from it by the divine decision. It is impossible for any other being to occupy the position of God. In that position it can only perish. It can only be made to realise that it is not God. Placed there in its creatureliness, it cannot continue as a creature. It is poison for any being to have to stand in the place of God. Placed there, it can only pronounce and execute its own sentence—not because it is evil, but because God alone is good. This is the threat which is necessarily incurred with the realisation of this possibility. It is from this threat that God wills to protect man. But even God can do this only if man for his part recognises and accepts the judicial office of God; if man allows God to be the Judge and does not himself become a judge and therefore the lost and impotent bearer of divine responsibility; if the knowledge of good and evil, and the choice between the two, really continues to be the affair of God alone. Even God cannot do anything against Himself. Even He cannot alter the fact that He alone is good; that He alone is competent to judge good and evil; that every other being will necessarily fail in the attribute and function of judge, and thus pronounce and execute sentence upon itself, because it is incapable of looking into the abyss of the divine freedom, and is not participant in the divine wisdom and righteousness. God would have to cease to be God to alter this difference between Himself and every other being. Because the threat cannot be averted, because man will really have to die if he eats of this tree and therefore attains possession of the knowledge of good and evil, he must be prevented from doing so. It is for this reason that God prohibits grasping at this fruit as a usurpation which will entail his destruction. It is for this reason that God in His fatherly concern tries to keep man from this second tree. The door to this possibility was opened when God planted the second tree. But above this door there stands the inscription "No entrance." This possibility is not to be realised. It is shown to man only as the divine possibility of which God can and did and does make proper use as He was and is and continues to be the Judge. In this possibility He and He alone wills to be recognised and praised. That man should be summoned to do this is the positive meaning of the second tree. That he should appropriate this divine possibility, becoming even if only secondarily like God, is what he is denied if we rightly understand the positive meaning of this tree, being warned against it by the express prohibition linked with its existence and by the notice written above this open door.

The second question is more difficult to answer. If the meaning of the prohibition, i.e., the connexion between the knowledge of good and evil on the one hand and the death of man on the other, and the will of God to prevent the former in order to avoid the latter, is plain enough in itself, the question is [263] posed all the more insistently: Why was not this divinely given prohibition more effective? Why did it merely take the form of a prohibition which could be transgressed and made ineffective by man? Indeed, we might go back even further and ask: Why did the revelation of God's judicial office take a form which could bring man into danger, leading him into a temptation against which the prohibition was a warning but which it only served to strengthen? Why is there opened a door in a direction which is closed to man? Would it not have been better to close this door than to write this prohibition upon it?

If we keep to the passage, it is to be noted first that it does not see any threat to man in this arrangement. It certainly sees that a problem is involved. There can be no mistaking the fact that with the existence of this tree and with the utterance of the prohibition man is brought to a cross-roads; that in the midst of Paradise, and therefore of the act of his creation, a question is put to him which he must answer with his existence. In face of the tree of the knowledge of good and evil the divinely given life of man assumes the nature of a task. It is to be lived in acknowledgment of the judicial office of God, in conscious gratitude, and to that extent in the form of decision and obedience. But the passage obviously does not imply that a shadow has now fallen, that man has been given opportunity to transgress and therefore occasion to lose his life, that in certain respects a snare has been laid for him. On the contrary, it obviously does imply that in this transaction the Creator is in every sense faithful to Himself and that man is thus well protected and exalted; indeed, that this second tree too is a special ornament of paradise, so that its glory, and therefore the glory of the man created by God, would not have been complete without it. God Himself planted it, and this excludes the thought that what we have here is, as it were, a bridgehead left to the kingdom of darkness by indifference or weakness on the part of God. The teaching of the passage is that we have to do at this point too with a well-planned arrangement of the divine wisdom and justice. In planting this tree and therefore opening this door, God acted here too as the Lord who knows how to distinguish between good and evil, who both can and does achieve that which is right. It is true that, although the acknowledgment of the judicial office of God in its sovereign freedom, and therefore conscious life in obedience to God, is offered to man in this arrangement, it is not made physically necessary. And it is also true that, although the eating of the tree of knowledge, and therefore the disastrous usurpation of the divine rights of majesty, is naturally forbidden, it is not made physically impossible. Thus it is true that some play is given to man, that freedom is ascribed to him. But his freedom is not, of course, a freedom of choice between obedience and disobedience. This is denied him by the fact that God makes Himself known to him as the One who, in and with his creation, has ruled as Judge over good and evil, who has made him good, who has therefore ordained and [264] equipped him only for what is good, and who, as his Creator, has cut him off from evil, i.e., from what He Himself as Creator negated and rejected. No play is given him on the edge of the abyss. He is not allotted a place midway between obedience and disobedience. His place is with and before the God who with his creation has chosen for him, deciding between good and evil, salvation and perdition, life and death. No other decision than that of obedience will correspond to this place; no other can be expected of him here; no other can be commensurate with his being; no other can be an act of the life given to him. In faithfulness to himself, and in continuance of the life given to him, he can only be obedient. That he has freedom to affirm this obedience has nothing to do with a temptation which overtakes him. How could God tempt him by expressly revealing Himself to him—this is what occurs in the planting of the tree of knowledge—as the One who as his Creator has ordained him for what is good and separated him from what is evil, and who even in forbidding him to eat of this tree demands of him only that he should honour His judicial office, and therefore for his part remain in the place which He has assigned to him? The honour of the indication, revelation and summons which comes to man in this respect is obviously the very opposite of anything that may meaningfully be described as temptation. But we must also abandon the idea that in granting man freedom to obey God put him on trial.

This presupposes that man might learn or not learn something; that he might pass or not pass a test with what he did. A test is an act of justified suspicion. But the passage is certainly not speaking of any suspicion on the part of God in relation to His creature. What was there in man to be the object of a testing suspicion or a suspicious test on God's part? What is he, and what does he have, which he does not owe to God's good decision taken at the time of his creation? If there is an adequate concept for the order of the relationship between God and man displayed at this point, it can only be that of confirmation. The purpose of God in granting man freedom to obey is to verify as such the obedience proposed in and with his creation, i.e. to confirm it, to actualise it in his own decision. It is obvious that if this is His will God cannot compel man to obey; He cannot as it were bring about his obedience mechanically. He would do this if He made obedience physically necessary and disobedience physically impossible, if He made man in such a way as to be incapable of a decision to obey. The existence of the tree of the knowledge of good and evil, and the prohibition attached to it, means that God has not created man in this way, but that He has created him with the capacity for a confirmation and actualisation of his obedience, for a personal decision to obey. This is not to say that God has given him, like a Hercules at the cross-roads, the choice of obedience and disobedience. If this were the case, we should certainly have to

[265] speak of a divine temptation or trial at this point. What is implied by the tree of knowledge of good and evil, and underlined by the prohibition, is simply that the given possibility of obedience is not the possibility of one choice as opposed to another, but of a free decision. Things are made no easier for man than this. He is taken no less seriously than this. God's decision for him as taken in and with his creation does not mean that he has not to repeat and affirm it by his own decision. On the contrary, this repetition and affirmation are expected of him, and the capacity and human freedom for it obviously belong to the structure of his peculiar creatureliness. This certainly does not consist in his standing between good and evil and being able to choose between the two. But it does consist in the fact that the man who stands thus before the God who in his creation has determined him for good is not only subject to this divine decision but can respect it in the form of his own decision. This is the freedom which God gave him at his creation. It is in this and no other way that He has determined him in His own decision for good. He expects and has made him capable of confirmation, of the obedience of his own free will and act.

There was no reference to human freedom in the description of man's creation from the dust of the earth and his animation by the divine breath. It is only here in the Garden of Eden, and with the description of the foundation of the relationship between God and man, that the question emerges. And it does not do so in the form of an expansion of the preceding anthropology, but in the form of the description of the second tree and the prohibition coupled with it. It is only to man confronted by the revelation of God that freedom is given as he is confronted by God in His Word. From this standpoint his creation is completed only as God makes Himself known to him as the sovereign Judge of good and evil, commanding him to cleave to Him as this Judge and forbidding him to try in any sense to be this judge himself. By reason of this address and summons, and the responsibility thus ascribed to him, man becomes and is free; free for what is expected and required of him; free to confirm, not himself, but God's decision accomplished in and with his creation.

This freedom assigned to man—not the freedom to choose between obedience and disobedience, which is excluded by the prohibition to eat of the tree of knowledge, but the freedom to obey—is obviously the true *tertium comparationis*[EN367], and therefore the sign of the fellowship already established between God and man at his creation. This freedom has nothing whatever to do with man's divine likeness or the foolhardy assumption of divine responsibilities. Nor can this freedom be dangerous to man. It is simply the freedom to be humble; his capacity to recognise and to praise the divine judicial office; his ability to side with God without assuming, even if only secondarily, a right of control. It is the freedom of the creature, keeping to its own place as such, affirming and maintaining it, to hold fellowship with the Creator—not merely [266] to have fellowship with Him like plants and animals and all the other creatures of heaven and earth, but to hold fellowship with Him in unassuming but conscious, spontaneous and active assent to His divine decision. The will of God when He gives man this freedom is supreme fellowship with Himself. It is thus to be noted that God does not in any sense will to exclude man even from His judicial office, but that on the contrary He wills quite definitely that man should participate in it and therefore in His own divine essence. In making use of the freedom given him, and therefore acknowledging the divine decision in the obedience of his own, man undoubtedly participates in the wisdom and righteousness in which God made His decision. The wisdom and righteousness of God are the rock on which he too can now stand; they are the mighty wings beneath which he too is sheltered. It is not without man but with him— and with him in his own decision and act—that God is wise and righteous, the sovereign Judge who judges rightly. This true union with man, this true exaltation of the creature, is what God wills when He gives him *freedom* to obey. And because this is His will, He gives him freedom to obey, and has not therefore made obedience physically necessary or disobedience physically impossible. It would not really have been a greater benefit if He had acted as the posing of the problem of a theodicy demands at this point, making things easier for man, sparing him the decision to obey, denying him freedom and therefore making a Paradise without any problems. This effective protection from transgression and its consequences would in reality have been proof of an inferior love. If God had protected man in this way, if from the very outset He had

---

[EN367] basis of comparison

exempted him from the clamant question of his existence, He would obviously not have called him to this fellowship and therefore to this true union with Himself. But if He did call him to this fellowship and union; if the determination of man for obedience was his determination for obedience in fellowship with God, He had to give him the freedom which He has obviously given him, not to tempt or test him, but to give him place for spontaneous obedience according to his creation. He had to be brought to the cross-roads; he had to be shown the possibility denied him for his salvation; that door had to be opened. In the freedom given him by God, man could not possibly will to make use of it. The transgression of man cannot be deduced from what God positively willed with it and with the freedom given to him. Not the fatal divine likeness of a personal knowledge of good and evil, but fellowship exercised in freedom with the God who had willed the good and rejected the evil, was the genuinely alluring and inviting thing in Paradise, the door which was not merely open but ordained for entry. The tree of knowledge could become a danger to man only if he faced it in a freedom appropriated in misuse of the freedom given him. In face of the realisation of this possibility, God the Creator needed no justification.

[267]   To look back for a moment, we are reminded by the double name of God that in this second and central section too we have to do with the decrees of the God who will choose, create, call and rule the people Israel. From this aspect as well creation has an inner basis, and this is the covenant which in the history which follows creation will take the form of the covenant of God with Adam, the Patriarchs, Abraham and the people of Israel. For the moment it is without form. But what is here recorded as creation history is in the last resort incomprehensible if we do not see that the form of this covenant is already prepared and outlined here, characterising both the totality and the individual constituents of the "pre-historical" origination described. Of course the writer fabulises, yet not accidentally, arbitrarily or at random. He does so with a definite intention and according to the definite law of a divination and imagination stimulated but also regulated by the revelation given to Israel. Hence he has neither the time nor the desire to be occupied with the origination of the world and man in general, but with that of the world and the man whose existence will receive its meaning in the execution of God's covenant. Already, then, in this origination as God's creation he can seek and find not merely the intention of a future covenant but its foundation and lineaments.

The first striking feature is that the creation of the earth and man finds its continuation in the planting of the special Garden in Eden and the placing of man in this Garden. The jump made is similar to that which the Genesis stories will later make when, among all the countries which call for consideration, they will arbitrarily (as it seems) single out the strip of fruitful land between the Mediterranean Sea and the Arabian desert—the land of Canaan. Between the two selections there is obviously an inner connexion. To be sure, Eden is not Canaan. The passage is careful to make this clear even geographically. It does so in such a way that we cannot localise it anywhere. Its precise localisation is a mystery. But, like the land of Canaan, it is a definite earthly place. Nor do we lack other and more precise points of comparison. It is a place chosen by God. It is not an elysian wonderland, but it is certainly fruitful, and eminently so in contrast with other strips of land. And its obviously supernatural characteristics have also to be taken into account. It is marked as God's sanctuary by its central point, where the will of God may be known both tacitly and audibly. It is the place where a stream rises which is the source of all the other rivers which fructify and bless the earth. Is it an accident that all these natural and supernatural attributes and functions of the special divinely created Garden in Eden should later also be those of the place, especially distinguished by God's revelation, where Israel will find its home and its history will be enacted? No Israelite hearer or reader of this saga could be surprised to hear of the act of God the Creator in establishing this place. For he himself was [268] the witness of an event closely corresponding to it. He lived in the midst of the fulfilment of the promise given to his fathers of a good land, good above all other lands, and destined to be the sanctuary of God. Indeed, he lived on its soil and was sustained by its fruits. With all his unfaithfulness he knew its destiny; he knew, sought and honoured its centre, where God in all His hiddenness was so revealed and so hidden in His revelation. At all events, Israel's prophets knew the universal significance of this particular place, and the river which was to proceed from it and bless not only this land but also the whole earth. It can hardly fail to be be noted that the whole actuality of Israel in Canaan in the course of salvation history is here projected backward, or better still, is here perceived and revealed as the meaning of creation. The creation story tells us that the particularity of God's revelation and salvation, as it emerged in the promise granted to Israel and in the gift of this land and its determination as the "holy" land, was not a mere coincidence but was deeply embedded in the nature of all things; that this "holy" land already had its prototype in God's creative act establishing all things; indeed, that the divine creative act had its meaning in the fact that it constituted this prefiguration.

But the comparison goes further. It is not just a striking coincidence that man was no more created or at home in the home assigned to him than Israel originated as a people in the land which it was allotted. Abraham, we remember, is led out of another country into this land which God will show him, and later Israel becomes a great people in a strange land and has to be redeemed as such and brought into its own place. So, too, it is with the first man. Paradise does not belong to him. It belongs to his Creator. Originally he is outside and not inside. It is his Creator who brings him into it and gives him rest. He as little chose this special place as the place could choose itself for this special function. But the divine choice of this place, and of man as its occupant, took place, and the creation of both was at the same time the execution of this choice. In this way man came to be in Paradise. And in exactly the same way it came about that Israel became and was allowed to be the occupant of that land. A further point of agreement is that the decree of the Creator was provisional; that the man who was placed in the Garden could be removed from it; that it could become to him an unknown and inaccessible place, a lost Paradise; and that this actually happened—just as Israel did not find any final abiding place in its country, but had to return to the exile from which it had been taken, yet without ever forgetting that country as the home given to it, without ever being able to shake off a longing for it, and without forfeiting the promise of a return to it. There is agreement, again, that the removal of man and of Israel from their respective places will be an act of divine judgment, but as such [269] also an act of divine grace; that that which God intends for man and Israel will be achieved, not in this particular place, but in and with their removal from it. To this extent the exile and the return from exile are no less prefigured in creation than Israel's occupation of the land.

But the decisive parallel has still to be mentioned. It consists in the relationship between the trees which form the centre of the Garden and the revelation of God which, according to Israel's history, formed the virtual centre of the "holy" land and the virtual centre of the life of the nation occupying this land. What does it mean that this nation in this land is God's nation? What does it mean that God wills to dwell in its midst, not just eternally but for this very reason temporally, not just omnipresently but for this very reason locally? What happens in this proximity between God and man? What does it mean that after the fashion attested by the Old Testament God meets man *hic et nunc*[EN368], and not in a general but in the unique *hic et nunc*[EN369], chosen by Himself, of His dealings which are these dealings, which have the specific form of His temporal and local dealings with Israel? What is it that we see as this divine order of the relationship between Himself and man? This question is answered by the account of the planting of the two trees in the midst of the Garden. It is an anticipation of the answer which will later be given by the rest of the Old Testament and therefore by the history of Israel. The account of the planting of the two trees tells us that the answer given later was already present in God's creative act; that God's creative act had its meaning precisely in the fact that it was the prototype of this answer; and that all that happened later could only be the unfolding of the wisdom already at work there, the fulfilment and confirmation of the prototype already present. It points us already to the content and range of the divine revelation in the possession of which Israel will live in the land promised and given to it.

On the one hand, this revelation will altogether be and mean to Israel what the tree of life in Paradise was and meant to man. The voice of God heard and attested by Moses and the prophets; the fact that it is so singled out among all nations by its service; the Law of God to which it can cleave; the tabernacle and later the temple and the special ministry entrusted to it; the sacrifice which is

---

[EN368] here and now
[EN369] here and now

to take place in the midst—the whole concrete centre of its being as this nation in this land will be to it the sign of the absolute goodness of God, i.e., the sign that it can live. The sign tells it that everything which could and had to be done for its sake has taken place and is accomplished. The sign places before it the accomplished fact of its deliverance and salvation. God has made it a nation; God has brought it to this place; God is present with it in this place: the wholly distant God is so wholly near it. As a reality without condition, reservation and limitation, the absolute faithfulness of God in which it may put its absolute confidence cannot fail. It is the hope which cannot be taken from it, [270] for it is sure in itself. While the sign of the covenant is there, everything is there—tacitly, self-evidently, needing neither explanation nor emphasis, exposed to no particular assault and therefore needing no prohibition, because the whole message of the sign is that this is given to Israel, that it actually lives by it and will definitely continue to do so. This sign demands only that it should be seen and heard; that it should not escape the eye and ear; that the gift to which it bears witness should be continually accepted; that Israel's existence should be an uninterrupted use of this gift; that it should really live by that by which it may and does live according to the promise of the sign. What is required of Israel is simply the freedom into which it is actually translated according to this sign. If it lives in this sign, it lives an absolutely secure and blessed life. This is the one thing which the revelation of God which it has experienced signifies to this people.

On the other hand, it has also the meaning which the tree of knowledge had for man in Paradise. It is also the warning sign of a possibility which, if realised, will necessarily be the opposite of the life and salvation promised to it, involving its destruction and ruin. It lives by God's election. It lives by the fact that God alone in His wisdom and righteousness has given to it this land. It has its promise and hope solely in the divine decision verified in this fact. For this people everything depends upon its acceptance of the sovereignty and uniqueness of this decision. It cannot, therefore, approach God and in its own knowledge of good and evil try to choose from His seat of judgment. It cannot do this even secondarily. This is not because God envies it the joy of its own choice and therefore its own decision, but because He knows that it can find true joy only in His divine choice and decision; that with every act of self-choice and self-justification, with every attempt to understand and to that extent accomplish its own distinction, even if only secondarily, it simply pronounces its own death sentence instead of living in it. Its distinction from other nations is that it is elected without having elected itself, without being able even secondarily to base its election on its own goodness and strength or other excellent attributes. The power of the promise given to it is that its content is the goodness of God, resting on Himself alone and not on anything else. To rejoice in it, Israel had to live on this goodness of His election which has no basis except in God, on the ground of His knowledge of good and evil. Hence the commandment to sanctify itself; not to make itself like other nations; not to serve their gods nor make gods of its own. The positive meaning of this commandment is simply that, without self-exaltation, self-election or self-justification, it should be satisfied with the grace of God; that, without desiring to know all God's ways and judgments, it should live on the basis of the good which, in virtue of His free choice and decision, God has addressed to it. This is what other peoples, left to their own devices, do not do. They live on their supposedly good qualities, on the estimation of their worth, on the self-satisfaction with which they call them (and therefore themselves) holy, and think they recognise and honour them (and therefore at bottom themselves) as their gods. Idolatry is the final result and clearest exponent of the knowledge of good and evil usurped by man; the sign of the mistaken path on which, according to the penetrating insight of the Old Testament, one nation after another rises and falls, blossoms and fades. It is from this path of all flesh that Israel is restrained by the commandment given to it. It is to hold fast to the glory which by the wisdom and righteousness of God it has before God on the basis of His election. It is not to ascribe glory to itself. For this reason it is to have nothing to do with idolatry as the sign of all self-exaltation. It has a very particular reason to hold fast to this commandment. What if it lacks altogether the good qualities to which it might refer on that mistaken path? What if God has chosen as His people, in preference to all others, a nation without any glory and power of its own, a foolish, stiff-necked and anxious people? What if it strives in vain after the idols of other nations, and in vain makes idols for itself, because it is quite futile for it to boast of its natural virtues or to magnify them into forms of idolatry? What if the chosen nation can find no consolation or help outside the God who chose it, and not even temporary mercy outside His judgment? What if every step on the road of self-exaltation, self-choice and self-justification entails at once the discovery of its nakedness and impotence, and its abandonment to them? How doubly forsaken and lost it would then be! How surely would its decline and ruin be sealed! What a dreadful fall from the supreme heights, what suicide, for Israel to try to live by anything but God's free goodness towards it, to try in any sense to live by its own goodness. It is against the realisation of this threat that the divinely given revelation seeks to guard and preserve Israel. On the day on which it eats of this tree it will surely die. The prohibition based on this warning is obviously the reverse side of the commandment given by the same revelation of God, according to which it is to live in the freedom which it is granted. In this freedom alone, says revelation, to the extent that it is commandment, i.e., the Law of Israel, which not for nothing is surrounded by so many promises and so many threats. At this point we meet the same questions as those which we can put in face of the prohibition and threat of the tree of knowledge in the Garden, and we must also give the same answers.

The first question is why Israel must suffer and vanish the moment it presumes to ascribe to itself that which is given to it by God's decision. And the answer is that at this moment it is involved in inevitable failure; that it can

[271]

reveal only its anger and folly, its weakness and helplessness; that in the strength of a good which it ascribes to itself it cannot continue either before [272] God or man, either spiritually or politically, either in the preservation of its national unity and freedom or the maintenance of the land given to it. *Yahweh* is the righteousness of this people. It is His righteousness which exalts this nation. But sin—the sin which consists in the surrender of this its only real righteousness for the sake of another, its own righteousness—this sin is in every respect the destruction of the people, i.e., the people which is directed solely to God's gracious judgment. Hence this people had to cleave to the Law of God which commands it to sanctify itself, i.e., to be content with the grace of God, to set its confidence solely in His judgment, without wishing to fortify itself by its own judgment, and to ascribe glory to itself, thus mortally weakening itself.

The second question is why God's grace is not so powerful, so triumphant and so penetrating, as to make superfluous the special sanctifying of Israel and therefore all injunctions and prohibitions? The answer is that God would not take Israel seriously if He were to make it easier than this, not giving it freedom in and with the revelation of His grace, and not demanding free obedience of it. The unreserved promise, the full hope, the confident trust of life given to this people, has its depth in the fact that it is a summons which awaits an answer, a divine decision which finds its confirmation in human decision. God does not will only to triumph over and in Israel. He wills this in fellowship, in covenant with Israel. This is why He gives it His Law, and demands its sanctification. This is why He wills its obedience. This is why Moses and the prophets speak warningly of a threat whose realisation an unsanctified and disobedient Israel necessarily brings upon itself. This is why the revelation of God given to it speaks of a way of life and death, as it did already at the heart of the Garden of Eden. The depth of God's grace, and the prophecy of disaster of which the Old Testament is so full, demands this too. *Yahweh* not only is Israel's righteousness, but Israel is to believe this in its heart and confess it with its lips.

It cannot be denied, of course, that the saga about the two trees of Paradise has also a general anthropological sense. We have tried to develop and maintain this. But it is only of the two trees that this can be said, or also said. All the rest, the whole conception of the planting and existence of the Garden, is a particular conception. This is true even though the river spreads out from it over the whole earth, for the fact that it proceeds from this place gives this universal relationship of Paradise a particular meaning and content. The meaning of Paradise as such can thus consist only in the fact that it is the type of the good land which *Yahweh* Elohim willed to give to His people. The account of the two trees opens up a further aspect. It is possible and necessary to understand it as the type of the order in which *Yahweh* Elohim and His revelation will encounter man, and in which man will always and everywhere [273] encounter Him. But it is a question of *Yahweh* Elohim and man, not of any deity and any man, and therefore primarily of the God of Israel and His people and their encounter. According to the saga, these trees are planted in this place, in the Garden of Eden and therefore in a particular region. Hence it is necessary to understand even this idea primarily in a limited sense, and only secondarily and derivatively in an unlimited. The whole force of the truth and validity of what is said generally in this account depends on the fact that it is said primarily with God and Israel in view. According to the tenor of the Old Testament as a whole, the covenant which God formed with all flesh on earth in the person of Adam and later again in that of Noah was actualised in and through the medium of this covenant. It is here that we have the promise of life, but also the threat of death for the sake of the promise of life. The grace of God is so profound that it condescends to call and receive man as His free covenant-partner.

And here the question of the final, objective Christological meaning of this passage is also necessarily raised, i.e., the question of the particular thing from which that to which it seems to point is really to be seen. The question of its subjective meaning, i.e., the meaning corresponding to the intention of the passage, might have been answered and exhausted by the reference to the history of Israel and the general anthropology secondarily and implicitly revealed in it. But here as elsewhere, beyond this question and answer there is raised a further question which is not directly answered by the Old Testament itself—that of the reality which confronts the statements of this passage, and therefore the account of the Garden of Eden, its rivers, and above all its two trees. The continuation of the text imposes this question. The Garden of Eden seems actually to have been planted in order that man might leave it again, and that it might become to him a lost Paradise. God's covenant with Adam is at once fulfilled in such a way that the latter stumbles at the tree of knowledge whose existence was to keep him warningly within his limits and therefore to keep him alive, so that instead of obeying the command of God he disobeys it, and lest a worse thing befall him has to be removed from the tree of life also. Immediate life from the fulness of God's goodness could now become a fact only in the form of human robbery, and a curse eternally perpetuating his dying would be the necessary consequence of this robbery. That he is prevented from this is the first act of the grace of God now granted to him. And what is now left to him is only life in the knowledge of good and evil, on the heights which he has reached, or rather the depths into which he has plunged, and therefore a life which has become inwardly impossible, a dying life subject to death. The grace of God, which in the form of the two trees constituted the centre of Paradise as the Gospel and the Law, is now in some respects dissolved into its components: the Gospel is one thing, the Law another; and Paradise, as the scene of the one grace, has become a place unknown and inaccessible to man. Therefore outside the Garden, God is now present with him and sustains him. On this presupposition, the covenant between God and man will now take shape. Where now is the reality to which the saga referred? Was the reference merely to a beautiful dream which dissolved on an evil awakening? But

[274]

even the reference to Israel and that which it typifies and signifies generally is of no help to us. For it is under these conditions that the covenant with Noah, Abraham and later Moses and the people of Israel is actually concluded and executed. Israel cannot and may not approach its God as the tree of life seems to promise. What precautions have to be taken to keep it at a safe distance from all immediate contact with the Holy One of Israel! What an absence of direct and simple and unreserved and inwardly assured life before and with God in all the relationships presupposed in the Law and the prophets and concretely displayed in the accounts of Israel's history! Everything now seems to be designed for the man who has eaten of the tree of knowledge, who constantly behaves as such, who step by step seems to be waiting for nothing but the opportunity to do what God prohibited and what he ought not to have done in any circumstances, i.e., to exalt himself, to call upon strange gods, or to make his own gods. From the very outset this people of Israel is at every point a chastised, suppressed, suffering and lost people, a dying and perishing people. It is with this people and under these conditions that *Yahweh* Elohim has formed a covenant. It is over it that first to last and step by step His grace undoubtedly rules. It is this people which He loves and commands to live. He does this even when He repeatedly puts it to death, when finally He leads it in its historico-political totality to destruction, and when all its tokens of mercy, its protection in the wilderness, its entrance into the land, and the kingdoms of David and Solomon are only steps on the road to death, at the end of which the Servant of the Lord appears as portrayed in Is. 53, and the good land belongs to strangers, and even the return to it is only a dim shadow of the promise which the prophets had unceasingly renewed even at the height of all the prophecies of destruction. To what extent can this antitype be understood as the reality of that type? To what extent are Gen. 2 and all the corresponding prophecies of salvation more than a dream if this is the truth, if things are so different from the real Paradise, from the real covenant historically accomplished? How could Ezekiel venture to renew the prophecy of the river of Paradise in his portrayal of the waters which issue from under the threshhold of the temple, become deeper and deeper, and finally sweeten even the waters of the Dead Sea? How can Proverbs venture to speak expressly of the tree of life as if it were still an attainable reality as before? Where were all these things to be found? What was Jewry in Palestine and the Diaspora? What was it for itself? [275] What did it signify for the world at the goal and culmination of history anticipated in Gen. 2? These are the tensions and difficulties in the relationship between Gen. 2 and 3, and between Gen. 2 and the rest of the Testament, which in respect of the Old Testament as such can be removed only when we either renounce altogether the question of the reality envisaged in Gen. 2 or take it to be the expression of a bold hope which was never actually fulfilled, i.e., as the document of a grandiose illusion. In this case we must assume the burden of proving how an illusion of this kind could be formed and maintain itself so tenaciously. The alternative answer is the Christian. It, too, necessarily proceeds from the fact that the meaning and reality of the history of Paradise are to be found in the history of Israel. Yet it does not understand the history of Israel as a reality which is self-enclosed but as one which from the very outset is open to the front, pointing to a goal beyond itself. What the history of Paradise indicates acquires its form in the history of Israel, but only its provisional form. The history of Israel controls in certain respects the problem of the covenant between God and man indicated in the story of Paradise. It shows how in accordance with the history of Paradise God will actually accept man, and how He wills to hold fellowship with him. It also shows the great gulf which is to be overcome. It shows God in all the glory of His goodness and man in all his sin, need and shame. It shows how God in all faithfulness conducts His will for the covenant to its realisation. It shows also how this realisation can only be the work of His incomprehensible mercy, and how it can only become an event through the passing and renewal of man and of the world; through a passing and renewal which from the standpoint of man are incomprehensible, in which God Himself will not only ultimately accept man but will Himself have to intercede for him, finally realising the covenant in His own person and thus enforcing definitively the judicial knowledge in which He was the Creator of all things. It shows how man and the world are conducted toward this goal. But it does not as yet show how this goal was reached, or how the covenant was accomplished and fulfilled. Hence it speaks of divine mercy and human sin, of life and death, of Gospel and Law, of election and rejection—but all so antithetically and in so self-contradictory a way that if we fail to see, or lose again, the sign which always points forward, we really have to doubt the unity and therefore the reality of the whole, and thus fail to see its agreement with the prototype of the history of the Paradise. And we can only say in conclusion that the history of Paradise, because it is itself a reflection of the history of Israel, can in its juxtaposition of the two trees present this unity only ambiguously and, as it were, dialectically so long as we do not read it with reference to one point where the covenant of God with man is accomplished and fulfilled, and

[276] where there is only one tree instead of two. This point lies beyond the history of Israel and beyond the Old Testament as the record of this history. But it can and must be said that it is envisaged here, i.e., that the creation saga is no illusion, and that the history of Israel recorded in the Old Testament is really more than the history of a contradiction, if it has actually and objectively found its goal, intended for it from the very outset, in the person and death and resurrection of the Jewish Messiah, Jesus of Nazareth, as proclaimed by the Evangelists and apostles of the New Testament, if it is true that it pleased God to become and be this person and in it Himself to actualise the passage and renewal to which the whole of the Old Testament bears such clear but disparate witness, thus ratifying the judicial recognition of His work of creation. If this is true, if the Christian reading of the Paradise saga is valid, its reference—and therefore the reference of the history of Israel prefigured in it—is to a reality: to the way in which the earth became a good land at a given

place; to the way in which the man created by God was given rest in this place by the same God; to the way in which the river which was mighty enough to flow through the whole land and fructify it had its source there; to the way in which the Gospel and the Law, the justification of life by God and its sanctification for God, were one and the same, as was also sinful, dying, lost man and man unreservedly loved and blessed and glorified. But if this is so, the history of the Garden of Eden and the history of Israel speak of the accomplished, real fellowship between God and man. Between the picture of Paradise in Gen. 2 on the one hand, and the form and work of Jesus Christ on the other, there lies the full, free and proper agreement which is not quite so obvious between Gen. 2 and 3 and Gen. 2 and the history of Israel. In the light of it, the agreement between Gen. 2 and 3, and that of Gen. 2 with the history of Israel, cannot be so obscure and contradictory and unnatural as would otherwise be the case. That already the history of Israel has its full share in the reality manifested in Jesus Christ will also be revealed, as the Evangelists and apostles never weary of reminding us. From this standpoint, we no longer look in vain from restricted Israel to humanity at large, from the particular to the general, nor do we ask in vain concerning the general anthropology so enigmatically proclaimed in Gen. 2. This is the Christian answer which we have to declare at this point. Whether it be accepted or not, it has at least the advantage of overcoming those tensions and difficulties. It is self-evident that in the sphere of the Christian Church the choice does not rest with us to accept or to decline it.

The literary unity of Gen. 2^{8-17} has been assailed. Must we reckon with an earlier form of the saga in which, instead of two trees, there was only one, namely, the tree of knowledge? The geographical relationship between the two trees is not very clear even in v. 9, and in Gen. 3^3 the tree of knowledge seems to be "the tree in the midst of the garden." But it may be asked whether we are not demanding too great precision from a passage of this kind if we allow ourselves to be so concerned about such obscurities that we are incited to break up the [277] sources. And it may also be asked whether the silence by which the "tree of life" is surrounded in Gen. 3, until it is mentioned again with great emphasis in 3^{22}, is not originally for an important purpose. Already at the commencement of the conversation with the serpent the tree of life is in a sense invisible, for in the presence of this first tree it would have been quite impossible to discuss the second. If we accept the view that the first tree, which in Gen. 2^9 was obviously *the* tree in the midst of the Garden, was added in a later redaction, the completed whole owes its present wealth and depth decisively to this addition. The same is true of the description of the river which flows out of Eden in vv. 10–14. This is often regarded as an addition for the sake of a suspected or desired uniformity of the picture. The geographical location of Eden needs to be outlined more exactly than in the passage (Zimmerli). But the passage does not help us very much in this respect. If an addition is discerned, its purpose is only to describe Paradise as a place richly blessed with water, and therefore as the fountainhead of all the rivers of the world. And it may be asked whether Paradise would really have been Paradise without this token; whether this token does not necessarily belong to a description of it. Account has also to be taken of other imaginary or real inconsistencies. Naturally it is of the very essence of saga to compose its portraits out of different elements. Hence these suspicions are not to be opposed by a strict affirmation to the contrary. But there are as good grounds for affirming that (originally or later) the text must have had a good coherent meaning in its present and not merely in certain underlying forms, so that it is legitimate and even obligatory to ask concerning it.

"*Yahweh* plants a park" (Gunkel). This interpretation of v. 8 is not incorrect, but it lays too great emphasis on the Persian root underlying παράδεισος EN370 and is thus misleading, since what is envisaged in v. 15 is not a place of leisure or luxury but a glorious sphere of activity. Its decisive determination consists in the fact that it was planted by God, and belongs to Him, and is thus assigned to man. In this sense the well-watered plain of Jordan (Gen. 13¹⁰) and the future Zion (Is. 51³) are compared with it as the "garden of the Lord," the latter being called the "garden of God" in Ezek. 28¹³ and 31⁸. Whether by "Eden" (delight) we are to understand a country in which this Garden was situated or the Garden itself does not seem to be of any moment, for the name does not purport to give us geographical information of any value. There are also references to "Eden" or the "garden of Eden" in Is. 51³ and Ezek. 36³⁵, and in Gen. 4¹⁶ we are told that Cain dwelt in the land of Nod "on the east of Eden"—an allusion which geographically is intentionally more puzzling than illuminating. According to v. 8, the Garden itself lay "in the East." Does not this settle all attempts to localise it in the region north of Mesopotamia? It must be conceded that in Ezek. 28¹⁴ᶠ· it is brought into close relation with the conception of the "holy mountain of God," which was usually sought in the North. But the East cannot be the North, and it is not easy to make of the one river with its four branches the fountainhead of the two Mesopotamian rivers. Is it not enough to assume that in pointing away from Palestine into the unknown distance of the desert the aim of the saga was to point to the sunrise? And is it not clear that (even in the reference to the river) it is trying to describe the locality of the Garden as a locality on earth but one which cannot be found? The whole description of this Garden—trees, a spring and even a resting place for man—is obviously that of an oasis. This is what God has planted, and it is to this that He has brought man. As the only clear biblical parallel for man's original habitation in this place reference must again be made to Ezek. 28¹¹⁻¹⁹, where it is said with remarkable explicitness of the king of Tyre that he had originally dwelt there in great majesty, in the midst of fiery stones, by the side of the covering cherub, "perfect in thy ways from the day that thou wast created"—until iniquity was found in him, until his heart was lifted up because of his beauty, until he himself corrupted his wisdom for the sake of his glory, so that his expulsion and destruction became necessary. This passage is obviously metaphorical. What happened to the first man happened to the king of Tyre. The fact that it was possible to use Gen. 2⁸ᶠ· in this way to describe the origin and destiny of a foreign kingdom indicates the universal significance which was obviously ascribed to the Genesis saga and undoubtedly intended by it. It translates the man created by God, "humanity" as such and absolutely, into a direct and specific divine sphere. It says that this specific divine sphere was his original home. It characterises man's fall as his unfaithfulness to the law of his original home, and his misery as his removal from the glory of this place. And it also says, of course, that this specific place will also be God's final goal for man.

[278]

We have emphasised that the description in v. 9 of the majesty of the trees in the Garden must not be opposed to the charge given to man in v. 15 to "till and keep" the Garden. Here, too, a contradiction is to be seen only if we demand from the saga a pragmatics which as a saga it cannot and will not offer. According to v. 5, God created man to "serve" the earth. This destiny is not cancelled by his translation into God's Garden, for only here can it find its confirmation. The fact that he is brought here does not mean that he is translated into the kind of fool's paradise that Moslems expect hereafter. He is "given rest," but this does not mean that he has not to act. According to the basic view of the saga, perfect joy and work are not yet divorced. It is only when man lives far from Paradise (3¹⁷ᶠ·) that the ground is cursed,

---

EN370 paradise

3. *The Covenant as the Internal Basis of Creation*

that it bears thorns and thistles and is tilled in the sweat of his face. It is obviously as useless to enquire concerning the practical necessity of "cultivation," and the foes and perils from which man is to guard the Garden of God, as it is concerning its geographical location. Food and defence have here a certain purpose and value in themselves and not in any external intention. To be a husbandman and warrior is a good thing in itself, irrespective of all considerations of utility or necessity. If we are content not to try to understand by it what cannot be understood outside it, we shall be hesitant to make Paradise a kind of island of the blessed, and thus to suspect that the reference to man's activity (v. 15) is a foreign body ("withered branches," Zimmerli) introduced from a context originally quite different.

In exposition of v. 10, Delitzsch has rightly observed that Luther's translation: "There arises a river ... " (so too the LXX and the Zürich Bible) is misleading, and that the *egrediebatur*[EN371] of the Vulgate is correct. It arose. What we have here is the description of a unique and miraculous event which has nothing whatever to do with the geographical concept of the continuous "rising" of a river. The river which took its rise here was *the* river whose waters fructify the earth. We are still in creation history. It necessarily belongs to the reality of an oasis that there is a spring there. But what we have here is *the* spring of *the* oasis. We are then told that this river which had its origin in the Garden of Eden was divided outside it into four branches, the names of which are given and can be partially identified by the countries which they encircled. But we cannot demonstrate this fact either geographically or hydrographically. Nor does it enable us to fix the location of Paradise. We have obviously missed the sense of the saga if we think that it is referring to a place of springs or a delta. It speaks of a river which miraculously divides itself rectangularly in the four directions of the compass. Ought not the system as such to warn us against trying to find it on any map? Of the names adduced in v. 14, Hiddekel (the Tigris) and Euphrates are familiar, but not as rivers with a common source as they need to be according to this passage. And two other rivers deriving from the same source are added. But no light is shed by the names Pison ("ariser") and Gihon ("bubbler") which they are given in vv. 11–13, nor is it a great help that there are references to the land of Havilah and Ethiopia (Cush) and various precious metals to be found in them. All that can be said of the various attempted solutions of these verses is that by now every philological and geographical possibility and combination has been explored (from Arabia to the Nile, the Indus and the Ganges), but that so far no one has succeeded in identifying convincingly the unknown quantities in this passage and putting them together with the known to form a satisfying picture *vis-à-vis* the whole. Until this is done, it is best to consider the scene portrayed here as an imaginary scene typically compounded of known and unknown ingredients. Even on internal grounds no other explanation than this can be considered for the Garden of Eden. What interested the saga was the rich water supply of the Garden of Eden and its central significance as a source of the rivers of all the four quarters of the earth. It mentions and describes the four rivers "as signposts pointing back to the lost Paradise, as *disiecta membra*[EN372] of the one river of Paradise no longer in existence" (Delitzsch). It says that all waters, and therefore all fruitfulness, and therefore all the gladsome abundance of the earth, have their origin in the source which by the miraculous creation of God springs up in this specific place which later became unknown and inaccessible to every creature. And the remarkable thing about these verses is that—with what is said in v. 5 f. about the humidity which the earth at first lacked and which was later given to it—they express the peculiar conception of water characteristic of this second creation saga and a whole series of other biblical passages. In the first saga and a whole series of similarly orientated biblical passages, water is the dangerous element of chaos and death hemmed in and

[279]

[EN371] it arose
[EN372] scattered members

held back by God. But here and in another series of passages it is the element of life necessary to the earth and man and granted to them by God in His mercy. It is the sum of the blessing for which man hopes in the cosmos and which again by the gracious power of God is actually granted to him. In this connexion reference may be made to the promise of Deut. 11[10-15]: "For the land, whither thou goest in to possess it, is not as the land of Egypt, from whence ye came out, where thou sowedst thy seed, and wateredst it with thy foot, as a garden of herbs. But the land, whither ye go to possess it, is a land of hills and valleys, and drinketh water of the rain of heaven: a land which the Lord thy God careth for: the eyes of the Lord thy God are always upon it, from the beginning of the year even unto the end of the year. And it shall come to pass, if ye shall hearken diligently unto my commandments ... that I will give you the rain of your land in his due season, the first rain and the latter rain, that thou mayest gather in thy corn, and thy wine, and thine oil. And I will send grass in thy fields for thy cattle, that thou mayest eat and be full." We may also refer to Ps. 65[9f.]: "Thou visitest the earth, and waterest it: thou greatly enrichest it with the river of God, which is full of water: thou preparest them corn, when thou hast so provided for it. Thou waterest the ridges thereof abundantly: thou settlest the furrows thereof: thou makest it soft with showers: thou blessest the springing thereof." Wells in a dry land, the digging of wells (by the servants of Isaac, Gen. 26[18f.]) and encounters at the well (such as that of Eliezer and Rebekah, Gen. 24[11f.]) are most important requisites in the history of the Patriarchs. The fact that Moses brought forth water from a rock in the wilderness (Ex. 17[2]) is one of the first miracles of grace in the journey through the desert. We read in Jud. 15[19] how God clave the hollow of the "jaw" for the benefit of Samson perishing with thirst, so that "there came water thereout; and when he had drunk, his spirit came again, and he revived." It is not for nothing that the prophetic demand of Am. 5[24]; takes the form: "Let judgment run down as waters, and righteousness as a mighty stream." Is. 8[6f.] is particularly interesting because it directly opposes the "waters of Shiloh that go softly" to the "strong and mighty waters" of the Euphrates which rise and threaten to engulf Judah; the holy and healing waters which represent the sum of the promised and expected help of *Yahweh* to the destructive waters which signify the Assyr-

[280] ian invasion. That springs, brooks and rivers of water break out and flow and are poured forth is a distinctive element in the prophecy of salvation applied in different ways in the later portions of Isaiah (e.g., 12[3], 30[25], 35[6], 43[19], 44[3], 49[10], 58[11]). As emerges dramatically in the story of Elijah, the God of Israel is the God who gives rain to the land and man. Against this we may ask with Jer. 14[22]: "Are there any among the vanities of the Gentiles that can cause rain? or can the heavens give showers? art not thou he, O Lord our God? therefore we will wait upon thee: for thou hast made all these things." Hence in Jer. 17[8] (cf. Ps. 1[3]) it is said of the man who trusts in the Lord and has his confidence in Him that "he shall be as a tree planted by the waters, and that spreadeth out her roots by the river, and shall not see when heat cometh, but her leaf shall be green; and shall not be careful in the year of drought, neither shall cease from yielding fruit." Similarly Ps. 23[2] says of the man who has the Lord as his Shepherd: "He maketh me to lie down in green pastures: he leadeth me beside the still waters." And all this is taken up in the New Testament, where Jesus is described (Jn. 4[10f.]) as the One who gives living water to drink, who even promises (Jn. 7[38]) to the man who believes on Him that from his body streams of living waters will flow, and who in heaven will not cease to lead His own to streams of living water (Rev. 7[17]). This is impressively repeated on the very last pages of the Bible: "I will give unto him that is athirst of the fountain of the water of life freely" (Rev. 21[6]). "And the Spirit and the bride say, Come. And let him that heareth say, Come: and let him that is athirst come. And whosoever will, let him take the water of life freely" (Rev. 22[17]). And the water from which Noah was saved has now become (1 Pet. 3[20]) the redeeming water of baptism as man's saving introduction to the quickening power of the death of Jesus Christ (Rom. 6[4]). The passages at the end and the present passage at the

beginning of the Bible agree particularly in emphasising that the waters which bring life and blessing proceed from one definite place and thence spread out in all directions. According to Rev. 22^1, it is from the throne of God and of the Lamb established in the heavenly Jerusalem that there proceeds the river of the water of life which is clear as crystal. Already in Joel 3^{18}, Zech. 14^8, Ps. 46^5 and above all in the great vision of Ezek 47$^{1-12}$, reference may be found to a fountain which breaks out in Jerusalem, and a river which issues from it. In the latter vision the threshhold of the temple is described as the source of a spring whose water first encircles the temple itself, then turns in an eastward direction and becomes deeper and deeper cubit by cubit, with trees on its lower banks whose leaves do not fade nor fruits fail (for the water which nourishes them "proceeds from the sanctuary"), until at last it reaches the Dead Sea and heals its water, so that it is full of swarming fishes and nets are spread "from En-gedi unto En-eglaim." We have here—in the distinctive prophetic declension—the most exact parallel to Gen. 2$^{10f.}$ And it is undoubtedly in this great biblical passage that we must seek the meaning of the hydrographically impossible and geographically indefinite river system described in our passage. It speaks of the river of life which first blesses the earthly sanctuary chosen and established by God, and then the whole face of the earth, fructifying it, quenching its thirst, healing its wounds, refreshing and renewing all creation. This is what has become of the universally destructive chaos-element of water in the second creation saga. This is what it now attests and signifies. It is no longer the water averted and restrained but the water summoned forth by God. It is no longer the suppressed enemy of man but his most intimate friend. It is no longer his destruction but his salvation. It is not a principle of death but of life. It may be that this change of view is to be explained by a different place of origin, but the true explanation is to be found in the fact that, unlike the first, this saga finds the inner basis of creation in the history of the covenant whose purpose is not only the preservation but the transformation of man and the cosmos, the divine lordship over all forces, and therefore their serviceability; the history, that is, at whose culmination life will swallow up death with all its menace and death itself, for all that it is menacing, will become life. This does not mean that the view of the first saga and the corresponding line of biblical teaching are opposed but that they are transcended and placed in a larger context of truth. It is true, of course, that God desires to keep and preserve man and the cosmos. But the second saga considers His purpose and intention in their preservation. It is also true that the existence of creation is threatened on its frontiers. But the second saga considers the fact that even this threat comes from God and to that extent is necessarily full of endless promise. It is also true that man must die. But the second saga considers the fact that even the death of man as the work of the divine wrath is from the very outset, in the true and final depth of its dreadfulness, the grace of God. It is also true that water is the sign of the end of all things. But the second saga considers the fact that on the far side of the end of all things the true will and act of God have their beginning, so that it is able to see in the sign of that end the sign of this beginning. It is also true that Jesus Christ will calm the storm on the sea and walk on its waves, and that His apostle will follow Him in the same way, and that finally the sea will become the crystal sea and thus cease to be dangerous, or even to be the former sea at all. But the second saga considers the fact that Jesus Christ will create living water, giving the thirsty drink and making them springs of water. Thus the second saga embraces and includes the presentation of the first. Its horizon is admittedly much narrower than that of the first, but in this respect it is wider. Being cosmologically particular, it can be eschatologically universal. From its distinctive narrowness and nearness it can really look to the final height and distance, and thus self-evidently admit this great change of meaning in respect of the sign of water. When we remember this, vv. 10–14 of this passage are better not described as "sterile Paradise-geography" (Zimmerli). They are full of prophetic content, and if they are later additions we cannot be too grateful that they were made.

[281]

Vv. 9b and 16–17 deal with the two special trees in the Garden of Eden. If we proceed with the picture which the saga offers in its existing form, we must first affirm that this picture is as much dominated in the foreground by the tree of knowledge as it is in the background by the tree of life. The crucial thing in the history of the first human pair which begins in $3^{1f.}$ is, of course, the tree of knowledge. Reference will be made to the tree of life (3^{22}) only as an element which will make man's stay in the Garden dangerous under the changed conditions, i.e., only as the reason for his expulsion from this Garden. But this does not alter the fact—indeed 3^{22} confirms it—that the tree of life, otherwise mentioned only in 2^9, is really the more distinctive of Paradise and man's existence in it and the act of creation as such. The place in which God gives rest to man when He creates him, and which even when it becomes totally unknown and inaccessible will still be the original starting point toward which, when he has left it, his history must genuinely strive under the government of the same God, is the Garden in the centre of which the tree of life is planted. It is the genuine tree of Paradise, whereas the tree of knowledge, as the second tree alongside the first, and on account of the problems indicated by it even in Paradise, points to the fact that the covenant between God and man will be realised on the road which is to run from the Paradise at the beginning to that at the end. The road outside it will come under its sign. But the act of creation, the divine establishment of human existence as such—in contrast to its own beginning—stands under the sign of the tree of life. Hence it is the latter which returns triumphantly in the picture of the last kingdom (Rev. 2^7): "To him that overcometh will I give to eat of the tree of life, which is in the midst of the paradise of God." According to Rev. $22^{2f.}$, which obviously points back to Is. 47^{12}, this one tree will have become many trees, and their meaning is made very clear by the context "In the midst of the street of it (of the heavenly Jerusalem), and on either side of the river, was there the tree of life, which bare twelve manner of fruits, and yielded her fruit every month: and the leaves of the trees were for the healing of the nations. And there shall be no more curse: but the throne of God and of the Lamb shall be in it; and his servants shall serve him. And they shall see his face; and his name shall be in their foreheads." On this way from the beginning to the end the tree with its many fruits and unfading leaves corresponds necessarily as it were to the living waters. What does this mean in Gen. 2? The fact that it stands in the midst of God's Garden surely indicates that it stands in a special relation to the Lord of this Garden, and that man as its creaturely occupant cannot overlook it as such. The tree in the midst of the Garden indicates that the Garden is God's sanctuary. Here, in what the tree both represents and offers, the Creator is present with the creature which He has placed in it. God wills to be recognised, honoured and loved by man in what this tree represents and offers. While He gives man the enjoyment of the whole Garden and all its trees, by the planting of the tree of life in its midst God declares that His primary, central and decisive will is to give him Himself. "Behold, the tabernacle of God is with men, and he will dwell with them, and they shall be his people, and God himself shall be with them, and be their God" (Rev. 21^3). In the Garden the tree of life occupies the position and fulfils the function which the tabernacle will later occupy in the camp of Israel in the desert, and the temple in Jerusalem in the land which it is promised and given, and the Holiest of Holies in the tabernacle and the temple. Moreover, in the midst of the Garden in the unique place assigned to the tree of life, what is prefigured is that there can and will be only one sanctuary in the holy land and on the whole earth, i.e., that which is chosen by God Himself. If it is called the tree of life, we must first think of the process of v. 7 where God breathed the breath of life into man's nostrils. In this most direct and immediate act God raised man from the dust of the earth to be a living creature, and in so doing bound him to Himself. Thus God created man, or began to create him, as the being which lives in virtue of this divine action, and depends for its life on a repetition of this action. His creation is as yet incomplete. To the mode of his existence already described,

[282]

278

there is added by his translation into the Garden whose centre is occupied by the tree of life the fact that God grants him His own presence, i.e., Himself as the Co-inhabitant of this place. The tree of life has obviously the function to give man the guarantee and certainty that God, and therefore the One who quickens him and is his Deliverer, is near to him in face of the death which threatens him as a thing formed from dust. He is not only bound to God, referred to Him and dependent on Him. God is there for him. And God does not will that he should die but live. It is with this intention that He has given man peace in His Garden, and Himself made His abode in this Garden. As the other occupant of this Garden, man need have no fear of death or anxiety about the renewal and therefore the preservation of his life. This is guaranteed to him by his translation to the place which has this centre. There are a number of verses in Proverbs from which it emerges that the notion of the tree of life later acquired proverbial significance as a description of that in which the highest guarantee of a secure human existence was thought to be found. According to Prov. 3[18], wisdom is a tree of life to those who lay hold of it. The "fruit of the righteous" (Prov. 11[30]), fulfilled yearning (in contrast to deferred hope (Prov. 13[12]) and a "wholesome" (in contrast to a false) tongue (Prov. 15[4]) are all called "a tree of life." Similarly, the "mouth of the righteous" (Prov. 10[11]), the "law of the wise" (Prov. 13[14]), the "fear of the Lord" (Prov. 13[27]) and "understanding" (Prov. 16[22]) are called a wellspring, a fountain of life. It is clear that in all these places we not only have an important confirmation of the connexion between fountain and tree, but also a derivative and indirect use of the notion of the tree of life in the Garden of Eden. Linguistically, this is brought out by the fact that this tree alone is called *'etz hahayyim*, the tree of Proverbs being connected with life but having no article. The only true [283] parallel is in Ps. 36[9], which says of God that with Him is the fountain of life. The tree of life of Gen. 2 is the presentation and offer of life, for it describes God Himself, the source of life, as the Co-inhabitant of the Garden, the One who is present in the midst of it, and therefore the guarantee of human existence. Even the saying about wisdom in Prov. 3[18] cannot be regarded as a true parallel because there can be no question of an "apprehension" of that which the tree of life in Paradise represents and offers. On the contrary, it seems to belong to its nature to fulfil its function by being there in the midst and as a background, so that in normal circumstances the question of a necessity and need to eat of its fruit does not arise. Seen in connexion with v. 7, it can be said that the necessary renewal and preservation of life can take place only where it was originally given and originated, namely, in God Himself. That God does actually renew and preserve it can, of course, be attested and guaranteed by the tree of life as a presentation and offer of God's presence. Yet it cannot be effected by this creaturely medium, but only by God Himself. And as the tree attests and guarantees this event, and its witness and guarantee are accepted, it is obviously superfluous to try to appropriate, by grasping and enjoying its fruit, that which is already possessed in the present and assured for the future. It is only when the relationship between God and man is abnormal, and the witness and guarantee given and objectively present to man with the existence of this tree are no longer accepted by him, that there can arise any question of a desire for its fruit, of a grasping and enjoyment of it. When the relationship is normal—and the act of creation as such produces a normal relationship—it does not even need to be prohibited. The purpose in the act of his creation is to live in absolute certainty, and therefore without any fear whatever of the threat of death and therefore without any hunger for life. The fear of death and the hunger for life do not correspond to his destiny. His real destiny is given him as he is given rest in the place whose centre is constituted by the tree of life; in the place in which the fear of death and the hunger for life are mutually excluded because he knows that he is protected from death and assured of life. From Gen. 3[22] we do, of course, learn something apparently different, namely, that the eating of the tree of knowledge will give man the knowledge of good and evil and therefore make him like God. And when this actually happened, when the abnormal relationship between God and man commenced, man might have stretched out his hand to the tree of life and therefore "lived for ever"— *wahay le'olam.* It would be quite inept to compare this verse too directly with the conceptions of the wonderful elixirs of life, rejuvenation or immortality familiar to us from the general history of religion. It tells us, in fact, that there is no such elixir. The fear of death and care of life in an abnormal relationship make man grasp at such elixirs in an attempt to save himself from death and create life. But this is not merely forbidden him but actually denied to him. He cannot actually do it, and it is his salvation that he cannot do it, and that he is expelled from the Garden of Eden where in a normal relationship *vis-à-vis* God, life, rejuvenation and immortality were certainly promised. In the abnormal situation the punishment meted out to him by God has become his only salvation—to wit, that he may die. Everlasting life, rejuvenation and immortality as they were promised him in the Garden were the outcome and gift of God's immediate presence. In this divine presence, as he received and accepted the witness and the guarantee of the tree of life, he could not die at life's beginning any more than at the end of his day when he is raised from the dead and again in the divine presence. But when he broke God's commandment, this presence became intolerable. When he had become like God in the knowledge of good and evil, he could not possibly endure before Him but had to die. The abnormal relationship and the arbitrary grasp after the gift of His presence would necessarily have turned its blessing into a curse. Had he taken what was promised him as God's gift, the promise would have been fulfilled in the sense that in God's presence he would have had to be the eternal sinner and transgressor subject to constant dying. The abnormal relationship into which he had fallen would then have assumed the nature of finality, his curse the nature of a definitive determination, and his death the character of eternal death—an unceasing existence in death. But because God did not will him to fall so deeply, he had to be removed from the tree of life and therefore from God's immediate presence. That access to Sinai and therefore direct participation in God's revelation are denied to the people (Ex. 19^{24}); that Moses himself, hidden in the cleft of the rock, is allowed only to see the Lord from the rear (Ex. 33^{18}); that the Holiest of Holies in the tabernacle and the temple is accessible to the High Priest only once a year (Lev. 16^2); that according to 1 Sam. 5–6 the ark of the covenant can bring nothing but death and destruction to the Philistines who, in their possession of it, thought they could rejoice in the aiding presence of the God of Israel—all this is bound up with what is described as the promise of the tree of life now transformed into a threat. "God is not mocked" (Gal. 6^7). It would be to mock God, and thus to bring upon himself eternal destruction, if man were to make use of the gracious presence of God to satisfy the fear of death and the hunger for life to which he fell victim when he disobeyed God. It would be to mock God if in his opposition to God he tried to enlist God's aid in meeting the consequences of this opposition. Even then God would not refuse His help. But this very help would actually be a final rejection of man. The one true elixir of life, of which he had no need in the normal relationship, could only become a more extreme form of death in the changed relationship. His only hope, the only guarantee in face of death, is that grasping at the tree of life should be made impossible to him; that the matter should simply end in death; that he should be allowed to die in order that, dying, he may at least fulfil without resistance the will of God as he must encounter it after his transgression; in order that in death at least he should be in His hand, and therefore should not be rejected, but should have his hope in God. The passage in Gen. 3^{22}; thus confirms the nature of the first tree as a tree of life, i.e., as a sign of the presence of God which guarantees life to man. But in some sense it confirms it negatively, not in relation to an operation of this sign purposed and executed by God, but in relation to an operation restrained rather than willed and executed by Him. It tells us that the sign of life would have to be the sign of death to man fighting God unless God willed it altogether otherwise; unless

[284]

He willed to prevent the man who fights against Him from being under this sign—his final and definitive sign. In the light of Gen. 3^{22}, the parallel to the sanctuary of the same God of Israel cannot be missed. And it is to be noted that the nature of the tree of life as such remains actually untouched by what is said about it in Gen. 3^{22}. Since it was not actually permitted to become a tree of death, since the presence of God was not permitted to have this truly destructive effect upon man, it is still the case that in this sanctuary, which had naturally become unknown and inaccessible to man in himself, the promise of life awaits him in full and unequivocal clarity even as and though he must die. That which man cannot expect there, but which is a fact and comes, is not at any point or time a real threat, and has not at any point or time really destroyed, but is always the promise of life and hope. It is for this reason that Israel ventured to speak as it did of the tree, at least figuratively and proverbially. And it is for this reason, too, that the Apocalypse called it the tree of which those who overcome do not eat in their own right but will be given to eat by their Lord.

To the tree of knowledge there are no parallels either in the Old Testament or in the general history of religion. The result has been an even greater variety of attempts to explain it. The most venerable is that of Augustine (*De civ. Dei*, XIII, 20, XIV, 12, *et freq.*), Luther (*Ennarr. in Gen., W.A.*, 42, 73 f., 80 f.) and Calvin. On this view, the tree itself has nothing whatever to do with evil, but like the prohibition connected with it is appointed *propter* [285] *commendandum purae et simplicis oboedientiae bonum, quae virtus in creatura rationali mater quodammodo est omnium custosque virtutum*[EN373] (Augustine), as a *signum externum cultus et reverentiae*[EN374] (Luther), and as an *examen obsequii*[EN375] (Calvin). Thus the prohibition of the fruit of the tree was a kind of test. Everything depended on its formal fulfilment, so that there is no need to ask concerning its meaning and content and therefore the nature of the tree. Jacob and to some extent Gunkel too share this opinion. Without any reasons man is required to obey with a childlike obedience, as Abraham did later when he left his father's home and when he offered up Isaac. Luther gave to the thought an acute and surprising turn: *hic textus vere ad ecclesiam seu theologiam pertinet*[EN376]. By the one tree there is really to be understood a small orchard of trees of the same species. Here Adam was to gather with his descendants on the Sabbath, and when they had together eaten of the tree of life, to preach, i.e., to proclaim God, and His praises, and the glory of creation, and particularly of the divine likeness, and to exhort them to a holy and sinless life and to a faithful tilling and keeping of the Garden: the *religio nudissima, purissima et simplicissima, in qua nihil laboriosum, nihil sumptuosum fuit*[EN377], and the relics of which were to be restored through Christ, though in relation to the worship of Paradise they are only *miserae reliquiae*[EN378], until one day, united with the angelic choirs, we shall be permitted to return to its entirety and perfection. Thus, founded *sine muris et sine pompa in loco spatiosissimo et amoenissimo*[EN379], the Church is obviously older than husbandry and the state. And it is this intrinsically good commandment of the pure worship of God which man has transgressed by his own fault. This interpretation rightly recognises that the point at issue in the planting of the tree of knowledge is the establishment of a proof of obedience and faith and the initiation of a relationship between man and God accomplished in man's conscious decision. But the fact

---

[EN373] so that the good of pure and simple obedience would be preserved, since that virtue is in rational creatures in a certain manner the mother and protector of all virtues

[EN374] outward sign of worship and reverence

[EN375] test of obedience

[EN376] this text actually refers to the church and theology

[EN377] the barely, purely and simplest religion, in which there was nothing either burdensome or extravagant

[EN378] wretched remnants

[EN379] without walls and without pomp in a most spacious and delightful place

that it is called the tree of knowledge of good and evil and mediates this knowledge, that this is the tree which is denied to man with all that this implies, that in spite of this he grasped after it, and that finally his mortality was connected with this prohibited grasp—all this deserves much fuller consideration than is given to it on this view. What does "knowledge of good and evil" mean? The expression is obviously too concrete to allow us to accept the interpretation of Wellhausen (*Prolegomena*, 300 f., etc.) that its reference is to science and our general knowledge of things. Indeed, if this were so, it would be impossible to see why God should prohibit this to man and thus prohibit progress from childish ignorance to culture, or why the saga should regard this progress as deadly. For this reason other writers (e.g., Delitzsch) have thought in terms of the problem of progress from childish innocence to moral decision. Knowledge of good and evil characterises intellectual maturity and moral decision. "As the tree of life was to mediate life to man as a reward for obedience by its enjoyment, so the tree of knowledge was to give man a right use of freedom by its avoidance." The aim of the pre-historical *mitzwah*[EN380] was "to give man occasion to proceed from the given freedom of choice to an autonomously attained freedom of power." But why should this be done by the prohibition of this tree? Why is the enjoyment of this tree described as deadly when according to this passage it is the eating of this tree (and not its avoidance) which undoubtedly mediates this knowledge and therefore makes this progress possible? According to another interpretation—included by Gunkel in his exposition of Gen. 3—the fruit of this tree was aphrodisian in character, and the consequence of man's eating was the discovery of sex differentiation and the corresponding libido. Indeed, one English scholar has jumped to the conclusion that by *tobh* we are to understand the normal heterosexual and by *ra'* the abnormal or homosexual libido. It must be admitted that the passages in 2^{25} and 3^7 which speak of the nakedness of the first human pair in the Garden before and after the fall give us to understand that the deadly knowledge of good and evil,

[286] illegitimately acquired, works itself out immediately and primarily in the perversion of their mutual relationship, namely, their sexual relationship, so that they now feel shame at something of which they should not be ashamed—their differentiation and mutual relationship. With the transformation of something which is natural into a *pudendum*[EN381], there is immediately issued from the seat of judgment occupied by man a perverted sentence. And it is to be noted that this verdict, and the impotent moral self-help (fig leaves!) to which it gave rise, are disowned by the fact that according to 3^{21} God makes them coats of skin, thus bringing order into the disorder which has arisen, and which has not been resolved by his moral effort. Yet neither here nor anywhere else in the Old Testament can there be even the slightest suggestion of discrediting an awareness of the sexual relationship. And it is wholly arbitrary to overlook the fact that this first visible blunder of man is a consequence—even if the first—of the fatal knowledge acquired, but that the knowledge itself and as such is deeper and more embracing and cannot possibly be equated directly with sexual knowledge or its perversion. An explanation which avoids the arbitrariness of all these attempts and leads us to solid ground must find its starting-point in what is meant by the knowledge and differentiation of "good and evil" in the rest of the Old Testament. In the first instance, we have to take account of a number of passages in which the capacity for it simply means the capacity—not yet possessed in childhood and perhaps no longer possessed in old age—to be responsible and to act. "Your little ones, which ye said should be a prey, and your children, which in that day had no knowledge between good and evil, they shall go in thither (the promised land), and unto them will I give it, and they shall possess it" (Deut. 1^{39}). Or again, with reference to Emmanuel in Is. 7^{15-16}: "Butter and honey shall he eat, that he may know to refuse the evil,

---

EN380 commandment
EN381 embarrassment

and choose the good. For before the child shall know to refuse the evil, and choose the good, the land that thou abhorrest shall be forsaken of both her kings." Or on the other hand the aged Barzillai says in 2 Sam. 19³⁵: "I am this day fourscore years old: and can I discern between good and evil?" Jon. 4¹¹ may also be cited in this connexion with its reference to the great city of Nineveh wherein were more than sixscore thousand persons "that cannot discern between their right hand and their left." But there are other places with a more pregnant use of the concept. The distinction between good and bad is described in Lev. 27³³ as the ability to choose between worthy and less worthy cattle and sheep. In Gen. 31²⁴ Laban the Syrian is told in a dream to beware and not to speak "either good or bad" to Jacob about the latter's flight, i.e., not to summon him to a defence or to judge him, because the flight corresponds to the will and plan of God. And in 1 K. 3⁹ we have the petition of Solomon at the commencement of his reign: "Give therefore thy servant an understanding heart to judge thy people, that I may discern between good and bad: for who is able to judge this thy so great a people?" Here knowledge of good and evil has obviously become the necessary predicate of a good ruler and judge. It was with reference to this predicate that the woman of Tekoah (2 Sam. 14¹⁷) addressed David: "The word of my lord the king shall now be comfortable: for as an angel of God, so is my lord the king to discern between good and bad." It is to be noted how in both these passages this capacity to discern is referred to God, for in the former it is the subject of a prayer and in the latter it is compared with the capacity of an "angel of God." A whole series of further passages may be adduced to show that primarily and ultimately it is to God alone that this capacity belongs. God controls this knowledge, and God accomplishes the distinction between good and evil, because He stands in His being and ruling over the things which have to be distinguished, and they are both in His sight and might. "Shall we receive good at the hand of God, and shall we not receive evil?" (Job 2¹⁰). "Whether it be good, or whether it be evil, we will obey the voice of the Lord our God, to whom we send thee; that it may be well with us, when we obey the voice of the Lord our God" (Jer. 4²⁶). It is the fact that God knows both, that He forms the light and creates darkness, makes peace and creates evil (Is. 45⁷), which distinguishes Him from the idols of the nations, which in Is. 41²³⁻²⁴ are addressed sarcastically: "Yea, do good, or do evil, that we may be dismayed, and behold it together. Behold, ye are of nothing, and your work of nought: an abomination is he that chooseth you." And Jer. 10⁵: "Be not afraid of them; for they cannot do evil, neither also is it in them to do good." Whereas, according to Zeph. 1¹², God could not be worse misunderstood than He is by those who say in their hearts: "The Lord will not do good, neither will he do evil." It is characteristic of both His being and His doing that both are in His sight and in His hand. Both good as good and evil as evil receive their nature from Him and are subjected to Him in the realisation of their disposition which then also becomes their judgment. He it is who hardens and destroys Pharaoh and frees Israel (Ex. 7²ᶠ⁻). He "killeth, and maketh alive: he bringeth down to the grave, and bringeth up. The Lord maketh poor, and maketh rich: he bringeth low, and lifteth up" (1 Sam. 2⁶⁻⁷). He is the God of David and the God of Saul. Around His throne are assembled the good and evil spirits, the sons of God and Satan also among them (1 K. 22⁹ᶠ⁻, Job 1⁶ᶠ⁻). For this reason it lies utterly in His power to set before His people "life and good, death and evil" (Deut. 30¹⁵), to set before them the warning: "If ye forsake the Lord, and serve strange gods, then he will turn and do you hurt, and consume you, after that he hath done you good" (Josh. 24²⁰), but also the promise: "As I thought to punish you, when your fathers provoked me ... so again have I thought in these days to do well unto Jerusalem and to the house of Judah" (Zech. 8¹⁴⁻¹⁵). Hence it follows for man—and strangely it is in a saying of Balaam (Num. 24¹³) that this deduction finds classical expression: "If Balak would give me his house full of silver and gold, I cannot go beyond the commandment of the Lord, to do either good or bad of mine own mind" (lit. "after my own heart"). From the point of view of all the other passages, this

[287]

obviously brings us into decisive proximity to Gen. 2^{16-17}. To transgress the Word of the Lord means to do good or evil after one's own will. But this is something which must not be done because it is God who must decide concerning good and evil, commanding the one and prohibiting the other, whereas man, choosing after his own heart, cannot attain good but will do evil. This, then, is what God prohibited. This is the possibility indicated by the tree of knowledge in the Garden of Eden but also prevented by the commandment. This is the possibility whose realisation delivers man to death by removing him automatically from the One with whom is the fountain of life. It makes him like this One. It thus means that, choosing and deciding for himself, he must now be the fountain of life himself. But he is unable to be the fountain of life himself. Hence he can only forfeit his life and die. Being like God and yet not God, he can only perish before the One by whom he was created and by whose breath he could live. That God knows and really controls good and evil, salvation and perdition, life and death, is something which man must experience to his sorrow now that he is like Him. It is this that the prohibition to eat of the tree is designed to prevent. The question frequently raised whether we are to understand by "good and evil" what is morally right and wrong, or useful and useless, or pleasant and unpleasant, cannot be answered as though these were alternatives. The Old Testament concepts of *tobh* and *ra'* embrace all these things in the instances adduced. To know good and evil is to know right and wrong, salvation and perdition, life and death; and to know them is to have power over them and therefore over all things. The Genesis saga in its account of the fall, and in agreement with the rest of the Old Testament, undoubtedly tells us that man has seized this knowledge and power to his own undoing, and that he must now live in the possession of this knowledge and power. But in its account of creation it tells us that this does not belong to him; that if he is not to use it merely to destruction he must ask it of God like Solomon, and that instead of following his own [288] inclinations he must learn it from God like Balaam. What God has made good is good, and what God has made evil is evil, i.e., neither the one nor the other in and for itself, or according to the decision of man, but in keeping with His commandments which point him wholly and exclusively to the God who commands and binds him to His decisions. T. C. Vriezen is surely right when he sees recorded in Gen. 2^{16-17} the great delimitation of the Old Testament from the "polytheistico-magical outlook of the ancient East" (*Onderzoek naar de Paradijsvoorstelling lij de oude semietische Volken*, 1937, 147). Knowledge of magic is a pretension of the divine knowledge and distinction of being, i.e., of divine power over it. In Gen. 2 this knowledge and power are denied to man as a mark of his creatureliness, whereas in Gen. 3 they are granted to him as a mark of his alienation from God and therefore his enslavement to death. And Vriezen is probably right when he points out that it is not for nothing that it is the serpent, the magical animal *par excellence*, which in Gen. 3 is opposed to this delimitation and is man's tempter and counsellor in this transition to alienation from God and enslavement to death. It may be noted in conclusion that there is no reason to share the surprise of Gunkel that the prediction of Gen. 2^{17}: "In the day that thou eatest thereof thou shalt surely die," was not fulfilled at once, so that the serpent was right after all when he stated (3^4): "Ye shall not surely die." In point of fact, the man who was later called Adam was not stricken down when he ate of the tree of knowledge, but according to 5^4 lived for another eight hundred years. The saga is not to be understood in this pragmatic way. There is something far worse than the onslaught and the actual moment of death, and that is an existence in the fear of death, in the hunger for life, and under the sentence of death which invariably follows disobedience. And this is the existence which man commenced that day.

In Gen. 2^{18-25} the second account of the creation is brought to its climax and conclusion. This third and most explicit section is marked by the greatest inner and outer concentration. It has only one theme—the completion of the creation of man by the adding to the male of the female. There is also an account of the creation of animals, but this has only an incidental significance in the framework of that decisive event. Again, an account is given of the origin of human language, but this has no weight except in the larger context and must not be given a false prominence in our exposition. Everything aims at the one fact, to wit, that God did not create man alone, as a single human being, but in the unequal duality of male and female. What was said in one short sentence in the first account in Gen. 1^{27}—although in highly significant connexion with the divine likeness—is now developed at large. In the light of this development, there can be no further doubt concerning the emphasis of that short sentence. The account of the creation of man as male and female now forms the climax of the whole. The fact that the earth received its cultivator; that God formed him of the dust of the earth and gave him life by His breath; that God planted the Garden of Eden and gave man rest in it; that in this sanctuary there were two trees with their similar but wholly dissimilar function and meaning—all this acquires life and substance only when we learn how God created man in the basic form of all association and fellowship which is the essence of humanity. And this account is put immediately before the transition from the "pre-historical" history of creation to the "historical" history of the covenant, i.e., to the account of the event in which man will perform his first responsible action, and will do so at once in this twofold form, both the man and the woman being conjoined as the doubtful heroes of this event. Hence the account of man's coming into being as male and female is of supreme importance from this standpoint too. The peculiar light which is thus shed on the brief statement of Gen. 1^{27} cannot be an accident but was surely intended by the redaction which combined the two sagas.

[289]

A first point to notice is that the record is again introduced by the account of a kind of reflection on the part of the Creator Himself: "And the Lord God said, It is not good that the man should be alone; I will make him an help meet for him." The correspondence with Gen. 1^{26} must not be overlooked. At this point, and at this point alone, immediately prior to the climax of the creative act, we have in both sagas a kind of divine pause, a Word directed by God Himself to Himself. The effect is the same in both cases, for the hearer or reader will observe that the climax has now been reached, and that the reference is now to the decisive moment in the whole creative act. The difference consists in the fact that in the one case the divine reflection has as its theme and result the being that is to rule over the beast and is godlike as such, and that this finds its correspondence in the creation of man as male and female; whereas in the other it is addressed at once to man and the necessity to create him in dual rather than single form, as male and female. But in the emphasis on this duality the two accounts are at one. When we are told that God saw that it was not good for man to be alone, what is meant is simply that the saga did not consider the creation of man to be completed by what had been so far said.

There is, of course, no thought of a successive constitution of the being of man now reaching its completion. In the references to man's formation from the dust of the earth, to his animation, to his commission to cultivate the earth, to his translation to the Garden of Eden and to his confrontation with the two trees, the concern has always been with distinct elements in the whole man. But who and what the whole man is must now be stated, and it must be told in the genre of saga because man did not exist from eternity as God did, but was made in time by God's creative act. The whole man, i.e., the whole man whom God forms and animates, who is to cultivate the earth, whom He translates into the Garden of Eden, who has to keep his specific creatureliness in face of the sign of the two trees, is not solitary man. In isolation man would not have been good. That is, he would not have been created good. He would not have been the being with whom God later willed to enter into relationship and to have intercourse. He would not have been a good goal of creation, and to that extent creation as a whole could not be called good. Supplementing the sec-

[290] ond account from the first, we might say that it would not be good because solitary man would not be man created in the image of God, who Himself is not solitary. In the account itself, however, the reason is to be sought in the future. Solitary man would not be good because he would not as such be the subject presupposed as the partner of God in the history which follows. But if created man were solitary, creation as a whole would not be good, because it would then lack its internal basis in the covenant. It is with male and female that God will have dealings in the history which follows. This is what God the Lord considers in His soliloquy. The content of this Word was the covenant, determined already though not yet instituted, in which God the Lord willed to have dealings with a twofold being. To be God's partner in this covenant, man himself needed a partner. Partner is perhaps the best modern rendering for the term "helpmeet." What is sought is a being resembling man but different from him. If it were only like him, a repetition, a numerical multiplication, his solitariness would not be eliminated, for it would not confront him as another but he would merely recognise himself in it. Again, if it were only different from him, a being of a wholly different order, his solitariness would not be eliminated, for it would confront him as another, yet not as another which actually belongs to him, but in the way in which the earth or tree or river confronts him as an element in his sphere, not as a fellow-occupant of this sphere fulfilling the duty allotted within it. To be created good, man needs a being like him and yet different from him, so that in it he will recognise himself but not only himself, since it is to him a Thou as truly as he is an I, and he is to it a Thou as truly as it is an I. It is in this way that God Himself will confront man, having intercourse and dealings with him. Man's own existence must thus correspond to this mode if it is to be good for God; if it is to be serviceable for His dealings with it. It must be an anticipation or type—the term image is unavoidable if we are to explain the matter—of what the form of God's relationship to it will be in the coming covenant between them. In virtue of his

nature man must be formally prepared for grace. This takes place as he is not left alone but is given a creaturely helpmeet. It can happen only in one way—he must be given this helpmeet. "I will make him an help meet." This most important requisite of his existence is the completion of his creation by God. How can it be otherwise when it is a question of his preparation for God's grace? Who but God, who in this covenant with man will give everything its true reality, can accomplish this anticipation or establish this pattern—the co-existence of man with a helpmeet, the relationship between I and thou? The creation of this necessary helpmeet thus belongs to the history of creation.

In order to understand what follows, we must turn at once to the final goal: "This is now bone of my bones, and flesh of my flesh," is the cry of man when God brings him the woman. This exclamation, the expression of a recogni- [291] tion, the proclamation of a choice and decision made by man—the first saying of man expressly recorded in the saga—is not just a kind of epilogue to the creation of the woman, and therefore the completion of man's creation, but it is with this express saying of man that the latter reaches its goal. In this matter everything hinges on the fact that this being—the helpmeet, the Thou to the I—does not only exist like the earth and trees and river and later the beasts of the Garden of Eden; that it is not only known to man and named by him, but is recognised as this being and named in this recognition. The whole story aims at this exclamation by man. In this, and this alone, the creative work of God reaches its goal, for only now has man really been given the necessary help designed by God. He himself has had to seek and find it. He himself has had to accept it as it was given. He himself has had to recognise it for what it is. He himself has had to choose and decide. Apart from this act of human freedom, the supreme and final gift of God would not be what it is.

This is the goal even of the episode which at first seems to disturb or at least delay the consummation of that of the animals who have not so far been mentioned by the second saga. The account of their creation is now introduced. God formed them—cattle, birds and beasts of the field are all mentioned, but aquatic creatures are characteristically ignored—as He did man, out of the ground. In harmony with Gen. 1^{24}, they too are called "living creatures" like man in Gen. 2^7, except that in regard to them there is no reference to a quickening by the breath of God as in the case of man. But as this account is only incidental, it does not have the independent significance which falls to this section in the structure of the first account. The reason why the creation of animals is mentioned is simply to show, by way of contrast, what is really meant by the helpmeet ordained for man, and to prove that none of the animals—as hearers or readers might think in view of that Word of God—can possibly be this helpmeet. As living creatures, animals too were created by God, being fashioned from the earth, and then brought to man by God as was later the case with woman. But the account goes on to say that they were not what he needed, what God sought and found for him, and what he for his part was to seek and to find. Thus the creation of animals is mentioned here only as a dark background to the true work towards which the narrative hastens.

Similarly, if we are to be true to the meaning and purpose of the text, we must not ascribe any independent significance to the fact that it says that God brought the animals to man "to see what he would call them: and whatsoever Adam called them, that was the name thereof." It is true that formally this is a clear parallel to the statement of the first saga (1²⁶, ²⁸) concerning the lordship of man over the animals. It tells us that animals at least, if not other things as well, were by divine decree to be called what man would name them. It is in [292] their relationship to him that they are what they are. His thoughts about them decree their being. But to be precise the reference is rather to the allowing of this naming than to the express command which we might have expected (but must not import) from Gen. 1²⁸. And in any case the permission has no independent purpose in the context of the passage, and must not be made a subsidiary centre of interest in the course of the narrative.

The same is also true of the fact that incidentally we are here told something about the origin of language, namely, that it had its origin in the nouns by which man was allowed to name the animals according to his own insight, choice and decision, so that it is not of divine but human origin, having its true basis in the freedom given to man by God in relation to his environment. It would be quite wrong to assume that the point of the passage is to give us this information, although there can be no doubt that it does this in passing.

On the contrary, when the context is taken into consideration, the emphasis obviously falls on the fact that man was placed by God before a choice and decision which he was consciously to make and verbally to confess. Not only was he to receive his partner or helpmeet, but he was to discover this helpmeet as such, and freely accept her. She was to become to him in his own recognition what she really is, and to be acknowledged and welcomed as such by his own free word. The recognition of the I in the Thou which rests on this recognition is possible only in freedom, and it is by a free word that this recognition must be revealed as a responsible decision. In order that he might discover his partner, his Thou, God first brings the animals to man. In so doing He asks him what he thinks of each of them, what he has to say to each of them, and finally what he will say when he sees them. In naming them he will express what they are to him; what impression they make on him; what he expects and hopes and fears of them. In this way—in execution of a well-considered plan of God—it is to be revealed that man cannot recognise any of the animals as belonging to him; that he cannot address any of them as Thou; that he cannot ascribe to any of them the nature of an I. It might almost be said that the completion of God's creation is conditioned by the fact that man cannot do this; that though he can recognise in the animals objects which are near and lovable and useful, or perhaps strange or even ugly and terrifying, he cannot recognise his helpmeet ; that here at the heart of the rest of creation there is a gap which must be filled if man is really to be man and not in some sense to be so only potentially, and in the presence of which, even though surrounded by the superabundance of the rest of creation, man would always be solitary, always in a vacuum and not among his equals. But it is better to express it the other way round. The divine creation is finished in such a way that even in the animal kingdom and as its lord, even in the exercise of his dominion by the [293] giving of names, man does not find the similar but different being which he needs to be man, to be created good; that all the superabundance of the animal kingdom and his own sovereignty over it can eventually serve only to reveal this lack. At any rate, this is what actually happened: "And Adam gave names to all cattle, and to the fowl of the air, and to every beast of the field; but for Adam (for himself) there was not found an help meet for him." The whole transaction is not a divine experiment which failed. God had to act in this way if the gift which He had for man was not to be his undoing, if man was to recognise, choose and confirm the helpmeet ordained and created for him. He was not to be compelled to accept her merely because there was no possible alternative. He could not find her without having honestly sought elsewhere. To seize freely the right possibility, he had to see and consider and reject other possibilities. He had to be led into the impasse portrayed in the passage; to be brought to the yawning gap in the whole of creation, and to recognise it as such. And this is just what happened. What if he had not recognised the chasm? What if he had been content with the company of an animal for the lack of anything better? The passage does not tell us why man did not do this, and its meaning is surely that the only possible reason is that he was man, i.e., that he was created by God as the one who in the full exercise of his freedom could give the beasts their names and co-exist with them in love or fear, but could not recognise in them his equals or choose them as his helpmeets. As man, man was free to prefer solitude to the exchange of his solitude for false company. He was free to accept the impasse, rejecting every ostensible offer and waiting for the true helpmeet. Having seen, understood and named all the animals, and ordered his relationship to them, he was free to remain unsatisfied, for it is better to be unsatisfied than to be half-satisfied or wrongly satisfied. Why is this the case? Again, it is because he is man, and because only in this attitude, in this use of his freedom, can he be brought to the climax of his creation. A being which in this position could have thought otherwise would no more be man than God would be God if He could lie. Thus the choice and decision which we here see him make negatively are not by his own free disposition, and are not to be confused with the forbidden judgment of good and evil, but are simply a confirmation of his own creation in which God disposed concerning him and made him man. He chooses the fact that he is elected. He decides for the decision which has been made concerning him. He remains man. And for this reason he remains unsatisfied. For this reason he can and will be prepared to remain unsatisfied. For this reason he cannot recognise his helpmeet in earth, tree, river or beasts. For this reason he remains free for the helpmeet which will really be given him. For this reason

[294] he can and will have to wait at the risk of waiting in vain. And this is his genuine freedom and most proper choice and decision.

It is significant that the witness introduced the account of the creation of woman in this way. In so doing he did not put woman on the same level as the animals. He ascribed to her in advance the highest humanity. He did not merely describe her creation as the climax of creation which had not yet taken place with the formation of solitary man or that of the whole animal kingdom, but from the very outset denied to solitary man every other possibility of an appropriate helpmeet even in the exercise of his genuine freedom. He said of God Himself that with the creation of woman He expected man to confirm and maintain his true humanity by the exclusion of every other possibility. The way could not have been more gloriously cleared for the creation of woman.

And this creation of woman is described in the following way. The Lord God caused a deep sleep to fall on man. While he was in this condition He took one of the ribs, replacing it with flesh, and formed woman from this rib taken from man. He then brought her to man, who joyfully recognised, greeted and acknowledged her as the true helpmeet now at last granted to him. Each element in this description has its own importance.

We note that the whole episode reaches its climax in this confession of man's positive choice and decision, as is only to be expected in view of the introduction. God has created man in such a way that in the exercise of his genuine freedom he must will to confirm his humanity with this unequivocal Yes to the woman given to him as to the helpmeet corresponding to him because both similar and dissimilar. But the provision or realisation of this helpmeet, and therefore the completion of his own creation, is not his work but God's. Again, it is God's wisdom and omnipotence, God's sovereignty and creation, and therefore God's choice and decision, that he himself will finally have to choose and for which he himself will have to decide. Thus in the first instance the passage speaks again of a new and final putting forth of the divine hand, and only when this has attained its goal will the moment have arrived when in the exercise of the freedom given to him man will terminate the whole process of activity with this confession, praising his Maker.

That man was caused by God to fall into a deep sleep has first the simple meaning that he did not actively participate in the creation of woman and therefore in the completion of his own creation. He did not even know positively what it was that he lacked within the rest of creation. It was not he who thought of woman as his helpmeet. He was just unsatisfied. He could affirm his humanity only by not allowing himself to be tempted to seek this helpmeet elsewhere, where he would not really have found it. What was done was not his
[295] idea but actually and exclusively the plan of God. God saw that it was not good for man to be alone. He knew the true and effective remedy. He knew the true helpmeet which could be man's true counterpart and therefore his genuine helpmeet. There would thus be no question of man being able to bring her to himself, or even to have a share in doing so. It had to happen in this way. He

had to sleep while she was introduced. This sleep, moreover, means that he knew as little about the event as he knew about his own creation and the creation of earth and heaven. The question is still one of the pure emergence of the creature, which as such cannot be an object of its own observation and perception. We are still in the history of creation, which as such can only be a saga of creation. And there can be no doubt that this is very strongly emphasised in this place. The completion of all creation described here, i.e., the completion of man by the creation of woman, is not only one secret but *the* secret, the heart of all the secrets of God the Creator. The whole inner basis of creation, God's whole covenant with man, which will later be established, realised and fulfilled historically, is prefigured in this event, in the completing of man's emergence by the coming of woman to man. Man will then become a witness to the corresponding reality. He will then be in a position to recognise and affirm what God has here willed and done. As the history prefigured here begins, man will himself be participant in the covenant which is here the internal basis of creation. But it could not and cannot be his affair to know about creation itself, and thus to know how God accomplishes his creation and existence with this covenant in view. The preparation of his nature for God's grace, and the basis, concealed in his creaturely existence, of God's merciful good-pleasure in him, is the secret of God. It is sufficient that this preparation has taken place and that this basis exists. It is sufficient that man can say Yes to the result of this preparation and foundation and therefore to his own humanity and nature as the pattern of the divine grace offered to him. That he may do this is a matter of his knowledge and confession. To this end he will have to use positively the freedom given to him. But in the divine act which creates the presupposition of his knowledge and confession he does not participate either actively or consciously. That it has taken place he may gratefully realise as he emerges from it. How it happens can be told only by saga—and in the form of an attestation of the fact that it has taken place. And at this point the saga itself must confirm the necessary limitation of all saga by telling us that at the moment of man's completion God caused a deep sleep to fall upon him, thus taking from him the possibility of knowing how it happened. The strong anthropomorphism with which the saga speaks in this passage—more powerfully than anywhere else in the two accounts of creation—corresponds to the knowledge of this nescience. For how can we speak of this matter? In the face of all kinds of uncertainties, man evidently knows four things about the How of his completion on the basis of its result. Four things respecting his emergence [296] stand so clearly before him in this result that he can and must recognise and express it, and the saga cannot fail to describe it (in saga form).

The first is that in woman man finds not only another being of another and alien origin, not merely another human being, but a being which he can and must recognise as part of himself, "bone of my bones, flesh of my flesh," as is said later. She is not himself but something of and from himself. He is related to her as to another part or member of his own body. She is as little foreign to him as any part or member of his own body can be foreign. With her special existence she fulfils something which he himself ought to fulfil in this special part or member but cannot, so that it awaits fulfilment in her existence. So close is she to him. This is what the saga has in view when it speaks of the rib which was taken from man and from which God formed woman.

The second thing is that he cannot himself divest himself of this part or member of his body. He cannot himself produce woman of himself, not even in the way in which he will afterwards beget or woman bear children. Woman, then, does not come into existence in such a way that man can rule this part or member as his own lord, or disinterestedly separate himself from it. In some sense he must be robbed of himself. It has simply to happen that woman is what she is as something from and of himself. The saga makes this point by telling how God took from him a rib without any activity on his own part and even at the risk of death (for he lies in a deep sleep and a mortal wound is apparently inflicted on him).

The third thing is that with this removal of a part of his body, and the consequent formation of woman, man suffered something. He experienced a loss. He is no longer wholly himself, but has had to yield a part or member of his body. Is it not really death which has befallen him? But he does not have to die. He does not have to suffer because of his loss. He bears no wound, not even a cicatrised wound. He has not ceased to be wholly himself because woman was taken out of and from him. Indeed, is it not only now in contrast to woman, in whom he recognises something of himself, that he is wholly man, as man in relationship to woman? The saga makes this third point by telling how God covered with flesh the part from which the rib had been removed, thus saving the life which was apparently destroyed, and restoring the harmony which had apparently been disturbed.

The fourth and most important and decisive point is that man can not only recognise in woman something of himself, but even in this relationship of hers to him necessarily recognises a being with its own autonomous nature and structure. What has now become of the part or member taken out of him? It is no longer simply what it was in its former relationship to him, and what he [297] knew it to be in this relationship. If it is still the same, it is the same in a new and very different way, quite autonomously, in its own form and being. If it is unmistakeably his, it is also unmistakeably hers. If it is unmistakeably of man, it is also unmistakeably woman and not man. For she has not just remained but has been fashioned out of what was taken from man and can still be recognised in her. The saga makes this fourth point by telling how God made woman from a rib taken out of man. God used man for the creation of woman just as He used the dust of the earth for the creation of man. In both cases He fashioned the new out of the old.

Is not the saga rather too presumptuous at this point? With all this concrete information has it not tried to unveil the secret of creation? On a closer examination we cannot really say this. It is only repeating—and repeating very precisely—what is already suggested to man in this matter by God's completed work. We have still to consider the wider contexts in which it does this. But it is already clear that on a proper understanding of God's finished work, and therefore a proper understanding of woman and the relationship between man and woman, we can and must say of the emergence of this work, and therefore of woman and this relationship, exactly what the saga does say. The four points attested by the saga are not concealed from man, from male and female in their actual co-existence, but revealed to them. They are the four basic pillars of their relationship. And it is of these that the saga can and must speak in its witness to what is manifest. Not only does it not unveil the real secret in and behind all this; it does not even touch it, but makes it quite plain that it is a secret. The real secret consists in the fact that everything is as it is, i.e., that by the will of God and in virtue of His work it is thus and not other-wise. Has not the saga made this perfectly clear? It has described the whole process, not as a natural process, but as a divine action, thus indicating that it escapes all our observation and concepts. And in detail it has described it in such a way that all questions concerning its How are not only not answered but are posed all the more acutely, and its inability to answer stands out the more clearly. Within this framework, however, it is not silent about the essence of the matter, but gives it expression. What is said in the very remarkable verses 2^{21-22} is essentially that the real secret is no easier than this, nor is the riddle actually propounded by woman in her relationship to man less difficult. Woman and this relationship could not have been described less dialectically even if the saga had refused to give any account of its emergence or narration of the creation of the woman as such. All that the saga does when it boldly ventures the anthropomorphism of its account of the act of creation which took place during the deep sleep of man is to point to the reality and multidimensional depth of the unmistakeable mystery of the existence of woman and the sex relationship.

It was as this special miracle, then, that she stood before man when in the [298] words of the saga God "brought her unto the man." It is here obviously—and subsequently, as is only right—that the noetic basis of the whole matter emerges. It is of the one whom God brought to him that man knows so exactly how she was formed during his deep sleep and without his knowledge. It is her mystery, the mystery of the one brought to him by God, that the saga ventures and is compelled to describe so concretely, because it is now a reality in this concrete form. It is to be noted that this reality with its concrete witness to its emergence is not exhausted by the mere existence of the woman. It also belongs to this reality that she is brought to man. The account does not merely introduce woman, leaving her to be discovered, incidentally recognised, greeted and welcomed by man when he incidentally wakens from sleep and as he sees fit. God Himself brings her to him. God Himself brings and gives her to him. Without this link, everything which precedes and follows is unthinkable. It is God's relationship to man, His mercy toward him, which brings about this completion of his creation, giving meaning to the existence of woman and disclosing her secret. Naturally the completion of man's creation in the relationship of I and Thou, of male and female, in the mutual encounter and duality of the two, is the work of God. It is in His will and plan that it all has its original basis. And in order that man might realise it, in order that it might be established for him and therefore livable, God must enter in again. He creates not only the I and Thou, man and woman, but also their mutual relationship. This is not a matter of chance or human arbitrariness. If it were a matter of chance or arbitrariness, it could not be a subject of joy, or of revelation and knowledge, as it is later depicted. It would simply be blunt, sealed and blind actuality. Hence the bringing of woman to man is an integral part of the whole act of creation as described in this saga.

But this does not exclude the fact that it is analogous to what is said earlier about the animals. The freedom in which man is to receive this gift is not taken from him even now. In bringing the woman to man, God undoubtedly wills to know again "what he would call her." He again asks him what he thinks of this work of His, what he has to say about it. He again waits for man's exclamation at the sight of His own work. And only with man's exclamation, with the declaration of his free choice and decision, will God's own work have reached its goal. What follows has thus been rightly described as the climax of the narration. As previously he uttered a responsible No, man must now utter—subsequently, but necessarily—his responsible Yes to what God has willed and done. He must be present with his knowledge and confession at the completion of his own creation. He must recognise and welcome the woman who will be the true helpmeet now given to him. It must be shown again that she is not a [299] destiny suspended over him. With his own free thought and word he must confirm that God has created her for him and brought her to him. He is not compelled to do this even now. The question must also be asked: What if he had not done so? What if he had not recognised that the gap in creation had now been closed, and that what he had lacked, the better thing which he had previously awaited, was now present? What if he had still remained unsatisfied? The text again does not give us any reason why this time things were different. It is again simply the case that the saga can only record that this time things were different. Man was the man created by God and endowed by God with freedom. When God wakened him out of his deep sleep, and brought woman to him, and showed and gave her to him, in the exercise of this freedom he could only say Yes as previously he could only say No when he failed to recognise a helpmeet in any of the animals. As man he was free to recognise and accept a helpmeet in the woman created for and brought to him by God. He was free to see himself saved from his previous difficulty. He was free to be satisfied. A being not free for this, acting otherwise than described in this passage, would no more be man than God would be God if He could lie. And freedom to act otherwise would be the worst and most radical bondage. Again, therefore, he does not dispose of himself, or judge concerning good and evil.

He merely confirms his own creation, the decision which God has taken concerning him, God's choice of him and therefore his own humanity. Because he is man he recognises and rejoices in woman as the helpmeet given to him. The mystery of her being and the mystery of her creation is obvious to him in all its concreteness. Thus we can now see from the opposite side to what heights woman has been exalted. The biblical witness causes man for the first time to affirm positively his humanity in the recognition and welcoming of woman as the helpmeet given to him. And he finds the basis of this recognition and welcome in the fact that man can and does find in her something of himself, and yet not only something of himself, but a new and independent being planned and moulded by God. At the sight of her, God caused man to think of a grievous wound inflicted on him but also healed; of the nearness of death but also—and much more so—of protection from death. The witness tells us that the particular address to man with which God completed as He had commenced his creation, reached its climax in the bringing of woman to him. And he causes man to say an unequivocal Yes to this whole work of God. This Yes he clearly distinguishes from the statements with which he previously ordered his relationship to the animals. He causes man to recognise and welcome in woman the being which belongs to him and is therefore itself human and the necessary partner of his own humanity. From this standpoint, too, it can be said that woman could not have been introduced with greater honour.

In what man says in Gen. 2²³ note should be taken of the thrice used demonstrative pronoun: "This is now bone of my bones, and flesh of my flesh: this (A.V. she) shall be called Woman, because this (A.V. she) was taken out of Man." Above all, it is to be noted that the grammatical form of the statements makes it plain that they are more than a bare assertion of facts. Formally there is still the express giving of a name as in v. 20. Formally it is still a question of the ordering of man's relationship to his environment. But something takes place which has nothing more to do with the mere giving of a name, but which fulfils the purpose of naming and in so doing transcends it. There takes place here something which could not take place between man and animals. Association gives way to fellowship. There is choice and therefore personal relationship. The being of man becomes being in the encounter in which man receives and will always have a neighbour. His last objective assertion about another becomes his subjective confession of *this* other. He still speaks of it, as of himself, in the third person. But the next, the first historical word after this last objective word, can only be the word "thou" which seems already latent in the reflective "this." The decision has already been made that his helpmeet is not only present but is recognised as such. The free thought of man is thought. The free word for which God waited is uttered. And God has heard it. It had to be directed to God, and God had to hear it because it is in this that God's work comes to a climax. This is evidently the deeper reason for the reserve with which it is still spoken. What constitutes this climax is not the fact that man says Yes to woman, but that in this affirmation he says Yes to God in the presence of

[300]

woman. It is in this way that he really welcomes and receives her. It is in this way that he honours her as the one whom he will now be able to address as "thou," and before whom he will commence to say "I." The supremely subjective thing aimed at here has its creative ground and truth in the supremely objective, because, regarding and indicating woman, man gives the glory neither to himself nor woman, but to God and His finished work. Even subjectively, even as the establishment of his own relationship to woman, his confession could not have greater force than it has in virtue of the fact that materially it is a simple recapitulation of the divine work.

Who is woman? The "this" certainly refers to the helpmeet which according to the view of God expressed in Gen. 2^{18} man needed for his own humanity but could not find in the animal kingdom. "This," this *femininum*[EN382], indeed this *femina*[EN383]—for what distinguishes her from the beast is the fact that she is not only *femininum*[EN384] but *femina*[EN385]—supplies this need. "This" means the banishment of his want. It makes him what he could not be in his solitariness— a man completed by God. The simplest and most comprehensive definition of woman is that she is the being to which man, himself becoming male, can and

[301]   must say in the exercise of his freedom that "this" is now the helpmeet which otherwise he had sought in vain but which had now been fashioned and brought by God. From the standpoint of our text we can only say of those who do not know this "this" that they are merely giving rein to theory and fancy and do not really know what they are saying when they speak of woman. They would do better to say nothing at all, for they can only speak incompetently. Whatever else may have to be said can be only an explanation of this demonstrative, which is twice solemnly repeated.

But why "this"? Because "this" is itself human, yet not another human being, but "bone of my bones, flesh of my flesh"; because man finds in her a lost part or member of his own body and being; because she is not strange to him but as familiar as he is himself; because he can partake of his lost part again only when he partakes of her; and because he can only fully partake of himself when he partakes of her. He is not himself without her, but only with her. She is as near to him as this. This, then, is woman—the one who is so near to the man who through her existence has become man, and is therefore so indispensable to him for his own sake. If she were not this to him; if she were neutral, distant and dispensable in relation to him; if she were to him another being, human but only feminine, she would not be woman. Again, from the standpoint of this passage, those who do not see and understand woman as the one who is near and indispensable to man, as a part of himself which was lost and is found again, are merely giving rein to theory and fancy.

The naming to which we now come has the same significance. It is not always

---

EN382 female
EN383 woman
EN384 female
EN385 woman

easy to give an adequate rendering of *'isha* in other languages, since it is necessary to try to keep the assonance as well as the meaning. The point of the name given by the saga is that woman is of man. This does not mean that she is really mannish. Nor does it mean that she is man's property. Nor does it mean that unlike him she is not a human being in the full sense. What it does mean is that in her being and existence she belongs to him; that she is ordained to be his helpmeet; that without detriment to her independence she is the part of him which was lost and is found again—"taken out of him." It is proper to her to be beside him. This is her humanity, and in this place and the consequent form it is no less than that of man but surpasses it in a definite and decisive respect, although she surrenders and forfeits it if she tries to exchange it for that of man. The fact that the relationship is not one of reciprocity and equality, that man was not taken out of woman but woman out of man, that primarily he does not belong to her but she to him, and that he thus belongs to her only secondarily, must not be misunderstood. The supremacy of man is not a question of value, dignity or honour, but of order. It does not denote a higher humanity of man. Its acknowledgment is no shame to woman. On the contrary, it is an acknowledgment of her glory, which in a particular and decisive respect is greater even than that of man. Again, from the standpoint of this [302] passage, we can only say that those who do not know woman in this relationship to man do not know her at all. A whole host of masculine and feminine reflections concerning woman completely miss her reality because this element is either not taken into consideration at all or is not taken into consideration properly.

And if we finally ask: Why "woman"? Why "bone of my bones, and flesh of my flesh"? Why "this"?, attention must be particularly paid to the reason given: "Because she was taken out of Man." Behind the special existence and being of woman is to be found the divine initiative and attack upon solitary man. For his completion God causes him to fall into a deep sleep in which a part is taken out of him by the infliction of a mortal wound. It is to be noted that there is an analogy here to his own creation. As he was taken out of the earth, so now at the creation of the woman, in which his own creation is completed, he is himself what the earth was in his own case—the material which quite apart from its merits or suitability is used by God for His work and impressed into His service. What is meant by the statement that woman "was taken out of Man" is that God willed to complete man of and through himself irrespective of any capacity of his own. In this way man receives an incomprehensible honour and distinction, and woman is this honour of his in her own person. She is the witness and embodiment of the free favour in which—without detriment to the miraculous nature of His own work and the sovereignty of His glory and power as Creator—God willed to complete him as man, not without himself, but of and through himself. It is, of course, a strange honour. It came by God's initiative and attack. Without even being asked, man had to yield up something of what belonged to him by divine and natural right. He had to allow the infliction upon himself of a mortal wound. For one who was not a lump of dead earth but a living soul it entailed sacrifice, pain and mortal peril as God marched to this climax of His work. God spared him, and yet the strange mixture of the perfect joy of finding and the never-absent pain of deprivation in his relationship to woman is the constant reminder of that from which he was spared. Woman is his great but also his strange glory. She is this because her creation signifies the completion and to that extent the declaration of his own creation, and because it is her existence which signifies the completion of the humanity of his own creation. She is this also because by his Yes to woman, by the recognition of his free thought and the confession of his free word, man participates a second time in her creation and therefore in his own creation, and in this way—honourably enough—in the completion of creation as a whole. Woman now stands before him as his glory, and it is her glory to be his glory in this multiple sense. It is for this reason that she is called "woman," that she is "bone

[303] of his bones, and flesh of his flesh," and therefore "this." Hence she does not stand before him either accidentally or arbitrarily. She is his glory as he himself is the glory of God (1 Cor. 11⁷). Without her he would be without glory. Without her he could not be the glory of God. It is the peculiar glory of her creation, i.e., that she was "taken out of man," that she completes the creation of man from man himself and that this is crowned by his own recognition and confession—it is this distinction, insurpassable in its own way, which, not for her humiliation but her exaltation, specifically and inexorably assigns her to this position. Only in this position does she possess her true humanity, but in this position she really does possess it.

From this standpoint we can understand something which is very strange on any other presupposition, namely, that the text makes no mention of any corresponding declaration on the part of woman. Woman is as little asked about her attitude to man as was solitary man about his attitude to God when after his formation from the dust of the earth God animated him by His breath. She does not choose; she is chosen. She is not asked to decide between the beasts and man. Unlike man and the animals, she was not taken from the earth; she was taken "out of Man." Because she is in some sense human from the very outset, because she is the glory of man and marks the completion of his creation, it is not problematical but self-evident for her to be ordained for man and to be for man in her whole existence. Thus she is not called upon first to prove her humanity or to confirm it by any special recognition or confession. Being herself the completion of man's humanity, she has no need of a further completion of her own. Her Yes in this matter is anticipated by that of the man, which as we have seen is not directed to her but to God, but which as regards content is uttered with her in view. His recognition and acknowledgment imply hers as well. As man chooses her, she has chosen him. For as God has made her out of and for man, as man has to confirm this by his choice and explanation, she is this, and in her case the question of choice or explanation does not arise. She would not be woman if she had even a single possibility apart from being man's helpmeet. She chooses that for which God has chosen her. She thus chooses herself by refraining from choice; by finding herself surrounded and sustained by the joyful choice of the man, as his elect. In the sense of the creation saga, this does not involve anything strange, or humiliating, or detrimental, or restrictive of the true humanity of woman, or prejudicial to her position in relation to man. From the standpoint of creation, her true humanity according to the will and purpose of God consists simply in the fact that she is the elect of man, acknowledging and realising in her election by man the will and purpose of God for her.

The account of the creation of woman, and therefore the whole of the second creation narrative, concludes with two observations which stand formally apart. The first (v. 24) is obviously a reflection of the editor concerning the [304] preceding confession of man: "Therefore shall a man leave his father and his mother, and shall cleave unto his wife: and they shall be one flesh." The importance assigned to this reflection by later New Testament readers of the passage is shown by the fact that this saying is described in Mt. 19[4] as a Word of the Creator Himself. And there can be no doubt that it had for the editor himself the significance and character of a revealed Word of God. This does not mean that it is incompatible with the view which with reference to this verse describes the whole passage as the "classical illustration of an aetiological myth"—except that it is better to keep to the more relevant concept of "saga." Not every saga, but certainly every creation saga, and therefore this one too, is essentially "aetiological," i.e., a poetic vision of the becoming which underlies being. This passage makes it very plain that genetically the whole text is undoubtedly to be understood as a prophetico-poetical retrospect from the being of the creature to its becoming, i.e., from existence to creation. But if we are to say this in the sense of the passage itself, we must add that it is to be understood as a retrospect from the being of the creature as it stands in the light of divine revelation, to its being as illumined by this revelation; and therefore as a retrospect from the history directed by God to God's creation. For this cause—because woman was made by God as described, and the relationship between man and woman was established and fashioned at that time, in primal history—the present love between man and woman, and the marriage based upon it (it is only now that we can meaningfully introduce these two terms into our exposition), take place in such a way that a man shall "leave his father and his mother, and shall cleave unto his wife: and they shall be one flesh." If what preceded has been carefully read and correctly understood, we are rather startled by this continuation. This description of the being of man and woman is hardly expected immediately after the description of their becoming. In the first two statements at least everything seems to be topsy-turvy, and even in the third it is different from what was previously intimated. Man is now the follower and adherent of woman, and the two are an absolute unity. We may well ask what has happened to the emphasised supremacy of man. We may well ask in what sense the passage can connect with a "therefore" the becoming in God's creation and this actual being of the relationship between man and woman? But the contradiction is only in appearance. There is good reason for the puzzling "therefore." We must attempt to think the matter through from its two angles—for twofold reflection is proper to aetiological saga.

From the first angle the author wishes to say that the mutual relationship of man and woman in historical reality, their mutual love and adherence in marriage, conform to that which is laid down concerning them in the creation narrative. When a man forsakes his father and mother, i.e., his first and nearest [305] and closest ties; when he cuts himself loose from his most natural roots and thus becomes an independent man; when he finds in this woman the Thou without which he cannot be I, this man; when he "cleaves" to this Thou, i.e., is related to it with the same power with which he is I; when he turns to this woman with the same necessity with which he is this man; when with this other, an apparent stranger yet no longer a stranger to him, but his nearest and dearest, he becomes one flesh, an absolutely integrated whole; when he can now be man only in conjunction with her—then it is true that she is "woman," "this," "bone of his bones," because she is "taken out of Man." In this unheard of process, by which woman assumes so decisive and transcendent a meaning for man, it is confirmed that it was not good for man to be alone; that he really needed a helpmeet, and that without the existence of this helpmeet his own creation would really not have been complete. It is also confirmed that woman is his true glory: his radiant glory; but also—as indicated by the fact that he severs his roots and leaves his father and mother—his strange glory, to be realised only in sacrifice, pain and mortal peril. It is also confirmed that man had to complete his own creation according to the will and purpose of God by electing woman and saying Yes to her existence before him, thus also saying Yes to God's whole creation, and finally and supremely to his own humanity. What we have here, then, is simply a revelation of the fact that the will and purpose of God in this matter were no game but deadly serious, and that His creation was the basis of all reality. Things have to happen as they do when man and woman love each other and are married; man has to be the one who seeks, desires, sacrifices and is utterly dependent on woman for the fulfilment of his relationship to her, so that to this extent he is the weaker half, because all this is rooted and grounded in the divine creation and therefore in the divine will and purpose. The meaning of the author is thus that in its historical reality, in its actual realisation in mutual love, the relationship of man and woman is intended and has to be understood, established and inwardly fashioned as described in the account of their creation. This is the prototype from which it cannot depart without risking its destruction. Hence if it takes place that a man leaves his father and his mother, and cleaves to his wife, to become one flesh with her, this is not something arbitrary or accidental but conformable to what begins in creation. Everything depends, therefore, upon man's really seeking and finding the good thing without which his own humanity is incomplete, and on woman's being this good thing for him. This act, then, must really be the act which completes the emergence of man, and the decision and choice of his free thought and word. Man's tearing himself away from his roots must not be a rebellious self-emancipation, but the offering of the required sacrifice, the realisation of the autonomy attained and granted at this cost. He must not seek his I but his Thou—his "help meet." He must be sure that she is [306] "this," "bone of his bones, and flesh of his flesh." In the manifold meaning of the concept he must really seek and find in her his own glory. And she for her part must desire only to be his glory. The will and purpose of God for both must find realisation in this event. It would bode ill for both man and woman if the event rested on accident and arbitrariness or blunder and misunderstanding.

But the author had something very different to say from the opposite angle. He also wished the creation narrative to be understood from the standpoint of the historical reality, which for him stood no less but even more than creation itself in the light of the divine revelation. Thus he also wished to say that, as the relationship between man and woman is realised in the historical reality, this is what was envisaged at the creation of man and woman, and it is in this light that we have to understand what we are told concerning the primal event. If it is the case that God found that it is not good for man to be alone and decided to give him a helpmeet, then this is the pattern of the restless necessity which now drives a man to leave father and mother and seek his own companion. The goal of the act of creation in which woman is taken from man and becomes "bone of his bones, and flesh of his flesh," "woman," is the lack and fulfilment by which man is bound to his elect as he has bound himself to her by his own choice. The goal of his recognition and definition of woman, of his "this," is the unity in which alone man and woman can be together, twice man, in love and the marriage based upon it. The goal of the whole supremacy shown at this point is his subordination to this arrangement. It is only in this arrangement that it can and will be revealed and validly operative that he alone is the one who chooses. Only in the humiliation which he must experience in this event; only in the fact that—as the one who seeks, desires, sacrifices and is referred to her—he confronts the woman as the weaker partner, can he be her lord and stronger than she. Only in the consummation of this event does he gain and have the right, in virtue of his free thought and with his free word, to speak for the woman and in the express confirmation of his own humanity to acknowledge hers too. His whole pre-eminence stands or falls with his assertion of it in the self-determination rooted and grounded in the nature of his actual relationship to woman. From this standpoint it may be seen that in practice woman need not fear this pre-eminence. As man's supremacy by creation is brought into relationship by this "therefore" with the historical reality of love and marriage, man does not really lose anything of what is assigned to him. But he is shown for what purpose it is given. There is thus taken from woman the last pretext for anxiety, self-seeking or rejection. In the simple historical reality of love and marriage there can be no place from either angle for any misunderstanding of its basis in creation.

[307]   After this reflection the second of the two concluding remarks (v. 25) resumes the narrative: "And they were both naked, the man and his wife, and were not ashamed." In the second saga this is the final saying in this matter, and indeed in respect of creation generally. Coming from the hands of his Creator and entering on his way, man finds himself in the state described. And the cosmic sphere of heaven and earth is from creation one in which this is the case with him.

In face of this verse it may be asked whether we do not have here a kind of doctrine of the primal innocence of man in his first estate. It is evident that what is said here gives us an image of the man created by God which is very different from that which he will later present when the beginning of his history, his first act, is his transgression. The immediate consequence of the transgression of man and woman will be an awareness of their nakedness as something disgraceful and shameful, and an attempt to overcome their embarassment. But if we are to use the term state (*status*), we must observe that they had a very different "standing" in their innocence from what they had in their guilt. The difference consists in the fact that in the former—and this was their innocence—there could be no question of a standing of their own with which they had in a sense adorned themselves. Their innocence consisted purely and simply in the fact that they omitted to do something which they never even dreamed of doing prior to their disobedience. It consisted purely and simply in the fact that nothing like shame even entered their heads or lay in their capacity. They only began to "stand" after they had "fallen"! And the fall was their determination to "stand." And now they had to "stand," but in so doing could only confirm their guilt. In this "state" they had primarily and supremely to be ashamed. Prior to this God had stood for them: God with His will and plan as Creator; He their glory and their innocence. Their own "standing" could consist only in the fact that they accepted this; that they found nothing to add of their own to the work and gift of God, because they lacked nothing; that in this way their free act was simply a confirmation of the fact that they allowed God to be wholly for them, without wishing to improve or complete His purpose and the work of His hands by their own purpose and work. Their later guilt belonged to them, and so did their later shame because of their nakedness. Their earlier innocence was true, genuine and pure innocence because it did not belong to them, because they had not endowed or adorned themselves with it, because it was the natural garment with which God had clothed them at their creation and in which they were concealed as long as they were satisfied with Him. If this is to be called their "first estate," it must not be separated from God's creative act as such, nor must it be compared with the first estate of God as the original and true estate of man, as his own achievement and the proof of his virtue. In fact the true estate of man, his achievement and the proof of his virtue in contrast to the first estate of God, [308] was immediately his state of guilt. The fact that man was good and innocent is not a part of his own history but the consummation and climax of the history of his creation. It stands under the view of the first saga (Gen. 1³¹) that God saw all that He had made—including man—and, behold, it was very good. Its most exact parallel is the divine observance of the Sabbath (Gen. 2²⁻³) in which man is at once given a share, so that his course can actually commence in and with the rest of God.

To understand the declaration of v. 25 it is to be noted that for the first time there is a reference to "both," and then to "the man and his wife." The problem with which the final section of the saga opened is now resolved and removed. Man is no longer single but a couple. He no longer lacks the good thing which he lacked according to the judgment of God in v. 18. His creation is now completed. He now exists in the plural. The I has now found its Thou, and that means "both." Both together are now the acting and responsible subject man. With the creation of woman as the climax of his own creation, and his acknowledgment of her, man has lost his position of sole responsibility. He is no longer the only spokesman as in v. 23. From now on woman will be there, and with him she will be "man" and will stand before God as such. God's whole intercourse with man will now be strictly related to man conjoined as male and female and existing as I and Thou, and therefore to humanity. But woman will be there as woman. The encounter of man and woman is not in any sense an encounter of two freely disposing or disposable factors which can be shaped or reversed at will. Only as ordered by God at creation can this encounter be normal and good in its relationship to God. Any other form of the mutual relationship of man and woman alters their relationship to God. And every alteration of their relationship to God is betrayed by the disturbance and reversal of their normal and good mutual relationship. The striking expression "the man and his wife" points already to the definite order of this relationship. According to v. 23, this means man generically and his wife. It does not simply say male and female, for the subject of what follows is man: man with his wife; man who is now no longer alone but man with his wife; man whose own creation was only completed, who only became "man," as he became and is "man with his wife," with woman. The relative supremacy of man is brought home to us by this expression. But it is to be noted that its relativity is secured by the fact that the reference is not to the male as such but to man. Man does not exist as a male in abstract masculinity, but as the man to whom woman belongs, who has woman at his side as "his" wife. On the other hand, the possessive "his" does not describe woman as the wife of the male, but as the wife of man. It is as the wife of man and not as the wife of the male that she is called "his" wife. The force of the possessive is to include the humanity of the woman. It is valid in the framework of the numeral "both," which puts man and woman [309] together, denying any humanity to man without the presence of woman. But in this framework it really is valid. Woman is his, i.e., she is the wife of man. And this man is the male. She is taken out of him, "bone of his bones, flesh of his flesh." Before God he has chosen and welcomed her with the words: "This is now." She is there for him, as the answer to his question, as his true helpmeet. She is I as his Thou. She is man as the completion of his humanity. What would she be as "female" if she were not his "female," given and brought to him, recognised, addressed, and accepted as such by him? In him, the male, she has her man, and with and in him her own humanity. As there is no abstract manhood, there is no abstract womanhood. The only real humanity is that which for the woman consists in being the wife of a male and therefore the wife of man. Nothing of all this is to be seen alone, and nothing overlooked. Nothing must be emphasised at the expense of something else, or suppressed or neglected for the sake of something else: neither the humanity of man and woman, nor their manhood and womanhood; neither the supremacy of man nor its relativity; neither the rights of woman nor the connexion of these rights with the man's just claim to her help. This is how it was with man and woman in the act of their creation and as God stood for them as the Creator. They were in this differentiation, totality and unity. They stood in this way before they fell by trying to create their own estate, which could only be that of their guilt.

They were naked, i.e., they saw with open eyes what they were—the man, the man; the woman, the woman. And they were not ashamed, i.e., they were this without any embarrassment and disquietude, recognising themselves as such, i.e., the man recognising the woman as woman and the woman recognising the man as man. They were blind to every possibility that their existence as man and wife might entail embarrassment and disquietude. They had nothing to hide from each other, because as God created them both were right before God and therefore for one another. What had they to blame or to hide? Humanity was not for them an ideal beyond masculinity and femininity. But masculinity and femininity themselves, in their differentiation and unity, constituted humanity. Thus neither masculinity nor femininity could be sub-human—a weakness which had to be endured and concealed. So long as neither tried to assert itself *in abstracto*EN386, both were valid *in concreto*EN387. So long as man's supremacy was only the expression of a claim first raised, not by himself, but by God and therefore legitimate, it could not be blamed and he was not compelled to hide it from woman. And so long as the subordination of woman to man was only the expression of the help which in her person made the male man and man a male, this did not involve any humiliation for her, nor did she have to reproach man that she was wholly and exclusively his helpmeet. How could one work of God be ashamed as such before another? How could there be accusation and therefore shame within this one interdependent work of God? Shame is possible only where there is disgrace. In God's work

[310]

EN386 in the abstract
EN387 concretely

as such there is neither shame nor even the possibility of it. The sphere of disgrace and therefore of accusation and shame is the sphere of the alien work of the creature, i.e., where the creature seeks to stand by itself instead of allowing God to stand for it.

The meaning of the passage is not, of course, that it was their innocence as created by God to be naked and not ashamed. Their innocence was in God and their being before and with Him; in the sign of the "tree of life"; in the freedom in which they rejoiced in the life given by Him and to be given back to Him; in their self-evident restriction from the "tree of knowledge" as a frontier which they had no desire to cross and the prohibition of which was only a confirmation of what they could not possibly will of themselves. Their innocence was their creatureliness, in which there could be no place for disgrace or shame. And because there was nothing disgraceful in this innocence in which God had robed them as in a garment, they were necessarily naked, and could be so, without needing to be ashamed. The nakedness and holy shamelessness of man and woman, which the passage concludes by affirming, are thus the correlate and expression of their innocence. Because they were innocent, they were naked and were not ashamed, their nakedness as such being manifest and yet concealed as a cause of offence. With their innocence this correlate had also to be lost. When they had eaten of the tree of knowledge, their first act of knowledge was the opening of their eyes and an awareness of their nakedness. In the glory of the divine work they had to see disgrace, and to be ashamed of it, and impotently to try to find help in their disgrace. When their knowledge became the inappropriate knowledge of good and evil, it was corrupted. And when it was corrupted, their nakedness was also corrupted. Coming under the divine accusation, they had to accuse themselves. When their relationship to God was disturbed, their mutual relationship was also disturbed; everything that belongs together disintegrated; everything that was created in a definite order was thrown into confusion. Humanity became a sexless and therefore an anæmic and finally a soulless ideal hopelessly confronting abstract masculinity on the one side and abstract femininity on the other, and leading to the conflicts between the blind dominion of man and the jealous movement for feminine emancipation; between an evil eroticism and an evil absence of eroticism; between demonic and bourgeois views of love and marriage; between dissipation and respectability. But this is not the place to pursue these topics. There can be no doubt that the condition of man as fallen from God is betrayed first and foremost by the fact that it is the condition of secret and open, conscious and unconscious, organised and unorganised [311] shame at the relationship between man and woman; the condition in which one or other of the constituent elements in the order of this relationship is either over-emphasised or neglected, so that the whole order as such is lost.

It may well be said that the corruption of man's judgment of good and evil cannot be revealed more crassly than in the fact that in its verdict it stumbled first at this most intimate sphere of humanity and human glory and freedom;

that it first discovered shame at this point; that here first it conceived it to be its duty to frame moral codes, thus causing and introducing corruption and shame. Where, from the standpoint of God's creation, everything is pure and holy and harmless, there the impure eye of disobedient man sees nothing but impurity, unholiness and temptation, and in so doing defiles, dishonours and destroys everything. It has to be said, of course, that it is the genius of the sin which entered the world to declare the relationship between man and woman, or sexuality, the *pudendum*[EN388] of humanity, and thus to make it its real *pudendum*[EN389]. The history of creation as such knows nothing of this *pudendum*[EN390]. Indeed, its presentation of the divine work culminates in the radiant assertion that at this very point where the sin of man had to unveil his darkness, and in so doing to actualise it, the glory of God the Creator, and therefore the glory of the creature, the glory of humanity, is at its greatest. It declares unequivocally that the necessity of shame, however great it may have become as a result of man's disobedience, does not derive from his nature as established by God but is contrary to it. It opposes to all the human disorders and orders which have become necessary in the sphere of this relationship the original divine order which is not in any sense denied or abrogated. It proclaims that this relationship in all the corruption in which alone we now know it stands under an unparalleled promise and command. At this very point it shows us a light which no darkness has overcome and by which all the darkness which has arisen through man's disobedience is surrounded. This is the sense of this final statement of the saga which is also the final statement of the first two chapters of Genesis devoted to God's creation. In Gen. 1 we were told that God created man in His image, i.e., as man and woman. In Gen. 2 we were told how He fashioned this image. And now in the final statement we are told that it was without blemish, that, as male and female, man had nothing to be ashamed of, because, as male and female, he was right in the sight of God and therefore in his own sight, because it was God's will that he should not be alone, because in the woman God had created and brought him his helpmeet.

But what have we actually been told? If we try to read the passage in isolation, we can only conclude that what we are offered is an account of the divine basis of love and marriage as the fulfilment of the relationship between [312] man and wife. But what is the meaning and purpose of the emphasis on this foundation at the commencement of the Bible? Why is it that even the first creation narrative describes the creation of man in God's image as the creation of male and female? And why is it that the second narrative presents them in this form as the climax of the whole work of creation? What is the precise relationship between this determination and problem of human exist-

---

[EN388] embarrassment
[EN389] embarrassment
[EN390] embarrassment

ence and the theme of the Old Testament, the revelation and dealings of God in the midst of the people of Israel? As the passage sees it, it has a great deal to do with it. Here too, and particularly, we find ourselves before the mystery of the divine covenant of grace as the inner basis of the divine creation. There can be no doubt of this if we really have to reckon with an analogy with everything preceding. Indeed, it is imperiously suggested by the explicit reference in Eph. 5³². Paul undoubtedly saw the mystery in this light. But what is the connecting link? Where are the outlines of this mystery to be seen?

To understand this, we must first consider what seems to be a surprising gap in the text. What is envisaged and elucidated is undoubtedly the foundation of love and marriage, and the relationship between man and wife as established and decreed in creation. But the missing feature is what the rest of the Old Testament regards as the heart of the matter, and many a later treatment has more or less seriously and successfully made the main issue, namely, the problem of posterity, human fatherhood and motherhood, the family, the child and above all the son. In this respect Gen. 2 occupies an almost isolated position within the rest of the Old Testament. The *eros* of both sexes, the fulfilment of humanity in its encounter and relation, has as such only an incidental significance in the rest of the Old Testament (with only a single exception). The sexuality of man is considered almost exclusively in connexion with the procreation of the holy seed and therefore the hope of Israel, and therefore its determination and Messianic expectation. It is for the sake of a son that a man must seek his wife, the future mother of his children and above all of the heir of his body. It is for this reason that marriage must be considered sacred. The turbulent impulse of man to leave his father and mother and cleave to his wife, becoming one flesh with her, is expressed and presented only in one other part of the Old Testament, although here in a form which is almost terrifyingly strong and unequivocal. This is in the Song of Songs, which not without reason is ascribed to King Solomon, who is surrounded by so much anticipated eschatology. It is in this book alone—and this exception proves the rule—that Gen. 2 is developed. It is here that we see that the picture given in Gen. 2 is not just incidental or alien to the Old Testament, but that it played a specific, although for the most part unseen, role in the thought of Israel: to wit, the delight, not of the potential father or head of the family, but simply of man as such, not in the potential bearer of his children but simply in the woman as such; the *eros* for which there is no such thing as shame according to v. 25 of this passage. [313]

Indeed, we have here a note which cannot be heard in Gen. 2. For woman is now portrayed in the same rapture—one might almost say with the same eager: "This is now"—in relation to man. She now answers just as loudly and expressly as she is addressed by him. She now praises him no less than she is praised by him. It is she who now seeks him with pain and finds him with joy. The famous inversion is now found on her lips: "My beloved is mine, and I am his" (*Song of Sol.* 2¹⁶); "I am my beloved's, and my beloved is mine" (*Song of Sol.* 6³).

It is almost incredible that this should be found so unreservedly in the Bible. It may well be said that by taking up so definitely the thought of Gen. 2, and even enlarging on it, in its isolation from the rest of the Old Testament, the Song of Songs merely gives sharper point to the question which arises in connexion with Gen. 2. The Song of Songs itself rightly calls for explanation. In the upshot it only shows that Gen. 2 does not really offer an isolated riddle, and that we must really try to find a solution for it. A comparison of Gen. 2 and the Song of Songs does at least reveal that what interested the authors of the creation saga and these love songs was the fact that in the relationship between man and woman—even prior to its character as the basis of the father-mother-child relationship—we have to do primarily with the question of an incomparable covenant, of an irresistibly purposed and effected union. The Song of Songs is one long description of the rapture, the unquenchable yearning and the restless willingness and readiness, with which both partners in this covenant hasten towards an encounter. Gen. 2 is even more radical in its great brevity. It tells us that only male and female together are man. The male alone is not yet man, for it is not good for him to be alone; nor can the female alone be man, for she is taken out of the man: "They twain shall be one flesh." Hence Gen. 2 speaks of the covenant made and irrevocably sealed. It sets at the beginning that which in the Song of Songs is the goal. It was for the sake of this covenant that God first created man as male and female. And the Song of Songs agrees. With this covenant in view, man and woman must and may and will hasten toward an encounter in spite of any hindrance and restriction.

In connexion with both passages we may well ask where the authors found the courage—or perhaps we should ask how the redactors of the Canon came to choose these passages whose authors, ignoring the well-known disturbance and corruption in the relationship of the sexes, obviously had the courage—to treat of the matter in this way, speaking so bluntly of *eros* and not being content merely with the restrained and in its own way central reference to marriage and posterity. Did they not realise what is involved? Did they not see with what almost hopeless problems the amatory relationship between man and woman [314] is actually burdened? Ought they not to have been afraid that by concentration on this relationship they would merely add fresh fuel to a fire which is destructive enough without it? Who, then, is innocent enough to write these innocent passages? And who has eyes so innocent as to read them as innocent passages? But the author of Gen. 2 knew well enough of the ruin of that relationship. He himself described it quite plainly. And we can hardly complain that the rest of the Solomonic literature suffers from illusions regarding the true state of affairs as between man and woman; that it has not seen the abysses and morasses by which this relation is criss-crossed. If in the existence of these passages we do not have a mere accident, and therefore an alien blot on the Old Testament witness to revelation, the only explanation is that the authors of the creation saga and these love songs had in mind another covenant, stained and spotted, almost unrecognisable in historical reality, and yet concluded, sealed, persisting and valid (and thus necessitating a movement towards its realisation); and that the existence of this covenant inescapably compelled them to see and present in a supremely positive light the sphere of the relationship of the sexes even on its dangerous and corrupted aspect, taking this second covenant with childlike seriousness in the knowledge of the first.

It is certainly no accident that in the strict sense this is to be found only in these two passages in the Old Testament, at any rate expressly and explicitly. For it can be ventured only in relation to God's creation, and then again in the eschatological context of the portrayal of Solomon's royal glory. But in this connexion it obviously has to be ventured. An inner necessity breaks through every reservation. God the Lord and sexual *eros*, well known in Israel especially as a dangerous dæmon, are brought into close relationship. The "flame of the Lord" and the very different flame of love (Song of Songs 8[6]) are necessarily mentioned together and openly and distinctly compared and related. For at these points the witnesses to God's revelation think not only of the covenant as such, broken and denied by Israel's disobedience, but of the covenant firmly established, preserved and executed by God's free grace. At these points they necessarily venture to look away from all that their nation for its part was and did in this covenant, to the God who had elected it, and therefore to look upon their nation as elected by Him, i.e., to look upon that which on the basis of His election it may properly be before and for Him in the eyes of His love in spite and in defiance of its disobedience. It is of this covenant, this God and this Israel that the witnesses to *Yahweh's* revelation had to venture to think when they thought of the beginning and goal of this covenant. What lies at the back of the creation saga is the thought of its commencement, and what lies at the back of the Solomonic love songs is the thought of its goal. The authors of Gen. 2 and the Song of Songs speak of man and woman as they do because they know that the broken covenant is still for God the unbroken covenant, [315] intact and fulfilled on both sides; that as such it was already the inner basis of creation, and that as such it will again be revealed at the end. Their particular and remarkably free knowledge of love and marriage as proclaimed in these passages corresponds to their particular knowledge of the covenant, of its origin before all the unfaithfulness of Israel and its completion after it.

The Old Testament looks only infrequently in this direction. As a rule, it does not do so at all. Its gaze is normally fixed on the centre, on the history of the covenant actualised as a covenant broken and despised by Israel, so that God's faithfulness is necessarily manifested more in threats than promises, in chastisement than rewards, and men and women are better thought of only as fathers and mothers in Israel, and it is comforting to be able to think of them hopefully at least in this direction. In this context it is better to say nothing at all about *eros*. References to marriage will largely be in the form of warnings and threats against adultery. In sad contrast to the Song of Songs 2[11f.], the winter is not yet passed, the rain is not over and gone, the flowers have not yet appeared on the earth, the time of singing has not yet come. The call: "Arise, my love, my fair one, and come away," could have only a suspicious, deceptive, lascivious, or at least supremely indifferent, worldly connotation. The first woman's welcome to the first man, and the nakedness and shamelessness of both, are better ignored. The Song of Songs had better not be written, or not read if already written. But the Old Testament does occasionally look in the other direction. Its whole witness to God's covenant is shot through by the knowledge that this centre where it is broken and despised, and persists only in this form, is not the whole story, and that it has its frontiers in a very different beginning and end, where *Yahweh* and His people are together and are "one flesh." And when its gaze rests on these frontiers, and to that extent on the reality of the covenant, the Old Testament witnesses can and must also think and speak of man and woman very differently from what they usually do. The vision of the incomprehensible nearness, intimacy and sweetness of the relationship between *Yahweh* and Israel can then actually break through the caution, the care, the legitimate severity and anxiety, which otherwise cause them to speak so non-erotically of the erotic. They must speak out freely. Love and marriage between man and woman become to them in some sense irresistibly a parable and sign of the link which *Yahweh* has established between Himself and His people, which in His eternal faithfulness He has determined to keep, and which He for His part has continually renewed. In this way they irresistibly see even this most dangerous sphere of human existence in its old and new glory.

[316]   The remarkable fact that the prophets always described the alliance between *Yahweh* and Israel in terms of love and marriage is reflected in the necessity with which this takes place. It is true that as a rule at the heart of the Old Testament witness *Yahweh's* love for Israel is compared with a man's love for a woman who was from the very outset unworthy of Him, whom He raised out of the dust (Ezek. 16$^{1-14}$), whom He undeservedly honoured by turning to her, and whom He adorned with His gifts. What is Jerusalem to Him? Is it not "by birth and nativity of the land of the Canaan, thy father an Amorite, and thy mother an Hittite?" And even more bitterly it is said in Hos. 1 and 3, in the very strange action required of the prophet, that she whom *Yahweh* chose and elevated to be His wife did not merely become a harlot but was one already when He found her. And it is as such that she now deports and behaves herself—Israel here, Judah there and even Jerusalem. It is by the punishment and misery of such that she is irresistibly visited. And terribly forthright descritions are given in Hos. 2, Jer. 3 and Ezek. 23. As *Yahweh's* partner had been unworthy from the very outset, she now proved herself to be unworthy. She forgot the "days of her youth," and the condition in which *Yahweh* had found her and loved her. She never really occupied the position at His side for which He had raised her. She at once became an adulteress with the idols of the nations, a public prostitute. She was never anything but unfaithful to her husband. She never brought Him anything but shame. And so He rejected and abandoned

her. Numerous direct and indirect references remind us again and again that the covenant which is the prototype of human love and marriage is the covenant which in its historical reality was broken by Israel; the covenant in which, as is re-echoed even in the New Testament, Israel, Judah and Jerusalem showed themselves to be "an evil and adulterous generation," a nation which could only ignore, despise and ridicule the grace of God addressed to it. In view of this we can understand the shadow which necessarily lies over the relationship between man and wife as such. We can also understand why it is only seldom that the Old Testament can refer positively to the erotic sphere, and this only in relation to the frontiers of the historical reality of the covenant. But all this, far from altering, proves finally even in its negativity that the covenant, as God willed, concluded and now maintains it, is a covenant of love and marriage. Love is always love even if it is not deserved or reciprocated by the beloved, even if she rejects and disgraces it by unfaithfulness. Similarly, marriage is always marriage even though broken by *Yahweh's* partner. *Yahweh* is always the Lover, Bridegroom and Husband. And His lost people is always His beloved, His bride and His wife. Nor do the prophets fail to make this continuity plain in spite of their exposure of the discord. We have to reckon with the unfaithfulness of the wife, but never with the unfaithfulness of the Husband. We have to reckon with her rejection and abandonment, but not with a bill of divorce. If the one partner has forgotten the days of her youth, the Other has not forgot- [317] ten them. The call for her return, and above all the assurance of His love and faithfulness, are not abrogated.

"I will not cause mine anger to fall upon you: for I am merciful, saith the Lord, and I will not keep anger for ever" (Jer. 3^{12}). "If thou wilt return, O Israel, saith the Lord, return unto me: and if thou wilt put away thine abominations out of my sight, then shalt thou not remove" (Jer. 4^{1}). The assurance remains: "I will even deal with thee as thou hast done, who hast despised the oath in breaking the covenant. Nevertheless I will remember my covenant with thee in the days of thy youth, and I will establish unto thee an everlasting covenant ... but not by thy covenant" (Ezek. 16$^{59f.}$). "And I will betroth thee unto me for ever; yea, I will betroth thee unto me in righteousness, and in judgement, and in lovingkindness, and in mercies. I will even betroth thee unto me in faithfulness: and thou shalt know the Lord" (Hos. 2$^{19-20}$). The expectation remains: "And it shall be at that day, saith the Lord, that thou shalt call me Ishi; and shalt call me no more Baali. For I will take away the names of Baalim out of her mouth, and they shall no more be remembered by their name" (Hos. 2$^{16-17}$). And the whole promise of the covenant remains: "Fear not; for thou shalt not be ashamed: neither be thou confounded; for thou shalt not be put to shame: for thou shalt forget the shame of thy youth, and shalt not remember the reproach of thy widowhood any more. For thy Maker is thy husband; the Lord of hosts is his name; and thy Redeemer the Holy One of Israel; The God of the whole earth shall he be called. For the Lord hath called thee as a woman forsaken and grieved in spirit, and a wife of youth, when thou wast refused, saith thy God. For a small moment have I forsaken thee; but with great mercies will I gather thee. In a little wrath I hid my face from thee for a moment; but with everlasting kindness will I have mercy on thee, saith the Lord thy Redeemer" (Is. 54$^{4-8}$).

"But not by thy covenant," is written right across it. What is envisaged is really the beginning and end of the historical reality, and both at the beginning and the end it is God's love and faithfulness alone which gives this alliance with Israel its authority. At the centre, where the question of Israel's own position and preservation arises, this alliance has been completely destroyed by Israel. But even so, in the light of its beginning and end, and therefore from the standpoint of God's decision and disposal, it cannot cease to be love and marriage. We cannot note or feel too strongly the weight of the fact which stands immovably in the background and is always presupposed over and over again—that *Yahweh* is the Husband and Israel the wife, i.e., that *Yahweh* is Israel's Husband and Israel *Yahweh's* wife. This is the fact which the authors of Gen. 2 and the Song of Songs had in mind. And as and because they had it in mind, they ventured to make this great and free exception in touching on the sphere of the erotic. We naturally miss their meaning if we regard their presentation merely symbolically, for they undoubtedly meant to speak and did speak of man and woman as such, and love and marriage as such. Again, we do not understand them if we fail to realise that they spoke of this sphere as they did because they had in mind, as a prototype of the events in this sphere, the love which *Yahweh* addressed once and for all to Israel as her Husband and which

[318]   He Himself initiated and preserved with Israel. Similarly, we miss the meaning of the prophets if we understand what they say about *Yahweh's* love and marriage only symbolically, as if they were merely trying to illustrate and clarify *Yahweh's* relationship with Israel in terms of an ideal picture from the erotic sphere. What they described as *Yahweh's* love and marriage is quite incomparable in this sphere, transcending every comparison with what has ever taken place between husband and wife. For such love and marriage is not the affair of a human husband, but only that of the Husband *Yahweh*. We have here the unattainable prototype of what is realised in the human sphere between husband and wife. Yet it is the prototype of this event. Because the election of God is real, there is such a thing as love and marriage, and seen from the standpoint of this election human love and marriage in the emancipated and total form in which they are depicted in Gen. 2 and the Song of Songs. The picture that these passages offer is the clear and necessary reflection of the covenant of grace; not of that kept by Israel but of that kept by God. Because God as Creator, Lord and King of the whole terrestrial sphere did not will to be alone in relation to it, but to have His concrete counterpart in this terrestrial sphere in a people of His possession, He found it not good for a man to be alone, and therefore ordained for him a helpmeet or counterpart in woman. Because in His divine freedom He found in no other people on earth what He needed; because as the One He is, *Yahweh* Elohim, He willed to ignore the rest and to choose this people alone, without any merits of its own but solely on the basis of His own being, necessarily acknowledging it in the wisdom of His will, man as man could not recognise the completion of his creation in the fellowship of any of the beasts but only in that of woman.

It is because it is grounded in the utter mystery of God's deity that He is *Yahweh* Elohim, the Holy One of Israel, that in the act which completes his humanity man is placed in a deep sleep, and on awakening finds that the divine work has taken place. It is because in and with Israel's election God has from the very first offered, surrendered and sacrificed no less than something of Himself, in some sense hazarding Himself, so that from the very first the existence of Israel includes in itself the existence of the Son of God on earth, that the helpmeet of man is "bone of his bones, and flesh of his flesh," earthly as he is, yet not just taken out of the earth but taken out of him, not formed from the earth but "fashioned" out of something which man had to yield and surrender. It is because in free decision God has said Yes to the Israel created not only by but of Himself, to the compromising and jeopardising of His own divine being, that man jubilantly exclaims: "This is now." When a man leaves his father and mother and cleaves to his wife, when he and she become one flesh, it is because God has so irrevocably united Himself with His people, and so unconditionally declared His solidarity with it, as was the case in the establishment of the covenant, in their "time of youth" together. When man and his wife were naked and not ashamed, it was because the Husband *Yahweh*, "the Lord of Hosts," the "Lord of all the earth," had first—really first—revealed Himself wholly as He is to that poor and wicked harlot, just as she for her part was known and revealed to Him in all her utter misery, and because in this mutual but divinely grounded [319] revelation there was nothing but love, good-pleasure and delight, because the Husband *Yahweh* was really not ashamed of the harlot Israel, and because He willed to allow and promise her that ultimately she would not have to be ashamed before Him even in all her nakedness.

These are the outlines of the covenant of grace in the history of the creation of man as male and female. And because it exhibits these outlines it is not really so isolated and alien in the Old Testament as appears at first sight. It is to be noted again that it is not an "allegory"—nor is the Song of Songs. It says exactly what it says. It is undoubtedly and unequivocally an erotic history. But it exists in this concrete context and cannot be detached from it. It must be understood in conjunction with it. As an absolutely pure and holy erotic history it has a meaningful place in the Old Testament because its background and context is the history of the covenant, i.e., the history of the love exercised by God Himself, of the marriage unreservedly instituted and unfalteringly preserved by Him. Having this background and standing in this context, it knows what it ventures, and is compelled to make the venture.

On this basis it is comparatively easy to understand the message of the New Testament as the fulfilment of the Old. In this respect, too, the Old Testament waits for a fulfilment which is not apparent in the framework of its own message. As we have seen, in the Old Testament there is a twofold correspondence in covenant history to Gen. 2[18f.] The first may be seen in the Song of Songs, the second in the prophets. Each conditions and supplements the other. If the object of the presentation on the one side is a perfect relationship of love between man and woman, on the other, again in the form of a love relationship, but now a one-sided relationship established and preserved by the faithfulness of the Husband and never realised but always broken by the wife, it is the relationship between *Yahweh* and Israel.

According to the Song of Songs, the Old Testament knows finally a proper meaning and seriousness of the sexual relation as such. That is why it ventures, in the voice of the prophet, to describe the connexion between *Yahweh* and Israel in terms of the relationship between man and wife. It knows equally well the disturbance to which the sexual relationship has fallen victim in historical reality. For this reason it can present the relationship between *Yahweh* and Israel as perfect on the part of *Yahweh* but only as devastated on that of Israel.

On the other hand, according to the same voice of the prophet, the Old Testament hopes for a perfect expression of the relationship between *Yahweh* and Israel to be brought about by the Husband *Yahweh*. It looks for a "betrothal in justice and righteousness, in kindness and compassion." Therefore, at least on the fringe of its message, it can and must see the relationship between man [320] and woman in the very different light of the Song of Songs, and occasionally give free expression to *eros*. But it sees equally clearly that this perfect form of relationship between *Yahweh* and Israel is a matter of its hope and can only be a matter of its hope. For this reason it does not usually listen to *eros* when it speaks of the sexual relationship. For this reason it usually sees man and woman in the role of father and mother, begetting and bearing posterity, i.e., not directed towards themselves but towards the future Son.

Are these converging or diverging lines? Do they involve agreement or contradiction? Looking at the message of the Old Testament in and for itself, we can only say that all the lines obviously seek to converge, but actually diverge, so that for all the apparent agreement in intention and general substance the expression and details end only in unresolved contradiction.

How does the Old Testament know of the dignity of the sexual relationship as such? How does it come to paint the relationship between *Yahweh* and Israel in just these colours? On the other hand, how does it know so exactly the actual disturbance of this relationship ? By what bitter necessity is it thus compelled to portray the relationship between *Yahweh* and Israel only as a devastated erotic relationship?

What is the source of its hope for a restoration of this relationship to its perfect form? And where does it get the courage, in view of this hope, occasionally to give such free expression to sexual *eros*? Again, why is there this restriction on its hope? Why does it so wholly remain a hope and therefore a vision of something future? What is the source of the sober discipline which usually confines itself to the problem of fatherhood and motherhood, so that it causes man and woman to look beyond themselves, and exclusively to the future Son? It is not impossible that all these lines might intersect at a single point; that a single answer might offer a solution to all these questions. Indeed, it forces itself upon us in view of the plenitude of obvious interconnexions. But it is equally clear, or even clearer, that in this point it is not to be found as such in the Old Testament, nor is this answer directly given, so that in this as in so many other places the final word of Old Testament exegesis can only be an insoluble riddle.

It can—and in the Christian Church must—be maintained, however, that the correspondence to Gen. 2$^{18f.}$ in covenant history is not exhausted by what is to be seen along these two lines, in the Song of Songs and the prophets. It can and must be maintained that the Old Testament as a whole forms a single material context with the New, and that it is in this context, and beyond the confines of the Old Testament, that Gen. 2$^{18f.}$ must be seen if it is to be rightly understood. It can and must be maintained that we are forced to affirm convergence rather than divergence, harmony rather than contradiction, once we [321] see the focal point which is outside the Old Testament and identical with the central point of the message of the New. Instead of being arbitrarily ignored, Eph. 5^{25} can and may and must be taken into account as a commentary on Gen. 2$^{18f.}$, and therefore on the Song of Songs, and therefore on those passages from the prophets. "This is a great mystery, but I speak concerning Christ and the church" (Eph. 5^{32}). If this is accepted, it cannot be denied that even the obscure language of the creation saga takes on a wholly different form and colour, acquiring indeed a very concrete meaning.

Why could not man be alone? Why had he to acquire in woman a helpmeet ? Why could his creation, his emergence as man, be completed only with the creation of woman? In the wider context we may answer that it is because the man Jesus, the Son of God, whose earthly existence was envisaged at the creation of heaven and earth, and the Son of Man whose manifestation and work were envisaged in the election of Israel, was not to be alone; because in His own followers, in the Church which believes in Him, He was to have His counterpart, His environment, His helpmeet and servants. It was not apart from them but with them that He was the firstborn from the dead. And therefore it was not without but with them that He was already the firstborn of creation. For His own incarnation was completed only with the bringing of these "others" and their reception into the Church.

Why could not man be content with the co-existence of the animals? Why could he recognise in the woman alone the helpmeet which he lacked? From the standpoint of the New Testament we must answer that it is because the calling and ingathering of the Church of Jesus Christ, for whose sake He was born and crucified and raised again from the dead, was to be a matter of His own free election; because His own were to become His own followers in virtue of the fact that He recognised them as such, that He decided for them, and called them, and formed of them His own *entourage*. Like had to come to like, and He Himself had to decide who were to be like Him; He Himself had to be the measure by which they could be like Him and therefore His followers, described as such. As the Son of God and Son of Man He Himself had to recognise and address them as such.

Why did the first man have to fall into that deep sleep when the work of God was done in which the woman had her origin? From the standpoint of the New Testament it is because the Church of Jesus Christ was to have its origin in His mortal sleep and to stand complete before Him in His resurrection.

Why had the woman to be taken out of the man—bone of his bones and flesh of his flesh, i.e., be "formed" from his rib? Because the death of Jesus was to be His sacrifice for His Church, and its reconciliation an exchange between divine glory and human misery. The Church of Jesus Christ emerges when He endures the pain of death, allowing a part of His own life to be taken from Him; when it is "formed" from that which is wholly His and which

315

He now surrenders; when it receives from His its own essence and existence. And He in turn receives its flesh, accepting its weakness and making it a part of His own body. Hence it is not without Him nor He without it. Hence He recognises it as His body, formed from what was taken from Him, and alive through His death. Hence He acknowledges it, its weakness being enfolded and borne by His glory, and itself quickened by His death.

Why can man jubilantly exclaim: "This is now …? Because the Church of Jesus did not first recognise Him but was first recognised by Him, being created for Him by divine omnipotence in the power of His resurrection, and brought to Him, and given Him out of the world; [322] because He was to rediscover Himself in it, in "another," a counterpart; because in its existence His own was to be completed; because with it—only with it, but with it truly—He was to be altogether Himself; because with its service He was to become and be the Lord and King of the whole universe. In and with its election, His own election is complete; in and with its revelation, His own revelation is finally accomplished.

Why does a man leave father and mother and cleave to his wife, so that they become one flesh? Because Jesus will leave the glory of His Father for the sake of His own followers; because His mother and brothers and sisters will be those, and only those, who as His followers do His will; and because He will declare His full solidarity with them, genuinely uniting Himself with them.

And why were man and woman naked and not ashamed? Because between Jesus and His followers there will take place an unreserved—and as such merciful and salutary—disclosure of man; because He will stand and not need to be ashamed before them in absolute poverty, humiliated and rejected by God, and therefore the Bearer of every honour and the Elect of God; and because they too will be seen and discovered in their own poverty, humiliation and rejection, and will not be ashamed or judged, because He will not be ashamed of them, because He will call them His brothers and sisters, and because, as the Elect of God, He will defend them with His riches.

There again emerge, but more concretely, the outlines of the covenant of grace already concluded with Israel. And the fact that everything essential in the Old Testament along the lines of Gen. 2[18f.] recurs in supreme concretion at the central point in the New is a clear indication that this is also the focal point of these Old Testament lines, and that they and their origin in Gen. 2 are really to be understood from this angle. If the man Jesus Christ is the fulfilment of what is prophesied in the Old Testament in respect of the Husband *Yahweh*, the questions which crowd in upon Old Testament exegesis as such are not unanswerable.

When the Old Testament gives dignity to the sexual relationship, it has in view its prototype, the divine likeness of man as male and female which in the plan and election of God is primarily the relationship between Jesus Christ and His Church, secondarily the relationship between *Yahweh* and Israel, and only finally—although very directly in view of its origin—the relationship between the sexes. It is because Jesus Christ and His Church are the internal basis of creation, and because Jesus Christ is again the basis of the election and call of Israel, that the relation between *Yahweh* and Israel can and must be described as an erotic relationship.

When the Old Testament so inexorably describes the relationship between *Yahweh* and Israel as a disrupted relationship; and when it normally describes the relationship between man and woman only in the light of its disorder and infinite danger, its real aim is the covenant between God and man which in the plan and election of God already included the surrender and death of His Son, which could be accomplished only at this cost, in which God and man, and God and the two sexes, confront each other as do Jesus Christ and His followers to the extent that Jesus Christ had to be offered up for their sins and to die for their reconciliation with God. In this confrontation how can they be anything but adulterers before God and between themselves? From this standpoint, how can there be any different or milder view of their relationship to God and to one another? If the price which had to be paid for them was so costly, their sin and need could not be less than that described by the prophets in words which sound almost intolerably harsh. If the rejection and crucifixion of its King was the end of Israel's history, there was obviously a bitter necessity to speak in this way of and to Israel. From this standpoint the relationship of the sexes had to be seen in the way in which the Old Testament usually sees it.   [323]

If in face and defiance of all appearances the Old Testament proclaims the hope of a restoration; if it expresses confidence that the betrothal in justice and righteousness between *Yahweh* and His people will yet be realised; and if it can thus dare to speak so positively about love and marriage as such, its true aim is the event in which, purified in baptism and sactified by His Word (Eph. 5²⁶ᶠ·), the Church of Jesus will be presented to Him in glory without spot or blemish, holy and inviolable. His betrothal and marriage to this woman, unlike that of *Yahweh* to Israel in the Old Testament, is made by His action alone a relationship of mutual love and faithfulness, in which "mercy and truth are met together; righteousness and peace have kissed each other. Truth shall spring out of the earth; and righteousness shall look down from heaven" (Ps. 85¹⁰⁻¹¹). Here is a realm where the fall of man is arrested and made good, so that the accusation against him can and must be silenced. Here, then, is a realm where it is the duty of men "to love their wives as their own bodies." "He that loveth his wife, loveth himself. For no man yet ever hated his own flesh; but nourisheth and cherisheth it, even as the Lord the church: for we are members of his body" (Eph. 5²⁸⁻³⁰). Here for the first time the relationship between man and woman is honoured as such, and not merely in the light of fatherhood or motherhood or posterity—which fade into the background in the New Testament. Here this relationship is again given its own glory as glowingly asserted in the Song of Songs.

And if the Old Testament limits this hope and presents it strictly with a view to the future; if in connexion with it it gives great prominence to fatherhood and motherhood, in so doing it points beyond all the generations of Israel to the Son, the Son of Man, who in His person was to be the Lover, Bridegroom and Husband of His own people sanctified by Himself. It can and must be said that with its normal observance of strict sobriety in this sphere the Old Testament pointed most powerfully beyond itself to the King given to Israel and rejected by it but exalted by God, the Son of God and Son of Man, Jesus Christ. Because they had Him objectively in mind, passages such as Gen. 2 and the Song of Songs could only form the fringe and not the centre of its witness, its central witness being to the Son, the expected One. But in view of this it may be seen that that centre could and had to have this fringe and the creation saga this climax—the creation of man as the creation of male and female who were both naked and were not ashamed.

[324]

That it is not good for a man to be alone (v. 18) is also clearly stated—although less emphatically than appears to be the case—by Ecclesiastes: "Two are better than one; because they have a good reward for their labour. For if they fall, the one will lift up his fellow: but woe to him that is alone when he falleth; for he hath not another to help him up. Again, if two lie together, then they have heat: but how can one be warm alone? And if one prevail against him, two shall withstand him; and a threefold cord is not quickly broken" (Eccl. 4^9–12^). But the present passage is not concerned merely with the general misery of loneliness (Vriezen) or the fact that man is "created for company" (Jacob), but with the radical, sexual duality of man which is the root of all other fellowship, without which he would not be "good" as a creature, and without the establishment of which his creation as man would thus be incomplete. *In mulieris persona tandem absoluta fuit humanum genus*^EN391^ (Calvin on v. 22). It is worth noting that in the divine statement: "I will make him an help meet ... " the LXX uses ποιήσωμεν^EN392^ and the Vulgate *faciamus*^EN393^. So strongly was the parallel to Gen. 1^26^ felt even at this early time that it was thought necessary to introduce here too that mysterious plural. But it is quite enough that here too, and in a very striking way, we have reference to special divine reflection and decision. The question why man needed a helpmeet cannot, of course, be answered concretely in the sense of the saga. We need agree neither with Augustine (*De Gen. ad. lit.*, IX 3) and others in thinking of procreation, with Delitzsch in referring to what man has to do in the Garden (v. 15), nor with Ecclesiasticus 36^26^ that woman is a pillar "on which he can lean." The helpmeet which he needs is—generally and comprehensively—the helpmeet necessary for human life as such. He is not helped to this by self-help. What he needs—and it is best not to try to translate the phrase—is an *'etser knegdo*^EN394^. Zimmerli comments: "Apart from the help which he has in the Lord, he is to receive help appropriate to him." But this antithesis is artificial, and the idea of appropriateness (so also the Zürich Bible) is too anaemic. It is a matter of the creature which is essentially similar but also relatively different, so that it can be his counterpart or partner, forming a duality with him. A creature of this kind will be his intended helpmeet. Jacob advances the following consideration: "Man is not to be able to say that he would not have been deceived if he had found his life companion himself. He himself recognises woman as the only one suitable." But this rather hostile exposition hardly corresponds to the simple sense of the saga, which merely implies that man can only be regarded as good and fully created in this twofold state, i.e., with his helpmeet. It is he and he alone who is really helped.

The ensuing description of the creation and naming of the animals (vv. 19–20) is the better understood the more clearly it is seen to be an episode, i.e., the more definitely it is incorporated into the obvious process of the whole narration. It is sheer invention to affirm that the second creation saga is trying to explain the existence of animals, or to recall an original kinship and vital fellowship between man and beast, or to present a doctrine of the

---

EN391 But in the person of the woman that the human race was completed
EN392 let us make
EN393 let us make
EN394 a helper fit for him

origin of language. That these things are done incidentally cannot be denied, but the saga is not really concerned about them. What it is trying to show is how the way to the completion of man's creation led past and beyond the creation and existence of the animal kingdom. What it is trying to bring to light in connexion with the creation of woman is the humanity of man in contrast to all mere animalism. It does this by telling how the creation of animals gave man the opportunity to take stock of his attitude to them, the result being that he could give each animal its name but was unable to find in this obviously lower sphere his true [325] helpmeet and therefore the completion of his humanity. That God experimented with different creations until He finally succeeded (Gunkel), so that we have in this passage a proof of "God's irrational, merciful vitality" (Zimmerli), can be said only to the extent that God allowed man to make actual use of the freedom given to him. As will later be described even more drastically, man himself is to participate in his creation; he is to decide for his humanity, to discover, protect and acknowledge it as he "tries it out" in his encounter with the different animals, i.e., as he applies it. He himself is to establish that no animal is adequate to give the necessary duality which is the foundation of all community. This is what happens: "But for man was there was not found (by man) an help meet for him." This rejection and negation as the affirmation of man's humanity is the successful experiment recounted by the saga (vv. 19–20), and therefore positively the decision described in Ps. 73[21–23]: "Thus my heart was grieved, and I was pricked in my reins. So foolish was I, and ignorant: I was as a beast before thee. Nevertheless I am continually with thee: thou hast holden me by my right hand."

The "deep sleep" into which man fell according to v. 21 is the kind of deathlike "divine sleep" in which the Word of God came to Abraham (Gen. 15[12]), to Samuel (1 Sam. 3[3]), to Job (4[13], 33[15]) and to Daniel (8[18], 10[9]). The LXX translated the word by ἔκστασις[EN395], Aquila by καταφορά[EN396], Symmachos by πάρος[EN397] and the *Graec. Venet.* by κῶμα[EN398]. According to Is. 29[10] and 1 Sam. 26[12], it could also have the force of a divine closing or sealing. To talk as Jacob does about a "narcotic," or to say with Delitzsch that God's creative activities take place in the region of the unconscious, is foreign to the passage. The occurrence means that at the decisive point man's actual participation in the creation of woman was not active but purely passive. There was a place for man's activity both before it in the rejection of the animals and after it in the welcoming and recognition of the woman created by God, but not at this central point—as little here as in the act in which his own creation had its beginning. The widespread idea that woman is the creature of man is implicitly rejected by this part of the account. Woman is indeed taken out of man, but only during his deep sleep, as he himself is created out of the earth which is incapable of independent action. Woman—and therefore the climax of his own creation—is the new creation of God. This creation takes place in relation to him, and he thus has a passive part in it in the form of his confession and the freedom given to him. But since it is a creation, he cannot in any sense accomplish it, but can only confirm and recognise it. As the helpmeet brought to him, woman is to him a mystery, as he is to himself in his co-existence with her. Only by the confirmation and recognition of the divine work (negatively by the rejection of the animals and positively by his choice of the woman brought to him) does he actively participate in this work.

The description of the creation of woman in vv. 21–22 induced even from Calvin, who has few Christological references in his exegesis, the observation: *In eo perscipimus veram nostrae*

EN395 trance
EN396 swoon
EN397 an help meet for him
EN398 coma

cum Filio Dei unitatis effigiem; nam et ille debilis factus est, ut membra haberet virtute praedita[EN399]. Properly this is the final word of exegesis rather than the first, but there can be no doubt that both the context and the independent features of these verses force us to look in this direction from the very outset. The foreground can be meaningfully understood only if it is seen against its existing background. We ascribe too much to the creation saga if to the absurd question of Zimmerli why the ribs break off so suddenly, or Delitzsch what has happened to the thirteenth rib, we give the equally absurd answer that the gap reveals the divine hand and its initiative. It cannot be denied that we have to do here with the basis of the inner connexion and mutual inter-relationship of man and woman, and perhaps of the linguistic kinship of the words *'ish* and *'isha*[EN400], and to that extent with aetiology. But we must make a

[326] sober distinction between what the saga says incidentally and its main intention, recognising that its intention is not the impartation of this or that information in relation to all kinds of familiar facts, nor a rationalisation of puzzling realities, but the presentation of the establishment of man's bi-sexuality as a mystery—as a "great" mystery, according to St. Paul (Eph. 5[32]). What we are taught in these verses has to do with the execution of the programme of creation described in v. 18 by the concept of the divinely created helpmeet. In order that woman might be a help to human life, she must be human in the deepest sense, i.e., a part of man. Hence she is formed out of his rib. Because she is to be his divinely created helpmeet, his rib must be taken out of him during his deep sleep, not by his own volition or action, but forcibly by God's disposal and activity. To receive in her his helpmeet, he must suffer, but in the mercy of God not to his destruction. A deadly wound must be inflicted, but it must at once be healed. And to be his true counterpart, to be an autonomous being for all her similarity to him, in her essential being as part of him, she has to be specially made of what was taken out of him. The word used by the LXX is ᾠκοδόμησεν[EN401], and as we know Paul describes as οἰκοδομή[EN402] the erection of the community on the one foundation laid in Jesus Christ. The reference here, of course, is exclusively to man and woman, but to them as the crowning mystery of the divine work of creation, and therefore inclusively the inner basis of the relationship between *Yahweh* and Israel. And when we think through the riddle of this relationship, and do not arbitrarily regard the New Testament as a closed book, we find ourselves actually face to face with the *effigies*[EN403] of the realisation in Jesus of this relationship which also proves to be the final basis of the relationship between man and woman. It is strange, but unmistakeable, that properly the whole dramatic description of vv. 21–22 reassumes concrete meaning only when we do not shut our eyes to the reference given in Eph. 5. Without this reference we have finally to accept it as strangely contingent. The main point of the verses is the plain declaration that the woman is of man (ἐξ ἀνδρός[EN404], 1 Cor. 1[18]) and thus the wife of man and the climax of his creation. But this irreversible declaration is the quintessence of the whole history of the covenant and salvation in both Old and New Testament. It is quite out of the question that there should be no significance in the fact that, wholly irrespective of its concrete content, it forms the climax of the whole history of creation. It is thus quite out of the question to read and expound these verses properly without taking this significance into consideration.

The fact that God brings woman to man (v. 22) expresses the truth, as Calvin has rightly observed, that man *proprio arbitrio non sumpsit uxorem, sed oblatam a Domino sibi addictam*

[EN399] In it we see the true image of our unity with the Son of God; for He, too, was made weak, so that He might have members provided by power
[EN400] man and woman
[EN401] built
[EN402] upbuilding
[EN403] image
[EN404] of man

accepit[EN405]. The content of the saying is not really deepened if we say that in some sense the role of God is to give away the bride. Too many important features are lacking for us to see here the simple portrayal of a betrothal or marriage. We are still in the realm of creation and therefore primal history, and what is related is not the story of the first love and marriage, but the laying of the foundation which makes possible what is later actualised in history as love and marriage. Not for nothing—but very obscurely and unrealistically if this were a real story of love and marriage—it is not to the male but to man that woman is brought by God for the completion of his humanity with this divine gift. The male does not encounter woman but is encountered by her. What happens in this bringing, as the presupposition, not the actualisation, of their encounter and future love and marriage, is that God steps in and blesses His finished work, i.e., man in his duality, man in his relationship to the other, man as male and female, commanding him to be what he is in this relationship of man and fellow-man. The point at issue in this presupposition is in fact a divine *addicere*[EN406] to which there can correspond only an *accipere*[EN407] and not a *sumere*[EN408] on the part of man. God has finished man; and so man can only accept the fact that he is this finished man, i.e., man in duality, man who has received a helpmeet. On the other hand, we must not go too far in the direction so well indicated by Calvin, and wholly overlook the importance peculiar to the explanation given concerning man. Calvin was right again when he observed that it was not of himself but *ex arcana revelatione Dei*[EN409] that man spoke of himself as we now hear him speak. It was not he who brought it about that "this" is his helpmeet, "bone of his bones, and flesh of his flesh," and is thus to be called and to be "woman." And as he has not done it himself, he does not know it himself, but speaks prophetically when he makes this confession. But it is in his own freedom that he speaks prophetically, repeating what he has not discovered of himself, but what God has revealed to him in and with his accomplished work as the necessary positive affirmation of his humanity. It is in fact the companion created for him by God, and now introduced to him, who now speaks for herself by her being and existence, i.e., by her ἀναστοφὴ ἄνευ λόγου[EN410] as the κρυπτὸς τῆς καρδίας ἄνθρωπος ἐν τῷ ἀφθάρτῳ τοῦ πραέος καὶ ἡσυχίου πνεύματος, ὅ ἐστιν ἐνώπιον τοῦ θεοῦ πολυτελές[EN411] (1 Pet. 3¹ᶠ·) in the σιγή[EN412] (1 Cor. 14³⁴) and ἡσυχία[EN413] (1 Tim. 2¹²), in which the New Testament does not see a lack but the distinctive features of woman. The *arcana revelatio*[EN414] which man perceives and reproduces according to v. 23 is this still, quiet, soft and silent message of the work finished and presented by God. Woman created by God and brought to man reveals herself by her existence. She convinces by her presence. She cannot be mistaken, but can be recognised without any effort on her part.

For this reason, although the knowledge and confession with which man welcomes her are not his, but are dependent on the power of their object, they must be recognised as the work of his most proper freedom. His own creation is completed in an act of responsibility when, keeping to the fact created by God, and instructed by it, he now acknowledges woman

[327]

EN405 did not take a wife by his own will, but received an offering delivered by the Lord Himself
EN406 delivery
EN407 reception
EN408 taking
EN409 by the secret revelation of God
EN410 wordless conversation
EN411 the hidden man of the heart, in that which is not corruptible, even the ornament of a meek and quiet spirit, which is in the sight of God of great price
EN412 silence
EN413 quiet
EN414 secret revelation

as the "this" (*haec tandem aliquando*[EN415]), as the helpmeet granted to him for the removal of the lack still present in his own humanity. There is an echo of these words in Prov. 18[22]: "Whoso findeth a wife findeth a good thing, and obtaineth favour of the Lord." And it is worth considering whether the famous description of the "virtuous woman" in Prov. 31[10ff.] is not also to be understood against this background. Of course, to understand that this saying is really meant to be prophetical, and that it has power because it rests on revelation alone, we shall have to take into account the opposing passage in Eccl. 7[26f.] Here the final result of the exertions of human wisdom in this matter is formulated very sharply: "I find more bitter than death the woman, whose heart is snares and nets, and her hands as bands: whoso pleaseth God shall escape from her; but the sinner shall be taken by her. Behold, this have I found, saith the preacher, counting one by one, to find out the account: which yet my soul seeketh, but I find not: one man among a thousand have I found; but a woman among all those have I not found. Lo, this only have I found, that God hath made man upright; but they have sought out many inventions." A glance at Gen. 3 shows that this dark aspect was not foreign to the Yahwistic tradition either. In Gen. 2, however, the reference is to woman created by God, and to the knowledge of woman given to man by God's revelation, and not to this painful result of his own wisdom. Hence it is possible for man to make this positive confession. It is to be noted that it does not contain any value judgment. It is also to be noted that it does not contain the declaration of love which has often been sought since the days of Herder. For all the unmistakeable change of language, for all the note of joy, it is a very sober and factual assertion. The helpmeet is there, and in a form in which man cannot fail to recognise, in spite of every difference, a being of his own kind which is related to him as he is to it, and which as *'isha*[EN416] he has to accept and honour and treat as belonging to him. This plain truth is the foundation of love and marriage in the creation of God to which testimony is here given. Whatever follows—every favourable or unfavourable judgment, all love or failure to love, every selection or rejection in the historical reality of the relationship between man and woman—has its source in this basic truth.

[328]   The saying in v. 24 ("For this cause shall a man leave ... ") is taken by Delitzsch to be a continuation of Adam's speech: "In her countenance he divines the nature of marriage; in the creation of woman he sees the idea of God realised." This is a correct and profound interpretation of the verse. But from analogous passages like Gen. 10[3], 26[33] and 32[33] it may also be concluded that the narrator (Calvin: *Mose pro doctoris officio*[EN417]) is the spokesman. Either way, the verse gives the important exegetical hint that in the reading of this whole passage its true meaning is to be sought beyond its concrete content—in the time following creation. It is here that creation reaches its goal. Conversely, the goal of creation is to be seen here. The apparent contradiction of what precedes, to wit, that man is now described as one who for the sake of woman will leave father and mother and become her follower and adherent, has occasioned the suspicion that matriarchal relationships are here presupposed and expressed. Zimmerli thinks that in some respects this is done as a counter-weight, in order "to reveal the divinely given dignity of woman in face of all one-sided notions of her utility." But surely it is simpler than this. The process of courtship and marriage in historical reality—and it is to this that v. 24 refers—is what is described here whether under matriarchal or patriarchal relationships. The fact that man encounters woman—his wife—means that he begins a new life with new ties instead of the old. He thus makes a break which is not self-evident. And in so doing he confirms everything which was said about the creation of woman and everything he had confessed in face of this finished divine work of creation. She

---

[EN415] this now at last
[EN416] woman
[EN417] Moses in the role of a teacher

is his "helpmeet." Whatever his father and mother might be to him, they cannot be this. He remains their son, and must still honour them as his father and mother. But in the encounter and confrontation with his wife, he becomes a man, the independent head whose own glory is his wife. It would not be true that woman was taken out of man, that she is "bone of his bones, and flesh of his flesh," that she was brought to him by God and acknowledged by him as the needed helpmeet now given to him, if he could do other than sever his roots and become one flesh with her (thus finding himself). It is instructive to note the context in which the matter is taken up again in Eph. 5[29]. The verse is as follows: "No man ever yet hated his own flesh, but nourisheth and cherisheth it, even as the Lord the church, for we are members of his body .... For this cause shall a man leave his father and mother ...." The basis of love and marriage is not, then, the creation of woman out of man, but behind and above creation the co-existence of Christ and His community. These are the "great mystery" of Gen. 2. The view which sees in the words "shall be one flesh" only a reference to physical sexual intercourse (Gunkel) is far too crude, although this is certainly not excluded but included. What is at issue, however, is the totality of life-fellowship, the establishment of personal unity between man and woman. The aim of creation was the completion of one man in his existence as man and woman. This is what is fulfilled in their love and marriage when this takes place according to the will of God. On the other hand, it is over-subtle to try to find in the words "shall be one flesh" a reference to the necessity of monogamy (Calvin). The necessity of monogamy follows only from the fact that the one Christ and His one community are one flesh in the one fulfilled covenant. It is thus no coincidence that in the Old Testament, as is well known, monogamy does not emerge either directly in the marriage customs and marriage laws of Israel, or indirectly in the relation of *Yahweh* to Israel, which does not take the form of one but of many covenants, and in which the partner of *Yahweh* is not single, but according to the prophets has the double form of Israel and Judah. If we refuse to take the passage in conjunction with the Song of Songs and finally the New Testament, it is hardly possible to make any deduction from it in respect of monogamy as the perfect and ultimately the only possible and legitimate form of love and marriage, because, although it answers the problem implicitly, it does not do so explicitly. The same is true, of course, of the Song of Songs if we refuse to link it with Gen. 2 (and with Eph. 5). Seen in this narrower and wider context, the necessity of monogamy follows compellingly from this passage and therefore from v. 24. But only in this context!

[329]

In relation to v. 24, Jacob recalls passages like Hos. 2[3], Job 1[21] and Eccl. 5[14], where nakedness is regarded as the sign of man's dependence at birth and death, and passages like Am. 2[16] and Job 24[7, 10], where it is also regarded as an element of human need and misery. But it would be a mistake to understand the nakedness of the first couple affirmed in this passage as the "nakedness of poverty." Even among passages like 1 Sam. 19[24], Is. 20[2] and Mic. 1[8], which speak of certain prophets temporarily going about naked as signs, only the last points in this direction. And v. 25, as Jacob knows and admits, is plainly connected with Gen. 3. But in this chapter it is not their poverty of which the first couple begins to be ashamed before one another and God, but their sexuality, as is shown by the remedy they seek. That they were not ashamed of it in the act of their creation is stated in Gen. 2[25]. Again, it is too crude to say, with Gunkel, that they were not ashamed because they were still children, in a state of prepuberty which they later lost, i.e., exchanged for a state of sexual maturity—the knowledge of good and evil. The preceding verse points far too plainly to sexuality and its legitimate use to make this possible. To be naked together—and it is on the latter that the emphasis falls in v. 25—means not to be concealed from one another, but to be revealed and known without any cover. And "not to be ashamed" means not to be any embarrassment, burden or reproach to oneself or the other in this mutual knowledge, revelation and familiarity. V. 25 says that man and woman as they were created by God and proceeded from His hand had no occasion for it—indeed that it was quite impossible. Their innocence did not consist in this, but that they were innocent was revealed in it, and decisively so as the saga understands it. They were not poor in their nakedness. But they were rich in things in which later they became poor. And from this standpoint their later riches could be their real poverty. They were justified before God and each other because they were what they were. To be and to continue to be this, not of themselves but as the work of God, was the only necessity in which they stood, i.e., the necessity in the recognition of which they were free. Lacking every other justification but this, they were really justified and therefore free. Every other justification with which they later sought to protect and adorn themselves, and in so doing delivered themselves up to captivity, could only from this standpoint reveal their transformation, and at the same time the accusation brought against them without any possibility of escape or excuse. God did not create them as transgressors. There was thus no need for them to flee or to excuse themselves, even if they could have done so. They were thus free, and in the exercise of their freedom good—the good work of God. They were thus under no condemnation. And therefore they were both naked, the man and his wife, and were not ashamed.

THE YES OF GOD THE CREATOR

The work of God the Creator consists particularly in the benefit that in the limits of its creatureliness what He has created may be as it is actualised by Him, and be good as it is justified by Him.

1. CREATION AS BENEFIT

We have so far been considering the work of creation in the context in which it is the content of the divine revelation attested to us in Holy Scripture and the object of Christian faith. Its meaning and purpose as the first of all the divine works and the beginning of all things distinct from God, are to be seen in the covenant of God with man fulfilled in Jesus Christ. From this point we will now return to the question of its distinctive nature in itself and as such. What does creation mean as a divine work undertaken and completed to this end and in this sense?

One thing at least is assured by our recognition of the context, and must be presupposed in any relevant consideration of the questions. This is that divine creation is a work of a very definite character. It is not a happening on which a character is later impressed from without by a particular interpretation, so that it may in any given case be disregarded or questioned. On the contrary, a specific character is intrinsic to it (in virtue of its purpose and meaning) in its very occurrence. The revelation and perception of creation means necessarily and at once the revelation and perception of this intrinsic character. The creation of God carries with it the Yes of God to that which He creates. Divine creation is divine benefit. What takes shape in it is the goodness of God. This is the character without which it would not be a work of God.

We have already considered at an earlier point the thesis of the Early Church and the Reformation that creation is to be understood as an act of divine *gratia, misericordia, bonitas*[EN1]. This statement is not made in the void, nor need it be used with such reserve as is sometimes the case, but it is of essential importance if it is referred to the character proper to creation in virtue of its connexion with the covenant. The process whose fundamental purpose, as we have learnt from the biblical testimony to creation, is the history of salvation which culminates in Jesus Christ, cannot itself be hostile or indifferent, but can only be a benefit and can only be understood as such.

[EN1] grace, mercy, goodness

God the Creator did not say No, nor Yes and No, but Yes to what He created. There is, of course, a divine No as well: the necessary rejection of everything which by His own nature God cannot be; and consequently the necessary rejection of everything which again by His own nature God cannot will and create, and cannot even tolerate as a reality distinct from Himself. But the power of this twofold No is only the recoil of His equally twofold Yes: His Yes to Himself and to the reality which, although not identical with Him, was willed and created by Him. The latter is the divine Yes to creation. Creation is not, then, rejection. It is not the wrathful positing of the non-real by the recoil of the divine No. Creation has to do with this non-real element only in so far as it consists inevitably in its exclusion. Creation as such is not rejection, but election and acceptance. It is God's positing in accordance with His nature of a reality which is distinct from Him but willed by Him. As a work of God turned outwards it participates in the right, dignity and goodness of the Yes in which He is God by Himself. As God in creation manifests His inner being outwardly, as in supreme faithfulness and not unfaithfulness to Himself He says Yes not only to Himself but also to another, creation is divine benefit. For it is the essence of all divine and therefore all true benefit that in supreme faithfulness to Himself God rejoices in another which as such has not shared in the divine being; that He honours and approves this other within the limits of its distinct being. Creation is benefit because it takes place according to God's beneficence, and therefore according to the supreme law of all benevolence and *bene esse*[EN2]. Creation is blessing because it has unchangeably the character of an action in which the divine joy, honour and affirmation are turned towards another. What God has created is as such well done. What He has not created—the whole sphere of the non-real—is clearly to be recognised by the fact that it is not good. And if something is not good, it can be clearly recognised not to have been created by God, but to belong to the kingdom of the non-real. Only the creation of God is really outside God. And only that which really exists outside God is the creation of God. But the creation of God and therefore what really exists apart from God is as necessarily and completely the object of the divine good-pleasure, and therefore the divine benefit, as that which has not been created by God and is not therefore real must be the object of divine wrath and judgment.

This affirmation is not an irresponsible venture. It is not only permitted; it is commanded. We cannot understand the divine creation otherwise than as benefit. We are not free to think and speak in this matter otherwise or even uncertainly and equivocally. The Christian apprehension of creation requires and involves the principle that creation is benefit. It shows us God's good-pleasure as the root, the foundation and the end of divine creation. It suggests the peace with which God separated and protected what He truly willed from what He did not will, and therefore from the unreal. It implies that God Him-

[EN2] well-being

326

self, in and with the beginning of all things, decided for His creation and made Himself the responsible Guarantor of it. Creation, as it is known by the Christian, is benefit. To talk otherwise it is necessary to revoke the whole insight afforded by the biblical testimony to creation and to draw upon some other source. We can, of course, arrive at a different view if we try to learn what creation is from human conjectures concerning the beginning of all things. But we are presupposing a willingness to stand by the insights given by the biblical witness to creation. From this standpoint we have no option but to adopt the present line of thought. We may add in explanation that this statement is demanded and supported by the Christian knowledge of the Lord who alone can be the Creator at the beginning of all things. Who is this Lord? He is the God of Israel who in Jesus Christ has loved man, and sought and found him in his lostness and drawn him to Himself, averting from him the suffering of His righteous judgment, and in grace giving him life with the promise of eternal life. If the God who has expressed and revealed His nature in this way is the Creator, He has already expressed and revealed the same nature as the Creator, not saying No, or Yes and No, but an unqualified Yes to what He has really willed and created. What this God has created is good as such. Only if we lose sight of this God and His nature can we say otherwise. On the other hand we may also add in explanation that the Christian understanding of the creature renders this statement unavoidable and unshakeable. Whatever the creature be, it cannot be gainsaid that God has entered into solidarity with the human race in the history of Israel, and that in Jesus Christ He has even become a creature Himself, the Son of Man of the seed of Abraham and David. If He did not find this impossible and unworthy of Himself, then for all the difference between creaturely being and His own the former was at least an object of His good-pleasure. With a creature negated and rejected by Himself, He obviously could not enter into a covenant and even unite Himself as He has actually done in the history which finds its consummation in Jesus Christ. The fact that this covenant and union came into being shows the benefit enjoyed by the creature as such because bestowed in the act of creation. We necessarily overlook this decisive aspect of creation if we deny or even question this benefit. Our own presupposition is that this aspect cannot be overlooked and therefore that the statement is confirmed from this angle. [332]

We have to realise that any loosening or obscuring of the bond between creation and covenant necessarily entails a threat to this statement, and that it collapses altogether if this bond is dissolved. That God's creation has the character of benefit derives everywhere, as we have seen, from the fact that its fundamental purpose lies in the covenant between God and man. This is made a compelling insight by the revelation of God in Jesus Christ as the Fulfiller of the covenant attested already by the Old Testament witness to creation. But doubt falls on this character in proportion as we dissociate covenant and creation (and previously, simultaneously or subsequently the Old and New Testaments), seeking either a particular knowledge of creation alongside or outside [333]

the Christian knowledge of the covenant, or a special knowledge of the covenant alongside or outside the Christian knowledge of creation. The more firmly
such a dissociation is carried through, the less firmly our affirmation is
grounded. How can it be seriously demanded and sustained except by the
Christian knowledge of creation and covenant in their inner connexion? The
more this connexion becomes merely outward and nominal; the more the
insight into the inner unity of the works of God is replaced by the idea of a
step-like succession or juxtaposition of two intrinsically separate spheres, the
more the statement that God's creation is God's benefit becomes outward and
nominal, a mere assertion, and the more apparent it is that this character is
only incidental to the divine creation, perhaps only the result of a specific
interpretation. Whatever we may say in support of this statement apart from
the inner and real connexion between creation and covenant—the well-meant
arguments of a predominantly positive attitude of the Christian subject in face
of existence, or even the Nevertheless of Christian faith, or the simple assertion of the identity of God the Creator and God the Redeemer—does not
suffice to give the statement more than a hypothetical certainty. Grounded
only in this way, it assumes more and more the character of a mere interpretation. And it is then necessarily an irresponsible venture. But the genuine venture of this Christian affirmation is distinguished from all similar ventures by
the fact that it can be made responsibly. And the possibility of uttering it
responsibly disappears in proportion as it does not rest on the clear insight
that the truth of the covenant is already the secret of creation, that the secret
of the covenant includes the benefit of creation. The confident certainty of
this affirmation stands or falls with the fact that it is not grounded upon a good
opinion or conviction of the Christian subject, but upon this objective reality.
Only then can it also be the content of the good opinion or conviction of the
Christian subject, and therefore ventured, i.e., as a statement of faith which
implies knowledge and of which an account can be given. On the other hand,
if the weakening and obscuring of this connexion are followed by its dissolution, and the question of creation is raised independently of the knowledge
of the covenant, or the question of the covenant in abstraction from the knowledge of creation, it is left hanging in the air and can only fall. For although it
can have indirect validity where the connexion is externalised and nominal-
ised but has not completely disappeared and is not utterly denied, it is rendered quite ineffectual when the divorce between the two spheres is logically
carried through. The biblical witness both to creation and the covenant is then
weakened and can only seem uninteresting and unfruitful, being discarded,
outmoded and unimportant. For this witness lives in virtue of this inner con-
[334] nexion, and cannot be heard where the view of this connexion is fundamentally repudiated and disappears. In such circumstances the notion of benefit
cannot be attained. For God as the Benefactor is visible neither in creation nor
in the covenant. But the concepts of creation, Creator and creature, from the
correct interpretation of which this statement derives, are also robbed of their

content; for what distinguishes them from neutral categories (such as operation, cause and effect, or art, artist and work of art) is the fact that they are filled out by their connexion with the operation of a God who unassailably exists and can be regarded as a Benefactor. Where the covenant is no longer seen in creation, or creation in the covenant, the affirmation that creation is benefit cannot be sustained.

In relation to the early stages as well as the final outcome of the error to be avoided, it is worth recalling the ancient heretic Marcion and more recently Arthur Schopenhauer—a philosopher who can still be called modern when we think of F. Nietzsche, J. Burckhardt, R. Wagner, R. Steiner, S. Freud, M. Heidegger and A. Schweitzer.

The thesis of Marcion (cf. for what follows A. v. Harnack, *Marcion: Das Evangelium vom fremden Gott*, 2nd edn, 1924) stands in diametrical opposition to the principle that creation is beneficent. As he sees it, creation and benefit are mutually exclusive ideas. Only the antithesis is tenable that creation is not beneficent but maleficent. Creation as such is the origin of sheer darkness and horror, of falsehood, shame and evil. And its product, the creature, can only look forward to the dissolution corresponding to and merited by this depravity. The good activity of God not only begins when creation ceases, but is the negation and opposition of the latter. The message which announces this, the Gospel of Jesus Christ, confronts as a new and alien truth man and his world as they exist on the basis of creation and are determined by it. The salvation it promises consists in man's release from the wholly disastrous work of creation. In these circumstances there can be no question of an identity between the author of creation and the true God revealed and active in Jesus Christ; the God of salvation. Creation is the work of an inferior God only too well known to man as profane and evil; a God who even used bad material. The mark of this God is the "justice" of an envious tyrant concerned only about His own honour, rewarding submission to His will and avenging rebellion, and in all His undertakings—primarily in the creation and determination of man, but also in the organisation and equipment of the cosmos, and the direction of history—revealing himself as a crude, ignorant and petty bungler, supremely suspicious and unkind, and in the last resort care-ridden and impotent. This bad Creator-God with His justice is the God of the equally bad Jewish people which He chose with blind particularity; the God of the Old Testament. His bad spokesmen and servants are the Old Testament patriarchs and prophets. His bad revelation in the Law, with its external, fleshly, capricious and cruel demands. His bad Christ is the Old Testament Messiah, the long-awaited world-ruler of the Jews. In Jesus this inferior God was confronted by the superior and true God, who was quite unexpected by the man created by the former, whose way was quite unprepared by the world and history as ordered and ruled by Him, who was indeed hampered by the whole economy of the Old Testament—a *Deus alienus*[EN3] whose nature is the pure, generous, non-violent, patient omnipotence of love and whose it is to espouse in pure mercy the cause of a wholly alien creature man, freeing him—all men—from the power of his Creator and enabling him to participate in a new and eternal life. He did this by anticipating, in the person of His Son, the Son of the world-Creator, i.e., the Jewish Messiah, and by refusing to become a man of flesh—which would have meant approving the creation of the bad God— but by taking a human form and thus being in a position to act and suffer as a man among men and on their behalf. He became the Friend of publicans and sinners, who were the enemies of the Old Testament God. By His Word and will alone He healed countless people who were forced to suffer by the Creator-God. And when He penetrated to the underworld,

[335]

[EN3] alien God

He freed the prisoners of the Jewish God who longingly welcomed Him: Cain, the Sodomites, the Egyptians and all the Gentiles, but not Abel, Enoch, Abraham, Moses, who were excluded from salvation by their positive relationship to the inferior God. After suffering on the cross the death accursed by the God of the world and the Jews, and thus paying the ransom price of creation, He raised Himself from the dead, and as the One who has overcome the evil world He is the future Saviour of all those who, united in the Church which is the new creation founded by Him, believe in Him already in this world, and prove their faith by the fact that as they are able (e.g., by abstinence from sexual procreation, from flesh and wine and worldly lusts, etc.) they oppose the Creator-God, as Jesus Christ Himself did in the realm of creation, and again in His discipleship know how to love their enemies and to reward evil with good in contrast to the Old Testament Law, bringing forth the fruit of good works in freedom from all fear. Their hope lies in the world judgment which will be executed by the alien God in Jesus Christ and by which non-believers, those who are only "righteous," are not of course punished—for this would contradict the nature of the true God—but must perish in accordance with their nature, as the Creator and His whole age and work will also perish, whereas believers, having finally discarded the earthly body, will share the gracious gift of eternal life.

Side by side with this we must set the doctrine of Schopenhauer as presented particularly in the fourth volume of *Die Welt als Wille und Vorstellung* (1st edn 1819, revised and expanded 1844 and 1859). Here, too, we find diametrical opposition to the statement that creation is beneficent. The world is object in relation to subject, formed on the one hand by space and time as the principle of individuation, and on the other through ideas as the external forms of things. It is an object of knowledge to the extent that by its submission to the principle of causation it can be investigated; and it is an object of art to the extent that in detail, and outside that causal relationship, it can be contemplated. Such is the world as idea, as phenomenon, as the veil of Maya. But the objectification of knowledge and art, and therefore the world as idea, is itself only the reflection of a very different kind of objectification and a very different world, the real world, that of will, which is immediately known to me in the action of my own body not merely as idea but in each present, and in which (if I am not to be guilty of a fantastic sceptical egoism) I have to recognise the thing in itself, the key to the essence of all phenomena. This is the will for life, whose proper, intelligible and therefore free, powerful and undying Subject is hidden in the will of empirical individuals who are subjected to necessity and who come into being and perish. It is active as the true source of their *agens*[EN4], and can always be more or less apparent in man. The nature of the world of phenomena may be known in man, and his will is faced by the question whether it is going to follow the motives offered by the world of phenomena, or whether it will serve the recognition of the true nature of the world along the path of quietism, i.e., whether it is prepared to affirm or deny itself as the will which wills and conceives this world. The nature of the phenomenal world can and must be seen in the action of our own body, and therefore in the will for life itself to the extent that this is an object of our conception, and decisively and comprehensively in its form as sexual desire ("the genitals are the real focal point of the will"). And it is revealed as the boundless and intrinsically aimless striving of the human race towards its own continuance and renewal; a longing which springs from need and discontent, and which can be fulfilled only in further need and discontent. In great things as in small, life offers itself to us as perpetual deception. It does not keep its promises except to show how little desirable was that which we desired. If it gave it was only to take. Happiness always lies in the future or the past. The present is comparable to a small dark cloud which the wind drives over a sunny surface. Everything is bright before it and behind it. But wherever it goes, it can

[336]

[EN4] agency

only cast a shadow. Life is thus essentially suffering. It is the constant bearing of a great pain which can only be increased by wishes and their fulfilment. Life is a continuous oscillation between unrest springing from what we lack and tedium flowing from the objects of our desire which perish as they are grasped. Life is a matter of care and conflict with the certainty that we shall finally lose it. It is a sea full of rocks and whirlpools with the certain prospect of shipwreck. Even when conducted happily and cleverly it is a walking on ground which is undermined. Art itself can redeem it only for a small minority, and for this minority only in the form of passing dreams. It can picture to us only the struggle for happiness, not happiness itself. Every melody consists only in the abandonment and resumption of the basic note, which would only be the more painful if it were persistently maintained. Life is merely death delayed and restrained—the death which must finally conquer, seeing we are its victims from birth. Life plainly carries the stamp of something to be suffered by us. In detail it is a comedy of petty errors and confusions. As a whole it is a real tragedy shaped by the will for life at its own expense; one of the many imperfect and transient dreams of the infinite spirit of nature. Such is each individual human life. Are we not happiest when we are least aware of our own existence, and does not this prove that it would be better not to be at all? Who would wish to live his life a second time? Is not the best part of life the fact that it is so short? Life a gift? Who among us, if only we could have surveyed and tested it beforehand, would not have declined the gift? Only a blind, unseeing will could place itself in the position in which we are. And so the whole as a whole, and human history, is one great sphere of accident and error, of folly and evil, in which what is excellent is only an exception proving the rule. Thus we can only say of the world in general—and this is shown already by its theoretical problems—that in effect it ought not to exist. In the words of Mephistopheles: "For all that comes to be deserves to perish. Hence it were better, it had not come to be." Where did Dante derive his vision of hell if not from the real world? No, life in this world is not a gift; it is a debt which we contract with our birth, the interest having to be paid during our life-time, and the capital with our death. "The best of all possible worlds?" On the contrary, the world is as bad as it possibly can be if it is to be at all. Optimism ? It is the unjustified self-praise of the real originator of the world, the will for life, complacently viewing its own image. It is not just an absurd mode of thought, but positively outrageous in its scornful disregard for the inexpressible suffering of humanity. There is indeed an eternal justice, but it consists only in the fact that on the whole the misery of man is not greater than his unworthiness, that his guilt and pain are on the whole equally balanced. Hence right can only mean the necessary prevention of the attempts of some to exercise too egotistically their will for life by impeding and destroying the will for life no less essential to others. Goodness is the recognition and corresponding respecting (*tat tvam asi*: That art thou!) of the will for life in the alien appearance known to us only by conception. Love is compassion (even to the point of renouncing one's own rights) as opposed to the self-seeking of *eros*. If we adopt radically and consistently the perception of the world of ideas and the constituent principle of individuation which begins in right, goodness and love, we are led to a pacification of the will, and the affirmation of the will for life is converted into its denial. Desire is thus replaced by renunciation, striving by quietude and ambition by resignation, as taught in the New Testament, and even more profoundly in Christian asceticism and mysticism, and most profoundly of all in the religious ethical wisdom of the Indians as the "second way" of self-denial. This cannot be [337] fulfilled by suicide, by which we negate life but not the will for life, and evade the sacrifice which is really required, but by the voluntary renunciation of sexuality, by voluntary poverty and self-castration, etc. But it is not to be attained by any theorising, because, arising from the most inward relationship of insight and will, it suddenly strikes the empirical individual like a blow from without, and with the increase of age the decline of energy naturally promotes the surrender of illusions and the diminution of the will. To this extent it is grace, and the first and also the last act of the will itself, the sole direct manifestation of its freedom. In it the veil of Maya is torn asunder. The thing in itself emerges. We then see—and this is not frightening, but the source and essence of all comfort—that the whole of this real world of ours, with all its suns and milky ways, is nothing. As the will fades, conception also fades. The world is no more. Nothingness, as it arose from nothing, returns to nothing. Redemption has become a fact. Understood in this way the doctrines of original sin (the affirmation of the will symbolised in the person and act of the empirical man Adam) and of redemption (the denial of the will symbolised in the person and act of the intelligible man Christ) are the great truth of Christianity, while everything else, and especially everything connected with an individual (non-docetic) interpretation of Christ, is only its vesture, veil, vehicle and Jewish accretion.

For all their differences, the views of Marcion and Schopenhauer have at the decisive point, namely, in the opposition to the affirmation that divine creation is benefit, a common origin as well as a common conclusion. Both derive their force from a consistent abstraction at the place where, for the Christianity which keeps to revelation, there exists a close and clear connexion. Both stem from a basic and definitive separation between creation and the divine covenant, though they develop this in opposite directions. Thus, although at their point of departure they seem to face opposite ways, they necessarily agree in the mistaken antithesis that creation is an evil.

The obvious intention of Marcion is to look wholly and exclusively to the covenant. If only he had seen the real covenant! But the fact that his abstraction has this in view is what seems to render his doctrine so plausibly Christian. God is for him wholly and utterly the love manifest in Christ. There are few Christian theologians who refer faith so strictly to God's revealing work in Christ, who so earnestly try to connect it with Christ alone, as this heretic did. That is why Harnack thought he could speak, in obvious commendation, of Marcion's Pan-Christism. But all that glitters is not gold. Marcion's Christology is in fact docetic. He maintains that the unknown God did not become man in Christ, but only the likeness of man with an illusory body. But this means that the uniqueness of the revelation and work of this unknown God becomes at this point only an empty conceptual assertion not corresponding to any observation. And this means above all that there cannot be a Gospel of this unknown God because even in Christ He has confronted man in alien form, and remained alien, not entering into solidarity with him. The whole gracious and merciful love for which Marcion praises Him was not so great that it could even be truly revealed to man, let alone save him. This Christ—and here too Marcion could only assert the contrary—could not speak, act, suffer, die and rise again. Deprived of their natural connexion with a real man, these statements are all irrelevant. If they do not say that a man did all these things, they say nothing at all. And it depends on just these statements whether we can believe that it was the true Son of the true God who freed man and brought him eternal life. The God who remains aloof—although He is the epitome of love, but only its epitome—can only exclude and not include man and the creature. The creature cannot in truth believe in Him. If He is incapable of Himself becoming man, He is also incapable of entering into real fellowship with man, of being the resurrection and life of man. This is implied by the statement which [338] Harnack is so fond of quoting and which is supposed to have formed the beginning of Marcion's *Antitheses*: "O wonder of wonders, rapture, might and astonishment, that man can neither say nor think anything concerning the Gospel, nor compare it with anything!" Marcion's whole message of joy and emancipation has a hollow ring against this background. There is no doubt that Marcion's gaze is directed towards the covenant. And his aim is to look in this direction with the eyes of the one apostle Paul and in accordance with a New Testament purified from all Jewish accretions and misunderstandings. But his view is too radical, and in the last analysis too secular, for him to be able to see what is really to be seen here. He purifies the New Testament so drastically that he cannot appreciate its true Christ, and His existence even in Israel, and the connexion of the whole of the New Testament with the whole of the Old. He apprehends the witness of Paul the Jew only in a violently distorted form. In his view, therefore, the covenant becomes a fruitless antithesis between the fixed idea of pure Godhead and a humanity *a priori*[EN5] excluded from it because in view of its sheer novelty and transdencence the former cannot concern it, much less enter into a covenant with it in accordance with the assertion that it is love. In Marcion's view the covenant is not really a covenant at all. The result is obvious. Because he refuses to see the true humanity of Christ, and therefore cannot understand the covenant, he can interpret true man and creation as a whole only independently of fellowship with the true God revealed in Christ. Hence he cannot understand this true God as the Creator. And in the Creator he can see only another and inferior God who is only just and not loving. Hence in creation (since this God is its author) he can see only an evil deed which cannot possibly be described as beneficent and the reversal of which is the only concrete form of the hope of redemption. Where the humanity of Christ is denied and by implication the covenant, Israel and the Old Testament, the Creator and creation, are all necessarily placed on the left hand and cast into outer darkness. And this result is all the more certain, the more insistently the divinity of Christ is also proclaimed. Hand in hand with his denial of Christ's humanity, Marcion laid the greatest possible emphasis on His divinity, and with a supreme logical consistency hardly attained by any other Docetic he grasped and stated the consequent position of Israel and the Old Testament, the Creator and creation. The aim and fulfilment of the real covenant is Christ as very God and very man in one person. Thus the real covenant does not exclude but includes Israel and the Old Testament, the Creator and creation. If we see the real covenant, things which for Marcion are outside Christ and in darkness are set in the light of Christ. The merit of Marcion is not to have evaded the consequences of negating this connexion, and therefore to have exposed the true basis of every denial of the statement that creation is benefit—a basis which is no less effective and menacing even in less consistent negations of the connexion.

Schopenhauer succeeded in reaching the same result by abstracting in the opposite direction and focusing his attention on creation. His concentration of vision is admirable. But the truth to be apprehended is necessarily concealed from him because his view too is far too radical and secular. The revelation and work of God in Christ and therefore the covenant do not exist at all in the picture which he draws. Thus his view of the world is inevitably as godless as Marcion's view of God is world-less. His intention is the very opposite of that of Marcion. But its fulfilment brings the two together. When subsequently and incidentally, in illustration of his very different view of creation and redemption, he comes to speak of Christ, he emphatically guards himself against ascribing any saving meaning to the empirical individual man Jesus, and confesses himself a Docetic (with express reference to the Marcionite Apelles). The only thing is that he obviously has a truer appreciation than Marcion of the secret of Docetism—that the divinity of Christ is not bound up with His appearance in the flesh, but essentially independent of it, and perceptible at other points [339] as well. Hence he does not argue either from God in Christ or even from God at all, but in free contemplation from a being freely described as such—the being of man. God is not denied outright. But the fact that He remains aloof and unknown is implied in the self-evident presupposition of his teaching, that He is obviously absent. It is the world which is present, and this not as the creation of God but as an objectification of will and idea, of human will and human idea. What remains of Creator, creature and creation in

---

[EN5] unconditionally

Schopenhauer's worldview is simply man himself, whose will has its focal point in the genitals, and whose power of conception is at once the author and weaver and the bearer and contemplator of the veil of Maya. The world and his life within it is produced and shaped as a work, but both as regards its intelligible archetype and its empirical image it is his own work, the proper work of the man who exists both intelligibly and empirically, both freely and necessarily. Man himself is both creator and creature, and in the affirmation of the will for life he is continually involved in the work of creation. He has to thank himself alone, and is responsible only to himself, for the existence and apprehension of the world and himself. It is thus his business, by the exercise of right, goodness and love, to draw nearer and nearer to the proper recognition that the world and he himself are in the last resort nothing. And it is his duty to give effect to this insight, and thus become his own saviour as well as his own creator, by the negation of the will for life which overtakes him in disruptive grace supported by the natural process of growing old. As Marcion excludes man from the covenant, so Schopenhauer excludes God from creation. And as in Marcion's scheme creation is lost sight of in the covenant, so in the scheme of Schopenhauer the covenant is lost sight of in creation. And again the result is obvious, and it inevitably agrees with the view of Marcion. When creation is viewed in isolation from God, as the world of human will and idea, it can only be shrouded in the darkness in which Marcion envelops it by his isolation of God from creation. It is obviously no great gain to man that according to Schopenhauer he has usurped the place of God, and it is significant that, in contrast to Hegel and other recent philosophers who agree with him in this, Schopenhauer perceived, and not merely admitted but proclaimed with a wealth of invective which only increased as he grew older, that man the creator-god is as such fundamentally foolish, wicked, guilty and condemned; that the fault of this creator-god with all his fictions and illusions is to have been born at all; that the creature which is its own creator can as such and essentially be only the inhabitant of a vale of tears, punished with constant disillusionment and the immediate victim of mortality; and that the creative process as the ontic and noetic producing and fashioning of this man (subjective and objective genitive) is nothing but the work of a bungler, wholly maleficent and not beneficent. Excellently seen and stated! This is what man has to thank himself for! It only remains for him to appreciate this state of affairs, and to draw the practical conclusion that a bungler's job of this kind must be undone and finally destroyed. It deserves only to perish. Man must return whence he has come, not beginning all over again, or doing again what he has done, but renouncing all further ontic and noetic creative activity and retiring from the post of creator-god, so that he has no longer to be his own creature. Confronted by his view of the evil character of creation, Schopenhauer obviously finds that he is not in a position to help himself out by a reinterpretation *in meliorem partem*[EN6]. Why not? And how does he really know what he pretends to know? In the last resort he can arrive at this knowledge only because he has viewed the being of the world and life and man without and apart from God, so that he has not seen the real but the unreal creation in all its abstractness and unreality because divorced from the covenant and the divinity of the man Jesus, and has necessarily had to understand it and speak of it in those terms. What he knows, he knows finally on the basis of the ignorance of God presupposed in his conception of the world and life and man. He knows what he knows after negating the nexus of creation and covenant, and facing honestly (more honestly than so many others who directly or indirectly deny this nexus) the (unreal) state of affairs which consequently fills the field of his vision. Schopenhauer did not shrink from this honesty, although he might easily have sought refuge in an aesthetic world-view. This is his greatness. For an honest gaze the creation from which God is excluded can only be evil. And its author—the man who is guilty of the caprice of trying to

[340]

[EN6] in a better light

replace God Himself as Creator—can have no more ardent wish than to see his own creation, which is nothingness and arose from nothingness, return as quickly and radically as possible to nothingness, and thus redeem himself (ironically) by participating in a redemption which comes upon him from without. It is Schopenhauer's great merit to have faced and stated this unflinchingly. His pessimism cannot be refuted once his presuppositions are granted.

Where we think abstractly instead of concretely at the decisive point we are already on the way to the result which Marcion and Schopenhauer both, attained—that creation is evil and not good. And it is only a question of logical consistency and honesty whether we reach this conclusion or evade it. That is why a warning must now be given against taking the first step.

The character of divine creation consists materially, as we shall see in the two sub-sections which follow, in the fact that what God willed to create and has created may be, and be good. The creation of God is the actualisation and justification of the creature. In this it is benefit. We conclude this introductory consideration with an observation which in the light of this applies to the Christian doctrine of creation as a whole.

Its theme is the work of God which is characterised by the fact that—because the covenant is its basic purpose and meaning and God in Jesus Christ is the Creator—it is divine benefit. The character of its theme, established in his way, is what distinguishes the Christian doctrine of creation from all the so-called world-views which have emerged or may conceivably emerge in the spheres of mythology, philosophy and science. It differs from all these by the fact that it is based on God's revelation. But this is not merely a formal difference. It is also material. The Christian doctrine of creation does not merely take its rise from another source. It also arises very differently from all such world-views. It not only has a different origin, but has a different object and pursues a different course. The divine activity which is its object can never become the theme of a world-view.

The truth of this assertion is seen at once from the fact that none of the world-views so far known to us has attained to the concept of creation by following to the end the way from noetics to ontology and geneseology, but has usually remained stuck either in noetics or at most in ontology. The philosophical equivalent for the theological idea of divine creation would have to be at least that of a pure and basic becoming underlying and therefore preceding all perception and being. But the world-views normally take their point of departure within the circle of perception and being, subject and object, and are content to describe it according to the relationships determined by a particular [341] view, the variations and differences, progressions and retrogressions, between the individual systems being so great that on the one hand the universe seems to be more like a great thought, and on the other more like a great machine. In some cases the basic problem of becoming, the question of the whence of the universe, whether it be conceived as thought or machine, is not even noticed but naively ignored. In others it is not overlooked but consciously left open, with a resigned or emphatic assertion of its inherent unanswerability. In others again there may be an attempt to answer it, but only in the form of a geneseologically deepened noetics or ontology, so that it is not really answered but only distorted. For the problem of becoming as opposed to that of knowledge or being is a new and independent problem which cannot be answered by any interpretation of knowledge and being and their mutual relationship. It must be viewed independently if it is to escape the suspicion that it has not really been viewed at all.

If we survey the history of the world-views so far advanced it cannot be disputed that the independent problem of the nature of pure becoming is objectively present in them all, whether perceived, distorted or ignored, and that it lies within their field of vision (intentionally or otherwise) at least as a disturbing margin and border to their picture. The Christian doctrine of creation destroys itself if it accepts the possibility of a world-view which does not have objectively this disturbing margin. It can thus concede that all the world-views which have emerged and found some measure of recognition have been objectively concerned with an equivalent for the theological idea of divine creation, at least to the extent that the question of the whence of the circle of knowledge and being which is their main concern is for them too a boundary and mysterious background. And by its very existence, by its representation of the idea of divine creation, it will also remind them that this background of theirs is still mysterious, that they have not yet answered the question prior to all the questions to which they have given their different answers, and that to this extent they have built their systems in the air.

It is inadvisable, however, to affirm that from the standpoint of the Christian doctrine of creation this prior question is essentially unanswerable, or to contest in principle the possibility that the independent problem of pure becoming might be seen in undistorted form and positively answered even in a mythical, philosophical or scientific world-view, and therefore that at least a discussable equivalent might be advanced—which has not so far been the case—alongside the theological concept of creation in an independent geneseology, instead of remaining obscurely in the background. It cannot be the business of theology to decide in what new "dimensions" myth might one day be able to express itself, philosophy to think, or science to investigate; and [342] it is quite improper for theology to assume *a priori*[EN7] an attitude of scepticism. If a future philosophical system ventures an answer to the prior question, hitherto disregarded or left open or distorted, which underlies all other philosophical questions, then from the standpoint of the Christian doctrine of creation it has not only to be said that this attempt is motivated by genuine necessity, but that it cannot be refused the keenest interest and attention.

But a new doctrine of pure becoming advanced as an equivalent for the theological concept of divine creation can be admitted only if this doctrine is able to show as unequivocally as is the case in the Christian doctrine of cre-

---

[EN7] unconditionally

ation that this pure becoming is pure divine benefit preceding all knowledge and being and underlying all knowledge and being. Thus the idea of pure becoming to be developed by this future system cannot be that of an event which is neutral in face of the weal and woe of the evolving and evolved cosmos. It cannot be a blank page still to be covered by specific interpretations. Like the theological concept of divine creation, it must be characterised from the very outset as the epitome of pure benefit. As a concept of pure becoming it must be an affirmation both of that which becomes and of that which has become. No less is required of this future system if it is to be of real interest to theology. Whether it has achieved this or not must first be investigated before it can be granted that it is really dealing with divine creation (although in other terms), and that the latter is not exclusively the theme of the Christian doctrine of creation.

We have seen, however, that the statement that creation is divine benefit is rooted solely and exclusively in the connexion between creation and covenant, and therefore in the recognition that God is the Creator in Jesus Christ. Only from this standpoint can it be decisively affirmed that creation is benefit, and to what extent this is the case. There can obviously be no question of a philosophical equivalent to this basis. The statement has this basis, or it has none at all. A future philosophy in its doctrine of pure becoming would have to decide on this basis, or it would not be able to make this decision. We have seen that this decision cannot be reached on any other basis. On any other basis a future scheme of thought is logically doomed to end up with Marcion and Schopenhauer. But if this is the case, a future world-view distinguished by a clear and genuine geneseology must necessarily cease to be a mere worldview. At the decisive juncture it must necessarily become identical with the Christian doctrine of creation. If it does not become theological at this point, and base itself on the datum of divine revelation, then, in spite of the disclosure of its new dimension, even as a doctrine of pure becoming it is not a securely based and necessary doctrine of the benefit of this becoming or of this becoming as the epitome of all benefit, and therefore it is still as different as ever—not merely in words but in substance—from the Christian doctrine of creation, being addressed to a different object.

Clearly we are faced at this point by the fundamental difference between the [343] Christian doctrine of creation and every existent or conceivable world-view. The formal difference that the former, as theology, is concerned only with divine revelation, whereas the latter, as non-theological thinking, reckons only with such apprehension of the cosmos as is possible to unaided reason, is materially confirmed on both sides by the fact that theology has to recognise and confess creation as benefit because it is the work of God in Jesus Christ, whereas philosophy is intrinsically incapable of doing this. In order to treat—even in other words—of the divine creation which has this character, a worldview must itself become theology, just as theology ceases to be true to itself, necessarily becoming a type of philosophical thinking, if it concerns itself with the problem of pure becoming without this character. In view of the decision regarding this character, it is no less essential to philosophy than to theology that the objects as well as the grounds of knowledge are different. Hence it follows that the Christian doctrine of creation must pursue its own path according to its special ground and object and independently of any and every established or future philosophical system. The implications may be briefly noted.

1. It cannot itself become a world-view. If it tries to do so, it abandons its special object, which is distinguished by the special character of divine creation from the object of every world-view. And if it can try to do so, in order not to remain without object it must renew contact at once with its proper object, and thus transmute itself afresh from a philosophical scheme into theology.

2. It cannot base itself on any world-view. For there is no world-view, ancient or modern, established or conceivable, which is capable of supporting it in the grounding and accomplishment of its investigation and representation of creation as divine benefit. Those already established inevitably mislead it by their inadequate handling of the problem of pure becoming; and those conceivable will always seduce it by their inevitable hesitation to maintain that creation is benefit. Hence it cannot allow itself to attach itself to any of them.

3. It cannot guarantee any world-view. For if a world-view which has grown conscious of the problem of pure becoming conies closer to it than one which ignores this problem, or leaves it an open question, or can only gloss it over by noetics or ontology, and if one which comes to grips with it as an independent problem comes closer to it than all those which think they can elude the necessity of this step, it is under no obligation to lend its support to any of them, because in face of the question which it regards as of decisive importance, even the better ones which come closest to it necessarily hesitate.

4. It cannot come to terms with these views, adopting an attitude either of partial agreement or partial rejection. On the one hand, it does not contradict them at all, for it sees them pursue to the end their chosen path in the responsibility which they have undertaken and in which it can have nothing to say to them. But, on the other hand, it contradicts them radically, for in the last resort it necessarily considers their choice of method and principle to be mistaken.

5. Its own consideration of these views is carried out in such a way that it presents its own recognition of its own object with its own basis and consistency, not claiming a better but a different type of knowledge which does not exclude the former but is developed in juxtaposition and antithesis to it. From its encounter with these views it expects for itself an increasing elucidation and precision of its own attitude to its own theme, and for the systems that, as their exponents hear the uninterrupted witness to God the Creator and are thus brought to realise that their restricted positing of the question is fundamen-

[344]

tally superseded, they will be invited at the very least to improve them, and finally to abandon them altogether.

6. As a part of Christian dogmatics it pursues its own special task, which is imposed upon it in the service of the Church's proclamation, and which consists in an increasing unqualified and full apprehension, and faithful and exact reproduction, of the self-witness of the Creator in His revelation, and therefore of the biblical witness to creation. If the world-views cannot help it in this, neither will allow itself to be disturbed by them in it. Understanding the creation of God as benefit, it proceeds independently, and is not embarrassed to confess that in regard to the creation sagas of Genesis, for example, it expects no material and direct help from any world-view, ancient, modern or future.

It is for these reasons that the problems posed in natural theology and the philosophy of religion cannot be taken into account in this exposition of the Christian doctrine of creation. Our conversation with the exponents of world-views will be conducted directly.

2. CREATION AS ACTUALISATION

That God as Creator has not said No, or Yes and No, but unequivocally Yes to what He has created, means in the first place that He has actualised it. The benefit of creation consists in the fact that the creature may be, and therefore is, through its Creator; that it is in its own creaturely mode, conditioned and determined by its dependence on the being of the Creator, and therefore distinct from and not to be compared with Him; but that it really is, that it is not not, or not merely an appearance, or the subject of an illusion or dream. There are such things, of course, as appearances, illusions and dreams. And on a closer view, much that is described in this way is a special form of reality. But in the divine creation there is no such thing as mere appearance, no illusion which is mere illusion, no dream without an object, no form which is only a [345] form of nothingness. God has created nothing to which He could only say No because of its inherent unreality. God's creation is affirmed by Him because it is real, and it is real because it is affirmed by Him. Creation is actualisation. Hence the creature is reality. No creature is rooted in itself, or maintained by itself, but each is willed, posited, secured and preserved by God, and therefore each in its place and manner is genuine reality. The reality of God Himself stands protectively above and behind it. The creature may be because God is. The creature is because God is its Creator. And because God is, and is its Creator, the creature may say after Him: I am also, and to his fellow-creature: Thou art also, and of this creature: He, or she, or it is also. Creaturely existence is the benefit of creation. And therefore recognition of creaturely existence means recognition of the benefit of creation on the ground of the self-disclosure of the Creator.

Only in this way can this recognition be attained and securely grounded and successfully maintained. Our consciousness of ourselves and the world, i.e., our awareness and conception of our ego, and of people and things existing outside ourselves, might well be a matter of mere supposition, of pure appearance, a form of nothingness, and our step from consciousness to being a hollow fiction. It is not true that we have an immediate awareness of our own or any other reality. It is only true that we immediately suppose that we have such an awareness. It is only true that we instinctively suppose that we and other beings exist, and that our consciousness implies actual existence, that of ourselves and of others. The negative assertion that it does not do so naturally goes too far. On what grounds can we know that nothing is real, that supposed reality is nothingness? Why should not our consciousness actually imply existence? The supposition that it does so is irrefutable. On the other hand, the positive assertion that it does so also goes too far. How can we be sure that supposed reality is real? When, where and how do we take the step by which our consciousness is in fact able to control our own being or that of others? The supposition pointing in this direction is irrefutable; but it is also unprovable. In support of the positive hypothesis we can only point out that as a rule we behave as if it were valid and the negative hypothesis invalid. The difference is in truth not inconsiderable. We assume being and not appearance or non-being. We live in the strength of this and not the opposite supposition. We live in and by the healthy opinion that we are, that something is. But in itself this is not better founded than the morbid idea that we are not, and that nothing is. We are certainly not in a position to verify our healthy idea and raise it into a certitude. We can persuade ourselves that we are certain on this point but it is only a matter of persuasion. Always beneath our feet there yawns the gulf of the possibility that our healthy opinion might be deceiving us, that it might actually turn out that nothing is real, that supposed reality is nothingness. And bound up with this is the fact that not even the principle that we behave "as if" is altogether unambiguous. For in fact how far do we really conduct ourselves as those who at least honestly confess their healthy opinion? Is not our conduct to a large extent that of people who live as if they were not, and for whom the world too is as though it were not? When and where, even in the light of our actual "as if" conduct, do we become indubitable guarantors of this good opinion, this irrefutable but also unprovable supposition? The nihilism which is implicit and often enough explicit in the human mode of life, which can never be quite suppressed and which it is better not to deny, calls in question the validity of this supposition. Thus in point of fact we live without knowing that we are or that anything is. We may well attempt to persuade ourselves that the world is real. But such an attempt cannot deliver us from the vicious circle of consciousness and being which might equally well be the circle of pure appearance. In making this attempt, we might be engaged in a constant repetition of this circle.

To affirm that we are, that something is, with any sense of security, we have

[346]

340

not merely to say this, but to be authorised and inescapably compelled to say it. Such an affirmation has to be based on and guaranteed by the fact that we say it because it has first been said to us. A higher Judge must have intervened between our consciousness and our supposed intrinsic and extrinsic being, and decided that our consciousness does not deceive us, and that our being is no imaginary being. That we are and that something is, instead of being a probable truth in the circle of our consciousness and being, has to become overwhelmingly and compellingly clear from the standpoint of the source from which it is objectively true; from the place where the noetic-ontological X, in which we suppose our existence grounded, is securely proved to exist; and thus from an originally and intrinsically and therefore indubitably exist-ent being, which as such is the ground of everything else that exists, and there-fore of our own existence. If we are the creation of a real Creator, we ourselves are real. Our consciousness would not deceive us either about ourselves or what exists outside us. The life of which we are conscious both in and outside ourselves is not a mere supposition, but within its limits (in its distinction from the life which is its basis) a true life. And if we are informed by this real Creator that we are His creatures, we do not merely suppose but know that on the basis of this information we really are. Our I-consciousness and world-consciousness is then removed from the sphere of appearance. In this case our being is pres-ent in the form of the information given. We are forbidden to doubt existence and ourselves. It is incumbent on us to be conscious of being and to recognise the reality of existence. We no longer live as if a positive hypothesis were valid and a negative one invalid. We are no longer dependent on the validity or [347] otherwise of any hypothesis. We no more live as if matters were thus or thus. We have no other choice but the decisive recognition, without any shadow of ambiguity, of the reality of the created world and ourselves, and the life founded upon this recognition.

We have to be told by our Creator that we and all that exists outside us are His creatures. Then in assured recognition we can and must and may and will also say that we are, that something is. This has to be said to us. Thus we are not referring to the content of an immediate consciousness of God which is bound up with our consciousness of ourselves and the world and originally underlies it. Let us suppose that there is such a thing; that it is characteristic of the essence of the created spirit; that apart from its self-consciousness and consci-ousness of the world it possesses also the capacity (perhaps to be exercised *via negationis, eminentiae*[EN8] and *causalitatis*[EN9]) to form the idea of a most perfect being; or more, that this is the most characteristic and all-comprehensive fac-ulty of spirit; that in the formation of this idea it develops its own deepest essence; and finally that this idea deserves to be called the idea of God, and the

---

[EN8] the ways of negation, eminence
[EN9] causation

341

peculiar consciousness from which it springs deserves to be called the consciousness of God. All this does not materially help us to cross the bridge from mere consciousness to the apprehension of the truth of being, to the recognition of existence. If our consciousness of God has to guarantee for our ego and our consciousness of the world that we are concerned with being itself and not mere appearance, then obviously the idea of God has also to be something more than a mere idea. God Himself has to exist if the idea of God is required to vouch to us for the real existence of what is otherwise known to us only in consciousness; if our sense of God is really to raise our self-consciousness and consciousness of the world into an apprehension of objective reality. But how are we to know that God really exists, and that our idea of God is more than a mere idea? The famous argument from the perfection of the being of God to His existence seems far too much like our hypothesis that we are and that something is. It resembles far too closely the problem which it is meant to solve. It is too much involved in the vicious circle of consciousness and being (which might equally well be a matter of appearance) for us to be able to derive much comfort from it. It may well be that it belongs to the essence of the creaturely mind to conceive this idea and indeed the idea of the existing God which in itself implies this existence. It may well be the case that in such an argument we have to do with the most characteristic and immediate act of the creaturely mind. There is no question that we always desire to be certain of existence, reality and being. Our very self-consciousness and consciousness of the world with its grand conceptions is a witness to this. And so it may well be that our consciousness of God—or, if we like to put it this way, our consciousness of a perfect being which as such also exists—is the crowning testimony to [348] this supreme desire which in itself is obviously deep rooted and inescapable. Why should it not be so? But to desire and to attain our desire are two different things even when the desire is thought to be so deeply rooted in our inmost being, and to be the most proper and immediate act of the creaturely mind. The fact that existence is integral to our idea of God as the most perfect being does not at all distinguish it from our ideas of the self and the world. Our idea of God unfortunately has it in common with our ideas of the self and the world that the mere assertion of the existence of its object is just as irrefutable but also just as unprovable as the assertion of the existence of the objects of the latter—and no doubt less profound or exalted—ideas. This perfect being, too, may be the subject of the hypothesis that it is, but it is also subject to the suspicion that it may not be. But if this supreme idea has not the power to vouch for the reality of its special object, it obviously does not have the power to guarantee the reality of the objects of those other ideas, the reality of creaturely existence. We do not at all escape the sphere of the ambiguity of our intrinsic and extrinsic being if we attempt to broaden it by pointing to the validity of our immediate apprehension of God. By so doing we can only circle round it once more and illustrate it at a greater depth. We are in a sense occupying ourselves with the highest and deepest things, but we are still only trying to persuade ourselves that we ourselves are and something is even though we attempt to base this assertion on the idea of God. Hence we have only re-emphasised and reiterated the supposition which is so necessary to our life, and given expression to our immediate and inescapable desire. But even in view of our consciousness of God we are thrown back upon the necessity of living "as if" we knew what in fact we do *not* know.

The fact that we are told by our Creator that we and what is outside us are His creatures is not, therefore, interchangeable with the immediate consciousness of God, however things may stand with the latter. Our reference is to the divine self-disclosure which corresponds to the reality of the Creator. Hence we are not concerned about an extension of our consciousness, but about a vital confrontation of our consciousness, and about the new insights to which this alone gives rise and which we can acquire only as we acknowledge this confrontation. Just as the reality of the Creator differs from all other reality in that it alone is self-existent and therefore original, so its self-disclosure differs from that of all other beings and every creaturely mind in that it and it alone is able to reveal its existence with authenticity, truth and effectiveness, and in this revelation to affirm the reality of its being. And as everything which exists outside the Creator owes its existence to Him and Him alone, so any knowledge of existence which arises outside Him can only come to be because He does not conceal but reveals His infallible knowledge of His own existence (which is the ground of all other existence). This self disclosure of the Creator, [349] i.e., this revelation of His own infallible knowledge of His existence (the ground of all else that exists) is the living confrontation which meets the creaturely consciousness and in virtue of which knowledge of existence, reality and being is possible and real even outside God, in the order of the creature which is distinct from Him. This knowledge begins with knowledge of the existence of God, and then, descending from this its primary and proper object, it becomes knowledge of the existence of the knower and his environment. For the primary content of the divine self-disclosure, and therefore the primary object of the knowledge based upon it, is God Himself and His own existence. But this content and object include the knower and his world, and assure him of the existence of the same. For God Himself, whose existence is disclosed in His self-revelation and recognised in the knowledge to which this revelation gives rise, is the ground of the existence of that which is distinct from Him and outside Him. The one who knows God by His self-revelation is distinct from and outside God, as is also the world which surrounds him. If, taught by God, he comes to know God Himself and His existence, this implies that he also knows himself and his own existence, and that of his world. In declaring to him His own existence, God has also declared to him the existence of his ego and the world. Because God declares: "I am," he not only can and may and must repeat: "Thou art," but also its complement: "I also am, and that which accompanies me is." God vouches to him—the ontological order demonstrates itself in the noetic—for His own divine existence, and by implication for that of the knower, and of the alien being distinct from God but allied to Him.

We emphasise that this awareness of creaturely existence rests wholly and exclusively upon God's self-communication in revelation. It is wholly and exclusively an echo and response of the creature to what is said to him by his Creator. It is neither a spontaneous nor a receptive accomplishment of the creature, for it does not rest upon any of his inherent faculties, nor is any of these faculties capable of this recognition. It merely takes place. It is a sheer fact that the creature whose faculties in themselves do not suffice to achieve this recognition, orientating himself according to God's self-revelation, is compelled to adopt this recognition. It is recognition in the form of acknowledgment; recognition under the law of faith and obedience. This character formally distinguishes it from all recognition based upon the consciousness of the ego, the world and God.

For this very reason it must also be emphasised that it has no share in the dialectics of the mode of apprehension rooted in the consciousness of the ego, the world and God. It does not move within that circle of consciousness and being, and therefore under the determination that the question of being or appearance must finally remain open. It is not merely a strengthened and [350] deepened supposition that this question might well have to be answered in favour of the reality of being. It is authentic, true and effectual recognition of the reality of being. It is assured recognition, for it answers to the self-disclosure of Him who exists originally in His self-existence, and is thus the ground of all other existence, merely echoing what has first been said by the Creator. It can know no fluctuation or doubt, because it does not depend upon any choice of the creature, but upon the choice of the Creator which is implicit in His self-disclosure, and in view of which the choice of the creature cannot be a matter of uncertainty, since the possibility that he and his fellow-creatures might equally well not be is excluded from the very outset and definitively. Such a possibility is as impossible as that God Himself might not be, or that He might err with regard to the knowledge of His own being, or that He might withhold His self-disclosure from the creature, or that in making it He might wish to deceive the creature with regard to Himself. It is ontologically excluded by the fact that God is, and is not not; that He knows Himself, and does not not know Himself. And it is noetically excluded by the fact that God is not hidden from the creature but revealed in His self-disclosure, and authentically revealed. The creature is forbidden to return to it by the law according to which he has moved on to the ground of God's self-disclosure. Only if he is a fool can he return to it. And only if he is a fool can he treat the opposite possibility as a mere possibility, as the object of a mere supposition, imagining that he has to live on the ground of a mere hypothesis. No, the only normal thing here is full, unlimited and unreserved certainty. The only normal thing here is the grateful rejoicing of the creature at the existence of his Creator, and also at his own existence and that of his fellow-creatures. We may be, and so we may live, and so we do live. Just because we cannot say this to ourselves except as it is declared to us, just because we have no capacity in ourselves to achieve this certainty, just because we can here give an echo and answer only in the realisation of our total incapacity, it is obvious and necessary for us to make this affirmation, and as we do so we find ourselves altogether outside and above the region of doubt. The creature is. We say this because God is, and we are told by God Himself that He and therefore the creature is. God is real. His creation is actualisation. Hence His creature is real.

In this discussion, we touch very closely on the theme of René Descartes' *Meditationes de prima philosophia* (1641).

It is worth noting that this radical question of the reality of that which is stands at the very beginning of modern philosophy as it was decisively shaped by the renaissance of ancient humanism and the rise of the exact natural sciences.

In the title of this work, in its dedication to the Sorbonne, and in the summary of its contents, Descartes spoke of it as though its theme were *De Deo et anima* and its essential content consisted in a proof of the existence of God and the immortality of the soul which would be irrefutable even for unbelievers. I do not know on what material or strategic grounds he made this claim. But it is palpable that it does not fit the facts. In the third [351] Meditation the proof of the divine existence is no more than a buttress for the proof of the self-existence of the thinking subject, and in the fifth it is only an inference from the latter. And we can hardly see a proof of the immortality of the soul in the casual remarks of the sixth Meditation concerning the indivisibility of the mind as opposed to the divisibility of the body. Thus the question of God and the soul, important as the answer to the first undoubtedly is, belongs methodologically only to the margin of what is actually attempted in this writing, viz. an answer to the question of the reality, or the certainty of the reality, of a being which is not identical with God. It is impossible to deny the reader the right to hold in view the purpose which is plainly visible in the contents of the book. (My quotations refer to the numeration of the German edition of A. Buchenau, *Phil. Bibl.*, Vol. 27.)

Everything is subject to doubt, is the declaration of Descartes in the first of these Meditations. "The fact that I am now here, that I sit by the fireside in my winter coat and hold this paper in my hand ... that these are my hands, that this whole body is mine"—all these things might be a dream (I, 6). And although he can comfort himself with the thought that there is an element of indubitable certitude at least in arithmetic, geometry and similar branches of knowledge which deal with universals, with the corporeality, extension, structure, quality, size, number, space and time of things which are possible irrespective of their reality, yet he is disquieted by the further thought that his real creation and that of all things by God is only an ancient opinion (*vetus opinio*), that God might equally well have willed and effected the non-being or the mere appearance of earth and heaven and extended things, so that even the addition of 2 and 3, or the counting of the sides of a quadrangle, necessarily reposes upon an illusion (I, 10). Supposing that instead of the all-wise God, the source of truth, an evil spirit who is both all-powerful and cunning has employed all his industry to ensnare my credibility by the illusion of the whole external world and my own sensuous existence (I, 16)?

Hence Descartes opens the second of his Meditations with the declaration that "he has fallen into doubts which are so serious as to be insuperable" (II, 1). "As though I had unexpectedly plunged into a deep whirlpool, I am so confused that I can neither find a firm footing nor swim up to the surface." What truth then remains? "Perhaps only that there is nothing certain," is Descartes' first reply (II, 2), but he then adds at once: "How do I know that there is not something ... which I have not the slightest reason to doubt?" (II, 3). But what can this be? The answer is obvious: I myself, even though I am deceived by a demon, am not completely deceived, for I am a being which can at least doubt, which can at least partly see through deception, and which therefore thinks. "Let him deceive me as much as he will, he will never be able to annihilate my existence as long as I think that I am something." If and in so far as I think this, I also am. What am I? Body or soul? All this may be an illusion created by the all-powerful deceiver, but it certainly presupposes a thinking being (*res cogitans*) and as such one that is not non-existent, but existent. The fact that, deceived or not, I discover, affirm, deny, desire, fear, imagine, perceive and above all doubt is my thinking, and in so far as I think, I also am (II, 14). I am in the position to watch a piece of wax both in the modification of its various qualities of colour, shape, warmth, hardness, etc., and also in the persistent identity of its being (II, 19). I do this as a thinking subject, and in the accomplishment of this thinking I am.

Descartes' third Meditation treats of the existence of God (*De Deo, quod existat*). Naturally it does not escape the notice of Descartes that in the second Meditation he had not so much proved the conclusiveness of his self-demonstration of the thinking subject as assumed it. He now proposes to prove it. And the idea of God serves his purpose at this point. He is aware that he has kept to a general principle in asserting that the certainty of the existence of a *res*

[352] *cogitans*[EN10] is deducible from the activity of thought. This principle is that "everything is true that I can clearly and distinctly perceive" (*valde clare et distincte*). Later in his *Principia Philosophiae*, 1644, I, 45, Descartes says concerning the meaning of these terms that a *perceptio* is *clara*[EN11] when it is in some way present and obviously impressive (*praesens et aparta*) to the percipient mind, such as a feeling of pain, whereas a *perceptio* is *distincta*[EN12] when it is distinguishable in its peculiarity from all others, as, for example, the specific localisation and causal explanation of this feeling. The awareness of my being as a thinking being is a *perceptio clara et distincta*[EN13]. But how do I arrive at the point of regarding a perception of this kind, and above all this perception, as true? It is certain that I do regard it as true. But how do I convince myself that I do so rightly? There is always the possibility that a demonic god has endowed me with such a nature that I am deceived even in what seems to me the most obvious of truths, e.g., in the result of the sum of 3 and 5. Everything in me protests, of course, against this possibility. "As often as I turn to those objects which I think I can clearly grasp, I become so fully convinced that I involuntarily burst out into the exclamation 'Deceive me who can! No one will ever bring it about that I am nothing so long as I have the consciousness of being something, or that I have never really been when it is now true that I am, or that 2 and 3 are more or less than 5, etc., which I see to be an obvious contradiction'" (III, 6). And what reason is there for me to concern myself about a deceiving god "when I do not adequately know that there is a god at all"? (III, 7). But in order to justify this protest, and to dispel this final if intrinsically feeble doubt, and thus to rebut our original hypothesis, we shall now attempt to investigate "whether there is a god, and if so whether he can be a deceiver" (III, 7). In other words, the proof of God's existence must now be undertaken. It takes the following form. The content of our ideas does not enable us to discover whether they proceed from any real object outside ourselves (III, 18). In themselves our ideas might only be fantasies. But even as ideas they may be more or less perfect to the extent that as such they have more or less real content (*realitas obiectiva*[EN14], III, 19). The idea of a substance has

---

[EN10] thinking being
[EN11] perception is clear
[EN12] perception is distinct
[EN13] clear and distinct perception
[EN14] objective reality

more real content than the idea of a mode or of a mere accident of a substance. And thus "the idea by which I conceive a supreme God, who is eternal, infinite, omniscient, omnipotent and the Creator of all things existing outside Himself, has in truth more objective and intrinsic reality than the idea by which finite substances are conceived" (III, 19). If now, seeing that I am a finite substance, the reality and perfection of my idea of God transcends my own reality, the former cannot flow from myself and my own conception. There must be something else outside myself which is the cause of this conception of mine (III, 23). "By the name of God, I understand a substance which is infinite, independent, of supreme insight and power, by which I myself and everything existent have been created, if there is in fact such a substance. And indeed the nature of everything created is such that, the more carefully I consider it, the more impossible it seems that it could have proceeded from myself. Hence it must be concluded from what we have said that God necessarily exists. For although the idea of a substance is intrinsic to me (by the fact that I myself am a substance), it cannot be the idea of an infinite substance (since I am finite) unless it proceeds from a substance which in truth is infinite" (III, 27). If we could suppose "that such a being does not exist, yet we cannot suppose that the idea of it represents to me nothing real" (III, 30). It is "the most true, clear and evident" of all the ideas present to me (III, 31). In a certain sense, it even precedes the idea of my own being. For "how could I understand that I doubt, that I desire something, i.e., that something is lacking in me and that I am not perfect, if there were no idea of a perfect being within me, by comparison with which I recognise my own need?" (III, 28). It thus transcends myself, or rather it proves to me by its existence as my idea the reality of its content which transcends myself—the existence of God. I myself, who [353] have this idea, could not exist at all if no such being existed (III, 35). I always exist, from one moment to another, only in my imperfection, and therefore solely in my relation to this perfect being, in my frailty continuously sustained or rather created afresh by this perfect being (III, 36), in which therefore, since I exist (and especially as I exist in doubt), I must recognise the ground and origin of my own being (III, 38). By the very fact that I exist and that I have an idea of a perfect being, i.e., of God, it is most clearly proved that God also exists (III, 40). But whence do I derive this authoritative idea? Clearly it is not conveyed to me through my senses, for when and where could my sense-organs have occasioned in me its formation? But just as little could I have invented it, for I certainly cannot either augment or diminish it (III, 41). Hence the only alternative is to recognise that it is innate in me (*innata*[EN15]) like the idea of my own existence; that in creating me God has implanted it in me as a token, "like the seal which the artist stamps upon his work." And thus it comes about that "when I direct my attention to my own being, I not only realise that I am an imperfect creature dependent upon another and aspiring to what is increasingly greater and endlessly better, but also that that on which I depend infinitely contains this greater in itself, and is therefore God. The whole cogency of this proof lies in the fact that I myself with this nature of mine—in so far as the idea of God is intrinsic to me—could not possibly exist if God Himself did not also really exist—the God, the idea of whom is innate in me, i.e., who possesses all the perfections which I do not comprehend but can in a sense reach in thought and which cannot possibly be subject to any lack. For this reason it is sufficiently clear that He cannot be a deceiver; for it is obvious to me by natural insight that all deception and cheating is conditioned by a lack" (III, 42). But God is a perfect being, without the imperfection of a lack. If He exists—and since I myself exist, I must be convinced that He also exists before me—then there is no obstacle to my accepting that general principle, justifying the assumption made in the second Meditation, and therefore regarding as true all that we

---

EN15 innate

347

perceive clearly and distinctly, and thus putting my confidence in the self-demonstration of the thinking subject.

When we come to the fourth Meditation, we find that on the basis of the achieved recognition that there is certitude of reality Descartes takes up the question of truth and error, i.e., the possibility of error and the equal possibility of overcoming it by the truth. God does not deceive me, so certainly as I know myself and therefore God as the perfect being (IV, 2–3). If I make the correct use of my capacity for judgment, this judgment cannot fail (IV, 4). How does it come about that in spite of this I err, and am therefore fallible, so that apart from the real and positive idea of God which does not deceive me, I can also have the negative idea of nothingness? (IV, 5). Could not God, who as the perfect being wills only the best, have so created me that I never deceive myself? (IV, 6). But this is to pose the question of ultimate ends, which in face of God is a frivolous undertaking. My imperfection, consisting in the fact that I can actually be deceived, may very well belong from God's standpoint to the perfection of the whole which God has created (IV, 7–8). The actual reason for my fallibility lies in the tension between my understanding and my will, not to the extent that both have been given me by God, but to the extent that my will is my own (IV, 9). If my understanding is limited, my freedom of choice is so great "that I am unable to conceive the idea of a greater, so that it is by this pre-eminently that I understand that I am an image and likeness of God." I am unfree only in proportion as I am undecided (IV, 12–13). Error arises from the fact that, affirming or denying in this freedom, I am also able to pass judgments about ideas which I have not yet perceived to be clear and distinct and therefore true (confirmed by the God who cannot deceive me). My judgment should keep within these limits. In so far as it does not do so, it becomes erroneous, although this is not inevitable, but might well be quite otherwise. To be sure, God gave me both will and understanding, and the functioning of both is good and true to the extent that both depend on God. It is my imperfection that again and again I do not rightly use this freedom and pass judgment upon what I do not correctly understand (IV, 21). Nevertheless I can protect myself against this imperfection. If I cannot know all things and everything clearly and distinctly, I can adopt the rule "so to restrain my will in judgment that it is exercised only with regard to what the understanding presents to it clearly and plainly." Within this limit, I cannot and will not go astray. And the fact that I cannot do so constitutes "the greatest and most conspicuous perfection of man" (IV, 24). "I shall attain it if only I pay adequate regard to what I perfectly appreciate, and distinguish it from all the things which I see in a confused and obscure manner" (IV, 35).

[354]

Descartes' fifth Meditation has the remarkable title "Concerning the being of material things, and again concerning the being of God." Before he turns his attention to the question which now arises concerning the existence of material things, Descartes wishes to apprehend their essence (*essentia*), i.e., the ideas of them, in so far as they present themselves to the Christian consciousness (V, 3). Their conceptual definition clearly consists in their magnitude, their capacity to be measured and counted (V, 4). It is not in their reality, but in this their conceptual definition, that they are "plain and manifest to me" even before they are known to me directly, i.e., through the senses. Mathematical ideas, which are a conceptual definition of material things, are not ideas of nothingness, whether anything outside me corresponds to them or not. Even as such they are immutable and eternal. A triangle, for example, may or may not exist outside me, but in any case three angles are equal to two right angles, and the biggest angle is opposite the biggest side, etc. (V, 4–5). "Whatever is true is also something." Certain relationships of figures and numbers are true, clear and plain, and therefore they are something (V, 6). Just at this point, to the surprise of the reader, Descartes breaks off with the question: "But if it is to be concluded solely from the fact that I cannot dismiss the idea of a thing from my consciousness, that everything which I plainly and clearly grasp as intrinsic to a thing does indeed belong to it, does not this give us again a proof of the existence of God?" (V, 7). On the basis of the axiom that what I clearly and plainly see to be intrinsic to the nature of a thing (as happens in mathematical apprehension) does in fact belong to this thing, Descartes takes up again the proof of God's existence. On the basis of this assumption, the proof is as follows. Like a selected mathematical conception (figure or number), I find that the idea of God is also present to my consciousness. And as I clearly and distinctly realise that certain relationships are integral to the very nature of specific figures and numbers, so also I plainly see that it is of the very essence of God always to exist in pure actuality (V, 7). This is only apparently a sophism. For if in regard to all other things I must distinguish essence and existence, and have set alongside the necessary determination of their essence the not so necessary idea of their existence, yet I can as little separate the existence of God from His essence as from the essence of a triangle the definition that the sum of its three angles is equal to two right angles, or from the essence of a mountain the idea of the proximity of a valley. A god who lacks the perfection of actual existence contradicts my innate idea of God as the supremely perfect being (V, 8). Although from the fact that I cannot conceive of a mountain without a valley there does not, of course, follow the existence of mountain and valley, yet from the fact that I can conceive of God (the sum of all perfection) as existent, it follows necessarily that existence is inseparable from His essence, and therefore that He does in truth exist. If I am free to imagine a winged horse without troubling about the question of its existence, yet I am not free to think of God without existence, i.e., to think of the most perfect being apart from total perfection and therefore apart from that of actual existence (V, 9). It is certainly not necessary that I [355] should ever conceive any thought of God, just as it is not necessary that I should ever think of a triangle. "But as often as it pleases me to conceive of a primary and supreme being and to produce this idea, as it were, out of the treasury of my mind" (*eius ideam ex mentis meae thesauro depromere*), it is necessary to ascribe to it fundamentally (although perhaps not always in fact) all possible perfections including that of existence, just as in the case of the conception of a triangle, once it is formed there is fundamentally bound up with it the recognition of all its attributes as such (V, 10). Why do I not always do this? Only the darkening of my mind by prejudices, only the mastery of my consciousness by the images of bodily things, can prevent me from doing so. Nothing is more obvious in itself than that the highest being conceivable to us exists and that to Him alone and fully does there accrue the unity of essence and existence, and this from all eternity. And once I grasp this most secure of all truths, then I notice in addition "that the certainty of all other things depends so utterly upon it that without it we can never know perfectly anything at all" (V, 12, 14). If I did not actually know that there is a God, I should constantly be liable to regard even my most clear and distinct apprehensions—e.g., the knowledge that the sum of the angles of a triangle is equal to two right angles—as uncertain and changeable opinions, and myself as a victim of deception at the very heart of my thinking (V, 15–16). "But once I have realised that there is a God, and that everything depends on Him, and that He is no deceiver, then I infer that everything which I clearly and distinctly perceive is necessarily true," and I have no further reason to doubt it. I thus possess a true and secure knowledge. I can, may and must comfortably consider as true all truth which I can plainly and evidently demonstrate (V, 1). "And thus I come to appreciate clearly the fact that the certain truth of all knowledge depends solely on the recognition of the true God; so much so that before I apprehended Him I could have no perfect knowledge about anything whatever. But now countless matters both concerning God Himself and other purely intellectual points, as also concerning the physical universe which is the object of pure mathematics, can be fully and certainly known to me" (V, 18). "As also concerning the physical universe which is the object of pure mathematics," is obviously what Descartes was aiming to prove in all his previous reflections. It was his aim to show that, if not everything in physical nature, innumerable things in their individual characteristics may be known to us as a genuinely existent external world, and this was to be generally guaranteed by the proof of the existence of God.

In Descartes' sixth Meditation the following proof of the reality of an external world is given. That material things can exist is to be inferred (1) from the fact that they form the object of pure mathematics and (2) from the capacity which I constantly exercise of imagining their existence (VI, 1). From the idea of a physical universe which actually arises in the mind there may be deduced at least the high probability of its existence as the most suitable explanation of the idea (VI, 4). Only, of course, its probability! Yet it must be maintained that this idea comes to me, always mediated by my senses, in any event without the intervention of my will and concurrence, in a much more vivid and significant way even than all the ideas of my pure thinking. Can it possibly spring from myself? (VI, 8–9). Does not the question arise whether I can have any idea at all in my mind which does not first arise through sensuous experience? (VI, 10). Descartes will not, of course, go so far as to assert this. But he does insist ever more strongly on the partial determination of the intellectual life of man by an external world which is distinct from him and which he conceives through the medium of the senses. Why do I inevitably react to specific sensations with sadness or joy? Obviously because "nature has taught me so to do" (VI, 12). Only without the recognition of God could I suppose "that my nature is so made as to render it possible for me to be self-deceived in what seems to me to be the most evident of all truth" (VI, 14). Certainly I cannot immediately accept as valid everything which I suppose my senses to suggest to me. Just as little may I systematically doubt it all (VI, 16). I at least know that I exist as a thinking being, and that as such I exist in distinction from my body as a non-thinking, extended essence (VI, 17). I also know that I have a passive capacity to feel, i.e., to receive and recognise the idea of sensuous things (VI, 20). Now since God has given me a great propensity to believe (*magnum propensionem*) that these ideas were truly emitted (*emitti*) by material things, I do not see how He could be anything but a deceiver if this were not in fact the case. But God is not a deceiver. Hence material things do exist (VI, 21). If they perhaps exist in a different mode from that which I perceive by my senses, it is still possible for me—again because God cannot be a deceiver—to correct my interpretation, and I have the secure hope of attaining an ever more solid recognition of the truth (VI, 23). What my nature teaches me is at least securely true so far as it goes. "For by nature I understand nothing other than God Himself or the coherence (*coordinatio*) of created nature as determined by God; by my own nature in particular, I understand nothing other than the sum total (*complexio*) of what God has imparted to me" (VI, 24). It is just nature itself (in a general and particular sense) which instructs me. *Natura docet*[EN16]. This is the crowning affirmation of the sixth Meditation. But it teaches me nothing more emphatically than that I have a body with its feelings and needs, that I am not merely present to it as is the pilot to his compass, but that for good or evil I constitute with it a certain unified totality, and that there exists in its environment a multiplicity of other bodies (VI, 25–27). My nature as that of a finite being is naturally not omniscient (VI, 31). In spite of the goodness of God even my judgments may be false through my own fault (VI, 35). But it is also to be affirmed that I am both an indivisible mind and a divisible body, the link between the two being the brain, or more precisely a special small part of the brain which is the seat of the intelligence (*sensus communis*[EN17], VI, 36–37) and which will normally convey to me precisely the feeling which supremely and most frequently contributes to the maintenance of my well-being. This feeling is something which nature has imparted to me—a proof of the power and goodness of God. And while the truth of it is obscured, it is not cancelled by the ever present possibility of error (VI, 39–42). It is not to be denied that in what is useful

[356]

[EN16] Nature teaches
[EN17] common sense

to the body all my feelings do more often suggest the true than the false. And to test any particular point, I can almost always make use of several of my senses, and also of the link of memory and the insight of reason, thus subjecting my perceptions to constant control. Hence I need not fear that what the senses convey to me will be wholly false (VI, 43), but I may repudiate excessive doubt as ridiculous, and need not give way to the suspicion that all my perceptions of objects have no other basis than that of a mere dream. For if I notice whence and where and when certain things offer themselves to my perception, and am able unremittingly to combine the observation of them with the whole of the rest of my life, then they cannot be a dream. For God is not a deceiver (VI, 44–45). It is thus the case that many if not all things are "perfectly certain and known to us" even about the physical world and therefore a real external world.

But what is this, and what are we to say to it? We may surely begin by noting that any unprejudiced reader will be relatively least convinced by the sixth Meditation. The mere fact that Descartes adduces such varied considerations is disquieting. What is the real proof of the reality of an external world, or its certainty? The continuity of my memory and the rational supervision of my supposed observations? The connexion between the mysterious *sensus communis*[EN18] and the health of my body in that equally mysterious and very small part of the brain? The observation of my *facultas passiva*[EN19] of assimilating sensuous impressions? Or my undoubted *magna propensio*[EN20] of crediting the latter? The distinction between my mind which is asserted to be indivisible and a world of extension asserted to be divisible? Or the new and startling idea of an instructing nature as the *complexio*[EN21] of the two aspects [357] of my existence? Or only the greater degree of probability with which mathematical truths point to the existence of an external world independent of my thinking? Or in the last resort the existence of God as the One who guarantees to me both the trustworthiness of my thought and the existence of an external world? Can all this be convincing either in detail or as a whole? We do not raise the query in opposition to Descartes but in co-operation with him. For he himself says in the synopsis which precedes his work that he does not suppose the *rationes*[EN22] adduced in the sixth Meditation to be *valde utiles ad probandum id ipsum quod probant, nempe revera esse aliquem mundum et homines habere corpora et similia, de quibus nemo umquam sanae mentis serio dubitavit*[EN23]. Yet it is just this—the true existence of his winter coat, of the paper on which he was writing, of his own hands, of his body, etc.—which according to the first Meditation he was doubting even in the exercise of sound common sense. But did he act as if he really doubted? There are also other considerations which cause the reader to doubt whether Descartes really had any doubt. But it was in his doubting and therefore in his thinking that he sought to build the whole structure of his certitude in the second Meditation. How can that be when according to his own declaration he cannot entertain such doubts if he is exercising sound common sense and therefore does not seriously doubt but merely plays with doubt in the first Meditation? Is the edifice of his system equally solid on the basis of a merely pretended doubt? But however that may be, in view of the result of the sixth Meditation it is quite impossible to agree, and he himself cannot maintain, that he has won even the game he had in mind. For whatever we may think of the weight of his

---

[EN18] common sense
[EN19] passive ability
[EN20] great propensity
[EN21] sum total
[EN22] reasons
[EN23] particularly useful for proving that very thing which they are supposed to prove, namely, the idea that there is a world, and that human beings have bodies and the like, which no one in their right mind has ever doubted

rationes[EN24], there can be no doubt that they are not covered by the rule of the clear and distinct as the criterion of truth. For good reason Descartes no longer invoked this canon in the sixth Meditation, when it was a question of proving the real existence of his winter coat and his own hands. What then is really covered by this criterion, the excellence of which is for the moment presupposed? What is it that according to his Meditations Descartes has clearly and distinctly and therefore truly apprehended?

Properly and directly, the only obvious answer is mathematical truths as such, as indicated at the beginning of the fifth Meditation. At the same time Descartes rightly pointed out in the first Meditation that in themselves even these, although true, might well be only dream-truths, elements of truth in the nexus of a monstrous theo-cosmic illusion. Even in the sixth Meditation he did not in any way show that they could imply the existence of a real external world except with a high degree of probability. And the *rationes*[EN25] which in this connexion he brings forward to support this hypothesis—however important they may be in other respects—have nothing to do with the clearly and plainly recognised mathematical truths.

The second point which Descartes asserts that he has apprehended clearly and plainly, and therefore truly, is the fact of his own existence as a thinking being. To what extent? As a being who doubts everything existing outside himself? This is what he says. But does he not also say that in the exercise of sound common sense he cannot doubt so very seriously, that at most he can only proceed as if he doubted? Can he then be clearly and distinctly and therefore truly certain of himself and his doubts? Or is the thinking being, certain of itself, the subject of clearly and distinctly realised mathematical apprehensions? But if the latter as such have been dreamed, if an external world corresponding to them may be accepted only as extremely probable, how can the subject which possibly only dreams them be certain of itself in any other way or in any higher degree? And even accepting the rightness of the act of thought, however performed, by which self-certainty is attained, how can even true thinking escape its own circle and reach the certainty of the true being of the thinking subject, penetrating clearly, distinctly and confidently to that "I am"?

[358] The third and most important application of the criterion of truth suggested by Descartes is the proof of God's existence by means of the key-thought introduced in the fifth Meditation: "What I apprehend as intrinsic to the nature of a thing, is indeed one of its attributes." I understand that the idea of a perfect being innate in me necessarily involves its existence outside me. Hence there exists of necessity a perfect being outside myself. But obviously it is involved necessarily only in my idea of such a being. Even the insight that the sum of the angles of a triangle is equal to two right angles, with which Descartes formally links his proof of God in the fifth Meditation, points only to the essential character of every triangle conceivable by me, but not to the actual existence of a triangle outside my thinking. What this proof of God demonstrates is the nature of the perfect being as conceived—necessarily, we may concede—by me. Its power to prove the existence of a God outside and above me is no smaller but also no greater than its cogency in regard to the external world, or the power of my thought to prove my own existence as a thinking subject. We have seen what the limits of this cogency are. In no sense does it attain to certitude. Thus the proof of the existence of God may carry us far within its essential limits. It may be very useful to bring about a noteworthy deepening of the hypothetical consciousness of myself and the world. But it does not serve to give us strict certainty in regard to a perfect being actually existing outside myself, a Creator whose perfection involves also the assumption that He cannot deceive me. But it was for this purpose that it was introduced into the third Meditation, and declared again at the close of the fifth Meditation to be useful and in fact indispensable. The

---

[EN24] reasons
[EN25] reasons

criterion of truth itself and as such was not accepted unthinkingly. We had to be shown the fact and extent that we may and must place supreme confidence in it. This was effected in the third Meditation to the extent that this demonstrated that the imperfect existence of the thinker, necessarily pointing to a perfection which is complementary to it, infers the existence of a very different and perfect being, and therefore of God. We see on what a slender thread the proof again hangs. If in the fifth Meditation the idea of God is produced out of the treasury of the human mind, in the third it is deduced from its deficiency. In the former case it resembles mathematical apprehensions as a positive work of my mind and thought; in the latter it is its negative presupposition, the power which is reflected in a weakness. But in both cases it is linked to my thought, and the asserted real existence of its content stands or falls with the asserted existence of myself as thinking subject.

But can this proof of God's existence have power to guarantee the truth of the criterion which guides my thinking? Can we accept Descartes' specific declarations that every truth, even the truth of mathematical apprehension (on the basis of which the proof of God's existence is again undertaken in the fifth Meditation), is dependent on the existence of God demonstrated in this way? Can we be persuaded by the existence of God demonstrated in this way that our instructing nature as a *complexio*EN26 of our capacity of understanding and feeling does not deceive us with regard to the existence of an external world, but is a trustworthy guide? For this is the one guiding thread in the confused argumentation of the sixth Meditation. Our nature in its complexity has been given us by God. Behind it stands the physical universe as the divinely controlled *co-ordinatio*EN27 of thinking and extended substances. And behind nature lies the nature of God by which, as the nature of the most perfect being, we are obviously to understand a pre-eminent co-ordination of these two aspects, and perhaps their unfathomable identity. It is for this reason that we must pay attention to the teachings of nature. But Descartes does not tell us what he knows—clearly and distinctly according to his own standard—about these three levels of nature. Indeed, he cannot tell us, although following his own line of argument he undoubtedly ought to instruct us about this *co-ordinatio*EN28 and *complexio*EN29 of the two aspects. But on this point he can only make assertions, notwithstanding his appeal to the existence of God. The only thing which he [359] knows positively is mathematical truth as such. But he does not know either a real external world corresponding to it, himself a thinking subject, or especially the actual existence of a perfect being who is the basis of, and evinces and demonstrates, the trustworthiness of his own thought, and his own existence, and the reality of the existence of an external world. It does honour to Descartes' understanding—and it casts a remarkable light upon the whole of modern philosophy inaugurated by him—that he considers it necessary and possible to assert the existence of God in order securely to ground the certainty of the human consciousness of the ego and the world. But one cannot fail to see that although he maintains the existence of God according to his own presuppositions and method, he does not prove it, so that his attempt to ground all other forms of certitude fails. The circle of the *cogitare*EN30 is never broken through. He never penetrates to the region of the *esse*EN31. Even the self-demonstration of the thinking subject, and the proof of mathematical truths, and supremely and finally the proof of God's existence, takes place within this circle. It is not demonstrated that God exists quite independently of my idea of Him, and hence it is not proved that I myself exist quite otherwise than in my own thinking, nor that the external world exists

---

EN26 sum total
EN27 co-ordination
EN28 co-ordination
EN29 combination
EN30 thinking
EN31 being

beyond my own conception of it. We already knew that sound common sense encourages us to trust our consciousness of the ego and the world, that we have a *magna propensio*^{EN32} to follow this encouragement, that in fact we constantly make use of the hypothesis of the *co-ordinatio*^{EN33} and *complexio*^{EN34}, that in this connexion we must guard against certain errors, but that we are also in a position to guard against them. To establish the point that *natura docet*^{EN35}, no Descartes is needed. Indeed, it is Descartes who poses it as a problem. He ought not to dismiss us with this observation when he begins by calling it in question. He promises to establish for us the fact and extent that this instruction on the part of nature does not give us only convention and probability but certainty. Descartes does not keep this promise. He cannot keep it. In so far as he expressly sees in the fact of God's existence the appropriate means for carrying out his enterprise, he is not far from the possibility of keeping it. But the very way in which he proves the existence of God, the very existence of the God proved to exist in this way, can only serve to make apparent the complete failure of his whole undertaking. For since his demonstration of certitude is not adequate at this point, it cannot be adequate at all.

Why is it not adequate at this point? Not because, as any child can see, his proof of God in the two forms in which he presents it contains a circular argument. Man would have to be God Himself if he were to speak of God otherwise than in the form of circular arguments. Even the Christian in his teaching can never demonstrate the existence of God to himself and others except in faith and by summoning to faith. Nor can we find any fault with the fact that by his own confession Descartes' initial datum is the idea of God, the human thought picture of a supremely perfect being. For beings who are not themselves God there is in practice no other possible approach. Even a Christian who in his confession thinks he is able to demonstrate in faith and the summons to faith the existence of God refers to his idea of God conceived in faith and expressed in confession. But the circular argument and the human conception without which even Christian faith cannot prove God's existence are not to be regarded as powerful instruments in the hands of man. Descartes uses them as such. He needs only to produce the idea of God from the treasury or deficiency of his mind and at once it stands at his disposal with no less but no greater power than the idea of a triangle. And equally well, and interchangeably with the existence of God, he can demonstrate the validity of his criterion of truth, just as on the basis of the latter he can prove the existence of God. The very power which he wields in this matter also shows his powerlessness. The idea and existence of this God produced from his mind, and alternately demonstrated and demonstrating, used by him and serving him, clearly remain within the circle which Descartes' Meditations are intended to break. From within it, it is quite impossible to reach out either to the transcendence of a God who confronts man in sovereign omnipotence, existing for Himself and therefore existing for man, to the transcendence of a subject of human thought which is not exhausted in the act of thinking, or to the transcendence of a real external world attained by our thought but not included within it. The God of Descartes is hopelessly enchained within the mind of man. Neither in the description given of Him nor in the role ascribed to Him does He bear the divine character which would distinguish Him as the being to whom objective existence beyond all human imagining must be ascribed, for the simple reason that it is He Himself who has inexorably and inescapably prescribed these thoughts for man. How can the objective existence of God be demonstrated so long as the supreme force of the proof consists in the necessity under the pressure of which man cannot

[360]

---

^{EN32} great propensity
^{EN33} co-ordination
^{EN34} combination
^{EN35} nature teaches

help attributing objective existence to the object of one of his ideas, so that its force is only that of the one who proves and not of the self-demonstration of the One whose existence is to be proved? Anything less than the latter cannot be required in a proof of God's existence. For by anything less the existence of *God*, the existence of the One who exists originally, necessarily and essentially, beyond all human constructs and conceptions, cannot be demonstrated. By anything less the divine character of this being is not respected. How, then, can it be *this* being whose existence is proved?

The validity of any proof of God's existence depends on its basis in the power of God's self-demonstration; on the fact that it gives this scope; on the fact that the description given of God and the role ascribed to Him, not merely do not conceal but reveal the divine character to the extent that the proof attempted by man ascribes existence to God because it is prescribed that he should do so and he is obedient to this command. Only in this way, by his obedient activity, does man show that he is aware of the divine existence and can prove it. Only in this way can it really be proved by him. It was on this (the only possible) basis, and in this (the only possible) way, that the existence of God was proved by Anselm of Canterbury in the 11th century. In *Prosl.* 2–4 Anselm showed that the God who is revealed and believed in the Christian Church, cannot not exist, or even be thought of as not existing, because by His self-revelation as the being *quo maius cogitari non potest*[EN36], by His self-revelation as the Creator, He forbids man his creature to entertain such a thought, making it logically and morally impossible for him to think it, because only the "fool" (the *insipiens*) who does not hear or heed the divine voice can actually say in his heart that which is logically and morally impossible: There is no God. The man who knows God by God Himself, on the basis of His revelation and by faith in it, is necessarily aware of God's existence, so that there can be no question of His non-existence.

The God of Descartes does not bear this divine character. His divinity has nothing to do with the fact that He has revealed Himself and is therefore to be believed. This idea of divinity is innate in man. Man can produce it at will from the treasury or deficiency of his mind. It is made up of a series of preeminent attributes which are relatively and primarily attributes of the human mind, and in which the latter sees its own characteristics—temporality, finitude, limited knowledge and ability and creative power—transcended in the absolute, contemplating itself in the mirror of its possible infinitude, and yet remaining all the time within itself even though allowing its prospect of itself to be infinitely expanded by this speculative extension and deepening. By transcending myself, I never come upon an absolute being confronting and transcendent to me, but only again and again upon my own being. And by proving the existence of a being whom I have conjured up only by means of my own self-transcendence, I shall again and again succeed only in proving my own existence. But if, as is the case in Descartes, it is intended to prove indirectly, by the demon- [361] stration of the existence of God, my own existence and that of an external world transcending me, then by a proof of God conducted in this way I have in fact proved nothing, for when the proof is completed in regard to the question of my own existence and that of a real external world I find myself in exactly the same position as that from which I set out. The circle in which my thinking has moved has definitely been a *circulus vitiosus*[EN37].

If the case is to be otherwise, I must believe the Word of the God who evinces Himself authoritatively in His revelation, and subject myself to His commands and prohibitions. By such an attitude I prove and confirm my awareness of the divine character of the being whose existence is to be demonstrated. By such an attitude I do not merely assert but genuinely recognise the eternal being of the God who transcends me. This attitude shows that in

---

[EN36] than which none greater can be conceived
[EN37] vicious circle

my function as a thinker I behave in harmony with what I assert I know about God. My thinking itself and as such—if I think in this attitude—is a thinking moulded and penetrated by the transcendent reality of God to the extent that it is a thinking in obedience to this God. In the subjection in which it is itself formally a witness to the transcendent existence of God, it can then develop the recognition of His existence as an element of the acknowledgment in which it is confronted by God, and therefore order its proof of God as Anselm did with great clarity and fulness. Without this subordination, in any other attitude but that of obedience to the divine self-demonstration, there can be no question of any proof of God's existence. And this is the point where Descartes fails. It may well be that originally and properly a proof of God on these lines hovered before his imagination. The third Meditation closes with a passage in which he explains that before exploring the consequences of the insight he has attained into the reality of God, he will be pleased to linger in the consideration of God (*placet hic aliquandiu in ipsius Dei contemplatione immorari*EN38), to ponder His attributes, to contemplate, admire and adore (*intueri, admirare, adorare*) the splendour of that unfathomable light, in so far as the sight of the dazzled human mind may bear it. "For as by faith we believe (*fide credimus*) that the highest bliss of the future life consists solely in the *contemplatio divinae maiestatis*EN39, so already here below we experience (*experimur*) that we derive our highest joy in this life from our present, even if much more imperfect, vision of God." It is for this reason that some scholars have dared to speak outright of a mystical element in the thought of this great (perhaps the greatest) rationalist. Unfortunately it is not possible to speak of more than mysticism in Descartes. The God here contemplated, admired and adored is not the God of whom our recognition is to be grounded in His own self-demonstration and made in obedience to Him, so that it may be a recognition of the God who really exists. If only he had once really made use of this *fide credimus*EN40! But Descartes' Catholic faith, unlike that of Anselm, is active in a region outside his philosophy and not within it. Hence it does not cause the latter with genuine modesty to become at its climax a theology. Nor does he feel compelled, in virtue of his Catholic faith, to demonstrate the existence of God out of veneration for the divine character of the being whose existence is to be demonstrated. It is for this reason that his proof cannot prove what it sets out to prove. And for the same reason his unconvincing proof not only does not support but radically threatens the enterprise in the interests of which it is made, viz. the demonstration of the certainty of our own existence and of that of a real external world.

It is a feature of Descartes' enterprise which demands constant attention, and gives him relevance in our present context, that he so closely combined this demonstration with the recognition of God and the proof of God's existence. In this we must say he was right. The knowledge of the reality of the created world, and therefore the legitimation of our consciousness of the ego and the world, depends essentially on the knowledge of God; on the recognition that the created world is affirmed in and through its creation by God, which means primarily that it has been posited as real. As and because we believe in God, we believe—and as we believe, we also recognise—that we are, and are not not, and that the world which surrounds us also is, and is not not. Descartes is right. Nature in itself and as such, the actual conjunction of our thinking with the other than ourselves which our senses suggest to us as similarly existent, is able to convey this truth to us only because it is created by God and because the God who is its Creator Himself bears witness to us that this is so. But the testimony of God on which everything depends must not itself be the testimony of our own mind, but the witness of God Himself to our minds, if it is to convey to us certainty

[362]

EN38 he is pleased to linger awhile in the contemplation of God Himself
EN39 contemplation of the divine majesty
EN40 by faith we believe

regarding what is in itself the problematical teaching of nature. Without this fundamental certitude we can, of course, calculate, construct, experiment, experience, compare, summarise and utilise. But in spite of and in all this activity, we cannot truly live without inner assurance and confidence. We can live truly only when we are certain about the presupposition, which we all constantly use, that our own individual existence and that of the surrounding world is real. All the wretchedness of human life is bound up with the fact that sound common sense and the *natura docet*[EN41] have no power at all firmly to plant our feet on the ground of the confidence that the created world is real. The Cartesian proof of God's existence, which indirectly is meant to demonstrate this certainty, has not this power either. Thus it is no wonder that in the last resort Descartes has to appeal to sound common sense and fall back on the *natura docet*[EN42] as though he had never doubted these presuppositions.

We know, for it is quite obvious and Descartes himself expressly says so, that in fact he never does doubt these presuppositions, and this being the case he invalidates the proof of his own existence which is based upon this doubt. Let us suppose for a moment that he had seriously doubted and not just pretended to do so; that he had doubted not merely the reality of his winter coat and his hands, but that of his own existence. Let us suppose that he really considered the possibility of the nothingness of his whole life as a scholar dedicated to the service of reason, with all his attempts at theoretical destruction and construction, with all the Catholico-humanistic equipment with which, "between the times," he orientated himself and carried through his work, with all his plans and achievements, his hopes and fears. Let us suppose that he really could not resist the conviction that this might indeed be so. Let us suppose that in view of this possibility, he not only seriously doubted but fell into despair. Obviously this did not happen. Equally obviously this could not happen. But it would obviously have had to happen if the self-examination of the first Meditation had been undertaken in the *contemplatio divinae maiestatis*[EN43]; not in the contemplation of the inoffensive product of his own mind, but really in the contemplation of the God of Holy Scripture who reveals Himself as the Creator. In the contemplation of this divine majesty Descartes' doubt could not possibly have been or have remained a mere pretence. In the recognition of this God the possibility of his own nothingness, and then also of the nothingness of his own thinking and of the whole external world, must have irresistibly impressed him. In the recognition of this God the whole problem of the existence of the created world alongside that of the Creator must have seemed to him colossal, and consequently—and not merely in play—the question of reality and certitude must have engaged his attention. In this way it would have become the serious problem which in his first Meditation it certainly is not. And the fact that it is not, that it is not genuinely necessary and serious, is closely connected with the inadequacy of his answer, and the failure of his attempt to prove the existence of God. By the genuine posing of the question in awareness of the living God, there would have emerged a genuine and satisfying answer, the presupposition of a real proof of God, and therefore the presupposition of a real certitude and a genuine legitimation of the human consciousness of the ego and the world. If in contemplation of the majesty of the living God he had been [363] genuinely moved by the possibility of the nothingness of creation, then at once he must have experienced gratitude that this God has repudiated the nothingness of creation, that He has rescued it from annihilation and affirmed it and endowed it with reality. In this gratitude for the grace of creation—and therefore at the very point where the whole problem necessarily becomes serious—the latter would have found a radical solution, and we should not finally

---

[EN41] nature teaches
[EN42] nature teaches
[EN43] contemplation of the divine majesty

have had to be referred back to the *natura docet*[EN44]. A serious answer would have corresponded to the serious question, as the serious answer for its part would always have evoked the serious question. In Descartes, unfortunately, neither the question is serious nor the answer. Neither can become serious for him. But as and because his philosophy attributes an important function to the question of religious faith, it is a good example of the fact that we cannot with impunity seek the reality of the created world anywhere but at the point where it is undoubtedly given, namely, in the revelation of God the Creator.

But our arguments in support of our thesis still lack their final point and precision. It is, of course, the *Christian* understanding of creation, the Creator and the creature, which promotes and sustains the principle that creation is actualisation. And it is with this that we have actually reckoned in the considerations so far adduced. But so far we have not made this clear, and we must now try to do this. The God who posits and guarantees creaturely existence, and by whose self-disclosure it is revealed and secured to the creature, is He who in and through His creative activity has established His covenant with the creature.

As Creator He does not exist as a monad, but in the overflowing plenitude of His life as Father, Son and Holy Ghost, in the desire and love in which He does not will to keep His glory to Himself but also to magnify it outside Himself, in which He does not will to live only for Himself but also for another distinct from Himself. He lives eternally, working and creating beneficently in this desire and love. He lives as the God who so loved man that He condescended to become man Himself in His only begotten Son. He lives as the Creator who was both able and willing to perform this act of self-giving. Hence His creation is not the mere positing and guaranteeing, the mere actualisation of this other. It is no characterless creation and event, but one which is characterised as the affirmation, election and acceptance of the creature. It is the positing and guaranteeing of the other to whom God wills to manifest His glory, to confirm His good-pleasure and thus to bind and commit Himself. Creation is a benefit because it establishes the presupposition of the execution of this divine will and plan, because it provides a sphere and object for the divine affirmation, election and acceptance, for the divine goodness and providence. Creation is a benefit inasmuch as it is based upon and attains its end in the divine covenant with man. Thus even the creature does not merely exist, but does so as the sphere and object of the covenant, as the being to whom God has devoted His good-will and whom He has destined to share in the overflowing of His own [364] fulness of life and love. To be a creature means to be determined to this end, to be affirmed, elected and accepted by God. To be a creature means to exist after the manner of Israel; after the manner which God in His own Son has not deemed it unworthy to adopt as His own. To be a creature means to be prepared for the place where His honour dwells. The creature is a beneficiary because his being does not arise without this intention and end. And finally

---

[EN44] nature teaches

even the self-revelation of the Creator to His creature is not the mere making known of the fact that He, and therefore His creature, is real, and that creation is actualisation. It is this too; it includes it. But it is not only this. It embraces the Creator not only as such but also as the sovereign Lord of the covenant of His grace; creation not only as such but also including the covenant which underlies it; and the creature not only as such but including his determination as a covenant-partner with God. It takes place in the course of the history of the covenant. It is the impelling factor in this history; the Word of God to His people, to Israel and the Church; the Word of grace for lost and saved sinners spoken in the course of God's dealings with men. Its content is the good news that God in His Son is not against them but for them. Proclaiming this to man, it meets him in sheer confrontation, but it also wins his heart and at the same time wins authority over him, awakening him to faith and obedience, placing him in a position of pure thankfulness, compelling him with the compulsion which excludes all choice and gives him freedom for the only true choice, viz. the acceptance of his election. As the glad tidings of Jesus Christ, God's self-disclosure is the work of the Holy Spirit by which man is inwardly assured of the grace of God and his own existence in grace, being both captured and liberated in God.

But as the glad tidings of Jesus Christ, it is also the disclosure of the real existence of the Creator and the creature, and thus includes the revelation that creation is actualisation. The gracious God is, and the creature which receives His grace is. For the God of grace discloses Himself to the creature as the One who is, and in so doing discloses the fact that the creature also is. He is real, and, actualised in creation, His creature is also real. It is permitted to be. This is the more precise Christian formulation of the existence of the Creator and the creature, and of the recognition of their existence. And it is the recognition of this co-existence of the Creator and the creature, characterised by the mutual implication of creation and the covenant, which we have had in mind in all that we have so far said. Only on this basis can there be a clear distinction between what we say to ourselves on the ground of our awareness of ourselves and the world, and what must be said to us by a higher Judge if it is to be valid; between assumptions and probabilities rooted in our own mind, and self-grounded certitude and truth; between our consciousness of God and God's unfailing self-disclosure; between the human idea of an existent God in [365] whom all existence is grounded and the existence of this God Himself implying that of man and his world; between the circle of our consciousness and being and the confrontation of this circle by the God in whom consciousness and being are not two but one. It is clear that the unconditional superiority of being over appearance, of recognition over doubt, can become apparent only in the light of this distinction; that the step from doubt to recognition can be taken only in the dynamic which this distinction suggests. But the dynamic of this distinction implies the mutual involvement of creation and covenant by which creaturely existence is characterised as permission to be.

It is only from this standpoint that the Cartesian proof of existence is really left behind. It is only from this standpoint that a better and genuine proof of existence can be made. We have attempted to give such a proof from this standpoint. It is only from this standpoint that the Christian Church can and will always offer such a proof. When it does this, it is always on solid ground. It apprehends the existence of the Creator and the knowledge of His creature in the fact that the Creator is gracious to His creature. It also sees this element of the wisdom of creation in the fact of the covenant which is the basis and goal of creation; in Jesus Christ "through whom" the existing Creator has created a truly existing creature. In Him creation is actualisation. In Him it is recognisable as such. If the covenant of grace is no illusion, if the love of God and the fact that we are loved in Jesus Christ is no dream, neither is the existence of God, nor our own existence, nor that of the world around us; neither is our consciousness that we are and that things outside us also are; neither is our consciousness of self or the world; neither is even our consciousness of God, however problematical this may be in itself. As a sure revelation of the covenant, the self-disclosure of the Creator is also a sure revelation of His reality as the Creator and therefore of our reality as His creatures. It thus means the basic end of all doubt either of that primary reality on the one hand or this secondary reality on the other. In affirming the created world as the sphere and object of His own glorification, and therefore of His good-will, God has affirmed it as such. And in proclaiming to us that first Yes, He also places the second in our hearts and on our lips—the recognition that He is and that we are—so that we can and must live in being and not in illusion, in trust and not in doubt. We doubt His word, and the reality of Jesus Christ dying and rising again in the real created world, if we still entertain suspicions about the reality of God and ourselves and our world. A command and a prohibition are issued at this point which radically cut off our retreat.

[366]

3. CREATION AS JUSTIFICATION

The affirmation of the creature by God the Creator implies in the second place that God has justified it. In this second and decisively important part of our statement, we take up that which we have so far formulated only in negative terms, viz. that the creature does not "merely" exist. The reality which it has and is, is not just any reality. Its being is not neutral; it is not bad but good. Because it is, and is thus distinct from nothingness, it is distinct from the bad and evil. In the words of the Genesis saga, it is separated from the darkness of chaos. Because it is affirmed and not denied, elected and not rejected, it is the object of God's good-pleasure. Because it may be by God, it may also be good. Its creation by God implies not only its actualisation but also its justification. Under whatever aspect it may present itself, whatever it may make of itself, whatever may become of it, however it is to be interpreted in detail and as a whole, it is good to the extent that it is, and it is therefore right for God and before Him, in the judgment of the One to whom it owes its existence. This is valid without reservation or qualification: naturally within the limits which divide the creature from the Creator, what is affirmed from the One who affirms, and therefore its goodness from His goodness; but within these limits absolutely without qualification. Gen. 1^{31} applies here too: "God saw every thing that he had made, and, behold, it was very good." The only thing which can be better than what is by God (apart from God Himself) is what is to develop out of what is in its communion and encounter with God. The only thing which can be better than creaturely existence is the goal of the covenant for which the creature is determined in and with its creation. But in the order of created existence as such there can be nothing better than what is. What is by God and is thus well pleasing to God, what is elected, accepted and justified by God, is for this reason not only good, but very good, perfect. Even the good and the best, which awaits its fulfilment at the goal of its fellowship and dealings with God, can add nothing to the perfection of its being as such. Even its future glorification presupposes that it is already perfectly justified by the mere fact of its creation. At this point there can be advanced only the affirmation of creaturely existence in this sense. Creation may be good, and is good, because the judgment with which God confronts it is good, because the God is good who in actualising it also justifies it. In echoing this divine judgment, in acknowledging and accepting the justification achieved in its actualisation, the creature may recognise himself and his fellow-creature as good. Creaturely goodness is the benefit of creation. Hence the recognition of creaturely goodness is the recognition of the benefit inherent in creation on the basis of the self-disclosure of the Creator.

It is clear that this recognition too, and particularly, cannot be attained or [367] firmly based and maintained in any other way. The statement that creation means justification and is thus a benefit in this precise sense, that that which is by it is good as such, is a more audacious and hazardous affirmation than that of creation as actualisation. If the creature cannot know of itself that it is, how can it know of itself that it is good? By what means, by what standard, is it to reach a solid judgment in the matter? How can it have on this point anything but opinions and suppositions, or advance anything but hypotheses? And how can these opinions, suppositions and hypotheses fail to be more distantly or closely limited by others? How can we justify a situation in which a difficult choice is continually demanded between one clear-cut affirmation and another which is opposed to it or neutral? How, then, can man persuade himself that at this vital point he knows something definite and has something definite to say? If he is to know and confidently to affirm that creation is justified and therefore good, he must receive an intimation to this effect from the source which has justified it. The basis and essence and criterion of the good must step in and so speak in the hearing of the creature that there can be no negative decision or neutral recession from the positive affirmation, the positive being so commanded that even in its freedom the creature has to appropriate it and make it without doubt or hesitation. If the clash of opinions is not to have the last word here too, we have to be enabled, authorised and compelled to perceive and declare that creation is justification, that creaturely being is good.

But here too the mere introduction of the thought of God is quite inadequate to bring us to this decision. It is, of course, an obvious temptation to strengthen the positive view, the optimistic thesis, by bringing it into immediate connexion with the being of a kindly God. But it has to be considered that the idea of a kindly God might only be the last and supreme expression of a scheme of valuation in which we think that from any accidental point of departure and with any arbitrarily chosen criterion we can reach unaided the conclusion that creation is justified. Or again, it might be the last and supreme expression of our desire to lend an absolute character to our own scheme of valuation, thus imparting a categorical emphasis to our justification of creation. Or finally, it might be the last and supreme expression of the certainty with which, absolutising our own valuation, we think we can proceed in our judgment of creation. It is certainly tempting in this valuation, desire and supposed certainty, to try to procure for our procedure an ultimate guarantee by invoking a supreme name. Its force will certainly not be less than that of our valuation, desire and certainty. How seriously we take it all will undoubtedly appear in the fact that we now venture to speak plainly of the kindness of a

[368]   God. But how can the force of this guarantee be greater than the intended force of our valuation, desire and opinion? What can we really attain in this way apart from a comforting and expressive underlining to convictions already formed and established? To what extent, for example, can it be the basis of a state of affairs which exists in any case? Can the invocation of a *Deus Optimus Maximus*[EN45] be in itself more than the pathetic asseveration of a thesis which as the product of a creaturely mind can have only the force of a hypothesis even with the help of this asseveration? It cannot and will not. Even when it is expressed in the form of this asseveration, it is an element in the self-conversation of the creaturely mind which even in the invocation of the *Deus Optimus Maximus*[EN46] is only another and more emphatic appeal to the right, dignity and authority of its own valuation, desire and confident opinion, and in which, in attempting to justify being, it does not omit first and foremost to justify itself. For this very reason it is only with relative certainty that it can assert and maintain itself against other and opposed theses and hypotheses, against all kinds of more or less radical complaints about life, and especially against various attempts at qualification. Its vindication of being is always open

---

[EN45] Best and Greatest God
[EN46] Best and Greatest God

to attack, and has in fact been attacked, on the very same ground on which it thinks it can and should justify life. It can never affirm the goodness of life without in the same breath having to doubt it. However emphatically it expresses its Yes, it will always accompany it with a secret No, or even with a Yes and No. Even in the invocation of the idea of God, in the appeal to the *Deus Optimus Maximus*[EN47], and therefore in the extreme intensification of its assertion, it is still itself in supreme need of justification. It cannot escape the disquieting consideration that unfortunately the same idea of God can also be invoked in support of other theses and hypotheses. It unfortunately cannot be said of the unaided mind of man that it can be filled with the idea of the goodness of God, for its optimism may easily turn into pessimism and even indifference, and again it will also feel it necessary and possible to find for its judgments and fears, but also for its weariness and half-heartedness, and finally for its own attempts to absolutise its corresponding judgments concerning being, something like an objective basis and background by trying to anchor all this in an ultimate reality described by the name of God or a term ostensibly equivalent to this name. Divinity is in this respect only the monstrous concave mirror in which the most various opinions of the creaturely mind are reflected and can be recognised. In this matter it does not stand above but within the conflict, just as the creaturely mind itself does not find itself above but within the dialectic of Yes and No, so that while it would like to prefer the Yes it must also leave some place at least for the No, and can never cling to an unequivocal Yes with the certitude necessary for a life lived in faith.

It is in this situation that we again take as our point of departure the self-disclosure of God the Creator. When we do this, our move has nothing whatever to do with the introduction of the thought of God for the purpose of rescuing the optimistic thesis. God's self-disclosure and faith in it are not an underlining of the creature's self-understanding, or the hypostatisation of a human opinion, but, in opposition to various competing human opinions, the revelation and recognition of the divine judgment on creaturely being. For it is of this, of the light of the divine good-pleasure resting on the created world, that the *valde bonum*[EN48] of Gen. 1^{31} speaks. This is something quite other than the lights which man may here and there see or fail to see in his own being and essence and that of the world. Neither is it a light like that which, with the help of the idea of a good God, man may as he sees fit discover in the world of creaturely being, only to find out later that this light is uncertain, and that in the created world even the thought of God throws as much shadow or even more shadow than light, and possibly universal darkness. The light of the Creator is not something which can be controlled either objectively or subjectively

[369]

[EN47] Best and Greatest God
[EN48] very good

by the creature. In face of all the attempted interpretations by optimists, pessimists and sceptics, it shines out in its own manner and strength. It can neither be kindled nor put out, neither dimmed nor concealed. It shines in its own power, and even the fact that its light is seen is always its own doing. While all creaturely being as such attests and reflects it, it is objectively and subjectively the result of the free action of the Creator Himself who is the basis of creation and the measure of its goodness. It shines authoritatively and thus liberates us from all human opinions. It decides the conflict of thesis and hypothesis before it has begun. It makes it quite impossible.

The self-revelation of the Creator, which must be our point of departure for an understanding of the goodness of His creation, implies the revelation of the truth that created being is justified by Him, and is therefore right as it is. It is to be noticed here too that the latter truth is given only by implication. Hence we must not try to grasp it abstractly and in isolation from the essential and chief content of divine revelation. We do not adequately appreciate what it tells us if, for example, we try to consult it only incidentally and with half an ear in this one respect, i.e., in seeking an answer to our question about the meaning of existence. In so doing, we inevitably confuse it with a human idea of God, and we need not be surprised if we find that in the last resort it is just as profitless for our purposes as the latter. Even in Gen. 1[31] the assertion that God found all that He had made to be very good cannot be understood in isolation from its context as a description of the cosmos. Of course, the Creator justifies the cosmos as such. But He does so only because the latter is created according to His will and plan, and therefore with the purpose of instituting and fulfilling the covenant between the divine Creator and man. He justifies it in view of this meaning and end of its creation and of His own dealings with it as the sphere and object of His activity. The created world is, therefore, right as it is, because in its essence and structure it is an appropriate sphere and instrument of the divine activity, and because man at the heart of it is the true object of the divine work which has its beginning, centre and end in Jesus Christ. Its rightness, goodness, worth and perfection spring from its correspondence to the work of God's own Son as resolved from all eternity and fulfilled in time. Because the divine self-disclosure has as its content the covenant of grace and therefore the work of the Son of God, it carries within itself the adequate and conclusive and incontestable answer to the question of the rightness of creaturely being as such. Inasmuch as this revelation speaks to us of Jesus Christ, it also tells us that the action of the Creator towards His creation is genuinely and in the widest sense of the term beneficent, and is for us the unambiguous and indisputable reason why we for our part should be pleased with what was well-pleasing to Him, being not merely content with creaturely being but unconditionally glad because of it. What is creaturely exists in order to be serviceable to the glory of God in the work of His Son. Because it lies under this determination, it is not evil but good, and not imperfectly but perfectly good. This is the decision actualised in and with the activity of God as Creator, and revealed in and with

[370]

God's self-revelation. It bids defiance to the darkness and dialectics in which the goodness of creation is hidden from us and from our thinking, and this darkness and dialectics is also defied by faith, which is the awareness of the reality of the Creator disclosed in His self-revelation. What *we* consider to be the truth about the created world is one thing. Quite another is the covenant of grace, the work of Jesus Christ, for the sake and in fulfilment of which creation exists as it is. The latter is the proper and principal content of the Creator's self-revelation. It is the latter which, revealed to us, relieves us of the task of having to form our own opinion about creation and either acquitting it with the optimists or condemning it with the pessimists. It is the latter which also and particularly relieves us of the false attitude of resignation or neutrality in face of the question of its goodness, or of involvement in the whole clash of opinions. For in face of this it gives us the most definite and secure position. It is our duty—and this is what we are taught by the self-revelation of God in Jesus Christ—to love and praise the created order because, as is made manifest in Jesus Christ, it is so mysteriously well-pleasing to God. And we must do this no matter what our own opinion about it may have been yesterday, or may be to-day or to-morrow.

Created order has what we may call its brighter side. But its justification by its Creator and His self-disclosure is not bound up with this brighter side. It is not connected with the fact that the sun shines, that there are blossoms and fruits, pleasing shapes, colours and sounds, realities and groups of realities which preserve and foster life, purposeful relationships and order, intelligible, controllable and serviceable elements and powers, which enlighten the cre- [371] ated mind of man, speak to his heart, and in some way correspond with his will for life and foster it. The righteousness of creation is not identical with this Yes, with the exultation of which it is undoubtedly capable, and man within it. It is certainly not the denial of this Yes. Indeed, it confirms it. Its own Yes includes this Yes. And only in virtue of its own Yes can the latter have any force. The joyful voice of the creature rings out where the self-revelation of God has been apprehended. Its word, too, is valid. An affirmative judgment on creation has its foundation and rightful place. The recognition of its direct and immanent goodness is demanded from the man whom the Creator in His revelation has confronted with Himself. In this very process of divine encounter he is placed before the reality of the created world, and to this reality belongs also this direct and immanent goodness. And to the praise of the Creator there definitely belongs gratitude for an order, beauty and purposefulness which speak for themselves, and a world-affirming attitude directly and genuinely grounded, not in illusions, but in actual phenomena and relationships. Thus the call that we should seek joy is not merely a concession or permission but a command which cannot be lightly regarded by one who has appreciated the divine justification of creation. We need not be ashamed before the holiness of God if we can still laugh and must laugh again, but only if we allow laughter to wither away, and above all if we have relapsed into a sadly ironic smile. The latter especially is excluded, for it surely conceals an evil superiority, a wholly inadmissible resistance to the divine revelation, which so illumines the created world that it demands our brightest and not an obstinately clouded Yes. But the divine self-revelation is not dependent on this illumination and brightness of the created world. If it gives us reason to rejoice in creaturely being, this does not spring from the fact that the latter in itself and as such gives cause for rejoicing. If it requires our gratitude for all that is undoubtedly characteristic of the created world in the way of direct and immanent goodness, its requirement is not confined to this demand for gratitude. If it forbids us to be blind and hardened or even indifferent in this matter, it bids us primarily and above all to be always perceptive and mindful of itself, directing our attention primarily to the transcendent reason of all reasons for being grateful. It shines primarily and essentially in its own light. If the created world shines, it does so in reflection of this light. But the light of revelation shines even where the created world itself is without light because the same God who gives it light at one point refuses it light at another, willing to reveal Himself here but to conceal Himself there. God is free to deal in this way with creation. It is still His work and witness, though His silent witness. For His Word also implies His silence; what He says implies what He does not say; His Yes implies His No; His [372] grace His judgment. His self-revelation as Creator also contains, as a true Word, His silence, No and judgment. Hence we must not be surprised if it is not identifiable with the Yes which we find in the created world. And however brightly this reflected light may shine, we must not refuse to go back to the source which knows a very different and the only unambiguous light. We do well to adhere to the supreme transcendence of divine revelation if only because we are obviously not in a position to rejoice in its reflection in the positive declaration of the direct and immediate goodness of creation, or to estimate in a way which even remotely corresponds to its objective value. What is there even in the created world which may not be infinitely better and more beautiful than we can possibly suspect? Who is able to do justice to its intrinsic value in quality only (to say nothing of the quantitative wealth all around us), and to be genuinely and correspondingly joyful and thankful? What would be our position if the revelation of the grace of God were tied to this witness of the created world, and we were dependent on our wretched understanding of this witness? From this standpoint, too, it is as well to remember the independence of the divine revelation, for the witness of the created world itself and as such is not objectively exhausted in the affirmation of its direct and immanent goodness, because in fact it does not offer us only a positive but also a negative aspect, thus placing a negative as well as a positive judgment on our lips. We are not in a position altogether to elude the shadow which is also characteristic of existence. Sooner or later, in one way or another, we shall have to give ear to this sad voice. And what becomes then of the vital recognition that everything is good as it is? In every respect, therefore, it is as well that, notwithstanding the truth and power of its attestation by the intrinsic goodness of creation, the divine self-disclosure should also shine in its own light, going its own way, and thus making us independent of the weakness and hesitancy of our own judgment and enabling us to do justice to the reality of the created world even on its darker aspect, to accept its silent or negative testimony, and thus to recognise its perfection not only in individual details but in its totality.

We have cause to remember on this side too that the justification of creaturely being by the self-revelation of the Creator is certainly not bound up with the darker side of human existence. The matter has been represented as if the true meaning of creation begins only where its direct and immanent goodness is to some extent negated, and revealed as apparent only where its nothingness emerges, where it says No to itself and therefore where it can only be denied by man. This point of view is not justified. The justice of creation is not compromised by the fact that the heavens grow dark, that harmony is engulfed in disharmony and teleology obscured by senselessness. It does not begin only at its frontier. And its revelation is not one with the announcement of the destruction of what is, with the contradiction and extinction of the human will for life, [373] or with the sentence of death. It does not attain credibility only as it discloses the falsehood and shame and misery and lostness of all existence. It is not identical with the No which does, of course, also characterise the created world, and which it also expresses in the form of self-accusation and self-pity. At this point, too, we have to say that it does not deny this but affirms it. Its Yes echoes and underlines this No. It is its Yes which first gives force to this No. And therefore this negative voice is also heard and its word is valid. This negative verdict on being is also justified—more so than it can possibly realise as a purely human judgment. The discovery of the inner lostness of being, despair of the meaning and strength of the human will for life, a sober realisation of his limits and of the frailty and end of all things, the unconditional admission of all this is undoubtedly required of the man whom the Creator confronts with Himself in revelation. How can a man stand before his Creator without realising that he is lost and must perish? When with the Creator the reality of the created world is also revealed to him, he necessarily sees that in comparison with the goodness of the Creator the latter is not good, and he cannot with conviction close his eyes to its riddles, paradoxes and contradictions. And to the praise of the Creator there belongs an unqualified readiness to confess that as creation owes everything to Him it cannot discharge the debt, but in its guilty creatureliness it is dust and ashes before Him. Again there is no illusion. Again we are faced by serious reasons. Again there is a divine requirement, not merely a concession and permission for particularly humble and troubled hearts, but a command which whether it is obeyed or not is issued to every one. It is also true that the Creator is to be sought and found at the end as well as the beginning of all the inner perfection of creation. Hence the man who must and will weep has no need to be ashamed when faced by the Creator's goodness. The only man who has cause for shame is he who motivated by a false pride refuses to weep, or perhaps for simple lack of insight has lost the capacity to do so. The very last thing which ought to happen is the attempt to elude the misery of life. It is in fact the heaviest curse which can strike a man if he really eludes it, and it is doubly heavy if he masters it in a painless mingling of joy and sorrow. It is the revelation of God which, when He is silent and says No and exercises judgment, clouds the created world and wills to be honoured in this too, demanding human complaint and accusation. But the revelation of God is as little bound up with the confining darkness of being as with its light. While it gives us cause for complaint and accusation, and places in our mouth a negative judgment on being, it does not in any sense consist in what creation can and does reveal in this way. It is not in any sense to be identified with the darkness of the created world. It challenges us not to evade the sighing of the created world. It challenges us not to evade the sighing of the creature. It gives power and life to this sighing. But its command is not exhausted in bidding us share in this sighing. If in this respect too it forbids obduracy or blindness, indifference or heedlessness, its primary command is attention to itself as the ground of all grounds for sorrow before God and therefore to salvation. Again we have to remember that it illuminates primarily with its own light and reveals primarily its own truth. This applies even when it casts shadows. It is true even of the No which accompanies its Yes, of the judgment which accompanies its grace, of the silence without which the divine Word could not be spoken. Even when we are enwrapped in shadow we have to consider that the same God who brings darkness upon us is always free to act quite differently towards us. We must not charge Him with the fact that He now enfolds us in darkness. We must not fondly imagine that we have to seek Him only in the shadow. He does not dispose only of the witnesses of His silence, No and judgment which now surround us. He can replace them in a moment by very different witnesses. And even though they are not replaced, even though we are continually hidden in shadows, they are only witnesses. Their silence, No and judgment in themselves and as such is in no way identical with the God who is their Lord. And the sorrow which they cause us is not in itself identical with the sorrow into which He plunges us as He takes up our cause to make us glad. His self-revelation takes place in the heights, above all the misery of life, and radically beyond even the greatest convulsions caused by the discords and meaninglessness of life. It can and does use these convulsions. But we should not be truly and deeply shaken, as we must be in the saving encounter with the divine self-revelation, if the latter were exhausted in this aspect of our experience of the created world. To our salvation it is not actually exhausted in this. For again it is subjectively the case that our senses and thinking are far too blunted for us even to realise what we experience of the created world in this respect. Just as we hear the exultation of being only partially and confusedly, so too and especially do we hear its complaint, against which we naturally shut our ears more tightly and readily. For this reason the judgment of God, without which we cannot experience His grace, would certainly never strike us if God had imposed upon Himself the limitation of committing the No which we must

[374]

368

hear wholly and utterly to the riddles and contradictions of life, to sorrow and pain and death. One can blind oneself even to the terrors of death—and of all who have died only one man has not done this. But objectively again it must be said that the witness of existence itself and as such is not unequivocal. Its voice is never so plainly negative and therefore serious, disturbing and humbling as to be able to bring and bind us to the sorrow which God has determined for us in order to make us truly glad. Our disquietudes, objectively considered, are never so great and crushing as to make us ultimately disturbed and therefore ready to find peace in God. For it is palpable that they are always followed by [375] pacifications which easily enable us to recover our poise—which has nothing whatever to do with the peace of God. As for death, its significance is nowhere so obvious in the world of creation that the thought of it necessarily induces reflection on the divine judgment. For as far as we can see, in spite of all the terrors which it may impress upon us, death does not usually meet us except in association with new life. Hence we cannot establish eternal truths even from a consideration of the negative aspect of existence and our own negative judgment on it. Even along these lines, *via negativa*EN49, we cannot reach the knowledge of God and therefore the vital recognition that everything is right as it is. If our share in the misery of life has the power to bind us to God, and thus to assure us of the justification of being, that is not due to the power of creaturely existence itself, and therefore to our own power, but to the independent power of divine revelation which transcends all creaturely power. It is as well that it has this independent and intrinsic power and goes its own way even though it is evinced in the creaturely testimony to its truth which can also serve it. And it is as well that we ourselves are made independent of the question concerning the depth and emphasis of our seriousness, the profundity of our capacity to suffer, our susceptibility to genuine disturbance and assault. We are never altogether serious if the revelation of the Creator is not serious in and by itself, and does not therefore make us ready to do justice to all reality and to recognise its perfection not merely in detail but at every point.

Thus far, however, we have only asserted and not explained that the creation of God is the justification of creaturely being, so that His self-revelation discloses its affirmation by God, and therefore His good-pleasure resting upon it, and therefore its perfection.

It is necessary to explain (1) the fact that the divine revelation not only transcends the two contradictory aspects and thus relativises the contrasting judgments of existence but implies primarily and particularly a confirmation of these two aspects and judgments (as opposed to their neutralisation by doubt). Why and to what extent is it the case that the divine revelation manifests both the sorrow and joy of life, and therefore not only permits but commands us to laugh and weep, to be glad and sorrowful, precluding only the attitude of indifference, the judgment of the sceptic? The answer is to be

---

EN49 by the way of negation

found in the fact that the revelation of God the Creator so closely binds the life which He has created with the covenant in which He willed to make Himself the Lord and Helper and Saviour of man; with the reconciliation of the world with Himself to be accomplished in Jesus Christ. In this intention of the Creator and therefore this final goal of the creature as manifested in the divine revelation, there is implied from the very outset, as far as the nature and essence of the creature are concerned, a twofold determination: on the one [376] hand an exalta tion and dignity of the creature in the sight of God (for otherwise how could it be His partner, or be accepted by Him?); and on the other hand the equally clear need and peril of the creature before Him (for otherwise how could it be so exclusively referred to His lordship and help in the covenant, and to reconciliation with God in the person of His Son?). God created man to lift him in His own Son into fellowship with Himself. This is the positive meaning of human existence and all existence. But this elevation presupposes a wretchedness of human and all existence which His own Son will share and bear. This is the negative meaning of creation. Since everything is created for Jesus Christ and His death and resurrection, from the very outset everything must stand under this twofold and contradictory determination. It is not nothing but something; yet it is something on the edge of nothing, bordering it and menaced by it, and having no power of itself to overcome the danger. It is destined for God as certainly as it is actual by Him alone; yet it is not incapable of being unfaithful to its origin and destiny and becoming the instrument of sin. It has subsistence; yet it does not have such subsistence as it can secure and maintain for itself. It lives; yet it does not live in such a way that its life is guaranteed in its own strength against destruction and death. It may hope in its Creator; yet it must also despair of its own ability to build for itself a future. And it is in this way that it stands in the presence of its Creator according to His self-revelation. This is how He wills it to be. This is how He has created it. This is what underlies the two aspects of its being—something more profound and radical and essential than may be descried by human vision or expressed in human judgment. Hence the joy and the misery of life have their foundation in the will of God. The two contrasting interpretations may be only opinions in human thought and speech, and as such they may be as little able as any human opinions to do justice to the real situation. But they have their root in the will of God and in the truth of being. It is really the command of God that we should rejoice with them that do rejoice, and weep with them that weep. Those who rejoice are justified and so too are those who mourn and protest. They are not intrinsically right but they are made right—more so than they themselves can imagine. The only ones who are wrong are the indolent and neutral, who in their wisdom do the less justice to the real situation the more they oppose it in their wisdom and therefore in their indolence and neutrality to the twofold determination of existence.

A further fact needing explanation is (2) that the self-disclosure of God the Creator does not merely confirm but transcends these two aspects, and therefore these two views of life. It includes them, but it is also superior to them and independent of them. It can use them, but it is not tied to them. It speaks of a very different exaltation than that which the greatest exultation of being can proclaim. But it speaks also of a very different misery than can be attested by the most vocal complaint about life. It is exhausted neither in the positive nor in the negative verdict of the creature. It pronounces an unconditional Yes and unconditional No as the voice of being itself never does. In what does its superiority consist? The answer is that it consists in the fact that the self-revelation of God is His own Word; that in it the Creator Himself has become creature. The secret, the meaning and the goal of creation is that it reveals, or that there is revealed in it, the covenant and communion between God and man, and therefore the fulfilment of being as a whole, which is so serious and far-reaching that the Word by which God created all things, even God Himself, becomes as one of His creatures, being there Himself like everything else, like all the created reality distinct from Himself, and thus making His own its two-fold determination, its greatness and wretchedness, its infinite dignity and infinite frailty, its hope and its despair, its rejoicing and its sorrow. This is what has taken place in Jesus Christ as the meaning and end of creation. His humili-ation and exaltation as the Son of God are the self-revelation of God the Cre-ator. What is all the majesty otherwise evinced by the creature when compared with the exaltation which it has been granted here? And what is all the lowli-ness otherwise disclosed by it when compared with the lowliness to which it has stooped here? For here the majesty and lowliness of God Himself are mani-fested. Here God Himself in His Son has made its majesty His apparel and its lowliness His shame. But it is evident that the Yes and No heard here are as distinct from every other Yes and No as are the heavens from the earth. It is evident that here both are proclaimed unconditionally and compellingly, being limited neither by the relativity which otherwise confines their expres-sion, nor by human incapacity to do justice to them. And it is evident again that here both go out in radical independence of the content and power of the revelations which creaturely being may otherwise convey concerning its two-fold determination, of the various judgments with which we more or less sin-cerely react to these revelations, and of the various opinions which we are accustomed to form in this connexion. Since it is God Himself who here goes His way rejoicing and sorrowing, everything that we think we know about this matter is not just relatively but absolutely transcended. Since it is God Himself who authenticates the matter in His own person, making Himself the Subject of this twofold determination of being, both aspects are unmistakeable, and it is clear that we cannot wholly escape either the one or the other. Since it is God Himself who assumes both aspects of existence, we are unambiguously sum-moned to take life seriously in its twofold determination, and unambiguously forbidden to evade either His No or His Yes, either sorrow or joy, the indo-lence and neutrality in which our human wisdom might seek its last refuge

[377]

[378] being so plainly forbidden us that this last possibility can only appear to us as the most impossible of all courses. In the light of God's own participation in the splendour and misery of created being, we can only say that even the most superficial joy in life and the most facile sorrow are better than indifference to reality. Indifference alone—if the accursed were capable of it—would be genuine ungodliness.

There is need also to explain the fact (3) that the self-revelation of God the Creator, in confirming and transcending the two aspects of being and the corresponding judgments, discloses the perfection of being, the divine good-pleasure resting upon it, its justification by its Creator, and therefore that it is right as it is, that it is good in its totality, indeed that it is the best. Here we are obviously confronted by the decisive point in the whole question. What is the mutual relationship between the two aspects confirmed and transcended by the revelation of the Creator? Is the one the limit of the other? Are they both valid alongside each other? Is there an equilibrium of Yes and No, in and for which God has created the reality distinct from Himself? Is this reality dual in character? And is this duality its eternal destiny? If so, we obviously cannot speak of a perfection of being. We can know nothing of its justification and right. We are undoubtedly compelled to seek this justification by chance or caprice, and therefore according to the dictates of subjective opinion, which is necessarily exposed to the contradiction of different opinions. And in these circumstances it may well be that the sceptic, the moderate man who keeps to the middle of the road, the man who no longer cares either to laugh or weep, the genuine and perfidious godless man, is the one who is really justified. It is as well to realise the true situation in respect of this third question. We cannot actually find a human basis on which a legitimate co-ordination of the two aspects and interpretations can be established. It is understandable that this coordination has been constantly sought and attempted in different ways. But apart from divine revelation this has always been at the expense of the full seriousness of one or other aspect, at the expense of the necessary rigour of the judgment demanded on both sides. For instance, the No heard in this matter may be rendered innocuous by bringing it into peaceful continuity with a much more triumphant Yes. Conversely, the Yes may be slurred over and made only the syllable before a much more crushing No. And *via positiva*[EN50] or *via negativa*[EN51] there is attained a justification of being, an affirmation of its inner perfection, or of the perfection which limits it outwardly, and this will have force and balance so long as we are not subjectively disturbed by the objective pressure exerted from the opposite side, and so long as we are not prevented by the divine revelation with its unqualified and disruptive emphasising of the antitheses. And if it is not the divine revelation but only an opposing consideration of a different origin which is responsible for the

---

[EN50] by way of affirmation
[EN51] by way of negation

disturbance, we may yield to the pressure of this counterbalancing factor, per- [379]
haps arriving at a different distribution of the various elements in the truth,
becoming a pessimist instead of an optimist or *vice versa*, but always with the
proviso that the second or any future decision is no more secure and definitive
than the first. And there will then present itself as the final conclusion of wisdom the possibility of placing ourselves at some neutral point midway
between, and thus coming to rest in the sphere of radical ungodliness. Perhaps
in the last analysis the only real choice is between ungodliness and faith in the
divine revelation. But let us suppose that we have no choice even between
these two; that the divine revelation forbids us either to ignore the exultation
of being on the one side or to minimise its misery on the other. Let us suppose
that it is from this angle that we have encountered the problem, and that once
we have become aware of them we cannot escape either the severity of the Yes
or the no less evident severity of the No. Let us suppose that we have been
obliged to ask concerning the righteousness of what is because the question
has been raised inescapably and unconditionally from both standpoints. In the
light of what we have said it is strange and yet true that in these circumstances
and on these presuppositions we not only can but must give a positive answer
to this question. When the name of God is heard in the conflict of these two
aspects of being, this does not only mean that they now gain full seriousness
and rigour, or that they are both radically transcended. For the name of God is
the name of the Lord of all life. To hear His voice is to be confronted by the
decision which has been taken on life as a whole, and by which it is determined
and ruled in both its aspects. And to hear God and assent to this fulfilled decision is to be forced to recognise the goodness of existence as determined and
ruled by Him. At this point everything depends on whether it is really the
name of God which is heard and the decision taken by Him to which assent is
given. A surrogate cannot perform for us the service which is necessary if we
are to achieve a positive attitude to creation and therefore to our own and all
created being. We speak of a God who has given us authentic information
about Himself as Creator. It is not enough, therefore, if we try to persuade
ourselves that the goodness of God is in some sense a valid philosophical proposition, and that by clinging to the thought of it we can bear the insoluble
conflict of the two aspects of being, maintaining with closed eyes, as it were,
the essential goodness of the reality created by God. This programme is quite
impracticable. The defiance of Christian faith without which no progress can
be made is not a blind defiance. As translated, explained and applied in the
New Testament, the Nevertheless of the Old is a Therefore. Christian faith sees
and knows to what it holds. It does not need to persuade itself of anything. It
has nothing to do with a tense clinging to the consequences of an idea, with
the laborious systematisation of a concept of God. It does not consist at all in
the resolve and exertion of enduring that conflict. It consists basically in the
recognition that it has already been endured, i.e., by God Himself who for our [380]
sakes endured and overcame it. On this basis, then, it is the defiant confidence

that we too can and will endure it. Its defiance springs from its sure confidence in this basis. For that reason it is not an obstinate and therefore a weak defiance. It is not a mere assertion, or idealistic postulate, or acceptance of resigned homage before the unfathomable, or subjection to the actuality of unresolved antinomies. On this basis it sees through the imperfections of being to its perfection. That this is not direct vision, but a seeing through, makes it a struggle—the struggle in which the decision fulfilled by God may be continually recognised as fulfilled by us. Yet the fact that on this basis it can and may be a true seeing, makes it a free and lighthearted struggle untainted by any toil or self-will. It can be this because it has its origin and object in God's self-revelation; because it has not to create a basis for what it sees and knows; because it has not to cling to an idea of God which it must first construct and systematise; because it has not to shoulder any kind of theoretical responsibility for the perfection of the created world, not even that of blind assertion. The Nevertheless is already spoken. God has spoken it. This divine Nevertheless is not only permitted but necessary for Christian faith because it is the required and legitimate justification of creation, the freedom in which man may become and be before God the Creator not only passively but actively at peace with Him and therefore with the world of His creature, in which he may himself be a mirror of the divine good-pleasure, and in which he may and must echo the divine affirmation of the creature in all humility, but also with definiteness.

That the Creator Himself willed to endure, and has endured, and still endures the contradiction in creaturely life is the first point to be noted in the foundation revealed in His self-revelation. For the real goodness of the real God is that the contradiction of creation has not remained alien to Himself. Primarily and supremely He has made it His own, and only then caused it to be reflected in the life of the creature. His rejoicing and sorrow preceded ours. For before light could gladden us and darkness torment us, He was aware of both, separating and thus co-ordinating them. Before life greeted us and death menaced us, He was the Lord of life and death, and bound them both in a bundle. And He did not do all this in such a way that He confronted it in mere superiority, so that it was alien and external to Him, but in such a way that in the full majesty of His Godhead He participated in these antitheses and their connexion, in eternal mercy causing them to be internal to Himself, and to find their origin in His own being. This is how we must put it if on the basis of His self-revelation we affirm that His covenant with man is the meaning and the goal and therefore the primary basis of creation. If this is so, He has taken [381] the creature to Himself even before it was, namely, in His own Son, who willed to live and die as a man for all men, as a creature for all creatures. He thus took it to Himself even in its very contradictions. He made His own both its menace and its hope. He did not spare Himself. He first placed Himself under the stern law of the twofold aspect of being. What are all the severity and relentlessness of its contradiction as known and experienced by us in comparison with the relentlessness and severity which He caused to be visited on Himself, on His own heart, even before He acted as Creator? What charge can we bring against the Creator in respect of this contradiction which He does not know first and infinitely better than we can ever do? We are inevitably too late even with the most careful and complete representations of the problem of being which we might attempt. It was and is primarily God's own problem. This means already that we are absolved from the necessity of having to solve it ourselves. We may really let it be the divine problem, and therefore keep to the divine solution. Naturally, this does not mean that the problem is to be relegated unsolved to the darkness of a secret divine counsel. As God's own problem it is precisely not a hidden problem, but one which is revealed to us and therefore posed with supreme urgency. It is, of course, the problem of Jesus Christ, His Son, our Lord, and as such it is not a dark dispensation, or a dark self-disposition of God, but in all its mystery a clear and clearly apprehensible fact which can be grasped with certainty and seen and understood. The self-revelation of God as our Creator consists in the fact that in Jesus Christ He gives Himself to us to be recognised as the One who has made our cause His own before it was or could be ours, who does not stand aloof from the contradiction of our being as a stranger, who has willed to bear it Himself, and has in fact borne it from all eternity. Thus it is not we who have discovered the problem of existence. Nor do we make any postulate regarding its solution. This does not mean that we refer it to a secret mystery of the being of God unknown to us. We do not snatch at an uncertain way of escape from a reality which we know into a sphere of which we have no knowledge. But we keep to the knowledge which God Himself has given us of Himself in order that we should keep to it. Thus the problem of existence is integral to us. But we must also confess that it was primarily and essentially God's own problem and only then and as such our own, so that it cannot be solved by us, but we have to recognise that it is solved by God. That as the Creator He intervenes and stands surety for us too is not an unknown fact but one which is known on the basis of the divine revelation.

That He stands surety for us in making the problem of existence His own affair is the next point calling for consideration. It did not happen casually or in obscure caprice that God's eternal mercy showed itself in the fact that from the very outset He willed to make His own, and did make His own in the person of His Son, the joy and sorrow, light and shade and life and death of creation. This took place on our behalf. It was the work of His eternal love that it was resolved and executed. We live by the fact that God Himself willed to be the Bearer of our contradiction, that in the full majesty of His Godhead He so deeply condescended to us. We live by the death and resurrection of Jesus Christ, by God's own suffering and triumph, sorrow and joy, by His original participation in the twofold nature of our being. Enduring to be what we are and as we are, He bears us. What would the creature be without the confidence [382]

375

that it is allowed to exist for the sake of the covenant, and for and in the covenant, which is the inner basis and meaning of its creation? What would it be as the creature of God if God willed to have nothing to do with it, if He did not will it for Himself, if He did not have dealings with it to win it for Himself, for existence in fellowship with Himself? The fact that this involves something so great and costly that the miracle of creation may almost seem to be dwarfed by the miracle of reconciliation at which it aims, nothing less than God's own intervention for the creature being sufficient to execute this counsel of love, is the real mystery at this point in which we can share only with blind faith because this relationship of God to us is absolutely incomprehensible, and can be known only in its actuality. But from the realised intervention of God for His creation we have to learn that no less than this was in fact sufficient to bring creation to this goal; or conversely, that this goal is so high that its attainment demanded nothing less than this intervention of God Himself. The counsel of divine love, which as such we can only reverence as it is revealed to us, involves His own participation in our life, and therefore in the antinomies of our life, His condescension and entrance into the imperfection of the created world. For love of us, God has made the problem of existence His own. When we realise this clearly, we cannot deny that there is a transparency, meaning and even perfection of creaturely imperfection. This is not intrinsic to it. It has gained this perfection from the fact that God in His Son has for our sakes appointed it His own vesture and nature. From this standpoint—and in all the imperfection unsparingly revealed from it—it is sanctified, blessed, affirmed and set in relation to God's own perfect being. How can we dispute this when God Himself has affirmed by His own condescension and entrance into its sphere, in the work of the love which He has addressed to us? What objection can we raise when God saw no objection to loving us so much, and therefore intervening so unreservedly on our behalf? Must not creaturely being be good, and are we not called to admit its goodness, in view of the revealed fact that on our behalf God willed to make it His own being? Is there any more decisive goodness than that which is assigned to it by this revealed action of God? Is there any more perfect world than that which, in its imperfection, is the arena, instrument and object of this divine action? To assert the contrary,

[383] it would be necessary to overlook this divine action, and thus to miss the central content of the divine self-declaration.

But a further step has necessarily to be risked. Can the contradiction of life, its dread aspect, and therefore the imperfection of creation really be a final word? Can its perfection remain in a certain sense behind and above it? In God and therefore in the world of His creation can we acquiesce in a juxtaposition of two spheres and therefore of two antithetical verdicts about its perfection? If our thinking starts at God's self-declaration, we cannot accept this position. For this declaration definitely does not speak of an ultimate antithesis of two spheres, of a parallel infinity of the two aspects, of a stable balance or absolute symmetry of these two factors, of an eternal dualism. It speaks of a dually orientated, but not of a dual reality. It speaks of one way and work, of one living action of God. Hence it does not permit us to systematise the relationship of these two dispensations of His will, as though we were dealing with the two pillars on which an edifice rests rather than with two successive events. It is quite clear that in appointing His Son to be the Bearer of creaturely existence and its contradictions God did not in the same way will and accomplish His humiliation and death on the one side and His exaltation and resurrection on the other. He pronounced the Yes and No with differing emphases. He took to His own heart very differently in Jesus Christ the infinite hope of the creature and its infinite peril. He is mighty in different ways in its power and weakness. In both cases the creature is subject to His power. In both directions His will is accomplished. His action, His own participation in light and darkness, life and death, implies either way the justification of creation. But this does not alter the profound difference with which the same end is accomplished in the two cases. In the person of Jesus Christ God has not definitively, let alone eternally, but only transiently shared the pain and death of creation. It is an act of providential care which He performs when He surrenders His own Son to the lowliness and misery of creaturely existence. He sees the hopeless peril of the created world which He has snatched from nothingness but which is still so near to nothingness. He sees that it cannot and will not check itself on the edge of this abyss. He sees its weakness and the power of temptation. And yet in this created world He wills to manifest His own glory. The man who forms its focal point must confirm and fulfil His will. He must stand firm and secure with Him in face of nothingness. He must say Yes with Him, and because of this he must also say No with Him, and therefore truly stand in covenant with Him. In order that this No should be spoken by man in his weakness and frailty as it was spoken by the Creator from all eternity, God Himself willed to become man, to make His own the weakness and frailty of man, to suffer and die as man, and in this self-offering to secure the frontier between His creation and the ruin which threatens it from the abyss. God is [384] gracious to man. He has appointed him to stand firm on this frontier, to say No in covenant with Him to what He has not willed but negated. But He knows man's incapacity to fulfil this destiny. And because He is unwilling to leave him unaided in the attempt to fulfil this destiny, He takes up his cause at this point and shares his creatureliness. He does this in order to rescue and preserve His creature. He does it because it is unable to rescue and preserve itself. It can be seen at once that there can be no question here of an end in itself. The No is not said for the sake of the No but for the sake of the Yes. We cannot stop at the suffering, death and burial of Jesus Christ. This is not a final word. The cross is followed by the resurrection, humiliation by exaltation, and the latter is the true, definitive and eternal form of the incarnate Son of God. This is the Yes for the sake of which the No had first to be spoken. This is the construction for the sake of which there had first to be a defence and securing of the frontier. This is the manifestation of the positive will of God for man. God gave Himself

377

up to the lowliness and misery of creaturely existence because otherwise the latter could not share His divine glory. By investing it with His glory, by raising and empowering weak and erring man in the person of His Son to say Yes with Him, He abandoned the prior and necessary No and cast the lowliness and misery of man behind Him, so that His participation in this negative aspect of existence became only a transient episode. It was the affair of a moment. The moment has now passed. Christ dieth no more. He lives eternally: not only as the Son of God but also as the Son of Man; not only as Creator of all things, but also as the creature whom He assumed to Himself, whose nature and cause He made His own, whose nature and cause He defended for a short time and conducted to eternal victory. Here we are at the end of the divine way. Here the final word is spoken. This explains the difference in the ways in which the one will of God is expressed and the one God is in control; the divergence between the two aspects of existence in the one work and living action of God; the asymmetry and disproportion, the polarity between the two determinations of created reality at the level of the covenant between God and man which is the meaning and end of creation. This is the form of the relationship between Yes and No in the created world according to the authentic revelation of God its Creator. It is clear that from this point of view it is impossible to speak of an eternal dualism of aspects, but only of a dualism which is dissoluble. If on this basis it is impossible to deny that they both actually exist, on the same basis they cannot be interpreted as two spheres which definitively limit each other and are similarly self-contained and secured. On the contrary, their juxtaposition is in terms of the movement and action of the strange battle in which "life and death wrestle together" and of which is to be said: "Life is

[385] victorious and has swallowed up death." The occurrence of this strange conflict is the justification of creaturely being. Not, then, a static perfection of God beyond and above creaturely imperfection, but the contesting and overcoming of the imperfection of the creature by God's own intervention on its behalf. In the interests of this divine conflict and victory, it may be imperfect, and even in its imperfection it already shares in God's own perfection. It does so in God's living action in Jesus Christ. It is the divine conflict and victory which forms the climax of the covenant and therefore the meaning and end of creation. And in Him the created world is already perfect in spite of its imperfection, for the Creator is Himself a creature, both sharing its creaturely peril, and guaranteeing and already actualising its hope. If the created world is understood in the light of the divine mercy revealed in Jesus Christ, of the divine participation in it eternally resolved in Jesus Christ and fulfilled by Him in time; if it is thus understood as the arena, instrument and object of His living action, of the once for all divine contesting and overcoming of its imperfection, its justification and perfection will infallibly be perceived and it will be seen to be the best of all possible worlds. How could it be better when it stands in the light and under the control of this divine action, and its conflicting aspects are thus co-ordinated by the Creator Himself? And how could we wish

378

it to be better if we have seen and understood the divine co-ordination of its antitheses?

In Christian faith it is a matter of apprehending the justification of creation accomplished in this divine action. It is clear that its reaffirmation in Christian faith has as little to do with the Yes of optimism as with the No of pessimism. Christian faith naturally says Yes to the created world—a secure, definitive and absolute Yes. What is it essentially but an echoing and mirroring of the divine Yes which God Himself spoke in this matter when He raised Jesus Christ from the dead? And if it conforms to this archetype, how can it say even a partial or provisional No when God has spoken His unqualified and everlasting Yes? But the point is that in echoing and repeating this divine Yes, and not (optimistically) on the basis of any human judgment, it will say Yes and not No. It will realise better than any pessimism that man is not capable of a well-founded and certain judgment in this matter, of a genuine assurance and elevation of the creature in face of the infinite perils which surround it, of its real rescue and deliverance and ultimate glorification; that all this can be accomplished only by God's own action and truly appropriated only in acknowledgment of this divine action; and that apart from this relationship it can only be an obstinate and ineffective assertion which man is quite unable to prove. Christian faith lives by the Yes which God Himself has spoken. This is the certitude, joy and peace of the positive decision which it makes, and which it must dare to make because if it does not do so it is not Christian faith. But even Christian faith is conscious of a No spoken to the created world, and repeats this No. [386] God Himself has said No in the sacrifice of His Son for us: No to the danger which threatens it from the neighbouring sphere of nothingness; No to its weakness and frailty; No to the imperfection which clings to it, to its subjection to sin and death, and to the ruin which consequently awaits it. How can the divine Yes be rightly repeated if it does not include a repetition of this No? But it is distinguishable from the No of pessimism by the fact that like the divine No it is never addressed to creation as such but to the nothingness by which creation is surrounded and menaced, to the sin and death by which it is mastered; and especially by the fact that when it was originally spoken by God it was superseded by His Yes, so that it can only be a No surrounded by and concealed in a Yes, and therefore a retrospective and secondary No: a No to that which has already been negated and cannot therefore have any force or merit independent attention; a No which can only be uttered and valid as it is enclosed and concealed in the greater Yes; a No which cannot in any way challenge the positive decision already made, but can only indirectly confirm it. As penultimate, implying the judgment already executed in the cross of Christ, it too is God's Word and is to be repeated in faith. But Christian faith realises better than any optimism that the final Word about creation is positive and not negative. For that reason it can and will take in all seriousness the penultimate negative word which is also true in this connexion, but only within its own limits, because it is only in its penultimate character that it is the Word of God.

Hence it will have nothing whatever to do with a pessimism which tries to represent the No obstinately and ineffectively as an ultimate word. And it will have even less to do with the neutral wisdom which is unwilling either joyfully to affirm an ultimate Yes or seriously to accept and repeat a penultimate Yes, but with equal obduracy ignores both the cross and the resurrection of Jesus Christ. If any conception is denied by Christian faith, it is certainly that in virtue of which the co-ordination of opposites achieved by God's own suffering and triumph can be left aside in favour of a neutral attitude meritoriously imputed to our own superior insight. As and because this co-ordination has been achieved in Jesus Christ, in Him it certainly is behind us, but in Him it is also before us as a hope which we have continually to grasp. In no case is it in us in the form of a position to be attained by us. And it is not before and behind us as a neutralisation of opposites, but as God's living action in them. As Christian faith follows this divine action, sharing its movement and imitating Jesus Christ, it makes the same decision and recognises the justification and therefore the righteousness of creaturely being.

It is necessary to explain the fact (4) that as God's self-declaration to us confirms and transcends the two aspects of being, and reveals in their co-ordination the perfection of creation, it mediates a secure, decisive and binding knowledge of all this. It might almost be said in answer to this final question that this is so by the very nature of the case. And it is indeed true that in its very occurrence the divine self-declaration as such cannot do other than illuminate conclusively and compellingly, leading to an unambiguous and secure knowledge. But it is as well to realise, above and beyond this very general statement, how far and in what sense it is true in this particular matter. Our point of departure is the fact that the living action of God in Jesus Christ, by which the two aspects of existence are confirmed and transcended and thus reveal the perfection of creation, makes it quite impossible for the man who knows it to maintain an attitude of neutrality in face of it. For it is he who is envisaged in this event. He himself is concerned in it from the very outset. He is the creature whom God has taken to Himself, whose peril and hope, death and life, woe and weal, God has made His own, and in whose interests He has conducted this strange warfare and gained this victory. The history of Jesus Christ as the end and meaning of creation is not a drama which is played out at a remote distance and which he can view as an interested or disinterested spectator. For he is the one whom God in His own Son has eternally taken to His heart of love. His cause is pleaded in the heart of God. He is defended against the menace of nothingness. Eternal life is won for him. He has been clothed in the glory of God. Christian faith does not merely contemplate what God has done; it receives it as done for us. It is our own participation in this divine event, as the latter is God's participation in our own being and nature. We are loved in the course of these events of the divine activity. We are His covenant-partners. And we cannot abstract from the fact that this is the case. We cannot arbitrarily reflect and argue on any other basis. We can do so only if we arti-

[387]

ficially seal our eyes to God's revelation. When we open them, we find that we ourselves are those who exist in the light and power of God's love and in the order of the covenant. There is no retreating from this to another sphere where we can be something different. We are as we are here addressed and treated. We have no possibility of forming the opinions and judgments of which we would be capable, and which we would be inclined to form, if we were otherwise. In so far as we are what we are, we cannot possibly entertain an optimistic or a pessimistic or a neutral view of existence. We have no other choice but that of appropriating and accepting as it stands the communication made in the revelation of this divine action. We are constrained to do so, not by the compulsion of force, but by the compelling power of divine love exerted in our favour. We could evade force but we cannot evade love. And the truth about our existence in its confrontation by God's self-revelation is that we are those who have been loved and sought and found by Him, won for Him and called to faith in Him—nothing else and nothing more. In this encounter we are those to whom salvation has come, whose being has been healed and sanctified, not by ourselves but by the action of God, by the divine justification [388] directed towards us in Jesus Christ, healing and sanctifying without possibility of demur. In this confrontation we have ourselves become those who have the stern divine No behind them and the liberating divine Yes before them, who must echo and repeat the two in this order and in this relationship. Thus we are not mere hearers of the divine revelation. We are ourselves its witnesses. With the decision which it proclaims to us, a decision is taken concerning us and our attitude and the content of our own judgment. We are thus placed under the command of God to affirm what He affirms and deny what He denies in the order and relationship in which He does so Himself. We are forbidden to make false and ineffective and arbitrary judgments. Especially are we forbidden to think and speak in neutral terms. How can the justified creature be witness to anything but the divine justification of creation? It denies itself if it tries to refuse recognition to the revelation of God the Creator which so clearly points in this direction. It is already committed as it is freed from all *a priori*EN52 conceptions; committed to think without prejudices and to stand for freedom from prejudice. No one can snatch it from this commitment: itself least of all, for it is itself made free and therefore set in this commitment. For this creature there remains only openness to the whole of reality in its twofold determination. There remains only a great confidence in the whole of reality. This is the necessary and therefore the sure confidence of those whom God has first drawn into His confidence, and repeatedly draws into His confidence, by the revelation of His activity, in view of which this confidence is continually renewed and its certainty continually achieved and confirmed. We are in a circle in which we may and must move, but in which we can do so only

---

EN52 unconditionally

in one direction, and which we can no longer leave. Hence the general statement is true that God's self-revelation as such can mediate only a sure and decisive and binding knowledge even in this matter. We need only remember this to note that the knowledge conveyed to Christian faith concerning the justification and perfection of being is an unshakeable knowledge.

Here, too, our theological enquiry must be set in relationship to a philosophical counterpart. The Christian thesis that the world was willed and created good by God its Creator bears a close resemblance to that of the well-known writings in which Leibniz (particularly in his *Essays de Theodicée*, 1710, but already in his *Discours de métaphysique*, 1686, in the treatise *De rerum originatione radicali*, 1697, and elsewhere) crowned his metaphysical, scientific, ethical but also theological work, and in which he at once founded and shaped and expounded and represented the religious consciousness of his age. Leibniz, too, in the question which here concerns us, resolutely and with a most emphatic appeal to the name of God made a positive choice and decision: *Ceux qui sont d'humeur à se louer de la nature et la fortune et non pas à s'en plaindre, quand même ils ne seroient pas les mieux portagés, me paroissent préférables aux autres. Car outre que ces plaintes sont malfondées, c'est murmurer en effet contre les ordres de la Providence. Il ne faut pas être facilement du nombre des mécontents dans la Republique où l'on est, et il ne le faut point être du tout dans la Cité de Dieu, où l'on ne le peut être qu'avec injustice*[EN53] (*Theod.*, I, 15). The gentle firmness with which this is explained is characteristic of the optimism, in its way theologically grounded, not only of Leibniz but of his whole period. We have it here in what is in a sense classical form.

Why does it appear *préférable*[EN54] to be contented rather than discontented with nature and destiny? The first and last and decisive proof which Leibniz gives of this thesis is the reference to God as the being which unites in Himself all perfections in their highest degree. He is the being which on the basis of its perfections has the distinction before all others that it must exist if possible. But there is nothing to prevent the possibility of a being free from all contradiction. We may thus recognise *a priori* that it exists. And the fact that it exists is to be inferred *a posteriori* from the existence of contingent beings who can have a sufficient ground only in the necessary being which has the ground of its existence in itself. This necessary and therefore existent and therefore perfect being is as such the ontological ground and noetic pledge of the goodness of the world, i.e., of the universe of all other beings. In virtue of His perfection, of the supreme wisdom, power, freedom and goodness united in Him, He can do no other than act perfectly in every respect. But the things distinct from God are not merely good in their nature, or in the ideas which God has of them, because this is willed and effected by God. The work praises its author in the fact that it is good in itself. As the work of God it is characterised by a proper and inward excellence which is recognisable as such and can be known on closer inspection. This applies even to the world of bodies: *Theatrum mundi corporei magis magisque ipso naturae lumine in hac vita elegantiam suam nobis ostendit, dum systemata macrocosmi et microcosmi recentiorum inventis*

[389]

EN53 Those who are of a disposition to praise nature and fortune and not to complain about them, even though they might not appear ideally distributed, seem to me preferable to those who do the opposite. Because, even disregarding the fact that such complaints are ultimately groundless, to complain is nothing less than to grumble against the dictates of Providence. One should be cautious about swelling the number of the discontented in in the earthly Republic where one lives, and such behaviour is even less permissible with respect to the City of God, where one cannot be discontentedother than unjustly

EN54 preferable

coepere[EN55]. (*Theod., Causa Dei,* 143). It applies even more to the beauty of the spiritual world fully to be revealed to us only in a future life. Again from the perfection of the being and action of God, it may be inferred that God could not have acted better than He has done in relation to beings distinct from Himself. What God chose, willed and performed, He chose, willed and performed on the most rational grounds. This necessary hypothesis finds its *a posteriori*[EN56] confirmation in a progressively increasing knowledge of the actual general harmony of the universe. The reason for the love which we owe supremely to God is that He always acts in the most perfect and desirable way possible. In regard to the circumstances in which we are placed according to His will, we must not only make every effort to be patient—for in this case we might be secret rebels—but we must be genuinely content, because as the One who loves us He seeks and finds His own satisfaction in the happiness and perfection of those who are loved by Him. *Idem velle et idem nolle vera amicitia est*[EN57] (*Disc. d. métaph.,* 4). And, of course, we for our part shall do our best to act with all our power according to the presumed will of God, each fulfilling his duty and promoting the general good in his sphere. In this way we shall serve the glory of God and attune ourselves to Him, so that whether our efforts are successful or not we may be certain that God as the best of all masters is concerned only with the heart, and that He well knows the hour and the place best adapted to crown our intentions with success. From the perfection of the being and action of God there follows the basic and comprehensive principle that from the inexhaustible possibilities of creation He did not choose just any world but the best, i.e., the most perfect within the limits of its creatureliness, and the most easily recognisable as such within the same limits. And this best possible world is our own, the real world in all its extension, parts and determinations, and in all the possible and actual changes and developments of its condition. If it had been possible for a better world than this to exist, God's wisdom must have recognised it. His goodness willed it and His omnipotence created it. Since God has not done so, but in His wisdom, goodness and omnipotence brought this world into being, we must and can recognise that it is the best. It is impossible for us to know why God has willed it [390] as the best in its present form. We are slow to recognise how far it is the best. This defect, however, is not to be imputed to the world, but to our imperfect insight, and we are not to doubt that it is in fact the best. For every advance in true knowledge can and will only confirm and reveal this.

Leibniz did not dispute that we are confronted at this point by an objective conundrum grounded in the reality of the creaturely world. But he consistently denied that the riddle is ultimate and insoluble, that the actual contradiction can persist. That the real created world is the best does not mean that it is absolutely good and perfect. If this were so, it would not be the created world. From its being as such, the non-divinity of its existence, there follows necessarily its imperfection. *Dieu ne pouvait pas lui donner tout, sans en faire un Dieu*[EN58]. (*Theod.,* I, 31). From its creaturely nature there thus follows the necessity of the metaphysical evil which is the basis of the possibility of physical evil, i.e., pain, and of moral evil, i.e., sin or wickedness. No serious objection can be raised on this score against the relative perfection of creation and the absolute perfection of the Creator because (1) the relative perfection of creation and therefore its very existence is impossible apart from these limits. Metaphysical evil, the imperfection of creation as such, confirms the good will of God to reflect His glory in the best and most perfect way in this other being, and we dispute both this good will of

---

[EN55] The theatre of the corporeal world shows us its elegance more and more in this life by the light of nature, as modern discoveries have begun to show the systematic organisation of the world on the large scale and the small

[EN56] conditional

[EN57] To agree in wanting and not wanting is true friendship

[EN58] God could not give it everything without making it another God

God and the actual but limited perfection of creation if we try to dispense with metaphysical evil. The latter provides no reason for substantial objection to the perfection of God and His creation because (2) its character is privative rather than positive. It is essentially a *limitation originale*[EN59] which cannot affect the inner perfection of creation but can only indirectly confirm it. Nor is there any objection for the further reason (3) that from the beginning God has co-ordinated the existence of evil with that of the created world, and therefore imperfection with perfection, in such a way that the former necessarily contributes to the increase of the latter. All this is basically true even of the physical and moral evil, the pain and sin, which are not necessary but only possible, though actual. Since these are involved in the necessary metaphysical evil, their existence cannot be the ground of complaint against the Creator or even against the relative perfection of creation. For they have to be understood as privation, and they are interwoven into the web of that transcendent continuity of perfection and imperfection.

What is pain? It is the sorrow which is essentially possible to created spirit, and actually experienced by it in its existence, being necessary along with pleasure because it is bound to a material body and therefore shares its positive and negative sensations, being what it is only in this association. There is good reason why this evil should now be more acute and now less, affecting some more than others. It is connected with the fact that our various positions and functions are not the same in the continuous texture of total creaturely existence, but that in this totality we occupy different spheres in which different portions of pleasure or pain are allotted at different times and to different people according to a plan which we can only occasionally and partially divine but which really exists as the plan of the world-totality willed and effected by God, so that it is good and salutary even though the detailed aspects of its execution may not always seem good, but may have the appearance of physical evil and cause us pain. In this connexion we must consider (1) that in practice this evil often has the character of a punishment necessary to us, or more generally of a means of instruction which as such partakes of the goodness of the whole. And reason and patience make every pain basically tolerable, even the most bitter. We have to consider (2) that the grounds for joy and happiness in our creaturely condition are more numerous and powerful than those for unhappiness and pain, and when we take into consideration the vastness of the partially [391] unknown spaces surrounding us, even to the farthest planetary systems, we have reason to suppose that all in all the proportion of pain is nothing in comparison with the fulness of creaturely happiness. Above all we must cling to the fact (3) that all pain is to be understood as only a temporary and partial privation in the inherently perfect system of things controlled by the perfect government of the perfect God, even though at times we were not in a position to appreciate this in detail.

But what is moral evil, i.e., sin? Here obviously it is supremely difficult to make an adequate answer, but here optimistic confidence is also strongest. Why has the perfect God given to His perfect creation the possibility of sinning? Why does He actually allow it to make use of this possibility? Leibniz thinks that He has given it this possibility because if He had not done so man would not have had the power of self-determination, the spiritual and moral being, which is what constitutes his perfection. God has no positive share in evil. He does not will man to sin. He does not compel him to do so. He only permits him to sin. But this permission as such is as necessary, purposeful and good as everything which He does. For the man in whose nature it lies to be able to sin, and whom God does not prevent from sinning, is the free man who is not compelled to sin, who can equally well obey the voice of his reason, fulfilling his duty and living and acting for the general good and the glory of God, and not lacking the necessary grace of God if he does so. He could not be such a

---

[EN59] original limitation

man—the one whom divine grace meets and assists—if he were not also the man who can and does sin. Thus the presupposition of the fall and of sin itself, without implying that God wills and does evil, is rooted in the original imperfection of creation. It is not, therefore, unconnected with its relative perfection. Sin, too, is a privation. It may become actual, and does so when man's conception lack true clarity and his free decision does not hit the mark. But in the harmony of the whole, and for the sake of it, sin has to exist in its negative mode, because without its possibility there would be no good in creation, and because even when it is actualised—although it is not good in itself or excusable and exempt from punishment— evil necessarily serves to increase the sum of total good and therefore redound in its own way to the glory of God. As actual pain is necesary from time to time to this or that individual in given circumstances, so is actual sin. If he did not commit certain sins, he would not be this or that man, and the universe would be something other and not the best which it is. Similarly the action and even the being of God Himself would be something different, and could not be the perfect being and action which they are. Since this is impossible, we have to say, for example, that God from all eternity sees that at a given time a man named Judas will exist, the conception of whom as borne in the mind of God involves certain future free actions and therefore the betrayal of Jesus. He will not do this under the compulsion of God's will or according to His Law, but as the free decision of his sin. And yet in so doing even he and his action will not be outside but inside the divine world-plan. Why such as Judas is not only possible but exists will always be incomprehensible to us. But since he exists, the evil he has wrought is necessarily cancelled by the dividend it yields, God bringing a greater good out of the evil, and the perfection of the whole always being demonstrated, even in respect of the sinner, in the totality of the nexus which includes the existence of the sinner (*Disc. de métaph.*, 30).

In the *Considérations sur la doctrine d'un esprit universel* (1702) Leibniz advances an explicit doctrine of death. It stands against the background and in association with the view that— always in the order of the universe as posited and ruled by God—individual souls and their bodily organisms have always existed, if only in diminutive form, and that the conception of living creatures is to be understood only as a kind of unfolding and enlargement. Accordingly death is only a constriction and transition to another form of development in which the organism actually continues in the parallelism of its dual existence, so that the immortal soul retains a delicate and in its way organised body which one day, at the resurrection, may [392] even be able to resume the visible form wherein it formerly dwelt. Like sleep and swooning, death is not the cessation of all the functions of an organism, but only the interruption of certain more obvious functions. Not only, then, is it not an extinction of individual souls (or their mere persistence in God), but also it is not a destruction of the organism as such. But as each individual soul in its special association with the world of bodies is in its own way a perfect mirror of the whole universe, contributing by its existence to its perfection, it remains this even in the transformation of death. Nowhere can a real vacuum arise through death. Death does not, therefore, provide any serious reason for opposing the perfection of the created world.

Properly to understand this, it is not unimportant to remember that the problem of evil particularly treated in the *Theodicy* plays, in its various forms, only an incidental part in the system of Leibniz as a whole, and that even in this work the discussion has only an esoterically apologetic character. The author tells us that the *Theodicy* arose out of his religio-philosophical conversations with Queen Sophia Charlotte of Prussia. It is also clear that it was shaped by his slight annoyance with certain statements made by the sceptic Pierre Bayle, whose death in 1706 moved him to conclude his introductory essay on the harmony of faith and reason with the words: *Il est à espérer que M. Bayle se trouve maintenant environné de ces lumières, qui nous manquent ici-bas: puisqu'il y a lieu de supposer, qu'il n'a point manqué de bonne volonté*[EN60]. Under the pseudonym Pacidius, Leibniz was ready enough for controversy, but he always adopted the mildest tones. He explained, and it was obviously his real opinion, that truth was more widespread than is supposed, and that with the exception of what was clearly illusory he approved almost everything he read. This is no doubt profoundly connected with the fact that at bottom he hardly had any serious interest (and from the practical standpoint none at all) in the problem of evil; that he had either in some way settled it or never really begun to tackle it; and that it was only in the context of other matters that he found occasion to touch upon it incidentally. Evil in every form really was for him what he called it, namely, a mere *malum privativum*[EN61] which is unfortunately present as such and can only confirm the perfection of the universe. His optimism stands on its own feet and does not need to do battle. It is founded and maintained irrespective of any considerations advanced by pessimism. From the very first it has nothing whatever to do with the clash of good and evil, but is nourished by a view which the problem of evil cannot affect or shake or even attack—the view that the perfection of the universe is rooted in God and therefore in itself. In what does it consist? First, in the fact that its order, corresponding to the divine being itself, is at once the simplest in presuppositions and means and the richest and most manifold in phenomena, ends and effects. But this is only a preamble which does not occupy him long. The perfection of the universe is to be found particularly in the fact that it exists in the fulness of absolutely individual, unique, incomparable and self-contained substances or functional unities of varying degree, each of which is at the same time analogous to God Himself and a compendium and mirror of the whole universe, and yet between all of which there exists the most perfect harmony, as complete, original and indestructible as between the working and rhythm of two clocks constructed with such utter precision that we can count on their constant harmonious functioning without any need for a third mechanism to regulate them, or for a man to rectify and control them, in short without any kind of direct relationship between them. The machinery of the world praises its divine Author because it consists in an infinite number of timepieces harmoniously functioning in this way. This full co-ordination between perfect existence in the individual and the perfect harmony of the totality of being, this unity, juxtaposition and intermingling of freedom and community as it is plainly taught by the *Discours de métaphysique* and clearly perceptible in the background

[393] even in the *Theodicy* (not to speak of the *Monadology* and related writings), is the real Leibnizian justification of the Creator and His creation. In regard to evil, it is only apologetically, subsequently and incidentally that we can add to all this that no matter in what form it exists and makes its presence felt, it can never negate this system, but as the limit of creaturely perfection can only confirm it. Leibnizian optimism was not a fighting and victorious optimism, but a pure monistic optimism, unbroken from the start, incapable of any break, self-contained and *a priori*[EN62] transcendental. It is as such that it has become so representative and constitutive for the whole period, and so exemplary for all time. It could not have been stated with greater purity. But its purity could be made more obvious than in Leibniz himself by receiving more simple and systematic expression.

This was given to it by Leibniz' younger contemporary, pupil and friend, Christian Wolff of Halle. In the preface to a book which appeared in 1719 (nine years after Leibniz' *Theodicy*), *Vernünfftige Gedancken von Gott, der Welt und der Seele des menschen, auch allen Dingen überhaupt, den Liebhabern der Wahrheit mitgeteilt*, he expressly boasted of the fact that he had set in a new light and made even more intelligible "the predetermined harmony of Mr. Leib-

---

[EN60] It is to be hoped that M. Bayle now finds himself surrounded by those lights which we lack here below: for there are grounds for thinking that he was never lacking in good will
[EN61] evil of privation
[EN62] unconditionally

niz." In this claim, he was not altogether wrong. The idea of perfection is tersely and well denned in his book (§ 152) as the "coherence of the manifold." If a clock is so constructed in its many parts that the hand correctly shows the hours and their divisions, it is perfect. When the manifold activities of a human being are collectively grounded in a general intention, his way of life is perfect. The prevailing intention is the basis, and this and the adjustment of the constitution of a thing to it form the measure of the perfection of that thing (§ 157). There are various degrees in which a thing can be perfect. And one and the same thing can have varying perfections which in an ideal case will be harmoniously adjusted and will yield a composite perfection (§ 162), but which may also conflict, in which case the greatest possible perfection of the whole must result from the necessary compromise between them (§ 166), etc. In reference to the perfection of a world this means that it consists in the fact that everything which exists contemporaneously and successively in a world coheres harmoniously (§ 701). Now it belongs to the essence of a world as a coherent totality that we are not able to know all these things, and even less their internal harmony as a whole. Hence this perfection remains incomprehensible to us (§ 702), and, since the imperfection of the parts can be compatible with the perfection of the whole, it is possible that at times we regard a part of the world totality as imperfect, although the latter has the supreme perfection possible to it as a world (§ 703). We may have the same experience in regard to the individual components of such a part in so far as their internal adjustment is hidden from us, e.g., when in our own life we see only the present and do not consider how it harmonises with the past and the future (§ 704 f.). There are various rules affecting world-perfection and therefore its internal coherence, as, for example, the rule which states that there are no leaps in nature, "so that in detail at least everything is comprehensible and pleasurable to us," or the rule that the quantum of the reaction of a body corresponds to the influence exerted upon it, which is the basis of all the laws of motion, or the rule that nature prefers the shorter to the longer way, or that the quantum of its power remains constant, etc. (§ 709). But in a world there is also the clash of different perfections and their systems, and there are, therefore, exceptions and necessary compromises. A world will be the more perfect the more these compromises actually bring out the underlying rules (§ 712). And it will be the more perfect the greater the manifoldness of the things subjected to these rules, for harmony in the relationships of manifold and divergent things is obviously greater than if there are only a few and analogous things (§ 715). It will also be the more perfect the greater the order and the fewer the exceptions (§ 716 f.). But we must remember that in a world there may be concealed a good deal of order which we cannot perceive because our perspective is too limited and we see too dimly and therefore do not grasp clearly enough the similarities and series which are present (§ 722). It is for this reason that in proof of the perfection of the real world Wolff, too, goes back to the idea of God. He does not need this, of course, for his definition of perfection. What perfection is in general, and what the perfection of a world is, he is able to declare independently long before the final section of his work devoted to the doctrine of God. But in this section (§ 977) we are taught as a kind of secondary basis that all worlds and all things therein gain their perfection from the mind of God, the Source of all that is perfect. And the Leibnizian doctrine that the actual world is the best of all possible worlds (§ 980 f.) is now given the following very clear and characteristic form. The dictum that nothing happens without sufficient reason applies also to the fact that God has preferred one world to the many possible worlds, and given it reality. But since the various possible worlds are all of one species, they can be distinguished only by the varying degrees of their perfection, and therefore God's sufficient reason to choose this particular world for realisation can only be the supreme degree of perfection which He has contrived in it. "Hence the supreme perfection of the world is the motive force of His will …. If a better than this one had been possible, He could not have preferred to it the more

[394]

imperfect." The perfection of the knowledge of God with regard to all possible worlds makes it impossible that He should have preferred the less to the more perfect in ignorance. The same conclusion follows from the perfection of the divine will, the freedom of which is expressed in the fact that He willed what He saw to be the best, whereas a less perfect world could not possibly have pleased Him. He could not and cannot will (§ 1004) anything contrary to His own perfection, or to the perfection of the world, or even to that of individual things in their coherence. We can thus read the will of God from what happens in the world, in the mutual relationship and harmony of all things (§ 1007), while by direct revelation He certainly will not convey to us anything which we cannot also know by reason or anything which contradicts reason or the laws of nature (§ 1010 f.). What is possible is once for all determined in the mind of God (§ 975), and it is no part of His omnipotence to make impossible things possible (§ 1022). And because He can will nothing but that which in relation to the totality of things is the best. He wills and effects only the latter, and not everything that is possible (§ 1023). "Every rational being behaves according to intentions. God is the most rational of all beings. Hence He must behave entirely in accordance with intentions" (§ 1026). What His intentions are can be discovered from the nature of the things created by Him (§ 1027 f.). In their coherence, and therefore in the coherence of the perfect world chosen by God, both good and bad fortune are seen to be part of God's intentions (§ 1030). The essence and nature of things are always the means by which God's wisdom fulfils His intentions in the world (§ 1031 f.). But it is the essence and nature of things to be "machines." "A machine is a composite mechanism whose movements are based on the mode of its composition. The world is likewise a composite thing whose changes are dependent on the mode of its composition. Accordingly, the world is a machine" (§ 557). "And so the world and all things in it are means by which God carries out His intentions, because they are machines. Hence it is clear that they are a product of the divine wisdom, because they are machines. Thus if we explain the universe intelligibly as we usually do in the case of machines, we lead directly to the wisdom of God; and if we do not do so, we lead away from the wisdom of God" (§ 1037). In proportion as the world were not a machine, but the sphere of supernatural and miraculous happenings, it would be only a product of the power and not of the wisdom of God. Hence a world where miracles are rare is to be more highly valued than one where they occur frequently (§ 1039). But what is God's chief intention for this world machine or mechanical world which is only infrequently disturbed by miracles and then in strict connexion with the natural order? What else can it be but to represent as in a [395] mirror the divine perfections (of which His wisdom is greater than His power)—"and this is usually called the revelation of the glory of God" (§ 1045). For the attainment of this goal God has not produced an imperfect world but the best, and not another world but this real world (§ 1047), in which everything happens most expediently and according to predetermined harmony (§ 1049 f.), His creative and sustaining activity confining itself to the production and maintenance of the reality of souls, things and elements as such, whereas their changes, as in the case of the work of a clockmaker, are the result of their essence and nature, and do not need His direct intervention (§ 1054 f.). The alteration of things or their states is identical with the interchange of their limits and the various modifications of their finitude (§ 107, 121, 585, 783). Consequently their limits and the imperfection bound up with them do not exist through God but only through the things themselves. And since everything which we call evil or wicked arises from the limitations of things, God has nothing to do with the evil and wicked, but they belong wholly to the creature (§ 1056). He permits both only as He creates and maintains things (§ 1057). Why does He permit them? This world is the best. In it there is much that is evil and wicked. Hence the best world cannot exist without that which is evil and wicked. God therefore maintains more good by permitting evil and wickedness than by not doing so (§ 1058). He can thus have no reason to render it impossible by means of miracles. Since He prefers the course of nature to miracles, He cannot will the reality of the world without also willing that its events should take place according to the implications of their nature and essence. Otherwise the world would not be the mirror of His wisdom which it is meant to be (§ 1059). He thus proves His wisdom by the harmonisation of the evil which derives from the creature and is permitted by Him with all the good which derives from Himself. He has not constituted the essence of things according to His pleasure but according to His intelligence; hence He cannot change it capriciously (§ 994). If He willed to place men on the earth, He could not deny them the capacity to sin. Or should He have created a world without men? Since the world is a machine, this would be as unreasonable as saying "that the clockmaker could have made the clock just as efficiently if he had left out certain wheels but not changed the rest of the machinery" (§ 1061). In actual fact God has conveyed as much perfection as possible, and therefore shown as much good as possible, to each thing (§ 1062). He could not show more goodness than is possible, and has thus displayed the utmost goodness and shown that He is supremely good to creation (§ 1063). And since He comprehends His own perfection and that of all other things simultaneously and completely, He must have pleasure, and indeed perfect, constant and unchangeable pleasure, in the whole process (§ 1065 f.). Who and what is this God? He is the being which, like our own soul but perfectly, has the power plainly to conceive all worlds at once. He does so impassibly except for His pleasure in the wellbeing of the creature whose inner perfection has induced Him to confer reality upon it; "and to this extent I can also ascribe love to Him" (§ 1067 f.). We need only to leave out of account the limitations of the nature and qualities of our own soul to gain a true idea of the nature and attributes of God (§ 1076 f.). And since everything that is possible and real can have only one sufficient ground and not several, there can only be one God. But this insight, too, is bound up with the fact that everything in the world is interlocked; that the world is a machine (§ 1080 f.). Thus God dwells "in perfect contentment." "Since He has everything to a supreme degree, there remains nothing which He could wish further" (§ 1089).

This was the philosophy in which Leibnizian optimism was systematically developed and disseminated in the 18th century, and in which the spirit of the time found classic expression. We can see at a glance the change which it has suffered. The doctrine of the monads, which envelops Leibniz' outlook with a certain formal mystery and magic, has been abandoned as a kind of superfluous flourish. What need was there of the monads when the perfection of the world was in any event guaranteed by the clockwork character affirmed by Leibniz himself? But we can also appreciate, especially in the development of the theodicy, the complete agreement and fidelity of the pupil who succeeded in developing the thoughts of the master into a system by elaborating the connecting details with which the latter did not concern himself.

[396]

To illustrate the same outlook at a higher or lower level, we shall select from a whole literary genre a work which may be described as characterising the practical application of this theory of Leibniz and Wolff. The proof of the perfection of the created world, which had been presented in abstract terms by the philosophers, could now be set out in concrete form by other scholars. This was attempted and performed with particular virtuosity by the Lutheran pastor Friedrich Christian Lesser in his book "*Insecto-Theologia*" oder: *Vernunfft- und schrifftmässiger Versuch wie ein Mensch durch aufmerksame Betrachtungen derer sonst wenig geachteten "Insecten" zu lebendiger Erkänntnis und Bewunderung der Allmacht, Weissheit, der Güte und Gerechtigkeit des grossen Gottes gelangen könne.* This was not a joke, for in the same style and dimensions the same author has also given us a theological lithology and testacaeology. It was an undertaking carried out with great stringency and logic. "The great God has placed before reasonable men for their intelligent consideration all kinds of creatures including the insects as a mirror and testimony of His infinite power and wisdom" (2nd Ed., 1740,

p. 3). Why not? Certain insects had presented difficulties enough to the older theology as regards the question of divine goodness. Lesser assures us sympathetically that "in his sermons he not only leads men to the natural knowledge of God, but also preaches Christ crucified" (p. 38). But: "It is incumbent upon me to seek traces of the divine attributes not only in the revealed book of Scripture but also in the great open book of nature, and to extol them to others" (p. 14). He quotes from Brockes' *Irdisches Vergnügen in Gott*:

> "It is regrettable that even theologians
> (Excepting some, for I do not speak of all)
> Have often taken not the smallest pains
> To seek the works of the Creator. How can it please God
> To see His servants silent about His marvels,
> Of all the glory, might and majesty,
> And the high perfection of the Creator,
> Reflected in His creatures,
> Showing us not the smallest trace,
> Because they do not know the same themselves?"

But "when we survey nature, nothing in it is to be regarded as superfluous and futile" (p. 11). Not even the insects! Lesser's book—apart from the information which he gathered "with and without magnifying glasses"—is not without certain elements of purposeful ingenuity. In the first and greater section it offers us a kind of complete phenomenology of this chosen department of natural science, which obviously had contemporary merits as a scientific compendium and could be read with pleasure. But the author with his philosophico-theological interests knows exactly where he wants to lead the reader, and he never forgets to make his thesis clear. "Since insects demonstrably do not take their rise from any primal generation, but by the maintenance of their species through sexual procreation, one main pillar and cornerstone is snatched from atheists." The honour of creation remains with an omnipotent and wise being "which has so ordered everything in the insect world that one species constantly leads to the generation of another, and this being we call God" (p. 49). God's greatness is extolled by the very smallness of insects (p. 59), and by the fact that

[397] in relation to its end their complex structure shows neither lack nor superfluity (p. 72). The same is to be said in relation to their inconceivable numbers (p. 78); their capacity to breathe the same air as man (p. 82); the manner of their propagation (p. 92); their transformations (p. 108); their sex distinctions (p. 115); the extraordinary places where they are sometimes found (this point gives Lesser occasion to remember the expelled Salzburgers, to point to the heavenly mansions awaiting souls dearly purchased by the blood of Christ, and finally to quote Jn. 14^{23}, p. 144); their astonishing freedom of movement, which necessarily causes us to infer a First Mover (p. 158); the fact that they are fed, which gives rational ground for every right-minded Christian to place a childlike trust in the gracious providence of God His Father (p. 183); their capacity for self-protection and defence, which reminds the author of everything written in the Psalms about God's protection of the just (p. 189); their love for their young, in connexion with which sharp words are spoken about the very different behaviour of child murderesses (p. 196); and finally their intelligence, i.e., their practical skill, which is very real although not directed by any intrinsic reason, and which finds illustration particularly in bees and spiders, the poem of a "pious *Doctor medicinae*[EN63]" being quoted with reference to the former, which opens with the following lines:

[EN63] Doctor of medicine

3. Creation as Justification

"What sayest thou now, thou hardened atheist,
With all thy doubts of the Creator's being and might
When the polity of bees strikes thy sight?"

What mathematician, huntsman, weaver, dyer, statesman, lawyer or general has instructed them? "But consider, O man, that all wit and wisdom spring from God! What a shame it is that we take such little pains to instruct ourselves and our children! Consider what wrong thou hast done! Well then! Thank God for thy intelligence, and use it to honour Him who has imparted such grace to thee! See that thou trainest thy children to be wise, and to know the good and perfect will of God!" (p. 240 f.). But this phenomenology is not yet ended. The insects have senses, if very imperfect sense-organs, and they use them (what a lesson for us!) solely for that end for which the overflowing goodness of God has designed them (p. 252). They have external and internal organs, and they are all so purposeful that we have to confess that a supremely wise being must have been their Author (p. 318). A further chapter deals with "some special qualities of certain insects." While mentioning an ant said to have appeared in Turkey "which was as large as a medium-sized dog," it first recalls the amazing smallness of many species in this kingdom, from which is to be inferred that "matter can be divided into almost innumerable parts." Reference is also made to the capacity of other insects to gleam at night or to emit sounds and smells, to the known phenomenon of mimicry, to the conflicts which arise between various species, to the astonishing fact that certain spiders contain stones, etc.—extraordinary qualities which are well calculated to awaken "many men out of the sleep of their inattention when by the more ordinary qualities of these tiny animals they refuse to be encouraged to pay a Christian attention to the works of God." For "when one realises that all such special capacities have their intended aim and usefulness, then one infers that there must be a wise being who has ordered and prescribed the same" (p. 339 f.). In a final chapter "Concerning the beauty of most Insects," Lesser thinks primarily of the well-distributed and always characteristic colouring of many species, from which he concludes "that these small creatures, even though they are not always useful, are sent for the purpose of observation, and if they do not always minister to our bodily needs, they refresh the eye and the spirit." We are taught that they remind us of the even greater beauty of the Creator, and that all human vanity about dress is contemptible if only because it rests "on the noxious excrement of a poor silkworm," and in any case cannot be compared [398] with the beauty of many insects (p. 355). In the second part of the work the problem of theodicy is vigorously tackled. Insects are partly useful and partly injurious. They are useful "because in the whole of nature nothing takes place which is not calculated to show that it springs from the government of a supremely wise being, from which it is to be inferred that the utility of creatures, including insects, has been predetermined, so that the real value and use of insects are not casually perceived by man" (p. 357). In particular there are certain insects (e.g., locusts) which can be eaten. Again, it is commonly known "that bees give us honey, whose sweet juice has many uses in cooking," and from which mead is also made in Moscow and other countries (the recipe is given in detail), not to speak of its useful by-product wax and the many ways in which it can be applied. Again, other insects such as the silkworm provide material for clothing and have always contributed to the prosperity of trade and commerce, as also in the case of beehives, honey and wax. Others again yield colours. Others serve as nature's barometers. Others purify the air of foul smoke and mist. Others are useful as baits for fishermen and huntsmen. And it is related of a pastor whose house was to have been stormed in the Peasants' War of 1525 that he unhesitatingly threw some beehives into the crowd, "which had so fortunate an effect that the rebellious peasants were driven away from the vicarage by the raging bees and they had to desist from their attack." Who, then, would dare to assert that insects have no use? Their theological significance—apart from the general purpose to which the whole book is devoted—emerges in the fact that honey plays a certain part in the ordinances of the Israelite law of sacrifice, as also in the fact that God often makes use of locusts, flies and gnats to execute His just punishments on the ungodly. They thus pose certain problems for legislation and therefore for jurists. But they are also of interest to medicine, as in the case of the leech and according to 18th century practice earthworms and even lice, scorpions, flies, wasps and cockchafers, while it is to the praise of ant-spirit to have excellent qualities for not only ear noises, catarrh and stomach pains, but also for the strengthening of the senses and the memory. Insects are also mutually beneficial, and they serve as food for many other species. "Great whales consume nothing but sea-lice, and it is astonishing that these monsters become quite fat from their enjoyment of these sea-lice" (p. 407). If we consider all this without prejudice, we can conclude that the Creator of creatures which serve such very different purposes, and are so well equipped to serve them, must be an omnipotent and very wise being. There are no useless insects, but only those whose utility which is not yet known to us and has still to be discovered. Even when they are not directly useful to man, they are indirectly of value: "Do not many supply food for fish, birds and other animals which are later consumed by man, from which it may be seen that by means of these animals *insecta*EN64 can still be of use to man?" (p. 417). A short note about the rearing and tending of bees and silkworms fittingly concludes this part of the book. But the author knows perfectly well that insects can also be harmful, and he faces the fact unflinchingly. They play an undesirable part in the consumption of plants and their fruits primarily intended for man. Flies besmirch the cleanest books, the finest clothes and the faces of kings no less than peasants. Fleas, bugs and mosquitoes do not scruple to disturb man in his sleep. Insects can sting and poison and cause and spread internal maladies. They can also harm animals that are useful to man, annoying and endangering cows, horses, dogs and sheep. But in this we may see the justice of God, for such may often be regarded as the well-merited punishment of wanton sins; the wisdom of God, since harmful insects inevitably serve to make men cautious, industrious, clever and hygienic; and also the goodness of God, seeing that these insects fortunately live only a short time and ravage only at specific times, and especially that there are so many natural means of master-

[399] ing them, and that in the animal kingdom there are many animals to counteract the increase of insects, e.g., spiders to eat flies, cockroaches gnats, swallows to cleanse cattle-stalls, etc. "Thus the one works constantly against the other, and yet it may be seen that there must be an omnipotent though kind being which has arranged everything in this way" (p. 465). A whole chapter, which is both instructive and encouraging, is devoted to an account of the successful fight against insects. It is impossible to wipe them out completely, "partly because there is such a huge quantity of them, partly because they multiply so rapidly." But it is quite possible, as is shown in an enthusiastic description, to prevent or mitigate the damage they do by various means beginning with prayer and ending with a "curious flea-trap" and "bug-mixture." The wisdom and goodness of God are shown in the fact that He has given man the intelligence to discover and use preventative means of this kind. Nor can it be a valid objection to the divine wisdom and goodness that there are so many examples of human misuse of insects, e.g., the superstitions associated with them, or the use of their products for courtly apparel and adornment, "from which all Christian and honourable persons of the feminine sex must freely keep themselves," or idolatry, quackery and so forth. Why has God not prevented this misuse? A good Wolffian reply is made to this question. For it is pointed out that free will is an essential part of the reason with which God in His goodness has endowed man. Hence it would contradict His wisdom if by His omnipotence He prevented the misuse of

---

EN64 insects

creation and therefore of insects. "As reason now requires that we should ascribe all the profit by which insects benefit man to their Creator, it would be very wrong to try to make Him responsible for the misuse of insects, which is rather to be imputed to man" (p. 506). A chapter "Of certain miracles recounted in Holy Scripture concerning certain *Insectis*," concludes and crowns the whole work, and in it we find a full enumeration, with commentary, of all the relevant miracles from the Egyptian plagues and Jonah's gourd to the miserable death of Herod Agrippa (Ac. 12¹³), the author everywhere presupposing the truth of Holy Scripture "because this has already been proved against atheists by others before me" (p. 508).

It must be confessed that in the light of everything here said concerning them, the existence of insects is fully and precisely justified. And it is obvious that many other spheres of creation could be justified in the same way, and hardly surprising that attempts were made to do this, not only in this semiscientific style, but also in a wide variety of more popular forms which bring out even more plainly the nature of the underlying optimism. A famous work of this kind, to which we have referred already, was that of the Hamburg Senator, B. H. Brockes, *Irdisches Vergnügen in Gott, bestehend in physikalisch- und moralischen Gedichten* (first published in 1721, and then in many editions, and even set to music by various composers, e.g., by the Zürich theologian, J. K. Bachofen), in which the four periods of the day and year, the twelve months, heaven, earth and sea, light and shade, sun, moon and stars, air, fire and water, garden, meadow, forest and mountain, a series of animal species, and finally the five senses, with all their capacities and functions, by which these things are happily mediated to man, are all described in detail and with fond enthusiasm, and in their astonishing nature brought into the most direct connexion with the almighty and wise Creator. Reflections on a grazing herd of kine conclude as follows:

"Mowing down the fresh grass
With their sharp tongues
Each bite causes a cutting sound
Mingling alternately with a fierce snorting,
So that for him who reclines on the cool turf
A not unpleasant music sounds.
In their dreamy eyes
Gleam gentleness and peace [400]
Calm and free from care, in joy they dwell.
Oh that man with tranquil mind
More often gazed upon you and took heed!
Jaws moving limply
Some sleek kine roamed
And from their overflowing udders
Spurted rich milk for our needs."

Aria:

"Sweet kine, standing here
I see thee milked
And I wonder how it is possible
That in thy body thus marvellously
Grass becomes meat and drink for me
And as in living kilns distils itself.
Speak now, O man! and say
Is it not meet to give eternal praise
To Him who made it thus?"

In a poem on the earth, its circular shape gives rise to the following reflections:

> "As well for us to note
> How the finger of the Almighty
> As in all His works
> Shows unsearchable wisdom
> In the making of this ball.
> For a perfect circle
> Is by nature's rule
> The most perfect figure.

All parts of a circle
Are equally at rest and poised
Upon its focal point
Whence they aid each other,
Each other press, yet buttress,
Whence the mighty burden of the world
Is balanced and upheld.

"Yet more, the circle serves
That even when sea and flood
Are lashed by wind and storm
They do less harm,
But flow from the rounded earth
Or else the world long since
Were engulfed by raging waters.

"Were the earth with its weight
Angular instead of round
Then the grim mountains' towers
For man and beast and worm
Unscaleable were found.
Nay, it could not turn
Nor balance learn."

But the problem of theodicy is also treated where relevant. The phenomenon of foggy and wet weather gives occasion for the following consoling lesson:

"When the world takes this unpleasant guise
We feel a something that not displeasingly
Moves softly through skin and nerves.
Something around us hovers,
Especially when we are dry and warm,
Which if we heed it rightly   [401]
Procures us shuddering pleasure,
And the damp air of dismal days
Can even give us joy.
A kind of delight steals through the breast
And the world is full of radiance bright
Above all when our pipe is a-light.
And a gentle, repeated shrug gives sign
Of the joy which is mine and thine."

When the winter is cold and inclement we are encouraged by the reflection:

"O wise and marvellous power of God,
Which claims our awe to measure,
That where there is greatest need of wood,
Of such is found a treasure:
For aye in the bleak north,
It has come supremely forth
Who thinks of this,

395

When like a sword, we feel the piercing blast?
Or who reflects,
That clothed in warmth and comfort,
'Tis only by God's grace and favour,
That we such clothing round us cast?
That His grace so far above us soars
To wrap us in hemp and wool and feathers and furs?
Awake! my heart and mind,
Take courage that He is so kind."

And in the same situation:

"When in the warm room at my window I stand,
And see the cold blast relentlessly blowing
The bent figure of many a traveller.
Bereft of warmth and breath
Hair snow-sprinkled and knees bent,
Neck drawn in and limbs benumbed,
Eyes almost shut,
Cheeks, nose and chin, shiveringly blue
Piercing the snow storm, laborious and slow,
Then with reason I ponder,
The blessing of my snug and sheltered room,
What comfort God upon me pours!"

And on seeing a bird-trap with dead and living prey a wise young man can soothe his troubled sweetheart as follows:

"Thy complaint seems just, but must birds
Be less useful to us than other beasts?
Should we not profit thereby? Or should they alone
Become the booty of the fierce claws of the hawk,
Or multiply unchecked? Must they not all die
And then no doubt with bitterer moan?

Therefore take comfort,
And if thou wouldst grant
Liberty to some,
Do so with unmixed pleasure.
Let the most splendid fly
Or free them without measure!"

Aria:

[402]

"To hunt and fish and shoot
Are pleasures innocent
To him who thinks anent:
These pleasures are God-given,
And God is well content
If only we have striven
Gladly to honour Him
And bless Him with heart and soul!

Hills, valleys, meadows, woods,
Ploughland and plain,
To us are pleasant goods,
When we can raise the strain,
That all things come from God,
Who made this beauteous earth,
He gives us joy and food,
We praise Him with our mirth."

And since many ancient and modern problems have undoubtedly found their simplest and plainest solution in Switzerland, we must not fail to mention in conclusion a rather discordant Swiss voice in the chorus belonging to the same decade, the *"Theologia naturalis et experimentalis" eingerichtet auf die Verrichtungen, Geschäfte und Handlungen der Einiwohneren des Hohen und Niederen Schweizerischen Gebirgs, um sie dadurch zu GOTT ihrem obersten Guttäter zu führen. Zur Vermehrung der Erkantinis, der Liebe und des Lobes Gottes unter diesem Volk herausgegeben von Abraham Kyburtz* (1753). The whole work can be sung to the tune of "Now thank we all our God." In his younger days its author had been a keen and militant pietist, a friend of S. Lutz and Jerome Annoni, who had served as a pastor in Bümpliz, Schwarzenegg and Saanen, but unfortunately did not meet with acceptance and finally became a military chaplain in the imperial army beaten at Rossbach. As is only proper, his loudest praises are for the Swiss mountains. It is like a prophecy of the *Réduit* of 1940, and of the theological comment to be made on it, when at the very beginning he sings:

"Came now a potentate
With all his mighty train
Against our mountain walls
He would hurl himself in vain,
And must his host withdraw,
His purpose quite undone,
Because he has no power
To throw thy ramparts down.

But peasant, mark it well!
In vain to make thy praise
Of these gigantic walls
If evil are thy ways:
Should God Himself depart
Thy strong defence would fail
And thou should'st have no strength
To cause thy foes to quail."

But his real praise of the mountains and the Creator is obviously in respect of more concrete things. For his second song treats of the uses of the mountains—milk, cheese and whey, etc.—to be sung to the same charming melody:

"Ye peasants, thank your God,
From whom the wit descends,
To find on Alpine slopes
The sustenance He sends,
For what avail is grass?
You cannot chew the cud,
But praise and thanks for cows,
By which God gives you food."

[403]

The third song gives us a picture of the life of the cowherds, including the Sunday sports of vaulting, putting the stone and hornblowing. The fourth directs our attention to the solid and fluid mineral substances that we owe to the mountains. Then in a series of poems we are introduced to the splendours of central Switzerland from Emmenthal to Schaffhausen. And finally we attain our goal in an explicit account of vegetables and roots (to be sung to the same tune) "for the honour, delectation and profit of doctors, apothecaries, and all connoisseurs of the highly celebrated arts of medicine and gardening," the spiritual interpretation being now pushed to the periphery but not suppressed altogether:

"A varied chemist's store
Upon the hills God sets:
Poor Christian is the man
Who all this love forgets.
For if His grace is poured
On our poor flesh and blood,
How much more to the soul
He will be kind and good.

Through outward things, O Lord,
Turn to Thyself the heart,
Until it finds in Thee,
The Giver, all its part,
Unending joy and bliss,
Awaits it at Thy side,
More than the whole wide world
Could anywhere provide."

Looking back, we cannot fail to see that for all the descending quality of the various presentations there is a unity of theme and approach. It is a long way, to be sure, from the perfection of the world which Leibniz found in the predetermined harmony of antitheses primarily actualised and developed in the original divine monad and secondarily in the plenitude of all other monads, to the machine-like character of creation in Wolff, its utility in Lesser, its ability to give pleasure to man in Brockes, and its direct or indirect edibility in A. Kyburtz. There are very real differences when God the Creator is understood and honoured in one case as the free but perfect primal being who in His perfection wills and creates only what is definitely the best, in another as the clockmaker who happily invents the best of all mechanisms, faultlessly constructing and delightedly setting it going, in another as the all-wise Author necessarily to be inferred from the marvels disclosed in the kingdom of ants and bees, in another as the praiseworthy maximum of all the observable greatness and joy and utility and pleasure of the universe, and finally as the supreme Giver of so much cheese, vegetables and root products. And there are differences again when the evil not to be overlooked in the world is regarded in one case as its unavoidable *de facto*[EN65] but not *de jure*[EN66] circumference, in another as a soberly calculable element in creaturely perfection, in another as a series of minus signs in the sum total of our calculations about life and the world—minuses which in practice cancel each other out and are therefore tolerable and indirectly pleasurable—and finally as a mere occasion for moralistic exhortations. Yet for all the obvious differences we are always in the same sphere and on one and the same ground. [404] The continuity on which this type of optimism lays such stress is at least demonstrated in its own downward evolution. For if it is unfair to make Leibniz responsible for the pedantries of

---

[EN65] as a matter of fact
[EN66] as a matter of right

Wolff or the trivialities of Brockes or Kyburtz, we cannot fail to recognise that Wolff is the faithful disciple of Leibniz, that Lesser only applies industriously what he learns through Wolff, and that the type of thought expressed by Brockes or Kyburtz cannot be refuted or even seriously criticised from the standpoint of Leibniz and Wolff. Once we have boarded this train, we find that it is a non-stop express and we must accept the fact that sooner or later we shall reach the terminus. And we can take comfort in the principle of the school—if the application may be permitted—that imperfection is integral and even essential to creaturely perfection, and serves only to increase it. As the world would not be the world, and God Himself would not be God, without metaphysical, physical and moral evil, so even according to his own teaching Leibniz would not have been Leibniz without Brockes and Kyburtz.

It is worth considering this historical phenomenon, because in all its forms it approximates closely to the doctrine of creation as justification as it must be represented in dogmatics, and this approximation cannot be overlooked, and is not so simple to explain as might at first sight appear.

We, too, have had to state clearly the principle that the nature as well as the existence of the created world is affirmed by God its Creator, so that to this extent it is justified and perfect. We, too, have even adopted and used the formula that the actual world of God's creation is not simply bad or good, but the best of all worlds, seeing that the good-pleasure of God created it and rests upon it. Hence we, too, have unquestionably espoused a definite optimism, and we cannot be ashamed of the company in which we find ourselves, whether we like it or not. It is notable that in the whole history of ideas there is hardly a single verdict which verbally corresponds so closely to the Christian verdict as that of 18th century optimism. We are forced to concede that we have here a triumphantly asserted confidence that creation is right as it is. We are dealing with a radical and scrupulous attempt to take it seriously on the basis of this presupposition. Doubt with regard to this presupposition is treated precisely as it is formally to be treated according to Christian doctrine—as an attitude which can never finally or seriously be independent, or harden into a negation, or be absolutised, because it has already been refuted and overcome from a higher point. Hardly a hundred years after the horrors and miseries of the Thirty Years War, there is sounded and sung to a finish a hymn in praise of the Creator which is in its own way powerful and certainly persistent, which is not just abstract but concrete, which is not just vague and general but has direct reference to the manifold realities of creation, and which displays an intensity of concentration and in many cases a moving gratitude which are almost exemplary in comparison with the inattention and ingratitude, resentment and indifference, sheer blindness and ignorance characteristic of so many other periods, e.g., with the sardonic sneering of Voltaire. It cannot be denied that Leibniz and all his stronger and weaker followers proclaim glad tidings, and thus display a formal affinity to the proclamation of the Gospel. Nor is it an accident that this century of all others produced the finest music—J. S. Bach and G. F. Handel, Gluck and Haydn, and the incomparable Mozart. And from this source there gushed out in other directions too a whole stream of natural joy in life in the strength of which we still live to-day and which it would be out of place to bring into downright discredit. All this must be remembered before we frown and grumble; otherwise we might easily put ourselves in the wrong even in relation to Kyburtz, let alone Leibniz. Optimism is not to be dismissed just because we cannot study its products without having to smile. Was it not a conscious and seriously executed part of its programme to show that smiling and even laughing are necessary and justified? Is it not a relative justification of the doctrine of the earthly pleasure of the soul in the God who Himself finds pleasure (according to Wolff) that this teaching does in fact give us pleasure even if in a different sense from what its author foresaw?—something [405] which cannot always be said of the apparently or genuinely more important products of other times and other minds. Must we not reckon with the fact that it needed the Christian

Gospel to make this phenomenon possible and even necessary at the appropriate time, for all its disconcerting audacity? And conversely, what would have been the fate in ecclesiastical and secular history of the radiance of God, the ultimate source of which we know to be the resurrection of Jesus Christ, if this phenomenon had not shone out so unequivocally right up to the present day? In "Go, my heart, seek joy … " P. Gerhardt had already anticipated something of the spirit of this outlook. And when it is a question of recognising the radiance of God in this world, all of us and the whole of Christendom must think and feel and speak more or less plainly and tastefully according to the insights, expression and tone of the 18th century, being constrained to seize their harps and lyres, and involuntarily smiling or laughing with them as well as at them, and admitting that we are right to do so. It was good and even necessary that this note should be sounded with the unbroken purity achieved in this period.

Nor is optimism to be lightly dismissed because it was only a phenomenon in the history of ideas like any other, and as such had its day, and when that day was over had to abandon the field which it had almost completely dominated for some decades, giving place to other views. That is what happened, of course. The Lisbon earthquake of 1755 marked the turning-point, and although the change was slow it was irresistible. Optimism itself had to become more reserved, critical and mature. The next milestone in philosophy after Leibniz bears the name of David Hume. The life and work of Rousseau, who cannot exalt too highly the goodness of nature and man, developed in fact into one long lament and accusation. And in Voltaire the type of the neutral, oscillating between merriment and bitterness, begins to take a form which is basically if novelly optimistic for all the scorn lavished on optimism in *Candide*. Maintaining the same background, but emerging from it, even Christian preaching must take up again the theme of the stern and unmistakeable judgments of God, and learn to proclaim rather more radically and restrainedly what it means that all things work together for good to them that love God. Then Kant (according to Goethe's peevish judgment), "wantonly sullied his philosopher's mantle with the shameful stain of a philosophy of radical evil, when he had spent a lifetime in cleansing it from every defilement of prejudice." After the rise and overthrow of the idealistic optimism of Hegel, the world then became both theoretically and practically a kind of machine which would have horrified even the satisfied Wolff with his satisfied God, and which even with the best will in the world could hardly be made out to be the best of all possible worlds. That this whole world of thought had vanished was not perceived, or only tardily, by many at the time and later, so that we need not be surprised to find traces of it until well on in the 19th century. But the fact that optimism was superseded does not suffice to invalidate it. That its structure was historically conditioned and historically dissolved shows only that it was not a final word and that it could be displaced. But Kant and Hegel, Schopenhauer and Nietzsche, Ibsen and Strindberg and Bernard Shaw, have all come and gone in the same way. And that which disappears may return in a changed and sometimes better form, and usually has returned in some degree. We are certainly not secure against the eventual return of Leibniz and his optimism in a new guise. And in its own way it would perhaps be good to live again in a Leibnizian age. At any rate, there is from this standpoint no reason not to take him calmly and seriously, however little he harmonises with the spirit and outlook of our own time. He must be taken seriously in dogmatics because he too, although in a very different way, tried to sing, and in his own way did in fact sing, the unqualified praise of God the Creator in His relationship to the creature.

[406]   We will now see the differences between what is said in optimism and what must be said in dogmatics.

The most striking feature of optimism, and at the same time its clearest weakness, is to be found in the way in which it does not so much eliminate as assimilate the shadowy side of human existence, i.e., its limitation by evil, sin and death, transforming it into a kind of margin to the sphere of light. The superiority with which Leibniz surveys the matter as from an eminence, the cold-bloodedness with which Wolff includes it in his calculations, the cheerfulness with which the popular exponents disposed of it, the art with which they all of them eluded it with open eyes, speaking of it with apparent frankness and yet not really speaking of it at all—all this is admirable and almost enviable. But in this whole scheme it is obvious that reality is only half seen, and therefore in the strict sense not seen at all. For it has two aspects. Earlier and later periods appreciated and expressed this truth. But 18th century optimism did not appreciate it at all. Why not? Was it already walking in the kingdom of God where there will be no more pain and tears and crying? Was it still walking or had it relapsed into the heathen fields of the blessed? Who can finally say? The astonishing fact is that the 18th century knew illness and poverty, lying and deceit, error, vice and violence, in their most repulsive forms. Nor can we say that these optimists had not read deeply enough in the book of nature or of history; that they did not know the relevant facts in this respect. Leibniz had a complete intellectual understanding of evil in its various forms. Lesser knew as precisely as Darwin about the struggle for existence which goes on in the kingdom of insects and elsewhere. And in Brockes, under the ironic title "Hero's Song," we find a poem in which he anticipates Berta von Suttner and inveighs sharply against the folly and horrors of militarism. He also gives us a New Year poem which takes the form of a conversation and in which all the arguments of scepticism, pessimism and atheism are collected and victoriously refuted. What is missing is not a knowledge of the facts or the intellectual possibility, but a compulsion to face this other aspect of life without running away. In other words, there lacks the restraint which this aspect might exercise, interrupting the direct line and hardening and deepening the praise of life. The skeleton is missing, and so the feast goes on—very decorously, respectably and religiously, but all the more vigorously and firmly. The spectator in the cosy warm room, watching the traveller outside lashed by snowstorm and bitten by cold, is content to draw the conclusion that he has much cause to be grateful to God for the comforts bestowed on him. The German student of the time, "filled with joy from high Olympus," regards others only as Philistines with "their pale envy which disturbs our youthful joy," and considers it a most sacred task to bid defiance to them. It would seem as though all these people were enclosed in a glass case through whose walls they can certainly see the pain of the world but are hopelessly precluded from being genuinely moved even when it finally affects themselves. No doubt they all speak of a future life and eternal glory, but it does not lie within their grasp to see in this a deliverance from the tragic contradictions of the present, or their cancellation. They do not need deliverance either for themselves or for others. As can still be seen in Lavater's *Aussichten in die Ewigkeit,* they hope only for an infinity of the same perfection which they already know and enjoy here below. They do not suffer under any contradiction, and therefore their teaching cannot disclose any, and half creation, and therefore perhaps the whole, is actually hidden from them and their disciples. Only the great earthquake, the mockery of Voltaire and later the guillotine began to draw the attention of some to the fact that there exists a disharmony and enigma which cannot be ignored. But we know there were others who as true children of their century were able to approach even the guillotine with wholehearted optimism and, as it were, in a sprightly minuet. No power on earth could make good the lack, and least of all were the arguments of a worldly scepticism and pessimism able to change the mind of these men whose eyes were wide open but who failed to see. As against this, however, the Christian way of affirming the Creator's justifying Yes to His creation obviously has another dimension and a wider scope. It includes what is palpably missing in optimism—a true and urgent and inescapable awareness of the imperilling of creation by its limits, of sin and death and the devil. Unlike optimism, it has a compelling reason to view reality as a whole and therefore in this dimension

[407]

too, and to take it seriously as a whole and therefore with an eye to this aspect too. For this reason it cannot be equated with 18th century optimism. That is the first point of difference.

The second is closely related, for if Leibnizian optimism passes too lightly over the problem of evil, sin and death, the same is true of its treatment of the positive aspect of the world. Incapable of weeping with them that weep, it is also incapable at bottom of rejoicing with them that rejoice, i.e., profoundly, calmly and definitively. This is suggested by the superlatives which it constantly and necessarily employs. The Leibnizian monads must be recognisable as no less than pure compendia and mirrors of the whole universe and the divine central monad. The clockwork of Wolff must be seen to be no less than the optimum of the divine intelligence which chooses and the divine omnipotence which executes. And the popularisers with their maximal expressions can never assure us enough how unsurpassably good and beautiful are all things in this world. If they had been sure of their cause they would never have had to protest so much. The same impression is left by the suspicious zeal for completeness of enumeration with which the arguments in favour of the optimistic thesis are assembled and accumulated. Would not a few instances from the life of bees or ants, calmly and impartially considered for themselves without this significant striving for completeness, have vouched far more credibly for the optimistic thesis that the attempt to make this whole department of zoology tally with theological truth? One can hardly read the *Insecto-Theologia*, the *Irdisches Vergnügen* and similar works without asking the disturbing question whether this is not an attempt to make a "one" out of the greatest number of noughts. This is also implied by the fact that it is characteristic of this whole literature continuously to exhort and admonish and implore, constantly to take the reader by the coat button and to challenge him—sometimes with violent scoldings for his hard-heartedness—to such monotonously repetitive reflection in the form of the acknowledgment of the intelligent design, beauty and utility observable in creation, the inevitable inference from creation to the wise, almighty good and providential Creator, and the gratitude which this necessarily evokes. These writers are clearly unable to make their insights plausible either to themselves or others without vigorous and constant moralising. And this arouses a certain feeling of oppression in face of their positive arguments, descriptions and praises. Their Gospel has so strongly legal a tone and colouring. One can almost detect a kind of gasping for breath behind their cheerfulness, and the fact that they never admit it makes it all the more noticeable. It is hard to conceive that Lesser was not heartily weary of insects when he had finished his *Insecto-Theologia*, that Wolff did not heave a sigh of relief and even yawn a little on completing the 1089 paragraphs of his *Vernünfftige Gedancken*, and that Leibniz himself did not gladly turn to other matters after so exhaustively justifying the Creator and His creation. There is thus an inner reason for the slightly comic effect indisputably exercised by what was thought and said so seriously. But why is it that there is this reason? What is the source of the unmistakeable weakness even of the stronger side of 18th century optimism? It surely springs from the fact that the horizon to which it looked on both sides, the sphere in which it thought it could seek and find both good and evil, was fundamentally restricted; that the measure which it used in both cases was in both cases inadequate for the attainment of an impartial and solid judgment. The judgment of optimism is the judgment of the creature about himself and the world that surrounds him—nothing more. It stands or falls objectively with the existence of the creaturely world as such and subjectively with the human capacity to see its actual character in the best light. It presupposes that the perfection and justification of the world is a quality which is radically and continuously intrinsic to it, and that man has at his command the criterion by which to establish it. We have seen that the determination and therefore the use of this criterion was variable. The thought of Leibniz was too lofty to permit him to seek the goodness of the creature in the fact that it is a perfect

[408]

machine. Wolff was too lofty to equate this goodness simply with utility. Lesser and Brockes were too lofty to identify the good merely with the edible. But when a man like A. Kyburtz was not too lofty to do so, there merely came to the surface a point which was weak and trivial even in the system of Leibniz, viz. the presupposition that the goodness which justifies creation must be intrinsic to it and as such amenable to human judgment. Moving in this circle, one could not be as certain of goodness as so obviously desired. And evil could not be squarely faced without evasion. It could be interpreted only as a natural and unavoidable defect, and therefore balanced by the good. It could not be regarded as an unconditionally serious reality in any of its forms. Nor could the judgment of the good have the inner conviction and consistency which it was desired to give it but which could obviously be given only with much strain and exertion and with no final certainty. It was their abstract this-worldliness and anthropocentricity, descending at its lowest to gastrocentricity, which prevented the optimists not merely from seeing the darker side of existence but even from speaking of its lighter side without monotony, making it impossible for them to see things straight, and therefore to be cheerful in deeds as well as words, and to radiate genuine cheerfulness. There is no escaping a question which cannot be answered within this circle of ideas—the question of the goodness of this good, of the ultimate meaning and purpose of this harmony or mechanism or useful apparatus. This question is aimed at man for whose benefit all this supposed good exists. And it is the more acute the more he thinks he can place himself at the centre of things. Within this circle of thought there is no freedom, and therefore no real joy, but only concealed pain. This is the second point which differentiates the thesis of the optimists from the Christian affirmation of the goodness of creation. We have seen that the Christian affirmation includes the two aspects of life and the twofold human judgment corresponding to them. But it does so because it transcends them. Another being than the contemplated and contemplating creature primarily and properly sorrows and rejoices. And it is in this other-worldly context that the voice of the rejoicing and sorrowing creature becomes living and powerful, and the two aspects of life are so eloquent and meaningful, so urgent and compelling, that they evoke our genuine participation. This other-worldly dimension is lacking in 18th century optimism. That is why it is only half-sure of its cause. That is why it has constantly to represent itself as stronger than it really is, speaking in superlatives, over-busy and so concerned to moralise. It would like to accomplish what can be accomplished only in this transcendent context. It would like to add a cubit to its stature. For this reason it wears a tall wig, as its exponents did in real life. But it cannot feel quite at ease under this wig. Christian optimism, which is obedient on both sides to a higher necessity, does not need any such wig.

The third point of difference is decisive. It is the greatness of 18th century optimism that like Christian truth it has made a choice between the two aspects of being, declaring the perfection of creation to be true and its imperfection illusory. It is its greatness, too, that like Christian truth it has made this choice with reference to, and in the name of, God. But at this point, although there is verbal coincidence, it is obvious that the two are not really saying the same thing. The system of Leibniz may be described as theocentric because, constructively considered, it undoubtedly has its origin and centre in the idea of God as the central monad   [409] and the Guarantor of the predetermined harmony of creation. But when we come to Wolff this idea loses its central position and function both in the external consequence and internal logic of the system. The first step in Wolff is to show that rational man and the ordered world are an integral whole. Only then does he think it necessary or desirable to crown the whole by the doctrine of God as the Inventor and Author of this finished machine; and it is open to question whether in its completeness it really needs this crown. However, a place is found for it, and better late than never. In the popularisers the idea is rhetorically re-emphasised as the culminating point in their view, and it cannot be too passionately acclaimed in their moralising apostrophes. Yet between the innumerable appeals to the divine name and a certain holy superfluity in the examples they quote, there is a contradiction which is not easily explained. Atheism, which knows all that the optimists know but can dispense with the almighty and wise Creator, is lurking somewhere at the doors, and the obvious excitement and sharpness with which the atheistic position must be refuted shows that the optimists themselves are more immediately sure of the perfection of the world, of the skill and intelligence of ants and bees, of the globular shape of the earth, of the pleasantness of a cosy room in winter, of the excellence of Swiss milk products, etc., than of the very different Figure who is so frequently referred to as the basis of all these things. But even if we admit that there is justification for buttressing or crowning the edifice of optimism by the idea of God, we have still to ask who or what this Figure is whose existence must be proved by the perfection of the world but must also prove its perfection. Remember that it is by reference to this Figure that the choice is made between the two aspects of being and preference is given to the affirmative over the negative judgment of the character of the world. How far can this dim Figure invite, encourage or compel this choice? Who or what is the God of the optimists? Why does He point imperiously in oné direction rather than another? The reply given is that He is the perfect being, all-powerful, wise and good, and as such supreme. In His perfection and plenitude He is the negation of everything imperfect, and therefore, since He is the Creator of all other beings as His creatures, He is to be understood as the Negator of their imperfection, and an adequate reason for regarding that imperfection merely as lack or defect. Among all possible worlds the one created by Him is necessarily the best, and therefore comparatively the most free from imperfection, because in His perfection it is impossible that He should will to create anything but this relatively best world. We for our part are thus compelled to think and speak the very best we can of it. But the point is that when we count on this being, and affirm that our choice is made under this divine constraint, we do so because we think ourselves justified in inferring such a being from the character of the world or "nature of things" (Wolff)—which is the very point at issue. There can thus be no doubt that we are using as a proof that which is itself in need of proof. And if we prove that which proves in this way, we have to assume as given and known that which is to be proved—the perfection of existence. But this raises the question why the latter has to be proved by the divine perfection when it is assumed to be known apart from this and therefore self-proved. And even if we leave that point we are still faced by the question how far the perfection of creation really is given as a self-evident fact on the basis of which we can know the perfection of God and thus be confirmed in our recognition of the perfection of creation. Where and how does one enter this circular argument? To this question the only possible answer is that of ourselves—in virtue of our reason as the kernel of our intellectual capacity—we are always in a position and free at any moment to enter it. The human soul with its rational faculty forms with the world and God a kind of triangle. As one of the angles of this triangle it is open to the other two, and they to it. It is related and similar both to the universe and God. What constitutes its own perfection must also constitute that of the universe and God. It only needs to consider and analyse its own perfection to be capable of appreciating, not quantitatively but qualitatively, the perfection of the universe and of God. Therefore, assuming its own perfection and applying the understanding to be derived from it, it can enter that circular argument, inferring and proving either the divine perfection from that of the universe or the perfection of the universe from that of God. The whole optimistic thesis obviously depends on the legitimacy and force of this mode of entry. But this mode of entry is purely and simply an act of human self-confidence. We must have the courage and confidence to stand in that triangular relationship with the universe and with God, and in our way to be perfect, and in the correct understanding of our own perfection to have in our hands the measure of the perfection of the universe and of that of God. The

[410]

classical man of the 18th century has this self-confidence, or he believes that he should behave as if he had. The optimistic thesis stands or falls with his absolutism (*L'état, c'est moi*EN67). For its sustaining it does not really need either the universe or God. It is valid *a priori*EN68. Its only primary and essential need is man, who as such stands on the same level with the universe and God, who is able to treat with both on equal terms, and who therefore takes it upon himself to declare the world good in the light of his own goodness. Does he need God in this task? Obviously, only in the second place. The optimists *did* make use of God, and to their annoyance and disgust the atheists did *not*. But the optimists, as the system of Wolff reveals, made use of Him only as an afterthought and not essentially. At a pinch human perfection could be content to be reflected only in the perfection of the world. God could be used but He was not essential. For in spite of all the superlatives there was not to be found in the perfection of God anything basically new or different from that of man. It is undoubtedly the central weakness of the optimistic thesis that as it is undertaken in this sovereignty of man it must really be sustained in the same way. It cannot possibly be presented on the basis of divine power and authority, but at best only with a maximum of human self-confidence. Trusting confidently in himself, regarding his five senses and reasoning intelligence and emotional sensibility as his only and secure guide, optimistic man was bold to take the step which according to his philosophy he had to take on this basis, not only distinguishing between good and evil, salvation and perdition, life and death, but also co-ordinating all things, defining and proclaiming the superiority of the one to the other, the victory of light over darkness, and thus rolling away the stone from the entrance to the tomb. That the whole darker side of life consists only in a lack of that which is perfect in itself, that its essential insignificance can be recognised ever more plainly in the freedom of growing knowledge—this triumphant assertion had to be maintained and proved and lived out on his initiative and in his own strength. Nothing could be expected from the Bearer of the divine name, for He had played only an incidental and non-essential role in the framing of the assertion. We recall that in face of the world and man His position is only that of a clockmaker rejoicing in his craft. He has nothing to do directly with the changes in the world within which the life of man is lived. It is a part of the perfection of man and the world that God should be content with a minimum of direct participation in the historical process. Why did not Wolff say point blank that God will refrain from any direct participation? There is certainly no compelling reason to count on it, nor can any promise be given of divine participation in the world of becoming. All that man can be told is that he must use his reason, express his feelings and exercise his will. In fact, the Gospel of optimism can be preached to him only as a system of Law. God will help him only as and to the extent that he helps himself. He is placed in a position of fearful loneliness. For whether he believes in God or not, his relationship to the world is poised on his self-confidence. Existence is rational as and to the extent that he himself is rational. Once he doubts himself, the abyss yawns. From this [411] standpoint we can understand the puppet-like respectability of this man, his stiff rectitude, the outward constraint and narrowness which are so little in keeping with his inner absolutism, the artificial dignity of his bearing. In all these things there is plainly betrayed the anxiety which inevitably accompanies his fundamentally godless self-confidence and its audacities. The scorn and ridicule which the "Sturm und Drang" and the Romantics later heaped upon this attitude were quite uncalled for. Liberation from the conventions of fathers and grandfathers was one thing, but what about the underlying anxiety which had made these conventions necessary? And what about the godless self-confidence which was

EN67 I am the state
EN68 unconditionally

the real root of this anxiety? But however that may be, the Christian affirmation of the goodness of creation is not menaced by anxiety, and does not need to express itself with this
rigidity, because it has nothing whatever to do with that sort of self-confidence. It is based
unequivocally on the judgment of the Creator God. It simply expresses that which in obedience to His will must be expressed in relation to His self-revealing activity in the created
world. It is not a spontaneous exclamation of man proving the world, himself and God, but
man's response to God's self-authentication in which he knows both himself and the world
to be grounded. For the God whom it invokes is not the supreme being who may or may not
be drawn into the reckoning and referred to, but the free Lord of man and the world who
makes Himself responsible for their character, and has disclosed Himself as the Bearer of
this responsibility. It is on the basis of His revealed decision that in Christian faith Yes is said
to the world, a Yes which is deeply aware of the No and includes it, but also overcomes and
transcends it. It is on this basis that the Yes is preferred to the No, the No being contradicted
as the nothingness which it is recognised to be. It may well be that ultimately the optimists of
the 18th century meant to echo this divine Yes, this divine overcoming of the No by the Yes.
In so far as that was the case, they unconsciously and involuntarily proclaimed an imperish-
able truth. But in any event they did so most confusedly. And to that extent the Christian
affirmation stands out in marked distinction.

The fourth and final point of difference is related to the third. We have already seen that
optimism was not sure of itself. For all its absolutism, its insights were not secure, decisive or
compelling. It was unable to speak with divine force and authority. The man of the 18th
century who was so powerfully controlled by it for a time could change again. When its time
came it could go as it had come. What is the inner reason for its insecurity and temporary
validity? Part of the explanation is that its God merely reflected a perfection which man first
thought he could ascribe to himself, so that he had only an optional use for this God, and
could have no real and final security in Him. But it has also to be taken into account that
these optimists are incorrigible spectators, and that as such they successfully evade and resist
(to their own detriment) the necessity for decision and action. They sit at their telescope or
in their cosy studies or on the turf among the cows, observing and then reflecting on what
they have seen. They do not allow themselves to be personally affected, for all their interest
in these things. They it is who decide and regulate the distances and relations between themselves and things. They it is who observe and experiment and note the interconnexion of
things and their detailed and general harmony and usefulness. They are the masters who are
able to put everything to rights. But like oriental despots in relation to their subjects, they
have no personal interest in things. Things do not really touch them, either for evil or for
good. And so they cannot really make contact with things or be sure of good or evil. Everything remains in the sphere of views and opinions and persuasions. Everything is a
panopticum[EN69]. Even God and they themselves are mere figures in this *panopticum*[EN70]. If the
glasses were different, everything would change. Hence while the optimistic thesis is self-
evident for them, it is not vitally necessary to the exclusion of all others. They have and
exercise the power of choice. But they are not elected to choose in this way. The loftiness of
their attitude is dearly bought. It betrays the fact that the man who adopts it is not held in it,
but that where he stands to-day he may fall to-morrow. He possesses much, but nothing
possesses him, and the fact that this is so calls in question all that he has. Behind his self-
confidence stands his impotence. This impotence in self-confidence is the real disease of the
18th century. For all that it was felt so deeply and proclaimed so loudly its confidence was
vulnerable. An earthquake could set everything in a new and different light. And it is sym-

[412]

[EN69] panopticon
[EN70] panopticon

bolical and symptomatic that of all possible disasters it was an earthquake which brought about this change. It was fatal for these eternal observers and spectators that they should suddenly feel shaking beneath them the earth on which they thought they could calmly make their observations. What were they, what was the significance of their interpretation, when they were no longer sure of themselves? Real certainty depends on whether the ground on which we see and think is solid or unstable. We have seen that the Christian affirmation of the justification of existence gains its certitude from the fact that those who utter it have themselves been so seized upon and transformed that they cannot do other than affirm this belief. They have been brought to the point of decision. They are not just spectators but sworn witnesses to the perfection of the created world. They have been reached and pierced by the self-declaration of their Creator. They have been sought and found and chosen and called by Him. At the heart of creation He Himself has come to them, and grasped them, and committed them to the verdict of His good-pleasure, so that their minds and lips can know no other. Confronting God, they must also confront the truth of all things. And this fact implies the freedom of their judgment in face of shattering disturbances which inevitably affect observation and reflection that are free only in appearance. In this sense, too, the Christian affirmation says something different from that of pure optimism. It has its own word, and there can be no equating the one with the other.

We draw to a close. There is a common denominator under which all these points of difference may be grouped. The 18th century, too, was a Christian century. And the exponents of its spirit whom we have studied more or less seriously intended to be Christians. The difficulty is to decide how far this had any significance for the foundations of optimism. The interest which Leibniz took in the churches as in so many other matters, and the respect with which he approached the Bible and dogma, deserve attention. In his *Theodicy* he tried to come to terms with Paul, Augustine, Calvin and especially Luther's *De servo arbitrio*, i.e., to explain them in his own sense. But in the sequence of his thought we seek in vain one specifically Christian element—with an exception still to be mentioned. Again, in the philosophy of Wolff a carefully delimited and guarded sphere is reserved for divine miracles, and therefore for Christian faith, and subjectively he can hardly have felt that he deserved the threat of execution for atheism once made against him by Frederick William I of Prussia. But we seek in vain for a genuinely Christian note in his *Vernünfftige Gedancken*. Again, in Brockes' *Irdisches Vergnügen*, while in theory the book of nature is placed solemnly side by side with that of revelation, in practice the former alone is used. He hardly discusses the fact that this is where he really is, and although he entertains all due respect for the latter book, he makes no use of it at all. But the Christian element which is not denied in all this literature, which is admitted and sometimes greeted from afar, but which is not put to any profitable use in the establishment and interpretation of the optimistic thesis, is simply Jesus Christ Himself, on the knowledge of whom absolutely everything depends in the establishment and interpretation of the corresponding Christian thesis. The meaning and truth of Christian optimism consist in His lowliness and exaltation, in His death and resurrection as the secret of the divine will in creation and the divine good-pleasure in the created world. It is the fulfilment of the covenant in Him which shows us that the two opposites of life both [413] have their necessity and seriousness since they are both grounded in an eternal dimension; that their mutual relationship is that of the overcoming of the one by the other, and that man is in no position to come to a different decision from the divine decision made in this relationship. In the light of the name of Jesus Christ, everything that has to be said in this connexion in the dogmatics of the Christian Church becomes quite different. This, then, is the common denominator of all the differences between the Christian view and the optimistic thesis, and of all the objections which we must raise against the latter. It is, of course, understandable that in spite of the alleged and to some extent, no doubt, genuine Christianity of its exponents, it was unable to make the name of Jesus Christ its starting point in this matter, and had to argue about Christianity as it actually did. We have seen how the good Lesser assured his readers that as a preacher he did not proclaim "merely" the natural knowledge of God but also "Christ crucified." But that even the natural knowledge of God, the knowledge of God in and from the created world, and therefore the knowledge of its perfection, can clearly, solidly and necessarily be reached only through the medium of Jesus Christ the Crucified, was a possibility of which he does not seem ever to have dreamed. When he is treating of the natural knowledge of God, and therefore of the justification of existence, he reads in a very different book, gazing through his glasses into the *panopticum*[EN71] as though there were no such thing as Good Friday and Easter instead of looking at creation through the message of Good Friday and Easter. The result is the weakness which vitiates his optimism as well. We are confronted at this point by what can be described only as the deep Christian ignorance of this optimism. It missed the one and only thing which could make its intended thesis possible, necessary and strong.

It is to the special credit of Leibniz, however, that at least once to my knowledge he found a place for this one essential thing. In the Latin conclusion to his *Theodicy* (*Causa Dei*, 49) there stands the following reflection (independently of what precedes and follows): *Optimae autem seriei rerum (nempe huius ipsius) eligendae maxima ratio fuit Christus θεάνθρωπος, sed qui, quatenus creatura est ad summum provecta, in ea serie nobilissima contineri debebat, tanquam Universi creati pars, immo caput, cui omnis tandem potestas data est in coelo et in terra, in quo benedici debuerunt omnes gentes, per quem omnis creatura liberabitur a servitute corruptionis, in libertatem gloriae filiorum Dei*[EN72]. Hence it is in relation to Christ, to His position as Member and Head of creation, as Lord and Saviour and Hope of the world, that God chose this world as the best; and it is in the divinity and humanity of Christ that we are to recognise the *maxima ratio*[EN73] as the supreme principle of the perfection of the universe and therefore of the perfection of God Himself. Are we to regard the passage as an incidental expression of the Christian piety of the author, or as the type of concession to the teaching of the Bible, the Church and Christian doctrine which is often found in almost every philosopher of the period but has no real significance, or as an element in the Leibnizian universalism which in its task of describing the divine choice of the best of all worlds did not want to leave out this element as well? However that may be, Leibniz did actually write it, and it is not to be overlooked how differently his system might have developed if he had realised the full implications of what he wrote and found himself compelled to rethink his whole system from the standpoint of this *maxima ratio*[EN74] of all perfection. This did not happen. We can only note that it might have happened. It was not that the optimism of this period lacked altogether the knowledge of Jesus Christ. The real trouble was that it did not know how to exploit this knowledge. It allowed it to remain only as a thing apart. It had no practical use for it. All its weaknesses are rooted in this fact. We cannot go into the historical causes of this state of affairs. We can only say that they also and primarily include the weakness which at this cen-

---

[EN71] panopticon
[EN72] Now the supreme ground of the choosing of the best series of events (and especially of this particular one) was Christ the God-man; and since He has been raised on high as a creature, He had to be contained in this most excellent series, inasmuch as He is a part of the created Universe, indeed its head, to whom all power in heaven and on earth has been given, in whom all nations have been blessed, through whom every creature will be set fee from the servitude of corruption for the freedom of the glory of the children of God
[EN73] supreme ground
[EN74] supreme ground

tral point was inherent already in the theological orthodoxy of the 16th and 17th centuries. [414] This was gravely at fault in the fact that, although it still spoke very fully and loudly about Christ at some points, in many others—as, for example, its doctrine of God and predestination, its natural theology, its doctrine of the state, its whole doctrine of creation and providence and its explanation of the Mosaic *valde bonum*^{EN75}—it hardly knew what to make of Him at all, but was far more at home with Aristotle and Descartes. In this respect, too, the Enlightenment was the not unmerited judgment on the dual system of book-keeping adopted (in Roman Catholic fashion) by the Lutheran and Reformed fathers and even to some extent by the Reformers themselves. If we approve of and use this system because we cannot free ourselves from the Roman Catholic tradition; if we tear asunder nature and grace, creation and covenant, the revelation of creation and the revelation of salvation; and if we finally introduce this whole tension even into the Holy Trinity, we have no right to throw stones at Leibniz and the movement associated with him. The sun of the Enlightenment ruthlessly exposed what must always come to light sooner or later when this double system is used. When the two books are juxtaposed as sources of our knowledge of the Creator and creation, it is quite useless to recommend the book of grace. The very fact of this juxtaposition means that the book which is actually read and from which the knowledge of the Creator and creation is actually gained is only the one book, i.e., the book of nature. The co-existence of an earthly pleasure with the heavenly necessarily makes the latter superfluous. To set that which is human, wordly and rational alongside that which is Christian is inevitably to expel the latter. No man can serve two masters. And if we once serve another master alongside Christ, as will always be the effect of this procedure, we must not be surprised to see bad fruit growing on the bad tree. A choice is thus demanded in respect of the knowledge of the justification of existence. It can be achieved as the knowledge of Him *cui omnis potestas data est in coelo et in terra*^{EN76}. But it cannot be achieved if it does not really find a place for confessing Him. This is the lesson which we have finally to learn from a survey of 18th century optimism.

EN75 very good
EN76 to whom all power in heaven and on earth has been given

INDEX OF SCRIPTURE REFERENCES

INDEX OF SUBJECTS

INDEX OF NAMES